family relationships

Edited by

Gladys K. Phelan

Colorado State University
Fort Collins, Colorado

Burgess Publishing Company
Minneapolis, Minnesota

Editor: Kay Kushino
Production Editor: James Montgomery
Production Manager: Morris Lundin
Art Director: Joan Gordon
Designer: Paula C. Gibbons
Compositor: Tjody Heitz
Sales/Marketing: Travis Williams

Cover design by Paula C. Gibbons

Dedicated to my own family.

G. K. P.

contents

PART 2
Parent-Child Relationships

PART 3
Sibling Relationships

PART 4
Extended-Family Relationships

PART 5
Toward a Total View of Family Relationships

preface

As a rule, most books of readings about the family focus on premarital and marital relationships very heavily and include a few readings concerning parent-child relationships. The experience of teaching an upper-division family relationships course without a book which covered research literature on marital, parent-child, sibling, and extended-family relationships prompted the literature search and the editing tasks which have culminated in this book. The book should prove most useful in courses taught at the upper-division undergraduate and the beginning graduate levels.

The purpose of this book is to bring together under one cover material pertinent to the study of family relationships. In this book, the term *family relationships* refers to those interactional patterns which comprise the internal family processes taking place within various traditional and nontraditional family settings.

The introductions to each of the book's five parts briefly discuss the selected readings within the context of other salient research on related topics. The additional sources cited in the introductions are valuable because of the obvious limit to any book of readings; no attempt was made to include readings on every topic in family relationships. These additional sources may provide the instructor with ideas for class lectures and discussions and give the student ideas for class projects or additional reading assignments.

The readings in this book are drawn from reviews of research, original research studies, theoretical papers, and clinical observations. This variety should make the book more readable, however, the reading material will vary greatly in terms of difficulty. A few highly technical research articles are included primarily because of the editor's belief that undergraduate students should learn how to read and interpret research articles. Students who graduate without this knowledge can be assured that their recently acquired degrees will be endowed with instant obsolescence.

After the manuscript was finally compiled, an obvious imbalance in the research literature became apparent. So much research has focused on marital and parent-child relationships that comparatively speaking, the study of family relationships is just beginning to explore other relevant areas in the field.

The authors and publishers of the individual readings reprinted in this book are acknowledged for granting the necessary permissions. These readings, which come from two books and 21 different journals, represent the variety of disciplines contributing to the interdisciplinary study of family relationships. In order to include a maximum number of readings, some tables, charts, figures, and photographs had to be omitted. It was generous of the authors and publishers to permit the necessary deletions. Additionally, the sabbatical leave program at Colorado State University should be acknowledged, since a one-semester sabbatical leave permitted the initial planning and early selection of appropriate readings.

Some colleagues who made valuable suggestions and were generally supportive of this endeavor deserve special recognition. Helpful suggestions regarding Part 1 (Marital Relationships) were made by Dr. Elizabeth Franklin. Dr. D. Bruce Gardner and Mrs. Margaret B. Hanson gave worthwhile guidance on parent-child relationships in Part 2 of the book. Dr. Jerry J. Bigner, a sibling researcher himself, offered valuable advice concerning the content of Part 3 (Sibling Relationships). Dr. Joseph G. Turner, a specialist in adult development and aging who has studied intergenerational relationships, brought considerable insight to Part 4 (Extended-Family Relationships). Also, special thanks to Mrs. Mary Rehn, who typed the original portions of the manuscript, and to Cathryn Brackett and Bonnie Mucklow, two graduate students who offered evaluative suggestions. Dr. George P. Rowe and Dr. Jay D. Schvaneveldt are thanked for their careful reviews of the manuscript. As many of their suggestions as possible were incorporated into the final manuscript. Mrs. Kay Kushino, home economics editor for Burgess Publishing Company, is recognized for the significant role she has played in making this book a reality. Deep appreciation is expressed to all these people for their valuable input.

introduction

Since most of us have grown up in a family, we often feel that personal observation and experience have taught us everything we need to know about the family and the interpersonal relationships that occur within it. Often, there is considerable disparity between what we think is true of family life and what empirical evidence suggests. Consequently, there have been sound reasons for the development of a body of scientific knowledge relevant to the family.

As Christensen (1964) pointed out in his history of the development of family study, the study of family relationships is a relatively new discipline, when compared to other fields of scientific inquiry. Christensen described the period before 1850 as the "Preresearch" period and characterized the thoughts regarding marriage and the family as primarily based upon superstition or speculation. Although the literature, religious writings, and philosophical works of this period contained much information about marriage and family life, the writings had no empirical base.

What was written from about 1850 to 1899 Christensen dubbed "social Darwinism." This period was characterized by evolutionary studies examining the social evolution of many institutions, among them marriage and the family. The period of what Christensen termed "emerging science" did not appear until the early 1900s, at which time many of the classical studies were published. The scientific method was applied to marriage prediction (Burgess and Cottrell, 1939; Terman, 1938), and family history was examined (Calhoun, 1917-1919; Frazier, 1948; Goodsell, 1915; Sirjamaki, 1953; Zimmerman, 1947). However, the predominant emphasis of research in the twentieth century was on the interpersonal relationships of family members. As early as 1926, Burgess described the family as "a unity of interacting personalities" (1926: 5) and thus assisted greatly the development of scientific research regarding internal family relationships.

Empirical research took on a new dimension in more recent times. Christensen (1964) referred to this phase in the development of family studies, which began about 1950, as the period of "systematic theory building." An early attempt at a theoretical explanation of family change was undertaken by Zimmerman (1947), who traced historical changes in power and control over family relationships. He explained the competition between the social institutions of government, religion, and family for control over family relationships. Since then, greater emphasis has been placed upon 1) providing a theoretical base for empirical family research and 2) designing empirical studies that contribute to theory development.

Nimkoff (1948), identifying trends in family research, noted that sociological contributions to the understanding of family relationships gained impetus during the 1920s. The foundation of family research was built on two bases. One was the theoretical contributions of Cooley, Mead, and Thomas. Their ideas were pushed forward by Burgess when he emphasized that the family was a unity of interacting personalities. This definition was modified later to "the family [is] a unity of interacting personalities, 'each with a history,' in a given cultural milieu" (Nimkoff, 1948:478). The initial version of the expanded definition focused upon the psychoanalytic contribution, whereas the later version pointed to the anthropological contribution. In this way, the interactional approach could be applied more broadly yet more precisely to specific dimensions of family research.

Increased knowledge of family trends also evolved during the 1920s, and this knowledge formed the second base for the foundation of sociological research. The momentum of contributions to family research was accelerated through studies of social change (Nimkoff, 1948).

A recent identification of research trends appeared in the introduction to Olson and Dahl's inventories of the literature related to marriage and the family (1975, 1977). Their computations were based on the contents of their own volumes, which cover publications for the years 1973 to 1975 and 1975 to 1976, and on the contents of two previously published volumes for the years 1900 to 1964 (Aldous and Hill, 1967) and 1965 to 1972 (Aldous and Dahl, 1974). All four volumes used the same major subject-matter headings, which allowed Olson and Dahl to make some comparisons.

For 1900 to 1964, a total of 12,610 published articles were listed, for 1965 to 1972 there were 6,346 listed, and for 1973 and 1974 the number of listings totaled 3,502. It has been estimated that more than 3,500 articles were published between 1975 and 1976. These figures illustrate the rapidly growing volume of literature pertaining to marriage and the family. Furthermore, more than one-fifth of the articles listed in the four volumes dealt with topics in the "Family as a Small Group" category, and this category contained the majority of articles relevant to family relationships. The family as a small group was the most frequently studied general topic, having the largest percentage of listings in all four volumes (Olson and Dahl, 1977). Thus it becomes obvious that a large amount of scientific literature on family relationships has been accumulating at an accelerating pace.

Since it is logical for a study of family relationships to begin with marital relationships, to move on to parent-child and sibling relationships, and to include relationships with in-laws and other extended kin, this book has been divided into parts which follow this sequence. Each part of the book examines a kind of family relationship. Each part begins with an introduction by the editor and then presents a group of readings which has been selected as representative of the present knowledge pertaining to the kind of family relationship under examination.

The readings tend to emphasize the interactional and developmental conceptual frameworks more heavily than other research approaches. Some of the readings may also be identified with social-change theory and systems theory. Since most contemporary researchers provide a theoretical base for their research reports, the reader will uncover theory as it is presented within the articles. The book will focus on the research articles, research reviews, clinical experiences, and interpretations of scholars in the field as contributions to the knowledge of family relationships rather than to family theory *per se*. The selections should help the reader to examine specific patterns of family interaction, since all have been selected as pertinent to family relationships within the historical and cultural context of contemporary American society.

REFERENCES

Aldous, J., and Dahl, N. *International bibliography of research in marriage and the family, volume II, 1965-1972.* Minneapolis: University of Minnesota Press, 1974.

Aldous, J., and Hill, R. *International bibliography of research in marriage and the family, 1900-1964.* Minneapolis: University of Minnesota Press, 1967.

Burgess, E. W. The family as a unity of interacting personalities. *Family 7* (1926):3-9.

Burgess, E. W., and Cottrell, L. S., Jr. *Predicting success or failure in marriage.* New York: Prentice-Hall, 1939.

Calhoun, A. W. *A social history of the American family from colonial times to the present.* 3 vols. Cleveland: Clark, 1917-1919.

Christensen, H. T. Development of the family field of study. In *Handbook of marriage and the family,* edited by H. T. Christensen, pp. 3-32. Chicago: Rand McNally, 1964.

Frazier, E. F. *The Negro family in the United States.* New York: Citadel, 1948.

Goodsell, W. *A history of the family as a social and educational institution.* New York: Macmillan, 1915.

Nimkoff, E. F. Trends in family research. *The American Journal of Sociology 53* (1948):477-82.

Olson, D. H., and Dahl, N. S. *Inventory of marriage and family literature, 1973 & 1974, volume III.* St. Paul: Family Social Science, University of Minnesota, 1975.

Olson, D. H., and Dahl, N. S. *Inventory of marriage and family literature, 1975 & 1976, volume IV*. St. Paul: Family Social Science, University of Minnesota, 1977.

Sirjamaki, J. *The American family in the twentieth century*. Cambridge: Harvard University Press, 1953.

Terman, L. W. with Buttenwieser, P., Ferguson, L. W., Johnson, W. B., and Wilson, D. P. *Psychological factors in marital happiness*. New York: McGraw-Hill, 1938.

Zimmerman, C. C. *Family and civilization*. New York: Harper, 1947.

part 1

marital relationships

INTRODUCTION

In this first part of the book, the focus is on marital relationships as a subsystem of relationships in the family system. In order to place the marital relationship briefly within the context (of the premarital dyad) from which it arose, some brief attention will be paid to mate selection before actual marital relationships are addressed. Consequently, this part is divided into three sections: 1) mate selection; 2) marriage typologies—variations among marital relationships; and 3) factors associated with the marital relationship.

MATE SELECTION

Since the marital relationship is actually a very complex relationship produced by the interaction of the personalities of both husband and wife, some attention should be paid to the process by which mates are chosen. No two marriages can be exactly alike because no two individuals are the same. Since our society lacks a system by which marriages are officially arranged, how then are the two individuals brought together to form a marital relationship?

Over the years, much information has been accumulated regarding the process of mate selection. As early as 1950, there was strong research support for social homogamy (the notion that like marries like) based on social characteristics such as race, age, religion, ethnic origin, and social class (Hollingshead, 1950).* Research interest in mate selection persisted during the 1960s. During recent years, however, there has been a decline in the percentage of family-related research studies devoted to mate selection (Olson and Dahl, 1977).

Undoubtedly some readers would expect to find a sampling of the original research studies within this section. However, since the emphasis in Part 1 is on the marital relationship and not on mate selection, only two theoretical articles are included. The first, by Eckland, is included because it offers a general overview of the most salient theories of mate selection and examines important issues of concern to geneticists as well as behavioral scientists (1).

From the content of Eckland's article, it becomes clear that a great deal had been theorized and explored by the late 1960s regarding the choice of mates. Since that time the bulk of research has reconfirmed or refuted the findings of earlier studies. For example, when DeYoung and Fleischer (1976) set out to explore the motivational and personality trait relationships in mate selection, they were attempting to test Winch's theory of complementary needs in mate selection. They found positive rather than negative correlations between husband and wife traits, except for the traits of

---

*In-text references to related research literature, which are by name and/or date, appear in a list at the end of each part's introduction. Italicized numbers 1 through 42 enclosed in parentheses refer to articles reprinted in this book.

1

fear and pugnacity. Therefore, this recent study supports homogamy theory more than it does Winch's theory of complementarity.

Alston, McIntosh, and Wright's (1976) national data regarding the extent of interfaith marriages of white Americans demonstrated that 83 percent of their subjects had spouses of the same religious preference. When they controlled for the variable of age, they found that those under thirty years of age were more likely to be in mixed religious marriages than those over thirty. Their data also lend considerable support to homogamy theory. Despite the fact that the younger subjects were more likely to be in mixed marriages than the older subjects, less than 33 percent of the 18- to 29-year-olds were in religiously heterogamous unions.

Just as there appears to be an increase in the rate of interreligious marriage, there is also evidence of an increase in the rate of interracial marriage (Monahan, 1976). The proportion of racially mixed marriages for the total population remains very low, less than .75 percent in any year from 1963 to 1970. However, if one overlooks the marriages of whites with whites and focuses on minority marriages, it then becomes clear that a substantial proportion of the marriages involving a member of a minority race are mixed. As Monahan concluded:

> The overall incidence of interracial marriage is small but it is rising, particularly the marriage of Negroes with Whites. From the point of view of the minority, biological amalgamation is considerable. As the phenomenon grows, more attention will be given to it, by the minorities if not by the majority [Monahan, 1976:230].

It appears that the homogamy theory, at least as it pertains to social characteristics, still receives considerable support on the basis of national surveys, despite the trends toward more mixed marriages. Perhaps at some time in the future, the United States will become the "melting pot" it is often believed to be. Presently, the homogamous tendency remains so strong in the white majority that mixed marriages are still most likely among minority-group members.

Perhaps one reason for the declining interest in research related to theories of mate selection is the fact that most researchers prefer to explore topics that have been studied less thoroughly. One does not usually develop an outstanding reputation by replicating someone else's research. Another possible explanation is that many studies of mate selection were initially undertaken in order to identify which premarital factors are most highly correlated with later marital satisfaction or adjustment. Such predictive studies have not led to the "pay-offs" desired (Hicks and Platt, 1970). Declining interest in mate-selection theories might also be attributed to a common belief among researchers that we now know all we need to know about the process of mate selection. However, Lewis points out that there remains the challenge to "social scientists to systematically draw together a well-articulated theory from all present empirical evidence by means of interdefined and interrelated concepts" (1975:222).

Since romantic love is so often characterized as the prime motivating factor for the majority of marriages in our society, it may seem peculiar that no mention of the word *love* is made by Eckland in his discussion of mate selection *(1)*. There are those who feel that the role of romantic love in mate selection cannot be overlooked, and, in the second article on mate selection, Goode discusses the theoretical importance of love *(2)*. He concludes that the love between two individuals in a society is controlled by families in various degrees based on social class. For example, Goode suggests that the upper-class group in our society tends to use social isolation of its children as a means of controlling their focus of affection and thus preventing undesirable matches, whereas the remainder of our population generally encourages the development of love and the selection of mates in a social environment formally free of choice restrictions.

Considerable support can be found for the belief that the upper class wields more power in controlling the mate-selection choices of its members. Scott (1965a, 1965b) has examined the American college sorority system and shown that it supports this upper-class practice by providing some control over the social class and ethnic background of the young men with whom sorority members associate. Thus, Scott's findings show that the sorority has played a role in class and ethnic endogamy. In a more recent study, by Blumberg and Paul, of wedding announcements appearing in the *New York Times* on Sundays in June for the decade 1932-1942 as compared to the decade 1962-1972, continuities and discontinuities in upper-class marriages were revealed. Although there was some evidence of horizontal and possibly vertical expansion among the upper-class pool of eligibles, "a great theme of continuity runs through these largely upper-class marriages" (1975:75). It would appear that the upper-class manages to keep itself remarkably intact through endogamy. These more recent research findings can be viewed as support for Goode's theoretical perspectives on love. Falling in love is a socially controlled process such that lovers are not chosen at random but rather from specific approved cultural groups.

A contrasting view has been offered by Greenfield (1965), who adopted a functional approach in explaining love. His premise was that romantic love motivates individuals to marry. When one is in love, one is irrational enough to move into husband/father and wife/mother positions, which are essential to the formation of nuclear families. Nuclear families, in turn, are essential for reproduction, socialization, and the maintenance of our economic system. Through the irrational behavior of loving, one takes on responsibilities that he would otherwise avoid.

Erich Fromm's *The Art of Loving* (1956) was a very important philosophical work in its day. In it, Fromm identified five kinds of love feelings, only one of which was erotic love. In a more contemporary work, Arieti and Arieti (1977) have built upon Fromm's earlier classification, including the five kinds of love, but the bulk of their writing related to the erotic or romantic love between a man and a woman.

In view of our society's preoccupation with love, it seems strange that love so seldom comes into the study of mate selection. Reiss (1960) formulated a theory regarding the heterosexual love relationship, but his wheel theory, however, did not explain why one potential mate (lovable person) was selected over another. Subsequently, Lee (1974) researched styles of loving and identified nine types or styles. Lasswell and Lasswell *(7)* found support for Lee's styles of loving in their concurrent research attempts. It appears that one of the important variables not considered by theories of mate selection and theories of the development of love is this new concept of styles of loving. To date, none of the theories of mate selection have addressed the issue of the probable need for styles of loving to be compatible.

MARRIAGE TYPOLOGIES—VARIATIONS AMONG MARITAL RELATIONSHIPS

Although there has always been diversity among marital relationships, recently it has become a well-publicized fact that numerous alternatives to traditional marriage exist. The mass media have communicated the idea that traditional marriage is no longer a viable life-style. So much attention has been given to all the choices available that some people perceive the number of alternatives as mind boggling and bewildering. The preponderance of alternatives motivated Broderick (1972) to write an article that might serve as a consumer's guide to contemporary pairing patterns. Also, in a recent marriage textbook, Burr (1976) identified a long list of alternative marriage styles. He summarized, in tabular form, what was known about each marriage type in terms of a series of variables associated with married life.

Among the marriage typologies given by Burr, the utilitarian (conflict-habituated, passive-congenial, and devitalized) relationships and intrinsic (vital and total) relationships have their origin in the research of Cuber and Harroff, who studied an upper-middle-class sample *(3)*. Rainwater's article on conjugal role-relationships examines the association between social class and marriage type *(4)*. He uses the terms *joint*, *segregated*, and *intermediate* to describe the conjugal or marital relationship. The portion of his work which is included in this section on marriage typologies includes examples of each

TABLE 1. DIMENSIONS IN ALTERNATIVE STYLES OF MARRIAGE

	Intrinsic	Utilitarian	Open	Swinging	Two-Step	Temporary	Judaic-Christian	Eternal	Group	Traditional
1. Value of stability	Very high	Varies*	Varies	High	Low/High	Very low	Very high	Very high	Varies	High
2. Disruptiveness of divorce	Very high	Low	Low		Low	Very low	High	High	Varies	High
3. Amount of companionship expected	Very high	Limited amount	Varies	†	High	Very high	Varies	Varies	High	Seldom high
4. Equality of the sexes	Varies	Varies	Equal	Equal		Equal	Unequal	Unequal	Varies	Unequal
5. Desire for children	Probably	Varies	Varies		No/Yes	No	Yes	Yes	Usually	Yes
6. Approval of extramarital sexual activity	Usually no	Varies	Yes	Yes			No	No	Varies	No
7. Importance of legal sanction	High	Varies	High	High	Ideally high	Low	High	High	Low	High
8. Importance of marriage compared to other aspects of life	Very high	Low	High	Usually high		Varies	High	Very high	Usually high	Varies
9. Intensity of the affect	Very high	Usually not high	Varies	Varies		High	Varies	Varies		High then low
10. Complexity of the marital relationship	High	Lowest	High	High	Low/High	Low	High	High	Highest	High
11. Amount of change expected in marital relationship	Low	Varies	High	High			Low	Low	Low	Low
12. Amount of personal development is valued	Varies	High	Very high			Varies	Varies	Varies	Varies	Low
13. Amount of involvement with kin	Very high	High		Low		Low	High	Very high		High
14. Intensity of marital bonds	Very high	Low	High	Usually high		Very low	High	High	Varies	Usually high

From Burr, Wesley R. *Successful Marriage: A Principles Approach.* Homewood, Ill.: Dorsey Press, 1976. pp. 22-23. Reproduced by permission of the author and the publisher.

*"Varies" means that there is considerable variation in this style of marriage on this particular dimension. Some want the marriage to be one way and some another.
†Column is left blank if the trait is not a distinguishing characteristics of a particular style of marriage and if the literature describing the style of marriage doesn't necessarily state that there is variation on this dimension.

conjugal role-relationship as described by upper-lower-social-class couples. The balance of the chapter from which the reprinted excerpt has been taken illustrates all three types of marital relationships in each of the social classes studied.

The next reading in this section by O'Neill and O'Neill (5), explains an alternative which continues to receive considerable professional attention (Leopard and Wachowiak, 1977). Even now, six years after O'Neill and O'Neill's book (1972) was published and became a best-seller, professionals and the public are still discussing the concepts involved in their theory of open marriage.

The remainder of the marriage types given by Burr are fairly self-explanatory. Interested readers are referred to Burr (1976), Gordon (1972), and Smith and Smith (1974) for additional information regarding specific alternatives.

Although Burr's listing is one of the most complete tabulations available, it excludes one important dimension that relates to a variety of marital alternatives. There is no mention made, in Burr's formulation, of the job or career commitments of either spouse. This appears to be a serious omission; however, there is a large body of research literature, recently completed, which examines traditional one-income families (9), two-person, single-career families (Papanek, 1973), two-income families (Burke and Weir, 1976; Ridley, 1973), and dual-career families. Due to present economic and social conditions, there has been a decline in the percentage of single-income families, while at the same time, the number of dual-career families has been increasing. The last reading in this section, an article by Rapoport and Rapoport that deals with dual-career marriage, illustrates the importance of alternatives within marriage and is representative of the numerous marriage types based on the employment status of one or both spouses (6). These authors have also written a monograph that includes case studies of dual-career families (Rapoport and Rapoport, 1971).

In a more recent article, Rapoport, Rapoport, and Thiessen (1974) have built on Young and Wilmott's (1973) concept of the symmetrical family. According to their research, the combination of the orientations of husbands and wives demonstrated a "six-fold typology of symmetry, ranging from low symmetry couples (whose pattern is the conventional one—husband 'career oriented,' wife 'traditional') to high symmetry (husband 'family oriented,' wife 'integrated')" (Rapoport, et al., 1974:590).

Ryder has also contributed to the study of marriage typologies. From interviews with 200 young couples, he derived 21 marriage patterns and organized them on five dimensions, which led to a topography of early marriage. This research was undertaken to "document and organize information about differences, not similarities" among marriages (1970:386).

Consequently, studies like Ryder's on the variety of marital relationships available may provide information relevant to the alternatives *within* the marital relationship, information of the type called for in 1975 by Clark Vincent, who, as president of the American Association of Marriage and Family Counselors, offered the following criticism of contemporary studies of alternative life-styles:

> There are two factors which are disturbing: The first is that the emphasis on alternate life styles is too limited—focusing on various patterns outside of marriage and ignoring far greater variety of alternative life styles within marriage. The second irritant is that so many of papers and discussions on alternative life styles seem to be overly concerned with the polarized issue of approval or disapproval of existing and emerging life styles. This implicit assumption of a gatekeeper function is not our domain, but may explain why we are five to ten years late in studying new or different life styles [Vincent, 1975:101].

FACTORS ASSOCIATED WITH THE MARITAL RELATIONSHIP

Marriage and family counselors have reported a variety of factors which contribute to the quality of the marital relationship. One such report (Burton, 1973) specified love, sexuality, money, aggression, and play as factors central to the marital relationship. This writer has modified the list by including readings relevant to love, sex, work, leisure, and stage of the family life cycle.

Although the concept of love has been written about for years, only recently has it been systematically researched. The article with which this section begins is by Lasswell and Lasswell *(7)*, who have based their work on Lee's (1974) styles of loving. This reading may well explain why so many people feel as though they are unloved or unloving, and it may also help to explain why many individuals feel that they are misallied, married to the wrong person (Cuber, 1974). A potential marital problem exists whenever the spouses' styles of loving are incompatible or the differences between their styles of loving are not understood.

The sexual relationship is often simplistically perceived as so closely associated with the marital relationship that it is assumed that the general nature of the marital relationship can be estimated from knowledge of the quality of the sexual relationship. However, Komarovsky has pointed out that "sexual satisfaction may turn out to be a more sensitive barometer of marital happiness in some classes than in others" (1962:111). She found that the degree of association between sexual adjustment and marital adjustment varied with the educational level of the blue-collar wives in her sample.

Considerable research evidence indicates that the nature of the sexual relationship is influenced by the social and cultural context within which the marriage exists. For example, social class is related to sexual expectations, values, and behaviors (Cuber, 1974; Komarovsky, 1962; Rainwater, 1964, 1965; Rubin, 1976). Rubin's (1976) study has shown that many working-class wives still tend to hold rather negative attitudes regarding sexual relations. Many of the attitudes voiced in this recent study are very much like those expressed in earlier studies by Komarovsky and Rainwater. Generally, in lower social-class groups, there is a higher level of segregation in the conjugal role-relationships, the sexual relationship is not close, and the wife does not find her marital sexual relations to be sexually fulfilling (Rainwater, 1964, 1965). In the lower classes, and particularly among the poor, sexual relations are more likely to be viewed as the man's pleasure and the woman's duty.

Cuber reported that slightly less than 20 percent of his upper-middle-class subjects maintained "a vigorous, meaningful, and fulfilling sex life even into their later years" (1974:31). He attributes the low percentage of sexually fulfilled individuals in this social strata to, in part, the high degree of career commitment among upper-middle-class males.

> *The commitment to career isn't all physical. Time, like money, can only be spent once. If a man spends 16 hours a day, and many do at his career and career-related activities, he not only isn't home much for "family life" but isn't the most scintillating husband, father, and lover when he is there [Cuber, 1974:18].*

Until recently, the sexual dimension of the marital relationship was not considered a suitable topic for conversation, let alone research. Alfred Kinsey and his associates (1948, 1953) made sex an appropriate topic for research, and Masters and Johnson's (1966) studies led to more extensive sexual research. The early 1970s were full of debate regarding female orgasmic response. *The Hite Report* (Hite, 1976) and other recent research should supply some answers to previously asked questions regarding female sexuality, and factual information regarding almost any aspect of marital or nonmarital sexuality can be found in a recently published volume by Sadock, Kaplan, and Freedman (1976). Arieti and Arieti (1977) have devoted one chapter to a discussion of the sexual dimension. The vast amount of literature regarding sexuality that has accumulated since the early 1960s suggests that we have moved from an avoidance of all discussion of sex to almost a preoccupation with the topic.

The overemphasis of the sexual dimension of marriage can create some misconceptions. According to Martin (1977), it is possible to read of happy, sexless marriages. There is considerable variation among sex drives and two people with low sex drives could live happily together with little or no coitus. In the presence of stable and secure marital bonds, a marriage does not necessarily become an unhappy one if a spouse becomes physically disabled and can no longer have sexual intercourse. In summary, Martin adds:

> *Neurotic mates whose lack of sexuality is a by-product of their illnesses may experience the marriage as happy because their needs are complementary. Careful observation of marriage reveals that it is an infinitely varied relationship, bringing homeostasis and a feeling of happiness not only to the mature and healthy, but also to the less mature if they happen to meet each other's needs [Martin, 1977:84].*

Some spouses who do not find sufficient sexual gratification within their marital relationship may find it outside of the marriage. Generally speaking, extramarital sex takes one of two forms. Either the spouses agree to extramarital sexual activity in the form of mate-swapping, or "swinging," in order to enhance the marital relationship, or one of the spouses enters a more secretive extramarital relationship, the affair (Cole and Spanier, 1973). Even though considerable research has focused on "swinging" as a part of experimental alternative life-styles, the affair is the more common form of extramarital sexual activity. Cuber concludes that "swinging" is "a lower middle-class, chiefly suburban-based phenomenon limited to couples in their late 20's to early 40's" and adds that, "the upper middle-class pattern, on the other hand, spawns endless anecdotes about men and their private secretaries or the buyer and assistant buyer" (Cuber, 1974:24). He indicates that the primary kind of extramarital relationship among upper-middle-class men begins as a nonerotic, empathic relationship with a coworker and then develops into a significant extramarital relationship.

Depending upon the couple's value orientation, extramarital sex may have a positive or negative influence on the marital relationship (Neubeck, 1969). Furthermore, Ellis (1969) has pointed out that involvement in extramarital relationships can be based on motivations that are either healthy or disturbed. Hunt (1969) discussed the prevalence of the desire for extramarital involvement in the form of sexual or romantic fantasies with people other than spouses.

> *There are some, of course, who neither feel the polygamous urge nor find themselves committing imaginary infidelities: they include the very few who remain thoroughly happy and satisfied in their marriages, and the much larger number who are so ruled by conscience that not only detailed fantasies but even desire itself are barred from consciousness. Such people, however, are in the minority; the majority of American husbands and wives do, whether only occasionally or very frequently, feel such yearnings and envision scenes of sex or romance involving themselves and people other than their mates [Hunt, 1969:27].*

It would appear that it takes more planning to become involved in "swinging" than to begin an affair. Henshel (1973), who studied the decision-making process involved in "swinging," found that it was usually the husband who suggested this experimental activity and that the wife became involved primarily to please him. However, it was the wife who was most often the one to suggest that the "swinging" activity cease. It appears that differential values of the sexes do play a significant role in sexual activity. Generally, the female tends to equate sex with love more than the male does. Therefore, the male can more often take part in sexual activity without feeling the need for an emotional or committed relationship. Recent sexual liberation explains the increasing numbers of women who are behaving more comfortably in multipartner situations (Rossi, 1977).

Because there is an extensive amount of literature dealing with the sexual aspects of marriage, it was difficult to choose one selection for inclusion in this section. Trainer's article was chosen because it examines sexual incompatibilities developmentally. He divides his discussion of sexual problems in marriage into those associated with the early, middle, and late phases of marriage *(8)*.

Although no readings are included regarding aggression, anger, and hostility in marriage, these negative emotional aspects, which can destroy the marital relationship, have been dealt with in a number of salient writings. Bach and Wyden's (1969) attempt to inform their readers on how to conduct fair fights with their lovers led many to the assumption that marriage partners should let their anger and hostility out. Yet, Straus (1974) found that verbal aggression was not a substitute for physical aggression. On the contrary, in his study of 385 couples, he found a positive correlation between verbal and physical aggression. The more verbal aggression expressed, the more physical aggression reported.

With knowledge of Straus's findings, Mace (1976) wrote of the potential destructiveness of mismanaging the intimate marital relationship. In such a close interpersonal relationship as marriage, the "deadly love-anger cycle" can create havoc. Those involved in intimate relationships are often in strong emotional states. It is to be expected that some emotional reactions will be positive and others negative. Instead of venting all of our anger, Mace suggests that one must 1) acknowledge the anger, 2) renounce it because it is inappropriate, and 3) ask one's spouse for help. He recommends the final step because it usually neutralizes the anger.

Given the high incidence of marital violence (Flynn, 1977; Gelles, 1976; Saunders, 1977), it appears that numerous modes of intervention are essential. Many marriage and family counselors are attempting to assist their clients in developing the skills necessary for handling marital conflict. For example, Strong (1975) presents a seven-step model for the resolution of marital conflict. Obviously, the intervention programs which are springing up in communities throughout this country are needed, and it is hoped that some evaluative research will indicate which approaches are most helpful.

Kemper and Reichler's article on work integration, marital satisfaction, and conjugal power has been included in this section because it centers on several issues of importance (9). They examine the relationship between the husband's work integration and marital satisfaction in families where the husband is the sole wage earner. When husbands were satisfied with their jobs, they and their wives were more likely to be satisfied with their marriages as well.

In another study (Burke and Weir, 1976), husband-and-wife pairs were questioned about their satisfaction with life, marriage, and job. Since 28 percent of the wives were employed outside of the home, comparisons were made between the husbands of working and nonworking wives, comparisons which have rarely been made (Axelson, 1970). Research findings showed that working wives were more satisfied with their marriages and their lives in general than nonworking wives. In contrast, husbands of working wives were less satisfied and performed less effectively than the husbands of nonworking wives.

Contrary to common belief, traditional marriage brings more rewards to men than it does to women. Bernard's (1972) study indicated that married men fared better physically, socially, and psychologically than did married women. Very similar findings, in relation to marital status, mental health, and mortality, have been reported by Gove (1972, 1973, 1974). Since wives usually have the less satisfying marital relationship as compared to their husbands, it is of interest to see the reverse occurring in two-income families (Burke and Weir, 1976). Perhaps, the wife involved in a traditional marriage lacks positive mental health because she has had to do most of the adjusting in the marriage (Bernard, 1964; Blood and Wolfe, 1960; Luckey, 1961). It appears that once women are employed, the husband-wife relationship becomes more symmetrical (Rapoport, Rapoport, and Thiessen, 1974), which allows wives to share the conjugal power more equally with their husbands.

Conjugal power was another factor examined by Kemper and Reichler (9). Blood (1976) has indicated that family power structure is one of a number of topics which has been overresearched. In his view, the many studies that have been carried out on this topic simply reconfirm again and again the findings of earlier studies, including those of his own classical study (Blood and Wolfe, 1960). In a review of the literature published during the 1960s which included power-structure studies, Safilios-Rothschild noted that although a large number of research studies had focused on this topic, there was a "lack of conceptual and methodological sophistication" (1970:539). Some progress, however, is being made, as evidenced in the monograph by Cromwell and Olson (1975). In a more recent work, by Rollins and Bahr, "it is assumed that: (1) power and control are social interaction constructs rather than attributes of individual persons; (2) power and control are relevant constructs only when a conflict exists between the goals of marriage partners; and (3) authority, resources, and power do not exist independently of perceptions" (1976:619).

Almost all marriage manuals and textbooks contain statements about money being a significant source of friction in today's marriages. "Money has both a real and a symbolic import. On the real basis, the woman has historically been dependent upon her husband for money, and he has in turn used it to control her and make her subservient" (Burton, 1973:1204). This background information on the importance of money in shaping the marital relationship may help to explain why research studies have found the employment status of the wife to be associated with the balance of power in the marital relationship.

There are some writings which deal more broadly with the relationship between the worlds of work and marriage. The interested reader will find that relevant literature has been reviewed comprehensively by Pleck (1977), Rapoport and Rapoport (1965), Renshaw (1976), and Safilios-Rothschild (1976). Of special interest will be the excellent research report by Kanter (1977).

The role of leisure in the marital relationship has been studied from a developmental perspective by Orthner *(10)*. Orthner's article has been included because his careful examination of leisure activity patterns and marital satisfaction over the marital career is one of the few contemporary studies dealing with leisure and marriage. The results from his sampling of upper-middle-class subjects clearly show that leisure patterns are associated with marital satisfaction but differentially for husbands and wives. He also found that period in the marital career was an important variable to control. Since it is well documented that leisure patterns vary significantly from one social-class group to the next (Cuber, 1974) and that lower-class groups are more likely to take part in sexually segregated activities (Rainwater, 1964, 1965), leisure activity patterns of lower-class couples may well contribute to the lower levels of marital satisfaction reported by women in the lower and working classes of our society.

The two remaining readings in this section, those by Glenn *(11)* and by Atchley *(12)*, have been chosen as examples of research that show how a couple's perceptions of marital and general life satisfaction may be influenced by the stage of the family life cycle it occupies. Although there is considerable disagreement among family scholars as to whether or not the concept of family life cycle should be discarded and replaced by the concept of marital careers (Feldman and Feldman, 1975), it is not necessary to become bogged down with questions of semantics. The purpose for including these readings—the desire to share some assessments of marriage at different points in the family development process—can be accomplished despite the debates. Through these readings one can learn something of the marital and life satisfaction of couples in the postparental stage *(11)* and of the life satisfactions of those who are widowed as compared to those who are married in the later years *(12)*.

Earlier studies of marital satisfaction over the life cycle results in conflicting findings. Blood and Wolfe (1960) reported a gradual decline in marital satisfaction over the years, whereas Burr (1970) and Rollins and Feldman (1970) generally found a decline in the earlier stages of the family life cycle followed by an increase during the later stages. In subsequent research (Rollins and Cannon, 1974), it was concluded that the U-shaped-curve description given originally by Rollins and Feldman was correct. This description despite the shortcomings of such research (Hicks and Platt, 1970), indicates that marital satisfaction is lowest during the child-rearing stages of the family life cycle. Recent research has linked the frequency of companionate activities positively with marital satisfaction and has also shown that the amount of companionship is negatively affected by the number of children and positively associated with social status (Miller, 1976), which brings us to the next area of family relationships to be examined.

REFERENCES

Alston, J. P., McIntosh, W. A., and Wright, L. M. Extent of interfaith marriages among white Americans. *Sociological Analysis 37* (1976):261-64.

Arieti, S., and Arieti, J. *Love can be found.* New York: Harcourt Brace Jovanovich, 1977.

Axelson, L. J. The working wife: Differences in perception among Negro and white males. *Journal of Marriage and the Family 32* (1970):457-64.

Bach, G. R., and Wyden, P. *The intimate enemy: How to fight fair in love and marriage.* New York: Morrow, 1969.

Bernard, J. The adjustments of married mates. In *Handbook of marriage and the family,* edited by H. T Christensen, pp. 675-739. Chicago: Rand McNally, 1964.

Bernard, J. *The future of marriage.* New York: World Publishing Company, 1972.

Blood, R. O. Research needs of a family life educator and marriage counselor. *Journal of Marriage and the Family 38* (1976):7-12.

Blood, R. O., Jr., and Wolfe, D. M. *Husbands and wives: The dynamics of married living.* New York: Free Press, 1960.

Blumberg, P. M., and Paul, P. W. Continuities and discontinuities in upper-class marriages. *Journal of Marriage and the Family 37* (1975):63-77.

Broderick, C. B. Man + woman: A consumer's guide to contemporary pairing patterns including marriage. *Human Behavior 1,* no. 4 (1972):8-15.

Burke, R. J., and Weir, T. Relationship of wives' employment status to husband, wife and pair satisfaction and performance. *Journal of Marriage and the Family 38* (1976):279-87.

Burr, W. R. Satisfaction with various aspects of marriage over the life cycle: A random middle class sample. *Journal of Marriage and the Family 26* (1970):29-37.

Burr, W. R. *Successful marriage: A principles approach.* Homewood, Ill.: Dorsey Press, 1976.

Burton, A. Marriage without failure. *Psychological Reports 32* (1973):1199-208.

Cole, C. L., and Spanier, G B. Induction into mate-swapping: A review. *Family Process 12* (1973):279-90.

Cromwell, R. E., and Olson, D. H., eds. *Power in families.* New York: Halsted Press, 1975.

Cuber, J. F. Sex in the upper middle class. *Medical Aspects of Human Sexuality 8,* no. 1 (1974):8-32.

DeYoung, G. E., and Fleischer, B. Motivational and personality trait relationships in mate selection. *Behavior Genetics 6* (1976):1-6.

Ellis, A. Healthy and disturbed reasons for having extramarital relations. In *Extramarital relations,* edited by G. Neubeck, pp. 153-61. Englewood Cliffs, N.J.: Prentice-Hall, 1969.

Feldman, H., and Feldman, M. The family life cycle: Some suggestions for recycling. *Journal of Marriage and the Family 37* (1975):277-84.

Flynn, J. P. Recent findings related to wife abuse. *Social Casework 8* (1977):13-20.

Fromm, E. *The art of loving.* New York: Harper and Row, 1956.

Gelles, R. J. Abused wives: Why do they stay. *Journal of Marriage and the Family 38* (1976):659-68.

Gordon, M., ed. *The nuclear family in crisis: The search for an alterantive.* New York: Harper and Row, 1972.

Gove, W. R. Adult sex roles and mental illness. *American Journal of Sociology 78* (1973):812-35.

Gove, W. R. The relationship between sex roles, marital status, and mental illness. *Social Focus 51* (1972):34-44.

Gove, W. R. Sex, marital status, and mortality. *American Journal of Sociology 79* (1974):45-67.

Greenfield, S. M. Love and marriage in modern America: A functional analysis. *Sociological Quarterly 6* (1965):361-77.

Henshel, A. M. Swinging: A study of decision making in marriage. *American Journal of Sociology 78* (1973):885-91.

Hicks, M. W., and Platt, M. Marital happiness and stability: A review of the research in the sixties. *Journal of Marriage and the Family 32* (1970):553-74.

Hite, W. *The Hite report: A nationwide study of female sexuality.* New York: Macmillan, 1976.

Hollingshead, A. B. Cultural factors in the selection of marriage mates. *American Sociological Review 15* (1950):619-27.

Hunt, M. *The affair: A portrait of extra-marital love in contemporary America.* New York: World, 1969.

Kanter, R. M. *Work and family in the United States: A critical review and agenda for research and policy.* New York: Russell Sage Foundation, 1977.

Kinsey, A. C., Pomeroy, W. B., and Martin, C. E. *Sexual behavior in the human male.* Philadelphia: W. B. Saunders, 1948.

Kinsey, A. C., Pomeroy, W. B., Martin, C. E., and Gebhard, P. H. *Sexual behavior in the human female.* Philadelphia: W. B. Saunders, 1953.

Komarovsky, M. *Blue-collar marriage.* New York: Random House, 1962.

Lee, J. A. The styles of loving. *Psychology Today 8,* no. 5 (1974):44-50.

Leopard, J. G., and Wachowiak, D. The open marriage O'Neills: An interview. *The Personnel and Guidance Journal 55* (1977):505-9.

Lewis, R. A. Social influences on marital choice. In *Adolescence in the life cycle: Psychological change and social context,* edited by S. E. Dragastin and G. H. Elder, pp. 211-25. New York: Wiley and Sons, 1975.

Luckey, E. B. Perceptional congruence of self and family concepts as related to marital interaction. *Sociometry 24* (1961):234-50.

Mace, D. Marital intimacy and the deadly love-anger cycle. *Journal of Marriage and Family Counseling 2* (1976):131-37.

Martin, P. A. The happy sexless marriage. *Medical Asects of Human Sexuality 11,* no. 5 (1977):75-84.

Masters, W. H., and Johnson, V. E. *Human sexual response.* Boston: Little, Brown, 1966.

Miller, B. C. A multivariate developmental model of marital satisfaction. *Journal of Marriage and the Family 38* (1976):643-57.

Monahan, T. P. An overview of statistics on interracial marriage in the United States, with data on its extent from 1963-1970. *Journal of Marriage and the Family 38* (1976):223-31.

Neubeck, G., ed. *Extramarital relations.* Englewood Cliffs, N. J.: Prentice-Hall, 1969.

Olson, D. H., and Dahl, N. S. *Inventory of marriage and family literature, 1975 & 1976, volume IV.* St. Paul: Family Social Science, 1977.

O'Neill, N., and O'Neill, G. *Open marriage: A new life style for couples.* New York: M. Evans, 1972.

Papanek, H. Men, women, and work: Reflections on the two-person career. *American Journal of Sociology 78* (1973):852-72.

Pleck, J. H. The work-family role system. *Social Problems 24* (1977):417-27.

Rainwater, L. *Family design.* Chicago: Aldine, 1965.

Rainwater, L. Marital sexuality in four cultures of poverty. *Journal of Marriage and the Family 26* (1964):457-66.

Rapoport, R., and Rapoport, R. N. *Dual-career families.* Harmondsworth, U. K.: Penguin, 1971.

Rapoport, R., and Rapoport, R. N. Work and family in modern society. *American Sociological Review 30* (1965):381-94.

Rapoport, R., Rapoport, R. N., and Thiessen, V. Couple symmetry and enjoyment. *Journal of Marriage and the Family 36* (1974):588-91.

Reiss, I. L. Toward a sociology of the heterosexual love relationship. *Marriage and Family Living 22* (1960):139-45.

Renshaw, J. R. An explanation of the dynamics of the overlapping worlds of work and family. *Family Process 15* (1976):143-65.

Ridley, C. A. Exploring the impact of work satisfaction and involvement on marital action when both partners are employed. *Journal of Marriage and the Family 35* (1973):229-37.

Rollins, B. C., and Bahr, S. J. A theory of power relationships in marriage. *Journal of Marriage and the Family 38* (1976):619-27.

Rollins, B. C., and Cannon, K. L. Marital satisfaction over the family life cycle: A reevaluation. *Journal of Marriage and the Family 36* (1974):271-82.

Rollins, B. C., and Feldman, H. Marital satisfaction over the family life cycle. *Journal of Marriage and the Family 26* (1970):20-28.

Rossi, A. S. A biosocial perspective on parenting. *Daedalus 106,* no. 2 (1977):1-31.

Rubin, L. B. *Worlds of pain: Life in the working class family.* New York: Basic Books, 1976.

Ryder, R. G. A topography of early marriages. *Family Process 9,* 1970, 385-402.

Sadock, B. J., Kaplan, H. I., and Freedman, A. M., eds. *The sexual experience.* Baltimore: Williams and Wilkins, 1976.

Safilios-Rothschild, C. Dual linkages between the occupational and family systems: A macrosociological analysis. *Signs 1,* nos. 3, 2 (1976):51-60.

Safilios-Rothschild, C. The study of family power structure: A review 1960-1969. *Journal of Marriage and the Family 32* (1970):539-52.

Saunders, D. G. Marital violence: Dimensions of the problem and modes of intervention. *Journal of Marriage and Family Counseling 3* (1977):43-52.

Scott, J. F. The American college sorority: Its role in class and ethnic endogamy. *American Sociological Review 30* (1965a):514-27.

Scott, J. F. Sororities and the husband game. *Trans-Action 26* (1965b):10-14.

Smith, J. R., and Smith, L. G., eds. *Beyond monogamy: Recent studies of sexual alternatives in marriage.* Baltimore: Johns Hopkins University Press, 1974.

Straus, M. A. Leveling, civility, and violence in the family. *Journal of Marriage and the Family 36* (1974):13-29.

Strong, J. R. A marital conflict resolution model: Redefining conflict to achieve intimacy. *Journal of Marriage and Family Counseling 2* (1975):269-76.

Vincent, C. E. Isms, schisms, and the freedom for differences. *Journal of Marriage and Family Counseling 1* (1975):99-110.

Young, M., and Willmott, P. *The symmetrical family.* New York: Pantheon, 1973.

mate selection

theories of mate selection

bruce k. eckland

This paper is devoted to a review and clarification of questions which both social and biological scientists might regard as crucial to an understanding of nonrandom mate selection. Owing to the numerous facets of the topic, the diverse nature of the criteria by which selection occurs, and the sharp differences in the scientific orientations of students who have directed their attention to the problem, it does not seem possible at this time to shape the apparent chaos into perfect, or even near-perfect, order and, out of this, develop a generalized theory of mate selection. Nevertheless, it is one of our objectives to systematize some of our thinking on the topic and consider certain gaps and weaknesses in our present theories and research.

Before embarking on this task, it would be proper to ask why the problem is worth investigating, a question which other speakers no doubt also will raise during the course of this conference. If the social and biological scientists had a better understanding of mate selection, what would happen to other parts of our knowledge or practice as a result? Despite the fact that our questions arise from quite different perspectives, there is at least one obvious point at which they cut across the various fields. This point is our common interest in the evolution of human societies, and assortative mating in this context is one of the important links between the physical and cultural components of man's evolution.

Looking first from the geneticists' side, at the core of the problem lies the whole issue of natural selection. Any divergence from perfect panmixia, i.e., random mating, splits the genetic composition of the human population into complex systems of subordinate populations. These may range from geographically isolated "races" to socially isolated caste, ethnic, or economic groups. Regardless of the nature of the boundaries, each group is viewed as a biological entity, differing statistically from other groups with respect to certain genes. To the extent that different mating groups produce more or fewer children, "natural" selection takes place.

In the absence of differential fertility, assortative mating alone does not alter the gene frequencies of the total population. Nevertheless, it *does* change the distribution and population variance of genes (Stern, 1960) and this, itself, is of considerable importance. Hirsch (1967), for example, has stated:

> As the social, ethnic, and economic barriers to education are removed throughout the world, and as the quality of education approaches a more uniformly high level of effectiveness, heredity may be expected to make an ever larger contribution to individual differences in intellectual functioning and consequently to success in our increasingly complex civilization. Universally compulsory education, improved methods of ability

assessment and career counseling, and prolongation of the years of schooling further into the reproductive period of life can only increase the degree of positive assortative mating in our population. From a geneticist's point of view our attempt to create the great society might prove to be the greatest selective breeding experiment ever undertaken. (p. 128)

Long-term mate selection for educability or intelligence increases the proportion of relevant homozygous genotypes which over successive generations *tends* to produce a biotic model of class structure in which a child's educability and, therefore, future social status are genetically determined. Since these propositions hold whether or not everyone has the same number of children with exact replacement, assortative mating would seem to have consequences just as relevant as any other mechanisms involving the genetic character of human societies.[1]

Also from the biological point of view, it is probable that assortative mating is becoming an increasingly important factor relative to others affecting the character of the gene pool. Infant mortality, for instance, does not appear to exert the same kind of selection pressure on the populations of Western societies today as it did a hundred, or even fifty, years ago. Likewise, accompanying the rise of mass education and spread of birth control information, fertility differentials appear to have narrowed markedly, especially in this country (Kirk, 1966). For example, the spread is not nearly as great as it once was between the number of children in lower and upper socioeconomic families. It is not altogether clear, of course, just how the relaxation of selection pressures of this kind would, in the long run, affect future generations. Yet, assuming, as some have suggested, that these trends will continue, then a broader understanding of the nature and causes of mate selection may eventually become one of the outstanding objectives of population geneticists. One reason is that the more the assortative mating, the greater the rate of genetic selection. If nearly all members of a society reproduce and most reproduce about the same number of children, and these in turn live to reproduce, it might then be just as important to know who mates with whom as to know who reproduces and how much.

The interest of social scientists in mate selection has been more uneven and much more diffuse. Some anthropologists undoubtedly come closest to sharing the evolutionary perspective of geneticists, as indicated by their work in a variety of overlapping areas which deal in one way or another with mating, e.g., genetic drift, hybridization, and kinship systems. In contrast, sociologists have been less sensitive to genetic theories. We share with others an evolutionary approach, but one that rests almost wholly on social and cultural rather than physical processes. Nonetheless, mate selection lies at the core of a number of sociological problems. These range, for example, from studies of the manner in which class endogamy is perpetuated from one generation to the next to studies in which endogamy is conceived as a function of marital stability. While sociologists have helped to ascertain many facts as well as having developed a few quasi-theories about assortative mating, it is rather difficult when reviewing our literature on the subject to distinguish between that which is scientifically consequential and that which is scientifically trivial. The general orientation of social scientists, in any case, is far from trivial and can be used instructively in the region of mate selection and in ways heretofore neglected by population geneticists. Some of their "theories" will be reviewed later in this paper.

EVOLUTION IN PARALLEL AND INTERACTION

Differences in the basic theoretical orientations of the social and biological sciences with respect to human evolution and assortative mating perhaps can best be understood in terms of the set of diagrams that follow. Fig. 1 illustrates the usual manner in which investigators in either field approach their subject matter. The course of human development is traced on separate but parallel tracks. Some textbooks and elementary courses in sociology begin with a brief treatment of genetics, but it is soon forgotten. In a like manner, students in a course in genetics are told that the expression of the genetic character of an individual depends largely on environmental influences, after which no further reference to environment seems to be necessary (Caspari, 1967).

Evolution viewed in parallel has allowed each field to articulate its own theories and perspectives. Mate selection is only one case in point, but a good one. The anthropologist or sociologist typically begins with some universal statement to the effect that in no society is mate selection unregulated and then he may proceed to analyze the cultural controls that regulate the selection process. As he has defined his problem, there perhaps has been no need to consider physiological processes. The geneticist, on the other hand, typically introduces the topic with some statement about how mate selection alters the proportion of heterozygotes in the population (as we have done) and then proceeds to a discussion of allele frequencies of consanguinity. Becuase he is concerned almost exclusively with the nature of the genetic material, he does not care, for example, why tall people seem to prefer to marry tall people. I doubt that sociologists especially care either. There are, however, traits far more relevant than these, like education, which serve as a basis of assortative mating and to which sociologists have given considerable attention and the geneticists relatively little.

The gap about which I am speaking also can be illustrated by the manner in which some geneticists define assortative mating. To repeat a definition which appeared recently in the *Eugenics Quarterly*, assortative mating is "the tendency of marriage partners to resemble one another as a result of preference or choice" (Post, 1965). The reference to individual "preference or choice" illustrates one of the major weaknesses in the geneticist's understanding of the nature of culture and society. (It is not just this particular statement that is troublesome, but many others like it throughout the literature.)

Mate selection is *not* simply a matter of preference or choice. Despite the increased freedom and opportunities that young people have to select what they believe is the "ideal" mate, there are a host of factors, many *well* beyond the control of the individual, which severely limit the number of eligible persons from which to choose. As unpalatable as this proposition may be, it rests on a rather large volume of data which suggests that the regulatory systems of society enforce in predictable ways a variety of norms and sometimes specific rules about who may marry whom. Perhaps the most important point I will have to make in this paper is that geneticists must begin to recast their assumptions about the nature of culture and society, just as sociologists must recast their thinking about genetics (Eckland, 1967).

Assuming that both geneticists and sociologists do reconsider their positions and assuming, too, that each discipline has a hold of some part of the truth, there still remains the unfilled gap in the kinds of knowledge needed to develop a set of interlocking theories between the social and biological sciences with regard to mate selection. I do not question that organic and cultural evolution can and, in many ways, must be studied as separate phenomena. The point is, however, that they do interact and this, too, should be studied; and to do so will require a much broader historical perspective than most geneticists and social scientists have exhibited up to now.

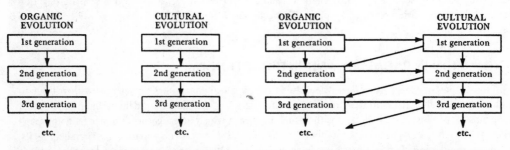

FIGURE 1. EVOLUTION IN PARALLEL.   **FIGURE 2. EVOLUTION IN INTERACTION.**

An interaction model of organic and cultural evolution must specify the precise nature of the relationships between the hereditary factors and environmental influences. Although certainly a very old idea, the notion of *interaction* has laid relatively dormant until recent years, probably largely due to the nature-nurture controversy and the racist arguments that covered most of the first half of the twentieth century. The expanded model in Fig. 2 suggests a more elaborate system of causal paths along which there is continuous feedback between the genetic and cultural tracks from one generation to the next. As before, we are dealing with the processes by which generational replacement and change occur. However, in addition to the duplication of most genes and most cultural traits in each succeeding generation, new patterns invariably emerge through the interaction of heredity and environment. Briefly, and with no intent on my part to intimate either purpose or consciousness, (*a*) genes restrict the possible range of man's development and (*b*) within these limits he alters his environment or cultural arrangements in such ways as to change the frequencies or distribution of genes in the next generation which (*c*) enables him to carry out further changes.

It is important to note here that the interaction of heredity and environment does not occur within the duration of a single generation, a point that social scientists, in particular, need to recognize. Holding for inspection a very short segment of the life span of a single cohort, as so often we do, it is not possible to observe, even to logically think about, heredity and environment in interaction. Within the span of one generation, the relationship appears only as a one-way process, with the genetic makeup of individuals determining the norms of reaction to the environment. The path from environment *back* to genetics which actually allows us to speak in terms of *inter*action appears only *between* generations, as in the above model. In other words, models of the sort abbreviated in Fig. 3 do not fit reality. The cultural environment, of course, may have an immediate and direct effect upon an individual's endocrine system, as well as other physiological and morphological structures, but it cannot, as far as we know, alter his genes. Environment can only alter their phenotypic expression and, owing to selective mating, the genes of one's progeny in the next generation.

We have now moved into a position whereby we might raise two rather crucial questions regarding the search for significant variables in mate selection, that is, significant in the context of an interaction model. The first is: What genotypes have social definitions attached to their behavioral manifestations or, conversely, what physical, personality, and social traits depend on our genes? The answer requires determining how much, if any, of the variance of a particular trait is due to heredity (and how much to environment). For example, taking the operational definition of intelligence we now employ, if none of the variance can be attributed to genetic sources, then no matter how intense assortative mating is for intelligence, we most certainly would exclude it from any further consideration in our model. Objections sometimes have been raised against partitioning the variance on the grounds that there is a strong interaction component in the development of most traits. It will be recalled, however, that our general model permits no interaction of this form between heredity and environment in the development of the intelligence or any other phenotype of an *individual*. Every character is determined during the lifetime of that individual, with genotypes determining part

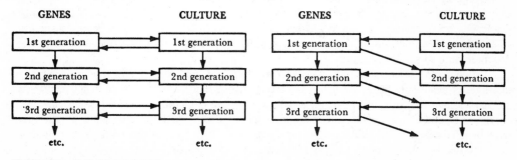

FIGURE 3. FALSE MODELS.

of the course of development and not the other way around. There are other problems to be encountered in any analysis of variance which attempts to sort out the hereditary component, but this is not one of them.

The second question is: What criteria for mate selection are *functionally* relevant within a particular population at a particular time? This question, of course, raises some long-standing issues in genetics regarding the "adaptive" quality of characteristics which are genetically variable. It appears, for example, that some traits like the O, A, B, and AB blood types for the most part are adaptively neutral or, at least, it is not known how they affect the biological or social fitness of their possessors in any significant way. Likewise, there are traits like eye color which apprently have no clear functional value and yet seem to be involved in the sorting which unites one mate with another. By this, I do not mean that the search for socially relevant traits in mate selection should be directed toward putting the science of genetics to the service of human welfare. Rather, it is my belief that the discovery of socially relevant biological dimensions of human variation is likely to be of the sort, such as intelligence, which may be treated simultaneously as Mendelian mechanisms in the reproductive process and as sorting and selecting mechanisms in the allocation of social status and in the maintenance of boundaries between social groups, the discovery of which may serve to further our general understanding of human evolution. Any delimiting, therefore, of the class of mate selection variables we eventually must take into account should deal, on the one hand, with traits which are understood in terms of genetic processes and partly in terms of social and other environmental processes and, on the other hand, with traits whose survival or social value is at least partly understood.

NOTES ON TERMINOLOGY

Two basic forms of nonrandom mate selection are *assortative* mating and *inbreeding.* Assortative mating usually encompasses all character-specific mate selection which would not be expected to occur by chance. Inbreeding, on the other hand, encompasses all mating where departures from perfect panmixia involve the relatedness or ancestry of individuals. While some authors have used the terms in essentially this manner (e.g., Spuhler, 1962; Post, 1965), others have not (e.g., Allen, 1965; Warren, 1966). The latter have not restricted assortative mating to refer only to character-specific situations but have included inbreeding as one of its forms. Another variation is that some authors have used the labels *genotypic* assortative mating to refer to inbreeding and *phenotypic* assortative mating to refer to the nonrandom, character-specific form (e.g., Fuller and Thompson, 1960). Also, the terms *consanguine* and *conjugal* sometimes are used to make the same distinction.

Attention to the rules governing the selection of a spouse has led to another set of terms: the first, representing conformity to the norms, called *agathogamy;* the second, involving prohibited deviations from the norms, called *cacogamy* (Merton, 1964). *Incest,* a special case of inbreeding, involves prohibited deviations from the rules controlling matings between closely related persons and is also a special case of cacogamy since the latter includes other forms of socially disapproved matings as well, such as *mesalliance,* a marriage with one of an inferior position. Special cases of mesalliance are *hypergamy* to denote the pattern wherein the female marries upward into a higher social stratum (the male marries the one in the inferior position) and *hypogamy* wherein the female marries downward into a lower social stratum.

In common use are the more general terms *endogamy* and *exogamy* which refer to in-group marriages of almost any kind. Inbreeding is a special case of endogamy; *hybridization* and *admixture* are special cases of exogamy in which "racial" features are the implied criteria. *Interbreeding* and *intermarriage* also have about the same meaning as above, except the latter term is more frequently used in reference to traits dealing with categories other than race, such as *interfaith* marriages. Miscegenation, another form of exogamy, is the term usually applied to interbreeding between white and Negro or other intergroup matings (legitimate and illegitimate) wherein the contractants have violated cultural proscriptions; and, in this respect, miscegenation is also a form of cacogamy, as well as a form of mesalliance.

Still another term commonly employed to describe assortative mating is *homogamy* which denotes something about the likeness or similarity of the married couples, with or without specific reference to any particular set of characteristics. Thus, one may speak in terms of racial homogamy or social homogamy or, simply, homogamous marriages. The antonym, *heterogamy,* is not widely used but could logically refer to mixed matings, the tendency toward random mating, or selection for "dissimilar" traits. The latter, however, is more often called *negative* assortative mating; all other forms are called *positive* assortative mating.

The above discussion probably comes close to exhausting the arsenal of terms we employ. However, with few exceptions, the concepts which arise from their meaning do not appear to be especially useful for classifying mating patterns in such a manner as to provide a sound basis for bridging the gap between the organic and social models presented earlier. It is quite probable that not only do we need more knowledge of assortative mating upon which to base more generalized theories, but we very well might find it necessary either to develop a new set of concepts (and terms) or to undertake a major revision of those now used. At present, they are confusing and often redundant, many do not appear particularly relevant to our problem, and few perhaps mean the same thing to both the geneticist and social scientist.

In the remainder of this paper, I shall review briefly some of the current theories of mate selection. By no means a complete review, I have neglected, for example, the very large body of work of anthropologists and population geneticists dealing with inbreeding. Studies of consanguineous marriages provide important information about genetic processes, such as the mutation load which is especially sensitive to inbreeding. Also reported in this literature, but not here, are a number of theories that attempt to explain the cultural development of kinship systems in which inbreeding is permitted or prescribed. However, most, although not all, of this work tends to deal with small populations which have been isolated for many generations. It is not convenient for explaining assortative mating in large, relatively open, and highly mobile cultures. The following discussion, therefore, involves a search for those psychological and structural features which best show how assortative mating operates in contemporary societies.

INDIVIDUALISTIC THEORIES

The disappearance of unilineal kinship systems in Western societies has led to a decline of kinship control over mate selection. The resulting freedom which young people now enjoy has brought about an enormously complex system. No doubt, the selection process actually begins long before the adolescent's first "date." Moreover, under conditions of serial monogamy where it is possible to have many wives but only one at a time, the process for some probably never ends. Determining the "choice" are a myriad of emotional experiences and it is these experiences, along with a variety of subconscious drives and needs, upon which most psychological and other "individualistic" theories are based.

The Unconscious Archetype

Some of the earliest and perhaps most radical theories of mate selection suggested that what guides a man to choose a woman (it was seldom thought to be the other way around) is instinct. Scholars believed that there must be for each particular man a particular woman who, for reasons involving the survival of the species, corresponded most perfectly with him. A modern rendition of the same idea is Carl Jung's belief that falling in love is being caught by one's "anima." That is, every man inherits an anima which is an "archetypal form" expressing a particular female image he carries within his genes. When the right woman comes along, the one who corresponds to the archetype, he instantly is "seized" (Evans, 1964). However, no one, as far as we know, has actually discovered any pure biologically determined tendencies to assortative mating.

The Parent Image

A psychoanalytic view, based on the Oedipus configuration, has been that in terms of temperament and physical appearance one's ideal mate is a parent substitute. The boy, thus, seeks someone like his mother and the girl seeks someone like her father. While it admittedly would seem reasonable to expect parent images to either encourage or discourage a person marrying someone like his parent, no clear evidence has been produced to support the hypothesis. Sometimes striking resemblances between a man's wife and his mother, or a woman's husband and her father, have been noted. Apparently, however, these are only "accidents," occurring hardly more frequently than expected by chance.

Like Attracts Like

Another generally unproven assumption, at least with respect to any well-known personality traits, involves the notion that "likes attract." Cattell and Nesselroade (1967) recently found significant correlations between husband and wife on a number of personality traits among both stably and unstably married couples. The correlations, moreover, were substantially higher (and more often in the predicted direction) among the "normal" than among the unstably married couples. As the authors admit, however, it was not possible to determine whether the tendency of these couples to resemble each other was the basis for their initial attraction ("birds of a feather flock together") or whether the correlations were simply an outgrowth of the marital experience. Although the ordering of the variables is not clear, the evidence does tend to suggest that the stability of marriage and, thus the number of progeny of any particular set of parents, may depend to some extent on degrees of likeness.

The Principle of Complementary Needs

Probably as old as any other is the notion that "opposites attract"; for example, little men love big women, or a masochistic male desiring punishment seeks out a sadistic female who hungers to give it. Only in the past twenty years has a definitive theory along these lines been formulated and put to empirical test. This is Winch's theory of complementary needs which hypothesizes that each individual seeks that person who will provide him with maximum need gratification. The specific need pattern and personality of each partner will be "complementary" (Winch, 1958). Accordingly, dominant women, for example, would tend to choose submissive men as mates rather than similarly dominant or aggressive ones. The results of a dozen or so investigations, however, are inconclusive, at best. More often than not, researchers have been unable to find a pattern of complementary differences. No less significant than other difficulties inherent in the problem is the discouraging fact that the correlation between what an individual thinks is the personality of his mate and the actual personality of his mate is quite small (Udry, 1966). Nevertheless, the theory that either mate selection or marital stability involves an exchange of interdependent behaviors resulting from complementary rather than similar needs and personalities is a compelling idea and perhaps deserves more attention.

No firm conclusions can yet be reached about the reasons for similarity (or complementariness) or personality and physical traits in assortative mating. (Even the degree of association or disassociation on most personality characteristics is largely unknown.) To state that "like attracts like" or "opposites attract," we know are oversimplifications. Moreover, few attempts to provide the kinds of explanations we seek have thus far stood up to empirical tests.

SOCIOCULTURAL THEORIES

In a very general way, social homogamy is a critical point in the integration or continuity of the family and other social institutions. It is a mechanism which serves to maintain the status quo and conserve traditional values and beliefs. And, because marriage itself is such a vital institution, it is not too difficult to understand why so many of the social characteristics which are important variables generally in society, such as race, religion, or class, are also the important variables in mate selection. Thus, most studies in the United States report a very high rate, over 99%, for racial endogamy, an overall rate perhaps as high as 90% for religious homogamy, and moderately high rates, 50% to 80% for class homogamy, the exact figures depending on the nature of the index used and the methods employed to calculate the rate.

One possible way of illustrating the conserving or maintenance function of social homogamy in mate selection is to try to visualize momentarily how a contemporary society would operate under conditions of *random* mating. Considering their proportions in the population, Negroes actually would be more likely to marry whites than other Negroes, Catholics more often than not would marry Protestants, and a college graduate would be more apt to marry a high school dropout than to marry another college graduate. In a like manner, about as often as not, dull would marry bright, old would marry young, Democrats would marry Republicans, and teetotalers would marry drinkers. What would be the end result of this kind of social heterogamy? A new melting pot, or chaos?

It seems that, in the absence of "arranged marriages," a variety of controls govern mate selection and, in the process, substantially reduce the availability of certain individuals as potential mates. Many structures in society undoubtedly carry out these functions, sometimes in quite indirect ways, such as, the subtle manner in which the promotion of an "organization man" may be based, in part, on how well his mate's characteristics meet the qualifications of a "company wife." Thus, despite the "liberation" of mate selection and the romantic ideals of lovers who are convinced that social differences must not be allowed to stand in their way, probably one of the most important functions of both the elaborate "rating and dating" complex and the ceremonial "engagement" is to allow a society to make apparent who may "marry upward" and under what conditions exogamy is permitted. We are referring here, then, not merely to a society's control over the orderly replacement of personnel, but to its integration and the transmission of culture as well.

Rather than reviewing any very well-formulated theories (since there may be none) in the remaining discussion, I have attempted to touch upon a fairly broad range of conditions under which homogamy, as a social fact, relates to other aspects of contemporary societies.

Propinquity and Interaction

Whether we are speaking about place of residence, school, work, or such abstruse features of human ecology as the bus or streetcar routes along which people travel, propinquity obviously plays a major part in mate selection since, in nearly all cases, it is a precondition for engaging in interaction. (The mail-order bride, for instance, is one of several exceptions.) A person usually "selects" a mate from the group of people he knows. Findings which illustrate the function of distance have been duplicated in dozens of studies. In Columbus, Ohio, it was once found that more than half of the adults who had been married in that city had actually lived within sixteen blocks of one another at the time of their first date (Clarke, 1952). Cherished notions about romantic love notwithstanding, the chances are about 50-50 that the "one and only" lives within walking distance (Kephart, 1961).

As many authors have pointed out, people are not distributed through space in a random fashion. In fact, where people live, or work and play, corresponds so closely with one's social class (and race) that it is not quite clear whether propinquity, as a factor in mate selection, is simply a function of class endogamy or, the other way around, class endogamy is a function of propinquity. Ramsøy's (1966) recent attempt to resolve this issue, I want to note, misses the mark almost completely. Investigating over 5,000 couples living in Oslo, Norway, she concludes that propinquity and social homogamy are "totally independent of one another" and, therefore, rejects the long-standing argument that "residential segregation of socioeconomic and cultural groups in cities represents a kind of structural underpinning both to propinquity in mate selection and to homogamy." More specifically, the author shows that "couples who lived very near one another before marriage were no more likely to be of the same occupational status than couples who lived at opposite sides of the city." This is astonishing, but misleading. The author equated the social status of the bride and, implicitly, her social class origin with *her* occupation at the time of marriage. No socioeconomic index other than the bride's occupation unfortunately was known to the investigator and, thus, it was a convenient although poorly considered jump to make. To most sociologists, it should be a great surprise to find in any Western society, including Norway, that the occupations young women hold before marriage give a very clear indication of their social status, relative either to the occupational status of men they marry or to their own places of residence.

Exchange Theory

An explanation often cited in the literature on mate selection, as well as in that on the more general topic of interpersonal attraction, deals in one form or another with the principle of exchange. A Marxian view, marriage is an exchange involving both the assets and liabilities which each partner brings to the relationship. Thus, a college-educated woman seldom brings any special earning power to the marriage, but rather she typically enters into contract with a male college graduate for whom her diploma is a social asset which may benefit his own career and possibly those of his children. In exchange, he offers her, with a fair degree of confidence, middle-class respectability. Norms of reciprocity might also help to explain the finding that most borderline mentally retarded women successfully marry and even, in some cases, marry upward, if they are physically attractive. This particular theory, however, has not been well-developed in regard to mate selection, despite its repeated usage. Also, it may be a more appropriate explanation of deviations from assortative mating or instances of negative mate selection than of positive selection.

Values and Belief Patterns

In contrast to the inconclusive evidence regarding assortative mating in terms of personality characteristics, numerous studies do indicate that married couples (and engaged couples) show far more consensus on various matters than do randomly matched couples. Even on some rather generalized values, as in the area of aesthetics or economics, social homogamy occurs. Apparently, our perception that other persons share with us the same or similar value orientations and beliefs facilitates considerably our attraction to them (Burgess and Wallin, 1943).

The importance of norms and values in mate selection, part of the social fabric of every society, also can be illustrated in a more direct way by looking at some of the specific sanctions that we pass along from generation to generation. Without really asking why, children quite routinely are brought up to believe that gentlemen prefer blondes (which may be only a myth perpetuated by the cosmetic industry), that girls should marry someone older rather than younger than themselves (which leaves most of them widows later on), and that a man should be at least a little taller than the woman whom he marries (which places the conspicuously tall girl at an enormous disadvantage). Simple folkways as such beliefs presently are, they nevertheless influence in predictable ways the "choice" of many individuals.

Social Stratification and Class Endogamy

We have already noted that the field of eligible mates is largely confined to the same social stratum to which an individual's family of orientation belongs. Social-class endogamy not only plays a significant part in the process of mate selection, it may also help to explain other forms of assortative mating. For example, part of the reason why marriage partners or engaged couples share many of the same values and beliefs no doubt is because they come from the same social backgrounds.

There are at least five explanations which can be offered for the persistence of class endogamy, each of which sounds reasonable enough and probably has a hold on some part of the truth.

First, simply to turn the next to last statement around, persons from the same class tend to marry *because* they share the same values (which reflect class differences) and not because they are otherwise aware or especially concerned about each other's background.

Second, during the period of dating and courtship most young people reside at the home of their parents. (Excluded here, of course, are the large minority in residential colleges and those who have left both school and home to take an apartment near their place of work.) The location of parental homes reflects the socioeconomic status of the family and is the general basis for residential segregation. With respect to both within and between communities, the pattern of segregation places potential mates with different backgrounds at greater distances than those with similar backgrounds. Thus, to the extent that the function of distance (or propinquity) limits the field of eligibles, it also encourages class endogamy by restricting class exogamy.

Third, class endogamy in some cases is simply a function of the interlocking nature of class and ethnicity. A middle-class Negro, for example, probably is prevented from an exogamous marriage with a member of the upper-class not so much because class barriers block it but because he (or she) is Negro. The majority of the eligible mates in the class above are whites and, in this instance, what appears to be class endogamy is really racial endogamy.

Fourth, ascriptive norms of the family exert a great deal of pressure on persons, especially in the higher strata, to marry someone of their "own kind," meaning the same social level. The pressures that parents exert in this regard sometimes are thought to have more than anything else to do with the process and certainly are visible at nearly every point at which young people come into meaningful contact with one another. Norms of kinship regarding the future status of a child may be involved, for example, in the parent's move to the right community, sending a child to a prep school, or seeing that he gets into the proper college.

Fifth, and an increasingly convincing argument, even as the structure of opportunities for social mobility open through direct competition within the educational system, class endogamy persists owing to the educational advantages (or disadvantages) accrued from one's family of orientation. Most colleges, whether commuter or residential, are matrimonial agencies. As suggested earlier, despite whatever else a woman may gain from her (or, more often, her parents') investment in higher education, the most important thing she can get out of college is the proper husband or at least the credentials that would increase her bargaining power in an exchange later on. Given the fact that men generally confer their status (whether achieved or ascribed) upon women and not the other way around (female proclamations to the contrary notwithstanding), marriage as a product of higher education has far more functional value for women than vocational or other more intrinsic rewards.

To carry this argument a bit further, access to college depends in large measure on the academic aptitude (or intelligence) of the applicants. Moreover, the hierarchical ordering of colleges which is based on this selectivity has led to a system of higher education which, in many ways, replicates the essential elements of the class structure. Differentiating those who go to college from those who do not, as well as where one goes to college, are *both* aptitude and social class. These two variables correspond so closely that despite the most stringent policies at some universities where academic aptitude and performance are the central criteria for admissions and where economic aid is no longer a major factor, students still come predominately from the higher socioeconomic classes. For whatever the reason, genetic and environmental, this correspondence facilitates the intermarriage of individuals with similar social backgrounds, especially on American campuses where the sex ratio has been declining. It is interesting to note in this context that Warren's recent study of a representative sample of adults showed that roughly half of the similarity in class backgrounds of mates was due to assortative mating by education (Warren, 1966).

Ethnic Solidarities

While intermarriage is both a cause and consequence in the assimilation of the descendants of different ethnic origin, various writers claim that the American "melting pot" has failed to materialize. Religious and racial lines, in particular, are far from being obliterated. In fact, the very low frequency of exogamous marriages across these lines itself underscores the strength of the cleavages. Most authors also agree that nationality is not as binding as either race or religion as a factor in mate selection. Nation-type solidarities are still found among some urban groups (Italian and Poles) and rural groups (Swedes and Finns), but our public school system and open class structure have softened considerably what were once rather rigid boundaries. There is some evidence, too, that religious cleavages have been softening somewhat, and perhaps are continuing to soften as the functions of this institution become increasingly secular and social-problem oriented. On the other hand, racial boundaries, from the view of mate selection, appear to be as binding today as at any previous point in history; at least I have found no evidence to the contrary. The gains that Negroes have made in the schools and at the polls during the past ten years apparently have not softened the color line with respect to intermarriage.

Explanations of racial endogamy in America, some of which would take us back several centuries in time, are too varied to discuss here. It might be well to point out, however, that cultural and even legal prohibitions, probably have relatively little to do with the present low rate of interracial marriage. As one author has stated, "the whole structure of social relationships between whites and Negroes in the United States has been organized in such a way as to prevent whites and Negroes from meeting, especially under circumstances which would lead to identifying each other as eligible partners. . . . Under these circumstances, the few interracial marriages which do occur are the ones which need explaining" (Udry, 1966).

For the population geneticist, too, it would seem that the deviant cases are the ones which require attention. Elsewhere I have suggested, for example, that genes associated with intelligence may simply drift across the white and Negro populations since it appears that only certain morphological features, like skin color, actually operate to maintain the color line (Eckland, 1967). In other words, if the skin of an individual with Negro ancestry is sufficiently light, he may "pass" (with no strings attached) into the white population. Even just a lighter-than-average complexion "for a Negro" probably enhances his chances of consummating what we socially define as an "interracial" marriage. In neither the first or second case, however, is intelligence necessarily involved.

If intelligence *were* associated in any predictable way with racial exogamy, the drift would not be random and we would then have a number of interesting questions to raise. For instance, do only the lighter *and* brighter pass, and, if so, what effect, if any, would this be likely to have on the character of the Negro gene pool? What, too, is the character of the inflow of genes from the white population? We do know that the great majority of legally consummated interracial marriages involve Negro men and white women. Does this information provide any clues? And, what about the illegitimate progeny of white males and Negro prostitutes? How often are they placed for adoption in white households and with what consequences? Before taking any of these questions too seriously, we would want to have many more facts. For obvious reasons, our knowledge is extremely meager.

PRECAUTIONARY NOTES

In conclusion, five brief comments may be made upon the present state of research and theories of mate selection as revealed in the foregoing discussion.

First, there is a great deal of evidence of homogamous or assortative mating but relatively few theories to explain it and no satisfactory way of classifying its many forms.

Second, nearly all facts and theories regarding mate selection deal with engaged or married couples and hardly any attention has been given to illegitimacy (including adultery) and its relationship to assortative mating. It may be, such as in the case of miscegenation, that some of the most important aspects of mate selection occur outside the bonds of matrimony.

Third, our heavy emphasis upon courtship and marriage has obscured the fact that people often separate, divorce, and remarry. Mate selection may be a more or less continuous process for some individuals, affecting the character of the progeny of each new set of partners.

Fourth, the relationships between fertility and assortative mating still must be specified. Are there, for example, any patterns of assortative mating on certain traits, like education, which affect the number of children a couple will have?

Fifth, most of the factors in mate selection appear to covary. We discussed some of the more obvious problems in this regard, such as the relationship between residential segregation (propinquity) and class endogamy. It would appear that much more work of this sort will need to be done.

In regard to the last point, it would also appear that it is precisely here that social scientists, and sociologists in particular, may best serve the needs of population geneticists. Through the application of causal (chain) models and multivariate techniques, it may eventually be possible to sort out the relevant from the irrelevant and to specify in fairly precise terms not only the distribution of assortative mating in the social structure with regard to any particular trait, but also the ordering of variables and processes which restrict the field of eligibles.

FOOTNOTE

[1] I have attempted in the early part of this paper to place mate selection in an evolutionary perspective. The discussion later will focus on explanatory theories, treating assortative mating as the dependent variable. In another paper, I shall discuss in much greater depth than outlined here the social-evolutionary consequences of mate selection. See Bruce K. Eckland, "Evolutionary Consequences of Assortative Mating and Differential Fertility in Man," in Theodosius Dobzhansky (ed.), *Evolutionary Biology,* Vol. IV, Appleton-Century-Crofts, in press.

REFERENCES

Allen, Gordon. 1965. Random and nonrandom inbreeding. Eugen. Quart. 12:181-198.

Burgess, Ernest W., and Paul Wallin. 1943. Homogamy in social characteristics. Amer. J. Sociol. 49:109-124.

Caspari, Ernst. 1967. Genetic endowment and environment in the determination of human behavior: Biological viewpoint. Paper read at the annual meeting of the American Educational Research Association, February 17, 1967.

Cattell, Raymond B., and John R. Nesselroade. 1967. "Likeness" and "completeness" theories examined by 16 personality factor measures on stably and unstably married couples. (Advanced Publication No. 7.) The Laboratory of Personality and Group Analysis, University of Illinois.

Clarke, Alfred C. 1952. An examination of the operation of residential propinquity as a factor in mate selection. Amer. Sociol. Rev. 17:17-22.

Eckland, Bruce K. 1967. Genetics and sociology: A reconsideration. Amer. Sociol. Rev. 32:173-194.

Evans, Richard I. 1964. Conversations with Carl Jung. Van Nostrand, Princeton.

Fuller, J., and W. Thompson. 1960. Behavior genetics. Wiley, New York.

Hirsch, Jerry. 1967. Behavior-genetic, or "experimental," analysis: The challenge of science versus the lure of technology. Amer. Psychol. 22:118-130.

Kephart, William M. 1961. The family, society and the individual. Houghton Mifflin, Boston.

Kirk, Dudley. 1966. Demographic factors affecting the opportunity for natural selection in the United States. Eugen. Quart. 13:270-273.

Merton, Robert. 1964. Intermarriage and the social structure: Fact and theory, p. 128-152. *In* Rose L. Coser (ed.), The family: Its structure and functions. St. Martin's, New York.

Post, R. H. (ed.). 1965. Genetics and demography. Eugen. Quart. 12:41-71.

Ramsøy, Natalie Rogoff. 1966. Assortative mating and the structure of cities. Amer. Sociol. Rev. 51:773-786.

Spuhler, J. N. 1962. Empirical studies on quantitative human genetics, p. 241-252. *In* The use of vital and health statistics for genetics and radiation studies. United Nations and World Health Organization, New York.

Stern, Curt. 1960. Principles of human genetics. W. H. Freeman, San Francisco.

Udry, J. Richard. 1966. The social context of marriage. J. B. Lippincott, Philadelphia and New York.

Warren, Bruce L. 1966. A multiple variable approach to the assortative mating phenomenon. Eugen. Quart. 13:285-290.

Winch, Robert. 1958. Mate selection. Harper and Row, New York.

2   the theoretical importance of love

william j. goode

Because love often determines the intensity of an attraction[1] toward or away from an intimate relationship with another person, it can become one element in a decision or action.[2] Nevertheless, serious sociological attention has only infrequently been given to love. Moreover, analyses of love generally have been confined to mate choice in the Western World, while the structural importance of love has been for the most part ignored. The present paper views love in a broad perspective, focusing on the structural patterns by which societies keep in check the potentially disruptive effect of love relationships on mate choice and stratification systems.

TYPES OF LITERATURE ON LOVE

For obvious reasons, the printed material on love is immense. For our present purposes, it may be classified as follows:

1. Poetic, humanistic, literary, erotic, pornographic: By far the largest body of all literature on love views it as a sweeping experience. The poet arouses our sympathy and empathy. The essayist enjoys, and asks the reader to enjoy, the interplay of people in love. The storyteller—Bocaccio, Chaucer, Dante—pulls back the curtain of human souls and lets the reader watch the intimate lives of others caught in an emotion we all know. Others—Vatsyayana, Ovid, William IX Count of Poitiers and Duke of Aquitaine, Marie de France, Andreas Capellanus—have written how-to-do-it books, that is, how to conduct oneself in love relations, to persuade others to succumb to one's love wishes, or to excite and satisfy one's sex partner.[3]

2. Marital counseling: Many modern sociologists have commented on the importance of romantic love in America and its lesser importance in other societies, and have disparaged it as a poor basis for marriage, or as immaturity. Perhaps the best known of these arguments are those of Ernest R. Mowrer, Ernest W. Burgess, Mabel A. Elliott, Andrew G. Truxal, Francis E. Merrill, and Ernest R. Groves.[4] The antithesis of romantic love, in such analyses, is "conjugal" love; the love between a settled, domestic couple.

A few sociologists, remaining within this same evaluative context, have instead claimed that love also has salutary effects in our society. Thus, for example, William L. Kolb[5] has tried to demonstrate that the marital counselors who attack romantic love are really attacking some fundamental values of our larger society, such as individualism, freedom, and personality growth. Beigel[6] has argued that if the female is sexually repressed, only the psychotherapist or love can help her overcome her inhibitions. He claims further that one influence of love in our society is that it extenuates illicit sexual relations; he goes on to assert: "Seen in proper perspective, [love] has not only done no harm as a prerequisite to marriage, but it has mitigated the impact that a too-fast-moving and unorganized conversion to new socio-economic constellations has had upon our whole culture and it has saved monogamous marriage from complete disorganization."

In addition, there is widespread comment among marriage analysts, that in a rootless society, with few common bases for companionship, romantic love holds a couple together long enough to allow them to begin marriage. That is, it functions to attract people powerfully together, and to hold them through the difficult first months of the marriage, when their different backgrounds would otherwise make an adjustment troublesome.

3. Although the writers cited above concede the structural importance of love implicitly, since they are arguing that it is either harmful or helpful to various values and goals of our society, a third group has given explicit if unsystematic attention to its structural importance. Here, most of the available propositions point to the functions of love, but a few deal with the conditions under which love relationships occur. They include:

(1) An implicit or assumed descriptive proposition is that love as a common prelude to and basis of marriage is rare, perhaps to be found as a pattern only in the United States.

(2) Most explanations of the conditions which create love are psychological, stemming from Freud's notion that love is "aim-inhibited sex."[7] This idea is expressed, for example, by Waller who says that love is an idealized passion which develops from the frustration of sex.[8] This proposition, although rather crudely stated and incorrect as a general explanation, is widely accepted.

(3) Of course, a predisposition to love is created by the socialization experience. Thus some textbooks on the family devote extended discussion to the ways in which our society socializes for love. The child, for example, is told that he or she will grow up to fall in love with some one, and early attempts are made to pair the child with children of the opposite sex. There is much joshing of children about falling in love; myths and stories about love and courtship are heard by children; and so on.

(4) A further proposition (the source of which I have not been able to locate) is that, in a society in which a very close attachment between parent and child prevails, a love complex is necessary in order to motivate the child to free him from his attachment to his parents.

(5) Love is also described as one final or crystallizing element in the decision to marry, which is otherwise structured by factors such as class, ethnic origin, religion, education, and residence.

(6) Parsons has suggested three factors which "underlie the prominence of the romantic context in our culture": (a) the youth culture frees the individual from family attachments, thus permitting him to fall in love; (b) love is a substitute for the interlocking of kinship roles found in other societies, and thus motivates the individual to conform to proper marital role behavior; and (c) the structural isolation of the family so frees the married partners' affective inclinations that they are able to love one another.[9]

(7) Robert F. Winch has developed a theory of "complementary needs" which essentially states that the underlying dynamic in the process of falling in love is an interaction between (a) the perceived psychological attributes of one individual and (b) the complementary psychological attributes of the person falling in love, such that the needs of the latter are felt to be met by the perceived attributes of the former and *vice versa*. These needs are derived from Murray's list of personality characteristics. Winch thus does not attempt to solve the problem of why our society has a love complex, but how it is that specific individuals fall in love with each other rather than with someone else.[10]

(8)   Winch and others have also analyzed the effect of love upon various institutions or social patterns: Love themes are prominently displayed in the media of entertainment and communication, in consumption patterns, and so on.[11]

4. Finally, there is the cross-cultural work of anthropologists, who in the main have ignored love as a factor of importance in kinship patterns. The implicit understanding seems to be that love as a pattern is found only in the United States, although of course individual cases of love are sometimes recorded. The term "love" is practically never found in indexes of anthropological monographs on specific societies or in general anthropology textbooks. It is perhaps not an exaggeration to say that Lowie's comment of a generation ago would still be accepted by a substantial number of anthroplogists:

> *But of love among savages? . . . Passion, of course, is taken for granted; affection, which many travelers vouch for, might be conceded; but Love? Well, the romantic sentiment occurs in simpler conditions, as with us—in fiction. . . . So Love exists for the savage as it does for ourselves—in adolescence, in fiction, among the poetically minded.*[12]

A still more skeptical opinion is Linton's scathing sneer:

> *All societies recognize that there are occasional violent, emotional attachments between persons of opposite sex, but our present American culture is practically the only one which has attempted to capitalize these, and make them the basis for marriage. . . . The hero of the modern American movie is always a romantic lover, just as the hero of the old Arab epic is always an epileptic. A cynic may suspect that in any ordinary population the percentage of individuals with a capacity for romantic love of the Hollywood type was about as large as that of persons able to throw genuine epileptic fits.*[13]

In Murdock's book on kinship and marriage, there is almost no mention, if any, of love.[14] Should we therefore conclude that, cross-culturally, love is not important, and thus cannot be of great importance structurally? If there is only one significant case, perhaps it is safe to view love as generally unimportant in social structure and to concentrate rather on the nature and functions of romantic love within the Western societies in which love is obviously prevalent. As brought out below, however, many anthropologists have in fact described love *patterns*. And one of them, Max Gluckman,[15] has recently subsumed a wide range of observations under the broad principle that love relationships between husband and wife estrange the couple from their kin, who therefore try in various ways to undermine that love. This principle is applicable to many more societies (for example, China and India) than Gluckman himself discusses.

THE PROBLEM AND ITS CONCEPTUAL CLARIFICATION

The preceding propositions (except those denying that love is distributed widely) can be grouped under two main questions: What are the consequences of romantic love in the United States? How is the emotion of love aroused or created in our society? The present paper deals with the first question. For theoretical purposes both questions must be reformulated, however, since they implicitly refer only to our peculiar system of romantic love. Thus: (1) In what ways do various love patterns fit into the social structure, especially into the systems of mate choice and stratification? (2) What are the structural conditions under which a range of love patterns occurs in various societies? These are overlapping questions, but their starting point and assumptions are different. The first assumes that love relationships are a universal psychosocial possibility, and that different social systems make different adjustments to their potential disruptiveness. The second does not take love for granted, and supposes rather that such relationships will be rare unless certain structural factors are present. Since in both cases the analysis need not depend upon the correctness of the assumption, the problem may be chosen arbitrarily. Let us begin with the first.[16]

We face at once the problem of defining "love." Here, love is defined as a strong emotional attachment, a cathexis, between adolescents or adults of opposite sexes, with at least the components of sex desire and tenderness. Verbal definitions of this emotional relationship are notoriously open to attack; this one is no more likely to satisfy critics than others. Agreement is made difficult by value judgments: one critic would exclude anything but "true" love, another casts out "infatuation," another objects to "puppy love," while others would separate sex desire from love because sex presumably is degrading. Nevertheless, most of us have had the experience of love, just as we have been greedy, or melancholy, or moved by hate (defining "true" hate seems not to be a problem). The experience can be referred to without great ambiguity, and a refined measure of various degrees of intensity or purity of love is unnecessary for the aims of the present analysis.

Since love may be related in diverse ways to the social structure, it is necessary to forego the dichotomy of "romantic love—no romantic love" in favor of a continuum or range between polar types. At one pole, a strong love attraction is socially viewed as a laughable or tragic aberration; at the other, it is mildly shameful to marry without being in love with one's intended spouse. This is a gradation from negative sanction to positive approval, ranging at the same time from low or almost nonexistent institutionalization of love to high institutionalization.

The urban middle classes of contemporary Western society, especially in the United States, are found toward the latter pole. Japan and China, in spite of the important movement toward European patterns, fall toward the pole of low institutionalization. Village and urban India is farther toward the center, for there the ideal relationship has been one which at least generated love after marriage, and sometimes after betrothal, in contrast with the mere respect owed between Japanese and Chinese spouses.[17] Greece after Alexander, Rome of the Empire, and perhaps the later period of the Roman Republic as well, are near the center, but somewhat toward the pole of institutionalization, for love matches appear to have increased in frequency—a trend denounced by moralists.[18]

This conceptual continuum helps to clarify our problem and to interpret the propositions reviewed above. Thus it may be noted, first, that individual love relationships may occur even in societies in which love is viewed as irrelevant to mate choice and excluded from the decision to marry. As Linton conceded, some violent love attachments may be found in any society. In our own, the Song of Solomon, Jacob's love of Rachel, and Michal's love for David are classic tales. The Mahabharata, the great Indian epic, includes love themes. Romantic love appears early in Japanese literature, and the use of Mt. Fuji as a locale for the suicide of star crossed lovers is not a myth invented by editors of tabloids. There is the familiar tragic Chinese story to be found on the traditional "willowplate," with its lovers transformed into doves. And so it goes—individual love relationships seem to occur everywhere. But this fact does not change the position of a society on the continuum.

Second, reading both Linton's and Lowie's comments in this new conceptual context reduces their theoretical importance, for they are both merely saying that people do not *live by* the romantic complex, here or anywhere else. Some few couples in love will brave social pressures, physical dangers, or the gods themselves, but nowhere is this usual. Violent, self-sufficient love is not common anywhere. In this respect, of course, the U.S. is not set apart from other systems.

Third, we can separate a *love pattern* from the romantic love *complex*. Under the former, love is a permissible, expected prelude to marriage, and a usual element of courtship—thus, at about the center of the continuum, but toward the pole of institutionalization. The romantic love complex (one pole of the continuum) includes, in addition, an ideological prescription that falling in love is a highly desirable basis of courtship and marriage; love is strongly institutionalized.[19] In contemporary United States, many individuals would even claim that entering marriage without being in love requires some such rationalization as asserting that one is too old for such romances or that one must "think of practical matters like money." To be sure, both anthropologists and sociologists often exaggerate the

American commitment to romance;[20] nevertheless, a behavioral and value complex of this type is found here.

But this complex is rare. Perhaps only the following cultures possess the romantic love value complex: modern urban United States, Northwestern Europe, Polynesia, and the European nobility of the eleventh and twelfth centuries.[21] Certainly, it is to be found in no other major civilization. On the other hand, the *love pattern,* which views love as a basis for the final decision to marry, may be relatively common.

WHY LOVE MUST BE CONTROLLED

Since strong love attachments apparently can occur in any society and since (as we shall show) love is frequently a basis for and prelude to marriage, it must be controlled or channeled in some way. More specifically, the stratification and lineage patterns would be weakened greatly if love's potentially disruptive effects were not kept in check. The importance of this situation may be seen most clearly by considering one of the major functions of the family, status placement, which in every society links the structures of stratification, kinship lines, and mate choice. (To show how the very similar comments which have been made about sex are not quite correct would take us too far afield; in any event, to the extent that they are correct, the succeeding analysis applies equally to the control of sex.)

Both the child's placement in the social structure and choice of mates are socially important because both placement and choice link two kinship lines together. Courtship or mate choice, therefore, cannot be ignored by either family or society. To permit random mating would mean radical change in the existing social structure. If the family as a unit of society is important, then mate choice is too.

Kinfolk or immediate family can disregard the question of who marries whom, only if a marriage is not seen as a link between kin lines, only if no property, power, lineage honor, totemic relationships, and the like are believed to flow from the kin lines through the spouses to their offspring. Universally, however, these are believed to follow kin lines. Mate choice thus has consequences for the social structure. But love may affect mate choice. Both mate choice and love, therefore, are too important to be left to children.

THE CONTROL OF LOVE

Since considerable energy and resources may be required to push youngsters who are in love into proper role behavior, love must be controlled *before* it appears. Love relationships must either be kept to a small number or they must be so directed that they do not run counter to the approved kinship linkages. There are only a few institutional patterns by which this control is achieved.

1. Certainly the simplest, and perhaps the most widely used, structural pattern for coping with this problem is child marriage. If the child is betrothed, married, or both before he has had any opportunity to interact intimately as an adolescent with other children, then he has no resources with which to oppose the marriage. He cannot earn a living, he is physically weak, and is socially dominanted by his elders. Moreover, strong love attachments occur only rarely before puberty. An example of this pattern was to be found in India, where the young bride went to live with her husband in a marriage which was not physically consummated until much later, within his father's household.[22]

2. Often, child marriage is linked with a second structural pattern, in which the kinship rules define rather closely a class of eligible future spouses. The marriage is determined by birth within narrow limits. Here, the major decision, which is made by elders, is *when* the marriage is to occur. Thus, among the Murngin, *galle,* the father's sister's child, is scheduled to marry *due,* the mother's brother's child.[23] In the case of the "four-class" double-descent system, each individual is a member

of *both* a matri-moiety and a patri-moiety and must marry someone who belongs to neither; the four-classes are (1) ego's own class, (2) those whose matri-moiety is the same as ego's but whose patri-moiety is different, (3) those who are in ego's patri-moiety but not in his matri-moiety, and (4) those who are in neither of ego's moieties, that is, who are in the cell diagonally from his own.[24] Problems arise at times under these systems if the appropriate kinship cell—for example, parallel cousin or cross-cousin—is empty.[25] But nowhere, apparently, is the definition so rigid as to exclude some choice and, therefore, some dickering, wrangling, and haggling between the elders of the two families.

3. A society can prevent widespread development of adolescent love relationships by socially isolating young people from potential mates, whether eligible or ineligible as spouses. Under such a pattern, elders can arrange the marriages of either children or adolescents with little likelihood that their plans will be disrupted by love attachments. Obviously, this arrangement cannot operate effectively in most primitive societies, where youngsters see one another rather frequently.[26]

Not only is this pattern more common in civilizations than in primtive societies, but is found more frequently in the upper social strata. *Social* segregation is difficult unless it is supported by physical segregation—the harem of Islam, the zenana of India.[27]—or by a large household system with individuals whose duty it is to supervise nubile girls. Social segregation is thus expensive. Perhaps the best known example of simple social segregation was found in China, where youthful marriages took place between young people who had not previously met because they lived in different villages; they could not marry fellow-villagers since ideally almost all inhabitants belonged to the same *tsu.*[28]

It should be emphasized that the primary function of physical or social isolation in these cases is to minimize informal or intimate social interaction. Limited social contacts of a highly ritualized or formal type in the presence of elders, as in Japan, have a similar, if less extreme, result.[29]

4. A fourth type of pattern seems to exist, although it is not clear cut; and specific cases shade off toward types three and five. Here, there is close supervision by duennas or close relatives, but not actual social segregation. A high value is placed on female chastity (which perhaps is the case in every major civilization until its "decadence") viewed either as the product of self-restraint, as among the 17th Century Puritans, or as a marketable commodity. Thus love as play is not developed; marriage is supposed to be considered by the young as a duty and a possible family alliance. This pattern falls between types three and five because love is permitted before marriage, but only between eligibles. Ideally, it occurs only between a betrothed couple, and, except as marital love, there is no encouragement for it to appear at all. Family elders largely make the specific choice of mate, whether or not intermediaries carry out the arrangements. In the preliminary stages youngsters engage in courtship under supervision, with the understanding that this will permit the development of affection prior to marriage.

I do not believe that the empirical data show where this pattern is prevalent, outside of Western Civilization. The West is a special case, because of its peculiar relationship to Christianity, in which from its earliest days in Rome there has been a complex tension between asceticism and love. This type of limited love marked French, English, and Italian upper class family life from the 11th to the 14th Centuries, as well as 17th Century Puritanism in England and New England.[30]

5. The fifth type of pattern permits or actually encourages love relationships, and love is a commonly expected element in mate choice. Choice in this system is *formally* free. In their teens youngsters begin their love play, with or without consummating sexual intercourse, within a group of peers. They may at times choose love partners whom they and others do not consider suitable spouses. Gradually, however, their range of choice is narrowed and eventually their affections center on one individual. This person is likely to be more eligible as a mate according to general social norms, and as judged by peers and parents, than the average individual with whom the youngster formerly indulged in love play.

For reasons that are not yet clear, this pattern is nearly always associated with a strong development of an adolescent peer group system, although the latter may occur without the love pattern. One source of social control, then, is the individual's own teenage companions, who persistently rate the present and probable future accomplishments of each individual.[31]

Another source of control lies with the parents of both boy and girl. In our society, parents threaten, cajole, wheedle, bribe, and persuade their children to "go with the right people," during both the early love play and later courtship phases.[32] Primarily, they seek to control love relationships by influencing the informal social contacts of their children: moving to appropriate neighborhoods and schools, giving parties and helping to make out invitation lists, by making their children aware that certain individuals have ineligibility traits (race, religion, manners, tastes, clothing, and so on). Since youngsters fall in love with those with whom they associate, control over informal relationships also controls substantially the focus of affection. The results of such control are well known and are documented in the more than one hundred studies of homogamy in this country: most marriages take place between couples in the same class, religious, racial, and educational levels.

As Robert Wikman has shown in a generally unfamiliar (in the United States) but superb investigation, this pattern was found among 18th Century Swedish farmer adolescents, was widely distributed in other Germanic areas, and extends in time from the 19th Century back to almost certainly the late Middle Ages.[33] In these cases, sexual intercourse was taken for granted, social contact was closely supervised by the peer group, and final consent to marriage was withheld or granted by the parents who owned the land.

Such cases are not confined to Western society. Polynesia exhibits a similar pattern, with some variation from society to society, the best known examples of which are perhaps Mead's Manu'ans and Firth's Tikopia.[34] Probably the most familiar Melanesian cases are the Trobriands and Dobu,[35] where the systems resemble those of the Kiwai Papuans of the Trans-Fly and the Siuai Papuans of the Solomon Islands.[36] Linton found this pattern among the Tanala.[37] Although Radcliffe-Brown holds that the pattern is not common in Africa, it is clearly found among the Nuer, the Kgatla (Tswana-speaking), and the Bavenda (here, without sanctioned sexual intercourse).[38]

A more complete classification, making use of the distinctions suggested in this paper, would show, I believe, that a large minority of known societies exhibit this pattern. I would suggest, moreover, that such a study would reveal that the degree to which love is a usual, expected prelude to marriage is correlated with (1) the degree of free choice of mate permitted in the society and (2) the degree to which husband-wife solidarity is the strategic solidarity of the kinship structure.[39]

LOVE CONTROL AND CLASS

These sociostructural explanations of how love is controlled lead to a subsidiary but important hypothesis: From one society to another, and from one *class* to another within the same society, the sociostructural importance of maintaining kinship lines according to rule will be rated differently by the families within them. Consequently, the degree to which control over mate choice, and therefore over the prevalence of a love pattern among adolescents, will also vary. Since, within any stratified society, this concern with the maintenance of intact and acceptable kin lines will be greater in the upper strata, it follows that noble or upper strata will maintain stricter control over love and courtship behavior than lower strata. The two correlations suggested in the preceding paragraph also apply: husband-wife solidarity is less strategic relative to clan solidarity in the upper than in the lower strata, and there is less free choice of mate.

Thus it is that, although in Polynesia generally most youngsters indulged in considerable love play, princesses were supervised strictly.[40] Similarly, in China lower class youngsters often met their spouses before marriage.[41] In our own society, the "upper upper" class maintains much greater control than the lower strata over the informal social contacts of their nubile young. Even among the Dobu, where there are few controls and little stratification, differences in control exist at the extremes: a child betrothal may be arranged between outstanding gardening families, who try to prevent their youngsters from being entangled with wastrel families.[42] In answer to my query about this pattern among the Nuer, Evans-Pritchard writes:

You are probably right that a wealthy man has more control over his son's affairs than a poor man. A man with several wives has a more authoritarian position in his home. Also, a man with many cattle is in a position to permit or refuse a son to marry, whereas a lad whose father is poor may have to depend on the support of kinsmen. In general, I would say that a Nuer father is not interested in the personal side of things. His son is free to marry any girl he likes and the father does not consider the selection to be his affiar until the point is reached when cattle have to be discussed.[43]

The upper strata have much more at stake in the maintenance of the social structure and thus are more strongly motivated to control the courtship and marriage decisions of their young. Correspondingly, their young have much more to lose than lower strata youth, so that upper strata elders *can* wield more power.

CONCLUSION

In this analysis I have attempted to show the integration of love with various types of social structures. As against considerable contemporary opinion among both sociologists and anthropologists, I suggest that love is a universal psychological potential, which is controlled by a range of five structural patterns, all of which are attempts to see to it that youngsters do not make entirely free choices of their future spouses. Only if kin lines are unimportant, and this condition is found in no society as a whole, will entirely free choice be permitted. Some structural arrangements seek to prevent entirely the outbreak of love, while others harness it. Since the kin lines of the upper strata are of greater social importance to them than those of lower strata are to the lower strata members, the former exercise a more effective control over this choice. Even where there is almost a formally free choice of mate—and I have suggested that this pattern is widespread, to be found among a substantial segment of the earth's societies—this choice is guided by peer group and parents toward a mate who will be acceptable to the kin and friend groupings. The theoretical importance of love is thus to be seen in the sociostructural patterns which are developed to keep it from disrupting existing social arrangements.

FOOTNOTES

[1]On the psychological level, the motivational power of both love and sex is intensified by this curious fact: (which I have not seen remarked on elsewhere) Love is the most projective of emotions, as sex is the most projective of drives; only with great difficulty can the attracted person believe that the object of his love or passion does not and will not reciprocate the feeling at all. Thus, the person may carry his action quite far, before accepting a rejection as genuine.

[2]I have treated decision analysis extensively in an unpublished paper by that title.

[3]Vatsyayana, *The Kama Sutra,* Delhi: Rajkamal, 1948; Ovid, "The Loves," and "Remedies of Love," in *The Art of Love,* Cambridge, Mass.: Harvard University Press, 1939; Andreas Capellanus, *The Art of Courtly Love,* translated by John J. Parry. New York: Columbia University Press, 1941; Paul Tuffrau, editor, *Marie de France: Les Lais de Marie de France,* Paris L'edition d'art, 1925; see also Julian Harris, *Marie de France,* New York: Institute of French Studies, 1930, esp. Chapter 3. All authors but the first *also* had the goal of writing literature.

[4]Ernest R. Mowrer, *Family Disorganization,* Chicago: The University of Chicago Press, 1927, pp. 158-165; Ernest W. Burgess and Harvey J. Locke, *The Family,* New York: American Book, 1953, pp. 436-437; Mabel A. Elliott and Francis E. Merrill, *Social Disorganization,* New York: Harper, 1950, pp. 366-384; Andrew G. Truxal and Francis E. Merrill, *The Family in American Culture,* New York: Prentice-Hall, 1947, pp. 120-124, 507-509; Ernest R. Groves and Gladys Hoagland Groves, *The Contemporary American Family,* New York: Lippincott, 1947, pp. 321-324.

[5]William L. Kolb, "Sociologically Established Norms and Democratic Values," *Social Forces,* 26 (May, 1948), pp. 451-456.

[6]Hugo G. Beigel, "Romantic Love," *American Sociological Review,* 16 (June, 1951), pp. 326-334.

[7]Sigmund Freud, *Group Psychology and the Analysis of the Ego,* London: Hogarth, 1922, p. 72.

[8]Willard Waller, *The Family,* New York: Dryden, 1938, pp. 189-192.

[9]Talcott Parsons, *Essays in Sociological Theory,* Glencoe, Ill.: Free Press, 1949, pp. 187-189.

[10] Robert F. Winch, *Mate Selection,* New York: Harper, 1958.

[11] See, e.g., Robert F. Winch, *The Modern Family,* New York: Holt, 1952, Chapter 14.

[12] Robert H. Lowie, "Sex and Marriage," in John F. McDermott, editor, *The Sex Problem in Modern Society,* New York: Modern Library, 1931, p. 146.

[13] Ralph Linton, *The Study of Man,* New York: Appleton-Century, 1936, p. 175.

[14] George Peter Murdock, *Social Structure,* New York: Macmillan, 1949.

[15] Max Gluckman, *Custom and Conflict in Africa,* Oxford: Basil Blackwell, 1955, Chapter 3.

[16] I hope to deal with the second problem in another paper.

[17] Tribal India, of course, is too heterogeneous to place in any one position on such a continuum. The question would have to be answered for each tribe. Obviously it is of less importance here whether China and Japan, in recent decades, have moved "two points over" toward the opposite pole of high approval of love relationships as a basis for marriage than that both systems as classically described viewed love as generally a tragedy; and love was supposed to be irrelevant to marriage, i.e., noninstitutionalized. The continuum permits us to place a system at some position, once we have the descriptive data.

[18] See Ludwig Friedländer, *Roman Life and Manners under the Early Empire* (Seventh Edition), translated by A. Magnus, New York: Dutton, 1908, Vol. 1, Chapter 5, "The Position of Women."

[19] For a discussion of the relation between behavior patterns and the process of institutionalization, see my *After Divorce,* Glencoe, Ill.: Free Press, 1956, Chapter 15.

[20] See Ernest W. Burgess and Paul W. Wallin, *Engagement and Marriage,* New York: Lippincott, 1953, Chapter 7 for the extent to which even the engaged are not blind to the defects of their beloveds. No one has ascertained the degree to which various age and sex groups in our society actually believe in some form of the ideology.

Similarly, Margaret Mead in *Coming of Age in Samoa,* New York: Modern Library, 1953, rates Manu'an love as shallow, and though these Samoans give much attention to love-making, she asserts that they laughed with incredulous contempt at Romeo and Juliet (pp. 155-156). Though the individual sufferer showed jealousy and anger, the Manu'ans believed that a new love would quickly cure a betrayed lover (pp. 105-108). It is possible that Mead failed to understand the shallowness of love in our own society: Romantic love is, "in our civilization, inextricably bound up with ideas of monogamy, exclusiveness, jealousy, and undeviating fidelity" (p. 105). But these are *ideas* and ideology; *behavior* is rather different.

[21] I am preparing an analysis of this case. The relation of "courtly love" to social structure is complicated.

[22] Frieda M. Das, *Purdah,* New York: Vanguard, 1932; Kingsley Davis, *The Population of India and Pakistan,* Princeton: Princeton University Press, 1951, p. 112. There was a widespread custom of taking one's bride from a village other than one's own.

[23] W. Lloyd Warner, *Black Civilization,* New York: Harper, 1937, pp. 82-84. They may also become "sweethearts" at puberty; see pp. 86-89.

[24] See Murdock, *op. cit.,* pp. 53 ff. *et passim* for discussions of double-descent.

[25] One adjustment in Australia was for the individuals to leave the tribe for a while, usually eloping, and then to return "reborn" under a different and now appropriate kinship designation. In any event, these marital prescriptions did not prevent love entirely. As Malinowski shows in his early summary of the Australian family systems, although every one of the tribes used the technique of infant betrothal (and close prescription of mate), no tribe was free of elopements, between either the unmarried or the married, and the "motive of sexual love" was always to be found in marriages by elopement. B. Malinowski. *The Family Among the Australian Aborigines,* London: University of London Press, 1913, p. 83.

[26] This pattern was apparently achieved in Manus, where on first menstruation the girl was removed from her playmates and kept at "home"—on stilts over a lagoon—under the close supervision of elders. The Manus were prudish, and love occurred rarely or never. Margaret Mead, *Growing Up in New Guinea,* in *From the South Seas,* New York: Morrow, 1939, pp. 163-166, 208.

[27] See Das, *op. cit.*

[28] For the activities of the *tsu,* see Hsien Chin Hu, *The Common Descent Group in China and Its Functions,* New York: Viking Fund Studies in Anthropology, 10 (1948). For the marriage process, see Marion J. Levy, *The Family Revolution in Modern China,* Cambridge: Harvard University Press, 1949, pp. 87-107. See also Olga Lang, *Chinese Family and Society,* New Haven: Yale University Press, 1946, for comparisons between the old and new systems. In one-half of 62 villages in Ting Hsien Experimental District in Hopei, the largest clan included 50 per cent of the families; in 25 per cent of the villages, the two largest clans held over 90 per cent of the families; I am indebted to Robert M. Marsh who has been carrying out a study of Ching mobility partly under my direction for this reference: F. C. H. Lee, *Ting Hsien. She-hui K'ai-K'uang t'iao-ch'a,* Peiping: Chung-hua p'ing-min Chiao-yu ts'u-chin hui, 1932, p. 54. See also Sidney Gamble, *Ting Hsien: A North China Rural Community,* New York: International Secretariat of the Institute of Pacific Relations, 1954.

[29] For Japan, see Shidzue Ishimoto, *Facing Two Ways,* New York: Farrar and Rinehart, 1935, Chapters 6, 8; John F. Embree, *Suye Mura,* Chicago: University of Chicago Press, 1950, Chapters 3, 6.

[30] I do not mean, of course, to restrict this pattern to these times and places, but I am more certain of these. For the Puritans, see Edmund S. Morgan, *The Puritan Family,* Boston: Public Library, 1944. For the somewhat different practices in New York, see Charles E. Ironside, *The Family in Colonial New York,* New York: Columbia University Press, 1942. See also: A. Abram, *English Life and Manners in the Later Middle Ages,* New York: Dutton, 1913, Chapters 4, 10; Emily J. Putnam, *The Lady,* New York: Sturgis and Walton, 1910, Chapter 4; James Gairdner, editor, *The Paston Letters, 1422-1509,* 4 vols., London: Arber, 1872-1875; Eileen Power, "The Position of

Women," in C. G. Crump and E. F. Jacobs, editors, *The Legacy of the Middle Ages,* Oxford: Clarendon, 1926, pp. 414-416.

[31] For those who believe that the young in the United States are totally deluded by love, or believe that love outranks every other consideration, see: Ernest W. Burgess and Paul W. Wallin, *Engagement and Marriage,* New York: Lippincott, 1953, pp. 217-238. Note Karl Robert V. Wikman, *Die Einleitung Der Ehe. Acta Academiae Aboensis (Humaniora),* 11 (1937), pp. 127 ff. Not only are reputations known because of close association among peers, but songs and poetry are sometimes composed about the girl or boy. Cf., for the Tikopia, Raymond Firth, *We, the Tikopia,* New York: American Book, 1936, pp. 468 ff.; for the Siuai, Douglas L. Oliver, *Solomon Island Society,* Cambridge: Harvard University Press, 1955, pp. 146 ff. The Manu'ans made love in groups of three or four couples; cf. Mead, *Coming of Age in Samoa,, op. cit.,* p. 92.

[32] Marvin B. Sussman, "Parental Participation in Mate Selection and Its Effect upon Family Continuity," *Social Forces,* 32 (October, 1953), pp. 76-81.

[33] Wikman, *op. cit.*

[34] Mead, *Coming of Age in Samoa, op. cit.,* pp. 97-108; and Firth, *op. cit.,* pp. 520 ff.

[35] Thus Malinowski notes in his "Introduction" to Reo F. Fortune's *The Sorcerers of Dobu,* London: Routledge, 1932, p. xxiii, that the Dobu have similar patterns, the same type of courtship by trial and error, with a gradually tightening union.

[36] Gunnar Landtman, *Kiwai Papuans of the Trans-Fly,* London: Macmillan, 1927, pp. 243 ff.; Oliver, *op. cit.,* pp. 153 ff.

[37] The pattern apparently existed among the Marquesans as well, but since Linton never published a complete description of this Polynesian society, I omit it here. His fullest analysis, cluttered with secondary interpretations, is in Abram Kardiner, *Psychological Frontiers of Society,* New York: Columbia University Press, 1945. For the Tanala, see Ralph Linton, *The Tanala,* Chicago: Field Museum, 1933, pp. 300-303.

[38] Thus, Radcliffe-Brown: "The African does not think of marriage as a union based on romantic love, although beauty as well as character and health are sought in the choice of a wife," in his "Introduction" to A. R. Radcliffe-Brown and W. C. Daryll Ford, editors, *African Systems of Kinship and Marriage,* London: Oxford University Press, 1950, p. 46. For the Nuer, see E. E. Evans-Pritchard, *Kinship and Marriage Among the Nuer,* Oxford: Clarendon, 1951, pp. 49-58. For the Kgatla, see I. Schapera, *Married Life in an African Tribe,* New York: Sheridan, 1941, pp. 55 ff. For the Bavenda, although the report seems incomplete, see Hugh A. Stayt, *The Bavenda,* London: Oxford University Press, 1931, pp. 111 ff., 145 ff., 154.

[39] The second correlation is developed from Marion J. Levy, *The Family Revolution in China,* Cambridge, Harvard University Press, 1949, p. 179. Levy's formulation ties "romantic love" to that solidarity, and is of little use because there is only one case, the Western culture complex. As he states it, it is almost so by definition.

[40] E.g., Mead, *Coming of Age in Samoa, op. cit.,* pp. 79, 92, 97-109. Cf. also Firth, *op. cit.,* pp. 520 ff.

[41] Although one must be cautious about China, this inference seems to be allowable from such comments as the following: "But the old men of China did not succeed in eliminating love from the life of the young women. . . . Poor and middle-class families could not afford to keep men and women in separate quarters, and Chinese also met their cousins. . . . Girls . . . sometimes even served customers in their parents' shops." Olga Lang, *op. cit.,* p. 33. According to Fried, farm girls would work in the fields, and farm girls of ten years and older were sent to the market to sell produce. They were also sent to towns and cities as servants. The peasant or pauper woman was not confined to the home and its immediate environs. Morton H. Fried, *Fabric of Chinese Society,* New York: Praeger, 1953, pp. 59-60. Also, Levy (*op. cit.,* p. 111): "Among peasant girls and among servant girls in gentry households some premarital experience was not uncommon, though certainly frowned upon. The methods of preventing such contact were isolation and chaperonage, both of which, in the 'traditional' picture, were more likely to break down in the two cases named than elsewhere."

[42] Fortune, *op cit.,* p. 30.

[43] Personal letter, dated January 9, 1958. However, the Nuer father can still refuse if he believes the demands of the girl's people are unreasonable. In turn, the girl can cajole her parents to demand less.

marriage typologies—variations among marital relationships

3   **five kinds of relationship**

john f. cuber

peggy b. harroff

The qualitative aspects of enduring marital relationships vary enormously. The variations described to us were by no means random or clearly individualized, however. Five distinct life-styles showed up repeatedly and the pairs within each of them were remarkably similar in the ways in which they lived together, found sexual expression, reared children, and made their way in the outside world.

The following classification is based on the interview materials of those people whose marriages had already lasted ten years or more and who said that they had never seriously considered divorce or separation. While 360 of the men and women had been married ten or more years to the same spouse, exclusion of those who reported that they had considered divorce reduced the number to 211. The discussion in this chapter is, then, based on 211 interviews: 107 men and 104 women.

The descriptions which our interviewees gave us took into account how they had behaved and also how they felt about their actions past and present. Examination of the important features of their lives revealed five recurring configurations of male-female life, each with a central theme—some prominent distinguishing psychological feature which gave each type its singularity. It is these preeminent characteristics which suggested the names for the relationships: the *Conflict-Habituated,* the *Devitalized,* the *Passive-Congenial,* the *Vital,* and the *Total.*

THE CONFLICT-HABITUATED

We begin with the conflict-habituated not because it is the most prevalent, but because the overt behavior patterns in it are so readily observed and because it presents some arresting contradictions. In this association there is much tension and conflict—although it is largely controlled. At worst, there is some private quarreling, nagging, and "throwing up the past" of which members of the immediate family, and more rarely close friends and relatives, have some awareness. At best, the couple is discreet and polite, genteel about it in the company of others—but after a few drinks at the cocktail party the verbal barbs begin to fly. The intermittent conflict is rarely concealed from the children, though we were often assured otherwise. "Oh, they're at it again—but they always are" says the high school son. There is private acknowledgment by both husband and wife as a rule that incompatibility is pervasive, that conflict is ever-potential, and that an atmosphere of tension permeates the togetherness.

An illustrative case concerns a physician of fifty, married for twenty-five years to the same woman, with two college-graduate children promisingly established in their own professions.

You know, it's funny; we have fought from the time we were in high school together. As I look back at it, I can't remember specific quarrels; it's more like a running guerrilla fight with intermediate periods, sometimes quite long, of pretty good fun and some damn good sex. In fact, if it hadn't been for the sex, we wouldn't have been married so quickly. Well, anyway, this has been going on ever since. . . . It's hard to know what it is we fight about most of the time. You name it and we'll fight about it. It's sometimes something I've said that she remembers differently, sometimes a decision—like what kind of car to buy or what to give the kids for Christmas. With regard to politics, and religion, and morals—oh, boy! You know, outside of the welfare of the kids—and that's just abstract—we don't really agree about anything. . . . At different times we take opposite sides—not deliberately; it just comes out that way.

Now these fights get pretty damned colorful. You called them arguments a little while ago—I have to correct you—they're brawls. There's never a bit of physical violence—at least not directed to each other—but the verbal gunfire gets pretty thick. Why, we've said things to each other that neither of us would think of saying in the hearing of anybody else. . . .

Of course we don't settle any of the issues. It's sort of a matter of principle not to. Because somebody would have to give in then and lose face for the next encounter. . . .

When I tell you this in this way, I feel a little foolish about it. I wouldn't tolerate such a condition in any other relationship in my life—and yet here I do and always have. . . .

No—we never have considered divorce or separation or anything so clear-cut. I realize that other people do, and I can't say that it has never occurred to either of us, but we've never considered it seriously.

A number of times there has been a crisis, like the time I was in the automobile accident, and the time she almost died in childbirth, and then I guess we really showed that we do care about each other. But as soon as the crisis is over, it's business as usual.

There is a subtle valence in these conflict-habituated relationships. It is easily missed in casual observation. So central is the necessity for channeling conflict and bridling hostility that these considerations come to preoccupy much of the interaction. Some psychiatrists have gone so far as to suggest that it is precisely the deep need to do psychological battle with one another which constitutes the cohesive factor insuring continuity of the marriage. Possibly so. But even from a surface point of view, the overt and manifest fact of habituated attention to handling tension, keeping it chained, and concealing it, is clearly seen as a dominant life force. And it can, and does for some, last for a whole lifetime.

THE DEVITALIZED

The key to the devitalized mode is the clear discrepancy between middle-aged reality and the earlier years. These people usually characterized themselves as having been "deeply in love" during the early years, as having spent a great deal of time together, having enjoyed sex, and most importantly of all, having had a close identification with one another. The present picture, with some variation from case to case, is in clear contrast—little time is spent together, sexual relationships are far less satisfying qualitatively or quantitatively, and interests and activites are not shared, at least not in the deeper and meaningful way they once were. Most of their time together now is "duty time"—entertaining together, planning and sharing activities with children, and participating in various kinds of required community responsibilities. They do as a rule retain, in addition to a genuine and mutual interest in the welfare of their children, a shared attention to their joint property and the husband's career. But even in the latter case the interest is contrasting. Despite a common dependency on his success and the benefits which flow therefrom, there is typically very little sharing of the intrinsic aspects of career—simply an acknowledgment of their mutual dependency on the fruits.

Two rather distinct subtypes of the devitalized take shape by the middle years. The following reflections of two housewives in their late forties illustrate both the common and the distinguishing features:

> *Judging by the way it was when we were first married—say the first five years or so—things are pretty matter-of-fact now—even dull. They're dull between us, I mean. The children are a lot of fun, keep us pretty busy, and there are lots of outside things—you know, like Little League and the P.T.A. and the Swim Club, and even the company parties aren't always so bad. But I mean where Bob and I are concerned—if you followed us around, you'd wonder why we ever got married. We take each other for granted. We laugh at the same things sometimes, but we don't really laugh together—the way we used to. But, as he said to me the other night—with one or two under the belt, I think—"You know, you're still a little fun now and then.". . .*
>
> *Now, I don't say this to complain, not in the least. There's a cycle to life. There are things you do in high school. And different things you do in college. Then you're a young adult. And then you're middle-aged. That's where we are now. . . . I'll admit that I do yearn for the old days when sex was a big thing and going out was fun and I hung on to everything he said about his work and his ideas as if they were coming from a genius or something. But then you get the children and other responsibilities. I have the home and Bob has a tremendous burden of responsibility at the office. . . . He's completely responsible for setting up the new branch now. . . . You have to adjust to these things and we both try to gracefully. . . . Anniversaries though do sometimes remind you kind of hard. . . .*

The other kind of hindsight from a woman in a devitalized relationship is much less accepting and quiescent:

> *I know I'm fighting it. I ought to accept that it has to be like this, but I don't like it, and I'd do almost anything to bring back the exciting way of living we had at first. Most of my friends think I'm some kind of a sentimental romantic or something—they tell me to act my age—but I do know some people—not very darn many—who are our age and even older, who still have the same kind of excitement about them and each other that we had when we were all in college. I've seen some of them at parties and other places—the way they look at each other, the little touches as they go by. One couple has grandchildren and you'd think they were honeymooners. I don't think it's just sex either—I think they are just part of each other's lives—and then when I think of us and the numb way we sort of stagger through the weekly routine, I could scream. And I've even thought of doing some pretty desperate things to try to build some joy and excitement into my life. I've given up on Phil. He's too content with his balance sheets and the kids' report cards and the new house we're going to build next year. He keeps saying he has everything in life that any man could want. What do you* do?

Regardless of the gracefulness of the acceptance, or the lack thereof, the common plight prevails: on the subjective, emotional dimension, the relationship has become a void. The original zest is gone. There is typically little overt tension or conflict, but the interplay between the pair has become apathetic, lifeless. No serious threat to the continuity of the marriage is generally acknowledged, however. It is intended, usually by both, that it continue indefinitely despite its numbness. Continuity and relative freedom from open conflict are fostered in part because of the comforts of the "habit cage." Continuity is further insured by the absence of any engaging alternative, "all things considered." It is also reinforced, sometimes rather decisively, by legal and ecclesiastical requirements and expectations. These people quickly explain that "there are other things in life" which are worthy of sustained human effort.

This kind of relationship is exceedingly common. Persons in this circumstance frequently make comparisons with other pairs they know, many of whom are similar to themselves. This fosters the comforting judgment that "marriage is like this—except for a few oddballs or pretenders who claim otherwise."

While these relationships lack visible vitality, the participants assure us that there is "something there." There are occasional periods of sharing at least something—if only memory. Even formalities can have meanings. Anniversaries can be celebrated, if a little grimly, for what they once commemorated. As one man said, "Tomorrow we are celebrating the anniversary of our anniversary." Even clearly substandard sexual expression is said by some to be better than nothing, or better than a clandestine substitute. A "good man" or a "good mother for the kids" may "with a little affection and occasional attention now and then, get you by." Many believe that the devitalized mode is the appropriate mode in which a man and woman should be content to live in the middle years and later.

THE PASSIVE-CONGENIAL

The passive-congenial mode has a great deal in common with the devitalized, the essential difference being that the passivity which pervades the association has been there from the start. The devitalized have a more exciting set of memories; the passive-congenials give little evidence that they had ever hoped for anything much different from what they are currently experiencing.

There is therefore little suggestion of disillusionment or compulsion to make believe to anyone. Existing modes of association are comfortably adequate—no stronger words fit the facts as they related them to us. There is little conflict, although some admit that they tiptoe rather gingerly over and around a residue of subtle resentments and frustrations. In their better moods they remind themselves (and each other) that "there are many common interests" which they both enjoy. "We both like classical music." "We agree completely on religious and political matters." "We both love the country and our quaint exurban neighbors." "We are both laywers."

The wife of a prominent attorney, who has been living in the passive-congenial mode for thirty years, put her description this way:

We have both always tried to be calm and sensible about major life decisions, to think things out thoroughly and in perspective. Len and I knew each other since high school but didn't start to date until college. When he asked me to marry him, I took a long time to decide whether he was the right man for me and I went into his family background, because I wasn't just marrying him; I was choosing a father for my children. We decided together not to get married until he was established, so that we would not have to live in dingy little apartments like some of our friends who got married right out of college. This prudence has stood us in good stead too. Life has moved ahead for us with remarkable orderliness and we are deeply grateful for the foresight we had. . . .

When the children were little, we scheduled time together with them, although since they're grown, the demands of the office are getting pretty heavy. Len brings home a bulging briefcase almost every night and more often than not the light is still on in his study after I retire. But we've got a lot to show for his devoted effort. . . .

I don't like all this discussion about sex—even in the better magazines. I hope your study will help to put it in its proper perspective. I expected to perform sex in marriage, but both before and since, I'm willing to admit that it's a much overrated activity. Now and then, perhaps it's better. I am fortunate, I guess, because my husband has never been demanding about it, before marriage or since. It's just not that important to either of us. . . .

My time is very full these days, with the chairmanship of the Cancer Drive, and the Executive Board of the (state) P.T.A. I feel a little funny about that with my children already grown, but there are the grandchildren coming along. And besides so many of my friends are in the organizations, and it's so much like a home-coming.

People make their way into the passive-congenial mode by two quite different routes—by default and by intention. Perhaps in most instances they arrive at this way of living and feeling by drift. There is so little which they have cared about deeply in each other that a passive relationship is sufficient to express it all. In other instances the passive-congenial mode is a deliberately intended arrangement for two people whose interests and creative energies are directed elsewhere than toward the pairing—into careers, or in the case of women, into children or community activities. They say they know this and want it this way. These people simply do not wish to invest their total emotional involvement and creative effort in the male-female relationship.

The passive-congenial life style fits societal needs quite well also, and this is an important consideration. The man of practical affairs, in business, government service, or the professions—quite obviously needs "to have things peaceful at home" and to have a minimum of distraction as he pursues his important work. He may feel both love and gratitude toward the wife who fits this mode.

A strong case was made for the passive-congenial by a dedicated physician:

I don't know why everyone seems to make so much about men and women and marriage. Of course, I'm married and if anything happened to my wife, I'd get married again. I think it's the proper way to live. It's convenient, orderly, and solves a lot of problems. But there are other things in life. I spent nearly ten years preparing for the practice of my profession. The biggest thing to me is the practice of that profession, to be of assistance to my patients and their families. I spend twelve hours a day at it. And I'll bet if you talked with my wife, you wouldn't get any of that "trapped housewife" stuff from her either. Now that the children are grown, she finds a lot of useful and necessary work to do in this community. She works as hard as I do.

The passive-congenial mode facilitates the achievement of other goals too. It enables people who desire a considerable amount of personal independence and freedom to realize it with a minimum of inconvenience from or to the spouse. And it certainly spares the participants in it from the need to give a great deal of personal attention to "adjusting to the spouse's needs." The passive-congenial ménage is thus a mood as well as a mode.

Our descriptions of the devitalized and the passive-congenials have been similar because these two modes are much alike in their overt characteristics. The participants' evaluations of their *present situations* are likewise largely the same—the accent on "other things," the emphasis on civic and professional responsibilities, the importance of property, children, and reputation. The essential difference lies in their diverse histories and often in their feelings of contentment with their current lives. The passive-congenials had from the start a life pattern and a set of expectations essentially consistent with what they are now experiencing. When the devitalized reflect, however, when they juxtapose history against present reality, they often see the barren gullies in their lives left by the erosions of earlier satisfactions. Some of the devitalized are resentful and disillusioned—their bitterness will appear at various points throughout this book; others, calling themselves "mature about it," have emerged with reasonable acceptance of their existing devitalized modes. Still others are clearly ambivalent, "I wish life would be more exciting, but I should have known it couldn't last. In a way, it's calm and quiet and reassuring this way, but there are times when I get very ill at ease—sometimes downright mad. Does it *have* to be like this?"

The passive-congenials do not find it necessary to speculate in this fashion. Their anticipations were realistic and perhaps even causative of their current marital situation. In any event, their passivity is not jarred when teased by memory.

THE VITAL

In extreme contrast to the three foregoing is the vital relationship. The vital pair can easily be overlooked as they move through their worlds of work, recreation, and family activities. They do the same things, publicly at least; and when talking for public consumption say the same things—they are proud of their homes, love their children, gripe about their jobs, while being quite proud of their career accomplishments. But when the close, intimate, confidential, empathic look is taken, the essence of the vital relationship becomes clear: the mates are intensely bound together psychologically in important life matters. Their sharing and their togetherness is genuine. It provides the life essence for both man and woman.

> *The things we do together aren't fun intrinsically—the ecstasy comes from being together in the doing. Take her out of the picture and I wouldn't give a damn for the boat, the lake, or any of the fun that goes on out there.*

The presence of the mate is indispensable to the feelings of satisfaction which the activity provides. The activities shared by the vital pairs may involve almost anything: hobbies, careers, community service. Anything—so long as it is closely shared.

It is hard to escape the word *vitality*—exciting mutuality of feelings and participation together in important life segments. The clue that the relationship is vital (rather than merely expressing the joint activity) derives from the feeling that it is important. An activity is flat and uninteresting if the spouse is not a part of it.

Other valued things are readily sacrificed in order to enhance life within the vital relationship.

> *I cheerfully, and that's putting it mildly, passed up two good promotions because one of them would have required some traveling and the other would have taken evening and weekend time—and that's when Pat and I live. The hours with her (after twenty-two years of marriage) are what I live for. You should meet her. . . .*

People in the vital relationship for the most part know that they are a minority and that their life styles are incomprehensible to most of their associates.

> *Most of our friends think we moved out to the country for the kids; well—the kids are crazy about it, but the fact of the matter is, we moved out for ourselves—just to get away from all the annoyances and interferences of other people—our friends actually. We like this kind of life—where we can have almost all of our time together. . . . We've been married for over twenty years and the most enjoyable thing either of us does—well, outside of the intimate things—is to sit and talk by the hour. That's why we built that imposing fireplace—and the hi-fi here in the corner. . . . Now that Ed is getting older, that twenty-seven-mile drive morning and night from the office is a real burden, but he does it cheerfully so we can have our long uninterrupted hours together. . . . The children respect this too. They don't invade our privacy any more than they can help—the same as we vacate the living room when Ellen brings in a date, she tries not to intrude on us. . . . Being the specialized kind of lawyer he is, I can't share much in his work, but that doesn't bother either of us. The big part of our lives is completely mutual. . . .*

Her husband's testimony validated hers. And we talked to dozens of other couples like them, too. They find their central satisfaction in the life they live with and through each other. It consumes their interest and dominates their thoughts and actions. All else is subordinate and secondary.

This does not mean that people in vital relationships lose their separate identities, that they may not upon occasion be rivalrous or competitive with one another, or that conflict may not occur. They differ fundamentally from the conflict-habituated, however, in that when conflict does occur, it results from matters that are important to them, such as which college a daughter or son is to attend; it is devoid of the trivial "who said what first and when" and "I can't forget when you...." A further difference is that people to whom the relationship is vital tend to settle disagreements quickly and seek to avoid conflict, whereas the conflict-habituated look forward to conflict and appear to operate by a tacit rule that no conflict is ever to be truly terminated and that the spouse must never be considered right. The two kinds of conflict are thus radically different. To confuse them is to miss an important differentiation.

THE TOTAL

The total relationship is like the vital relationship with the important addition that it is more multifaceted. The points of vital meshing are more numerous—in some cases all of the important life foci are vitally shared. In one such marriage the husband is an internationally known scientist. For thirty years his wife has been his "friend, mistress, and partner." He still goes home at noon whenever possible, at considerable inconvenience, to have a quiet lunch and spend a conversational hour or so with his wife. They refer to these conversations as "our little seminars." They feel comfortable with each other and with their four grown children. The children (now in their late twenties) say that they enjoy visits with their parents as much as they do with friends of their own age.

There is practically no pretense between persons in the total relationship or between them and the world outside. There are few areas of tension, because the items of difference which have arisen over the years have been settled as they arose. There often *were* serious differences of opinion but they were handled, sometimes by compromise, sometimes by one or the other yielding; but these outcomes were of secondary importance because the primary consideration was not who was right or who was wrong, only how the problem could be resolved without tarnishing the relationship. When faced with differences, they can and do dispose of the difficulties without losing their feeling of unity or their sense of the vitality and centrality of their relationship. This is the mainspring.

The various parts of the total relationship are reinforcing, as we learned from this consulting engineer who is frequently sent abroad by his corporation.

> She keeps my files and scrapbooks up to date.... I invariably take her with me to conferences around the world. Her femininity, easy charm and wit are invaluable assets to me. I know it's conventional to say that a man's wife is responsible for his success and I also know that it's often not true. But in my case I gladly acknowledge that it's not only true, but she's indispensable to me. But she'd go along with me even if there was nothing for her to do because we just enjoy each other's company—deeply. You know, the best part of a vacation is not what we do, but that we do it together. We plan it and reminisce about it and weave it into our work and other play all the time.

The wife's account is substantially the same except that her testimony demonstrates more clearly the genuineness of her "help."

> It seems to me that Bert exaggerates my help. It's not so much that I only want to help him; it's more that I want to do those things anyway. We do them together, even though we may not be in each other's presence at the time. I don't really know what I do for him and what I do for me.

This kind of relationship is rare, in marriage or out, but it does exist and can endure. We occasionally found relationships so total that all aspects of life were mutually shared and enthusiastically participated in. It is as if neither spouse has, or has had, a truly private existence.

The customary purpose of a classification such as this one is to facilitate understanding of similarities and differences among the cases classified. In this instance enduring marriage is the common condition. The differentiating features are the dissimilar forces which make for the integration of the pair within each of the types. It is not necessarily the purpose of a classification to make possible a clear-cut sorting of all cases into one or another of the designated categories. All cannot be so precisely pigeonholed; there often are borderline cases. Furthermore, two observers with equal access to the facts may sometimes disagree on which side of the line an unclear case should be placed. If the classification is a useful one, however, placement should *as a rule* be clear and relatively easy. The ease is only relative because making an accurate classification of a given relationship requires the possession of amounts and kinds of information which one rarely has about persons other than himself. Superficial knowledge of public or professional behavior is not enough. And even in his own case, one may, for reasons of ego, find it difficult to be totally forthright.

A further caution. The typology concerns relationships, not personalities. A clearly vital person may be living in a passive-congenial or devitalized relationship and expressing his vitality in some other aspect of his life—career being an important preoccupation for many. Or, possibly either or both of the spouses may have a vital relationship—sometimes extending over many years—with someone of the opposite sex outside of the marriage.

Nor are the five types to be interpreted as *degrees* of marital happiness or adjustment. Persons in all five are currently adjusted and most say that they are content, if not happy. Rather, the five types represent *different kinds of adjustment* and *different conceptions of marriage*. This is an important concept which must be emphasized if one is to understand the personal meanings which these people attach to the conditions of their marital experience.

Neither are the five types necessarily stages in a cycle of initial bliss and later disillusionment. Many pairings started in the passive-congenial stage; in fact, quite often people intentionally enter into a marriage for the acknowledged purpose of living this kind of relationship. To many the simple amenities of the "habit cage" are not disillusionments or even disappointments, but rather are sensible life expectations which provide an altogether comfortable and rational way of having a "home base" for their lives. And many of the conflict-habituated told of courtship histories essentially like their marriages.

While each of these types tends to persist, there *may* be movement from one type to another as circumstances and life perspectives change. This movement may go in any direction from any point, and a given couple may change categories more than once. Such changes are relatively *in*frequent however, and the important point is that relationship types tend to persist over relatively long periods.

The fundamental nature of these contexts may be illustrated by examining the impact of some common conditions on persons in each type.

Infidelity, for example, occurs in most of the five types, the total relationship being the exception. But it occurs for quite different reasons. In the conflict-habituated it seems frequently to be only another outlet for hostility. The call girl and the woman picked up in a bar are more than just available women; they are symbols of resentment of the wife. This is not always so, but reported to us often enough to be worth noting. Infidelity among the passive-congenial, on the other hand, is typically in line with the stereotype of the middle-aged man who "strays out of sheer boredom with the uneventful, deadly prose" of his private life. And the devitalized man or woman frequently is trying for an hour or a year to recapture the lost mood. But the vital are sometimes adulterous too; some are simply emancipated—almost bohemian. To some of them sexual aggrandizement is an accepted fact of life. Frequently the infidelity is condoned by the partner and in some instances even provides an indirect (through empathy) kind of gratification. The act of infidelity in such cases is not construed as disloyalty or as a threat to continuity, but rather as a kind of basic human right which the loved one ought to be permitted to have—and which the other perhaps wants also for himself.

Divorce and separation are found in all five of the types, but the reasons, when viewed realistically and outside of the simplitudes of legalistic and ecclesiastical fiction, are highly individual and highly variable. For example, a couple may move from a vital relationship to divorce because for them the alternative of a devitalized relationship is unendurable. They can conceive of marriage only as a vital, meaningful, fulfilling, and preoccupying interaction. The "disvitality" of any other marriage form is abhorrent to them and takes on "the hypocrisy of living a public lie." We have accounts of marriages which were unquestionably vital or total for a period of years but which were dissolved. In some respects relationships of this type are more readily disrupted because these people have become adjusted to such a rich and deep sharing that evidences of breach, which a person in another type of marriage might consider quite normal, become unbearable.

> *I know a lot of close friendships occur between men and women married to someone else, and that they're not always adulterous. But I know Betts—and anyway, I personally believe they eventually do become so, but I can't be sure about that. Anyway, when Betty found her self-expression was furthered by longer and longer meetings and conversations with Joe, and I detected little insincerities, not serious at first, you understand, creeping into the things we did together, it was like the little leak in the great dike. It didn't take very long. We weren't melodramatic about it, but it was soon clear to both of us that we were no longer the kind of pair we once were, so why pretend. The whole thing can go to hell fast—and after almost twenty years!*

Husbands in other types of relationships would probably not even have detected any disloyalty on the part of this wife. And even if they had, they would tend to conclude that "you don't break up a home just because she has a passing interest in some glamorous writer."

The divorce which occurs in the passive-congenial marriage follows a different sequence. One of the couple, typically a person capable of more vitality in his or her married life than the existing relationship provides, comes into contact with a person with whom he gradually (or suddenly) unfolds a new dimension to adult living. What he had considered to be a rational and sensible and "adult" relationship can suddenly appear in contrast to be stultifying, shallow, and an altogether disheartening way to live out the remaining years. He is left with "no conceivable alternative but to move out." Typically, he does not do so impulsively or without a more or less stubborn attempt to stifle his "romanticism" and listen to well-documented advice to the effect that he should act maturely and "leave the romantic yearning to the kids for whom it is intended." Very often he is convinced and turns his back on his "new hope"—but not always.

Whether examining marriages for the satisfactions and fulfillments they have brought or for the frustrations and pain, the overriding influence of life style—or as we have here called it, relationship type—is of the essence. Such a viewpoint helps the observer, and probably the participant, to understand some of the apparent enigmas about men and women in marriage—why infidelities destroy some marriages and not others; why conflict plays so large a role for some couples and is so negligible for others; why some seemingly well-suited and harmoniously adjusted spouses seek divorce while others with provocations galore remain solidly together; why affections, sexual expression, recreation, almost everything observable about men and women is so radically different from pair to pair. All of these are not merely different objectively; they are perceived differently by the pairs, are differently reacted to, and differently attended to.

If nothing else, this chapter has demonstrated that realistic understanding of marital relationships requires use of concepts which are carefully based on perceptive factual knowledge. Unfortunately, the language by which relationships between men and women are conventionally expressed tends to lead toward serious and pervasive deceptions which in turn encourage erroneous inferences.

Thus, we tend to assume that enduring marriage is somehow synonymous with happy marriage or at least with something comfortably called adjustment. The deception springs from lumping together such dissimilar modes of thought and action as the conflict-habituated, the passive-congenial, and the vital. To know that a marriage has endured, or for that matter has been dissolved, tells one close to nothing about the kinds of experiences, fulfillments, and frustrations which have made up the lives of the people involved. Even to know, for example, that infidelity has occurred, without knowledge of circumstances, feelings, and other essences, results in an illusion of knowledge which masks far more than it describes.

To understand a given marriage, let alone what is called "marriage in general," is realistically possible only in terms of particular sets of experiences, meanings, hopes, and intentions. This chapter has described in broad outline five manifest and recurring configurations among the Significant Americans.

4   social class and conjugal role-relationships

lee rainwater

Conjugal life is a highly variegated and complex experience, and each of its aspects can be examined in great detail; only a careful evaluation of the many aspects of family interaction can present a really full and valid picture of family life. Noting that "the general function problems facing the family are analogous to those facing the society as a whole," Bell and Vogel (1960:19ff.) delineate four broad functional problems of activity within the nuclear family: (1) task performance, (2) family leadership, (3) integration and solidarity, and (4) pattern maintenance. Hess and Handel (1959:4) outline five overlapping major processes that "give shape to the flux of family life": (1) establishing a pattern of separateness and connectedness, (2) establishing a satisfactory congruence of images through the exchange of suitable testimony, (3) evolving modes of interaction into central family concerns or theses, (4) establishing the boundaries of the family's world of experience, and (5) dealing with significant biosocial issues of family life. Studying total families with these kinds of questions in mind is obviously a large order and beyond the scope and practical requirements of the present study.

. . .

However, one central characteristic of families which differentiates them from each other and has important consequences for their actions lies in the nature of the role-relationship between husband and wife—their typical ways of organizing the performance of tasks, their reciprocal expectations, their characteristic ways of communicating, and the kind of solidarity that exists between them. We will take the concept of conjugal role-relationship as central in our characterization of the family life of the couples studied. We will use it to organize our presentation . . . of variations in marital relations. . . .

Following Bott (1957:3), we mean by a conjugal role-relationship those aspects of the relationship between husband and wife that consist of reciprocal role expectations and the activities of each spouse in relation to the other. Thus, a characterization of the conjugal role-relationship of a particular couple would involve many of the dimensions cited by Bell and Vogel and by Hess and Handel. Patterns of task performance and expectations about it are involved, as are the kinds of family leadership, the solidarity characteristic of couples, and the value systems used to legitimate marital role execution. Separateness and connectedness (one aspect of family solidarity) is an important theme in characterizing the role-relationship, as are the central family concerns and the way the couple establishes boundaries for its world. Consensus (congruence of images) between the partners is significantly conditioned by the acceptance each partner gives to the role-relationship as it has developed in the marriage.

Bott (1957:53-55) sees conjugal role-relationships as ranging along a continuum from the "jointly organized" to the "highly segregated." Following her conceptual approach, three types of conjugal role-relationships have been used in characterizing the couples in this study.

1) *Joint conjugal role-relationship* refers to relationships in which the predominant pattern of marital life involves activities carried out by husband and wife together (shared) or the same activity carried out by either partner at different times (interchangeable). In these relationships, husband and wife undertake many activities (including recreation as well as task performances) "together with a minimum of task differentiation and separation of interest. They not only plan the affairs of the family together but also exchange many household tasks and spend much of their leisure time together." In discussing family life they stress the value—and not just the functional efficacy—of sharing and the mutual interpenetration of the concern, understanding and interest of each in what the other does. Thus, even where there is a division of labor in task performance—husband as breadwinner and wife as housekeeper—each is expected to be interested in and sympathetic to the other in his assigned duty.

2) *Segregated conjugal role-relationship* refers to relationships in which the predominant pattern of marital life involves activities of husband and wife that are separate and different but fitted together to form a functioning unit or that are carried out separately by husband and wife with a minimum of day-to-day articulation of the activity of each to the other. Among such couples,

> *husband and wife have a clear differentiation of tasks and a considerable number of separate interests and activities. They have a clearly defined division of labour into male tasks and female tasks. They expect to have different leisure pursuits, and the husband has his friends outside the home and the wife has hers (Bott, 1957).*

Such couples tend to emphasize a formal division of labor in the family rather than a solidarity based on interchangeability of role activities, or the identification and empathy of each with the other's activities and concerns. While too much separateness can be disruptive to the family's stability, such couples do not see the positive value in "togetherness" shown by couples with less segregated conjugal roles.

3) *Intermediate conjugal role-relationship* refers to relationships that are not sharply polarized in either the jointly organized or highly segregated direction. Such couples value sharing and interchangeability of task performance but they do not carry this as far as do the couples with joint relationships. They preserve more of the skeleton of formally organized division of labor, particularly in connection with household tasks other than child rearing (fathers in this group want to be more occupied with the parental role than fathers in more segregated relationships). Among these couples, the statuses "father" or "husband," "mother" or "wife," are still very central to the functioning of the family rather than the somewhat more *pro forma* designations they represent for couples who emphasize joint organization. Among jointly organized couples of the latter type there is instead much more emphasis on husband and wife relating as persons, as individuals, and less as actors of normatively-specified and encompassing roles (cf. Goffman, 1961:150-52). For couples with intermediate relationships, separate leisure time pursuits (particularly evening activities) may be frowned upon and held to a minimum, but this does not carry with it the emphasis on active sharing of such interests that is characteristic of couples with joint relationships. In many ways the paradigm of the intermediate relationship is that of leisure time pursuits dominated by watching TV or reading magazines; the husband and wife amuse themselves alone, do not talk with each other about what they see or read, but still feel that such activities reflect their "togetherness." The integrity of the family is maintained in this way without requiring the couple to meet the emotional demands of joint relating.

The couples in the study sample were categorized in one of these three types on the basis of their responses to several general questions. They were asked first to tell something about their family

TABLE 1. SOCIAL CLASS AND CONJUGAL ROLE-RELATIONSHIPS

		Joint	Intermediate	Segregated
			Role-Relationships	
Upper-middle class	(32)	88%	12%	—
Lower-middle class	(31)	42	58	—
Upper-lower class*				
Whites	(26)	19	58	23%
Negroes	(25)	12	52	36
Lower-lower class*				
Whites	(25)	4	24	72
Negroes	(29)	—	28	72

*Whites and Negroes at each class level combined for test.
$X^2 = 100.34$ df = 6   P < .0005   T = .50

life and about the important things that happened during their marriage. Then they were asked how decisions were made in the family, about the main duties of husband and wife, about the interests and activities of each, and each respondent was asked to evaluate how his spouse felt about him. From all of this material a judgment was made as to which of the above three types the couple most closely approximated. Clearly no couple is a pure type; each represents a mixture of joint and segregated relationships, and the classification of a couple indicates simply the preponderant direction of role performances in the family and of the values emphasized by husband and wife in talking about their life together.

A more concrete idea of what these terms denote can be gained from an examination of what couples of each type say about their married life. First, however, an examination of Table 1 will indicate the variations in the distribution within our sample of conjugal role-relationship types by social class. Joint relationships are characteristic of 88 per cent of the upper-middle class couples, and segregated relationships of 72 per cent of the lower class couples. The two classes between have a more mixed distribution of the types. A majority of the lower-middle class couples have intermediate relationships, but 42 per cent of them share the joint role-relationship pattern that characterizes the upper-middle class. A majority of the upper-lower class couples also have intermediate relationships, but very few have joint relationships, and about one-third of them have highly segregated relationships.

At this broad level of characterization, marital relationships show sharp class differences, particularly in the distinctiveness of upper-middle and lower-lower class patterns. The former overwhelmingly emphasize sharing and joint participation in married life; the latter almost equally strongly emphasize separateness and isolation of the marital partners from each other. As we shall see, this latter pattern is comfortable for some couples and a source of friction for others (usually it is the wife who is unhappy with the segregated state of affairs). The intermediate pattern characterizes the majority of the middle group.*

To exemplify how couples characterized in these three ways speak of their married life we have chosen three couples at the same (upper-lower) class level in order to minimize class differences and highlight differences in the role-relationship. The first case is that of a thirty-four year old man and twenty-eight year old woman who have been married a little over a year. They have three children by her former marriage and she is pregnant. He has had some training as a commercial artist but has worked most recently as a dance instructor. Now they both work part-time while he studies to be a hairdresser. They live in a small apartment which the interviewer describes as bare but nicely maintained. Here is how they speak of their marriage:

*Herbert J. Gans, in a recently published study of an Italian-American working class group, notes these same class differences, and in surveying the findings of other studies of working and lower class subcultures he notes that most research on such groups comes to similar conclusions (1962:50-53, 229 ff.).

The husband:

> *The most important thing is that there must be a great deal of love and mutual understanding. One other thing is that the husband and wife should have some common interests in activities outside the home. They should have some future goal that they are working for. We are both working now so I can go to school and become a hairdresser. This will give us security which is very important in marriage; insecurity in money matters is probably what people fight over most. A satisfactory adjustment sexually is also important. I don't believe in one person making a decision. I believe that the people involved should have some say in the decision. I would say this is true of us in most areas. My main duty is to be the bread winner; you should make it a duty to do all you can for your family. I've never balked at doing the dishes. Even if the husband is tired he should help. . . . My wife is very nice. She's interested in dancing. She's very generous, understanding in certain areas. She's not as understanding in certain areas like finances but she's certainly not a spendthrift. . . . I'm very artistically inclined and I enjoy all types of sports. I believe I am very understanding and considerate. Sometimes I'm too emotional, with a tendency to drown my sorrows in a couple of beers. Being impulsive is my worst fault. . . . My wife thinks I'm pretty good with the kids. Actually I'm too easy with them, we both are.*

The wife:

> *I guess we're both looking for a future together, and making each other happy. My husband enjoys family life; there was no family life in my first marriage. My first husband made good money but he was never around. . . . My husband gives me his check and I pay the bills. With the children, except when they're very naughty and he tells them to stand in the corner and sees that they stay there, which ever one of us is nearest corrects them. We decide together if we want to go to the beach or go out. We relax together mostly. . . . He's very considerate. He hasn't got many bad points; he can't hurt people even with words. When he gets a bottle of beer he likes to talk. He's the type that anyone can get along with. He's independent, too. . . . I'm impatient and I'm independent. . . . We've had some financial problems but nothing much else. We haven't been married long so he wants lots of attention. He's the type of person who sits down and talks things out when there's a problem before it grows.*

Both husband and wife emphasize the twin theme of interchangeability of duties in the home and the importance of sharing interests and gratifications together. The husband is pleased that his wife is interested in dancing, as he is; the wife emphasizes that they want to "make each other happy," unlike the situation in her first marriage. There is probably more conflict between them about their economic situation than either hints at, but both seem to value mutual understanding and working together toward a solution to this problem. It is important to them that they spend time together, either by themselves or with the children. That they have not been married long perhaps encourages the joint relationship ("We haven't been married long so he wants a lot of attention"), but there are other couples in essentially the same situation in which the husband moves into a going household of mother and children and assumes either a segregated male role (often the case among lower-lower class Negroes) or an intermediate role in which little need is felt by either partner for an extended honeymoon period.

A second upper-lower class couple illustrates a segregated relationship. The husband and wife are twenty-three years old, have been married three years and have two children. The husband works as a machinist's helper. Both attended but did not finish high school. They live in a four-room basement apartment that the interviewer found rather dilapidated.

The husband:

> *I pay the bills and help with the kids when the wife needs help. I fix things around the house. She has to take care of the kids, clean the house, do the wash and like that. She keeps pretty busy. She usually gets the shopping done by herself OK. She's a good mother to the kids. She's a good cook, mostly she does cooking. . . . She's always lending things out which she generally never gets back; she's too good-hearted, people take advantage of her. . . . I like hunting, fishing, swimming. I try to take care of my family. . . . My bad points are going out sometimes and not coming home until late. I don't overdo it I guess, but sometimes I goof up. . . . We've had mother-in-law troubles, that's the main one. I guess you could say we've had money problems, too. We're pretty much over the mother-in-law problem now; she hasn't bothered us too much lately.*

The wife:

> *I worry about the children, the house, the shopping, meals and laundry. . . . My duties are to cook his meals, that's about all. . . . He helps with the kids, babysits for me, supports us, chauffeurs me around until I get a license. I hope to work when I get the opportunity. Oh, he takes out the garbage, that's a big thing around here. He's hard to talk to. He tries to be understanding. He likes fishing, hunting, cartoons on TV. He was so kind and nice when I met him and so courteous.* [Why "was",] *He's changed; he's not courteous at all; he's moody now. Bills bother him; he jumps when the bills are piling up. I'm always nagging at him because he throws his clothes around, and he's always late for everything. I like to take trips, even with the kids. I like to drink. I like to go shopping with money enough to spend. I like to cook; that is, bake. I don't like to clean or wash or scrub. I try to have supper ready when my husband comes home and I try to keep the house clean. Sometimes I'm moody and can't get up in the morning and I forget to do things—like I'll do part of the ironing and forget the rest. I don't keep up with things. . . . We've had it rough from the start; two months after we were married we separated because of in-law trouble. He was always going over to his mother's.* [Here followed an extended discussion of their problems at that time.] *But we got back together. We've had bill problems.* [When did that start?] *About an hour after we were married. When we had children it got worse.*

This couple present a sharp division of labor for task performances in the family, and not much sense of common interests and activities. The husband works, pays the bills, does maintenance work around the house and drives the car since the wife does not have a license. Occasionally he helps with the children as babysitter or when the wife is loaded down. The wife does the housework and looks after the children; she also does most of the shopping (he "chauffeurs" her but neither says that they shop together). She thinks of her responsiblity toward him mainly in terms of providing his meals. He likes masculine recreation—hunting, fishing, going out by himself. She probably would like to go out with him but they do not seem to do this very often. Apparently segregation has characterized their marital relationship from the beginning; only after a separation did he stop depending on his own family for companionship. And apparently he feels that she also is sometimes too loyal to others, since he criticizes her for lending things out and letting people take advantage of her.

As time goes on the husband may spend more time at home, and the sharp segregation which now marks their marriage may moderate. Older lower class couples often describe their marital history in terms of a gradual settling down of the husband and greater willingness on his part to give up separate leisure pursuits. Sometimes this is accompanied by a greater willingness to share activities with the family, but sometimes the husband seems rather to shift his isolated life from outside to inside the home—perhaps tinkering with his car in the back alley on weekends and watching TV programs of interest only to him (westerns and sports) in the evening.

A third upper-lower class couple, illustrating an intermediate degree of conjugal role-organization, have been married for seven years and have two children; the husband is thirty-seven and the wife twenty-seven years old. He works as a baggage room clerk. They live in a five-room, modestly furnished apartment in a building owned by his mother.

The husband:
I want to make my kids happy; I want a good education for them. I want a little money saved up; insurance policies paid up. I want to see the kids go to college to get a good education. It will give them more sense, more facts of life. It will give them a job easier; a good office job. . . . We make decisions together; we talk about them. Her and me make the decisions on money. I leave my check on the desk for her; we don't have no trouble over it. [Who makes decisions regarding the children?] *On certain things I do, on others she does. I make decisions on how long they should stay up and what TV programs they watch. I keep us in bread, keep the bills paid always. My wife sees that the kids go to school; she feeds them. We both do the shopping; if she can't, I do it. I clean the walls in the house and I do the painting. I don't help with the house cleaning or the dishes. . . . Well, she was raised by nuns in a Catholic boarding school. She's real swell. She likes to go to movies; I don't. She gets a little hot-headed. . . . I don't get hot like she does; She does the arguing, I keep quiet. I like fishing. I work; even when I'm sick I go to work. . . . I go to the corner saloon once in a while. I don't take my wife out enough.*

The wife:
I have a good marriage. My husband is a little more than ten years older than I am but sometimes I feel I'm older than he is. My husband is so calm he never gets angry. We make most decisions together. . . . We agree on the children. If I punish them he don't say anything and if he punishes them I don't say anything. He gives me the money and I pay the bills. We go on picnics to the park with the kids. I take care of the kids and I wash and iron and take care of the house. Between the kids and the dog and the fish and the birds I keep pretty busy. My husband helps me with the children; he washes them and puts them to bed. He is a great person; I don't have no complaints about him. He had a pretty bad temper when we got married but he's calmed down. He loves sports and he loves to tinker with his car. He's handy, he put up all my cabinets and he's putting up shelves for me in the basement so I can can peaches and tomatoes. . . . I'm hot-headed for one thing. I enjoy taking care of the family. . . . I like making those plastic models like rockets; I have the X-15 and the Redstone. I sew and make clothes for the girls. I knit, too. [How does your husband feel about you?] *My husband never complains about me.*

This couple seems to have a fairly elaborate division of labor and rather clear-cut notions of what are husband-tasks and what are wife-tasks. On the other hand, there is a good deal of sharing of child care, and making decisions together seems important to them. They share leisure activities in which the children participate but they do not seem to attach much importance to shared recreation in which only adults participate (he goes out by himself, does not take her out enough). Much of their activity at home is closely articulated and would require a good deal of joint planning; on the other hand, both seem to value a sense of separate roles and probably would not respond positively to the emphasis couples in joint relationships put on interchangeability. If this couple had a more complete division of labor we would classify them as in a segregated relationship; their emphasis on joint decisions and the value they place on whole family activity suggest that the intermediate category is more accurate. It is possible that this couple's relationship is becoming less segregated as time goes on—the wife's reference to the husband's bad temper earlier in marriage may be an allusion to his independence and lack of attention to his family responsibilities; he probably goes to the corner saloon less often than he used to. His children have become for him a new focus of interest which probably makes it easier for him to give up the saloon-car-sports way of life: "Kids keep families together; I enjoy taking the kids on picnics, swimming, and to the forest preserves. I take them up North for vacations, too."

As was apparent in Table 1, each of the role-relationship types is characteristic of particular social classes—the joint relationship is most characteristic of the upper-middle class, the segregated relationship of the lower-lower class, and the intermediate type of the lower-middle and upper-lower class. The role-relationship typical of a class is an integral part of the life style of members of that class and is closely articulated with the self-concepts and concepts of spouse that reflect these life styles.

. . .

REFERENCES

Bell, N. W., and Vogel, E. F. *A modern introduction to the family.* New York: Free Press, 1960.
Bott, E. *Family and social network.* London: Tavistock Publications, 1957.
Gans, H. J. *Urban villagers.* New York: Free Press of Glencoe, Inc., 1962.
Goffman, E. *Encounters: Two studies in the sociology of interaction.* Indianapolis: Bobbs-Merrill, 1961.
Hess, R. D., and Handel, G. *Family worlds.* Chicago: University of Chicago Press, 1959.

5

open marriage: a synergic model

nena o'neill

george o'neill

In the wake of increasing dissatisfaction with the prevailing pattern of traditional monogamous marriage, a number of alternative marriage styles have begun to emerge. These experimentations vary from those involving more than three persons in the basic pattern and include group marriage, communal life styles, and polygamous patterns (more often triadic, and more often polygynous rather than polyandrous) to modifications in the basic one-to-one monogamous configuration. This last group may be divided into those which are nonmarriage relationships (still monogamous but extra-legal) and those which represent innovations, changes, deletions, and additions to the standard expectations for those legally married. These modifications may include such various items as separate domiciles, extramarital sexual relations in group or partner-exchange contexts, or reversal of traditional role patterns; i.e., woman provides, man housekeeps. None of these patterns are particularly new in transcultural contexts since all have occurred elsewhere in other societies at one time or another. However, their proliferation and the motives which have impelled men and women in our society to increasingly seek innovations in our marriage style deserve closer scrutiny.

It is not enough to say that society is pluralistic and that these alternate patterns for marriage have appeared in response to the changes in our society and the development of different life styles. Even though one can foresee a future in which there is a range of marriage patterns to choose from, the questions still remain: Why have so many experimental forms appeared? And more important, what are the personal motivations for seeking these innovative styles? Compendiums of sociological explanations seemed somehow to pass over the personal dimensions involved. Yet these questions are exceedingly important for the future especially since that future will affect our styles of child-rearing and thus the perpetuation of those values we deem most humanistic and worthy of saving. Even excluding experimental family forms, Sussman (1971) has pointed out that even today some children may live in numerous variant forms of the traditional nuclear family during their formative stages. Under these conditions some changes in our value system are to be expected. The questions are which values and how many?

With the above questions in mind we began to explore contemporary marriage in 1967.[1] The authors' interviews began first with those who were involved in experimental structures and in the greatest variations from the norm in traditional marriage. It was felt that these innovators would have greater insight because they had already opted for change, and that they would perhaps be more articulate and perceptive about why they had chosen change. The interviewers then moved on to the divorced, the nonmarrieds,[2] the singles, the young, and to those who were either disillusioned or contented with traditional monogamous marriage. As research was carried out in a primarily middle class setting, Cuber and Harroff's (1965) delineations of types of marriage relationships (i.e.,

Reprinted, by permission, from *The Family Coordinator*, 1972, *21*, 403-9. Copyright ©by the National Council on Family Relations.

conflict-habituated, devitalized, passive-congenial, the vital, and the total) gained increasing validity. During the research in the anthropological literature it was found that little attention had been given to the interpersonal dimension of marriage or to the interrelation of the intrapsychic and ideological aspects of marriage. However, it was felt that the anthropological perspective gave a holistic approach to the problems of contemporary marriage that was considered valuable. While cultural ideologies and prescriptions for marriage behavior persisted, value orientation and actual behavior were changing, thus creating confusion for many.

THE PROBLEM

As exploratory insights to the problems evolved, the authors became increasingly convinced that the central problem in contemporary marriage was relationship. The attempt to solve the problem by moving into group and communal situations did not seem to mitigate the problems we discovered in interpersonal relationships. With the breakdown of many external supports for traditional marriage, the pressures on the interpersonal husband-and-wife relationship became intensified. There was a need for that relationship to provide more fulfillment and benefits both on a personal and interpersonal level. Problems in marriage were manifested by the inability of the majority of individuals to find in the marital relationship both intimacy and opportunity for developing their personal potential. Understanding of the problem concluded in addition that:

1)   Marital partners and those contemplating marriage expressed a need for intimacy and growth in a relationship where they could actualize their individual potential without destroying the relationship.

2)   Most people did not have the skills in relating and in communication which would allow for growth in a noncritical atmosphere. The typical dyadic marital role relationships had already been precut for them. They were locked into a negative involuted feedback system. This was their perception of their situation as well, although not with the same terminology.

3)   Many of the innovations and experimental forms, although not all of them or all of the people involved in them, were a reflection and indication of this lack of skills in interpersonal relations.

4)   Other important impediments to growth were the unrealistic expectations and myths stemming from the traditional marriage format of the past, in particular, overriding emotional dependencies, and possessive jealousy.

This left us as the observers and researchers with the options of reporting the alternate styles with their attendant disillusionments and problems, or of choosing another path in utilizing the research. While one can catalogue all the sociological and technological forces that are contributing factors to the breakdown of marriage and the family, it offers little in the way of ameliorating the problems each individual faces when he comes to grips on an interpersonal basis with the old mores and patterns of institutions that have not changed, while his needs and the external socio-cultural conditions affecting his behavior *have* changed. Therefore, the authors chose to present a model for personal change and value reorientation that individuals could utilize on an interpersonal basis within their own marital situation.

THE ACTION MODEL

The concept of open marriage, which is outlined elsewhere in detail (O'Neill & O'Neill, 1972), is primarily based on the expression of desires for change and the perceived routes to change drawn from the interviews conducted over a period of four years and upon the actual changes already made in many relationships that were observed. The research conducted was utilized to create a model for change. In so doing the authors have stepped beyond the role of objective researcher reporting the data and findings into the realm of what can be termed action anthropology: that is, delineating a model for change by placing the problem areas in their cultural context. An attempt has been made to present the traditional marital configuration in its societal setting and to delineate the cultural imperatives and values implicit in these imperatives for examination by those involved in marriage relationships. The purpose, then, is to make it possible for individuals to become aware of the idealized precepts of the institution of marriage and the forces influencing their attitude toward, and their behavior in, marriage. Without an awareness of the present conditions, they cannot perceive the pathways to change. It is to be fully understood that some will choose to remain within traditional marriage where the perimeters and dimensions are defined for them by the norms. But for those who feel a need for change, awareness and insight are a necessary first step to determining or discovering what pathways are available.

Action anthropology is a variation on the theme of action research. In the past, action research (Festinger, 1953; Selltiz, 1963) has been associated with institutional or organizational change directed toward finding solutions to organizational or social problems. The flow has been from the institutional level down to the individual in effecting change. More recently it has been recognized that individuals can initiate measures for change and reverse the flow to effect change on the institutional level. Weinberg (1965) has noted that this is a problem-solving, action-oriented society, and continues:

> *On this action level, society and the person are both symbolic systems with varying capacities for solving problems. Both society and the person can respond to problems in terms of their knowledge and their capacity for decision making and executive knowledge. Both can communicate, plan, and implement programs to solve problems. . . . The individual deliberates about alternatives before selecting a problem-solving response.* [4]

Today, the orientation toward methods of change must begin with the individual. The need for a measure of self-determination is paramount. Yet the individual is frequently overlooked as a primary force for change, the assumption being that his behavior is shaped by impinging social forces in the environment and that he has neither sufficient knowledge and perspective to perceive these forces, nor is adequately equipped to institute directive and self-motivated change. This attitude underestimates the individual. The sample encompassed a broad range of middle class informant-respondents. The majority expressed a desire for some feeling of self-determination and autonomy in their lives and marriage behavior. Many had already instituted it. Furthermore, most had a knowledge of what the problem areas were in marriage.

One quote is offered from an interview with a 23-year-old single woman, who was at that time in a nonmarriage relationship with a young man and seriously contemplating marriage:

> *I don't want to say yes, yes we are going to be in love forever. It's like saying, yes, yes you know the ocean—and the next wave is going to look like this one, but I can say it is worth the risk if I feel I can do something about it. I want to be understanding, and start out with the attitude of, well it ain't going to be bliss but if I do my homework I stand a very good chance, and knowing what the chances are and stepping into it with your eyes open, you got a chance of making your marriage work . . . and there is a lot more homework to do today because people have to make decisions they never had to make before in marriage, but those marriages will be better for it . . . it's not I'm doing this because I've got to do it, it's doing this because I chose to do it, and that's what it is, man is a thinking animal, therefore I am. Once you get down to this kind of foundation and you can build, you know, 'well begun is half done.'*

THE OPEN MARRIAGE MODEL

Open marriage is presented as a model with a two-fold purpose:

1)   To provide insights for individuals concerning the past patterns of traditional marriage, which has been termed closed marriage. Based on closed systems model, traditional marriage was perceived as presenting few options for choice or change.

2)   To provide guidelines, through an open systems model, for developing an intimate marital relationship that would provide for growth for both partners in the context of a one-to-one relationship. This does imply some degree of mutuality. It does not imply that growth will always be bilateral, but rather that there will be supportive assistance and tolerance during unilateral growth. Shostrom and Kavanaugh (1971) have delineated the rhythmic relationship which best exemplifies this pattern. These guidelines have been designed in answer to the needs expressed by the majority of our informant-respondents for a relationship which could offer them more dimensions for growth together than either could attain singly. The principle through which this mutually augmenting growth occurs is synergy. Many couples found that this synergistic self-actualizing mode of relating became possible only through the revision and deletion of some of the expectations of closed marriage.

Open marriage can then be defined as a relationship in which the partners are committed to their own and to each other's growth. Supportive caring and increasing security in individual identities makes possible the sharing of self-growth with a meaningful other who encourages and anticipates his own and his mate's growth. It is a relationship which is flexible enough to allow for change, which is constantly being renegotiated in the light of changing needs, consensus in decision making, in tolerance of individual growth, and in openness to new possibilities *for* growth. Obviously, following this model often involves a departure, sometimes radical, from rigid conformity to the established husband-wife roles and is not easy to effect.

In brief, the guidelines are: living for now, realistic expectations, privacy, role flexibility, open and honest communication, open companionship, equality, identity, and trust. The first step is for partners to reassess the marriage relationship they are in, or anticipate, in order to reevaluate expectations for themselves and for their partner. Couples in today's society are not educated for marriage or the requisites of a good human relationship, nor are they aware of the psychological and myriad other commitments that the typical marriage contract implies. The expectations of closed marriage—the major one being that the partner will be able to fulfill all of the other's needs (emotional, social, sexual, economic, intellectual, and otherwise)—present obstacles to growth and attitudes that foster conflict between partners. Awareness of these expectations and a realignment more in accord with a realistic appraisal of their capabilities are fundamental to instituting change and to solving their problems in relationship.

Living for now involves relating in the present rather than in terms of the past or in terms of the future goals which are frequently materialistic and concrete rather than emotional and intellectual in nature. The granting of time off, or privacy, can be used for examination of the self and for psychic regeneration. A way out of what many marital partners conceive as the role-bind involves working toward a greater role flexibility both in terms of switching roles temporarily or on a part-time basis, and as a therapeutic device for understanding the self and the position of the other partner. Open and honest communication is perhaps the most important element in an open relationship. The lack of communication skills creates a formidable barrier between husband and wife, yet these skills are the most important in sustaining a vital relationship, promoting understanding, and in increasing knowledge of self. Open companionship involves relating to others, including the opposite sex, outside the primary unit of husband and wife, as an auxiliary avenue for growth. Equality involves relating to the mate as a peer in terms of ways to achieve stature rather than through the status attached to husband and wife roles. Identity involves the development of the individual through interaction with mate and others and through actualizing his own potentials. Trust, growing through the utilization of these other guidelines and based on mutuality and respect, creates a climate for growth. Liking, respect, sexual intimacy, and love grow through the exercise of these elements.

Each progressive guideline becomes increasingly abstract. The system can be seen as an expanding spiral of evolving steps in complexity and depth in the marital relationship. The system operates through the principle of synergy, a concept drawn from medicine and chemistry, first utilized by Benedict (Maslow and Honigmann, 1970) in cultural, and later by Maslow (1965, 1968) in interpersonal contexts. In open marriage, the concept of *synergic build-up* is defined as a mutually augmenting growth system. Synergy means that two partners in marriage can accomplish more personal and interpersonal growth together than they could separately without the loss of their individual identities. Synergic build-up defines the positive augmenting feedback that can enhance mutual growth.

While only a limited few may be able to utilize all these guidelines in their totality and simultaneously, open marriage would best be considered a resource mosaic from which couples can draw according to their needs and their readiness for change in any one area.

The majority of the sample had already explored the possibilities for change in some of the areas covered by the guildelines. Many of these reflected only a change in attitude, while behavioral changes were acknowledged as difficult. The two areas of greatest difficulty were the conflicts arising from changing man-woman and husband-wife roles and the problems encountered in self-development.

The question of marital and extramarital sexual behavior, while ever-present, did not seem to be the central problem with which they were coping. While marital sex sometimes presented problems, many felt that the emphasis on sexual adjustment, in terms of manuals and the media, was exaggerated. Although many felt that they could not cope with sexual jealousy in terms of extramarital sex, they were on the verge of deciding that sex *per se* was not their central problem in the marriage. Numerous couples had already effected some degree of sexual latitude in their own relationships. Some had done so with tacit knowledge but without verbalized agreement. Others had done so in various types of consensual arrangements, including group sex and partner exchange. While some benefits were noted, it was observed that by and large these experiences did not occur in a context where the marital partners were developing their primary marriage relationship sufficiently for this activity to count as a growth experience. Frequently it obscured relationship problems, became an avenue of escape, and intensified conflicts. For some, however, it did become a means of revealing other problem areas in the marriage.

Underlying the marital couple's explorations into any area of nonconformity, whether it was extramarital sex or the equally important area of changes in typical role behavior (i.e., male-female, man-woman, husband-wife), was the central problem of relationship.[3] That is, how could the marital partners relate in terms of their changing needs and those of society in a mutually beneficial fashion? Open marriage presents some of the elements in interpersonal relationships that would allow for change, for increasing responsibility for the self and for others, and for increased understanding between husband and wife.

The open marriage model offers insights and learning guides for developing more intimate and understanding marital relationships. An open relationship in marriage, as well as in any interpersonal matrix, involves becoming a more open person. Since the open-minded personality is one which can perceive options and alternatives and make decisions about the paths to change (Rokeach, 1960), efforts to help the marital couple in perception and skills should increase their ability to solve many problems in marriage. However, it will not be easy for most couples. Emotional maturity, and the development of responsibility and confident identity cannot emerge overnight. But standing still, or merely exploring experimental structural forms without attention to the interpersonal factors only seems to be increasing the number of problems in marriage and decreasing the benefits to be gained from it. Open marriage is not intended to solve marital problems, but by using the open marriage model, the couple will at least be substituting problems which promote growth and learning for problems which are currently insoluable.

IMPLICATIONS

It is in the arena of interpersonal relations that marriage and the family will have to find new meaning and gain greater strength, no matter what the structural framework may be. Children cannot be taught the value of supportive love and caring, responsibility, problem-solving, or decision-making skills unless the parents have first developed these qualities in their own relationship. The inadequacy of organized institutions to instill these values and skills is only too apparent. Therefore, intimate, long-term relationships such as those of marriage and the family must provide them, and in order to do this they must be more rewarding and fulfilling for their members and there must be feedback and caring for each other's welfare.

Focusing on the methods for achieving a rewarding one-to-one relationship provides something that individuals can deal with and work with on a self-determining level. By encouraging personal responsibility, self-growth and bonding through the synergic relationship, the basic unit of husband and wife should become more rewarding and offer more avenues for fulfillment.

Building from within strengthens the individual, the couple, and then the family unit, and thus the entire social structure, since the fundamental unit of society is the family. Whatever form the family unit may be, its strength will still depend upon the rewards gained from interpersonal relationships. It is in this sense that the individual, and the married couple, can become not only a fulcrum for change but also a key factor leading to the strengthening of the social structure. Thus both family and society can be better equipped to cope with accelerating technological and cultural change. Hopefully, open families can evolve to an open society and eventually to an open world.

FOOTNOTES

[1] In developing the concept of open marriage, the authors interviewed approximately 400 persons from 1967 to 1971. Informant—respondents were 17 to 75 years of age, urban and suburban middle class in orientation and occupation, and approximately 75 percent were married or had been married. Thirty interviews, both formal and informal, with professional therapists and marriage counselors supplemented this data. The interviews included individual and couple in-depth sessions (frequently tape recorded), discussion in group settings, and short mini-interviews in a variety of social settings. While some topical and background questions were used (i.e., age, occupation, marital status, etc.: "What do you think the ingredients of a good marriage are?"), the interviews were primarily open-ended and exploratory in nature, focusing on eliciting information through face to face encounter, about values, feelings and attitudes toward marriage and changes they perceived as necessary for improvement.

[2] The term nonmarried applies to those relationships in which there is some commitment but which are not legalized. They can range in time from a few months to a life time. Premarital is an accurate term for only a portion of these relationships since some never intend to marry the nonmarriage partner, or the relationship is frequently considered only a temporary plateau before each has the sustaining personal resources to move on to another level, or another person. Formerly marrieds would probably comprise a separate category. The word cohabitation is also misleading as a coverall term for these relationships. Since cohabitation implies both a shared domicile and sex without legal marriage, it did not apply to some relationships encountered, e.g., a couple who did not share a domicile but did form a cohesive unit insofar as they shared all their spare time, vacations, and sex, and presented themselves as a couple in social situations. Therefore, the term nomarriage relationship is suggested.

[3] Concerning these two areas of change, the authors are least optimistic about the movement into group marriage and communal living situations which involve random or even structured sexual intimacy among many. No true group marriage, as it is being explored in our society, with equal sexual sharing among all partners has existed according to the anthropological literature. Among all societies where larger family structures exist, they are maintained by elaborate kinship ties and other supportive structures interwoven with the institutional framework of the society, thus goals are integrated for the group or extended family. Certainly communal or community situations where the goals are banding together to share economic, child care, or recreational activities have many advantages and hopefully will increase. But when couples and individuals in groups are pressed into situations of total intimacy—including the sexual dimension—for which they have not been prepared either emotionally by training or by conditioning, the strain of the multistranded relationships tends to fragment the group. The goals of cooperation and support are difficult to maintain under the pressure of emotional conflicts which are intensified by prescriptions for sexual intimacy.

REFERENCES:

Cuber, John F., and Peggy B. Harroff. *Sex and the Significant Americans.* Baltimore: Penguin Books, 1965.

Festinger, Leon, and Daniel Katz. *Research Methods in the Behavioral Sciences.* New York: Holt, Rinehart and Winston, 1953.

Maslow, Abraham H. *Eupsychian Management.* Homewood, Illinois: Richard D. Irwin, Inc., 1965.

Maslow, Abraham H. Human Potentialities and the Healthy Society. In Herbert A. Otto, (ed.). *Human Potentialities.* St. Louis: Warren H. Green, Inc., 1968.

Maslow, Abraham H., and John J. Honigmann (eds.). Synergy: Some Notes of Ruth Benedict. *American Anthropologist,* April 1970, 72.

O'Neill, Nena, and George O'Neill. *Open Marriage: A New Life Style for Couples.* New York: M. Evans and Company, Inc., 1972.

Rokeach, Milton. *The Open and Closed Mind.* New York: Basic Books, Inc., 1960.

Selltiz, Claire, Marie Jahoda, Morton Deutsch, and Stuart W. Cook. *Research Methods in Social Relations.* New York: Holt, Rinehart and Winston, 1963.

Shostrom, Everett, and James Kavanaugh. *Between Man and Woman.* Los Angeles: Nash Publishing, 1971.

Sussman, Marvin B. Family Systems in the 1970's: Analysis, Politics, and Programs. *The Annals of the American Academy of Political and Social Science.* July 1971, 396.

Thomlinson, Ralph. *Sociological Concepts and Research.* New York: Random House, 1965.

Weinberg, S. Kirson. *Social Problems in Modern Urban Society.* Englewood Cliffs, New Jersey: Prentice-Hall, Inc., 1970.

6

further considerations
on the dual career family

rhona rapoport

robert n. rapoport

The dual career family is one in which both heads of household pursue careers and at the same time maintain a family life together. The argument in favour of this becoming a more pervasive pattern is based on a complex of trends in our society and in the world generally—for example, more equality of opportunity and access to higher education for men and women. Given that careers themselves are increasingly a primary source of personal satisfaction for more and more people, it is reasonable to expect that women, too, will wish to commit themselves to the world of work as well as to that of family life.

Conversely, as the impetus for total commitment to work is reduced with increasing affluence, men may allocate more of their energies and interests to domestic and community activities of one kind or another.

The term career, sometimes used to indicate any kind of work, is defined here as those jobs which require a high degree of commitment and which have a continuous developmental character. For example, careers within large organizations are thought of in terms of a progression of posts leading upward in some kind of hierarchy: careers in professions are thought of as proceeding through stages of cultivation and experience, accumulating expertise.

Work, as distinct from career, may involve any kind of gainful employment. Dual *worker* families are more numerous than dual *career* families. It is assumed that they have a good deal in common. No research comparable to the kind reported here has been done on dual *worker* families generally. The non-career type of dual worker family is more likely to occur among people with lower formal qualifications. Where both husband and wife are highly qualified, the dual *career* pattern is more likely to arise, but even here it is only one of several patterns that emerge in such marriages.

Our research, and that of others in related fields, shows that highly qualified women develop different kinds of orientations to their careers because, unlike most men, they are constrained to reconcile their careers with prescribed family norms which are potentially incompatible. This is especially so at the family stage when there are small children (Fogarty, Rapoport & Rapoport, 1971).

Very broadly, the women graduates studied manifest three major groups of work/family patterns:

Conventional: The woman drops her career when she marries or has children and concentrates on being a housewife with no intention to return to work.

Interrupted: The woman may drop work for a period when her children are small but intends to resume it eventually.

Continuous: The woman interrupts her work only minimally or not at all if she has children.

All but a tiny minority of men are continuous full time workers. However, among the highly qualified women in our survey of British graduates, only about one-third are continuous workers, and only a small sub-group—5 per cent of the sample—are full time continuous workers with small children.

Within each of the three broad categories mentioned there are many variations. Women who remain conventionally domestic vary enormously in terms of how much they like what they are doing. The bored or 'captive' housewife is as familiar a figure in contemporary society as is the house-proud, happy wife. Variations are observable amongst non-career workers as well—interrupted or continuous—not only in terms of the meaning of work but the degree to which the individuals work reluctantly for economic or other reasons.

It is generally accepted that a man must work and men are socialized for this from infancy. For women, working is more usually viewed as an option and if a particular woman finds herself working against her personal wishes because of an incompetent, disabled or disagreeable husband, then her disgruntlement may be greater than that of a man in a similar situation.

Nowadays, the 'interrupted' worker is perhaps the most generally approved model, particularly for women with special skills or talents. It allows them to fulfill societal expectations about what a 'good wife and mother' does when her children are small and, at the same time, holds out the expectation that she will not 'waste' her skills in the long run.

The more 'continuous' pattern entails considerable sacrifice and strain but where it is in response to a genuine commitment to work it has its rewards, not only for the woman herself, who is striving for self-expression, but also for her family, to the extent that she achieves greater satisfaction from her work than would have been possible for her at home.

The dual career pattern for families with children is a minority pattern and as such tends to rouse disapproval and even envy from some who wish that they were fortunate enough to emulate it. The fact that such a pattern occurs with little precedent in recent social history and, to some extent, in the face of powerful counter beliefs makes its adoption particularly difficult.

The legitimation of creative patterns like that of the dual career family contributes to its social acceptability. Legitimation is, of course, a complex process and to some extent is rooted in values. However, to the extent that systematic information can be accumulated, pointing to the positive balance in the cost-benefit assessment that many families make in evolving their particular work/family structures, the research becomes a contribution to the legitimation process.

In our research, it became clear that it is difficult for women to rise into positions of senior responsibility once they have dropped out for a substantial period, however unprejudiced the work environment may be. Whatever amibition a woman may have had prior to child-bearing is often damped down in the experience of infant care, and there are few with sufficient resilience to overcome not only the strains of re-entry into the competitive world of work but the extra effort required to make up for lost time, missed information and the development of expertise. Wives in dual-career families have tended to sustain a continuous work pattern, making it possible for them to rise to senior positions.

Each dual career family is produced by a particular constellation of forces—personal, interpersonal and social—not only in relation to the woman but in relation to her husband, how they fit together as a couple and the social environment in which they live. We have examined a number of such constellations in an attempt to detect common features.

COMMON FEATURES OF DUAL-CAREER FAMILIES

What Produces the Dual-career Family

If the social system, its family norms and educational teachings incorporated a component of women's roles that prescribed continuous work—as happens for men—the career-oriented woman would not be extraordinary. In our society one must search for special circumstances that may have fostered a tendency which is divergent, for the norm is for a woman to be home-oriented, particularly if she has children. Women graduates, with their special skills and training, provide a population perhaps more than usually likely to be career-oriented. Within this population, what predisposes a woman to be career-oriented in contrast to her more conventionally oriented fellow graduates—and what differentiates the husbands of those who actually pursue active careers from the husbands of those who do not?

The following discussion is based on two kinds of data: The first is a cross-sectional sample survey of men and women graduates from British universities in 1960; the second is from an intensive interview study of 16 dual-career families selected on the basis of the wife having risen to a senior position in one of the organizations which was being studied as a specimen work environment (see Fogarty, Rapoport & Rapoport, 1971, for a detailed description of these sub-studies).

The cross-sectional sample consisted of about 1,000 men and women who were surveyed in 1968 so that the respondents had had a chance in the intervening eight years to have established a pattern of work and family life based on actual experience rather than on envisioned ideals only. Within that sample there are nearly 400 married women graduates of whom some 200 returned questionnaires filled out by their husbands as well, providing a sub-sample of 'couples'.

Comparing the intensively interviewed sample of dual-career families with the sub-sample of 25 conventional couples drawn from the cross-sectional survey sample, the first point of general interest is that the dual-career wives are more different from the conventional family wives than their respective husbands, though the latter are distinctive in crucial ways.

Social class background differentiated the wives but not the husbands. Proportionately more dual-career wives come from higher social class backgrounds (as indicated by fathers' occupations) than do their conventional counterparts. Mothers' occupational experience and attitudes were also important for the wives, though not for their husbands. Many more of the dual-career family wives had mothers who worked than did the conventional wives, and those dual-career wives whose mothers did not work showed a greater tendency to have been frustrated with their housewife roles than was true for the conventional wives.

The higher social class background women tend to be from smaller families. They are frequently only children, or first children, and even where they are part of a larger set of siblings they tend to be separated in some way, e.g. by a large age gap. This syndrome, which we call the 'only-lonely' child syndrome, encompasses these different possibilities. Added to this, the dual-career wives tended to experience longer separations from their parents during childhood than did their conventional counterparts—sometimes through evacuation during the war, sometimes through attending boarding schools. This finding is consistent with other research indicating that innovators and creative people in various fields tend to have this background of personal loneliness. Most of these studies, however, have concentrated on heavily 'masculine' fields.

Somewhat greater overall tension is reported in the early family backgrounds of dual-career wives as compared with conventional wives. This finding is consistent with the interpretation, first noted by Rossi, that in these families there was less basis for the idealization of family relationships or the development of an attitude of confidence in the conventional type of family relationships as fully sufficient for one's personal needs and aspirations.

The two sets of husbands, while differing from one another less than their wives, did contrast in at least one crucial aspect. The husbands of career-oriented wives tended to come from families in which they were able to develop close relationships and empathy with women. If there were other children, the others tended to be girls. They also tended to have closer relationships with their mothers than did the conventional family husbands, though this is somewhat obscured by the tendency for conventional family backgrounds to be generally warm and close.

Motivational Syndromes

Some of the early interpretations of what differentiated career-oriented women from their more conventional counterparts were based on clinical materials from psychiatry and paediatrics and they emphasized psychopathological elements. Women who wished to work were regarded as frightened of or rejecting their 'natural' maternal role, or, in more extreme forms, as 'castrating' women who envied men and took up destructive competitive attitudes toward them in work. However, our survey materials on highly qualified women show that the wish to combine work and family roles is increasing. Some kind of combination is now, in fact, the modal pattern. The only issue is: how much work and at what point in the family life cycle?

As this tendency becomes more firmly established, the assumption of a typical motivational syndrome with connotations of deviance and pathology becomes increasingly inadequate, and it becomes more important to see each individual and couple in complex terms of strengths and weaknesses. If one concentrates on the loneliness and insecurity of certain elements in the backgrounds of many of the dual-career wives, one gets a picture of uncertainty and a drive for security and self-realization underlying their career motivation. Yet, why is this thought of as deplorable in women and admirable in men? It is only against the background of conventional role expectations that these different connotations are given to the same kinds of behaviour and motivational patterns in men and women.

For men, the capacity to understand and sympathize with the aspirations of women is, if balanced by appropriate strengths and competencies in the man's own world, interpreted here as a point of strength rather than as an aberration. Men, in our survey samples, who had this capacity, supported their wives in whatever pattern they wished to pursue. They are more conspicuous among the career-oriented wives because without such husbands it is particularly difficult to develop the career pattern, whereas the conventional housewife has support for her pattern from many sources (see Rapoport & Rapoport, 1972 and Bailyn, 1970).

The dual-career wives in both the intensive study and in the survey tend to be 'only-lonely' children and they frequently come from tense family backgrounds. The case studies revealed, in addition, elements of support as well as tension in the early family backgrounds. For example, one wife had extreme tension in her relations with her father but support from her mother in a family with considerable overall tension; another had an important relationship with a maternal grandmother and a close relationship with her father who was home at a time when many fathers were away during World War II; another felt very removed from, and even rejecting toward, the values of her parents, but had an elder brother as a supportive figure. One implication of this early pattern for later behaviour is seen in the tendency for women of this type to be particularly responsive to the attitudes of the male who is the central figure in her life (Rapoport & Rapoport, 1971a).

The men, both in the survey and in the case studies, seem to show a picture of greater familial harmony in their early backgrounds, and in most cases, more social mobility than their wives.

One husband reports on early family experiences of poverty and unemployment; another felt that his mother was particularly ambitious for her children. In some instances the husband's encouragement of his wife's employment would seem to have had an element of insurances against economic difficulties as well as the wish for expediting a high family standard of living.

Many of the husbands had a particularly close and sympathetic relationship with their mothers and felt some distance from their fathers. Behaviourally, the husbands studied varied in their degree of involvement and participation in their wives' careers, some being directly and collaboratively involved with their wives' work, others encouraging their wives to work to some extent as a compensation for the guilt they feel for their own heavy involvement in their own very segregated careers.

In contemporary society, the dual-career family pattern emerges in each case through a series of accidents which may have a cumulative character rather than being based on a preconceived model, as may be more the case in future families. In contemporary dual-career families, the steps that are taken to achieve a given satisfaction or reward or to avoid given dissatisfaction may entail costs which become known only as they accumulate.

Marital Satisfaction

Marital happiness is something that can exist or deteriorate whether or not the wife follows a career. Many women who are highly committed to a career are less likely to experience family life as idyllic whether or not they work, because of their own family backgrounds of tension; this alone tends to predispose against idealizing the family.

Bailyn's analysis of the 220 couples in the survey has increased our understanding of the major patterns that exist. Prior formulations seemed reasonable but too simple and therefore inconsistent with observations. For example, on the one hand marital happiness was thought to decrease with a wife's commitment to work because she could not give the necessary attention to her husband and to her home, and data could be found to support this. On the other hand, marital happiness was also shown to increase when the woman goes out to work because she then avoided boredom and a sense of being 'captive' or exploited (Bailyn, 1970).

It seems to us that one must start from a more differentiated set of assumptions. *Some* women are not only positively oriented to a career, but would be miserable if not able to pursue one. Many such women will tend to take employment, shifting the family into the category of a dual-working family with a higher degree of marital satisfaction than if they had remained in the conventional pattern. Conversely, if a woman is not career-oriented and does not actually have to work, it may be assumed that she will tend to adopt the conventional pattern and show a higher level of personal and marital happiness with it than if she had worked unwillingly. These choices are not totally open, but depend on opportunities in the work environment, constraints at home as well as the personal motivation of the individuals concerned. A given work-family pattern may thus emerge against different environmental constellations as well as in response to different motivational syndromes.

What are the effects on marital happiness of these different types of work-family structures? There is, first of all, a very high general level of marital happiness among the graduate couples at this stage of their careers; over 85 per cent report that they have a 'fairly happy' or 'very happy' marriage as perceived *both* by husband and wife. Over 60 per cent profess to have 'very happy' marriages. To differentiate the effects of different work-family structures it is useful to concentrate on the *'very happy'* proportions in the different categories. In the analysis of the data available, a distinction was made among the men as to whether they emphasized career above family life as an area of satisfaction, and among the women as to whether they were committed to the idea of women's careers at all.

Combining these variables produces family types in which both emphasized career ('careerist couples'), couples in which the husband emphasizes career but the wife emphasizes *only* the family ('conventional' couples), and couples in which both husband and wife emphasize family as the major source of their satisfactions (the 'familistic' couple). There are also intermediate types, among them those that Bailyn calls 'coordinate' couples in which the wife has a career and family orientation but the husband values family life as well as career. The dual career families in this study represent the latter type.

One thing is immediately clear. Having a wife who works or intends to return to work is not necessarily disastrous for marital happiness in couples of the kind reported here.

The findings indicate that the level of 'very happy' marriages are not significantly different for any of the couple patterns except for the 'careerist' one, where there is a significant drop in level of marital happiness (Bailyn, 1970).

THE DYNAMICS OF DUAL-CAREER FAMILIES

In the preceding discussion, the emphasis has been on common features of the dual-career families. On the basis of the 16 intensively studied dual-career families it is possible to contribute a further understanding of dynamics in such families as well as to consider in greater detail 'strains and gains' that they seem characteristically to experience.

The families presented were selected on the basis of wives' contrasting occupations, so this source of variation is manifest in the materials. However, cutting across the actual occupational content are two other sources of variation that are important. First, the type of organizational environment is important. Business people in small entrepreneurial organizations, while taking greater risks, also enjoy greater flexibility in the organization of their time. This is not to say that the more highly structured 'bureaucratic' work settings make it impossible for a dual-career family wife to function. Aside from the fact that bureaucratic structures themselves vary in their norms and in the rigidity with which they are enforced, they also provide security of a known income which has advantages in planning and domestic organization, children's schooling and so on.

Husbands vary as to which work context they see as advantageous for their wives, assuming that they support the general idea of their wives having a career. If she has a career within a more formal bureaucratic organizational structure, he may feel that he can take greater risks in his own work, or at least that his economic responsibilities toward the family are being shared. Alternatively, he may opt for the more secure occupational situation for himself, encouraging entrepreneurial activity by his wife as a way of engaging as a family in the excitement of risk taking, but covering the hazards at the same time.

The way the couples integrate their two work situations is also important. One architect couple studied, for example, work together as partners with their offices in the same building as their home. They have the greatest degree of overlap of work and home activities. In addition, each performs many elements in both spheres. Another architect couple have considerable interchangeability in their domestic division of labour, but at work their tasks are not interchangeable.

Some couples who work at separate occupations, participate to some extent in the work interests of each other because of a degree of overlap in their training and experience. Other couples are employed in different occupations, different kinds of employing organizations, and thus their involvement in one another's work problems is minimal. They may share leisure activities, and the personal bond that has evolved in this sphere provides the basis for their being able to be sympathetic auditors rather than active participants in one another's work concerns.

In all cases there was domestic help which took on many of the less desired aspects of domestic work, freeing the two heads of the family for the activities they chose. There is considerable variation, however, both in the way domestic help is organized, and in the selection of activities to cultivate on a shared interest basis.

Child care is an area where the variations are marked not only in terms of general philosophy and practice of child-rearing but more particularly in relation to the conception held of the child's role in family life. In some of the families, the child was not involved in the chore aspects of family living; in others, by contrast, the children had definite family work roles, and were expected to help with what had to be done.

In all of the families, there was an emphasis on enhancing the children's independence and competence. Delight is expressed by the parents when the children show mastery and aspire to a high level of accomplishment. The emphasis on high standards and excellence at what one does is very marked, although this is not an emphasis on 'going higher' but rather on doing whatever one does as well as possible. This attitude is independent of the sex of the child. In no case was there a stereotyped conventional orientation to sex roles. Where a daughter favoured a more conventional role, this was not discouraged but was regarded as a personal choice.

Other variations are in terms of the personalities of the individuals—the styles the couples have shown in their interpersonal relations, for example, in decision-making and conflict resolution. In personality there seems to be a general tendency for the marital partners to see themselves as temperamentally complementary. The wives tend to be described as more expressive, volatile and moody and the men as calmer and steadier. These personality contrasts have provided complementarities and strains among the couples. We have been more concerned with social structural, as distinct from personality, sources of strains and satisfactions, and these have received considerable attention.

Strains

The families studied have shown a good many elements both of strain and satisfaction associated with the pattern of life they have evolved. We have isolated five dilemmas which in their nature set up strains. They are dilemmas arising out of the choice element because the dual career pattern once chosen entails particular strains and sustaining the pattern means confronting the strains.

The five selected dilemmas, common in varying degree to all the couples are:

1.   Overload dilemmas.
2.   Dilemmas of environmental sanction.
3.   Dilemmas of personal identity and self esteem.
4.   Social network dilemmas.
5.   Dilemmas of multiple role-cycling.

Overload

Sheer overloading is something that each of the families experienced though they differed in the ways they handled it. The domestic 'back up' work of home care or supervision, child care, social arrangements and so on has either to be redistributed or neglected. Although domestic help was available, it was rarely entirely satisfactory more particularly when it was in the form of adolescent *au pair* girls who, in acting out their own family rebellion problems on their temporary family substitutes, sometimes added to the strain on the family.

The husband or the wife or both therefore found it necessary to do quite a lot of work, even with domestic help, to accomplish the running of the household at the standard they required. Sometimes, standards are deliberately lowered. The children, too, are pressed into helping roles. But for the most part, the additional load tended simply to be absorbed, adding to the physical strains and diminishing the amount of free time available.

Free time was deliberately created. Two of the couples had weekend cottage retreats for the purpose, another couple made it a point *not* to take work home, another cultivated boating as a family hobby.

Families that do not work at creating and conserving leisure time find that their 'work' at home and outside can consume all of their time and leave very little for other pleasures.

Environmental Sanctions

Times have changed in terms of the pervasiveness of negative sanctions in relation to married women working. If anything, there is a swing in the direction of slightly disparaging the non-working housewife, particularly if she happens to be highly qualified. Still, working women know that, as with other minority groups in society, they must be especially good and especially careful lest any shortcomings be chalked up to their sex rather than treated as an individual matter. While there is a clear and definite tendency for this sort of environmental strain (arising from traditional sex-stereotypes) to diminish in the workplace, it is still active in domestic roles, particularly in relation to child-rearing.

Where couples choose not to have children, they may be considered odd or at best, unfortunate. If they have children (the majority) they are expected to provide conventional care with mother staying at home and exercising her 'natural maternal instincts' whether she feels that she is well endowed with these instincts or not. Women who have given up their own career aspirations to be housewives may express their resentment at others who seem to be managing an alternative pattern, by indicating that they consider the dual-career wives to be bad mothers, bad wives, and perhaps bad and selfish individuals.

Most of the dual-career mothers studied show considerable maternal wishes. The challenge for them is how to distribute the care in such a way as to allow enough highly involved 'mothering' (by the actual mother *and* father) to take place along with filling the long hours of more routine care with competent ancillary people. In addition, the father's greater participation in domestic life had led to an increase in the children's exposure to their father more than is usual in conventional families—and this may serve to correct the imbalance in the conventional child-care and socialization situation that has evolved in contemporary society.

One of the ways of handling negative environmental sanctions is to avoid them and to this end all of the couples developed friendships which supported them by providing positive sanction and legitimation for what they were doing. One couple treated the matter with humour and remarked that they were considered a bit mad by their neighbours, but they all had a laugh about it. Others worked out a special image for themselves so that they were considered as a pair, part of the interesting metropolitan scene, much like the famous couples in the art or entertainment world.

Personal Identity and Self-esteem

Aside from the environmental sanctions, the individuals themselves, having been socialized in conventional ways, were concerned about whether, in adopting this variant pattern, they were good human beings. Is there something bad, unfeminine, sick about a woman doing this? Is a husband sacrificing his 'manliness' in altering his domestic life to take on greater participation and responsibility?

The sources of these doubts and anxieties are clear enough. These couples were socialized in the terms of norms and values of 30 years ago. Variance from the stereotyped sex role interests and activities tended in the past to arouse negative reactions. This inevitably led to internal doubts and ambivalences persisting into adult life, giving rise to guilt, anxiety and tensions of various kinds. At work, the wife may hesitate to press herself at a crucial point and thus may be considered lacking in drive; at home, she may react in various ways, for example, by being overindulgent to a child because of feeling guilty about being out at work.

The husband may make great personal and career sacrifices to help achieve the dual-career structure for its value to both parties, but he may show irritation or resentment at having modified his own pattern against persisting internalized conceptions of himself in relation to masculine roles.

Most families develop what we have termed a 'tension line' which is set up more or less unconsciously between the pair and recognized as a point beyond which each will not be pushed. Compromises are worked out within its framework.

Some couples take special care with the sensitivities of their partners so as to balance the other's self esteem at points recognized to be vulnerable. One husband emphasized the importance of criticism in any work partnership, but where the partnership is a marital one as well, the criticism in work matters must be done 'with love'. Other couples sharply segregate their work and home roles. One woman when she returns home becomes 'cook' and 'my husband's wife'.

Social Network Dilemmas

In general, the dual-career families tend to make their network of relationships on a couple basis rather than an individual one. This is partly a matter of 'sharing ideology', but it also functions to insulate them from the kinds of environmental sanctions that would arise if, for example, couples based on the husband's occupational network were brought in with conventional-minded wives.

Their relationships with kin tend to diminish except where there are clear responsibilities and/or compatibilities. This is partly due to their mobility and the sheer paucity of kin because so many of them are only children. But, it is also a function of the kinds of insulating devices already mentioned.

Dual career families tend to increase the number of people in their networks who are in service relationships with them. Often they are friends of such service people as doctors, lawyers, accountants. In addition, the wife's associates are drawn into the social circle more than is perhaps usual in conventional middle class families because of the need for environmental supports to sustain the dual-career pattern.

Multiple Role Cycling

In most of the dual-career families studied here, occupational establishment for both husband and wife preceded child-bearing, a pattern which differs from the conventional family cycling in which many couples marry and begin to have children when the husband is trying to establish himself occupationally. In the conventional pattern the high demands on the husband in his own establishment phases do not conflict with demands placed on the wife because she concentrates her activities in the home. In the case of one of the dual career couples studied, it was the wife's career establishment which preceded her husband's and she supported his preparatory and early establishment phases through her own occupational activity. He was willing to provide support on the domestic front. Another couple jointly established their occupational and family roles at the same time, by incorporating their office into their home.

Couples in the series studied tended to have their children in a compressed period and wives interrupted their work minimally. By having deferred child-bearing until they were occupationally established, they tended to have achieved a sufficient level of income to support the domestic service side.

For younger couples, new patterns of dealing with role cycling dilemmas may emerge. Marriage nowadays is earlier and there is widespread recognition that different opportunities for stipends, training, occupational entry and so on will make for different timetables for the two marital partners. Child-bearing may take place earlier and there may be a return to work at an earlier point in the occupational cycle.

Gains

The central element of gain for most of the women in the sample can be subsumed under the general notion of *self-expression*. All the women in this sample have as part of their personal identities a sub-identity associated with a professional work role. Many indicated that if the satisfactions from work were to be removed, they would experience a major personal deficit. Though the particular jobs they do may represent compromises with their original idealized conceptions, in every case they are realizing in major degrees what they really want to do and feel is worth doing as human beings, in relation to using their capacities.

Another gain that is more important than is frequently acknowledged is *economic*. It has often been observed in research on working women that highly qualified people tend to state that they work out of intrinsic interest while those with lower qualifications tend to mention money as a motive. Be this as it may, the financial return is mentioned as an important element for the highly qualified women in our sample from several angles.

Dual-career families have relatively high standards for domestic living, child-care, clothing, transportation and so on; to pay out the extra that is involved in all this, their income must be relatively high, particularly as good help is costly. Many of the couples also indicated that the overloads experienced made it important to provide for leisure and holidays which could be relatively costly because of the need on such occasions to be looked after so that the marital pair can regenerate their energies.

One couple expressed the attitude that it is preferable to have both partners working somewhat less than 'flat out' rather than that the husband get the highest possible income. By having two workers less fully engaged in the 'rat race' they feel that they do not have to sacrifice some of the shared enjoyments of family life while at the same time maintaining a high overall family income.

Another couple felt it was important to accumulate savings for future financial security and against possible disasters. Some of the women who experienced early economic deprivation were very much aware that this factor has been important in driving them toward a goal of economic security. Now that they were successful in their careers they gave less emphasis to this aspect as a personal need and transformed it into a wish to give their children more security than they had had themselves.

So much has been written about the negative consequences of deprivations experienced by children separated from their mothers (based mostly on institutional or traumatic experiences quite unlike those provided by professional women going to work) that some countervailing statements are appropriate.

The case for damage to children as a direct consequence of mothers' working is unproven. Our data suggest, as do a number of earlier studies, that while there are indeed problems raised by mothers having careers, the kinds of competent individuals who are in dual-career families tend to make arrangements for child-care which compare favourably with what would have occurred had the mothers stayed at home.

On the positive side, parents report that their children show independence and resourcefulness. By helping with family tasks, they contribute to the overall family needs and this legitimates their right to have a share in the family goods. Often the children in these families show pride in their parents' accomplishments. This takes the form of special interest and knowledge in the family that arouses in the child a feeling of competence and involvement in the wide range of interests that both parents have. The very fact that *both* parents have work as well as domestic interests and roles allows a greater range of role models for children of both sexes.

Neurotic difficulties, confused identification, loneliness and disturbance seem to be products much more of bad management of child care and of some of the dilemmas (e.g. in relation to countering social disapproval) than of a particular family structure itself. The families studied differed in their talents in this regard, but there is no reason to believe that the same individuals would produce more psychologically healthy children if they sacrificed their own wishes and needs so as to operate the conventional family structure.

Enabling Processes: The Facilitating Husband

Given the difficulties that confront a married woman with children who wishes also to pursue a full-valued career, it is clear from our data (both survey and case studies) that the husband's support is a crucial element. There are doubtless couples in which the wife's career is pursued despite overt disapproval of the husband (Hunt, 1970, reports a fairly high proportion of such instances in the general population), and in some instances a woman may turn to a career as a compensation for an unrewarding marital relationship. By and large, however, the support of the husband is critical. The dual career families provide an interesting instance, theoretically, in which families function to facilitate rather than impede members' participation in the work sphere. Since early analyses by Weber, the general tendency has been for family influences to be seen by sociologists as antithetical to those of the workplace, the latter demanding more rational and universalistic behaviour, the former more personal and particularistic.

We term those family processes which, on the contrary, facilitate members' participation in the external structure 'enabling processes'. It is interesting to consider in the data on dual-career families what these enabling processes seem to be and to analyze why the husbands in these instances facilitate their wives' participation in the world of work.

The first point that is important to note is that for most of the dual-career husbands, the participation of their wives in work is not experienced, initially at least, as antithetical to their own or their families' interests.

In each of the couples it was important to the husbands, themselves, that their wives developed their work lives as they did. For example, one couple evolved a creative partnership which was seen by them to have advantages over other working relationships that each had known. They developed their partnership while they were very young and were able to tailor their working conditions to suit their personal needs to a greater degree than is usual for people at their career stage.

The entrepreneurial success of one wife was important to her husband because it expressed some of his own fantasies about risk-taking and public acclaim. Another husband had experienced the loss of his first wife whom he had seen as frustrated through not having had a career. The drive and determination of one wife were important in expressing a latent part of her husband's character and helped him in his search for an appropriate occupational career. Another woman's work was in the area of her husband's life-long avocation. The husband facilitated it, in this instance, by recognizing his own interests in it.

For the wives it was crucial that their husbands approved and facilitated their careers in various ways and, indeed, that they actually wanted them to work. This transformed a wish to continue a career from something that was selfishly desired by one member into something that was wanted for the overall family benefit.

The individuals' capacity to take a joint perspective on the occupational situation, i.e. to see the work of each member as contributing something to the whole in which both have major investments, is also a critical element in resolving conflicts that arise. It takes a husband who is either very strong or very identified with the efforts of his wife to allow her to equal or exceed his own accomplishments without major disruption in the relationship, and most of the husbands in the families studied seem to have some combination of these two attributes.

It is important to note that there are other enabling processes, and other enabling relationships than the marital one; and it is also important to note that it is possible for women to pursue careers in the absence of positive facilitating efforts. Bailyn showed, for example, how one type of marital relationship yielding dual-career family-work structures was based on a kind of exchange, the husband would say, in effect, that he wanted only to be left alone to get on with his career and he granted the wife the same privilege. While a workable basis for the dual-career structure, this kind of arrangement was conspicuously lacking in marital satisfaction as compared with the more positive forms of facilitation (Bailyn, 1970).

The understanding of enabling processes, particularly those involving positive facilitating elements, is of considerable importance. Previous discussions have tended to concentrate on behavioural manifestations of facilitation—such as help with domestic chores, or help with financial management on the work side. The underlying social-psychological mechanisms on which we have concentrated in our case study analyses have received less attention except in the clinical literature. The data described seem to suggest that the optimization of self interest in work and family relationships need not be analyzed in psychopathological terms. Dual-career families seem to optimize the self-interests of their members by recognizing overlaps of interest as distinct from complementarities based on exclusive domains of interest.

REFERENCES

Bailyn, Lotte. (1970). Career and family orientation of husbands and wives in relation to marital happiness. *Hum. relat.23*, 97-113.

Epstein, Cynthia. (1971). Law partners and marital partners. *Hum. relat. 24*, 549-564.

Fogarty, M., Rapoport, Rhona & Rapoport, Robert. (1971). *Sex, career and family.* London: Allen & Unwin for P.E.P.

Rapoport, Rhona & Rapoport, Robert N. (1969). The dual-career family: a variant pattern and social change. *Hum. relat. 22*, 3-30.

Rapoport, Rhona & Rapoport, Robert N. (1971a). *Dual career families.* Harmondsworth: Penguin.

Rapoport, Rhona & Rapoport, Robert N. (1971b). Early and later experiences as determinants of adult behaviour: married women's family and career patterns. *Brit. j. sociol. 22*, 16-30.

Rapoport, Rhona & Rapoport, Robert N. (1971c). Family enabling functions I: The facilitating husband in the dual-career family. In: R. Gosling (ed.), *Tavistock jubilee volume* (forthcoming).

Rossi, A. S. (1965). Equality between the sexes: an immodest proposal. In: R. J. Lifton (ed.), *The woman in America.* New York: American Academy of Arts and Sciences.

Weber, M. (1947). *The theory of social and economic organization* (transl. by A. M. Henderson and T. Parsons). London: Hodge.

factors associated with the marital relationship

7   **i love you but i'm not in love with you**

thomas e. lasswell

marcia e. lasswell

The concept of love presents a true paradox for clinician and client alike. Few venture to say that they are sure what love is. However, there is at the same time a marked tendency on the part of most to react negatively to certain definitions of love that have been proposed. There seems to be a popular belief that there *is* such a phenomenon as love. It is also commonly believed that there is *one* "true" or "perfect" kind of love that *ought* to be achieved before two people marry or otherwise commit themselves to each other. The suggestion that there may be other kinds of love is usually met with the reply that if there are, they must be "infatuations," "puppy-love," or they are labeled with some other apparently negative judgemental term which implies that it is not "real love."

The term "love" appears frequently in the sociological literature on marriage and the family as well as in questionnaires and interview schedules used to gather basic research data; yet attempts made to define love are confusing at best.

Even in this scientific age, many people feel that love should or must remain a mystery. Thousands of years ago, Solomon said: "Three things are too wonderful for me; four I do not understand: the way of an eagle in the sky, the way of a serpent on a rock, the way of a ship on the high seas, and the way of a man with a maiden" (Proverbs 30:18, 19).

More recently, others (e.g. Senator Proxmire) have suggested that analyzing or defining love may destroy it. We differ from both of these categories of critics in that we believe that there is perhaps as much to be gained from studying the way of a man with a maiden as has been gained from studying the way of an eagle in the air or the way of a ship on the high seas.

We also cannot believe that analyzing human phenomena makes them disappear or necessarily must change their effects in either harmful or beneficial ways. If this were so, the invention of thermometers would have stopped (or perhaps increased) fevers; the discovery that water is composed of hydrogen and oxygen might have made it stop quenching thirst or no longer drown people.

We believe that valid and reliable knowledge about *anything* helps people to live in more rational and more meaningful ways.

DEFINING LOVE

From contexts, definitions, and other clues, it seems safe to conclude that "love" refers to a sentiment—it involves affect (feeling, emotion), libido, and cognition (an idea, knowledge, conscious awareness).[1] The verb "to love" is transitive; it is invested in (cathected upon, attached to) an object, or some class or category of objects. Hence, human loving involves a human social relationship; it has significance for describing or comprehending the social organization of a dyad or a larger group.[2]

In one of the leading dictionaries of terms used by behavioral scientists, English and English (1958), love is defined as:

1) A feeling, varied in its behavioral aspects and in mental content, but believed to have a specific and unique quality; affection; a feeling of attachment for a person (sometimes a thing); strong liking. The feeling of love need not, though it often manifestly does, have an erotic *element; and some theorists hold that all love feelings are erotic in essence. 2) A* sentiment *whose dominant feeling is affection, and whose goal is the close association of another person (or personified object) with oneself, and the happiness and welfare of that person. The* feeling *of (1) is essentially a temporarily limited* event. The sentiment *of (2) is an enduring* structure *(see sentiment). Yet the attributes of one of these are often ascribed to the other, probably because the feeling is seldom experienced except as an expression of the sentiment. 3) (psychoan.) The primitive and undifferentiated pleasure- seeking emotion (=libido), or a specialization thereof which contains a large element of (often-disguised) lust. 4) (psychoan.) The feeling expression of Eros, the instinct which accepts and constructs, or integrates.—See libido, usually a close synonym. The psycho- analytic meaning of love has shifted as analytic doctrine has developed; the earlier view of (3) merged gradually (and incompletely) into that of (4). 5) A spiritual quality, possibly derived from sexuality but free of any sexual quality, which unites persons, giving them a sense of being interrlated. See* agapism. *This meaning—religious, mystic, and literary, rather than scientific—nonetheless refers to a kind of relationship and of inter- personal behavior which it is important for psychology as a science to consider.*

ANALYZING LOVE

Calling attention to the animal studies of Harlow and others, Bardwick (1974) defines love in behavioral terms as a sequence of developmental stages of interactive capabilities. She remarks that:

As with any other behavior capacity which develops, later stages depend on earlier ones; each form of love relationship prepares the individual for the one that follows. The failure of any of the love behavior systems to develop normally deprives the individual of the necessary foundation for the development of subsequent complex affectional relation- ships . . . I generalize from Harlow's primates to people . . . (p. 46).

Bardwick, in this passage, accepts the notion that there are several forms of love relationships.

A strictly behavioral definition of love as secondary reinforcement (Secord & Backman, 1974) is, of course, scientifically useful. Many people are satisfied to generalize on human and animal love in this way. Somatic and/or behavioral effects of love, so defined, are observable and measurable.

In reviewing the concept of love, Benson (1971) comments:

. . . A certain vagueness and arbitrariness is characteristic of all efforts to pin love down. We could overcome these difficulties by using a more detailed operational definition, *such as saying that love exists whenever two persons answer a series of questions about their relationship in a certain way, but then we would have to accept precision in method at the expense of intelligence in content (p. 105).*

Rubin (1973) devised a Love-Scale and a Liking-Scale made up of series of questions, just as Benson suggests. Through these two 13-item scales (later reduced to nine-item scales), Rubin summed up several different qualities that defined liking and loving in various ways to produce quantitative measures of both. The total score in Rubin's Love-Scale thus reveals *how many ways* a subject believes that he or she loves another person.

Lee (1974) also devised a scale for identifying a subject's "style of loving" which, unlike Rubin's scales, was directed toward discovering the extent to which a subject associates several different *meanings* of love with particular feelings, beliefs; and behaviors. His scale defines eight distinguishable concepts of love derived from a somewhat larger logical classification.

When we read Lee's "The Styles of Loving" in *Psychology Today* in October of 1974, we were struck with how often there is an uncritical acceptance of the popular, unidimensional, dichotomous concept of love—a concpet which many of our clients and colleagues seemed to share.

DIFFERENT CONCEPTS OF LOVE

What would happen if self-designated lovers were attempting to develop a relationship on the basis of substantially different understandings about the nature of love? Perhaps worse, should the therapist identify the concept understood by one of the couple as "better," and help the other partner to accept it? Worse still, should the therapist unwittingly define "true love" on the basis of his or her own cultural or philosophical grounds and try to influence the client to accept this ideal?

Even more complex questions began to arise. If definitions of loving behavior are different for two people in a partnership, what effect does this have on each one's self-concept and self-esteem? What happens to their self-concepts when each expects the other to respond in certain ways before the behavior can be judged to be loving (Secord & Backman, 1961)? With differing expectations of what loving behavior should be, incongruity is a predicted outcome. Theoretically, distress and ultimately either psychological, behavioral, or somatic changes in one or both parties can be expected to follow.

We believe that there are three general classes of responses the human mind-body can make to stimuli, whether the stimuli are genetic, physiological, psychological, social, or cultural (Lasswell & Bode, 1974). These three categories are psychological, behavioral, and somatic. We further postulate that all somatic and behavioral responses are potentially observable and hence, measurable.

Conative, cognitive, and affective responses to stimuli are observable and measurable only in terms of their somatic or behavioral effects. In other words, subjective feelings, knowledges, motives, volitions, and so forth are hypothetical constructs. They are not directly observable, but observable phenomena are hypothesized to be *effects* of their presence, absence, or variation (Lasswell & Bode, 1974). Unlike Skinner (1971), we believe that the evidence for some of these hypothetical constructs (love, in particular, to take the case in point) is sufficient to warrant more investigation through observation of their believed somatic and behavioral effects.

Our work seemed to be cut out for us: to examine the kinds of changes which might accompany the distress resulting from differing expectations of what loving behavior should be. In theory, if two persons are using a common symbol (the word "love" as in "I love you") to designate different sentiments for each we hypothesized that we could expect: 1) communication failure in this area; 2) system distress; and/or 3) personal distress (Selye, 1974).

First, we needed to validate empirically the assumption that people do have different concepts of love. Then we needed to look more carefully at distressed clients to determine whether incongruous concepts of love were present. Finally, we needed to propose and test a therapy for relieving such distress clinically.

At first, we were not fully aware of the extensive scope of Lee's research and undertook an investigation of our own of the hypothesis that more than one distinct, individually integrated concept of love existed. We developed and validated some scales of our own. From those we were able to construct individual profiles of concepts of love. Later, we found that many of our findings were essentially the same as Lee's, although there appeared to be some minor differences.

We found that we shared with Lee a lack of concern with measuring *how much* a person loves another, but rather we do want to know *what that love means* to him or her. We shared a hypothesis that love can mean different things to different people. We concluded that people are likely to expect others to love them according to the meaning of love that they themselves have rather than recognizing that others have invested this sentiment with different meanings.

In our initial examination of the idea that love means different things to different people, we accepted Burgess, Locke, and Thomes' (1971) classification of love as a sentiment. Leighton (1959) defined a sentiment as a human phenomenon which has both cognitive and affective qualities. One can *think about* love, *know* when it is happening, and *distinguish its meaning* from other information; that is its cognitive aspect. One can also *feel* love with varying degrees of intensity and observe subjectively somatic states (altering cardiac and/or respiratory functioning, producing subjectively observable sexual arousal, or the like) that are cognitively attributed to the presence of that feeling.

Our empirical investigation of the cognitive referents of love did not concern itself with the affective qualities of the sentiment of love or with the quantitative measurement of such affect. We are aware of the physiological measurements that are available for such measurement. They range from galvanic skin response, electroencephalographic responses, blood pressure, pupil dilation respiration rate, voice prints, and other observable responses of the organism correlated with hypothetical feelings of love as well as other feelings such as anger, fear, and guilt. We know that hypothesized affect can be measured by somatic indexes. What intrigued us, however was the thought that two people who gave similar readings on a polygraph when concentrating deeply on "feelings of love" could get into a heated argument on the definition of love—its cognitive aspect. Our attention, as a result, was directed to beliefs, memories, and information that we hypothesized to be related to subjectively experienced "love."

In our initial examination of the idea that love means different things to different people, we constructed definitions of six hypothetical types of love, defined them operationally, tested the operational definitions for their distinctness and exclusivity of meaning, and then constructed profiles of the six scales which measured the six types of love for 188 subjects. As expected, we found both individual and categorical differences among the profiles of the subjects.

A collection of 144 items indicating the presence or absence of behaviors, thoughts, or feelings hypothesized as characteristics of the six constructed types was prepared according to a system of logical exhaustion of the distinctive differences postulated between the various types. This collection was reduced to 95 items by a panel of three judges; and these 95 items were presented to 188 subjects in the form of a true-false questionnaire.

An item analysis of the correlation between each item and each of the six scales was carried out and 57 items were judged to be discriminators. The clustering of responses to these 57 items were analyzed by a Gutman-Lingoes Smallest Space Analysis procedure and it was found that both two-dimensional and three-dimensional clustering indicated that the six constructed types were conceptually distinct. The number of items was subsequently reduced to 50 as a result of a Gutman-Lingoes Multidimensional Scalogram Analysis.

The 188 subjects included a variety of Japanese, Indonesian, Japanese-American, Chinese, Chinese-American, native Hawaiian, and United States mainland Caucasian subjects, both male and female, with Buddhist, Christian, Protestant, agnostic, and atheistic religious identities.

A sample of 34 subjects from the original 188 agreed to write narrative descriptions of their styles of loving *after* they had completed the questionnaire but before they had seen their profiles. The hypothesized types of love were explained to them for the first time, and they were asked to predict the relative magnitude of their scores on as many of the six scales as possible. Thirty subjects predicted most of their scores in their correct order of magnitude, although not all subjects made predictions for each scale[3]; two subjects predicted equal numbers of scores accurately and inaccurately, and two predicted more scores inaccurately than accurately. These subjective predictions were accepted as tentative evidence of the validity of the profiles.

To date, nearly 1000 additional profiles support the hypothesis that persons have different concepts of love.

A personal profile was computed to show the extent to which each subject conceptualized "love" as each of the six types. This profile is called the SAMPLE profile, so named by using the initial letter of each of the six scales. . . .

CONSTRUCTED TYPES OF LOVE

A description of the constructed types follows:[4]

Storge (life-long friends)

The constructed type of storgic love is characterized by rapport, self-revelation, inter-dependency, and mutual need fulfillment (Reiss, 1960). Storgic lovers are essentially good friends who have grown in intimacy through close association, with an unquestioned assumption that their relationship will be permanent and that they will find a way to deal with their problems that causes them minimum pain. A storgic lover does not fantasize finding some other—perhaps unknown but ideal—lover in the future and abandoning the storgic partner. It never occurs to extreme storgic types that a romantic "knight on a white horse" or "femme fatale" will appear at some future time to solve their problems. It is more likely that even if this should occur to the storgic love, he/she would need the storgic partner around to discuss the romantic lover, to give advice, and to share the joys of discovery.

The storgic lover is not a person bored by routine home activity, but is more likely to find it comfortable and relaxing. Storgic lovers are not constantly on the search for new love experiences; rather they enjoy the security of being able to predict each other's responses to their behaviors.

If storgic lovers should break up, they would probably remain close and caring friends, perhaps continue corresponding with one another and actively caring about one another.

Physical intimacy, coitus, and the appreciation of their partners as sexual persons usually come relatively late in a storgic relationship, are accepted comfortably and joyously when they do appear on the scene, and are thus satisfying. Pure storgic types are extremely unlikely to "keep an eye out" for new or more romantic sexual partners.

Temporary separations are not great problems to storgic persons. Their mutual trust is such that separations are viewed as necessary inconveniences, needed diversions, or opportunities for personal growth which will either improve or at least not damage their relationship.

The storgic lover does not "fall in love" in the way that other types of lovers do. The storgic type is more likely to recognize that he/she has been in love for some time without realizing it earlier. As a result, anniversaries, birthdays, Valentine's Day, and like occasions are not important to them and may even be forgotten or overshadowed by other matters.

In many ways storgic lovers resemble siblings in their understanding of the love relationship. If they fight and argue, it is not an indication that they do not love each other. They are likely to feel that when their love has matured it will be permanent and that they cannot replace their relationship with each other any more than they can replace those that they have with siblings or with parents.

Agapic (totally "thou" centered)

An agapic lover is forgiving. This kind of love typically assumes that when the loved one causes pain to himself or herself or to someone else, that he or she is acting in ignorance, innocent error, or is the victim of forces not originating in the love-object's personality. A male agapic lover might, for example help his female love object arrange an abortion if she became pregnant by someone else during their love affair. Or he might easily love and accept a child conceived by some other man with deep concern for the anguish caused to his loved one and with tender affection for the child. An agapic lover would be more likely to help his or her love object to get medical attention for a venereal disease contracted from someone else during their love affair than to be angry or punitive toward the love object for having a sexual relationship with another.

Agapic persons never "fall in love." Their love for others is always available and they are simply given the opportunity by some of their love objects to show their love to a greater extent than they are by others. An agapic lover cares enough about his/her love object's happiness to understand and give up the loved one if that would seem to give him or her a greater chance for happiness elsewhere.

An agapic lover is patient with the behaviors of his or her love object to an extent that seems to border on masochism. The ideal agapic lover would wait indefinitely for a love object to be released from prison or from a mental hospital, would tolerate the behaviors of an alcoholic or drug-addicted spouse, and would be willing to live with a partner who was engaging in illegal or immoral activities, even though he/she personally disapproved of such behaviors. The agapic lover is always supportive of his/her partner.

Mania (possessiveness and intense dependency)

The constructed ideal of this type of lover is obsessed with his or her love object. A manic lover may be unable to sleep, eat, or even think logically around the loved one. The manic lover has peaks of excitement, but also depths of depression, with very few periods without a high or low.

This type of lover is jealous to an extent that might be described as irrational. A manic lover cannot tolerate loss of contact with a love object, even for short periods of time, and is distressed by a lack of the lover's presence or anticipated interaction. A manic lover is typically crushed by either real or fancied rejection, possibly to the point of suicidal ideation.

The manic lover often tries to manipulate the behaviors or feelings of the loved one, but because he or she seems to be bereft of logic, often succeeds only in looking foolish in his or her own eyes. For example, a manic lover may tell the loved one that they should spend a few days apart to think objectively about their relationship, and then go into a state of panic because the partner cannot be located during that period. Manic lovers do not tolerate separation at all well.

The manic lover has a tendency to review his or her abortive love affairs and speculate about what went wrong that terminated them.

Manic lovers frequently have sexual problems as well as problems in handling other forms of intimate interaction. Because of their high level of anxiety, manic lovers would be expected to have sexual problems related to anxiety, such as vaginismus or premature ejaculation.

Mania is probably associated with low self esteem and a poor self concept. Because of this, manic persons are typically not attractive to persons who have good self concepts and high self esteem. They become burdensome to more self-sufficient others. If they are rejected by them, their anxieties intensify, making them even less attractive.

Pragma (logical - sensible)

The ideal constructed type identified as pragma is that of a person who is unable to invest love in "unworthy" love objects. The pragmatic lover is keenly aware of the comparison level for alternatives that he or she has. Pragmatic lovers are inclined to look realistically at their own assets, decide on their "market value" and set off to get the best possible "deal" in their partners. Once the "deal" is made, the pragmatic lover remains loyal and faithful and defines his or her status as "in love" because the loved one is a "good bargain." Should the assets of either partner change, the pragmatic lover may feel her or his contract has been violated, and may begin to search for another partner.

A pragmatic lover typically assists the loved one to fulfill his or her potentials; for example, such a lover might make sure the love object finishes school, asks for deserved promotions, gets the attention that he or she "deserves" from physicians, stockbrokers, or employers.

Typically, a pragmatic lover maximizes his or her own assets before "putting them on the market." A male pragma may decide not to become involved with any females until he has $10,000 in the bank, or has gone through psychoanalysis, or has a secure job, or has assured himself by reading enough or consulting experts to be sure that he is sexually skillful, or the like. A sterile or impotent pragmatic lover may deliberately seek out a widow or widower with children if he or she wants a family.

Once a prospect is in sight, the prototypical pragmatic lover might check out future in-laws and friends systematically, find out if the couple's Rh factors are compatible, and obtain assurance that there is a minimal probability of hereditary defects showing up in their mutual children, and so forth.

Pragmatic persons break up or divorce or stay married for practical reasons. Divorce may actually be planned for some future date. For example, pragmatic partners may decide to finish school, to get a different job at another location, to put their youngest child through high school, or to reach some other such goal or state before they get divorced.

Pragma always looks at things *in context* and knows his or her basic values, scaling everything by them. (E.g., if sex life is mediocre, pragma may consult a sex counselor, but is more likely to assign sexual activity a low value in his or her value system and simply accept its mediocrity. "After all, he *is* a good provider, and being orgasmic isn't all that important." "She *is* a good mother, and I can get by on coitus once a week without getting too tense.")

While other types may have spontaneous orgasms or masturbate just from thoughts of the beloved, pragma probably learns to recognize sexual tension and relieve it when necessary for sleep or comfort (if sex is not devalued).

Pragma thinks ahead about family size (and probably even about what sex the children will be). If pragma is a schoolteacher, he or she may plan an October/November conception so the baby will arrive during vacation.

Ludus (self-centered game player)

The ideal constructed type of a ludic lover is that of a person who "plays" love affairs as he or she plays games or puzzles—to win, to get the greatest rewards for the least cost. A ludic lover hates dependency, either in himself/herself or in others. This type shies away from commitment of any sort (does not like lovers to take him or her for granted). The ludic lover enjoys strategies, and may keep two or three or even four lovers "on the string" at one time. A ludic person may even create a fictional lover to discourage a real one's hopes for a permanent relationship. He or she avoids long range plans, is careful not to date the same person often enough to create the illusion of a stable relationship. A ludic lover would rather find a new sex partner than to work out sexual problems with an old one. And yet, he or she may suddenly show up for a replay, even years later, with birthday flowers, a bottle of a favorite wine, a sentimental Valentine, or a record of a favorite song, and vanish just as suddenly. A ludic person usually enjoys love affairs, and hence rarely regrets them unless the threat of commitment or dependency becomes too great.

Dates with a ludic person are never dull, even though they may not happen with great regularity. He or she is never possessive or jealous. The ludic lover usually has good self-concept, usually is assured of current success in love as well as most other areas. Unlike a pragmatic lover, a ludic lover never reveals all of himself or herself nor demands such revelation by partners.

Ludic lovers are not likely to be very sophisticated sexually. As a rule, they have only one sexual routine; if the sex partner is not pleased by the ludic lover's sexual pattern, then the ludic one simply finds another partner rather than attempting to improve an unsatisfying relationship. If she does not like his sexual behavior, the ludic man moves on to someone who does; if he does not get an erection or bring her to orgasm on his own (with no help from her) the ludic woman looks for a man who will. Sex is self-centered and may be exploitative rather than symbolic of a relationship. A ludic lover does not listen to (or take time for) feedback; that suggests commitment, which is "scary." A ludic lover may not even *want* to be his or her partner's best sex partner because that might necessitate commitment or dependency that would be "awful." Physical appearance of the partner is less important than other qualities, such as self-sufficiency and lack of demanding behavior, to ludic persons.

Eros (romantic)

The constructed type of Eros is *romantic* love. Erotic lovers believe that love at first sight is possible if not mandatory. Falling in love is highly desirable. It is believed to produce an optimum state in the whole mind-body; persons in love feel 10 years younger, sleep well, wake up rested and refreshed. Impotent persons become potent; inorgasmic persons become orgasmic. Every gland and organ is believed to be operating at maximum efficiency.

Eros is monogamous although often serially. Erotic lovers remember exactly how their partners looked when they met; they remember exactly the day they met, the time they first touched, the time they first kissed, the day, hour, minute, place, smell, lighting effects of their first sex; and they expect their partners to remember and celebrate the anniversaries of such occasions.

An erotic lover is certain he or she is in love because the beloved has *exactly* the skin, fragrance, hair, voice, body build, eye color and style he or she likes the most. If that is not objectively true, it becomes easy to *believe* it is true.

The romantic lover must always have his or her best foot forward. Risks of losing the beloved cannot be afforded. On the other hand, erotic lovers constantly search for new ways to please their beloveds with ever-increasing delights—presents, new foods, new sexual techniques, and so on.

An erotic lover wants to know *everything* about the beloved from the first moment of their meeting, all of his or her experiences, joys and sorrows, who else he or she has loved in the past, how much and in what ways. At the same time, an erotic lover wants to *reveal* everything to the loved one—what she or he dreamed about last night, what happened on the bus today, how a second grade teacher embarrassed him or her.

Erotic lovers may like to wear matching T-shirts, identical bracelets, matching colors, order the same foods when dining out, find out that their blood types are the same; they typically want to be identified with each other as totally as possible.

Erotic lovers usually report having had a secure and happy childhood and believe that their parents were happily married.

If erotic lovers do not get jealous it is because they are rarely apart. There is thorough commitment. An erotic type can go quite comfortably without falling in love, sometimes for a long time, but when cupid strikes, it is hard, fast, and total. Break-ups are explosive and painful.

Erotic lovers initiate sex early in their relationship. It is always perceived as perfect, or becoming so, as indeed are all qualities of and experiences with the partner.

These six types are ideal constructs. Rarely is anyone a "pure" type. Rather, persons have varying degrees of each quality. They may be high in two or even three scales or they may have only moderate elevation in some categories and be very low in all of the rest. The cognitive component of each person's sentiment of love is best shown by the profile which shows the degree to which the subject fits each ideal type.

CLINICAL APPLICATIONS

Clinical application of the research finding is still quite limited; however, the results have been encouraging. Lee's analyses of the types have been consistently affirmed and have suggested several useful therapeutic approaches (Lee 1973).

The following case illustrates some of the possible clinical protocols that may lead to an awareness of differing concepts of love:

Claude (24 years of age) and Vicki (age 28) sought marriage counseling as the result of a crisis which had developed in their relationship.

> Counselor: *Vicki, you say Claude wants a divorce and you don't. Is that correct, Claude?*
> Claude (calmly): *Yes, it is.*
> Counselor: *Why do you want a divorce?*
> Vicki (interrupting): *That's what's driving me crazy! He won't say.*
> Claude: *I just don't love her anymore.*
> Counselor: *When did you come to this realization?*
> Claude: *Vicki took our son to visit her sister for two weeks, and I not only didn't miss her while she was gone, I actually felt very comfortable.*
> Counselor: *And is this different from the way you felt when you married Vicki?*

> *Claude: Well, I'm sure that I must have loved her very much. But I really married Vicki because I felt a lot of obligation. Not that she was pregnant or anything like that. It's just that I thought I didn't have much choice.*

Exploration revealed that Vicki had been previously married to a man who "really began acting strangely" after about three years of marriage. Claude—a close, unmarried friend of both of the couple—was literally seduced by Vicki in the fourth year of her marriage. They had a brief sexual affair and Claude was then sent overseas in the military service. During the year while he was away, Vicki obtained a divorce.

> *Claude: Vicki kept writing that she expected us to be married when I got back. I didn't really consider any alternative. My friendship with her ex-husband got uncomfortable because of what I had done and I felt really guilty that I had been responsible for the breakup. Vicki needed me, though, and I did seem to make her feel better about herself.*
>
> *Vicki: I don't understand you at all, Claude. You don't act any differently now from the way you did then. (Turning to the counselor.) He has a wonderful relationship with our son. He insisted that we buy a new home last year. He's been putting in the lawn and works on the house every night and every weekend. We have a good sexual relationship and he tells me I'm a good cook and housekeeper. He brings me his paycheck every week and never questions what I do with the money.*
>
> *Claude: I like the way you manage money. And all the other things you say are true. But I know I'm not in love with you.*

Vicki has had two husbands whose patterns of relating to her "didn't make sense" to her. She thought she was being a good wife and a good lover to each of them. She thought her first husband had "gone crazy." Now her second husband seemed to be behaving in a "crazy" way. Maybe (she thought) she was the crazy one. She said she had thought about suicide in her despair but had rejected the idea because "who would take care of our son?"

> *Counselor: Claude, do you like married life?*
>
> *Claude: Yes. I think I am a homebody—a family man, you know.*
>
> *Counselor: Do you think you would be happier married to someone other than Vicki?*
>
> *Claude: I don't have anyone in mind, but I know I probably couldn't stand to live alone for very long.*
>
> *Vicki: Then, if you don't want someone else and you do want to live with someone, why not me?*

Both Claude and Vicki were given the SAMPLE scale along with other tests. Each was interviewed once by the counselors' psychiatric consultant. There was no indication of significant psychopathology in either. Individual sessions with the counselor substantiated the material in the first conjoint interview, and both denied any extramarital activity since their marriage. Their SAMPLE profiles were quite different, however. Claude had markedly high scores in Agape and Storge. Vicki's highest scores were in Mania and Eros.

> *Counselor: Claude, do you think Vicki loves you?*
>
> *Claude: I'm pretty sure she does. And it's just not fair to her to be married to me when I don't love her. She ought to be free to find someone who does.*
>
> *Counselor: Do you still feel that Claude loves you, Vicki?*
>
> *Vicki: I don't know now. I'm confused. He acts like he does, but he says he doesn't.*

It is our hypothesis that Claude's Storgic-Agapic concept of loving was internalized during his years of being the only child of a widowed mother. The stress of loving Manic-Erotic Vicki resulted not so much from adapting to her style of loving, as from the dissonance produced by confrontation with the idea that her concept of loving was "right." Curiously, the inability to accept his own internalized style of loving as valid had led him to deny any affect whatsoever toward Vicki. Since Vicki obviously had missed him while she was away, he felt that his failure to be miserable while she was away must mean that he didn't love her. He did not understand that his concept of loving could be as valid as Vicki's because she seemed to show her love in more overt ways. Vicki also thought her concept of loving was *right,* but she seemed satisfied with Claude's way, too. Claude, on the other hand, knew he didn't feel the way Vicki did, so he concluded that he did not love her.

Some edited passages from Lee's *The Colours of Love* on Storgic-Agapic and Manic-Erotic were read to them, and they agreed that the passages were descriptive. The counselor suggested that they could understand each other better if they each understood the other's definition of love. It was also suggested that styles of loving can be modifed and that through an acceptance of the concept that there are several valid styles of loving, they might slowly move toward more compatible styles.

DISCUSSION

A number of scales for defining love operationally have been devised. Many of these are based on a unidimensional assumption—that is that love (or caring, or romantic love) is a unique, integrated variable which can be scaled on a single gradient. Scales such as Shostrom's "Caring Relationships Inventory," Rubin's "Loving Scale" (1973), and Knox and Sporakowski's "Attitudes Toward Loving" scale (1968) seem to make a unidimensional assumption.

On the other hand, there are instruments which incorporate more than one dimension, from which some profile of subscales or of distinct scales can be constructed, operationally defining distinguishable factors which can be grouped conceptually as kinds of love relationships. In some instances, these are simply reinterpretations or procedural variations or comparisons of unidimensional scales, as in Hinkle and Sporakowski's factor analysis of the "Attitudes toward Loving" scale (1975) and Rubin's comparison of the "Loving Scale" and the "Liking Scale" (1973). In other instances, the scales or subscales appear to be independent and not inherently related to any general scale score. These latter cases include Shostrom's "Pair Attraction Inventory" (1971), and Lee's "Styles of Loving" scales (1973, 1974). These latter do not imply that either a general score or any particular profile of scores indicates that the respondent is any more or any less "in love" or "mature" or enculturated or socialized (with the exception of Shostrom's "G" score, which he evaluates as predictive of a better adjustment in marriage). Instead, they emphasize that people can "love" with *different* concepts of their own behavior and feelings, and with *different* expectations of the "loving" behavior of others.

The clinical implications of the latter concept become apparent when one member of a dyad estimates the degree of "love" in a partner's behavior on any informal "scale" that is implicit in his/her concept of love, but which is inappropriate for the partner's concept. Not only is there a misperception of the partner's behavior and a basic communication failure, but a resultant stress which can only be reduced by somatic change, behavioral change, or some other kind of cognitive reinterpretation of the relationship between the members of the dyad (Lasswell & Bode, 1974). A cognitive reinterpretation might include lowered self-esteem ("I am wrong or bad or worthless") or reevaluation of the partner ("He/she is wrong, bad, worthless") or a change in behavior (avoiding interaction with the partner as much as possible) or any other of the mechanisms identified by Secord and Backman (1961).

Obviously, the first step in the clinical management of counseling for a couple who seem to have incongruous concepts of love is for the counselor and the counselees to gain some insight into what their concepts of love are in a nonjudgmental way. The counselor's own profile may be useful to him/her in that defining his/her own concept of love constitutes a safeguard against unwittingly imposing it as "right" on the counselees, when in fact it is only *different* from other concepts.

If the theory presented here is correct (or when it is appropriate to a case), the logical procedure indicated would be diagnosis, support ("Your understanding of love is *different* from your partner's, but that's ok and you're still a good person"), conjoint/insight therapy, and confrontation ("Now that you understand the problem, what do you want to do about it?") Although behavior modificiation techniques may well result in cognitive changes of partners in a less stress-producing direction, we see no reason not to deal directly with understanding. It has the advantage of not demanding pre-judgment of a "right" or "best" concept of love. . . .

FOOTNOTES

[1] For example, Burgess, Locke, and Thomes (1971) suggest that love is a *sentiment:* ". . . Love, like other sentiments, is a complex of attitudes, emotions, and desires organized around an object," (p. 275).

[2] Goode says, ". . . Love is defined as a strong emotional attachment, a cathexis. . . Verbal definitions of this emotional relationship are notoriously open to attack. . ." (p. 41).

[3] Three subjects made predictions for only one scale score, nine for only two scores, five each for three and four scores, one for five, and eleven made predictions for all six scales.

[4] We are deeply indebted to Lee (1974) for borrowing from his typology. We have used his terminology (largely drawn from classical literature) to label six constructed types: storge, agape, mania, pragma, ludus, and eros.

REFERENCES

Bardwick, J. M. Evolution and parenting. *Journal of Social Issues,* 1974, *30,* 39-62.

Benson, L. *The family bond: Marriage, love, and sex in America.* New York: Random House, 1971.

Burgess, E. W., Locke, H. J., & Thomes, M. M. *The family: From tradition to companionship.* New York: Van Nostrand Reinhold Company, 1971.

English, H. B., & English, A. C. *A comprehensive dictionary of psychological and psychoanalytical terms.* New York: Longmans, Green and Co., 1958.

Festinger, L. *A theory of cognitive dissonance.* Evanston, IL: Row, Peterson, & Company, 1957.

Goode, W. J. The theoretical importance of love. *American Sociological Review,* 1959, *24,* 38-47.

Hinkle, D. E., & Sporakowski, M. J. Attitudes toward love: A reexamination. *Journal of Marriage and the Family,* 1975, *37,* 764-767.

Holy Bible, Revised Standard Edition, Catholic Edition. Camden, NJ: Thomas Nelson & Sons, 1966.

Knox, D. H., & Sporokowski, M. J. Attitudes of college students toward love. *Journal of Marriage and the Family,* 1968, *30,* 638-642.

Lasswell, T. E., & Bode, J. G. *Sociology in context: Scientific and humanistic.* Morristown, NJ: General Learning Press, 1974.

Lee, J. A. *The colours of love.* Toronto: New Press, 1973.

Lee, J. A. The styles of loving. *Psychology Today,* October, 1974, 44-51.

Leighton, A. H. *My name is Legion: Foundations for a theory of man in relation to culture.* New York: Basic Books, Inc., 1959.

Reiss, I. L. Toward a sociology of the heterosexual love relationship. *Marriage and Family Living,* 1960, *22,* 139-145.

Rubin, Z. *Liking and loving.* New York: Holt, Rinehart, and Winston, Inc., 1973.

Secord, P. F., & Backman, C. W. Personality theory and the problem of stability and change in individual behavior: An interpersonal approach. *Psychological Review,* 1961, *68,* 21-32.

Secord, P. F., & Backman, C. W. *Social psychology,* 2nd Edition. New York: McGraw-Hill Book Co., 1974.

Selye, H. *Stress without distress.* Philadelphia: J. B. Lippincott Company, 1974.

Shostrom, E., & Kavanaugh, J. *Between man and woman: The dynamics of intersexual relationships.* Los Angeles: Nash Publishing, 1971.

Skinner, B. F. *Beyond freedom and dignity.* New York: Alfred A. Knopf, 1971.

Udry, J. R. *The social context of marriage,* 3rd Edition. New York: J. B. Lippincott Company, 1974.

Winch, R. F. Another look at the theory of complementary needs in mate selection. *Journal of Marriage and the Family,* 1967, *29,* 756-762.

8   sexual incompatibilities

joseph b. trainer

One approach of considerable utility in dealing with sexual incompatibility in marriage is to divide the complex into early, middle, and late marriage. I think of early marriage more or less as that of the first two or three years. Middle marriage is the longer childbearing and launching segment. Late marriage is the post-launching epoch where the pair are having to fall back on each other as prime sources of company.

EARLY MARRIAGE

Expectations vs. Realizations

Most of the replies to the counselor's question "When did your marriage first seem to go off the track?" can be put on the fingers of one hand.
"The day I got married."
"The first night I was married."
"The day after I got married."
"The first week I was married."
"The first month I was married."

It has often been said that a marriage in trouble was in trouble from the start. Clinical experience confirms this. I believe the basic problem is the discrepancy between the expectations of the two and their realizations. They found something or someone quite different from whatever they had planned for or anticipated. (I am discounting here the whole question of what I think of as spurious marriages. These are liasons undertaken for essentially an invalid reason, such as to escape from the parental household or to achieve the status of marriage or to acquire wealth or citizenship. These are almost certain trouble as one might expect they would be.)

The presenting complaint of the usual, validly undertaken marriage at the early stage is most frequently not sexual. It is more likely to be one of fatigue, or of depression, some area of easily admissible conflict. At this stage, the couple do not wish to admit to a sexual failure, often to themselves. They likewise inwardly expect to improve their sexual situation with time. The counselor should inquire directly into this area as a part of the history of the problem. His ease and directness will allow the patient to respond in kind. While the open ended approach is excellent for the marriage as a whole, (e.g., "Tell me about your marriage."), it is not so effective for a sexual inquiry. A better approach is to ask, "What kinds of problems have you found with your sex life?" and go on from there.

Reprinted, by permission, from *Journal of Marriage and Family Counseling,* 1975, *1,* 123-34. Copyright ©1974 by the American Association of Marriage and Family Counselors, Inc.

Sexual Problems Seen in Early Marriage

Drive level divergence.

Since the population falls along a bell shaped curve for almost any measurable characteristic, it is not surprising that it appears to follow this same pattern for sexual drive strength. The drive mechanism is centered in the hypothalamus and has the basic automaticity of other hypothalamic functions. If two people have similar positions on the drive curve, there is not much likelihood of trouble from that source. If one of very high drive is mated to one of very low drive, a disaster is predictable from the onset. If the drives are discordant, but to a lesser degree, a major problem will develop in the process of attempting to resolve or "adjust" the difference. The parallel with food appetite is exact, in terms of trying to change it; the consequences of food-drive differences are only less serious in the pair bonding.

The clinical problem is to determine the degree of drive of each and seek out extrinsic modifying factors contributing to the discrepancy. Sexual ignorance and prior attitudes are the most usual modifiers, with anatomic or pathologic abnormalities far behind. One word of caution about determining drive level: The female in particular may have a high innate drive level, but due to cultural conditioning also have a low rate of arousal and an inability to be aggressive in any way. Thus both of the pair may have a high drive, yet the wife is dissatisfied and the husband puzzled—"I'll never understand women."—and frustrated.

Sexual ignorance.

In contrast to the otherwise similar process of eating, sexual activity and the conduct of sex are almost never learned from adult models. Sexual experimentation is therefore a curious mixture of pleasure and abysmal bungling. If this kind of gradual experiment and learning has not been carried out before marriage, it must be undertaken at the very onset of it. A double load is placed on the participants. They are attempting to cement a pair-bonding and arrive at a comfortable degree of head-to-head intimacy, a considerable task in itself. On top of that, they are faced with making the most intimate and restrictive physiological conjunction with an almost absolute ignorance of both the structures and functions involved.

The characteristic gender sub-culture difference existing up to recent times has been a block to both processes. We mix most easily with those like ourselves. Males and females grow up in two divergent environments and may share very little in their world views, likes and dislikes, and essential interests. The male has a quality of sensuality, the female one of tenderness. One could multiply these cultural differences indefinitely. They become a block to the easy achievement of satisfactory sexual rapproachment between a pair, and if not broken down to a considerable degree remain as permanent dividers.

Cultural taboos.

There is a new relation of easy, egalitarian companionship between young men and women which appears to be spreading both overtly and covertly, depending on old family attitudes and proximities. It has been aptly called the "Hang Loose Ethic" and to the older group the most prominent characteristic, or at least the most obtrusive, is the acceptance of sexual activity. Intercourse is at once more prevalent among them and at the same time given more of the quality of an expected pleasant biological function without carrying an overburden of emotional value. It appears to be something of the transference of the old male attitudes onto the female, made feasible by the availability of adequate contraception.

Nevertheless, it is probably still true that the majority of young marrieds still come under the strictures of the old gender subcultures mentioned above. The burgeoning sexuality of the male may often take his bride by surprise and be a source of uncertainty, discomfort, and dismay to her. The new couple may well get into trouble on just that account. The brand new husband sometimes is willing to give this a try up to a half-dozen times a day for a bit, often to the point where he forgets entirely about the emotional, love making aspect. The upset or disappointed new wife may get accommodated to this part when his abrupt switch of having caught up takes hold. Meanwhile, an emotional and communicative gulf has had a chance to develop, from a failure to associate sex with either love or marriage.

Probably the preeminent taboo derives from the unfortunate fact that the genital system is so anatomically related with the excretory system. Excreta of any kind is early associated with unpleasing, dirty, or disgusting. The female child in particular is prone to these associations, since she cannot as readily distinguish one part from another. The sexual area then becomes a part of the folklore of the dirty and forbidden together and may be unacceptable as a part of the body to play with, to touch with the hands or with the mouth.

Cultural taboos are best disposed of by dealing with them directly. The counselor must take the lead in exploring the possibility of this being a block to satisfactory sexual partnership and carry out such education as necessary for giving new perspective.

Medication effects.

The anovulatory pill is a high demand medication in the early married population and one which produces an appreciable amount of depression. The depression is accompanied by a loss of libido, and often by the usual interpersonal relationship disruptions seen with this disease. While both effects may be relatively mild, they bear an importance out of proportion at this early stage of pair-bonding.

Tranquilizers, particularly the phenothiazines, are destructive to the sex drive at the hypothalamic level and probably at the level of the limbic cortex.

The remedy in these problems is a reordering of priorities in drug use.

Fatigue states.

Fatigue holds a special problem in the lives of the newly married. The divergence between expectations and realizations is often brought about by the fatigue itself. Goal-oriented young people are the usual victims, since by nature they overextend themselves. In the new marriage the degree of overextension is greater than either partner anticipated. The small amount of time together is spent in what seems to be necessary problem-solving, and does very little for their personal relationship. With the failure of the courting and cultivating pattern consequent to that, and the pervasiveness of the fatigue, a sense of "sexual neglect" may occur. This may hit one of the pair before the other, or it may seem to arise together in both. It is usually interpreted as a personal rejection.

The counselor can do a great deal with this problem by helping the couple analyze their situation and their disposition of time and energy. A readjustment of some part of the living conditions is almost always possible, even if it involves nothing more than a minor change in schedule.

New paired-relationship images.

A dismaying discovery occurs when one of the partners realizes that what they considered acceptable behavior as a pair of lovers, suddenly is not accepted when they become a married pair. This is the opposite of their expectation, in which traditionally the marriage ceremony suddenly was to make everything all right sexually which was not supposed to be before. What appears to happen is that the two see each other in a new image, that of Wife Image and Husband Image, and potentially now as Mother Image and Father Image. Since they had never associated sex or sexual behavior with the images of their own fathers or mothers, they tend to dissociate sex from this image when they put it on each other. The bounding sexual round which was such a joy in the premarital period suddenly is not quite proper.

The counselor can be helpful if he recognizes what has happened and helps the patient analyze the origin of these strange and seemingly inappropriate feelings. When the patient can see how these images are created in the very early life experience of the old household, the basis is established for dealing with them in a rational way. The image is built on a false perception of reality, and by making the true reality clear the counselor is able to make sexual activity all right for them again.

MIDDLE MARRIAGE AND ITS SEXUAL PROBLEMS

The period of middle marriage, defined roughly as the time of child rearing to early launching, is really the heart of the working period of the family in being.

During this time the presenting complaint, usually of one of the pair, is a sexual one and the nature of it will be some deficiency in the other. The important part of the complaint, of course, is that the defect in the other produces an unsatisfactory sex (or other) life in the complaining one. While the sexual complaint is voiced, the real problem is probably to be found elsewhere. For one thing, there is a terrible tangle of images, one of the other. Clark Vincent paraphrases Oliver Wendell Holmes so well in this regard. Instead of just two people, we find at least six mixed up. There is, for example, the Self Image of the Husband and his Image of the Wife, and in addition his Image of the Wife's Image of the Husband. None of these may much resemble each other, and perhaps even less than the real husband and the real wife. Then there has to be the Self Image of the Wife, the Image of her Husband, and her Image of the Husband's Image of the Wife. This signals the arrival of a crowd on the scene in a legal sense, and one can expect something of the same crowd behavior and the presence of many confused noises without!

Personal Incompatibilities

There emerges with the passage of time in the marriage a progressive discrepancy between the early expectations and the chronic realities. What was happily expected at the onset becomes something looked for in time, then still hoped for eventually, then gradually, regretfully relinquished, and finally perhaps discarded bitterly. The two persons yoked together by law, mutual responsibilities, mutual financial interest are in fact very badly suited to the close demanding business of living together.

They have a personality incompatibility. Their natures, world views, aims, ideals, practices, values, are so at variance as to make any meaningful personal conjunction impossible. They may appear in public to be a normal, well-matched pair, but this public face is a sham and a farce. It is usually apparent to the counselor if to no one else. Where they are not in overt conflict, they have learned to live on the narrow edge of an uneasy neutrality.

A satisfying sexual conjunction is almost impossible in these circumstances. As a consequence, the sexual hunger of one of the partners is likely to be the focal point of the incompatibility. The drive is there; its reduction is not. The male may find enough extramarital sex to keep his existence on a level keel, yet this is not satisfactory. Most males would much prefer to have a satisfying sex life in the comfort of their connubial bed than anywhere else. The female is more hampered. Her drive is active, the tension cries for reduction. But the fact still is, even in this mobile society, her opportunities are fewer. If she does manage to find an extramarital outlet that is satisfactory, she is hampered by an insistent feeling of guilt, because she associates sex with love far more than the male. If she fails to find such an outlet, she is frustrated. Any physician who looks over his case histories, will realize that the basic reason for a very high percentage of his female patient visits could be traced back to either guilt or frustration.

With this situation affecting either of the partners, the sexual hunger focuses as the central burden, and it is expressed in terms of the defects of the partner. Rarely will someone come in truly expressing a conviction that whatever is wrong sexually is wrong with themselves.

Progressive Alienation

The history of the middle marriage is frequently one of either progressive alienation or of living divided, parallel lives. The divergence between the personalities are now in full swing, adding bit by bit with the passage of time. Each defect in the other makes one conscious of the possibility of the next defect to show up. Husbands and wives do not make an effort similar to that seen in the young's efforts to compensate for the real deficiencies in the parent by trying to make the parent they have seem like the one they wanted. Marital dissatisfaction is more like compound interest.

Preoccupation is prominent in this stage. Rather than cultivating the other, each is busy about his or her own concerns. The husband is concerned with his work and his career, or even his hobbies. The wife finds herself wrapped up in the endless struggle of rearing infants into little children and trying to keep little children out of accidents until they become big enough to get into their own. Neither one of the pair has much time or spends much time with or concerned about the other. Some will take refuge in the ideas of traditional gender roles to support the simple fact that they individually don't care much about being together.

One quality of the human shines forth like a beacon here, however. We may be silent in every other respect, but we retain our ability to express disapproval or dislike. This eminent quality is clearly shown behind the wheel of an automobile, but is present in other circumstances as well. Husbands and wives of middle marriage tenaciously hold on to the quality, to the point of considering it an inherent right. Each is a veritable Sherlock Holmes at ferreting out the faults of the other.

One stage down, probably is the less active "bog in boredom." The two have either moved through the combative period, or never had the energy to get to it. They find they are just purely bored by the other. So they sit silently at the table, or grunt over the newspaper, or settle in self containment in front of the television tube. Life has no spring, no bounce, no love, no interest. This is John Cuber's "Dull, durable marriage."

Sex is an inevitable casualty of such a collection of living circumstances. It may be taken on as a matter of "duty," or it may come about as a kind of partner masturbation, with a fantasy picture operating to make it all work. It is a very dissatisfying kind of sex.

Psychiatric States

Nothing about being married keeps anyone from having a psychiatric disease or a psychiatric prone neurotic personality. Being married may well precipitate trouble that is well compensated in less demanding relationships.

Schizoid personalities are marked by withdrawness. But so are people in an unsatisfactory, and currently unsolvable, marital trap. The trick is to distinguish one from the other, some insight into which may be gained by exploring the relationships outside the marriage. Even more productive is close observation of the personality in a joint interview versus that presented in the individual session. If the person is alive in the individual session, and deadened during the joint one, the problem is in the relationship. But, on the other hand, if the withdrawing is seen to be occurring not only in the marriage, but in the outer fringe as well, a schizoid reaction is probably taking place. This does not at all mean it is not related to the marriage. Far from it. The probability is that the stress of the poor marriage broke down the compensations of the individual.

Depressive disease is unfortunately a more evidenced characteristic of the human than euphoria, so much so that one almost thinks of it as a normal parameter of personality at some time, in some circumstances, or even as a usual operational mode. To separate out endogenous depression from exogenous depression may tax one's diagnostic skills, yet it can be done if the search is patient and the history taking careful. The depressed wife or husband presents a baffling obstacle to the mate. He or she cannot be approached, having put an unresponding shell about the personality. A mood of gloom tends to penetrate the household, and no efforts at livening it, making it joyful, or injecting some degree of enthusiasm seems to work. Since the usual accompaniment of depression is loss of appetite both for food and for sex, neither the meals nor the bed of the house becomes a particularly attractive place. The depressed one may well complain of the loss of appetite but be unable to do anything about improving them or making things better for the other. The undepressed one becomes progressively more restive both personally and sexually and usually finds it necessary to withdraw from the daily encounter.

The hysteric presents the problems of the superficially attractive person who lives in an adolescent state of excitability. They like the furor of excitement, which makes them interesting both sexually and in other respects during the courting stage and even in the early married stage. However, they become overburdeningly tiresome to live with, for they are totally unable to provide periods of peace of mind for anyone around them. To get the excitement, they will do capricious things, inappropriate things, or malicious things. If it takes a fight, they fight. If it takes a bout of histronics, they become momentary great dramatic actors and actresses. They are usually poor sexual partners merely because they cannot be genuinely interested in anyone else enough to make such a partner, and because they are so self-centered they are too aware of their potential pains and too insistent on their own pleasures. The hysteric holds always the apparent promise of that which cannot be delivered.

The psychopathic personality is even more difficult, in the fleeting encounters of the counselor's office. The history must ordinarily be had from someone else, but in the case of the marriage problem, the right person is on hand to deliver the very essence of the history. This is the quintessence of the "con man." The patient is likely to be attractive, personable, have a notable degree of earnest friendliness, and a general air which prompts you to believe whatever he (or she) says. The pattern of the marriage will probably have been much the same from the outset, with the only difference being that the problems have become more dimensioned with time. There will be times seemingly remarkably good, interspersed with periods of neglect, desertion, jail, or any of the unhappy things that can befall one who immediately runs afoul of society's regulations. It is well to remember that one reason the psychopath can seem so good at times is that whatever he may do, he never has to go through the inconvenience of feeling bad about it. His self image is therefore perfectly fine, and he can afford to present a pleasant view to the world, even when he is not actively trying to do it out of something. The sexual existence of this creature matches precisely the other characteristics and may explain in part for the fact that the marriages often are far more durable than would seem reasonable. In the good stage, the attention, the lovingness, the expressed affection and desire, the sometimes ostentatious outgoing giving carryover into superb sexual experiences. The memory of these is strong enough to warrant hanging on to the situation in its worst aspect in the hope of reattaining some of the emotional heights.

Authoritarian personalities are a difficult problem in a marriage and not at all a difficult problem in diagnosis. As the counselor you may not be sure you are right, even when you have to act like it, but this patient has no doubt whatever. He (sometimes she, but certainly more often he) is certain he is right; black is black and white is white. Right is clearly distinguishable from wrong, and the way he thinks and does is right. Such personalities are devastating to whoever has to live with them. The husband or wife becomes in effect a continual victim. Since he is always right, the other necessarily is always wrong. Sexually, this kind will most often simply use the partner, as he uses her in other respects. He will have no complaints and she likely dares have none.

The obsessive or compulsive personality deserves a word at this point. The world view of this personality may well be likened to a series of boxes or cubby holes into which things must fit. If they do not fit, he tries to study them to find a way to make them fit and if they absolutely refuse to fit he is likely to end up ignoring their presence entirely. These people are careful detail tenders and go about their work with uncommon intensity and endurance. They are hard to disturb or divert from their self-appointed tasks and they expect their partners to be something of the same kind of person. If they have to square off the end of the butter cube on the table, they cannot see why everyone else does not square it off. The sex life of such people is likely to be a little too well organized and ritualistic. The old sex manual was really made for them and you could almost hear them tagging off the page numbers of the manual as they move from one place in the sexual encounter to the next. Some undoubtedly run down the index when they get to the end to make certain nothing was missed.

The importance of these personality types and psychiatric states is that they are not uncommon frequenters of the physician's office or that of the marriage counselor. It is often mistakenly assumed that the marriage gave rise to the apparent problem in the person that is in fact a facet of the interrelational trouble between the two.

The demanding closeness of the marriage relationship must be recognized as the precipitating stress which uncovers the compensated personality abnormality. The small signs shown early are too often dismissed simply as "domestic trouble" and since this is so ubiquitous a closer look is not given. It is imperative that the counselor spend enough time with any problem which presents itself as a sexual or marital problem to really determine the nature of the personalities involved. If one of the pair is the victim of an intrapersonal defect, then there is no use in playing about the edges of it by way of interpersonal counseling. The sexual trouble in such marriages is only an incident, however pressing, in the relation between the pair. Ameliorating the relation, if it can be done at all, will have to depend on adequate psychic improvement in the troubled self.

Disease States

Middle marriage is a time of emergence of our common heritage of disease. The occurrence of disease imposes a burden on any marriage even though the burden be gladly and willingly accepted. The old ground rules change, and they change in ways neither of the partners could predict. The pattern of living is upset, and the pattern of the personal relation is interfered with, as the following example will show.

Diabetes occurs in about five percent of the population. Much of it has its onset in the Middle Marriage period. A pattern of hypoglycemia, inducing a repetitive eating pattern with a consequent obesity may herald the appearance of the mild obese type of diabetes. The first definitive symptoms may be a loss of libido and erectile impotence. If this is not recognized at its onset as due to diabetes some serious disruptions may take place in the marriage. The subsequent weight loss and rapid changes in refraction should give the show away, but unfortunately the patient is unaware of this sequence of events. About a third of diabetics have the problems of impotence, and it is one of the types that can be readily corrected by bringing the diabetes under control, correcting the thiamine deficiency neuritis, and sometimes using gonadotropins. This example perhaps better than most emphasizes the need for a good medical evaluation of the patient with a marital problem.

Children

Children form the earliest occurring and the last discussed barrier to a good marriage. The occurrence of a child, while pleasant in so many respects, and the satisfaction of a basic parental urge, does serve to divide the couple. There is a division of time and attention away from the spouse and onto the child. The wife may very well take on far more of a mothering role in the household than she does a wifely role. This may even go so far as to have the husband calling her "mother" instead of using her name. Both see her in the mothering image. This alone raises some hobbs with the sexual possibilities in the pair; you cannot feel very sexual about anyone you call "mother."

However, discrepancies arise which provoke disagreement between the two on the methods of child rearing. Assumptive knowledge comes to the fore, each bringing to this task something learned by watching his or her own parents. They may have rebelled at the right time, but unless the parental relationship was impossible, they tend to grow up believing that the way they were reared was the right way. This is never called into question until they are faced with a real life child of their own, and it therefore becomes oftener than not a source of conflict.

Finally there is the physical inhibition of the child in the sex life of the parents. We go to such enormous lengths to keep the child from discovering that we are sexual creatures. One of the commonest explanations people will give for inadequate sexual activity in the home is the presence of the children. Here, of all places we should be modeling a behavior for them to follow. Instead, we carefully conceal our true natures, and force the child in turn to conceal its inevitable sexual nature.

Summary

Middle Marriage is indeed shot through with problems of all sorts, many leading to outright divorce, many more to devitalized marriages. Sexual problems are entrained in almost every one of these situations, and are a basic cause of the lack of success in about a sixth. The success of Masters and Johnson in treating sexual inadequacy is largely due to their great insight into all these other relational problems that affect the ability to perform sexually and enjoy it. They help make over the personal relationship of the estranged pair, and in the course of doing so repair the sexual potholes brought about by the constant freezing and thawing in their patient's lives.

ADVANCED MARRIAGE

This part of marriage moves from the late launching period to the empty nest syndrome and beyond into retirement. It corresponds with the current second peak in the biphasic divorce curve which occurs at 25 years. Someone called marriage "the incredible entanglement of the lives of two people," which seems fair enough and which implies that if one is to get a divorce at that late stage, a long period of simmering discontent had to precede it to overcome all the entanglements.

The fact is that people married over this length of time tend to stay married out of habit or necessity or both. They are either loath to change the other parameters of their life styles, to which they have grown accustomed, or else they have alternatives which seem to offer no substantial improvement. As one observes them, at least through the window of the medical office (for they may look just fine outside), the pair of people at these later stages have a high degree of autonomy; are held together with exceedingly loose, live and let live ties; and show an enormous degree of daily operational independence. Their lives touch at the minimum necessary at acceptable points.

What are some of the sexual problems they present?

THE AGGRAVATED INCOMPATIBILITIES

By the time most couples have been together for 20 years they have learned each idiosyncracy of the other personality. They have not necessarily learned to make room for them with the passage of time. Rather, they tend to be tired of the whole bit and in fact somewhat sensitized to the peculiarities of the other. They have learned to overreact, in many cases, to a trivial bit of behavior. The differences between the two have become magnified with time, rather than diminished or reconciled. The rewards in old marriage are too often very few. Neither gives a great deal to the other in companionship, sympathy, attention, or affection.

Sex is a universal casualty in this association and not because it is biologically dead, but only because it is hamstrung and unpracticed. I had one kindly and gentle couple, both of whom I had taken care of for years. At age 76 the man approached me timidly in the course of a general examination and asked what I thought about his attempting to resume sexual relations with his wife. I asked him how long it had been since they had had relations, and he replied it had been nearly 30 years. They had stopped with the menopause and while she had not seemed interested, he had been wishing for 30 years that they could take it up again. I assured him that it would be perfectly all right, but that it would require some lubrication and considerable care at the onset because of the kraurosis and contracture of her introitus. Nature obviated the situation, however, for she died shortly after. It subsequently turned out that she had recently changed her will, cutting him out of her share even in their home. She had developed paranoia in her later years and while she was actually very dependent upon him she was convinced that he was her enemy. He thus had a double disappointment at 76.

Another man age 86 came in one day and asked me if I were giving him something to interfere with his powers. I asked him what the trouble was. He said, "I just can't seem to cut the mustard more than once a week lately." (This despite having been on large doses of estrogen for some years for a carcinoma of the prostate.) It turned out that I had indeed cut his activity, by putting him on therapeutic doses of nicotinic acid and interfering with his erectile capacity. We agreed on stopping the treatment.

I cite these as indicators of the continuing presence of awareness of sexuality and the desire to carry on sexual activity well into advanced age, and therefore through the heart of Advanced Marriage. It is subject to more extra sexual buffeting through these years, and like any physiologic function thrives on action and deteriorates on inaction.

Disease States

While we have the longest average life span in history today, it is because of the reduction in early deaths. We live in an acceleration of later deaths in critical areas largely concerned with the loss of circulation in the brain, the heart, the pelvis, or the legs. The process is hastened by inactivity, obesity, alcoholism, and a horrifyingly high fat diet.

The occurrence of a stroke or a myocardial infarction will have a profound effect on the relationship of the two people. There may be a complete shift in dominance or dependency. There may be an increase or decrease in sexual drive with a decrease in capacity. Sexual activity may itself pose a hazard to wellbeing or even life. The physician must take the initiative in specific sexual counseling in these cases or his task is yet incomplete.

Iatrogenic Libido Loss

From time immemorial, man has gone to the greatest lengths to find an elixir of youth, which is to say, an aphrodisiac. Most of the successful tonics of the past second generation had two critical components: alcohol, which in the amount used in the usual dosages released the inhibitions, and strychnine, which is a potentiator of spinal cord reflexes. The combination had not a little sexual utility. It is a curious twist of pharmocological fate that despite the ancient search for an aphrodisiac which rivals the equally ancient one for the transmutation of lesser metals into gold, we should develop a series of potent and useful drugs, but which have supression of sexual activity as a side effect. Reserpine, finally found by Western medicine after four millenia of use in India, controls anxiety well and blood pressure better, but it deals the coup de grace to a faltering phallus. Phenobarbital has an old history of use for hypertension and nervousness and combats both by putting the patient partly to sleep and shutting down his hypothalamus. Atropine relaxes the gastrointestinal tract, the bladder, blocks the hypothalmus, and interferes with erection and vaginal secretion. Nicotinic acid has the saving grace of tending to make the patient a little euphoric, so he may not notice the defeat in his sex life so much!

The moral of all this is a warning to the physician to remember the sexual function in managing the patient who is in a long standing marriage or who has progressed to an aging state himself. The sex may have a major significance in his or her life and should not be diminished to treat a relatively minor physiologic abnormality. A mild hypertension treated at the cost of the individual's sex life amounts to treating a minor disease at the cost of a social or psychologic catastrophe. The ramifications of any such treatment should be discussed completely with the patient and the choices of management jointly made.

Specific Aging Characteristics Destroying Sexuality

The male who has become the fat and sleepy lover is likely to get fatter and sleepier with the passage of time. He usually cannot rouse himself, let alone sexually arouse himself. As a husband he may be passable when presentable, but as a lover he is a total loss.

The female has some psychologic problems that move along with the hormonal shift at the menopause. A state of anxiety is created, partly by the sudden shifts in metabolic arrangements and the control of circulatory beds. Partly, however, the anxiety is created by the unequivocal sense of the departing phase of life, usually associated with a period of peak attractiveness in a physical sense. One common and misplaced response to this is the attempt to recapture the appearance of youth by the cultivation of its least important properties. Rather than putting effort into making herself a better person and a more attractive personality she begins to go to the beauty parlor more often. A series of mud baths, chin lifts, hair dyes, false eyelashes, and the like follow, none of which accomplish much of what was desired. She begins to be for a time a restless, sleepless, and often incompetent mistress to her man.

The physician can do a great deal for the self image of the menopausal woman by seeing to it that she is well informed on the mechanisms of the change from ovarian to adrenal function. She should be assured that her sexual capacity is likely to increase following the acute stage of the menopausal onset, and that her symptoms during that time can be adequately controlled by accessory hormone. Cystic disease of the breast may be a contra-indication to such hormonal supplementation and if it is, this too should be carefully explained.

The actual situation just past the menopause is enough to make a strong man cry. The female reaches the peak of her sexual capacity and enjoyment at about age 50; the corresponding male, who has felt he was well behind in his sex life up to that point tends to have a decline set in. The tables have finally turned, but good counseling from the physician as to what is a reasonable expectation for any given pair at this stage may go a long way to smoothing the period and lengthening the active sex life of both.

Evolutionary and Involuntary States

With the passage of the years, personalities alter just as surely as do appearances. People do not only grow and change with circumstances and learning, but their genetic characteristics make an appearance at differing times throughout their lives. The pair who were personally suitable for each other at 20 may be less so (or more so) at 30, and each passing decade will make its imprint. It can often be that by the fifth or the sixth decade, the two are entirely unsuited to each other, having changed so much with time.

Involutional states are prominent in Late Marriage and the effect is disastrous, particularly if the partner does not understand the nature of the mental disease occurring. Involutional melancholia is a disaster in any household. All the aspects of ordinary depression are magnified by the helpfulness of the pair to meeting it singly or jointly. Paranoia expresses itself as an attack of one upon the other and is a tragedy in the case of two who have lived in harmony for many years. The mate is hurt and bewildered by the most outrageous accusations and the constant concealment and spying. Amnesia is our common fate if we manage to dodge the Grim Reaper long enough and is an easy way of having nature let us down the final slide. It imposes an enormous burden on the more intact member, since taking care of one with geriatric amnesia is as constant a chore as watching a two year old.

EMOTIONAL RESPONSES TO MARITAL FRUSTRATION

A sexual incompatibility means by definition a frustrated urge. If one has no means to reduce the urge and relieve the frustration a hostile and venomous indifference will follow. The responses of hostility, fear, anger, and so on are too difficult to sustain for most of us. We go over such a crest of activity and then it subsides. The subsidence is even worse than the activity. So far as the partner is concerned, we become quiet, withdrawn, and self-oriented. The whole personality divides into the usual pattern of one for the remainder of the world and the negative one for the partner. This is partly a social protective shell which sustains the face and the ego in the presence of assault. But it also becomes a tool for an intimate social dominance, the motto of which is—spoken or silent—"I'll show you!" Many are the households that sing a dissonant chorus to that unhappy tune.

We can describe many marriages in this set of terms. Frustration from unsatisfied urges, or from realizations that failed to match with expectations; fear, hostility, anger, even hate, the erosion of friends and love. The end result: two persons who sit at a table staring in different and silent directions; two persons who so readily think something derogatory about the other and so rarely something good. These end results cannot be undone or remade until a satisfying means can come about to examine each of them and be able to dispose of them. To reestablish a basis for living with each other again, a couple must take a whole fresh look, with the accumulated debris removed.

For the frequent problems due to sexual ignorance, the treatment is clear. It is sexual education. This is not only erotic physiology, but a reorganization of attitudes as well. This means an orientation into sexual behaviors in order to give the patient some sociologic and anthroplogic perspective on the entire subject. The educative process may also be gradually transferred to the couple in the form of a "self-administered" Masters and Johnson type program, which will allow them to learn each other both attitudinally and sexually.

9

work integration, marital satisfaction, and conjugal power

theodore d. kemper

melvin l. reichler

A pervasive interest in the field of family studies has been the search for correlates of marital satisfaction and adjustment. Closely connected are studies which seek to explain husband- or wife-dominance or "power." In attempting to account for variation in these marital characteristics, researchers have covered a very broad spectrum, from personality theory at one end to social structure at the other. Those who favor the social structural approach have most often examined marital satisfaction and dominance as a function of social class differences. Yet, while social class does frequently *predict* differences in the two types of dependent variables, it does little to *explain* the differences. This has led to a progressive refinement of the implications of social class membership, with some part of the burden coming to rest, theoretically, not alone on income and its correlates, but on the conditions of work, especially that of husband (See Kohn, 1969). The study reported here pursues this line of inquiry further, in an attempt to specify which aspects of husband's work integration affect both husband's and wife's marital satisfaction and the distribution of conjugal power.

WORK INTEGRATION AND MARITAL SATISFACTION

There are two somewhat conflicting theoretical and empirical views of the relationship between husband's work integration and marital satisfaction and adjustment. The first of these finds a positive effect of work integration when indicators such as job satisfaction are employed (e.g., Bullock, 1952; Ridley, 1973) or when job satisfaction can be inferred from occupational prestige (e.g., Kephart, 1955; Goode, 1962; Williamson, 1954; Blood & Wolfe, 1960; Centers, Raven, & Rodrigues, 1971). The relationship between occupational prestige and job satisfaction has long been known (Morse & Weiss, 1955; Blauner, 1966).

A relatively straightforward psychological theory can be employed to articulate husband's satisfaction with work and the marital satisfaction of both husband and wife. Holding aside purely economic aspects, although these are not to be discounted (see, for example, Carey, 1967), satisfaction with work implies that there is little residual discontent that is brought home to interfere with the performance and enjoyment of domestic roles, or for the availability of husband for "therapeutic utilization" by wife (Blood & Wolfe, 1960). Not only is husband unencumbered in his accessibility for family interaction when he is satisfied with his work, there also is evidence that wife and children of satisfied workers are also pleased with his work and the implications of it for family life (Dyer, 1956). There appears then to be a reciprocal facilitation of harmony in family relations when husband is satisfied with his occupational situation.

Reprinted, by permission, from *Human Relations,* 1976, *29,* 929-44. Copyright ©1976 by Tavistock Institute of Human Relations, Plenum Press.

Other studies relating work integration to marital satisfaction have examined somewhat different indices of the work setting. Wilensky (1960, 1961) has proposed that occupational prestige differences, as these contribute to social class standing, will become less important than such considerations as whether or not the work career is "orderly," or enables an articulated progression from lesser to greater responsibility, or whether the worker has control over the pace of work and discretion over methods. Wilensky finds that patterns of leisure and social participation are affected by these career contingencies, and these in turn, as Locke (1951) has found, are related to marital adjustment.

Further evidence for the relationship between work integration and family adjustment can be found in the work of Indik (1964) who reports that when workers in high-stress positions have the support of their bosses, this leads to a reduction in evidence of "strain," e.g., psychosomatic symptoms. The physical consequences of work have been shown to be related to marital happiness in the work of Orden and Bradburn (1968) who find that disagreements over husband's job are related to arguments about "being tired," as well as "being away from home," and "not showing love."

Yet another perspective on work integration is found in the study by Langhorne and Secord (1955), in which female respondents (but not males) expressed a "need" for their spouses to want to get ahead, be ambitious, enjoy working, be energetic, and have a high status profession. These needs by wife enter into the complex equation between marital satisfaction and husband's work integration as mediated by the higher rewards of a high prestige occupation, and by the presence of psychological characteristics that make work itself pleasurable.

It can be seen, hence, from a number of perspectives, that satisfaction with work and social support in the work setting are related to the ability both to perform adequately and to give and derive satisfaction in the marital context.

There are, however, some studies which shed a different light on the work—family relationship. Principally, they have examined the effects of work salience or depth of work involvement on marital satisfaction. Pineo (1961) has suggested that husband's disenchantment in the early years of marriage is related to increased pressures from the work role and the coincidence of pressure for career attainment with the period of greatest family stress, namely the birth of children and the early years of child-rearing. Baum (1971) and Scanzoni (1967) support this view. Ridley (1973) finds evidence that while job satisfaction is positively related to marital satisfaction, job involvement is negatively related. Higher income, which suggests higher commitment and salience of work is also found to relate to a somewhat lower level of expression of positive sentiments by wives (Blood & Wolfe, 1960). Rapaport and Rapaport (1965) and Aldous (1969) have also raised the question of job salience as it affects family roles.

Dubin (1956), reporting on working-class respondents, also proposes a reversal of the work integration—family adjustment pattern. He argues that the lesser satisfactions of working-class occupations provoke retreat from the boredom of work into the more satisfying expressive attainments of family life, leading, potentially, to the inference of greater marital satisfaction for such workers. Indeed, this pattern of familism (more in evidence for the wife than for the husband in the working class) can also be found, according to Wilensky (1960) at higher occupation levels, if the conditions of the work setting and the orderliness of career do not provide adequate job satisfaction.

A final study to be cited in this area suggests that there is no relationship between marital happiness and husband's work. Levinger (1964) found that an item relating to husband's work did not load the general happiness factor for either husband or wife, and that the expressive involvements of the marriage itself were the significant determinants of happiness. Indeed, it is easy to agree with the finding that more proximal predictors will be more effective than the more distal, such as husband's work. It is perplexing, however, given the demonstrated relationship between work and happiness found in the results of Orden and Bradburn (1968), why the relationship should also not be found in Levinger's results.

In general, the studies of work integration and marital satisfaction suggest that husband's satisfaction with work, regardless of the grounds, is positively related to marital satisfaction and adjustment of both husband and wife, while high job demands and intragenerational mobility aspiration—both of which may be unrelated to job satisfaction—are negatively related to marital adjustment and happiness.

WORK INTEGRATION AND CONJUGAL POWER

Studies of husband's work integration have also looked at the effects on conjugal power. Numerous studies support the view that the higher the husband's occupational prestige, the more likely he is to be dominant in the relationship with wife (Blood & Wolfe, 1960; Goode, 1964; Clausen, 1966; Centers, Raven, & Rodrigues, 1971). Since high-prestige occupations are related to higher satisfaction, income, authority, etc., there is some need to sort out exactly what underlies these results. Rapaport and Rapaport (1965) propose that there is a behavioral isomorphism between work-role and family-role. Thus the husband who has a high level of authority and decision-making precedence on the job may simply transfer this work-role pattern to the family, whether or not it is appropriate there (Aldous, 1969). This may even be a generalized trait (Strodtbeck, James, & Hawkins, 1952). At lower levels of work-prestige and authority, there is a lesser tendency for husband dominance. Studies of unemployed workers (Angell, 1936; Komarovsky, 1940) support this view. They show that husbands who lost their jobs also lost decision-making power in the family. Strodtbeck (1963) also reports that in experimental settings, there is lesser dominance by working-class husbands in interaction with their wives.

Proceeding to more refined analysis of the work setting than merely prestige of occupation, several researchers have looked at the family-role implications of bureaucratically organized occupations. Contrary to the view of Mills (1953) and Merton (1957), Kohn (1971) finds that men who work in bureaucracies, as opposed to other types of work settings, are *more* open to new experience, *more* flexible intellectually, and *more* autonomous. This provides a useful bridge for understanding the results of Gold and Slater (1958) who found that when husbands worked in "bureaucratic" as opposed to "entrepreneurial" settings (Miller & Swanson, 1958) their marriages tended to be more "autonomic," i.e., equality of power between husband and wife. The greater intellectual flexibility would permit bureaucratic husbands to move away from traditional conceptions of husband-dominance, and the greater autonomy would reduce the emotional dependency that might lead to conflictful power relations (Kemper, 1972).

Additional support for this view of the conditions of work as related to conjugal power is found in the data of Rapaport and Lauman (reported in Rapaport & Rapaport, 1965), which show that scientists are more likely than engineers to engage in "joint" decision-making with wives. Rapaport and Lauman believe this is due to the wider dispersion of universalistic norms among scientists. But Kohn's (1971) suggestion that job complexity may also explain the greater openness to new experience, intellectual flexibility, etc. of the bureaucratic types can also be brought to bear on these findings, viz., scientific work is more "complex" than engineering. Centers, Raven, and Rodrigues (1971) also find that, while husband dominance is positively associated with occupational prestige, among professionals—who are at the highest levels of prestige, and also of job complexity—there is greater sharing of power between husband and wife than at prestige and job complexity levels just below the professional level.

Inkeles (cited in Rapaport & Rapaport, 1965) also suggests that work-setting social relations, particularly in the domain of power relations, may serve as prototype for the pattern of husband's domestic power orientations. Hoffman (1960), too, develops a "chain reaction" model of family power-relations—if father uses power assertion on wife, wife will use power assertion on child, child will use power assertion on peers, etc. It would be logical to assume that if the work setting is disadvantageous to husband, in power-assertion terms, this will help to initiate the process.

In general, the results of these studies suggest that a variety of conditions of the work setting, including power relations and job complexity, affect the distribution of conjugal power.

In the work to be described below, an attempt is made to specify conditions of work integration and of marital satisfaction and conjugal power, and the relationship between these is shown.

METHOD

Sample

The study reported here used data collected from a sample of 219 university students in undergraduate sociology classes at Queens College, CUNY. Participants included 148 females and 71 males.

Information on various aspects of father's work integration and on marital satisfaction and conjugal power relations was obtained by self-administered questionnaire. There is evidence that adolescents' reports of parental behavior is adequately accurate (Allinsmith & Greening, 1955; Becker, 1964). Furthermore, Cox (1970) has shown that there is a stronger relationship between children's reports of parental behavior and independently measured criterion variables than between parental reports of their own behavior and the same criterion variables. Specifically in regard to father's work integration, Dyer (1956) found that adolescents whose father reported high job satisfaction were significantly different in their evaluation of father's job from adolescents whose father reported low job satisfaction. Harter (cited in Hoffman and Lippitt, 1960) and Herbst (1952) also suggest that adolescents can provide accurate depictions of the relationship between mother and father.

Father's Work Integration

A consideration of various materials dealing with work (e.g., Wilensky, 1960, 1961; Blauner, 1966) provided a set of nine items to measure work integration. These were factor analyzed and three factors emerged. These are shown in Table I.

Factor one shows high loadings on items dealing with the intrinsic satisfactions of the work itself as well as the gratifications of income and status, derived from the work position. These items represent the satisfactions that accrue from both competence and the meaningfulness of the work. We have labeled this factor *Job Satisfaction*.

Items which load factor two refer to social relations, particularly power relations, and sociability with coworkers. The item dealing with boss is clearly a matter of the power relationship on the job, and this is amplified by the item dealing with discretion over pace and style of work. The sociability item may also be referred to power relations, at least in part. A condition for liking others is that they be supportive, and that they do not use power against us (Homans, 1961; Kemper, 1972). We have called this factor *Power Relations*.

There is some ambiguity in the meaning of the third factor. The first item, referring to ambition to climb higher, may simply reflect continuing mobility interest on the part of those who are satisfied, or may reflect the mobility interest of those who are dissatisfied, or who have not attained enough income or status. The second item, concerning regrets for opportunities not taken, suggests that the factor is weighted in the direction of the dissatisfied. The two items are related in opposite ways to the remainder of the items in the set. The ambition item correlates positively with the remaining seven items, while the regret item correlates negatively with the other seven items. Yet the ambition and regret items correlate positively with each other, permitting the emergence of a separate, unipolar factor. We have named this factor *Mobility Aspirations*.

TABLE I. FACTOR ANALYSIS OF HUSBAND WORK INTEGRATION ITEMS

Items	I Job satisfaction	II Power relations	III Mobility aspirations	h^2
1. Work meaningful, important, worthwhile, a contribution to society.	.73[a]	24	29	68
2. Likes to do actual work, eager to get back to it, likes to tell people about it	74	23	33	71
3. Satisfied with level of income obtained from work and with opportunity for income in the future.	72	31	09	62
4. Likes people works with	31	71	-05	61
5. Has control over pace and style of work, decides when and how to do it, makes decisions without being told what to do.	22	74	26	66
6. Gets along well with boss, obtains respect and liking from him.	10	86	-02	75
7. As high up in profession, organization, or business as deserved, receives the proper amount of recognition.	57	50	02	58
8. Ambition to climb higher in profession, organization, or business.	19	02	83	73
9. Regret about interests, jobs, ambitions not realized, or about opportunities not taken.	-68	11	52	74

[a] Decimals omitted for other values

Marital Integration and Conjugal Power

Table II shows the results of the factor analysis of the nine items dealing with marital satisfaction and conjugal power. Two factors emerged. The first shows high loadings on the items dealing with amount of conflict, ratings of satisfaction for both husband and wife, and mutuality of rewards and punishments. We have called this factor *Marital Satisfaction*.

The second factor loads the two "power" items—who makes the major decisions, and who starts the conflicts—and also includes the relatively high loading on the item measuring the degree to which wife punishes husband. The pattern of loadings indicates that the spouse who tends to make major decisions is also the one who tends to initiate conflict. When wife is dominant in these two items, she also tends to punish husband; when husband is dominant in decision-making and conflict initiation, wife tends to avoid punishing husband. We have labeled this factor *Conjugal Power*. This appears to be a reasonable name, despite the fact that there is considerable debate over exactly what constitutes power in the family (Safilios-Rothschild, 1970; Turk & Bell, 1972; Olsen, 1969). Hoffman and Lippitt (1960) point out that despite variations in methods of measuring power, different measures have been found to relate in the same way to many other variables. This gives us some assurance that a fundamental domain of concern is being tapped by our measure of power.

TABLE II. FACTOR ANALYSIS OF HUSBAND–WIFE INTERACTION ITEMS

Items	I Marital satisfaction	II Conjugal power	h^2
1. Most major decisions are made by husband.	-.14[a]	57	34
2. Frequency of conflict.	- 83	10	70
3. Frequency of husband's punishment of wife.	- 76	-09	58
4. Frequency of husband's reward of wife.	72	25	58
5. Frequency of wife's punishment of husband.	- 62	-46	59
6. Frequency of wife's reward of husband.	66	16	46
7. Wife's satisfaction.	71	-19	54
8. Husband's satisfaction.	74	-34	67
9. Husband generally starts conflicts (instead of wife).	- 27	77	66

[a] Decimals omitted for other values.

RESULTS

The question to which the statistical analysis addresses itself is the relationship between husband's work integration on the one hand and marital satisfaction and conjugal power on the other. Correlations were computed between the items of the two domains and those significant at $p < .05$ are shown in Table III. In order to specify more closely the relationship between the two domains, items are grouped according to the factors they loaded.

We find that three items referring to what may be considered *intrinsic* satisfaction with work—i.e., work is meaningful, liking for work, and control over pace of work—are significantly related to four of the five items of marital satisfaction; negatively with amount of conflict and positively with both the explicit satisfaction items and the mutual reward items. However, only meaningfulness of work was related significantly to husband's reward of wife. Indeed the two highest correlations in the table are between meaningfulness of work and wife's satisfaction and her willingness to reward husband. The only item of the power relations factor to relate significantly to any of the indices of marital satisfaction is the most intrinsic of the power-relations items, namely control over pace of work.

The two work-integration items relating to income satisfaction and adequate recognition, which might have been expected to relate to marital satisfaction (e.g., Inkeles, cited in Rapaport and Rapaport, 1965; or the many studies relating prestige of occupation with marital satisfaction), do not do so here. This gives some unanticipated support to the finding by Levinger (1964) that at least some aspects of husband's work do not relate to marital happiness.

These results may be understood as follows: Husband's work may be seen to contain *extrinsic* and *intrinsic* features. The former would include such things as income, prestige, and the like. The latter would include meaningfulness of the work, basic liking for it, etc. Although job satisfaction as such requires a combination of both of these features—this may be deduced from their loading the same factor—the impact of these separate aspects of work may be quite different.

Indeed, husband's lack of satisfaction with his income and recognition may actually facilitate family activities that might promote marital satisfaction. Gold and Slater (1958) discuss marital arrangements that are specifically premised on wife's "collegial" assistance in the development of husband's career. Thus, husband and wife may work together to augment the income and status rewards for the family as a unit. Husband may thus be dissatisfied with his income and recognition he receives, but this does not necessarily decrease domestic harmony.

TABLE III. CORRELATIONS BETWEEN HUSBAND'S WORK INTEGRATION AND HUSBAND-WIFE INTERACTION

Husband work-integration factors	Husband-Wife Interaction Factors								
	Marital Satisfaction						Conjugal Power		
	Amount of conflict	Husband punishes wife	Husband satisfied	Husband rewards wife	Wife satisfied	Wife rewards husband	Husband starts conflict	Husband makes major decisions	Wife punishes husband
Job Satisfaction									
1. Work meaningful, etc.	-15		17	18	28	28			-24
2. Likes to do work, etc.	-15		22		22	22			-20
3. Satisfied with income									
7. Proper recognition, etc.									
Power Relations									
6. Get along with boss, etc.									
5. Control over work pace	-20	-17	15		23	15			-18
4. Likes people works with									
Mobility Aspirations									
8. Ambition to climb, etc.								-15	
9. Regrets opportunities, etc.			-18		-18				

Intrinsic gratifications on the other hand, such as the sense of the meaningfulness of work, would appear to operate on marital satisfaction, doubtless by producing a certain quality of interaction, which reduces not so much objective opportunities for conflict, as the psychological inducements to engage in conflict. In our data the benefits of work satisfaction are revealed most sharply not so much by the direct effect on husband's satisfaction, but by the indirect effect on wife's satisfaction. If husband likes his work and is eager to get back to it after time away, this means he is less dependent on wife to gratify his psychic whims and needs, and while this appears to enhance his own satisfaction with the marriage, since he probably does not demand so much from it, his intrinsic satisfactions with work enhance even further wife's satisfaction with the marriage, since demands on her are also less.

These findings appear to support the view of Wilensky (1960, 1961) that certain extrinsic features of work life, such as prestige, income, etc., are becoming somewhat less important than certain intrinsic features which produce satisfaction with the work itself, permit individual discretion over its pace and style, etc. (It is also well to realize, however, that these results may be due to the fact that the very bottom of the occupational prestige scale is missing from the sample obtained for this study. Since respondents were college students, parents were sufficiently high up in the occupational structure to afford to support their children, at least in part, during the college years. A restriction of range in the variables dealing with extrinsic satisfaction may explain, at least in part, the lack of relationship between these variables and marital satisfaction and conjugal power found here.)

Less susceptible to methodological vagaries, however, is the finding that neither good relationship with one's boss, nor liking for coworkers relates to marital satisfaction or conjugal power. We can note that having bad relations with boss or with coworkers may become a source of *good* marital relations through the "therapeutic utilization" of wife (Blood & Wolfe, 1960) by husband. At the end of a trying day of poor social relations, wife is actually an ally and a friend who can give sympathy and support, since she can easily comprehend the kinds of demands and pressures that autocratic bosses or mean-spirited coworkers can engender. But the intrinsic conditions of work, involving its meaningfulness, or ability to control the pace or style of it, are probably far less likely to surface explicitly in husband's discussion of his day and what happened at work. Yet, where these occupational conditions are satisfactory, it would appear that they operate to produce a good effect on the marital satisfaction of both husband and wife.

The third work integration factor provides an item—regret for opportunities not taken—which is negatively correlated with both husband and wife satisfaction. The item represents discontent, and the discontent appears to contaminate the relationship between husband and wife. Discussion of this finding will be deferred until conjugal power is considered below.

Turning now to the relationship between work integration and conjugal power, we find that, with the exception of the item dealing with wife's punishment of husband, only a single significant correlation is found between husband's work situation and the distribution of family power. This is the negative relationship between the ambition item of the Mobility Aspiration factor and husband making the major decisions. Since the ambition item does not correlate with any of the satisfaction items, we must conclude that for the given sample (average age of husband is 52.7 years), the maintenance of a strong drive to "climb higher" is either fostered by the need to demonstrate the level of occupational success that would lead to the opportunity to assert greater conventional dominance in the marital relationship (Clausen, 1966); or is, here, evidence that when husbands are perceived as committed to mobility, their level of work involvement actually brings wife into greater prominence in the home and, therefore, she may be perceived as dominant. Bowerman and Elder (1964) found that when mother was either dominant or equal in the power relationship with father, she was perceived by adolescent offspring as "autocratic" in the mother-child relationship. This may have invaded the view of mother's share of the major decision-making in the eyes of the adolescent respondents of this study, and may have given rise to the correlation between ambition and mother's dominance. This must be clarified in further research.

Somewhat unanticipated was the failure of any of the Job Satisfaction or Power Relations items to correlate significantly with the two most definitive items of conjugal power: who makes the major decisions? and who is generally the one to start conflicts. From the studies of Rapaport and Lauman (cited in Rapaport & Rapaport, 1965), Kohn (1969) and Wilensky (1960, 1961), it could be supposed that work integration would lead to greater shared power. This was tested more directly by recoding the two conjugal power items, decision-making and conflict initiation in order to make possible for both items a test of an egalitarian power structure against a structure biased in the direction of either husband or wife. The two recoded items were correlated with the nine work-integration items, without substantial change in the results previously achieved. Only a single correlation was found to be statistically significant. This was between the recoded "conflict initiation" item and the "regret" item of the ambition factor ($r = .16$). This result implies that the greater the equality of conflict initiation the more likely husband regrets opportunities not taken. Looked at from the complementary perspective, the more nearly wife equals husband's power (in terms of conflict-initiation) the more likely husband regrets opportunities not taken. This suggests that husband's regret is a function of wife's goading and, perhaps, increased argumentativeness. Supporting this interpretation is the fact that the "major-decisions" variable, which was significantly related ($r = -.15$) to the ambition item, (see Table III) no longer correlated significantly with ambition when it was run as a recoded item. This implies that husband's ambition is stimulated by wife when *she* makes the major decisions. When decision-making is more egalitarian, i.e., when husband is not dominated, his ambition is not as sharp. This, however, may be due to the fact that egalitarian households tend to be households in which husband is more successful, and requires, therefore, less additional mobility to content him (or his spouse).

The Effects of Social Class

Since the three sets of variables considered in this study—work integration, marital satisfaction, and conjugal power—have been shown to vary by social class, it was considered necessary to determine the extent to which the present findings are affected by social class considerations. Respondents had provided information about mother's education, father's education, income, and estimated social class rank of family. These social class indicators were applied one at a time to obtain partial correlations between work integration and marital satisfaction and conjugal power, while holding the indicator constant.

The results for all indicators show virtually no effect of social class on the relationship between the work-setting items and the family items, with the following exceptions: the relationship between setting one's own pace at work and husband's satisfaction ($r = .15$) decreases to a statistically nonsignificant magnitude when some of the social class indicators are controlled. Similar reductions to nonsignificance are manifested in the relationships between regret for opportunities not taken and both father's satisfaction ($r = -.18$) and mother's satisfaction ($r = -.18$).

The social-class effect on work pace appears to occur in terms of the fact that discretion over pace of one's own work, indicating relatively low levels of supervision, is associated with occupational prestige and therefore social class level (Reiss et al., 1961; Kohn, 1969). The social-class effect involved in regret for opportunities not taken would appear to be simply that such regrets are more prevalent at lower social class levels.

From these results of holding social class indicators constant, it can be seen that the effects of the *intrinsic* aspects of husband work integration are largely indifferent to social class. While work may be considered more meaningful, or work may be better liked, at higher social-class levels, if the individual, regardless of class level, does like his work and does find it meaningful, then greater marital harmony and satisfaction are also likely to prevail.

SUMMARY

Nine items dealing with husband's work integration were factor analyzed, producing three dimensions: Job Satisfaction, Power Relations, and Mobility Aspirations. Nine additional items concerning husband and wife interaction were factor analyzed separately and two dimensions were extracted: Marital Satisfaction and Conjugal Power. The items of the separate domains were intercorrelated. Intrinsic satisfactions obtained from work, such as the meaningfulness of it, control over pace and style, etc., were found to be related to marital satisfaction while such extrinsic benefits and gratifications as income, status, or social relations in the work setting were not. Above the very lowest income and status levels, deficits in the extrinsic factors may, indeed, be grounds for enhancing rather than depressing the shared life-orientations of husband and wife, and may just as easily as not lead to the development of a united husband-wife outlook, e.g., "They are unfair to *us*. They don't know how to deal with people like *us*."

There appeared to be virtually no relationship between such work integration dimensions as satisfaction or power relations with the distribution of conjugal power. Rather, conjugal power appears to determine mobility orientations to some degree, with wife's dominance apparently goading husband into greater striving.

Lastly, a relatively small effect of controlling for social class was noted. Principally, both husband's and wife's satisfaction were found to be unrelated to mobility orientation when social class was controlled.

REFERENCES

Aldous, J. Occupational characteristics and males' role performance in the family. *Journal of Marriage and Family,* 1969, *31 (November),* 707-712.

Allinsmith, B. B., & Greening, T. C. Guilt over anger as predicted from parental discipline: A study of superego development. *American Psychologist,* 1955, *10 (August),* 320.

Angell, R. *The family encounters the Depression.* N. Y.: Scribners, 1936.

Baum, M. Love, marriage, and the division of labor. *Sociological Inquiry,* 1971, *41 (Winter),* 107-117.

Becker, W. C. Consequences of different kinds of parental discipline. In Martin C. Hoffman and Lois W. Hoffman (Eds.) *Review of child development research, Vol. I.* New York: Russell Sage Foundation, 1964.

Blauner, R. Work satisfaction and industrial trends in modern society. In Reinhard Bendix and Seymour M. Lipset (Eds.) *Class, status, and power.* New York: Free Press, 1966.

Blood, R. O., Jr., & Wolfe, D. M. *Husbands and wives.* New York: Free Press, 1960.

Bowerman, C. E., & Elder, G. H., Jr. Variations in adolescent perceptions of family power structure. *American Sociological Review,* 1964, *29 (August),* 551-567.

Bullock, R. P. *Social factors related to job satisfaction.* Columbus, Ohio: Ohio State University Press, 1952.

Carey, A. The Hawthorne study: A radical criticism. *American Sociological Review,* 1967, *32 (June),* 403-416.

Centers, R., Raven, B. H., & Rodrigues, A. Conjugal power structure: A re-examination. *American Sociological Review,* 1971, *36 (April),* 264-278.

Clausen, J. A. Family structure, socialization, and personality. In Martin C. Hoffman and Lois W. Hoffman (Eds.) *Review of Child Development and Research, Vol. II.* New York: Russell Sage Foundation, 1966.

Cox, S. H. Intrafamily comparison of loving—rejecting child rearing practices. *Child Development,* 1970, *41 (June),* 437-448.

Dubin, R. Industrial workers' worlds. *Social Problems,* 1956, *3 (January),* 131-142.

Dyer, W. G. A comparison of families of high and low job satisfaction. *Marriage and Family Living,* 1956, *18 (February),* 58-60.

Gold, M., & Slater, C. Office, factory, store—and family: A study of integration setting. *American Sociological Review,* 1958, *23 (February),* 64-74.

Goode, W. J. A cross-cultural analysis of divorce rates. *International Social Science Journal,* 1962, *14 (5),* 507-526.

Goode, W. J. *The family.* Englewood Cliffs, New Jersey: Prentice-Hall, 1964.

Herbst, P. G. The measurement of family relationships. *Human Relations,* 1952, *5 (February),* 3-35.

Hoffman, L. W., & Lippitt, R. The measurement of family life variables. In Paul H. Mussen (Ed.) *Handbook of Research Methods in Child Development.* New York: John Wiley, 1960.

Hoffman, M. L. Power assertion by the parent and its impact on the child. *Child Development,* 1960, *31 (March),* 129-143.

Homans, G. C. *Social behavior: Its elementary forms.* New York: Harcourt, Brace and World, 1961.

Indik, B. P. Relations between job-related stress and strain in industrial workers. *Journal of Industrial Psychology,* 1964, *2 (March),* 22-27.

Kemper, T. D. Power, status, and love. In David Heise (Ed.) *Personality and socialization.* Chicago: Rand-McNally, 1972.

Kephart, W. M. Occupational level and marital disruption. *American Sociological Review,* 1955, *20 (August),* 456-465.

Kohn, M. L. *Class and conformity.* Homewood, Ill.: Dorsey, 1969.

Kohn, M. L. Bureaucratic man: A portrait and an interpretation. *American Sociological Review,* 1971, *36 (June),* 461-474.

Komarovsky, M. *The unemployed man and his family.* New York: Dryden Press, 1940.

Langhorne, M. C., & Secord, P. F. Variations in marital needs with age, sex, marital status and regional location. *Journal of Social Psychology,* 1955, *41 (January),* 19-37.

Levinger, G. Task and social behavior in marriage. *Sociometry,* 1964, *27 (December),* 433-448.

Locke, H. *Predicting adjustment in marriage: A comparison of a divorced and a happily married group.* New York: Henry Holt, 1951.

Merton, R. K. Bureaucratic structure and personality. In Robert K. Merton. *Social theory and social structure.* Glencoe, Ill.: The Free Press, 1957.

Miller, D. R., & Swanson, G. E. *The changing American parent.* New York: John Wiley, 1958.

Mills, C. W. *White collar: The American middle classes.* New York: Oxford University Press, 1953.

Morse, N. C., & Weiss, R. S. The function and meaning of work and the job. *American Sociological Review,* 1955, *20 (April),* 191-198.

Myrdal, A. *Nation and family.* London: K. Paul, Trench, Trubner, 1945.

Olson, D. H. The measurement of family power by self-report and behavioral methods. *Journal of Marriage and the Family,* 1969, *31 (August),* 545-550.

Orden, S. R., & Bradburn, N. M. Working wives and marriage happiness. *American Journal of Sociology,* 1968, *74 (January),* 392-407.

Pineo, P. Disenchantment in the later years of marriage. *Marriage and Family Living,* 1961, *23 (February),* 3-11.

Rapaport, R., & Rapaport, R. Work and family in contemporary society. *American Sociological Review,* 1965, *30 (June),* 381-394.

Reiss, A., et al. *Occupations and social status.* New York: Free Press, 1961.

Ridley, C. A. Exploring the impact of work satisfaction and involvement on marital interaction when both partners are employed. *Journal of Marriage and the Family,* 1973, *35 (May),* 229-237.

Safilios-Rothschild, C. The study of family power structure: A review 1960-1969. *Journal of Marriage and the Family,* 1970, *32 (November),* 539-552.

Scanzoni, J. Occupation and family differences. *Sociological Quarterly,* 1967, *8 (Spring),* 187-198.

Strodtbeck, F. L. Family interaction, values, and achievement. In David C. McClelland, et al. *Talent and society.* Princeton, N.J.: Van Nostrand, 1958.

Strodtbeck, F. L. The family in action. In Marvin B. Sussman (Ed.) *Sourcebook in marriage and the family.* (2nd Ed.) Boston: Houghton Mifflin, 1963.

Strodtbeck, F. L., James, R., & Hawkins, C. Social status on jury deliberations. In Guy E. Swanson, Theodore M. Newcomb, and Eugene E. Hartley (Eds.) *Readings in social psychology.* New York: Henry Holt, 1952.

Turk, J. L., & Bell, N. W. Measuring power in families. *Journal of Marriage and the Family,* 1972, *34 (May),* 215-222.

Wilensky, H. L. Work, careers, and social integration. *International Social Science Journal,* 1960, *12 (4):* 543-560.

Wilensky, H. L. Orderly careers and social participation: The impact of work history on social participation in the middle mass. *American Sociological Review,* 1961, *26 (August),* 521-539.

Williamson, R. C. Socio-economic factors and marital adjustment in an urban setting. *American Sociological Review,* 1954, *19 (April),* 213-216.

leisure activity patterns and marital satisfaction over the marital career

dennis k. orthner

The differential influence of leisure activities on the interaction between husbands and wives is certainly not well understood. It has become almost generally accepted that leisure activities somehow influence a marriage, that these influences are generally positive, and that marital recreation should be encouraged, especially if done together. Following this line of reasoning, the National Recreation Association developed the slogan "The family that plays together, stays together." Despite the bantering of this phrase, surprisingly little is known about the relationship between leisure activities and the degree of relational satisfaction perceived by marital partners.

Earlier claims of a decline in the recreational function of the family (Ogburn, 1934; Parsons and Bales, 1955) have largely given way to a position supporting a potentially important role for leisure in the modern family (Foote and Cottrell, 1955; Hobart, 1963; Edwards, 1967; Dumazedier, 1967; Kelley, 1972). Marital solidarity appears to be altering its source from economic cooperation to other sources generally found in discretionary time (Goode, 1962; Hobart, 1963). The increasing interest in the emotional support function of the family, especially for the marital dyad, would seem to make the question of the role of leisure central to any analysis of marriage. Kaplan (1960:59) states that leisure is more than simply diversionary activity; it has become "a cause, a clue, and an index of sources of respect, love, interdependence, and knowledge of the other."

Two concurrent trends appear to be reinforcing each other and are important to this analysis. On the one hand, the family is moving toward a more companionate form (Burgess and Locke, 1945) in which the role of leisure may be especially important in determining the patterning of marital adjustment. On the other hand, the possibilities for leisure have increased for many as the potential for discretionary activity has increased. This does not mean simply that the workweek has been declining. For many, it definitely has declined (Carter, 1971; Kaplan, 1971). For others, increased commuting distances and other responsibilities have simply increased work-related hours (DeGrazia, 1962; Walker, 1969). Nevertheless, there has been a shift in values toward an acceptance of leisure as a legitimate short- and long-term life goal (Wolfenstein, 1958; Reisman, 1958; Lobsenz, 1962; Dumazedier, 1971). This is supporting an increase in discretionary time for most workers in some of the following ways: an increase in the average length of vacations (Carter, 1971), the number of paid holidays has increased and five of these have been made effective on either a Monday or Friday, some companies offer sabbaticals for workers (Klausner, 1968), retirement ages are declining (Kaplan, 1960), and flexible workweeks, four-day, and even three-day workweeks are being attempted.

Reprinted, by permission, from *Journal of Marriage and the Family*, 1975, *37*, 91-102, slightly abridged. Copyright ©1975 by the National Council on Family Relations.

LEISURE AND MARITAL INTERACTION

A common criticism by persons who are attempting to investigate the relationship between leisure and the family is the lack of empirical studies on the subject (Neumeyer and Neumeyer, 1958; Cunningham and Johannis, 1960; Kaplan, 1960; Dumazedier, 1967; Kraus, 1971). Especially interesting is the fact that we know more about what people are doing in their free time, how many people are participating in the various activities, and how much they spend for leisure than we know about how it affects their lives, and those with whom they interact.

Initial investigations of the leisure factor in marital interaction emerged out of the attempt to understand the marital adjustment process. Locke (1951) found that happily married men and women were more likely to agree on recreation needs and the value of spending time together. The enjoyment of mutual activities was more associated with the happily married while individual activities tended to be associated with the unhappily married. Benson (1952) reported little or no relationship between the total number of common interests of the couple and either engagement or marital adjustment. This result was substantiated by Hawkins and Walters (1952). In a study of family recreational interests, they concluded that the total number of different kinds of leisure activities participated in by a family was not related to marital or family interaction patterns. Both Locke (1951) and Benson (1952) found that mutual interest in some activities was more related to "good" adjustment than other activities.

Gerson (1960), in a study of college married couples, reported that the total amount of leisure time was not important in determining marital satisfaction. He did find a positive relationship between marital satisfaction and the perception of satisfaction with the kinds of leisure pursuits in the relationship. Klausner (1968), also interested in the role of time available for leisure and family patterns, discovered that the increased time provided by sabbaticals for steelworkers had a positive influence on husband-wife interaction. In a study of a shorter discretionary time period, West and Merriam (1970) reported that family camping trips resulted in increased marital cohesiveness, especially among those with low initial cohesiveness.

The research on leisure and marital relationships, as noted above, is quite inconclusive. The participation of individuals in particular leisure activities seems to be related to the overall adjustment process in marriage but it would appear that no attempts have been made to determine by what means those activities influence, either positively or negatively, a relationship. The total number of leisure activities engaged in or the total number of common interests of a couple seem to only marginally influence marital satisfaction. However, the generalized perception of desiring to share one's leisure time with the spouse is related to overall relational satisfaction.

There are several limitations apparent in this literature. First, there are no theoretical or conceptual frameworks that have been delineated to guide the empirical investigations. This is largely a problem of family research in general (Klein, et al., 1968), but in the case at hand the studies tend to be either limited to particular free-time activities or reports of statistical associations only tangential to the primary purposes of other research. To make matters more difficult, no common definition of leisure is utilized in the various designs. The result is incomparability between the various conclusions and an inability to link the investigations to the larger body of marriage and family research and theory.

A second limitation lies in the lack of adequate controls to specify the conditions under which relationships are operating. Part of the problem is the small size of the samples utilized in the research. Nevertheless, studies have demonstrated that social class is a significant determinant of the use of leisure time (Clarke, 1956; Sussman, 1959; Simon et al., 1970), and this factor should have been controlled while often it is not. Also, the length of the marital relationship has not been con- trolled in leisure research. An assumption is made that generalizations that operate at one point of the marital period apply equally to all other periods. The present investigation is an attempt to deal with these limitations through the use of a seminal theoretical model and controls on social class and periods of the marital career. The marital career concept (Rodgers, 1973; Feldman and Feldman, 1973) is utilized because it denotes an element of continuity while recognizing change in the marital dyad over time.

CONCEPTUAL FRAMEWORK

A marital relationship can be viewed as a system of interacting roles and communication networks. Underlying this system is a perception of relational satisfaction that determines whether or not the system is able to maintain itself in its present form. While the patterning of marital adjustment is determined by specific relational goals and the means by which they are achieved (Cuber and Harroff, 1965), the existence or possibility for adjustment hinges on the perception of relational satisfaction. This is why marital satisfaction or the subjective evaluation of individuals regarding the relative condition of their marital relationship (Burgess and Locke, 1945) is such a critical variable and the focus of the present investigation.

Any significant shifts in communication and/or role patterns are likely to influence an alteration in the adjustment pattern of the relationship and affect perceived satisfaction as well. It has been noted in the literature that there is a tendency for these changes to occur over time in marriages (*cf.* Axelson, 1960; Pineo, 1961; Rollins and Feldman, 1970; Burr, 1970). It is during critical periods of interactional alteration that leisure patterns become especially significant. During leisure time, when anxieties are reduced, the individual is more free to redefine situations and open himself to new behavioral interpretations (Kaplan, 1960; Stone, 1963; DeGrazia, 1965; West and Merrian, 1971; Orthner, 1974a). Leisure activities may, therefore, act as shock absorbers during periods of relational change and as stabilizers over the entire relationship.[1]

Not all leisure activities are likely to have the same influence on a marriage. By definition, leisure is associated with a pleasureable definition of the situation and discretionary time (Orthner, 1974a) but these conditions can be derived either alone or with others, with one's spouse or with persons other than the spouse, and with little or no interaction, despite the presence of others. Interactionally, three leisure activity patterns would appear to characterize the parameters of this factor. *Individual activities* require no communication with others and may actually discourage interaction. *Joint activities* require a high degree of interaction for successful completion of the activity and tend to open communication and encourage role interchange. *Parallel activities* are little more than individual activities in group settings and a minimum of interaction is allowed among the participants.

Persons usually participate in each of these types of leisure, to a greater or lesser degree. In a particular relationship, however, the interactional consequences may be quite different if one pattern dominates the others. This is especially true because of the changing nature of the marital career. In a stable relationship, each of the relational leisure patterns could function quite well because there would be few alterations in situational definitions. A changing relationship, however, requires an ability of the marital partners to alter their perspectives over time. In this latter pattern, individual activities may not be able to encourage the kind of interaction required for meaningful adjustments and marital satisfaction should be lower as a result. Joint spouse activities should encourage marital interaction and increase understanding and, therefore, maintain a higher level of marital satisfaction. Conceptually, parallel activities should maintain a median position between individual and joint activities as an influential factor.

It should be noted that this relationship is not necessarily directional. For example, persons with low levels of marital satisfaction are likely to reduce joint leisure participation with their spouse and further reinforce their relational disparity.

The above framework and the cited literature suggest three issues that need clarification. First, are the three relational leisure activity patterns differentially related to marital satisfaction as the model would suggest? Second, are different periods of the marital career likely to generate changes in the relationship between leisure activity patterns and marital satisfaction? Third, is the relationship between marital satisfaction and leisure activity patterns different for husbands and wives?

The following hypotheses are to be tested in the present investigation:

(1)   Individual activities are negatively associated with marital satisfaction for both husbands and wives at each period of the marital career.

(2)   Joint activities are positively associated with marital satisfaction for both husbands and wives at each period of the marital career.

(3)   Parallel activities are not associated with marital satisfaction for either husbands or wives at each period of the marital career.

RESEARCH DESIGN

The data for this study were collected in March, 1973, from the population of nonstudent, intact, upper-middle-class husbands and wives living in moderate size urban areas in the Southeastern U.S. The sample was derived by means of a stratified area probability sampling design (Sjoberg and Nett, 1968). To control for social class, housing areas with median home values of at least $30,000 were identified by the 1970 census block statistics. These were grouped into 10 roughly equal areas with a range of 227 to 251 households per area. Each household in an area was consecutively numbered from 1 to N and, utilizing a table of random numbers, 30 households were then selected from each. Because of potential underrepresentation of younger married couples and those that preferred not to live in single-family dwellings, three large higher-rent apartment complexes were also sampled. Twenty households were randomly selected from each complex in the manner used for the residential areas. A total of 360 sampling units resulted from this design.

A structured questionnaire was used to gather the data from the respondents. The instrument had been pretested on a married college student population and then randomly selected households from within the identified sampling areas. The pretests resulted in minor changes in the wording of instructions and a reduction in the sampled leisure activity time period from one week to one weekend—Friday evening through Sunday evening. Memory loss over the longer period was greater than anticipated and the weekend period appeared to provide more opportunity for persons to engage in a greater range of family activities if they desired (Scheuch, 1960). It should be remembered that this investigation is most concerned with the patterns of activity-interaction selected during leisure time rather than with the particular activities engaged in.

A letter was sent to each of the 360 designated sampling units informing them of their selection and inviting them to participate. On the following Monday, a fieldworker stopped at each of the selected households and left a questionnaire for both the husband and wife to complete. The respondents were instructed to seal the questionnaires in the included envelopes after completion and an appointment was made to collect the instruments within a few days. Forty-three households did not qualify for the study because either the husband or wife were full-time students or the marriage was not intact at the time. Of the remaining 317 couples, 223 husbands and 228 wives completed usable questionnaires. This was a respectable response rate of 71 per cent for husbands and 73 per cent for wives. Insufficient information on the number of years married or the indication that the previous weekend was atypical reduced the sample for the present investigation to 216 husbands and 226 wives or a total of 442 respondents.

Median family income for the sample is $19,000. With regard to husband's occupation, 36 per cent listed one of the professions and 48 per cent were managers or proprietors. Eighty-nine per cent of the husbands had some college experience, 73 per cent had graduated, and 43 per cent indicated postgraduate training. Among the wives, 78 per cent had some college experience, 62 per cent had graduated, and 16 per cent had postgraduate training. The respondents appear to conform to upper-middle-class social configurations.

Each subject in the investigation responded to the Leisure Activity-Interaction Index (Orthner, 1974b) developed to measure the relative use of individual, parallel, and joint activities. The Index contains a listing of 96 possible activities and the respondents were required to list the number of hours spent alone, with their spouse, or with a person other than their spouse over the past weekend in each of the activities in which they had participated. The activity list was as exhaustive as could be developed and served to remind the subjects of previous behavior. It even included items such as marital intimacy, casual conversation, and other family related pastimes. Any listed activities engaged in but not enjoyed did not fit the definition of leisure applied in the investigation and these were circled by the respondents and subsequently removed from the data analysis. Only insignificant losses resulted from this restriction.

The list of 96 activities had been previously submitted to a panel of judges who had demonstrated expertise in the field of leisure and recreation. They were asked to help determine whether each activity tended to be interactionally parallel or joint if performed in a group setting. Parallel activities were defined as group activites in which interaction is either nonexistent or limited to reactions regarding the particular stimuli that generates their common interest. Joint activities were those that required significant interaction among the participants for the successful completion of the activity. Each of the 96 activities were so designated and all activity-hours shared with others were coded as parallel or joint depending on the particular activity and the judges determination of its interactional nature. For example, playing games, visiting friends, playing in a park, camping, or engaging in sexual or affectional activity were judged to be joint while attending church, watching T.V., hunting, listening to records, or visiting a museum were judged to be parallel. All activity-hours indicated as having been spent alone were coded as individual.

The present investigation is concerned with the proportion of available leisure time husbands and wives spend alone or with their spouse and perhaps others and the interactional patterns of their leisure activities. The total number of activity-hours listed by each respondent in individual, joint with spouse, and parallel with spouse was derived. These totals were summed and a proportion of the total time in each of the three leisure-interaction categories determined.

Because of the multidimensionality of the concepts of satisfaction and morale (*cf.* Levinger, 1965; Hicks and Platt, 1971), the index of marital satisfaction was derived from responses to four questions, each with five possible responses. These items were selected because they had demonstrated in previous research the ability to differentiate between high and low morale marriage. The first was abstracted from the research of Rollins and Feldman (1970) as a measure of general marital satisfaction: In general, how often do you think things between you and your husband (wife) are going well? The five responses ranged from all the time to never. Three items were selected from Burgess and Wallin's (1953) marital satisfaction index. These items are as follows: Have you *ever* considered separating from your mate? (Seriously to have never considered it); Everything considered, how happy has your marriage been for you? (Decidedly happy to decidedly unhappy); If you had your life to live over, do you think you would marry the same person? (Certainly to not marry at all). A Likert-type scale was developed giving five points each to the most positive response and one point to the most negative. This generated a possible range of scores from 4 to 20 for the index.

Five marital career periods were selected for analysis based on the number of years married. It was assumed that intervals of six years would provide indications as to perceptions and needs in early marriage, the periods of family expansion and contraction, and the middle years of marriage. The husbands and wives are distributed as follows: 26 husbands and 27 wives in Period I (0 to 5 years), 38 husbands and 40 wives in Period II (6 to 11 years), 48 husbands and 52 wives in Period III (12 to 17 years), 32 husbands and 32 wives in Period IV (18 to 23 years), and 72 husbands and 75 wives in Period V (24 or more years).

In the data analysis, Goodman and Kruskal's *gamma (G)* was used to measure the strength of association and verify the hypotheses (Freeman, 1965). This is a measure of ordinal association; a ratio of the amount of agreement between two sets of rankings. It may be interpreted as the proportionate reduction in error in the dependent variable when the independent variable is known. A significance level less than or equal to .05 in a two-tailed test is required or the measure of association will be rejected as statistically nonsignificant in this study.

RESULTS

Before considering the hypotheses of the investigation, it would be helpful to note the distribution of the respondents on the primary variables. The husbands' weekend discretionary activity-hours were found to be apportioned in the following manner: a mean of 31 per cent in individual activities, 34 per cent in joint activities with their wives, and 27 per cent in parallel activities with their wives. The mean activity-hours for wives were apportioned in the following manner: 36 per cent in individual activities, 32 per cent in joint activities with their husbands, and 25 per cent in parallel activities with their husbands. Table 1 denotes the percentage of husbands or wives that indicated they spent 30 per cent or more of their time in each of the activity patterns over the five marital career periods.

Several observations on the above results are in order. Wives, apparently, tend to spend a slightly greater proportion of their time in individual activities than husbands and this holds true over the marital career. This can be partly explained by the fact that more of the husbands are likely to work on weekends than wives and, therefore, the total number of discretionary hours are greater for wives. The proportion of time spent in individual activities also increases over the marital career for both husbands and wives but the proportional increase for wives is greater than for husbands. The percentage of time spent in parallel activities tends to remain relatively constant over the marital career for both spouses. The increase in individual activities would appear to have its greatest effect on joint activities as it is the latter activity pattern that generally declined for both husbands and wives over time.

In support of other studies, the marital satisfaction scores were relatively high (*cf.* Burgess and Wallin, 1953; Rollins and Feldman, 1970). Out of a possible score of 20 on the composite index, 63.7 per cent of the husbands and 64.9 per cent of the wives realized a value of 17 or better. Table 2 lists the percentage of husbands and wives that received scores of 19 and 20 in the index over the five marital career periods. It is interesting to note that in four of the five periods, the husband's level of satisfaction exceeds the wife's. The greatest difference in scores is found in the first period when it

TABLE 1. PERCENT OF HUSBANDS AND WIVES SPENDING 30 PER CENT OR MORE OF THEIR LEISURE TIME IN INDIVIDUAL, JOINT, OR PARALLEL ACTIVITIES BY MARITAL CAREER PERIOD.

Activity Patterns	Marital Career Period				
	I (N=53)	II (N=78)	III (N=100)	IV (N=64)	V (N=147)
	%	%	%	%	%
Individual Activities					
Husbands	19.2	47.3	35.4	53.2	44.4
Wives	33.3	50.0	55.7	71.9	61.3
Joint Activities					
Husbands	69.3	71.0	60.4	37.5	51.4
Wives	66.7	67.5	50.0	37.5	49.3
Parallel Activities					
Husbands	65.3	50.0	62.5	59.5	65.3
Wives	55.5	47.5	53.8	57.2	64.0

TABLE 2. PERCENT OF HUSBANDS AND WIVES RECEIVING SCORES OF 19 AND 20 (OUT OF 20) ON THE INDEX OF MARITAL SATISFACTION BY MARITAL CAREER PERIOD.

	Marital Career Period				
Spouse	I (N=53)	II (N=78)	III (N=100)	IV (N=64)	V (N=147)
	%	%	%	%	%
Husbands	46.2	28.9	35.4	21.9	47.2
Wives	33.3	30.0	32.7	15.6	44.0

appears that disenchantment enters the wives earlier than the husbands. There also seems to be more stability over time in the satisfaction scores of the wives than that of the husbands which is contrary to the results of Rollins and Feldman (1970). Nevertheless, the time periods and indexes selected in the two studies are quite different and that may account for much of the variation that exists. Generally, the subjects in the present investigation tend to maintain the highest marital satisfaction scores in early marriage and in the postparental period as other studies noted earlier have demonstrated.

Moving to the central purpose of this investigation, the data indicate that the three leisure activity patterns are differentially related to marital satisfaction. (See Table 3.) Individual activities, first of all, tend to be negatively related to marital satisfaction, although more so for wives than for husbands. The level of association (G), without consideration for marital career period, is $-.14$ for husbands and $-.21$ for wives. The proportion of time spent in joint shared leisure activities is positively related to marital satisfaction for both husbands $(G=.18)$ and wives $(G=.21)$. Parallel activities tend to be positively related to satisfaction for husbands $(G=.14)$ and wives $(G=.09)$ but their influence overall is not as great as that of joint activities.

With regard to the first hypothesis, the data do not support the contention of a significant negative association between the proportion of time spent in individual activities and marital satisfaction for each marital career period. The only statistically significant associations are found in Period I for husbands and Period IV for wives. In four of the five marital career periods, the wives'

TABLE 3. ASSOCIATION (GAMMA) BETWEEN LEISURE ACTIVITY PATTERNS AND MARITAL SATISFACTION FOR HUSBANDS AND WIVES BY MARITAL CAREER PERIOD.

	Marital Career Period				
Activity Patterns	I (N=53)	II (N=78)	III (N=100)	IV (N=64)	V (N=147)
	(G)	(G)	(G)	(G)	(G)
Individual Activities					
Husbands	-.59**	.01	.06	-.24	-.15
Wives	-.20	-.15	-.21	-.44**	-.17
Joint Activities					
Husbands	.56**	-.20	.09	.50**	.21*
Wives	.51**	.10	.04	.55**	.08
Parallel Activities					
Husbands	.23	.01	.09	.37**	.09
Wives	-.03	.10	.13	.31*	.02

*Significant at the .05 level
**Significant at the .01 level

participation in individual activities is more related to dissatisfaction than the husbands'. Especially interesting is the relationship in Period I for husbands. The negative association ($G = -.59$) is much more significant than that of the wives ($G=-.20$) suggesting that individual activities among husbands in early marriage may be a good indicator of relational dissatisfaction and potential marital problems for husbands but not necessarily for wives. This is not the case, however, in Periods II and III when little relationship at all is indicated between individual leisure activities and marital satisfaction among husbands. The critical period for wives, the data suggests, is in Period IV when individual activities are a good indicator of relational dissatisfaction. In Period V, the relationships tend to be only moderately negative for both husbands and wives.

The hypothesized positive association between the proportion of time spent in joint spouse activities and marital satisfaction also needs to be clarified by marital career period. In general, husbands and wives respond more similarly to joint than to individual leisure activities. The data initially point to the critical role of joint shared activities for husbands and wives in early marriage. A significant positive association was determined in Period I for both spouses. However, during Periods II and III a sharp drop in the level of association is noted for both husbands and wives indicating practically no association between joint shared activities and marital satisfaction over those periods. Period IV again appears to be a critical time for both spouses as the use of joint leisure is likely to indicate marital satisfaction among both husbands and wives. The relationship drops off again during the fifth marital career period although not as greatly for husbands. Apparently, in the postparental period, participation in joint spouse activities is more related to and indicative of marital satisfaction for husbands than it is for wives.

The hypothesis of no relationship between shared parallel leisure activities and marital satisfaction is demonstrated for both husbands and wives in four of the five marital career periods. In Period I, the early marriage years, it is interesting to note that while parallel activities are related somewhat positively to relational satisfaction among husbands ($G=.23$), wives are slightly negatively influenced by this activity pattern ($G=-.03$). While neither coefficient is statistically significant, the results indicate that wives, especially, need more than "shared" leisure in early marriage. Parallel activities are sufficient to raise the marital satisfaction of husbands at this time, but this is not the case for the wives in the sample. Periods II and III maintain a low positive relationship between parallel leisure and relational satisfaction. However, in the fourth marital career period, a significant positive rise in level of association is noted for both husbands and wives. Parallel activities appear to have their primary influence on marital satisfaction at that time although the relationship is not nearly as great as that influenced by joint activities. Again, the familiar drop in level of association occurs in Period V.

DISCUSSION

Several issues have been raised in this research. First, it is apparent that not all shared leisure activities are similar in their influence on marriage. Both parallel and joint activities are by definition participated in together by husbands and wives but, apparently, more than physical proximity is required to bring about a satisfactory relationship. A couple spending the evening watching T.V. or going to a play are communicating more with the source of their interest than with each other. When the interaction required of the participants is greater, as in joint activities, the communication within the relationship is probably enhanced, understanding is increased, and the individuals are given the opportunity to alter behavior that may have negative consequences for the marriage. Admittedly, shared activities per se are more functional in this regard than nonshared activities but more emphasis needs to be given to the type of shared activities. The evidence from this investigation suggests that asking couples if they are "doing things together" as an index of their marital adjustment is inadequate and certainly insufficient to bring about or indicate marital satisfaction. It is just as important, if not more important, to determine the particular activities that they are "doing" together.

As a caution, the research results do not suggest that any particular leisure activity, such as watching television or knitting, is harmful to a marital relationship. Rather, the data indicate that when a particular activity pattern, *i.e.*, individual, parallel, or joint, becomes a dominant pattern, other activities are reduced and this has interactional consequences that may be positive or negative for the relationship.

It is also apparent from this investigation that the leisure factor changes in its influence over the marital career. In the early years of marriage, when initial adjustments are required and husband-wife interaction is very important in making these adjustments, the patterning of leisure has a significant impact. In support of Locke (1951), a high proportion of individual activities at this time reduces interaction and is associated with marital dissatisfaction. Joint activities, however, facilitate inter-action and are highly correlated with marital satisfaction for both spouses. The influence of parallel activities is marginal in early marriage and, among wives, since these activities reduce the possibility of joint participation, their effect may be slightly negative.

The only other period when leisure activities appear to have a significant influence on the relationship is during Period IV (18 to 23 years). The association patterns are similar at that time to those of early marriage with individual activities negatively related and joint activities positively related to marital satisfaction for both husbands and wives. The primary difference between the two marital career periods lies in the importance of parallel activities. This activity pattern becomes much more important as an indicator of satisfaction for both spouses during Period IV compared to the earlier periods. While joint activities are still more highly related to marital satisfaction, the concept of "shared" activities takes on more meaning during this latter period than in early marriage.

During Periods I (0-5 years) and IV (18-23 years), a number of relational adjustments are having to be made and these probably generate a need for heightened interaction. For example, in the latter period children are being launched, the marital dyad is having to be reestablished, occupational adjustments may be made by the wife, physiological changes, such as menopause, are occurring, the husband may be anxious about reaching the peak of his career, and so on. In effect, a relational identity crisis is most likely to occur in the initiation phase of dyadic formation and in the reaffirmation of the dyad at a later period. The data indicate that it is at these times that leisure can be a most influential determinate of the ability of a husband or wife to arrive at a satisfactory adjustment.

Interestingly, between Periods I and IV, and after them as well, leisure activity patterns are only marginally related to marital satisfaction. Couples at these times may be defining satisfaction more in terms of meeting parental or occupational goals and place the marital relationship "on hold" until these critical needs are met. This suggests that the primary relational function of leisure for marriage is that of a facilitator of communication during times of potential stress and relational change. Once these adjustments have been made and the marriage is stabilized, other factors may demand attention of the marital partners reducing significantly the role of leisure as an influencing variable.

Husbands and wives are also differentially influenced by leisure, particularly in individual and parallel activities. A predominance of individual activities among wives is more likely to indicate marital dissatisfaction than it is for husbands. This is especially true in the above described leisure latency period and the critical Period IV. The data on joint and parallel activities indicate that there is no great shared activity need in either spouse during marital career Periods II and III but at least some of this activity is required for the wife to maintain a positive affect for the relationship. If she is forced to accept individual activities as the primary pattern, then she may feel rejected or deserted in the marriage. Husbands, however, who engage in individual activities during Periods II and III do not demonstrate any decline in marital satisfaction and may not perceive the needs of their spouses for interaction.

Almost the opposite of this pattern occurs in early marriage, according to the data. The husband's level of marital satisfaction is more negatively influenced by individual activities and more positively influenced by parallel activities at this time than the wife's. One explanation would be that the marriage condition is sufficient for wives initially and as long as some joint activities are participated in by both she perceives the relationship as satisfying. The husband, however, may need more early support in the relationship from the wife because the culturel norms and values supporting the husband's role are not nearly as strong and secure.

CONCLUSION

The present investigation should make it increasingly difficult to make generalized statements regarding the role of leisure in marriage. Individual activities have not been demonstrated to have significant negative consequences for husbands and wives over the entire marital career. The concept of shared activities is certainly questionable as the relational consequences of joint and parallel activities appear to be quite different for husbands and wives at different periods in the marriage. Husbands and wives also react differently in some cases to a particular leisure activity pattern. Overall, the data support the conclusion that the leisure factor is most critical in determining marital satisfaction during two marital career periods: the first years of marriage when the dyadic formation process is crystallizing in marital adjustment and after 18 to 23 years when the marital relationship is reestablishing itself and a new dyadic adjustment becomes necessary. At other times, the differential use of leisure is much less significant as an indicator of relational satisfaction. Categorized statements, such as "doing things together" indicates marital adjustment, cannot be supported by this study.

Further research is definitely needed to clarify the issues raised in this investigation. The population of this study has been limited to upper-middle-class families and may or may not reflect other socioeconomic status groups. Other marital career periods should also be selected in future studies to determine if important relationships are being hidden by the periods selected. Limitations are also incurred by the use of questionnaire data and it is recommended that alternate designs be utilized in future studies as a means of substantiating the results of this investigation.

In conclusion, the leisure factor appears to be worthy of more consideration than it has been given in the past by family scholars. While this study represents an initial thrust into some of the variables that demand consideration, it is hoped that one of its most significant impacts will be as a stimulator of alternate theoretical statements and further empirical investigation. It is time to consider the dimensions of leisure in addition to work as an influencing variable in family relations. The ability of leisure to influence the family may be increasing and if the family is moving toward companionship as a source of marital solidarity, then the leisure factor is of critical importance.

FOOTNOTE

[1] It might be argued that free time raises anxieties and is not pleasureable for many persons. At this point we must make the distinction between leisure time and discretionary time with the former only encompassing that part of the latter that conforms to the definition described above. This means that free time and leisure are not necessarily synonymous and may have quite different effects on persons and groups.

REFERENCES

Axelson, Leland. 1960. "Personal adjustment in the postparental period." Marriage and Family Living 22:66-68.

Benson, Purnell. 1952. "The interest of happily married couples." Marriage and Family Living 14:276-280.

Burgess, Ernest W. and Harvey J. Locke. 1945. The Family: From Institution to Companionship. New York: American Book Company.

Burgess, Ernest W. and Paul Wallin. 1953. Engagement and Marriage. Philadelphia: Lippincott.

Burr, Wesley R. 1970. "Satisfaction with various aspects of marriage over the life cycle: a random middle class sample." Journal of Marriage and the Family 32:29-37.

Carter, Reginald. 1971. "The myth of increasing non-work vs. work activities." Social Problems 18:52-67.

Clarke, Alfred C. 1956. "Leisure and occupational prestige." American Sociological Review 21:301-307.

Cuber, John F. and Peggy B. Harroff. 1965. The Significant Americans. New York: Appleton-Century.

Cunningham, Kenneth R. and Theodore B. Johannis, Jr. 1960. "Research on the family and leisure: a review and critique of selected studies." Family Life Coordinator 9:25-32.

DeGrazia, Sebastian. 1962. Of Time, Work, and Leisure. New York: Twentieth Century Fund.

Dumazedier, Joffre. 1967. Toward a Society of Leisure. New York: Free Press.

Dumazedier, Joffre. 1971. "Leisure and post-industrial societies." In Max Kaplan and Phillip Bosserman (eds.), Technology, Human Values, and Leisure. New York: Abingdon Press.

Edwards, John N. 1967. "The future of the family revisited." Journal of Marriage and the Family 29:505-511.

Feldman, Margaret and Harold Feldman. 1973. "The marital life cycle: some neglected areas of study." Paper presented at the meeting of the National Council on Family Relations. Toronto, Canada.

Foote, Nelson N. and Leonard Cottrell. 1955. Identity and Interpersonal Competence. Chicago: University of Chicago Press.

Freeman, Linton. 1965. Elementary Applied Statistics. New York: John Wiley.

Gerson, Walter M. 1960. "Leisure and marital satisfaction of college married couples." Marriage and Family Living 22:360-361.

Goode, William J. 1962. "Outdoor recreation and the family to the year 2000." Report to the Outdoor Recreation Resources Review Commission. Report 22, Washington D.C.

Hawkins, Harold and James Walters. 1952. "Family recreation activities." Journal of Home Economics 44:623-626.

Hicks, Mary W. and Marilyn Platt. 1971. "Marital happiness and stability: review of research in the sixties." Journal of Marriage and the Family 33:59-78.

Hobart, Charles W. 1963. "Commitment, value conflict, and the future of the family." Marriage and Family Living 25:405-412.

Kaplan, Max. 1960. Leisure in America; A Social Inquiry. New York: Wiley.

Kaplan, Max. 1971. "The 4-day work week, a symptom of change." The Call (Spring).

Kelly, John R. 1972. "The family and leisure: finding a function." Paper presented at the National Council on Family Relations, Portland, Oregon.

Klausner, W. J. 1968. "An experiment in leisure." Science Journal 4:81-85.

Klein, John, Gene Calvert, Neal Garland, and Margaret Polomo. 1968. "Pilgrims progress I: recent developments in family theory." Journal of Marriage and the Family 31:677-687.

Kraus, Richard. 1971. Recreation and Leisure in Modern Society. New York: Appleton-Century-Crofts.

Levinger, George. 1965. "Marital cohesiveness and dissolution: an integrate review." Journal of Marriage and the Family 27:19-28.

Lobsenz, Norman M. 1962. Is Anybody Happy? New York: Doubleday.

Locke, Harvey J. 1951. Predicting Adjustment in Marriage. New York: Holt.

Neumeyer, Martin H. and Esther S. Neumeyer. 1958. Leisure and Recreation: A Study of Leisure and Recreation in Their Sociological Aspects. 3rd Ed. New York: Ronald Press.

Orthner, Dennis K. 1974a. "Toward a theory of leisure and family interaction." Paper presented at the meeting of the Pacific Sociological Association, San Jose, California.

Orthner, Dennis K. 1974b. "Leisure activities and family interaction." Unpublished doctoral dissertation, Florida State University.

Parsons, Talcott and Robert F. Bales. 1955. Family, Socialization, and Interaction Process. Glencoe: The Free Press.

Pineo, Peter C. 1961. "Disenchantment in the later years of marriage." Marriage and Family Living 23:3-11.

Reisman, David. 1958. "Leisure and work in a post-industrial society." In Eric Larrabee and Rolf Meyersohn (eds.), Mass Leisure. Glencoe: The Free Press.

Rodgers, Roy H. 1973. Family Interaction and Transaction. Englewood Cliffs, N.J.: Prentice-Hall.

Rollins, Boyd C. and Harold Feldman. 1970. "Marital satisfaction over the family life cycle." Journal of Marriage and the Family 32:20-27.

Scheuch, Erwin K. 1960. "Family cohesion and leisure time." Sociological Review 8:37-61.

Sjoberg, Gideon and Roger Nett. 1968. A Methodology for Social Research. New York: Harper and Row.

Stone, Carol. 1963. "Family recreation, a parental dilemma." The Family Coordinator 12:85-87.

Sussman, Marvin. 1956. "Leisure: Bane or blessing." Social Work 1: 11-18.

Walker, Kathryn E. 1969. "Homemaking still takes time." Journal of Home Economics 61:621-624.

West, Patrick and L. C. Merriam, Jr. 1970. "Outdoor recreation and family cohesiveness: a research approach." Journal of Leisure Research 2:251-259.

Wolfenstein, Martha. 1958. "The emergence of fun morality." In Eric Larrabee and Rolf Meyersohn (eds), Mass Leisure. Glencoe: The Free Press.

11 psychological well-being in the postparental stage: some evidence from national surveys

norval d. glenn

According to the folklore, as well as many early social scientific impressions, the last child's leaving home leaves a void in the life of the typical mother which she cannot easily fill. The activities which have occupied most of her time for most of her adult life, and which have given purpose and meaning to her existence, either cease or occupy much less of her time. In sociological terms, she loses one of her major roles and thus loses the rewards, such as a contribution to her sense of personal importance, which go with the role.

This view that the "empty nest" or postparental stage of the family life cycle is a traumatic and unhappy period for the typical woman has not disappeared entirely from social scientific circles, but negative evidence from a few small-scale studies has lessened its credibility. Perhaps the most widely cited evidence is reported by Deutscher (1964), who interviewed one or both spouses in 31 postparental households in Kansas City. A large majority of the persons interviewed (71 per cent of the husbands and 79 per cent of the wives) said the postparental stage was better than or as good as the preceding stages of the family life cycle. Only six per cent of the wives, and none of the husbands, clearly considered the quality of their lives to be worse after the children left home. At least one other retrospective study with a local sample has yielded similar results (Axelson, 1960), and at least one longitudinal study (also with a local sample) has failed to indicate that women typically become less happy after their children leave (Clausen, 1972).

In addition to the studies on global happiness and satisfaction, several studies provide tentative evidence on the effects of the children's leaving home on marital satisfaction and adjustment (see Rollins and Cannon, 1974, and Rollins and Feldman, 1970, for reports of two of the studies and summaries of the findings of most of the others). These effects are not necessarily in the same direction as the effects on global happiness, of course, but marital satisfaction is likely to be a major determinant of global happiness. The evidence is not entirely consistent, but some of the studies reveal greater marital satisfaction in the postparental stage than in the immediately preceding stages of the family life cycle, and no study shows sharply lower marital satisfaction in the postparental stage.

Although the published evidence suggests that the children's leaving home does not typically have any enduring negative effect on the mother's psychological well-being, the evidence is by no means conclusive. All studies of the effects on global happiness, and most of those of the effects on marital satisfaction, are based on local or otherwise unrepresentative samples, some of which are very small. Furthermore, each study suffers from the inherent limitations of its methods. Retrospective studies suffer from possible inaccuracies in the recollections of the respondents (although it is unlikely that postparental persons would systematically remember the parental stages of their lives to

TABLE 1. PERCENTAGE OF MIDDLE-AGED FEMALES WHO SAID THEY WERE "VERY HAPPY," BY FAMILY CYCLE STAGE, U.S. NATIONAL SAMPLES, MID-1960'S.

Age	Parental		Postparental		Difference
	%	(N)	%	(N)	
40-49	45.6	(425)	60.6	(109)	−15.0
50-59	59.5	(140)	55.3	(228)	4.2
40-59	49.1	(565)	57.0	(337)	− 7.9

Source: Combined data from Gallup Surveys 675, 735, and 736.
Question Wording: "In general, how happy would you say you are—very happy, fairly happy, or not happy?"

TABLE 2. PERCENTAGE OF MIDDLE-AGED FEMALES WHO SAID THEY WERE "VERY HAPPY," BY FAMILY CYCLE STAGE, U.S. NATIONAL SAMPLES, 1972 AND 1973.

Age	Parental		Postparental		Difference
	%	(N)	%	(N)	
40-49	42.5	(167)	48.2	(56)	− 5.7
50-59	29.4	(85)	41.9	(117)	−12.5
40-59	38.1	(252)	43.9	(173)	− 5.8

Source: Combined data from the 1972 and 1973 General Social Surveys, conducted by the National Opinion Research Center.
Question Wording: "Taken all together, how would you say things are these days—would you say that you are very happy, pretty happy, or not too happy?"

TABLE 3. PERCENTAGE OF MIDDLE-AGED FEMALES WHO SAID THEY MOSTLY ENJOYED LIFE, BY FAMILY CYCLE STAGE, U.S. NATIONAL SAMPLE, 1971.

Age	Parental		Postparental		Difference
	%	(N)	%	(N)	
35-49	81.6	(136)	87.2	(39)	− 5.6
50-64	72.2	(36)	83.3	(108)	−11.1
35-64	79.7	(172)	84.4	(147)	− 4.7

Source: Roper Survey 524.
Question Wording: "Thinking of your life as you live it day by day, which of these statements best expresses the way you feel? (1) Mostly I enjoy life, although at times I just go through the days. (2) Half of the time I enjoy life, and half of the time I just go through the days. (3) Sometimes I enjoy life, but most of the time I just go through the days."

be less pleasant than they were); longitudinal studies confound the effects of passage from one stage of the life cycle to another with the effects of aging and of general changes in the society (period effects); and the cross-sectional studies of family stage effects on marital adjustment have confounded those effects with the effects of age, duration of marriage, and cohort membership.

Unfortunately, there is no flawless method to study family stage effects. The method used here—a cross-sectional comparison of persons in the parental and postparental stages, with age roughly controlled—has limitations. For instance, persons in the two stages may differ in other characteristics which influence their psychological well-being and which are not controlled. However, since its limitations are different, this method complements the other methods, and the combined results of studies using different methods can provide more nearly conclusive evidence than the results of studies using any one method. Furthermore, the problem of small and unrepresentative samples is largely overcome here by use of data from six national surveys.

METHODS

The data are from surveys of the noninstitutionalized civilian population of the United States conducted in 1963 (Gallup 675), 1966 (Gallup 735 and 736), 1971 (Roper 524), and 1972 and 1973 (the General Social Surveys conducted by the National Opinion Research Center). For reporting, the data from the three Gallup surveys are combined (Table 1), as are the data from the two NORC surveys (Table 2). Measures of psychological well-being are used to compare "parental" and "postparental" persons in the broad age ranges of 40-49 and 50-59 (35-49 and 50-64 in the case of the Roper survey, which does not have exact age codes). The measures from the Gallup and NORC surveys are responses to questions on personal happiness (see Tables 1 and 2 for the question wording). Although both the Gallup and the NORC questions asked the respondents to rate themselves on a three-point scale, few respondents chose the lowest degree of happiness, so little information is lost by dichotomizing the responses into "very happy" versus other responses. (The Gallup and NORC data are not comparable, since the Gallup question tends to elicit a larger percentage of "very happy" responses.) The Roper question asked the respondents to rate themselves according to what proportion of the time they enjoy themselves (Table 3). Again, few persons chose the lowest point on the three-point scale, so the responses are dichotomized into the highest rating versus the others.

None of the six surveys provides the information needed for precise separation of postparental persons from other respondents. For instance, the Gallup surveys give information only on number of people in the household under age 21 and age 21 and older, so respondents can be operationally defined as "parental" or "postparental" only on the basis of whether or not anyone under age 21 was in the household. Therefore, the "postparental" category contains a few persons who had never had children. The Roper data suffer from the same defect, except that only persons under age 17 in the household are reported, and thus a good many of the "postparental" persons were really in the launching stage. The NORC data allow exclusion of persons who had never had children but do not allow separation of postparental persons from those who had children age 18 or older still living at home. The effect of these "contaminations" of the postparental category should generally be to reduce observed differences between the parental and the postparental categories.

The effect of the last child's leaving home is likely to differ according to whether or not the woman is left alone. Since no survey provides enough cases for a separate study of postparental women living alone, only married Roper and NORC respondents and Gallup respondents in a household with at least one other adult are included in the study.

Although the principal concern is with the effects of the "empty nest" on women, corresponding data on males were computed and are briefly summarized below. Other data somewhat incidental to the main purpose of the study—the results of a comparison of parental and postparental respondents to the 1973 General Social Survey on a one-item measure of "marital happiness"—are also briefly summarized.

The working hypothesis, based on previous findings, is that postparental persons, as a whole, will report psychological well-being equal to, or greater than, that reported by parental persons in the same age range.

FINDINGS

The findings from the pooled Gallup data (Table 1), the pooled NORC data (Table 2), and the Roper data (Table 3) generally support the hypothesis; only the Gallup data for persons ages 50-59 show greater psychological well-being in the parental than in the postparental category. All six surveys show greater happiness or enjoyment of life in the postparental category in the 40-59 age range (35-64 in the case of the Roper data)—in spite of the fact that postparental persons averaged considerably older than parental persons in that broad age category, and age is negatively related to reported psychological well-being. At the 40-49 age level, one survey (the 1972 General Survey) shows a greater percentage of "very happy" persons in the parental category, but by only 3.0 points. If that difference did not result from sampling error, it may have resulted largely from the fact that even in a ten-year age range, postparental persons average somewhat older than parental ones. At the 50-59 level, two sruveys (Gallup 675 and 735) show greater percentages of "very happy" persons in the parental category, by 8.2 and 9.8 points. These differences vary so sharply from the differences shown by the other surveys—including the other Gallup survey, which shows a difference in the opposite direction of 9.4 points—that they are likely to have resulted from sampling error. Nevertheless, the evidence that psychological well-being is not greater in the parental stage is considerably stronger for ages 40-49 than ages 50-59.

The probability is quite small that sampling error accounts for the overall failure of the data to show greater psychological well-being in the parental category. If one assumes that the different questions tap the same basic variable, in spite of the differences in wording, a sign test can be applied to the parental-postparental differences from the six surveys. For the 40-59 (or 35-64) age range, a one-tailed test yields a probability of .016. This is the probability that all six comparisons would show greater psychological well-being in the postparental category if there were no difference in the universe. However, even if the null hypothesis of no difference were correct, there would be no evidence of a negative effect of the "empty nest." If psychological well-being in the universe were substantially greater among parental than postparental persons, the probability of all six surveys showing the opposite difference would be a great deal less than .016.

Of course, any positive relationship between being in the postparental stage and reported psychological well-being could be spurious; the women who are happier, for whatever reasons, might tend to reach the postparental stage at an earlier age than the less happy women. For instance, women in families with higher incomes generally report greater happiness than women in families with lower incomes, and the former might tend to reach the postparental stage at lower ages. An efficient way to test for spuriousness via family income is to standardize the reports of happiness or of enjoyment of life of both parental and postparental respondents to the income distribution shown for the two categories combined. Generally, the income-adjusted data show about the same parental-postparental differences as the unadjusted data, the greatest change being a reduction of about two percentage points in the difference at ages 40-49 in the combined data from the General Social Surveys. Adjustment leaves greater psychological well-being in the postparental category in the 40-59 (or 35-64) age range in the data from each of the six surveys.

It seems, then, that passage into the postparental stage probably has, on the average, a positive effect on mother's global happiness and enjoyment of life. Confidence in this conclusion is enhanced by its consistency with the evidence from studies using other methods (*e.g.,* Deutscher, 1964; Axelson, 1960; and Clausen, 1972). However, unlike the Deutscher study, this one indicates that any net positive effect of the children's leaving home on a cohort of mothers is probably weak or moderate rather than strong.

The male data differ from the female data in that they show less consistency in the direction of the parental-postparental differences, all of which are quite small. Both the combined Gallup data and the combined General Social Survey data for males ages 40-59 show a greater percentage "very happy" in the postparental category, by only 2.7 and 1.5 points, and the Roper data show slightly greater reported enjoyment of life among parental than among postparental males at both the 35-49 and the 50-64 age levels. Therefore, a net loss in psychological well-being as a result of the children's leaving home seems somewhat more likely for fathers, as a whole, than for mothers, but it is not likely that any such loss is substantial.

Any positive effect on psychological well-being of the passage of women into the postparental stage may result from an increase in marital happiness. According to the data from the 1973 General Social Survey, the percentage of postparental women ages 40-49 who said they had "very happy" marriages was 82.8, compared with 57.1 per cent of the parental women in the same age range—a difference of 25.7 percentage points. The corresponding percentages in the 50-59 age range are 70.8 and 45.5—a difference of 25.3 points. The direction of the differences is the same for males as for females, but the magnitude is substantially smaller, being 4.1 and 10.0 percentage points for ages 40-49 and 50-59, respectively.

Even though the Ns are small (and for the purpose of significance tests must be considered only two-thirds as large as they are, to take into account the increase in standard errors brought about by the cluster sample design), the female parental-postparental differences in reported marital happiness are statistically significant, the one-tailed probabilities being .021 and .023. Furthermore, standardization of the data to the same family income distribution (that for parental and postparental persons combined) has little effect, the adjusted difference being slightly greater than the unadjusted difference at ages 40-59 and slightly smaller at ages 50-59. It is possible, of course, that the relationship between family stage and marital happiness is spurious, via some uncontrolled variable, but in view of the magnitude of the percentage differences, a totally spurious relationship is highly improbable. It is much more likely that the children's leaving home typically has a positive effect on the wife's marital happiness.

Other studies have generally not shown such a pronounced apparent effect of the empty nest on marital happiness or satisfaction, perhaps in part because they have used different measures of satisfaction and, in most cases, less representative samples. However, the greater family stage effect indicated here seems to have resulted in large measure from controls for age, which were not used in the other studies. The wider the age range, the smaller was the parental-postparental difference in percentage of "very happy" marriages; for ages 40-59 it was 20.7 points, for ages 30-59 it was 13.8 points, and for ages 20-59 it was 11.3 points. The apparent reason for the smaller difference in the broader age ranges is a negative effect on marital happiness of age, of some close correlate of age such as duration of marriage, or of membership in the older birth cohorts (the effects of which are totally confounded with those of age in these cross-sectional data). Although the data for all married females show only a very weak negative relationship of age to reported marital happiness, the relationship was fairly strong among both parental and postparental women; for instance, the percentage of the former who said their marriages were "very happy" varied monotonically from 68.8 per cent at ages 20-29 to 45.5 per cent at ages 50-59. And since postparental persons are older on the average than parental ones, the effects of age (or of its correlates, or of cohort membership) tend to obscure any positive effects of being in the postparental stage unless age is rather precisely controlled.

CONCLUSIONS AND IMPLICATIONS

The findings of this study, considered in conjunction with those of retrospective and longitudinal studies, provide convincing, although not absolutely conclusive, evidence that the children's leaving home does not typically lead to an enduring decline in the psychological well-being of middle-aged mothers. Rather, the effects seem to be moderately positive, on balance. However, these conclusions should be tempered with the following qualifications and cautions:

1. The data reported here are only for women living with a husband or some other adult. If the mother is left living alone, the effects may well be distinctly negative in most cases.

2. The aggregate data indicating little apparent net effect of the passage of a cohort of married women into the postparental stage probably conceal many individual cases of pronounced negative and positive effects on personal happiness. Furthermore, since most of the postparental women in the samples had probably been in that stage for at least several months, widespread short-term negative effects might not be reflected in the data.

3. Although the findings of this and similar studies indicate that the so-called "empty nest syndrome" is not as prevalent among middle-aged women as was once believed, problems of the "empty nest" may be prevalent enough to warrant public concern and corrective action. However, the problems of widows and of women with children still at home would seem to warrant greater concern.

An incidental finding of this study which may be as important as the principal one is that the postparental female respondents to one national survey reported distinctly greater marital happiness, as a whole, than parental women in the same age range. This finding suggests that global happiness may typically not decline as a result of the children's leaving home only because of a typical positive effect on the marital relationship (at least from the wife's perspective). This finding also makes clear the inappropriateness and prematurity of the recent recommendation of Rollins and Cannon (1974:280) that family life cycle stage not be further pursued as an independent variable in research on marital satisfaction. Their curious recommendation comes at a time when most attempted studies of family stage effects have been conducted with inadequate samples and before there has been a single sophisticated attempt to distinguish family stage effects on marital satisfaction from the effects of age, duration of marriage, and cohort membership. It is to be hoped that the tentative evidence now available represents only the beginning, not the end, of research on this topic.

REFERENCES

Axelson, Leland J. 1960. "Personal adjustment in the postparental period." Marriage and Family Living 22 (February):66-68.

Clausen, John A. 1972. "The life course of individuals." Pp. 457-514 in Matilda White Riley, Marilyn Johnson, and Anne Foner, Aging and Society, Vol. III: A Sociology of Age Stratification. New York: Russell Sage Foundation.

Deutscher, Irwin. 1964. "The quality of postparental life." Journal of Marriage and the Family 26 (February): 52-59.

Rollins, Boyd C. and Kenneth L. Cannon. 1974. "Marital satisfaction over the family life cycle: a reevaluation." Journal of Marriage and the Family 36 (May):271-282.

Rollins, Boyd C. and Harold Feldman. 1970. "Marital satisfaction over the family life cycle." Journal of Marriage and the Family 32 (February):20-28.

12   dimensions of widowhood in later life

robert c. atchley

Widowhood has long been recognized as an important and widespread role change which occurs primarily in later life (Atchley, 1972). A great deal of attention has been paid to the problems of widows (Clark & Anderson, 1967; Lopata, 1966, 1970, 1971, 1973; Parks, 1972), while less attention has been paid to the impact of widowhood on husbands (Atchley, 1972; Berardo, 1968, 1970; Parks, 1972).

Various studies have shown that people are generally able to cope with the changes widowhood brings, but at the same time preoccupation with grief, greater worry, lower morale, and unhappiness are all more common among widows and widowers than among others of the same age (Riley & Foner, 1968).

It has also been suggested that widows and widowers face different situations. While widowers generally can remarry more easily than can widows, several studies found that widows are often better prepared to lead a life as a single, self-sufficient adult. Direct comparisons of widows and widowers are hard to find (Berardo, 1968; Clark & Anderson, 1967; Parks, 1972).

PURPOSE AND PLAN OF THE STUDY

The goals of the research reported here were to describe various social psychological and social differences which occur between married and widowed older people and differences which appear between widows and widowers, and to develop some hypothesis concerning adjustment to widowhood.

Two occupational groups were sampled as a part of an earlier study in retirement (Atchley, 1971; Cottrell & Atchley, 1969). Responses were sought via mail questionnaire from all retired employees of a large midwestern telephone company and from a random sample of 3000 retired public school teachers. Sixty-five per cent (N = 3704) of the total sample responded. The data used in the present study were derived from these questionnaires.

In order to control age to a small degree, only respondents who were 70 to 79 years of age at the time of the study were included. Also, separated, divorced, and never married respondents were excluded in order to allow clearer comparisons between married and widowed respondents. This procedure yielded a sample of 428 married men, 72 widowers, 169 married women, and 233 widows, all aged 70 to 79.

Marital status was self-assigned. Data were also available on age, sex, age identification, sensitivity to criticism, anxiety, anomie, loneliness, participation in organizations, contact with friends, car driving, income, job satisfaction, self-esteem, depression, labor force status, job commitment, attitude toward retirement, and job deprivation (Cottrell & Atchley, 1969). For information on scales and cutting points, see Cottrell and Atchley (1969).

In the analysis of the data gathered the dependent variables were separated into two groups: social psychological (age identification, anxiety, anomie, loneliness, and job commitment), and social (social participation, auto driving, and income adequacy). The general strategy employed in analyzing the data was to examine differences two ways: between widows and widowers and between married and widowed. Because industry groups varied substantially on many of the variables, comparisons were often made with industry group controlled.

SOCIAL PSYCHOLOGICAL IMPACT

On social psychological variables, there were as many significant differences between widowers and widows as between widowed and married persons of either sex. Among former phone company employees, widowers were more likely to see themselves as old compared to widows of the same age. This matches our earlier finding that men tend to identify themselves with respect to age in terms of the roles they play more often than women do (Atchley & George, 1973). Widows were more likely to be anxious and to have a low job commitment than were widowers. Among former teachers the only significant difference was the tendency for widows to have a lower prevalence of high job commitment. In general, then, on the social psychological variables measured, there were more differences between widows and widowers in the clerical and service occupations than among professional teachers.

Widowed people showed a higher prevalence of identification as old and of loneliness compared to married people of the same age. Among former phone company women employees, widows were significantly more likely to show high anomie compared to those who were married.

These results have several implications. First, the wide variety of differences observed in a fairly limited sample suggest that overarching generalizations about psychological reactions to or consequences of widowhood should be made with great caution for both sexes. For example, while it is true that widowed people are "worse off" than married people in terms of age identification and loneliness in general, they were not significantly different from married people in terms of sensitivity to criticism, anxiety, anomie, job commitment, self-esteem, self-stability, depression, attitude toward retirement, or job deprivation. Thus widowhood produces stress on certain dimensions and not others, and theories concerning the effects of widowhood must take this variability into account. Likewise, no generalizations about psychological differences between widows and widowers could be found that held even within our limited sample.

SOCIAL IMPACT

On social variables, there were again significant differences both between married and widowed people and between widowers and widows. On social variables, widowers generally fared "better" than widows. Compared with widows in the same industry group, former phone company widowers were more likely to have increased their participation in clubs or organizations following retirement, while widowers who were former teachers were more likely to have increased their contacts with friends. Thus, widowers were more likely than widows to have increased their level of social participation following retirement, but the direction this increase took varied by industry group. Men are generally more likely to drive automobiles than are women, but the gap between widowers and widows among former phone company employees is especially great, particularly since the gap between married men and women in this industry group was much smaller. Also, widowers were significantly more likely to have adequate incomes than were widows. Hence, it was particularly among former phone company employees that widowers fared better than widows on social variables. Differences between widows and widowers were fewer and of less magnitude among former teachers.

In terms of differences between married and widowed people, widowhood increases the incidence of social participation among men, but it decreases social participation among former women teachers. Widowhood affects car driving significantly only among former women phone company employees. Likewise, former phone company women are the only category whose income adequacy is affected by widowhood.

THE PRIMACY OF ECONOMIC IMPACTS

Among former phone company women, primarily former telephone operators, widows were significantly worse off than widowed people in the other three sex and industry categories. These widows were likely to have inadequate incomes which probably accounts in large part for their low incidence of auto driving and their lower social participation and loneliness. Likewise, in a category that is poor and isolated, it is unsurprising that many are anxious and anomic. This line of reasoning suggests that economic circumstances are a power factor influencing the social situation of widows. Widows and widowers who view their incomes as adequate are much less likely to encounter either social or psychological stress than are widowed people with inadequate incomes.

Lopata (1973) holds that participation and adjustment following widowhood is primarily a function of personality, attitudinal, and ethnic factors. While she reports that low income is related to low social participation and greater dependency on family, Lopata does not follow up the possible causal force of low income as a fundamental variable structuring the life situation of the widow. The data reported in this paper point to income adequacy as an essential component of any theory of adjustment to widowhood.

Berardo (1970) found that widowhood is more stressful for men than for women. He saw aged, widowed men as being isolated and stressed by the dual effects of loss of spouse and loss of job which, in Berardo's eyes, cuts men off from their customary patterns of friendship. The data reported here do not support Berardo's findings. Widowers were better off than widows on all of the dimensions save age identification. These data suggest that males have economic supports which for the most part tend to offset the effects of other social and psychological factors.

From the literature, it is clear that the impact of widowhood on income adequacy and the role of income adequacy in adjustment to widowhood represent sorely neglected areas for further research. Longitudinal studies which regard adjustment as a process and which include the economic impact of widowhood would be particularly useful.

The data reported in this paper suggest a set of relationships which may be useful in future research. Fig. I is a schematic of these hypothetical relationships. Widowhood combines with sex and

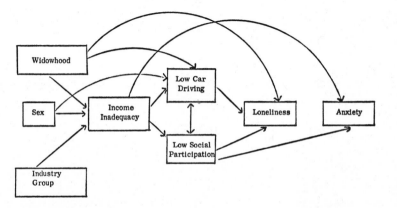

FIGURE I. IMPACT OF WIDOWHOOD.

industry group to produce income inadequacy. Income inadequacy in turn affects car driving and social participation (which also influence each other). Because American society is spatially structured on the assumption that everyone can get around by private car, widowed people with inadequate incomes become socially isolated and lonely. Income inadequacy and social isolation combine to produce anxiety. This theory assigns a high degree of importance to income inadequacy and its results. It deserves to be tested alongside theories of response to widowhood based on assumptions about personality or role relationships.

REFERENCES

Atchley, R. C. Retirement and work orientation. Gerontologist, 1971, 11, 13-17.

Atchley, R. C. The social forces in later life. Wadsworth, Belmont, CA, 1972.

Atchley, R. C., & George, L. K. Symptomatic measurement of age. Gerontologist, 1973, 13, 332-336.

Berardo, F. Widowhood status in the United States: Perspective on a neglected aspect of the family life-cycle. Family Coordinator, 1968, 17, 191-203.

Berardo, F. Survivorship and social isolation: The case of the aged widower. Family Coordinator, 1970, 19, 11-15.

Clark, M., & Anderson, B. Culture and aging. Charles C. Thomas, Springfield, IL, 1967.

Cottrell, F., & Atchley, R. C. Women in retirement: A preliminary report. Scripps Foundation, Oxford, OH, 1969.

Lopata, H. Z. The life cycle of the social role of housewife. Sociology & Social Research, 1966, 51, 5-22.

Lopata, H. Z. The social involvement of American widows. American Behavioral Scientist, 1970, 14, (Sept.-Oct.), 41-48.

Lopata, H. Z. Living arrangements of American urban widows. Sociological Focus, 1971, 5, 41-61.

Lopata, H. Z. Widowhood in an American city. Schenkman Publishing Co., Cambridge, MA.

Parks, C. M. Bereavement: Studies of grief in adult life. International Universities Press, New York, 1972.

Riley, M. W., & Foner, A. E. Aging and society, Vol. I, An inventory of research findings. Russell Sage Fdn., New York, 1968.

part 2

parent-child relationships

INTRODUCTION

Recent trends are having considerable impact on research productivity relevant to the parent-child relationship. With the emergence of some strong anti-parenting sentiments in our society, there has been considerable research on the voluntary childless state or nonparenting. Rossi (1977) has pointed out that recent research studies that emphasize innovative life styles focus more on the individual or the adult-dyad relationship than on the parent-child relationship. Once the lack of an adequate data base on the father-child relationship was articulated (Benson, 1968; Bigner, 1970; Walters and Stinnett, 1971), a shift occurred and more research focused on the father-child relationship. Even though a special issue of *The Family Coordinator* (October, 1976), published by the National Council on Family Relations, included 21 articles on fatherhood, research literature on the mother-child relationship continues to exceed in volume that which is published on the father-child relationship (Olson and Dahl, 1977).

Part 2 of this book is organized into three sections: 1) parenthood—a choice and an adjustment; 2) parent-child relationships in a variety of settings; and 3) parent-adolescent relationships. It is arranged so that readings pertaining to the most salient topics regarding the parent-child relationship can be drawn together for the reader's examination.

PARENTHOOD—A CHOICE AND AN ADJUSTMENT

The publication of Ellen Peck's *The Baby Trap* and Schvaneveldt's article *(13)* occurred in 1971. These publications attested to the rise of strong anti-child or anti-parenthood sentiments which thrived during the late 1960s. More serious questioning of the parental role, its advantages and disadvantages, has continued and has manifested its strength in the publication of an entire anthology (Peck and Senderowitz, 1974). Schvaneveldt's article is included as an introduction to the section on parenthood because it attempts to review the literature on both sides of the issue. Schvaneveldt not only examined the pros and cons of having children, but he also included a review of the literature, through 1970, regarding what was known pertaining to "parenthood as crisis" and marital adjustment during the childbearing and childrearing stages of the family life cycle.

Veever's article, which details a study of voluntarily childless wives, is included as an example of the type of research that she and other investigators have performed in this area *(14)*. Of the more recent studies on this topic (Cutright and Polonko, 1977; Movius, 1976; Poston, 1974, 1976; Renne, 1976; Veevers, 1974, 1975), Renne's study is highly pertinent. She concluded from her data that parental status had negative effects on health and marital satisfaction. She found that the former parents in her sample fared better than the active parents. The childless spouses appeared healthiest and reported the most marital satisfaction, even when the variable of age of the wife was controlled for in making comparisons.

Despite evidence of the negative effects of parental status, parenting will continue as an important role, particularly for many women. Rossi's article on the transition to parenthood is a classical work that explains the adjustments of married individuals to the parenting role *(15)*. Her work, as well as the recent replication study by Hobbs and Cole (1976), should finally put to rest the notion of parenthood as crisis. It appears more appropriate to refer to the adjustment to parenthood as involving a transition, not a crisis.

In one study (Ryder, 1973), longitudinal data were examined in order to investigate the relationship between marital satisfaction and parental status. The most salient finding was that mothers are more likely to report that their husbands do not pay sufficient attention to them. One of the transitions to parenthood obviously entails the change from a rather exclusive dyad relationship between husband and wife to a more complex triad relationship.

Despite all of the evidence that both mothers and fathers play significant roles in the parenting of their children, physical care of the young child remains the primary responsibility of mothers. When fathers take care of their children's physical needs, this form of parenting activity is perceived as helping or substituting for the mother. Androgyny, the blurring of sex roles, is given lots of verbal acceptance, but apparently only a minority follow a truly androgynous pattern of parenting. Rossi (1977) points out that during the first few years of life the physical care of the child falls primarily upon the mother, even in the communal living situations where liberation from sexually typed behavior is sought. Furthermore, evidence of the special role of the mother in multiple-parenting situations is provided by a reading *(38)* in a later section. One point remains clear: no matter who does the parenting, the transition to parenthood is not an easy one to make in our society and carries with it some serious responsibilities.

PARENT-CHILD RELATIONSHIPS IN A VARIETY OF SETTINGS

This section explores the variety of settings in which parent-child relationships take place. The readings cover only those cases of child-rearing in which one or both of the biological parents are present. However, much of what is included within these readings will be relevant to the adult-child relationships experienced by those children who do not have ongoing continuous relationships with one or both of their biological parents. Especially in the case of adoption, the genetic differences should not necessarily alter the parent-child relationship except in cases where attitudes may influence behavior.

One of the first variables to be researched in terms of an influence on parent-child relationships was that of social class. One of the earliest studies by Duvall of concepts of parenthood and how such concepts vary according to social class is included in this section because it is an outstanding classical study *(16)*. Duvall's findings were considered by Kohn (1963) when he examined and interpreted the association between social class and parent-child relationships. The article by Gecas and Nye *(17)* included in this section and a study by Wright and Wright (1976) reported elsewhere are examples of the numerous reexaminations of Kohn's hypothesis. Both of these studies reconfirm the earlier findings that values regarding parental expectations of children are significantly related to social-class differences. The Gecas and Nye study is reprinted in this section because both mothers and fathers were subjects for their investigation whereas Wright and Wright studied fathers only.

Wright and Wright (1976) indicated that although a substantial proportion of the variation in the responses regarding parental values could be explained by the variable of social class, additional research is needed in order to determine how much of the unexplained variation might be due to the influences of other social variables, such as race, religion, and ethnic group. It should be noted here that some earlier research did examine the influence of these other social variables. Duvall compared Negro and white and Jewish and non-Jewish respondents *(16)*, Baumrind (1972) made some black-white comparisons in regard to patterns of parental authority, and Lenski (1961) examined the influence of religion on family life by studying parental values and childrearing. In a

1958 survey of Detroit residents, he found that the percentage of respondents who valued intellectual autonomy over obedience was influenced by the interactional effects of race, religion, and social class since he had to control for all three variables simultaneously. He found that lower-working-class Negro Protestants and white Catholics valued obedience over intellectual autonomy, whereas upper-middle-class white Protestants, white Catholics, and Jews were the most likely to value intellectual autonomy over obedience.

Duvall's pioneering study is significant because of the labels she used to describe different parental orientations; specifically, she referred to traditional versus developmental concepts of parenthood. Since her article first appeared, such terms as *authoritarian, autocratic, democratic, permissive,* and *laissez-faire* have not only been applied to patterns of parental authority but also to the family or home environments which they create. These differential environments have their influence on childrearing and the socialization process.

More recently LeMasters (1974) has identified and described five parent models: 1) the martyr model, 2) the buddy or pal model, 3) the policeman or drill sergeant model, 4) the teacher-counselor model, and 5) the athletic coach model. It is obvious that if parents operate by one of these models, the resulting home environment will be quite different from how it would be if they followed another model.

Earlier there had been a strong interest in studying mother-child relationships and the effects of father absence on children. During the 1970s, however, a body of data has been accumulating on fatherhood, and there exists at present a large quantity of literature on the roles of fathers (Price-Bonham, 1976). The article by Lamb *(18),* a study of father-infant and mother-infant interaction during a child's first year of life, is included in this section for two reasons. First, it was selected over other studies because it is an excellent example of a carefully controlled observational study of the interaction patterns of both parents with their infant. For example, the study reveals that fathers and mothers hold their children for differing reasons. Fathers are more likely to hold a child in play situations, whereas mothers hold a child more often to take care of its physical needs. It is time that more studies of this type by pursued, for it is very difficult to make comparisons between the parental behaviors of mothers and fathers unless parents of both sexes are studied simultaneously. The second reason for including Lamb's article is that Lamb's sample included only subjects from intact nuclear families, hence this study can be viewed as representative of research on parent-child relationships within the nuclear family.

The traditional nuclear family has been defined very rigidly at times, so as to include only those intact nuclear families in which the father is the breadwinner and the mother is a full-time homemaker. If such a strict definition is applied, then it can be said that less than 33 percent of the families in the United States are traditional nuclear families (Cogswell and Sussman, 1972; Rossi, 1977).

The mother's employment outside of the home, in and of itself, should not be considered sufficient reason to categorize the family as a variant family form. It is a combination of economic and social factors which is causing more and more mothers to become employed outside of the home. The interest in the effects of maternal employment on children has been so great that no attempt will be made to summarize the findings of the many research studies which have dealt with this topic. The interested reader is referred to the extensive reviews by Hoffman (1974) and Howell (1973a, 1973b). For intact nuclear families in which both parents are employed outside of the home, the quality of the parent-child relationship will be determined by what takes place when the parents are with the child. Alternative child care during the mother's working hours may be seen as substitute or supplementary care, depending upon the arrangements that are made.

The next largest group of parent-child relationships takes place in partial families usually as a result of divorce, separation, desertion, or the death of one parent. These partial families are referred to as single-parent or one-parent families regardless of the actual reason for the absence of one parent. Bane (1976) carefully estimated that approximately 42 percent of the children who are being reared during the 1970s will spend some time in a single-parent family. She included percentages of children who will live with a divorced or widowed parent, with a never-married mother, and those whose parents will experience a lengthy separation or a legal annulment of their marriage. Bane's estimate illustrates the prevalence of marital disruption, a factor which is bound to influence the parent-child relationship.

The largest proportion of one-parent families are those resulting from divorce. A real problem in one-parent families which are headed by women, the vast majority, is inadequate financial resources.

> *In 1974, the median income for all female family heads was $6,400, less than half that of husband-wife families–$13,800. About 2.8 million female heads had a total family income of less than $5,000 and almost 3 out of 4 of these women had children under 18 in the home. . . . A larger proportion of black than white women heading families had less than $5,000 total family income–6 out of 10 compared with 3 out of 10 [McEaddy, 1976: 7].*

Three readings included within this section examine different aspects of the parent-child relationship in one-parent families. The first of these articles, by Glasser and Navarre, focuses on the structural problems of one-parent families (19). Since this article was written in the 1960s, its main emphasis is on the problems which, according to McEaddy (1976), continue to confront the one-parent families that are headed by mothers.

Since more fathers are now finding themselves as the single parent who has the responsibility of rearing one or more children, the article by Orthner and his associates (20) is included in order to cover the topic of single-parent fatherhood. It has been estimated that almost 1,400,000 children are living in single-parent families headed by fathers (Mendes, 1976). Although limitations of space prevented its inclusion in this book, the article by Hetherington, Cox, and Cox (1976) on divorced fathers who do not have custody of their children deserves mention because the majority of divorced fathers fall into this category.

The final reading pertaining to parent-child relationships in one-parent families is by Sorosky, who reviews the literature on the psychological effects of divorce on children (21). Although his article deals specifically with the effects on adolescents, the findings he reports usually hold true for children in general. These three readings permit one to see the differential effects of the one-parent family situation on mothers, fathers, and children.

Recent information on the topic of children and divorce has not been included in this section simply because the inclusion of one article from this ongoing research project could not possibly do it justice. Kelly and Wallerstein (1977), in their most recent publication on brief interventions with children in divorcing families, have described intervention strategies for use with children in the preschool, early latency, later latency, and preadolescent stages. In this article, the authors have cited all of their interrelated research reports on divorce counseling and on the effects of divorce on children from preschool-age through adolescence. Any reader who is highly interested in this topic should become familiar with their research project and the preliminary reports of their findings. Also, of general interest is a special issue of the *Journal of Social Issues* (Winter, 1976), which contains twelve articles on topics pertaining to divorce and separation.

A large proportion of one-parent families are only temporarily in that state. Many one-parent families become reconstituted families as a result of a parent's remarriage. It is through the remarriage process that stepfamily relationships are formed. Very little empirical research has focused on family relationships in reconstituted families, and what few studies do exist have been included in a recent review article on the special role of the stepfather (Rallings, 1976). Instead of including a research study on the stepfamily, it was decided to include in this section an article by Gerda L. Schulman, a family counselor, who examines the adaptation of the stepfamily (22). So far, the research data on stepfamilies comprise a "mixed bag"; studies have concluded that children in stepfamilies may experience a predominantly positive, negative, or mixed family environment just as they might in intact nuclear families.

Another kind of family environment in which some children are being reared is within a home which is headed by adults who have moved from a heterosexual relationship to a homosexual relationship and have brought their children with them. One published case study (Osman, 1972) reveals something of these family relationships in the case of a lesbian couple and their two male children. It appears that more research needs to be conducted on the parent-child relationship when same-sex partners rear children and when heterosexual parents rear children who have a homosexual orientation.

The next article, by Eiduson, Cohen, and Alexander, was chosen for this section because it examines three important emerging alternatives to traditional childrearing which are gaining support among those who have dared to be different and have broken away from traditional ideas regarding family life *(23)*. This article, which presents a progress report of an ongoing research project, focuses on three counter-culture alternatives: 1) the unmarried couple who lives together and has children but does not choose to legitimize the relationship by entering a legally contracted marriage; 2) the unmarried mother who neither marries in order to legitimize the child nor opts for abortion or adoption, but who chooses to rear the child as an unmarried mother; and 3) the contemporary communards who choose to rear their children in communal settings rather than in nuclear families. There are numerous studies on all three of these contemporary alternatives to the more traditional parent-child relationship, and the reader who wishes to learn more about these particular variant family forms has a growing body of research literature to examine. Of particular interest may be the special issues of *The Family Coordinator* (October, 1972; October, 1975) that have focused on alternative life styles.

This section concludes with an article by Brandt Steele which deals with a problem of concern to professionals, namely, the fact that a large number of children are reared in threatening environments and receive physical and/or psychological abuse from their own parents. Steele's article *(24),* which is written from a psychiatric perspective based on several years' experience of working with abusive parents, was published in a special issue of *Children Today* (May-June, 1975) that focused on a variety of related problems ranging from child neglect to sexual molestation. For the reader who would like to gain a perspective of a contrasting nature, Friedrich and Boriskin (1976) offer a review of the literature on the role of the child in child abuse. Early into the article, they point out that Helfer believes three factors or conditions must be present for abuse to occur: "(1) a very special kind of child, (2) a crisis or series of crises, and (3) the potential (in the parent) for abuse" (Friedrich and Boriskin, 1976:581). Other brief review articles on the subject of child abuse are easy to find since child abuse is a problem of great concern (Ackley, 1977; Gelles, 1973, 1976; Jayaratne, 1977).

PARENT-ADOLESCENT RELATIONSHIPS

As the family develops and parents find that they are living with teenagers, the nature of the parent-child relationship is altered. It is normal for young persons to assert their independence from their family in preparation for the adult relationships which lie ahead, often these will include marriage and procreation. A separate section that contains a few representative studies of parent-adolescent relationships has been included as a part of the study of parent-child relationships.

The first reading in this section, by Stinnett, Farris, and Walters *(25),* serves two purposes. In it, the authors review enough previous research such that the article can provide an overview of what is generally known about parent-adolescent relationships. Furthermore, these researchers have compared the perceptions of male and female high school students regarding parent-child relationships and obtained results which suggest that parents have differential impacts on their sons and daughters.

The second reading, by Curtis *(26)*, focuses on the comparative influence of parents and peers on adolescent orientations. Contrary to popular belief, he found no evidence that peers exert greater influence during the adolescent stage of development. His findings indicate that there is a growing independence in opinion rather than a shift from parents to peers in terms of significant reference groups. In a previously published article, Curtis concluded that we also need research on the role played by the total school community as a reference group. It may be inappropriate to make comparisons between the influences of parent and friend as individuals. Curtis suggests that "the school, *in toto,* may constitute a generalized reference field which takes on increasing importance once the adolescent has been socially incorporated into the school organization" (Curtis, 1974:368).

In a study of adolescent choices and parent-peer cross-pressures (Brittain, 1963), it was found that adolescents were influenced by those they felt knew most about a specific situation in which a decision had to be made. The peer group had more influence over choices with immediate consequences, such as what to wear, whereas parents had more influence over decisions with long-range effects.

Taken together, the findings of these studies do not seem to provide much support for the notion that peer influence causes most of the parent-teenager conflict in families. What then might be some of the other possible explanations of the cause of such conflict?

More than 35 years ago, Davis (1940) offered sociological explanations for parent-youth conflict in contemporary industrialized societies. He identified the following factors as the sources of the conflict: 1) the rapid rate of social change; 2) the combined effects of the birth cycle, decelerating socialization with advancing age, and parent-child relationships at different life stages; 3) physiological differences due to age differences; 4) the psychosocial differences, including adult realism versus youthful idealism; and 5) sociological differences, including the position of authority that the parent has over his teenage children.

Much has been written which supports the theoretical explanations offered by Davis. A recent article (Beiser, 1977) that focused on the sexual factors present in the antagonism between mothers and their adolescent daughters certainly coincides with Davis' discussion of the resentment or envy often experienced by parents as a result of the physiological differences between themselves and their teenage children. Just as the adolescent is reaching a high level of sex appeal, parents are becoming aware that they have entered a period of decline.

McArthur (1962) attributes some of the conflict between adolescents and parents to the fact that the developmental tasks of teenagers and their middle-aged parents do not coincide. Although the teenager is supposed to be striving for independence from his parents, the parents are, nevertheless, still held responsible for how the adolescent child conforms to society's expectations. Some of the conflict that arises between parents and teenagers is triggered not by the adolescents' peers, but rather by the indirect effect of the parents' peers. Many parents demand certain behavior of their children because of their concern for how friends and neighbors will judge them on the basis of their child's behavior.

LeMasters (1974) has pointed out that parents have no special training for their parental role, that they tend to parent as they were parented. This is fine in most areas, but in the areas of considerable social change today's parents find themselves trying to deal with situations with which their parents were not confronted. Middle-class parents, who have grown up in an environment where sexual experimentation was secretive and drug usage was limited to tobacco and alcohol, have difficulty coping with the present openness about sexual behavior and the fear that their children's lives might be ruined by a drug bust or a bad "trip."

One of these issues, parental views on teenage sexual behavior, is the subject of the article by Libby and Nass *(27)*. Although their sample consisted of only those parents who were willing to participate in the study (a fact that is bound to have influenced the results), the findings seem quite representative of the views of middle-class parents on this subject. Parents do feel that they have a responsibility for controlling teenage dating. Essentially all parents, regardless of democratic or autocratic life style, expressed conservative attitudes toward teenage sexual behavior.

In view of the rising rates of adolescent parenthood, one can see why so many parents are concerned about controlling the sexual activity of their teenagers. Furthermore, it has been a well-known fact that the act of becoming a parent, not just getting married, is what makes conservative and responsible individuals out of otherwise fun-loving, irresponsible people (LeMasters, 1974).

Although space has not permitted the inclusion of any readings on parent-adolescent relationships and juvenile delinquency, research indicates that, in general, the father-child relationship may be more significant than the mother-child relationship in terms of family background and its relation to juvenile delinquency (Lang, Papenfuhs, and Walters, 1976; Smith and Walters, 1975).

With the runaway problem reaching epidemic proportions, more and more parents wonder just how much parental power they can wield without losing their children. The last reading in this section, Wolk and Brandon's study of runaway adolescents' perceptions of parents and self, is one of the first empirical investigations of this contemporary family problem *(28)*. The general findings of this study include: 1) that runaway youths report more punishment and less control from parents than do non-runaway adolescents; 2) that runaway girls report the most parental control; 3) that runaway boys report the least parental control; and 4) that runaways have less positive self-concepts than non-runaways.

REFERENCES

Ackley, D. C. A brief overview of child abuse. *Social Casework 58* (1977):21-24.

Bane, M. J. Marital disruption and the lives of children. *Journal of Social Issues 32* (1976):103-17.

Baumrind, D. An exploratory study of socialization effects on black children: Some black-white comparisons. *Child Development 43* (1972):261-67.

Beiser, H. R. Sexual factors in antagonism between mothers and adolescent daughters. *Medical Aspects of Human Sexuality 11*, no. 4 (1977):32-47.

Benson, L. *Fatherhood: A sociological perspective.* New York: Random House, 1968.

Bigner, J. J. Fathering: Research and practice implications. *The Family Coordinator 19* (1970):357-62.

Brittain, C. V. Adolescent choices and parent-peer cross-pressures. *American Sociological Review 28* (1963):385-91.

Cogswell, B. E., and Sussman, M. B. Changing family and marriage forms: Complications for human service systems. *The Family Coordinator 21* (1972):505-16.

Curtis, R. L. Parents and peers: Serendipity in a study of shifting reference sources. *Social Forces 52* (1974):368-75.

Cutright, C., and Polonko, K. Areal structure and rates of childlessness among American wives in 1970. *Social Biology 24* (1977):52-61.

Davis, K. The sociology of parent-youth conflict. *American Sociological Review 5* (1940):523-34.

Friedrich, W. N., and Boriskin, J. A. The role of the child in abuse: A review of the literature. *American Journal of Orthopsychiatry 46* (1976):580-90.

Gelles, R. J. Demythologizing child abuse. *The Family Coordinator 25* (1976):135-41.

Gelles, R. J. Child abuse as psychopathology: A sociological critique and reformulation. *American Journal of Orthopsychiatry 43* (1973):611-21.

Hetherington, E. M., Cox, M., and Cox, R. Divorced fathers. *The Family Coordinator 25* (1976):417-28.

Hobbs, D. F., and Cole, S. P. Transition to parenthood: A decade replication. *Journal of Marriage and the Family 38* (1976):723-31.

Hoffman, L. M. Effects of maternal employment on the child: A review of the research. *Developmental Psychology 10* (1974):204-28.

Howell, M. C. Effects of maternal employment on the child, II. *Pediatrics 52*, no. 3 (1973a):327-43.

Howell, M. C. Employed mothers and their families, I. *Pediatrics 52*, no. 2 (1973b):252-343.

Jayaratne, S. Child abusers as parents and children: A review. *Social Work 22.*(1977):5-9.

Kelly, J. B., and Wallerstein, J. S. Brief interventions with children in divorcing families. *American Journal of Orthopsychiatry 47* (1977):23-39.

Kohn, M. Social class and parent-child relationships: An interpretation. *American Journal of Sociology 68* (1963):471-80.

Lang, D. M., Papenfuhs, R., and Walters, J. Delinquent females' perceptions of their fathers. *The Family Coordinator 25* (1976):475-81.

LeMasters, E. E. *Parents in modern America.* Rev. ed. Homewood, Ill.: Dorsey Press, 1974.

Lenski, G. *The religious factor.* New York: Doubleday, 1961.

McArthur, A. Developmental tasks and parent-adolescent conflict. *Marriage and Family Living 24* (1962):189-91.

McEaddy, B. J. Women who head families: A socioeconomic analysis. *Monthly Labor Review 99*, no. 6 (1976):3-9.

Mendes, H. A. Single fatherhood. *Social Work 21* (1976):308-12.

Movius, M. Voluntary childlessness: The ultimate liberation. *The Family Coordinator 25* (1976):57-63.

Olson, D. H., and Dahl, N. S. *Inventory of marriage and family literature, 1975 & 1976, volume IV.* St. Paul: Family Social Science, 1977.

Osman, S. My stepfather is a she. *Family Process 11* (1972):209-18.

Peck, E. *The baby trap.* New York: Pinnacle Books, 1971.

Peck, E., and Senderowitz, J., eds. *Pronatalism: The myth of Mom and apple pie.* New York: Crowell, 1974.

Poston, D. L. Characteristics of voluntarily and involuntarily childless wives. *Social Biology 23* (1976):198-209.

Poston, D. L. Income and childlessness in the United States: Is the relationship always inverse? *Social Biology 21* (1974):296-307.

Price-Bonham, S. Bibliography of literature related to roles of fathers. *The Family Coordinator 25* (1976):489-512.

Rallings, E. M. The special role of stepfather. *The Family Coordinator 25* (1976):445-49.

Renne, K. S. Childlessness, health, and marital satisfaction. *Social Biology 23* (1976):183-97.

Rossi, A. S. A biosocial perspective on parenting. *Daedalus 106,* no. 2 (1977):1-31.

Ryder, R. G. Longitudinal data relating marriage satisfaction and having a child. *Journal of Marriage and the Family 35* (1973):604-06.

Smith, R. M., and Walters, J. Fathers of delinquent males: A review of the literature. *Family Perspective 9* (1975):31-37.

Veevers, J. E. The moral careers of voluntarily childless wives: A note on the defense of a variant world view. *The Family Coordinator 24* (1975):473-87.

Veevers, J. E. Voluntary childlessness and social policy: An alternate view. *The Family Coordinator 23* (1974):397-406.

Walters, J., and Stinnett, N. Parent-child relationships: A decade review of research. *Journal of Marriage and the Family 33* (1971):70-111.

Wright, J. D., and Wright, S. R. Social class and parental values for children: A partial replication and extension of the Kohn thesis. *American Sociological Review 41* (1976):527-37.

parenthood—a choice and an adjustment

13   children: modern foes or friends?

jay d. schvaneveldt

The twentieth century has repeatedly been referred to as the century of the child. This label is not without justification when one considers the type and amount of child welfare legislation that has been passed since 1910, the educational facilities and variety of services now available for young children, plus the change in the daily routine of the child now as compared to seventy years ago. This paper sets forth interpretations of a new view of the child which has become increasingly popular since about 1960. Some will undoubtedly refer to this movement which will be called the "antichild view" as a backlash to "overpermissiveness."

The title of this paper asks the question whether children are foes or friends. The question is not answered, for the climate of each family depends on the personalities of its individual members. It has been portrayed in literature, poetry, song, and alluded to in research many times that the child is the unifying force, the fulfilling element in marriage, the reason for being. Specifically, a tender smile can be very rewarding as well as the experience of watching a baby develop physically and mentally. Also, there is something about babies which is hard to define but makes them just wonderful to have around. Lee (1948) remarked that the thing which always impressed him in regard to stable homes was a love for and a desire for children.

After the birth of a first child, a new life phase begins for husband and wife. They become a father and a mother, a fact which not even disruption or death will change. A man and woman by entering parenthood are forced to take the final step into the adult world, and one is expected to assume major responsibility for the physical and emotional welfare of a new and helpless human being. It has been the author's observation that college-age students express more willingness to marry a person who *cannot have* children than someone who *does not want to have* children.

Finally, this paper in no way attempts to demean children or parenthood, nor all the wonderful and fulfilling things which children bring to families and society. The goal in this paper is to illustrate that whereas childbearing was once a woman's most important function and mark of her success, it is now often regarded as a sign of resignation, of carelessness, or lack of ambition. The *why* of this statement is central to this paper and is illustrated in the "antichild" theme. This antichild theme will be interpreted and illustrated in four areas: (1) impact of parenthood on marital relations, (2) personal and societal attitudes toward parenthood and children, (3) child abuse and rejection, and (4) population crisis and fertility limitation.

Reprinted, by permission, from *Family Perspective*, 1971, 5, 27-35. Copyright ©1971 by Brigham Young University Press.

IMPACT OF PARENTHOOD ON MARITAL RELATIONS

Cooper (1957) studied 205 men and women at the University of Florida in testing the hypothesis that men were more negative toward children than women. This view was not supported by the data, but both sexes were more in favor of other parental tasks than they were in handling babies. The desire for having children only rated fourth with the men as being a reason for marriage. Men wanted a loyal companion from marriage and the women wanted love. These data imply that couples want to have children and rear a family, but that is not why they get married. Parenthood is far off and unreal.

Green (1946) was one of the first to postulate the destructive nature of the child in the upward, mobile middle-class home. The father classifies most things in terms of how they can help him further up the social scale. When the birth of a child occurs, it appears as a crisis situation. The child represents a direct interference with most of the dominant values and compulsions of the modern middle class. Because of the child, the parent gains more duties and obligations, while individual rights diminish. Christopherson (1960) expands this same view in suggesting that the main problems of the married college family are financial hardships, time shortage, and too much responsibility. All of these factors create the setting for further stress resulting when a child is born.

LeMasters (1957) began the series of studies which dealt with parenthood as crises. He assumed that since the family is a small social system, would not the adding of a new member force a reorganization of the system as drastic as does the removal of a member? In his study, thirty-eight of the forty-six couples reported crises at birth and only eight couples reported no crises. This implies that parenthood and not marriage is the real "romantic complex" in our culture. People are trained for husband and wife roles but not for motherhood and fatherhood.

Dyer (1963) in a restudy of parenthood as crises reported that the addition of the first child does constitute a crisis event for middle-class couples in his population. Most of these couples made a quite satisfactory recovery from the crisis and as would be expected, those couples experiencing the severest crisis had the hardest time recovering. In a third study, Hobbs (1965) reported divergent findings from LeMasters and Dyer. None of the couples in his sample reported "extensive" or "severe" levels of crisis. He concluded that more explicit information is needed in order to answer the question of the impact of children on the marital dyad.

Kluckholm (1950) believes that as the husband advances in his occupational direction and becomes more successful in his isolated economic sphere, and as the wife goes on running community affairs, their interests do not meet. This pushes the woman away from her husband and on to the children. Her belief concurs with the thesis of Green that a child causes goal disruption. Jansen (1952) reports that family solidarity varies with stage of the family life cycle, increasing somewhat as the first child arrives, decreasing from then on as more children join the group or as they become older. This pattern continues until the children leave home and then solidarity increases again, though not to the level as before the childbearing and childrearing period.

Cadden (1967) reviews literature which states that children were once thought to be the fulfillment of marriage, but research evidence suggests that the advent of a child is not necessarily the fulfillment of marriage. It may be the factor which separates husband and wife, and this separation widens with each child. Marital satisfaction is highest among the newly married couples who had no children and among older couples whose children had been completely launched. Rollins and Feldman (1970) report that stimulating common activity in marriage decreases from the onset of marriage and with no recovery. Wives specifically experience a decrease in general marital satisfaction and a high level of negative feelings in marital interaction during childbearing and childrearing phases of the family life cycle. These authors conclude that childbearing and childrearing not only have a negative effect on marital satisfaction for wives, but also on their assessments of self-worth in regard to their marriage. In assessing satisfaction with various aspects of marriage over the life cycle, Burr (1970) reports that the school-age stage is the most difficult and that satisfaction in parent-child relationships remains low through the adolescent years. Monahan (1955), in an extensive review of the literature on the relationship of marital stability and presence of children, concluded that marital stability, in the final analysis, may have no general relationship to childbearing. Christensen (1963) concurs with several of these studies in that both premarital and early postmarital pregnancy is followed by a higher-than-average divorce rate.

Some authors have suggested that pessimism of young people about marriage and family today is a reflection of marital and family instability. The body of thought presented in this section, while not so much advertised as divorce, but impactful nonetheless, suggests that pessimism about marriage and family is fostered by the burden and awesome task of having and rearing children in modern society.

ATTITUDES TOWARD PARENTHOOD AND CHILDREN

Chilman (1963) said that most doctors and friends act as if a newborn baby brings nothing but joy and seem to overlook the hard fact that mothers and fathers experience difficulty. A baby is a source of unbelievable bills, lost hours of sleep, intricate rites of feeding and bathing, and a general disruption of household order. Mendels (1966) agrees and believes that even good parents now and then resent their children. It is inevitable that a parent will sometimes resent his children, and the frustration, anxiety and fatigue they cause him.

Greene is most outspoken against motherhood and states openly that "I don't want to have any children. Motherhood is only a part of marriage, and I am unwilling to sacrifice the other equally important feminine roles upon the overexalted alter of parenthood" (1963:10). She expands the thesis that one need not be pressured into the state of parenthood just because society or some advice columnist states it is a sacred and noble duty, because the child, its care and demands are not enough for many women. Greene concludes her argument:

> *Too many men and women who don't really want children, who are selfish, immature, ill-prepared, hostile and baffled, are spawning youngsters with less thought than they would give to the purchase of a new car. These children must suffer. Whom do I harm by not having children? The nonexistent child? The world which already has too many? Surely having children for the wrong reasons or for no reason at all or bringing them into an atmosphere of resentment and neglect is the greater selfishness . . . (1963:11).*

Balchin (1965) states that the child is the sacred calf of the modern world and that one is continually told how unworthy he is to be a parent. The man who is negative toward children labels himself as a terrible monster. Balchin is father of five children and states, on the whole, that being a parent has been an expensive and unrewarding bore for him. He feels that children are not only wasteful and destructive of talent but that they are also destructive of the emotional life of the average man. Children do not keep marriages together, though many people use their children as an excuse for their own lack of courage in not parting. Balchin states his main thesis as

> *What emerges is that, whether we like it or not, children are fundamentally antisocial. They are cruel, ruthless, cunning, and almost incredibly self-centered, and they can conceal these qualities beneath a veil of careful charm. Hitler was a beautiful example of a man who could command the loyalty of a great nation by the simple process of never growing up. . . . What a relief it would be for 90 percent of humanity if the intolerable burdens of blood relationships were removed, and a man and woman could feel free of their children, and the children could feel free of their parents (p. 12).*

Balchin calls for a major scientific advance by which the growth and maturation of children could be greatly accelerated. He concludes that

> The world would be revolutionized if some means could be found by which the human child became fully grown and physically mature very young, as are the offspring of most other animals. But I suppose it is too much to ask that science undertake such a task. There are so many other more important things on which to spend our time, our genius and our money, such as going to the moon (p. 12).

Lear (1963) has elucidated the most extensive thesis against children and parenthood to date. Lear feels that many mothers and fathers have turned parenthood into a painfully competitive sport. America has thus produced parents which she calls child worshippers.

> Worshippers are compulsive parents. Their rallying cry, although they sometimes wish fervently they would stop shouting it, is "for the sake of the children"; and their goal, although they sometimes wish prayerfully they could forget it, is to be Good Parents in the eyes of child psychiatrists, the child guidance experts, the Parents' Club membership, and, of course, the neighbors (p. 14).

The plight of the suburban mother is portrayed by Lear in the following interaction between husband and wife:

> I come home from a hard day's work. I say, "What's new?" She says, "What could be new out here?" I say, "Why don't you get a job?" She says, "I can't. The kids need me." I say, "Why don't we move back to the city?" She says, "We can't. The kids need fresh air." I say, "Great. They've got you and they've got fresh air. You're all set." She says, "Thanks a lot" (p. 19).

Pediatricians also reflect the rejection against children and motherhood. Lear refers to data which revealed that more pediatricians wish they were in some other speciality than men in any other branch of medicine. Thirty-seven percent lament their choice, while psychiatrists are highest on the contentment scale. Lear reflects the hopelessness of parents in that they are slaves to their children. They are involved in car pools, supervision, talking about their children, in fact, "children, children, children . . . this is a middle-class disease" (Lear, 1963:135).

Lear concludes her book and thesis with the view:

> And for the child worship itself, the future looks grand. Today it is an American phenomenon; tomorrow, who knows? Freedom of the individual . . . is the core of our country. The parents have it, and so the children want it too . . . and it will spread. In this regard we are a laboratory for the world. Europeans and Asians still have the patriarchal system. They still like children in their place, but it won't last. They will come to our point of view . . . (p. 246).

CHILD ABUSE AND REJECTION

Since the concept or coinage of the term "the battered child syndrome" came out in the late 1950s, there have been a variety of research efforts launched in describing this phenomenon and attempting to explain correlates of this behavior. In 1965 the NSPCC investigated 39,000 cases involving more than 100,000 children. Just over one-half of the cases were of child neglect and about 10 percent of the cases involved assault and ill treatment. Walton (1968) reports that the essential feature of the "battered baby" is that the victim is too young to give an account of the injuries, while parents suppress the truth.

Not all child abuse is parentally inflicted but is manifest in some out-dated laws, welfare procedures, and communication breakdowns such as existed in the 22,000 impoverished children in Louisiana who were suddenly refused public aid during 1960 because of their misbehaved mothers. Bell (1965) discusses the critical nature of this state incident within the context of the time-honored eligibility condition for Aid to Dependent Children. In this particular situation, the birth of an illegitimate child or an out-of-wedlock pregnancy had been responsible for the ineligibility of 90 percent of the families affected by the statute.

Another example of broad child abuse and neglect is given by Gyorgy and Burgess (1965) who depict children in many countries of the world where 70 percent of those under five years of age are malnourished and have no chance of developing their full potential. These young preschool children constitute the major public health problem in such countries.

Elmer's work (1967) is representative of the detailed research on child abuse which has aimed at analyzing and describing current conditions of this problem in the United States. She included fifty children in her sample—over 25 percent of which turned out to have died or to be in institutions. There was a very high degree of dysfunction among the remaining children in the sample. Elmer reports that some abuse was inflicted by emotionally disturbed mothers, but in most cases, the mothers abused the children under the stress of a complex of unfavorable and personal circumstances. The most striking characteristic of her sample was the very young age of the child when abused. Fifteen were admitted to Children's Hospital at three months of age or less; nine were from four to seven months; and four were from seven to ten months. Fifty-six percent of the group were under ten months of age when they were found to have multiple bone injuries.

Fontana (1964) suggests that if complete and available statistics existed on the maltreatment of children, it could possibly turn out to be a more frequent cause of death than leukemia, cystic fibrosis, and a variety of other well-documented woes of childhood. Fontana reports that Cook's County Hospital in Chicago in 1961 saw, on the average, ten cases of child abuse per day. The neglect and injury to children in the United States range from deprivation of domestic needs, including parental love, to incidences where children are physically abused, causing trauma or even death. He feels that most parents who abuse children are quite rigid, compulsive, immature, suffer from depression, express antisocial behavior, and withhold warmth toward the abused child.

The 1968 book *The Battered Child,* by Helfer and Kempe, is one of the most comprehensive sources depicting this type of child rejection in America today. These authors feel that tens of thousands of children were severely battered or killed in the United States in 1967. Popular awareness of the widespread nature of this problem has also come about. All fifty states now have passed laws providing for mandatory reporting of suspected cases of child abuse.

It should be noted that some rejection and negativism are expressed to children by parents who are fatigued, saturated with feeding rituals, diaper routines, extra housework, and the constant supervision required by a child. This type of reaction may be considered "normal" unless these internal feelings are routinely overtly expressed. The point is that "A desire to get away from the kids and be free" can reflect a rather healthy expression of a captured mother.

POPULATION CRISES AND FERTILITY LIMITATION

The most recent theme reflecting an "antichild" orientation is contained within recent drives to curb population and reduce the number of children in society. Some feel that the great American baby boom is over. The postwar birth rate added nearly forty million citizens to the United States. The birth rate began to decline in 1958 and reached an all time low in the history of the United States with 17.9 births per 1,000 population in 1967. There is some evidence indicating that the number of children one has is a fad or fashionable thing. The third and fourth child were a form of status during the post-World War II era. Now fashion is swinging women to the view that it is desirable to have fewer children. Over 84 percent of married American women report that they have used contraception. Mass media have been very influential in making birth control more socially and ethically acceptable to the American public.

Time magazine (1966:20) refers to Margaret Mead who says:

> *Any and every drop in the birth rate is desirable. We've got enough people in the world and in this country so that there is no danger we'll ever run out. We have lots of people, but what we need is high-caliber individuals contributing as individuals. We need quality; quantity takes care of itself.*

Ehrlich (Hill, 1969) has the same goal and states that people have to be convinced that planet Earth must be viewed as a spaceship of limited carrying capacity. Ehrlich believes that 150 million people, or 60 million fewer than there are now, is the optimum number to live comfortably in the United States.

The vast avalanche of material published on the birth crisis in the United States and population problem reflects a feeling tone which calls for parents to change their desire for large families, to not have more children than are required to maintain the population equilibrium. The literature calls for a change in attitude which would modify the social and institutional pressures which tend to stigmatize the childless couples as abnormal.

Freeman (1969) calls for Americans to create a new land where they can live at ease with each other and with their environment. Gallup (1969) reports that 40 percent of a national sample said they would favor new law which would permit a woman to go to a doctor to end pregnancy at any time during the first three months.

Udall (*Salt Lake Tribune,* 1969) believes that Americans have to voluntarily and openly face the fact that most of our problems in the United States are directly due to population pressures. He believes that every family with two or more children should voluntarily decide not to have more children. Those couples with no children or one child would agree to stop with the second. Wiens (Halliday, 1970) favors an economic approach to birth control which would pay each male and female from puberty onward an annual payment of $1,000 per year as long as they remained childless. If a couple has a child, the annual reward for each parent would be reduced to $500. With the second child, there would be no reward and no penalty, but beyond two children, the couple would be obligated to pay the government the same type of annual rewards which they had received for remaining childless.

The last stanza of a recent poem (Viorst, 1968) quite accurately reflects the antichild theme which is reflected in fertility limitation proposals in America today:

> *Last year I had a shampoo and set every week and*
> *Slept an unbroken sleep beneath the Venetian chandelier of our discerningly electric*
> *   bedroom,*
> *But this year we have a nice baby,*
> *And Gerber's strained bananas in my hair,*
> *And Gleaming beneath the Venetian chandelier,*
> *A diaper pail, a portacrib, and him,*
> *A nice baby, drooling on our antique satin spread*
> *While I smile and say how nice. It is often said*
> *That motherhood is very maturing.*

SUMMARY AND CONCLUSIONS

This paper has reviewed a theme in the literature toward children which has been called antichild. It has been documented in four areas and various interpretations have been presented. Such a trend is not at all new. Rousseau placed his children in orphanages as he believed they would interfere with his work, and history has recorded mass rejection as well as specific family cases where children have been killed, sold, traded, exploited, or turned out into the streets to fair as best they could. The many methods of rejecting children depicted in this paper have occurred in an affluent society at a time when children are no longer an economic asset but in many ways an economic liability. Antichild literature also reflects the supremacy of the individual in the Western World, and the personal freedom which is sought by all. Perhaps it is also a reflection of the so-called "isolated nuclear" family which has few ties with the extended kinship system. Family and prenatal obligations restrict and restrain the mobile individual in an urban environment. It has been suggested that many parents cognitively "reject" their children briefly under the strain of daily care, but this is in sharp contrast to extreme abuse documented in the literature.

The antichild theme vividly illustrates the need for responsible parenthood; for loving parents; and for faith and determination to love, teach, and sustain the child. Richard E. Byrd, explorer of the South Polar regions, nearly died due to hardships of isolation in vast regions of ice and cold. While in this setting and facing the possibility of death, Byrd penned what he felt were the things that really matter:

> At the end only two things really matter to a man, regardless of who he is; and they are the affection and understanding of his family. Anything and everything else he creates are insubstantial; they are ships given over to the mercy of the winds and tides of prejudice. But the family is an everlasting anchorage, a quiet harbor where a man's ships can be left to swing in the moorings of pride and loyalty (1938:179).

Landis (1965) affirms this same point of view from an empirical base. In a study of people sixty-five years old and older, Landis asked them at what period in life they had been happiest and why they had been happiest at that time. After marriage and before their children had left home was mentioned most often as the happiest time. The things they most often mentioned as bringing greatest happiness had to do with marriage and parenthood. Bradford (1964) extends this theme by stating that the joy of being loved by our children, the joy of personal growth with children, and the joy of knowing that one is affecting the lives of others through children are the fulfilling nature of parenthood.

Unequivocally, most children are friends to society, to parents, to themselves; indeed, they are the very future of any society. Ambivalence expressed by many parents is only temporary or situational in nature, and in the course of the family life cycle, children entail both responsibility and fulfillment.

Children will continue to have and enjoy high status in the United States, but this author believes that the antichild theme presented in this paper is an important trend deserving of critical analysis. Our present societal structure and the removal of many traditional restrictions from the individual suggest that this theme will not come to a screeching halt.

REFERENCES

Balchin, Nigel. 1965. "Speaking out: Children are a waste of time." Saturday Evening Post (October 9):10-12.
Bell, Winifred. 1965. Aid to Dependent Children. New York: Columbia University Press.
Bradford, Reed H. 1964. And They Shall Teach Their Children. Salt Lake City: Deseret Book Company.

Burr, Wesley R. 1970. "Satisfaction with various aspects of marriage over the life cycle: A random middle-class sample." Journal of Marriage and the Family 32:29-37.

Byrd, Richard E. 1938. Alone. New York: G. P. Putnam's Sons.

Cadden, Vivian. 1967. "Most unexpected threat to a good marriage: Effect of children." McCalls 94 (July):94-95, 140-141.

Chilman, Catherine. 1963. "Baby puts a strain on marriage." Parents Magazine 38 (June):48-49, 113.

Christensen, Harold T. 1963. "Child spacing analysis via record linkage: New data plus a summing up from earlier reports." Marriage and Family Living 25:272-280.

Christopherson, Victor A., J. S. Vandiver, and M. N. Kruger. 1959. "The married college student." Marriage and Family Living 22:122-128.

Cooper, Lillian, 1957. "Predisposition toward parenthood: A comparison of male and female students." Sociology and Social Research 42:31-36.

Dyer, Everett. 1963. "Parenthood as crisis: A restudy." Marriage and Family Living 25:196-201.

Elmer, Elizabeth. 1967. Children in Jeopardy: A Study of Abused Minors and Their Families. Pittsburgh: University of Pittsburgh Press.

Fontana, Vincent J. 1964. The Maltreated Child. Springfield: Charles C. Thomas.

Freeman, Orville L. 1969. "Land to live in: Toward an urban-rural balance." Current 111 (October):33-39.

Gallup, George. 1969. "Sizable minority favors three-month abortion law." The Salt Lake Tribune (Sunday, November 30).

Green, Arnold W. 1946. "The middle-class male child and neurosis." American Sociological Review 11:31-41.

Greene, Gael. 1963. "Speaking out: A vote against motherhood." Saturday Evening Post (January 26):10-11.

Gyorgy, Paul, and Anne Burgess. 1965. Protecting the Pre-school Child. Philadelphia: J. B. Lippincott Company.

Halliday, Robert S. 1970. "Curb birth rate or perish, Savant warns." The Salt Lake Tribune (Monday, May 18).

Helfer, Ray E., and C. Henry Kempe. 1968. The Battered Child. Chicago: The University of Chicago Press.

Hill, Gladwin. 1969. "Birth rate zero: 'Great challenge of our time.' " The Salt Lake Tribune (Tuesday, November 25).

Hobbs, Daniel F. 1965. "Parenthood as crisis: A third study." Journal of Marriage and the Family 27:367-372.

Jansen, Luther T. 1952. "Measuring family solidarity." American Sociological Review 17:727-733.

Kluckholm, Forence R. 1960. "What's wrong with the American family?" Journal of Social Hygiene 36:227-236.

Landis, Judson T. 1965. "The family and social change: A positive view." Pp. 173-182 in Seymour M. Farber, Piero Mustacchi, and Roger M. L. Wilson (eds.), Man and Civilization: The Family's Search for Survival. New York: McGraw-Hill.

Lear, Martha W. 1963. The Child Worshippers. New York: Crown Publishers, Inc.

Lee, Harold B. 1956. "For strength and happiness." Pp. 154-159 in Harold Lundstrom (ed.), Motherhood: A Partnership with God. Salt Lake City: Bookcraft, Inc.

LeMasters, E. E. 1957. "Parenthood as crisis." Marriage and Family Living 19:352-356.

Mendels, Joe. 1966. "Do you resent your children?" Parents Magazine 41 (August):33-35.

Monohan, Thomas P. 1955. "Is childlessness related to family stability?" American Sociological Review 20:446-456.

Rollins, Boyd C., and Harold Feldman. 1970. "Marital satisfaction over the family life cycle." Journal of Marriage and Family Living 32:20-28.

The Salt Lake Tribune. 1969. "Father of 6 says 'Stop at 2.' " The Salt Lake Tribune (Friday, August 1).

Time. 1966. "Population: Welcome decline." Time 87 (May 6):20.

Viorst, Judith. 1968. It's Hard to Be Hip over Thirty. Cleveland: World Publishing Company.

Walton, Cynthia. 1968. "The battered baby syndrome." New Statesman (September 9):348.

14

voluntarily childless wives:
an exploratory study

j. e. veevers

Students of the family have generally tended to accept the dominant cultural values that married couples should have children, and should want to have them. As a result of this value bias, although parenthood (especially voluntary parenthood) has been extensively studied, the phenomenon of childlessness has been virtually ignored.[1] This selective inattention is unfortunate, for to a large extent the social meanings of parenthood can be comprehensively described and analyzed only in terms of the parallel set of meanings which are assigned to nonparenthood.[2] Although sociologists have occasionally discussed the theoretical relevance of voluntary childlessness, and have speculated regarding some empirical aspects of it,[3] virtually no direct research has been conducted. As a preliminary step towards filling this gap in the sociological study of the family, an exploratory study of voluntarily childless wives was conducted. The present article will not attempt to describe this research in its entirety, but rather will be concerned with brief discussions of four aspects of it: first, the career paths whereby women come to be voluntarily childless; second, the social pressures associated with that decision; third, the symbolic importance attributed to the possibility of adoption; and fourth, the relevance of supportive ideologies relating to concern with feminism, and with population problems.

SELECTION AND NATURE OF THE SAMPLE

Conventional sampling techniques cannot readily be applied to obtain large and representative samples of voluntarily childless couples.[4] Only about five per cent of all couples voluntarily forego parenthood,[5] and this small deviant minority is characterized by attitudes and behaviors which are both socially unacceptable and not readily visible. The present research, which is exploratory in nature, is based on depth interviews with a purposive sample of 52 voluntarily childless wives. Although the utilization of non-random samples without control groups is obviously not the ideal approach, and can yield only suggestive rather than definitive conclusions, in examining some kinds of social behaviors it is often the only alternative to abandoning the inquiry.

In the present study, respondents were solicited by three separate articles appearing in newspapers in Toronto and in London, followed up by advertisements explicitly asking for volunteers. Of the 86 individuals who replied, 52 wives were selected. Three criteria were evoked in these selections. First, the wife must have stated clearly that her childlessness was due to choice rather than to biological accident. Second, she must either have been married for a minimum of five years, or have been of post-menopausal age, or have reported that either she or her husband had been voluntarily sterilized for contraceptive purposes. Third, she must have affirmed that she had never borne a child, and had never assumed the social role of mother.

Reprinted, by permission, from *Sociology and Social Research*, 1973, *57*, 356-66.

The interviews, which were unstructured, averaged about four hours in length, and included discussion of the woman's life history, considerable detail concerning her marriage and her husband, and attitudinal and evaluative aspects of her responses to the maternal role. Data are thus available on the characteristics of 104 voluntarily childless husbands and wives, whose demographic and social characteristics may be briefly summarized as follows. The average age of the sample is 29, with a range from 23 to 71 years. All are Caucasian and living in urban areas, most are middle class, and many are upwardly mobile. Although educational experience ranges from grade school to the post doctoral level, most have at least some university experience. With the exception of one housewife, all are either employed full-time or attending university. Most individuals are either atheists or agnostics from Protestant backgrounds, and of the minority who do express some religious preference, almost all are inactive. Most individuals come from stable homes where the mother has been a full-time housewife since her first child was born. The incidence of first born and only children is much higher than would ordinarily be expected.

With the exception of two widowers, all of the subjects in the present research are involved in their first marriage. The average marriage duration is seven years, with a range from three to twenty-five years. Most couples have relatively egalitarian relationships, but still maintain conventional marriages and follow the traditional division of labor. Configurations of marital adjustment cover the entire continuum described by Cuber and Haroff,[6] ranging from conflict-habituated to total relationships, with many wives reporting vital or total relationships with their husbands.

All of the couples agree on the desirability of preventing pregnancy, at least at the present time. Most of the wives had never been pregnant, but about a fifth had had at least one induced abortion, and most indicate they would seek an abortion if pregnant. More than half of the wives are presently on the pill. About a quarter of the husbands have obtained a vasectomy, and another quarter are seriously considering doing so. Many of the women express positive interest in tubal ligation, but only one, a girl of 23, has actually been sterilized.

THE NATURE OF CHILDLESS CAREERS

In reviewing the processes whereby couples come to define themselves as voluntarily childless, two characteristic career paths are apparent. One route to childlessness involves the formulation by the couple, before they are even married, of a definite and explicitly stated intention never to become involved in parental roles; a second and more common route is less obvious, and involves the prolonged postponement of childbearing until such time as it was no longer considered desirable at all. These two alternatives will be elaborated.

Nearly a third of the wives interviewed entered into their marriages with a childlessness clause clearly stated in their marriage "contract." Although none of these women had a formal written contract in the legal sense of the word, the husband and wife explicitly agreed upon childlessness as a firm condition of marriage. The woman deliberately sought a future mate who, regardless of his other desirable qualities, would agree on this one dimension. Generally the negative decisions regarding the value of children were made during early adolescence, before the possibility of marriage had ever been seriously considered. In contrast, a few of the wives had indifferent or even vaguely positive attitudes towards childbearing until they met their future husbands. During their courtship and engagement, they gradually allowed themselves to be converted to the world view of voluntary childlessness, and by the time of their marriage were quite content to agree to never have children.

More than two thirds of the wives studied remained childless as a result of a series of decisions to postpone having children until some future time, a future which never came. Rather than explicitly rejecting motherhood prior to marriage, they repeatedly deferred procreation until a more convenient time. These temporary postponements provided time during which the evaluations of parenthood were gradually reassessed relative to other goals and possibilities. At the time of their marriages, most wives involved in the postponement model had devoted little serious thought to the question of having children, and had no strong feelings either for or against motherhood. Like conventional couples, they simply assumed that they would have one or two children eventually; unlike conventional couples, they practiced birth control conscientiously and continuously during the early years of marriage.[7]

Most couples involved in the postponement pattern move through four separate stages in their progression from wanting to not wanting children. The first stage involves postponement for a definite period of time. In this stage, the voluntarily childless are indistinguishable from conventional and conforming couples who will eventually become parents. In most groups, it is not necessarily desirable for the bride to conceive during her honeymoon. It is considered understandable that before starting a family a couple might want to achieve certain goals, such as graduating from school, travelling, buying a house, saving a nest egg, or simply getting adjusted to one another. The degree of specificity varies, but there is a clear commitment to have children as soon as conditions are right.

The second stage of this career involves a shift from postponement for a definite period of time to indefinite postponement. The couple remains committed to the idea of parenthood, but becomes increasingly vague about when the blessed event is going to take place. It may be when they can "afford it," or when "things are going better" or when they "feel more ready."

The third stage in the cycle involves another qualitative change in thinking, in that for the first time there is an open acknowledgement of the possibility that in the end the couple may remain permanently childless. The third stage is a critical one, in that the very fact of openly considering the pros and cons of having children may increase the probability of deciding not to. During this time, they have an opportunity to experience directly the many social, personal, and economic advantages associated with being childless, and at the same time to compare their life styles with those of their peers who are raising children. It seems probable that the social-psychological factors involved in the initial decision to postpone having children may be quite disparate from the social-psychological factors involved in the inclination to remain childless, and to continue with the advantages of a life style to which one has become accustomed. At this stage in the career, the only definite decision is to postpone deciding until some vague and usually unspecified time in the future.

Finally, a fourth stage involves the definite conclusion that the couple are never going to have children, and that childlessness is a permanent rather than a transitory state. Occasionally this involves an explicit decision, usually precipitated by some crisis or change in the environment that focuses attention on the question of parenthood. However, for most couples, there is never a direct decision made to have or to avoid children. Rather, after a number of years of postponing pregnancy until some future date, they gradually become aware that an implicit decision has been made to forego parenthood. The process involved is one of recognizing an event which has already occurred, rather than of posing a question and then searching or negotiating for an answer. At first, it was "obvious" that "of course" they would eventually have children; now, it is equally "obvious" that they will not. The couple are at a loss to explain exactly how or when this transition came about, but they both agree on their new implicit decision, and they are both contented with its implications.

CHILDLESSNESS AND INFORMAL SANCTIONS

All of the wives interviewed feel that they are to some extent stigmatized by their unpopular decision to avoid having children, and that there exists an ubiquitous negative stereotype concerning the characteristics of a voluntarily childless woman, including such unfavorable traits as being abnormal, selfish, immoral, irresponsible, immature, unhappy, unfulfilled, and non-feminine.[8] In addition, these devaluating opinions are perceived to have behavioral consequences for their interaction with others, and to result in considerable social pressure to become mothers. Some of the sanctions reported are direct and obvious, including explicit and unsolicited comments advocating child-birth and presenting arguments relating to the importance of motherhood. Other pressures are more subtle, and in many cases are perceived to be unintentional. For example, the childless frequently complain that, whereas parents are never required to explain why they chose to have children, they are frequently required to account for their failure to do so.

Childlessness is of course not always a disapproved state. Couples are rewarded, not punished, for remaining childless for the first several months of marriage, and thereby negating the possibility that they were "forced" to get married. After the minimum of nine months has passed, there is a short period of time when the young couple is excused from not assuming all of their responsibilities, or are perceived as having been having intercourse for too short a period of time to guarantee conception. The definition of how long a period of time child bearing may be postponed and still meet with conventional expectations is difficult to determine, and apparently varies considerably from one group to another. In most groups, the first twelve months constitutes an acceptable period of time. After the first year, the pressure gradually but continually increases, reaching a peak during the third and fourth years of marriage. However, once a couple have been married for five or six years there appears to be some diminution of negative responses to them. Several factors are involved in this change: part may be attributable to the increased ability of the childless to avoid those who consistently sanction them; part may be attributable to the increased ability of the childless to cope with negative and hostile responses, making the early years only seem more difficult in retrospect; and part may reflect an actual change in the behavior of others. After five or six years, one's family and friends may give up the possibility of persuading the reluctant couple to procreate or to adopt, and resign themselves to the fact that intervention, at least in this case, is ineffective.

It is noteworthy that although all wives report considerable direct and indirect social pressures to become mothers, most are remarkably well defended against such sanctions. Although on specific occasions they may be either indignant or amused, in most instances they are indifferent to negative responses, and remain inner-directed, drawing constant support and reaffirmation from the consensual validation offered by their husbands. Many strategies are employed which "discredit the discreditors"[9] and which enable the voluntarily childless to remain relatively impervious to the comments of critics and the wishes of reformers. One such strategy concerns the possibility of adoption.

THE SYMBOLIC IMPORTANCE OF ADOPTION

A recurrent theme in discussions with childless wives is that of adoption. Most wives mention that they have in the past considered adopting a child, and many indicate that they are still considering the possibility at some future date. However, in spite of such positive verbalizations, it is apparent that adoption is not seriously contemplated as a viable alternative, and that their considerations are not likely to result in actually assuming maternal roles. The lack of serious thought about adoption as a real possibility is reflected in the fact that generally they have not considered even such elementary questions as whether they would prefer a boy or a girl, or whether they would prefer an infant or an older child. With few exceptions, none of the couples have made even preliminary inquiries regarding the legal processes involved in adoption. Those few that had made some effort to at least contact a child placement agency had failed to follow through on their initial contact. None had investigated the issue thoroughly enough to have considered the possibility that, should they decide to adopt, a suitable child might not be immediately available to them.

For the voluntarily childless, the importance of the recurrent theme of adoption appears to lie in its symbolic value, rather than in the real possibility of procuring a child by this means and thereby altering one's life style. This symbolic importance is twofold: the reaffirmation of normalcy: and the avoidance of irreversible decisions. A willingness to consider adoption as a possibility communicates to one's self and to others that in spite of being voluntarily childless, one is still a "normal" and "well-adjusted" person who does like children, and who is willing to assume the responsibilities of parenthood. It is an effective mechanism for denying the possibility of considerable psychological differences between parents and non-parents,[10] and legitimates the claim of the childless to be just like parents in a number of important respects.

The possibility of adoption at a later date is of symbolic value, in that it prevents the voluntarily childless from being committed to an irreversible state. One of the problems of opting for a postponement model is that eventually one must confront the fact that childbirth cannot be postponed indefinitely. The solution to this dilemma is to include possibility of adoption as a satisfactory "out" should one be needed. The same strategy is employed by many couples who chose sterilization as a means of birth control, but who are not entirely comfortable with the absolute and irreversible solution. The theoretical possibility of adoption is also comforting when faced with the important but unanswerable question of how one will feel about being childless in one's old age.

THE RELEVANCE OF SUPPORTIVE IDEOLOGIES

The voluntarily childless appear to be in a state of pluralistic ignorance, in that they are unaware of the numbers of other individuals who share their world view. Although the deliberate decision to avoid parenthood is a relatively rare phenomenon, it is not nearly as rare as the childless themselves perceive it to be, especially among urban and well-educated middle class couples. A large proportion of wives indicated that until they read the article and/or advertisement asking for subjects for the present study, they had never seen the topic of voluntary childlessness discussed in the mass media. Many reported that they did not know any other couple who felt as they did about the prospect of parenthood, and many others reported having met only one or two like-minded people during the course of their marriage.

Feelings of uniqueness and of isolation are somewhat mitigated by the explicit agreement of husbands on the appropriateness of foregoing parental roles. However, regardless of how supportive the husband is in his reaffirmation of the legitimacy of childlessness, and how committed he is personally to avoiding fatherhood, because of cultural differences in sex roles he does not share an entirely comparable situation. He may be totally sympathetic, but he has a limited ability to em-pathize: The childless wife may be generally comfortable with her deicsion not to have children, and still express the wish that she could discuss her situation with other like-minded women who might have shared similar experiences within the female sub-culture, and who might provide a model for identification.

It is noteworthy that within the psychological world of the voluntarily childless, existing social movements concerned with population or with feminism have surprisingly little relevance, and provide relatively little intellectual or emotional support. The concern with population problems, especially as manifest in the Zero Population Growth movement, does provide a supportive rationale indicating that one is not necessarily being socially irresponsible and neglectful of one's civic obligations if one does not reproduce. However, although there is a clear statement that procreation is not necessary for all, most ZPG advocates are careful to indicate that it is not procreation *per se* they are opposed to, but rather excessive procreation. The slogan "Stop at Two" asserts that one should have no more than two children, but also implies that one perhaps should have at least one or two. Some of the childless wives are superficially involved in ZPG and sympathetic with its goals, but in all cases this identification is an *ex post facto* consideration, rather than a motivating force, and their satisfaction with being childless is related to concerns other than to their contribution to the population crisis.

It is sometimes suggested that an inclination to avoid motherhood is a logical extension of the new feminism. It is difficult to generalize about a social phenomenon as amorphous as the women's liberation movement, a rubric which incorporates many diverse and even contradictory attitudes. However, "A significant feature of the women's liberation movement is that, although its demands have been made on the basis of equity for women, it has not usually been anti-marriage or anti-children."[11]

In many instances, the ideological statements endorsed by the women's liberation movement are implicitly or explicitly pro-natalist. Motherhood is not perceived as an unfulfilling and unrewarding experience; rather, it is perceived as a positive experience which, although desirable, is not sufficient in and of itself for maximum self-actualization. Considerable concern is expressed with the problems involved in combining successful motherhood with comparable success in other careers. Rather than advising women to give up having children, the new feminist literature advises them to consider other careers in addition to motherhood, and advocates changes in society which would make the motherhood role easier. For example, there is considerable stress on the provision of maternity leaves, on increased involvement of fathers in childcare, on accessibility to adequate day care facilities. Although advocates of the new feminism may provide some support for the idea that motherhood is neither necessary nor sufficient for fulfillment, they do still advocate that normally it will be an important part of that fulfillment. Only a few of the voluntarily childless are at all concerned with women's liberation, and these few apparently came into the movement after their decision was made and their lifestyle was established.

Although none of the voluntarily childless are actively seeking group support for their life style, many would welcome the opportunity to become involved in a truly supportive social movement. The first example of such an association is the National Organization for Nonparenthood (NON) which was formed in California in 1971. Because of the state of pluralistic ignorance which surrounds voluntary childlessness, and because of the inadequacy of demographic and feminist movements in expressing the world view of the childless, such attempts to formulate a counter culture might be expected to be very successful.

SUMMARY

The present research on a purposive sample of 52 voluntarily childless wives is exploratory in nature. Although it is not possible to make definitive statements regarding the nature of childless couples, several tentative conclusions are offered. It is suggested that couples come to be voluntarily childless by a number of diverse paths beginning both before and after marriage, and that considerable diversity might be expected between those who enter marriage only on the condition of a clear childlessness clause in the marriage contract, and those who remain childless after a series of postponements of parenthood. Although considerable social pressures are directed towards the childless, most of the individuals involved appear to be very well defended against such sanctions, and the mechanisms of re-defining situations and of protecting themselves are worthy of further study. One such mechanism appears to be the use of the possibility of adoption to deny the status of voluntary childlessness while not seriously threatening the accompanying life style. Finally, it is suggested that existing social movements do not provide much relevant support for the voluntarily childless, and that an explicit counter-culture, such as the National Organization of Nonparenthood, might be expected to meet with considerable success.

FOOTNOTES

[1]J.E. Veevers, "Voluntary Childlessness: A Neglected Area of Family Study," *The Family Coordinator,* 22 (number 2, 1973), 199-205.

[2]J.E. Veevers, "The Social Meanings of Parenthood," *Psychiatry: Journal for the Study of Interpersonal Processes,* 36 (number 3, 1973), 291-310.

[3]Edward Pohlman, "Childlessness: Intentional and Unintentional," *The Journal of Nervous and Mental Disease,* 151 (number one, 1970), 2-12.

[4]Susan O. Gustavus and James R. Henly, Jr. "Correlates of Voluntary Childlessness in a Select Population," *Social Biology,* 18 (September, 1971), 277-84.

[5]J.E. Veevers, "Factors in the Incidence of Childlessness in Canada: An Analysis of Census Data," *Social Biology,* 19 (September, 1972), 266-74.

[6]John F. Cuber and Peggy B. Haroff, *Sex and the Significant Americans: A Study of Sexual Behavior Among the Affluent,* (Baltimore, Maryland: Penguin Books, 1966).

[7]Pascal K. Whelpton, Arthur A. Campbell and J.E. Patterson report in one study that nearly two out of three newlyweds do not start using contraception before the first conception. See their *Fertility and Family Planning in the United States,* (Princeton, New Jersey: Princeton University Press, 1966), 221.

[8]J.E.Veevers, "The Violation of Fertility Mores: Voluntary Childlessness as Deviant Behavior," in Craig L. Boydell, Carl F. Grindstaff and Paul C. Whitehead (eds.), *Deviant Behavior and Societal Reaction,* (Toronto: Holt, Rinehart and Winston, 1972), 571-92.

[9]J.E. Veevers, "The Moral Career of Voluntarily Childless Wives: Notes on the Construction and Defense of a Deviant World View," in S. Parvez Wakil (ed.), *Marriage and the Family in Canada,* (Toronto: Longmans Green, 1973), forthcoming.

[10]J.E. Veevers, "The Social Meanings of Parenthood," *op cit.*

[11]Commission on Population Growth and the American Future, *Report,* (Washington, D.C.: Commission on Population Growth and the American Future, 1972), 68.

15

transition to parenthood

alice s. rossi

FROM CHILD TO PARENT: AN EXAMPLE

What is unique about this perspective on parenthood is the focus on the adult parent rather than the child. Until quite recent years, concern in the behavioral sciences with the parent-child relationship has been confined almost exclusively to the child. Whether a psychological study such as Ferreira's on the influence of the pregnant woman's attitude to maternity upon postnatal behavior of the neonate,[1] Sears and Maccoby's survey of child-rearing practices,[2] or Brody's detailed observations of mothering,[3] the long tradition of studies of maternal deprivation[4] and more recently of maternal employment,[5] the child has been the center of attention. The design of such research has assumed that, if enough were known about what parents were like and what they in fact did in rearing their children, much of the variation among children could be accounted for.[6]

The very different order of questions which emerge when the parent replaces the child as the primary focus of analytic attention can best be shown with an illustration. Let us take, as our example, the point Benedek makes that the child's need for mothering is *absolute* while the need of an adult woman to mother is *relative*.[7] From a concern for the child, this discrepancy in need leads to an analysis of the impact on the child of separation from the mother or inadequacy of mothering. Family systems that provide numerous adults to care for the young child can make up for this discrepancy in need between mother and child, which may be why ethnographic accounts give little evidence of postpartum depression following childbirth in simpler societies. Yet our family system of isolated households, increasingly distant from kinswomen to assist in mothering, requires that new mothers shoulder total responsibility for the infant precisely for that stage of the child's life when his need for mothering is far in excess of the mother's need for the child.

From the perspective of the mother, the question has therefore become: what does maternity deprive her of? Are the intrinsic gratifications of maternity sufficient to compensate for shelving or reducing a woman's involvement in non-family interests and social roles? The literature on maternal deprivation cannot answer such questions, because the concept, even in the careful specification Yarrow has given it,[8] has never meant anything but the effect on the child of various kinds of insufficient mothering. Yet what has been seen as a failure or inadequacy of individual women may in fact be a failure of the society to provide institutionalized substitutes for the extended kin to assist in the care of infants and young children. It may be that the role requirements of maternity in the American family system extract too high a price of deprivation for young adult women reared with highly diversified interests and social expectations concerning adult life. Here, as at several points in the course of this paper, familiar problems take on a new and suggestive research dimension when the focus is on the parent rather than the child.

Reprinted, by permission, from *Journal of Marriage and the Family*, 1968, *30*, 26-39, slightly abridged. Copyright © 1968 by the National Council on Family Relations.

BACKGROUND

Since it is a relatively recent development to focus on the parent side of the parent-child relationship, some preliminary attention to the emergence of this focus on parenthood is in order. Several developments in the behavioral sciences paved the way to this perspective. Of perhaps most importance have been the development of ego psychology and the problem of adaptation of Murray[9] and Hartmann,[10] the interpersonal focus of Sullivan's psychoanalytic theories,[11] and the life cycle approach to identity of Erikson.[12] These have been fundamental to the growth of the human development perspective: that personality is not a stable given but a constantly changing phenomenon, that the individual changes along the life line as he lives through critical life experiences. The transition to parenthood, or the impact of parenthood upon the adult, is part of the heightened contemporary interest in adult socialization.

A second and related development has been the growing concern of behavioral scientists with crossing levels of analysis to adequately comprehend social and individual phenomena and to build theories appropriate to a complex social system. In the past, social anthropologists focused as purely on the level of prescriptive normative variables as psychologists had concentrated on intrapsychic processes at the individual level or sociologists on social-structural and institutional variables. These are adequate, perhaps, when societies are in a stable state of equilibrium and the social sciences were at early stages of conceptual development, but they become inadequate when the societies we study are undergoing rapid social change and we have an increasing amount of individual and subgroup variance to account for.

Psychology and anthropology were the first to join theoretical forces in their concern for the connections between culture and personality. The question of how culture is transmitted across the generations and finds its manifestations in the personality structure and social roles of the individual has brought renewed research attention to the primary institutions of the family and the schools, which provide the intermediary contexts through which culture is transmitted and built into personality structure.

It is no longer possible for a psychologist or a therapist to neglect the social environment of the individual subject or patient, nor is the "family" they are concerned with any longer confined to the family of origin, for current theory and therapy view the adult individual in the context of his current family of procreation. So too it is no longer possible for the sociologist to focus exclusively on the current family relationships of the individual. The incorporation of psychoanalytic theory into the informal, if not the formal, training of the sociologist has led to an increasing concern for the quality of relationships in the family of origin as determinants of the adult attitudes, values, and behavior which the sociologist studies.

Quite another tradition of research has led to the formulation of "normal crises of parenthood." "Crisis" research began with the studies of individuals undergoing traumatic experiences, such as that by Tyhurst on natural catastrophes,[13] Caplan on parental responses to premature births,[14] Lindemann on grief and bereavement,[15] and Janis on surgery.[16] In these studies attention was on differential response to stress—how and why individuals vary in the ease with which they coped with the stressful experience and achieved some reintegration. Sociological interest has been piqued as these studies were built upon by Rhona and Robert Rapoport's research on the honeymoon and the engagement as normal crises in the role transitions to marriage and their theoretical attempt to build a conceptual bridge between family and occupational research from a "transition task" perspective.[17] LeMasters, Dyer, and Hobbs have each conducted studies of parenthood precisely as a crisis or disruptive event in family life.[18]

I think, however, that the time is now ripe to drop the concept of "normal crises" and to speak directly, instead, of the transition to and impact of parenthood. There is an uncomfortable incongruity in speaking of any crisis as normal. If the transition is achieved and if a successful reintegration of personality or social roles occurs, then crisis is a misnomer. To confine attention to "normal crises" suggests, even if it is not logically implied, successful outcome, thus excluding from our analysis the deviant instances in which failure occurs.

Sociologists have been just as prone as psychologists to dichotomize normality and pathology. We have had one set of theories to deal with deviance, social problems, and conflict and quite another set in theoretical analyses of a normal system—whether a family or a society. In the latter case our theories seldom include categories to cover deviance, strain, dysfunction, or failure. Thus, Parsons and Bales' systems find "task-leaders" oriented to problem solution, but not instrumental leaders attempting to undercut or destroy the goal of the group, and "sociometric stars" who play a positive integrative function in cementing ties among group members, but not negatively expressive persons with hostile aims of reducing or destroying such intragroup ties.[19]

Parsons' analysis of the experience of parenthood as a step in maturation and personality growth does not allow for negative outcome. In this view either parents show little or no positive impact upon themselves of their parental role experiences, or they show a new level of maturity. Yet many women, whose interests and values made a congenial combination of wifehood and work role, may find that the addition of maternal responsibilities has the consequence of a fundamental and undesired change in both their relationships to their husbands and their involvements outside the family. Still other women, who might have kept a precarious hold on adequate functioning as adults had they *not* become parents, suffer severe retrogression with pregnancy and childbearing, because the reactivation of older unresolved conflicts with their own mothers is not favorably resolved but in fact leads to personality deterioration[20] and the transmission of pathology to their children.[21]

Where cultural pressure is very great to assume a particular adult role, as it is for American women to bear and rear children, latent desire and psychological readiness for parenthood may often be at odds with manifest desire and actual ability to perform adequately as parents. Clinicians and therapists are aware, as perhaps many sociologists are not, that failure, hostility, and destructiveness are as much a part of the family system and the relationships among family members as success, love, and solidarity are.[22]

A conceptual system which can deal with both successful and unsuccessful role transitions, or positive and negative impact of parenthood upon adult men and women, is thus more powerful than one built to handle success but not failure or vice versa. For these reasons I have concluded that it is misleading and restrictive to perpetuate the use of the concept of "normal crisis." A more fruitful point of departure is to build upon the stage-task concepts of Erikson, viewing parenthood as a developmental stage, as Benedek[23] and Hill[24] have done, a perspective carried into the research of Rausch, Goodrich, and Campbell[25] and of Rhona and Robert Rapoport[26] on adaptation to the early years of marriage and that of Cohen, Fearing *et al.*[27] on the adjustments involved in pregnancy.

ROLE CYCLE STAGES

A discussion of the impact of parenthood upon the parent will be assisted by two analytic devices. One is to follow a comparative approach, by asking in what basic structural ways the parental role differs from other primary adult roles. The marital and occupational roles will be used for this comparison. A second device is to specify the phases in the development of a social role. If the total life span may be said to have a cycle, each stage with its unique tasks, then by analogy a role may be said to have a cycle and each stage in that role cycle, to have its unique tasks and problems of adjustment. Four broad stages of a role cycle may be specified:

Anticipatory Stage

All major adult roles have a long history of anticipatory training for them, since parental and school socialization of children is dedicated precisely to this task of producing the kind of competent adult valued by the culture. For our present purposes, however, a narrower conception of the anticipatory stage is preferable: the engagement period in the case of the marital role, pregnancy in the case of the parental role, and the last stages of highly vocationally oriented schooling or on-the-job apprenticeship in the case of an occupational role.

Honeymoon Stage

This is the time period immediately following the full assumption of the adult role. The inception of this stage is more easily defined than its termination. In the case of the marital role, the honeymoon stage extends from the marriage ceremony itself through the literal honeymoon and on through an unspecified and individually varying period of time. Raush[28] has caught this stage of the marital role in his description of the "psychic honeymoon": that extended postmarital period when, through close intimacy and joint activity, the couple can explore each other's capacities and limitations. I shall arbitrarily consider the onset of pregnancy as marking the end of the honeymoon stage of the marital role. This stage of the parental role may involve an equivalent psychic honeymoon, that post-childbirth period during which, through intimacy and prolonged contact, an attachment between parent and child is laid down. There is crucial difference, however, from the marital role in this stage. A woman knows her husband as a unique real person when she enters the honeymoon stage of marriage. A good deal of preparatory adjustment on a firm reality-base is possible during the engagement period which is not possible in the equivalent pregnancy period. Fantasy is not corrected by the reality of a specific individual child until the birth of the child. The "quickening" is psychologically of special significance to women precisely because it marks the first evidence of a real baby rather than a purely fantasized one. On this basis alone there is greater inter-personal adjustment and learning during the honeymoon stage of the parental role than of the marital role.

Plateau Stage

This is the protracted middle period of a role cycle during which the role is fully exercised. Depending on the specific problem under analysis, one would obviously subdivide this large plateau stage further. For my present purposes it is not necessary to do so, since my focus is on the earlier anticipatory and honeymoon stages of the parental role and the overall impact of parenthood on adults.

Disengagement-Termination Stage

This period immediately precedes and includes the actual termination of the role. Marriage ends with the death of the spouse or, just as definitively, with separation and divorce. A unique characteristic of parental role termination is the fact that it is not clearly marked by any specific act but is an attenuated process of termination with little cultural prescription about when the authority and obligations of a parent end. Many parents, however, experience the marriage of the child as a psychological termination of the active parental role.

UNIQUE FEATURES OF PARENTAL ROLE

With this role cycle suggestion as a broader framework, we can narrow our focus to what are the unique and most salient features of the parental role. In doing so, special attention will be given to two further questions: (1) the impact of social changes over the past few decades in facilitating or complicating the transition to and experience of parenthood and (2) the new interpretations or new research suggested by the focus on the parent rather than the child.

Cultural Pressure to Assume the Role

On the level of cultural values, men have no freedom of choice where work is concerned: They must work to secure their status as adult men. The equivalent for women has been maternity. There is considerable pressure upon the growing girl and young woman to consider maternity necessary for a woman's fulfillment as an individual and to secure her status as an adult.[29]

This is not to say there are no fluctuations over time in the intensity of the cultural pressure to parenthood. During the depression years of the 1930's, there was more widespread awareness of the economic hardships parenthood can entail, and many demographic experts believe there was a great increase in illegal abortions during those years. Bird has discussed the dread with which a suspected pregnancy was viewed by many American women in the 1930's.[30] Quite a different set of pressures were at work during the 1950's, when the general societal tendency was toward withdrawal from active engagement with the issues of the larger society and a turning in to the gratifications of the private sphere of home and family life. Important in the background were the general affluence of the period and the expanded room and ease of child rearing that go with suburban living. For the past five years, there has been a drop in the birth rate in general, fourth and higher-order births in particular. During this same period there has been increased concern and debate about women's participation in politics and work, with more women now returning to work rather than conceiving the third or fourth child.[31]

Inception of the Parental Role

The decision to marry and the choice of a mate are voluntary acts of individuals in our family system. Engagements are therefore consciously considered, freely entered, and freely terminated if increased familiarity decreases, rather than increases, intimacy and commitment to the choice. The inception of a pregnancy, unlike the engagement, is not always a voluntary decision, for it may be the unintended consequence of a sexual act that was recreative in intent rather than procreative. Secondly, and again unlike the engagement, the termination of a pregnancy is not socially sanctioned, as shown by current resistance to abortion-law reform.

The implication of this difference is a much higher probability of unwanted pregnancies than of unwanted marriages in our family system. Coupled with the ample clinical evidence of parental rejection and sometimes cruelty to children, it is all the more surprising that there has not been more consistent research attention to the problem of *parental satisfaction,* as there has for long been on *marital satisfaction* or *work satisfaction.* Only the extreme iceberg tip of the parental satisfaction continuum is clearly demarcated and researched, as in the growing concern with "battered babies." Cultural and psychological resistance to the image of a non-nurturant woman may afflict social scientists as well as the American public.

The timing of a first pregnancy is critical to the manner in which parental responsibilities are joined to the marital relationship. The single most important change over the past few decades is extensive and efficient contraceptive usage, since this has meant for a growing proportion of new marriages, the possibility of an increasing preference for some postponement of childbearing after marriage. When pregnancy was likely to follow shortly after marriage, the major transition point in a woman's life was marriage itself. *This transition point is increasingly the first pregnancy rather than marriage.* It is accepted and increasingly expected that women will work after marriage, while household furnishings are acquired and spouses complete their advanced training or gain a foothold in their work.[32] This provides an early marriage period in which the fact of a wife's employment presses for a greater egalitarian relationship between husband and wife in decision-making, commonality of experience, and sharing of household responsibilities.

The balance between individual autonomy and couple mutuality that develops during the honeymoon stage of such a marriage may be important in establishing a pattern that will later affect the quality of the parent-child relationship and the extent of sex-role segregation of duties between the parents. It is only in the context of a growing egalitarian base to the marital relationship that one could find, as Gavron has,[33] a tendency for parents to establish some barriers between themselves and their children, a marital defense against the institution of parenthood as she describes it. This may eventually replace the typical coalition in more traditional families of mother and children against husband-father. Parenthood will continue for some time to impose a degree of temporary segregation of primary responsibilities between husband and wife, but, when this takes place in the context of a previously established egalitarian relationship between the husband and wife, such role segregation may become blurred, with greater recognition of the wife's need for autonomy and the husband's role in the routines of home and child rearing.[34]

There is one further significant social change that has important implications for the changed relationship between husband and wife: the increasing departure from an old pattern of role-inception phasing in which the young person first completed his schooling, then established himself in the world of work, then married and began his family. Marriage and parenthood are increasingly taking place *before* the schooling of the husband, and often of the wife, has been completed.[35] An important reason for this trend lies in the fact that, during the same decades in which the average age of physical-sexual maturation has dropped, the average amount of education which young people obtain has been on the increase. Particularly for the college and graduate or professional school population, family roles are often assumed before the degrees needed to enter careers have been obtained.

Just how long it now takes young people to complete their higher education has been investigated only recently in several longitudinal studies of college-graduate cohorts.[36] College is far less uniformly a four-year period than high school is. A full third of the college freshmen in one study had been out of high school a year or more before entering college.[37] In a large sample of college graduates in 1961, one in five were over 25 years of age at graduation.[38] Thus, financial difficulties, military service, change of career plans, and marriage itself all tend to create interruptions in the college attendance of a significant proportion of college graduates. At the graduate and professional school level, this is even more marked: the mean age of men receiving the doctorate, for example, is 32, and of women, 36.[39] It is the exception rather than the rule for men and women who seek graduate degrees to go directly from college to graduate school and remain there until they secure their degrees.[40]

The major implication of this change is that more men and women are achieving full adult status in family roles while they are still less than fully adult in status terms in the occupational system. Graduate students are, increasingly, men and women with full family responsibilities. Within the family many more husbands and fathers are still students, often quite dependent on the earnings of their wives to see them through their advanced training.[41] No matter what the couple's desires and preferences are, this fact alone presses for more egalitarian relations between husband and wife, just as the adult family status of graduate students presses for more egalitarian relations between students and faculty.

Irrevocability

If marriages do not work out, there is now widespread acceptance of divorce and remarriage as a solution. The same point applies to the work world: we are free to leave an unsatisfactory job and seek another. But once a pregnancy occurs, there is little possibility of undoing the commitment to parenthood implicit in conception except in the rare instance of placing children for adoption. We can have ex-spouses and ex-jobs but not ex-children. This being so, it is scarcely surprising to find marked differences between the relationship of a parent and one child and the relationship of the same parent with another child. If the culture does not permit pregnancy termination, the equivalent to giving up a child is psychological withdrawal on the part of the parent.

This taps an important area in which a focus on the parent rather than the child may contribute a new interpretive dimension to an old problem: the long history of interest, in the social sciences, in differences among children associated with their sex-birth-order position in their sibling set. Research has largely been based on data gathered about and/or from the children, and interpretations make inferences back to the "probable" quality of the child's relation to a parent and how a parent might differ in relating to a first-born compared to a last-born child. The relevant research, directed at the parents (mothers in particular), remains to be done, but at least a few examples can be suggested of the different order of interpretation that flows from a focus on the parent.

Some birth-order research stresses the influence of sibs upon other sibs, as in Koch's finding that second-born boys with an older sister are more feminine than second-born boys with an older brother.[42] A similar sib-influence interpretation is offered in the major common finding of birth-order correlates, that sociability is greater among last-borns[43] and achievement among first-borns.[44] It has been suggested that last-borns use social skills to increase acceptance by their older sibs or are more peer-oriented because they receive less adult stimulation from parents. The tendency of first-borns to greater achievement has been interpreted in a corollary way, as a reflection of early assumption of responsibility for younger sibs, greater adult stimulation during the time the oldest was the only child in the family,[45] and the greater significance of the first-born for the larger kinship network of the family.[46]

Sociologists have shown increasing interest in structural family variables in recent years, a primary variable being family size. From Bossard's descriptive work on the large family[47] to more methodologically sophisticated work such as that by Rosen,[48] Elder and Bowerman,[49] Boocock,[50] and Nisbet,[51] the question posed is: what is the effect of growing up in a small family, compared with a large family, that is attributable to this group-size variable? Unfortunately, the theoretical point of departure for sociologists' expectations of the effect of the family-size variables is the Durkheim-Simmel tradition of the differential effect of group size or population density upon members or inhabitants.[52] In the case of the family, however, this overlooks the very important fact that family size is determined by the key figures *within* the group, i.e., the parents. To find that children in small families differ from children in large families is not simply due to the impact of group size upon individual members but to the very different involvement of the parent with the children and to relations between the parents themselves in small versus large families.

An important clue to a new interpretation can be gained by examining family size from the perspective of parental motivation toward having children. A small family is small for one of two primary reasons: either the parents wanted a small family and achieved their desired size, or they wanted a large family but were not able to attain it. In either case, there is a low probability of unwanted children. Indeed, in the latter eventuality they may take particularly great interest in the children they do have. Small families are therefore most likely to contain parents with a strong and positive orientation to each of the children they have. A large family, by contrast, is large either because the parents achieved the size they desired or because they have more children than they in fact wanted. Large families therefore have a higher probability than small families of including unwanted and unloved children. Consistent with this are Nye's finding that adolescents in small families have better relations with their parents than those in large families[53] and Sears and Maccoby's finding that mothers of large families are more restrictive toward their children than mothers of small families.[54]

This also means that last-born children are more likely to be unwanted than first- or middle-born children, particularly in large families. This is consistent with what is known of abortion patterns among married women, who typically resort to abortion only when they have achieved the number of children they want or feel they can afford to have. Only a small proportion of women faced with such unwanted pregnancies actually resort to abortion. *This suggests the possibility that the last-born child's reliance on social skills may be his device for securing the attention and loving involvement of a parent less positively predisposed to him than to his older siblings.*

In developing this interpretation, rather extreme cases have been stressed. Closer to the normal range, of families in which even the last-born child was desired and planned for, there is still another element which may contribute to the greater sociability of the last-born child. Most parents are themselves aware of the greater ease with which they face the care of a third fragile newborn than the first; clearly, parental skills and confidence are greater with last-born children than with first-born children. But this does not mean that the attitude of the parent is more positive toward the care of the third child than the first. There is no necessary correlation between skills in an area and enjoyment of that area. Searls[55] found that older homemakers are *more* skillful in domestic tasks but experience *less* enjoyment of them than younger homemakers, pointing to a declining euphoria for a particular role with the passage of time. In the same way, older people rate their marriages as "very happy" less often than younger people do.[56] It is perhaps culturally and psychologically more difficult to face the possibility that women may find less enjoyment of the maternal role with the passage of time, though women themselves know the difference between the romantic expectation concerning child care and the incorporation of the first baby into the household and the more realistic expectation and sharper assessment of their own abilities to do an adequate job of mothering as they face a third confinement. Last-born children may experience not only less verbal stimulation from their parents than first-born children but also less prompt and enthusiastic response to their demands—from feeding and diaper-change as infants to requests for stories read at three or a college eduaction at eighteen—simply because the parents experience less intense gratification from the parent role with the third child than they did with the first. The child's response to this might well be to cultivate winning, pleasing manners in early childhood that blossom as charm and sociability in later life, showing both a greater need to be loved and greater pressure to seek approval.

One last point may be appropriately developed at this juncture. Mention was made earlier that for many women the personal outcome of experience in the parent role is not a higher level of maturation but the negative outcome of a depressed sense of self-worth, if not actual personality deterioration. There is considerable evidence that this is more prevalent than we recognize. On a qualitative level, a close reading of the portrait of the working-class wife in Rainwater [57] Newsom,[58] Komarovsky,[59] Gavron,[60] or Zweig[61] gives little suggestion that maternity has provided these women with opportunities for personal growth and development. So too, Cohen[62] notes with some surprise that in her sample of middle-class education couples, as in Pavenstadt's study of lower-income women in Boston, there were more emotional difficulty and lower levels of maturation among multiparous women than primiparous women. On a more extensive sample basis, in Gurin's survey of Americans viewing their mental health,[63] as in Bradburn's reports on happiness,[64] single men are less happy and less active than single women, but among the married respondents the women are unhappier, have more problems, feel inadequate as parents, have a more negative and passive outlook on life, and show a more negative self-image. All of these characteristics increase with age among married women but show no relationship to age among men. While it may be true, as Gurin argues, that women are more introspective and hence more attuned to the psychological facets of experience than men are, this point does not account for the fact that the things which the women report are all on the negative side; few are on the positive side, indicative of euphoric sensitivity and pleasure. The possibility must be faced, and at some point researched, that women lose ground in personal development and self-esteem during the early and middle years of adulthood, whereas men gain ground in these respects during the same years. The retention of a high level of self-esteem may depend upon the adequacy of earlier preparation for major adult roles: men's training adequately prepares them for their primary adult roles in the occupational system, as it does for those women who opt to participate significantly in the work world. Training in the qualities and skills needed for family roles in contemporary society may be inadequate for both sexes, but the lowering of self-esteem occurs only among women because their primary adult roles are within the family system.

Preparation for Parenthood

Four factors may be given special attention on the question of what preparation American couples bring to parenthood.

Paucity of preparation. Our educational system is dedicated to the cognitive development of the young, and our primary teaching approach is the pragmatic one of learning by doing. How much one knows and how well he can apply what he knows are the standards by which the child is judged in school, as the employee is judged at work. The child can learn by doing in such subjects as science, mathematics, art work, or shop, but not in the subjects most relevant to successful family life: sex, home maintenance, child care, interpersonal competence, and empathy. If the home is deficient in training in these areas, the child is left with no preparation for a major segment of his adult life. A doctor facing his first patient in private practice has treated numerous patients under close supervision during his internship, but probably a majority of American mothers approach maternity with no previous child-care experience beyond sporadic baby-sitting, perhaps a course in child psychology, or occasional care of younger siblings.

Limited learning during pregnancy. A second important point makes adjustment to parenthood potentially more stressful than marital adjustment. This is the lack of any realistic training for parenthood during the anticipatory stage of pregnancy. By contrast, during the engagement period preceding marriage, an individual has opportunities to develop the skills and make the adjustments which ease the transition to marriage. Through discussions of values and life goals, through sexual experimentation, shared social experiences as an engaged couple with friends and relatives, and planning and furnishing an apartment, the engaged couple can make considerable progress in developing mutuality in advance of the marriage itself.[65] No such headstart is possible in the case of pregnancy. What preparation exists is confined to reading, consultation with friends and parents, discussions between husband and wife, and a minor nesting phase in which a place and the equipment for a baby are prepared in the household.[66]

Abruptness of transition. Thirdly, the birth of a child is not followed by any gradual taking on of responsibility, as in the case of a professional work role. It is as if the woman shifted from a graduate student to a full professor with little intervening apprenticeship experience of slowly increasing responsibility. The new mother starts out immediately on 24-hour duty, with responsibility for a fragile and mysterious infant totally dependent on her care.

If marital adjustment is more difficult for very young brides than more mature ones,[67] adjustment to motherhood may be even more difficult. A woman can adapt a passive dependence on a husband and still have a successful marriage, but a young mother with strong dependency needs is in for difficulty in maternal adjustment, because the role precludes such dependency. This situation was well described in Cohen's study[68] in a case of a young wife with a background of co-ed popularity and a passive dependent relationship to her admired and admiring husband, who collapsed into restricted incapacity when faced with the responsibilities of maintaining a home and caring for a child.

Lack of guidelines to successful parenthood. If the central task of parenthood is the rearing of children to become the kind of competent adults valued by the society, then an important question facing any parent is what he or she specifically can do to create such a competent adult. This is where the parent is left with few or no guidelines from the expert. Parents can readily inform themselves concerning the young infant's nutritional, clothing, and medical needs and follow the general prescription that a child needs loving physical contact and emotional support. Such advice may be sufficient to produce a healthy, happy, and well-adjusted preschooler, but adult competency is quite another matter.

In fact, the adults who do "succeed" in American society show a complex of characteristics as children that current experts in child-care would evaluate as "poor" to "bad." Biographies of leading authors and artists, as well as the more rigorous research inquiries of creativity among architects[69] or scientists,[70] do not portray childhoods with characteristics currently endorsed by mental health and child-care authorities. Indeed, there is often a predominance of tension in childhood family relations and traumatic loss rather than loving parental support, intense channeling of energy in one area of interest rather than an all-round profile of diverse interests, and social withdrawal and preference for loner activities rather than gregarious sociability. Thus, the stress in current child-rearing advice on a high level of loving support but a low level of discipline or restriction on the behavior of the child—the "developmental" family type as Duvall calls it[71]—is a profile consistent with the focus on mental health, sociability, and adjustment. Yet the combination of both high support and high authority on the part of parents is most strongly related to the child's sense of responsibility, leadership quality, and achievement level, as found in Bronfenbrenner's studies[72] and that of Mussen and Distler.[73]

Brim points out[74] that we are a long way from being able to say just what parent role prescriptions have what effect on the adult characteristics of the child. We know even less about how such parental prescriptions should be changed to adapt to changed conceptions of competency in adulthood..In such an ambiguous context, the great interest parents take in school reports on their children or the pediatrician's assessment of the child's developmental progress should be seen as among the few indices parents have of how well *they* are doing as parents.

FOOTNOTES

[1] Antonio J. Ferreira, "The Pregnant Woman's Emotional Attitude and its Reflection on the Newborn," *American Journal of Orthopsychiatry,* 30 (1960), pp. 553-561.

[2] Robert Sears, E. Maccoby, and H. Levin, *Patterns of Child-Rearing,* Evanston, Illinois: Row, Peterson, 1957.

[3] Sylvia Brody, *Patterns of Mothering: maternal influences during infancy,* New York: International Universities Press, 1956.

[4] Leon J. Yarrow, "Maternal Deprivation: Toward an Empirical and Conceptual Re-evaluation," *Psychological Bulletin,* 58:6 (1961), pp. 459-490.

[5] F. Ivan Nye and L. W. Hoffman, *The Employed Mother in America,* Chicago: Rand McNally, 1963; Alice S. Rossi, "Equality Between the Sexes: An Immodest Proposal," *Daedalus,* 93:2 (1964), pp. 607-652.

[6] The younger the child, the more was this the accepted view. It is only in recent years that research has paid any attention to the initiating role of the infant in the development of his attachment to maternal and other adult figures, as in Ainsworth's research which showed that infants become attached to the mother, not solely because she is instrumental in satisfying their primary visceral drives, but through a chain of behavioral interchange between the infant and the mother, thus supporting Bowlby's rejection of the secondary drive theory of the infant's ties to his mother. Mary D. Ainsworth, "Patterns of Attachment Behavior shown by the Infant in interaction with his mother." *Merrill-Palmer Quarterly,* 10:1 (1964), pp. 51-58; John Bowlby, "The Nature of the child's tie to his mother," *International Journal of Psychoanalysis,* 39 (1958), pp. 1-34.

[7] Therese Benedek, "Parenthood as a Developmental Phase," *Journal of American Psychoanalytic Association,* 7:8 (1958), pp. 389-417.

[8] Yarrow, *op. cit.*

[9] Henry A. Murray, *Explorations in Personality,* New York: Oxford University Press, 1938.

[10] Heinz Hartmann, *Ego Psychology and the Problem of Adaptation,* New York: International Universities Press, Inc., 1958.

[11] Patrick Mullahy (ed.), *The Contributions of Harry Stack Sullivan,* New York: Hermitage House, 1952.

[12] E. Erikson, "Identity and the Life Cycle: Selected Papers," *Psychological Issues,* 1 (1959), pp. 1-171.

[13] J. Tyhurst, "Individual Reactions to Community Disaster," *American Journal of Psychiatry,* 107 (1951), pp. 764-769.

[14] G. Caplan, "Patterns of Parental Response to the Crisis of Premature Birth: A Preliminary Approach to Modifying the Mental Health Outcome," *Psychiatry,* 23 (1960), pp. 365-374.

[15] E. Lindemann, "Symptomatology and Management of Acute Grief," *American Journal of Psychiatry,* 101 (1944), pp. 141-148.

[16] Irving Janis, *Psychological Stress,* New York: John Wiley, 1958.

[17] Rhona Rapoport, "Normal Crises, Family Structure and Mental Health," *Family Process,* 2:1 (1963), pp. 68-80; Rhona Rapoport and Robert Rapoport, "New Light on the Honeymoon," *Human Relations,* 17:1 (1964), pp. 33-56; Rhona Rapoport, "The Transition from Engagement to Marriage," *Acta Sociologica,* 8, fasc. 1-2 (1964), pp. 36-55; and Robert Rapoport and Rhona Rapoport, "Work and Family in Contemporary Society," *American Sociological Review,* 30:3 (1965), pp. 381-394.

[18] E. E. LeMasters, "Parenthood as Crisis," *Marriage and Family Living,* 19 (1957), pp. 352-355; Everett D. Dyer, "Parenthood as Crisis: A Re-Study," *Marriage and Family Living,* 25 (1963), pp. 196-201; and Daniel F. Hobbs, Jr., "Parenthood as Crisis: A Third Study," *Journal of Marriage and the Family,* 27:3 (1963), pp. 367-372. LeMasters and Dyer both report the first experience of parenthood involves extensive to severe crises in the lives of their young parent respondents. Hobbs's study does not show first parenthood to be a crisis experience, but this may be due to the fact that his couples have very young (seven-week-old) first babies and are therefore still experiencing the euphoric honeymoon stage of parenthood.

[19] Parsons' theoretical analysis of the family system builds directly on Bales's research on small groups. The latter are typically comprised of volunteers willing to attempt the single task put to the group. This positive orientation is most apt to yield the empirical discovery of "sociometric stars" and "task leaders," least apt to sensitize the researcher or theorist to the effect of hostile nonacceptance of the group task. Talcott Parsons and R. F. Bales, *Family, Socialization and Interaction Process,* New York: The Free Press, a division of the Macmillan Co., 1955.

Yet the same limited definition of the key variable is found in the important attempts by Straus to develop the theory that every social system, as every personality, requires a circumplex model with two independent axes of authority and support. His discussion and examples indicate a variable definition with limited range: support is defined as High (+) or Low (-), but "low" covers both the absence of high support and the presence of negative support; there is love or neutrality in this system, but not hate. Applied to actual families, this groups destructive mothers with low supportive mothers, much as the non-authoritarian pole on the Authoritarian Personality Scale includes both mere non-authoritarians and vigorously anti-authoritarian personalities. Murray A. Straus, "Power and Support Structure of the Family in Relation to Socialization," *Journal of Marriage and the Family,* 26:3 (1964), pp. 318-326.

[20]Mabel Blake Cohen, "Personal Identity and Sexual Identity," *Psychiatry,* 29:1 (1966), pp. 1-14; Joseph C. Rheingold, *The Fear of Being a Woman: A Theory of Maternal Destructiveness,* New York: Grune and Stratton, 1964.

[21]Theodore Lidz, S. Fleck, and A. Cornelison, *Schizophrenia and the Family,* New York: International Universities Press, Inc., 1965; Rheingold, *op. cit.*

[22]Cf. the long review of studies Rheingold covers in his book on maternal destructiveness, *op. cit.*

[23]Benedek, *op cit.*

[24]Reuben Hill and D. A. Hansen, "The Identification of a Conceptual Framework Utilized in Family Study," *Marriage and Family Living,* 22 (1960), pp. 299-311.

[25]Harold L. Raush, W. Goodrich, and J. D. Campbell, "Adaptation to the First Years of Marriage," *Psychiatry,* 26:4 (1963), pp. 368-380.

[26]Rapoport, *op. cit.*

[27]Cohen, *op. cit.*

[28]Raush *et al., op. cit.*

[29]The greater the cultural pressure to assume a given adult social role, the greater will be the tendency for individual negative feelings toward that role to be expressed covertly. Men may complain about a given job but not about working per se, and hence their work dissatisfactions are often displaced to the non-work sphere, as psychosomatic complaints or irritation and dominance at home. An equivalent displacement for women of the ambivalence many may feel toward maternity may be felt toward the homemaker role.

[30]Caroline Bird, *The Invisible Scar,* New York: David McKay Company, 1966.

[31]When it is realized that a mean family size of 3.5 would double the population in 40 years, while a mean of 2.5 would yield a stable population in the same period, the social importance of withholding praise for procreative prowess is clear. At the same time, a drop in the birth rate may reduce the number of unwanted babies born, for such a drop would mean more efficient contraceptive usage and a closer correspondence between desired and attained family size.

[32]James A. Davis, *Stipends and Spouses: The Finances of American Arts and Sciences Graduate Students,* Chicago: University of Chicago Press, 1962.

[33]Hannah Gavron, *The Captive Wife,* London: Routledge & Kegan Paul, 1966.

[34]The recent increase in natural childbirth, prenatal courses for expectant fathers, and greater anticipation of men during childbirth and postnatal care of the infant may therefore be a *consequence* of greater sharing between husband and wife when both work and jointly maintain their new households during the early months of marriage. Indeed, natural childbirth builds directly on this shifted base to the marital relationship. Goshen-Gottstein has found in an Israeli sample that women with a "traditional" orientation to marriage far exceed women with a "modern" orientation to marriage in menstrual difficulty, dislike of sexual intercourse, and pregnancy disorders and complaints such as vomiting. She argues that traditional women demand and expect little from their husbands and become demanding and narcissistic by means of their children, as shown in pregnancy by an over-exaggeration of symptoms and attention-seeking. Esther R. Goshen-Gottstein, *Marriage and First Pregnancy: Cultural Influences on Attitudes of Israeli Women,* London: Tavistock Publications, 1966. A prolonged psychic honeymoon uncomplicated by an early pregnancy, and with the new acceptance of married women's employment, may help to cement the egalitarian relationship in the marriage and reduce both the tendency to pregnancy difficulties and the need for a narcissistic focus on the children. Such a background is fruitful ground for sympathy toward and acceptance of the natural childbirth ideology.

[35]James A. Davis, *Stipends and Spouses: The Finances of American Arts and Sciences Graduate Students, op. cit.;* James A. Davis, *Great Aspirations,* Chicago: Aldine Publishing Company, 1964; Eli Ginsberg, *Life Styles of Educated Women,* New York: Columbia University Press, 1966; Ginsberg, *Educated American Women: Self Portraits,* New York: Columbia University Press, 1967; National Science Foundation, *Two Years After the College Degree—Work and Further Study Patterns,* Washington, D.C.: Government Printing Office, NSF 63-26, 1963.

[36]Davis, *Great Aspirations, op. cit.;* Laure Sharp, "Graduate Study and Its Relation to Careers: The Experience of a Recent Cohort of College Graduates," *Journal of Human Resources,* 1:2 (1966), pp. 41-58.

[37]James D. Cowhig and C. Nam, "Educational Status, College Plans and Occupational Status of Farm and Nonfarm Youths," U.S. Bureau of the Census Series ERS (P-27). No. 30, 1961.

[38]Davis, *Great Aspirations, op. cit.*

[39]Lindsey R. Harmon, *Profiles of Ph.D.'s in the Sciences: Summary Report on Follow-up of Doctorate Cohorts, 1935-1960,* Washington, D.C.: National Research Council, Publication 1293, 1965.

[40]Sharp, *op. cit.*

[41]Davis, *Stipends and Spouses, The Finances of American Arts and Sciences Graduate Students, op. cit.*

[42]Orville G. Brim, "Family Structure and Sex-Role Learning by Children," *Sociometry,* 21 (1958), pp. 1-16; H. L. Koch, "Sissiness and Tomboyishness in Relation to Sibling Characteristics," *Journal of Genetic Psychology,* 88 (1956), pp. 231-244.

[43]Charles MacArthur, "Personalities of First and Second Children," *Psychiatry,* 19 (1956), pp. 47-54; S. Schachter, "Birth Order and Sociometric Choice," *Journal of Abnormal and Social Psychology,* 68 (1964), pp. 453-456.

[44]Irving Harris, *The Promised Seed*, New York: "The Free Press, a division of the Macmillan Co., 1964; Bernard Rosen, "Family Structure and Achievement Motivation," *American Sociological Review*, 26 (1961), pp. 574-585; Alice S. Rossi, "Naming Children in Middle-Class Families," *American Sociological Review*, 30:4 (1965), pp. 499-513; Stanley Schachter, "Birth Order, Eminence and Higher Education," *American Sociological Review*, 28 (1963), pp. 757-768.

[45]Harris, *op. cit.*

[46]Rossi, "Naming Children in Middle-Class Families," *op. cit.*

[47]James H. Bossard, *Parent and Child*, Philadelphia; University of Pennsylvania Press, 1953; James H. Bossard and E. Boll, *The Large Family System*, Philadelphia: University of Pennsylvania, 1956.

[48]Rosen, *op. cit.*

[49]Glen H. J. Elder and C. Bowerman, "Family Structure and Child Rearing Patterns: The Effect of Family Size and Sex Composition on Child-Rearing Practices," *American Sociological Review*, 28 (1963), pp. 891-905.

[50]Sarane S. Boocock, "Toward a Sociology of Learning: A Selective Review of Existing Research," *Sociology of Education*, 39:1 (1966), pp. 1-45.

[51]John Nisbet, "Family Environment and Intelligence," in *Education, Economy and Society*, ed. by Halsey *et al.* New York: The Free Press, a division of the Macmillan Company, 1961.

[52]Thus Rosen writes: "Considering the sociologist's traditional and continuing concern with group size as an independent variable (from Simmel and Durkheim to the recent experimental studies of small groups), there have been surprisingly few studies of the influence of group size upon the nature of interaction in the family," *op. cit.*, p. 576.

[53]Ivan Nye, "Adolescent-Parent Adjustment: Age, Sex, Sibling, Number, Broken Homes, and Employed Mothers as Variables," *Marriage and Family Living*, 14 (1952), pp. 327-332.

[54]Sears *et al., op. cit.*

[55]Laura G. Searls, "Leisure Role Emphasis of College Graduate Homemakers," *Journal of Marriage and the Family*, 28:1 (1966), pp. 77-82.

[56]Norman Bradburn and D. Caplovitz, *Reports on Happiness*, Chicago: Aldine Publishing, 1965.

[57]Lee Rainwater, R. Coleman, and G. Handel, *Workingman's Wife*, New York: Oceana Publications, 1959.

[58]John Newsom and E. Newsom, *Infant Care in an Urban Community*, New York: International Universities Press, 1963.

[59]Mirra Komarovsky, *Blue Collar Marriage*, New York: Random House, 1962.

[60]Gavron, *op.cit.*

[61]Ferdinand Zweig, *Woman's Life and Labor*, London: Camelot Press, 1952.

[62]Cohen, *op. cit.*

[63]Gerald Gurin, J. Veroff, and S. Feld, *Americans View Their Mental Health*, New York: Basic Books, Monograph Series No. 4, Joint Commission on Mental Illness and Health, 1960.

[64]Bradburn and Caplovitz, *op. cit.*

[65]Rapoport, "The Transition from Engagement to Marriage," *op. cit.;* Raush *et al., op. cit.*

[66]During the period when marriage was the critical transition in the adult woman's life rather than pregnancy, a good deal of anticipatory "nesting" behavior took place from the time of conception. Now more women work through a considerable portion of the first pregnancy, and such nesting behavior as exists may be confined to a few shopping expeditions or baby showers, thus adding to the abruptness of the transition and the difficulty of adjustment following the birth of a first child.

[67]Lee G. Burchinal, "Adolescent Role Deprivation and High School Marriage," *Marriage and Family Living*, 21 (1959), pp. 378-384; Floyd M. Martinson, "Ego Deficiency as a Factor in Marriage," *American Sociological Review*, 22 (1955), pp. 161-164; J. Joel Moss and Ruby Gingles, "The Relationship of Personality to the Incidence of Early Marriage," *Marriage and Family Living*, 21 (1959) pp. 373-377.

[68]Cohen, *op. cit.*

[69]Donald W. MacKinnon, "Creativity and Images of the Self," in *The Study of Lives*, ed. by Robert W. White, New York: Atherton Press, 1963.

[70]Anne Roe, *A Psychological Study of Eminent Biologists, Psychological Monographs*, 65:14 (1951), 68 pages; Anne Roe, "A Psychological Study of Physical Scientists," *Genetic Psychology Monographs*, 43 (1951), pp. 121-239; Anne Roe, "Crucial Life Experiences in the Development of Scientists," in *Talent and Education*, ed. by E. P. Torrance, Minneapolis: University of Minnesota Press, 1960.

[71]Evelyn M. Duvall, "Conceptions of Parenthood," *American Journal of Sociology*, 52 (1946), pp. 193-203.

[72]Urie Bronfenbrenner, "Some Familial Antecedents of Responsibility and Leadership in Adolescents," in *Studies in Leadership*, ed. by L. Petrullo and B. Bass, New York: Holt, Rinehart, and Winston, 1960.

[73]Paul Mussen and L. Distler, "Masculinity, Identification and Father-Son Relationships," *Journal of Abnormal and Social Psychology*, 59 (1959), pp. 350-356.

[74]Orville G. Brim, "The Parent-Child Relation as a Social System: I. Parent and Child Roles," *Child Development*, 28:3 (1957), pp. 343-364.

parent-child relationships in a variety of settings

16

conceptions of parenthood

evelyn millis duvall

This is a comparison of ideologies of parenthood found in mothers' groups in various subcultures in contemporary America. An attempt is made to describe the conceptions of "a good mother" and "a good child" in twenty-four groups representing four social class levels, Negro and white (Jewish and non-Jewish) and mothers of younger and older children in greater Chicago. Table 1 shows the number of groups in each classification and the number of mothers in each.

    The four social status levels. It is impossible to place any one group with certainty in the complex status system of greater Chicago, a system which has not yet been studied. It is, however, feasible to (1) select active groups on the basis of their participation in the status hierarchy; (2) plot their social characteristics . . . and (3) compare these latter roughly with class groups defined in other communities. Thus Level I resembles upper middle class and Level IV parallels upper-lowers of previous studies in other communities.[1] Levels II and III fall at recognizable intervals between I and IV.

    "Experienced" and "inexperienced" mothers. In anticipation of the fact that parents' expectations of themselves and their children may vary with the age of the children, a comparison was made between the "experienced" mothers whose first children were more than five years of age and the "inexperienced" mothers whose first children were five years old or less. . . .

TABLE 1. DISTRIBUTION OF THE SAMPLE

Class Levels	Jewish		Non-Jewish		Negro		Total	
	Groups	Persons	Groups	Persons	Groups	Persons	Groups	Persons
I	2	36	1	54	1	29	4	119
II	4	40	5	54	1	17	10	111
III	1	66	3	30	1	21	5	117
IV	3	27	1	23	2	36	6	86
Total	10	169	10	161	5	103	25	433

PROCEDURE AND METHOD

The original data, collected in every instance at a regular meeting of a mothers' group, consisted of minimal face-sheet information from each mother, and her free responses to two questions, "What are

Reprinted, by permission of the University of Chicago Press, from *American Journal of Sociology*, 1946, *52*, 193-203.

five things a good mother does?" and "What are five things a good child does?" This is a modification of a device used by Bavelas[2] in getting group ideologies of school children in the classroom. In formulating the categories, the original wording used by the subjects was kept, and the responses were finally grouped into twelve categories of "a good mother" and thirteen of "a good child." Two other judges, working independently, categorized the responses of all 433 persons in this study as well as the 36 others used in the pretest. Agreement between the three workers was 97.1 per cent.

Two types of responses were: (1) the traditional, that is, what used to be expected of a good mother and a good child (the roles are rigidly conceived); and (2) the nontraditional, which is characterized by expectations of mother and child in terms of growth and development rather than as specific behavioral conformities (the conceptions of role are dynamic and flexible). This developmental emphasis is so consistently strong in the nontraditional type of response that, at the cost of semantic purity, a dichotomy of "traditional" and "developmental" was recognized in the data and explored as follows.

The traditional-developmental division was devised by the investigator with the help of four other experienced workers. Two years later it was judged in its final form by three other social scientists, with complete consensus. Percentages of traditional and developmental responses for the various groups brought the differences into focus and provided a basis for observing trends. The categories with typical responses, in the original wording, follow.

Categories—A Good Mother

(With typical responses)

Traditional conception:
1. "Keeps house." (Washes, cooks, cleans, mends, sews, manages household.)
2. "Takes care of child physically." (Keeps child healthy, guards child's safety, feeds, clothes, bathes, sees that child rests.)
3. "Trains child to regularity." (Establishes regular habits, provides schedule, sees to regular hours for important functions.)
4. "Disciplines." (Corrects child, reprimands, punishes, scolds, demands obedience, rewards good behavior, is firm, is consistent, keeps promises.)
5. "Makes the child good." (Teaches obedience, instructs in morals, builds character, prays for, sees to religious education.)

Developmental conception:
6. "Trains for self-reliance and citizenship." (Trains for self-help, encourages independence, teaches how to be a good citizen, how to adjust to life, teaches concentration.)
7. "Sees to emotional well-being." (Keeps child happy and contented, makes a happy home, makes child welcome, helps child feel secure, helps child overcome fears.)
8. "Helps child develop socially." (Provides toys, companions, plays with child, supervises child's play.)
9. "Provides for child's mental growth." (Gives educational opportunities, provides stimulation to learn, reads to child, tells stories, guides reading, sends child to school.)
10. "Guides with understanding." (Sees child's point of view, gears life to child's level, answers questions freely and frankly, gives child freedom to grow, interprets, offers positive suggestions.)
11. "Relates self lovingly to child." (Shows love and affection, enjoys child, spends time with child, shares with child, is interested in what child does and tells, listens.)
12. "Is a calm, cheerful, growing person one's self." (Has more outside interests, is calm and gentle, has a sense of humor, laughs, smiles, gets enough recreation.)

Categories—A Good Child

(With typical responses)

Traditional conception:

1. "Keeps clean and neat." (Is orderly, is clean, keeps self neat.)
2. "Obeys and respects adults." (Minds parents, no back talk, respects adults.)
3. "Pleases adults." (Has good character traits, is honest, truthful, polite, kind, fair, courteous at all times.)
4. "Respects property." (Takes care of his things, is not destructive, hangs up his clothes.)
5. "Is religious." (Goes to Sunday School, loves God, prays, follows Jesus.)
6. "Works well." (Studies, goes to school, is reliable, takes responsibilities, is dependable in his work.)
7. "Fits into the family program." (Has an interest in his home, does his share, runs errands willingly, helps out at home.)

Developmental conception:

8. "Is healthy and well." (Eats and sleeps well, grows a good body, has good habits.)
9. "Shares and co-operates with others." (Gets along with people, likes others, is developing socially, tries to help, plays with other children.)
10. "Is happy and contented." (Keeps in good humor, is a cheerful child, is happy, is emotionally well adjusted.)
11. "Loves and confides in parents." (Responds with affection, loves his parents, has confidence in his parents, trusts and confides in them.)
12. "Is eager to learn." (Shows initiative, asks questions, accepts help, expresses himself, likes to learn.)
13. "Grows as a person." (Progresses in his ability to handle himself and different situations, enjoys growing up.)

The relative frequency of responses in any one or more of the categories was unknown while the categories were being formulated. These computed frequencies become the bases for comparison of the social status, religious and racial background, and experience of the parents.

Eighty-three mothers representative of each of the groups were selected for interviews. A guided interview, eliciting free responses to a few key questions, was used uniformly. Excerpts from these interviews are used to elaborate, corroborate, and interpret statistical findings, but there is no attempt to use interview material in judging a mother's conduct, since it is not her behavior that is being studied but rather the official ideology of the group to which she belongs.

FINDINGS

When mothers respond to the question, "What are five things a good mother does?" a great variety of replies are collected. Some are given much more frequently than others. . . . In general, the good mother is defined as one who "takes care of the child physically."

Mothers mention many things "a good child" does. . . . On the whole, the good child is described as one who "obeys and respects his parents" and "pleases adults."

In the comparison of the proportion of the individual responses, as found in the several groups, significant differences in the way the categories cluster were revealed. Clusters of categories emerge as characteristic of some social class levels, racial, religious, and experiential groupings. [Data clearly show] the tendency of categories 1, 2, 3, and 5 of "a good mother" (each of them traditional) to be characteristic of the two lower social class levels as compared with the two upper; the Negro as compared with the white mothers, and the experienced as compared with the inexperienced. Categories 8, 10, and 11 (all developmental) are characteristic of the two upper social class levels, the whites in the sample and the mothers of younger children (inexperienced).

Categories for "a good child" tend to cluster perceptibly in the same way. Categories 1, 2, and 3 (traditional) characterize the two lower class levels—and to a slight extent Level II as compared with Level I—the Negro as compared with the white, and the experienced as compared with the mothers of younger children. In addition, non-Jewish mothers mention items in category 2 significantly more frequently than do Jewish mothers. Conversely, categories 8, 9, 10 and 12 (developmental) tend to characterize the upper groups, the Jewish, the white, and the mothers of younger children.

Differences between the frequencies of the various categories . . . show consistent trends and seem worthy of further exploration.

By combining response categories into traditional and developmental, as described above, we are able to compare the frequencies of the two kinds of responses with results. . . .

. . . It is clear that the Negro mothers consistently mentioned traditional qualities both of a good mother and a good child appreciably more frequently than did either of the white groups. There is a very slight tendency in the non-Jewish white groups toward higher frequencies of traditional responses than in the Jewish groups. The trends for conceptions of a good mother tend to resemble closely those of the good child.

. . . It is evident that traditional responses are more frequent at the lower social class levels and less frequent at the upper levels. This is a straight line trend throughout the four class levels for both "a good mother" and, with a slight exception at Level III and IV, for "a good child." Conversely, developmental responses are consistently more frequent in the upper levels and less frequent at the lower levels.

Representative critical ratios show these observed differences in percentages of traditional and developmental responses between several of the social class levels to be significant within the Jewish, non-Jewish, and Negro samples.

Mothers of Level I speak of their children as developing persons: A Negro mother of three boys, six, eleven, and twelve years of age, says, "The principal thing is that I want to give them an opportunity to grow up strong and happy and capable and independent"; a North Shore white mother of a nine-year-old boy and a five-year-old girl says, "They are interesting and it is fun to watch them develop and grow and learn." These mothers speak of their children as having rights of their own: "If we call them and they are doing something, we don't expect them to drop what they are doing right that minute and come. Their activities are important, too, and they should be able to finish what they are doing. We try to respect the individual rights of the child" (Negro, Level I). These parents tend to be permissive and not to be greatly disturbed by the opinions and judgments of others. A Level I Jewish mother of an infant son and a four-year-old daughter says,

> You have to let them know that if they do something wrong, it's all right and not too important. J—— did something at Sunday School one Sunday, for instance. We got outside and she said, 'I made wee-wee.' She couldn't help it. She does sometimes, so I just changed her pants and we didn't worry about it.

In contrast, mothers at the other three levels are frequently embarrassed by their children's conduct. A Jewish mother in Level II with a girl of four-and-a-half and a boy of two years relates:

> I never taught G—— to wash her hands after completing her toilet and one day in school she went to the washroom and when she came back the teacher asked her if she had washed her hands. She hadn't, and when she told me I was so embarrassed! Before this I had always wiped them after she washed them. Well, believe me, I taught her right then and there. That teacher must have wondered what kind of home she comes from.

A mother at Level III with a boy of twelve and a girl of nine says, "I'm glad I have a yard to hang my clothes out in nice weather, so neighbors can see I do have clothing aplenty for them even if they do look messed up so much of the time." While a Level IV Jewish mother of a six-year-old girl expresses embarrassment over her child's behavior:

> *A few weeks ago a mother asked if I would let S——come up to her house and play with her little girl P——. I let S——go up to the house and she seemed to have had a good time. She didn't repeat her visit and the mother didn't repeat her invitation. I didn't wonder about this at all. Then the other day I was at a luncheon which P——'s mother attended and we were at the same table of bridge. She embarrassed me terribly. She asked me, "Who is S——'s boy friend?" I explained that S——didn't have a special boy friend; that all the little boys around the neighborhood she called boy friend. I asked her why she asked. "Well, S——paraded in front of P——like this [and Mrs. G jiggled her shoulders and squirmed her hips] and said to her, "P——, do you know what my boy friend calls me? Son of a b——." If there had been a hole around I would have fallen through. What a time to tell me! I'm ashamed to let S——play with P——. Imagine what her mother thinks! She must think we use that language around here. I put pepper on S——'s tongue.*

Several hundred pages of similar interview material give the impression of the striving of mothers at the lower levels for respectability, which tends to be related to "no smoking," "no drinking," and "good respectable company." They do not hesitate to "light into the kids" when the children do not mind, or to express their hostilities and rejections quite freely. There are evidences of considerable bewilderment and confusion. These mothers with more traditional concepts regret that children are not as obedient, as respectful, or as "mannerable" as they should be. The mothers find such behavior difficult to understand and to cope with and often speak wistfully of the old-fashioned virtues that are no more.

Differences between mothers of older and younger children. Responses of only mothers who gave the exact ages of their children were used, which accounts for the slight discrepancies of the number of responses in the various groupings.

. . . . It is clear that mothers of older children give consistently higher percentages of traditional responses to questions designed to elicit group conceptions of parenthood and of children than do mothers of younger children. This is true of the Jewish, the non-Jewish, and the Negro samples studied.

[Data show] the same tendency for mothers of older children to hold more traditional views than mothers of younger, in each class level as well as in the grand total.

CONCLUSIONS

Certain qualities of a good mother and a good child tend to be mentioned consistently more frequently than others by all mothers, whatever the social class (within the range studied), the age of first child, the racial background, or the religious affiliation. This common conception is in terms of taking care of the child physically. The good child is most frequently defined in terms of "obeys and respects his parents" and "pleases adults." All these conceptions are traditional rather than developmental as defined in this investigation.

Mothers of the lower class levels tend more consistently to the traditional responses than do mothers at the upper class levels. This is a simple trend with the highest percentages of traditional responses at the lowest levels and the greatest number of developmental responses at the upper levels. These class level differences remain for each age group, religious group, and racial stock studied and for conceptions of both the good mother and the good child.

Negro mothers lean more consistently and significantly to the traditional in their expectations of their children and their conceptions of their roles as parents than do white mothers. This racial difference is true at every level studied and for the two experiential groups.

There is a slight tendency in the Jewish mothers toward developmental responses, which is less marked in non-Jewish mothers. This is especially true in the highest social class level. Differences at the other three levels are inconclusive.

Mothers of older children tend to respond consistently more traditionally than do mothers whose first children are still five years old or younger. This tendency is noted in each class level and for each of the religious and racial groups.

Thus, while certain concepts are commonly held by all, mothers within the various subcultures of our society differ significantly in their conceptions of parenthood and in what they expect of their children. These differences tend to be most marked between social class levels, between Negroes and whites, and between mothers of older and mothers of preschool children. Slight differences are noted between the replies of Jewish and non-Jewish mothers.

The family, as the primary unit of our society, reflects and adjusts to industrialization, urbanization, and the secularization of life. In its transition from the traditional institution type of family to the person-centered unit[3] of companionship that it is becoming, conceptions of the role of the parent and the child are shifting. These changes do not appear all at once and with equal force throughout the total society, but are evidenced first in little islands of the new that break off from the mass of tradition and become established in subgroups within the culture. These developmental islands are characterized by such concepts as respect for the person (both child and adult), satisfaction in personal interaction, pride in growth and development, and a permissive, growth-promoting type of guidance as opposed to the more traditional attempts to "make" children conform to patterns of being neat and clean, obedient and respectful, polite and socially acceptable.

Traditional conceptions of parenthood remain in the lower-middle and upper-lower class levels, where recent migration, household drudgery, cramped living, and infrequency of opportunity to meet with other modes of adjustment keep both parents and children in line with traditional conceptions of role. The effort to achieve respectability so evident in the two lower class levels and among the minority racial group tends further to perpetuate conformity.

The tendency for mothers of younger children toward more developmental replies may be interpreted in a number of ways. The evidence points to the possibility that conformity is demanded of families with children old enough to have some life outside the family circle. As children become old enough to go to school and to range further afield in the community, the social pressures toward conformity are felt both by them and by their mothers.

Thus, we hypothesize a seesaw progress even within the more advanced groups. Some inexperienced mothers view their roles along new lines and break with the past in their efforts to make a more adequate adjustment to a changed social situation. As their children grow older and begin to represent them in the larger world, the earlier flexibility is modified by the demands of the more traditional mass. This theory of the shift in conceptions of role as a part of the adjustment to social change would bear further investigation.

FOOTNOTES

[1]Bernice Neugarten, "The Relation between Family Social Position and the Social Development of the Child" (unpublished Ph.D. dissertation, Committee on Human Development, University of Chicago, 1943). Also W. Lloyd Warner and Paul S. Lunt, *The Social Life of a Modern Community* ("Yankee City Series," Vol. I, 1941); *The Status System of a Modern Community* ("Yankee City Series," Vol. II, 1942) (New Haven: Yale University Press). Also Kenneth Eells, "Report on Refining and Testing the Validity of the Index of Status Characteristics" (unpublished MS, Committee on Human Development, University of Chicago, July, 1945).

[2]Alex Bavelas, "A Method of Investigating Individual and Group Ideology," *Sociometry*, V (1942), 371-77.

[3]E. W. Burgess and H. J. Locke, *The Family from Institution to Companionship* (New York: American Book Co., 1945).

17   sex and class differences in parent-child interaction: a test of kohn's hypothesis

viktor gecas

f. ivan nye

This paper focuses on styles of behavior utilized by parents to discipline their children or to elicit their compliance. Style, perhaps even more than content, is an important aspect of the *quality* of an interpersonal relationship, and in the rather vast literature on child socialization it has received considerable emphasis. For example, the degree to which parents are supportive, controlling, hostile, democratic, use reason or punishment in dealing with the child have been found to be consequential to the way in which the child develops (Baumrind, 1971; Becker, 1964; Gecas, 1971; and Hess, 1970). Two of the most frequently used analytical variables in these examinations of parent-child interaction are sex of parent and social class. The first is a major axis of structural differentiation within the family; the second is a major axis of social differentiation.

We approach parental disciplinary techniques with two objectives: (1) to describe and compare the reported behaviors of mothers and fathers in different social classes; and (2) to test Kohn's (1969) hypothesis of social class differences in parental response to the *circumstances* of the child's behavior.

Research dealing with social class variations in the *style* of socialization (childrearing) has consistently shown that since World War II, middle-class parents have become increasingly more permissive in childrearing than have lower-class parents. Bronfenbrenner (1958) attributed this trend to the influence of professional advice through mass communication, such as Dr. Spock's book on child care, and the differential exposure of mothers in different social classes to this source of information. Middle-class mothers would be more likely to seek out and be influenced by professional advice on childrearing than would lower-class mothers. This professional advice, Bronfenbrenner argued, reflecting strongly the neo-Freudian influence, stressed permissiveness coupled with love in childrearing, as opposed to the preceding philosophy emphasizing constraint, discipline, and the dangers of "sparing the rod and spoiling the child." Wolfenstein (1963) documented this shift in values from a "duty oriented" to a "fun oriented" socialization in her content analysis of advice to mothers given (from 1914-1951) in the Infant Care Bulletin of the Children's Bureau. And it is middle-class parents, better educated and typically more isolated from interaction with extended kin because of greater mobility, who were more likely to take this advice to heart. In terms of disciplinary styles this means that middle-class parents would be more likely to use reason with the child, verbal threats, or withdrawal of rewards to punish or solicit the child's compliance, while lower-class parents would be expected to rely more heavily on physical punishment of the child (*cf.* Bronfenbrenner, 1958).

But is there anything about social class per se which might affect the content and style of the socialization role? Kohn (1963, 1969) provides the most elaborate and theoretically convincing discussion of the link between the occupational structure (the most commonly used indicator of

Reprinted, by permission, from *Journal of Marriage and the Family*, 1974, *36*, 742-49, slightly abridged. Copyright ©1974 by the National Council on Family Relations.

social class) and the socialization role of the parent. He states that members of different social classes, by virtue of experiencing different conditions of life, come to see the world differently, develop different conceptions of social reality, different aspirations, and different conceptions of desirable personality characteristics (1963:472).

In discussing the conditions of life distinctive of these classes, Kohn (1969) identifies three ways in which middle-class occupations (white collar) differ from lower-class occupations (blue collar). First, white-collar occupations typically require the individual to deal more with the manipulation of ideas, symbols and interpersonal relations, whereas blue-collar occupations deal more with the manipulation of physical objects and require less interpersonal skill. Second, white-collar occupations involve work that is more complex, requires greater flexibility, thought, and judgment, while in blue-collar occupations the individual is more subject to the standardization of work. Third, the degree and closeness of supervision is less in white-collar than in blue-collar occupations. As a result of these differences between the conditions of white-collar (WC) and blue-collar (BC) occupational structures, two basic value orientations emerge. White-collar workers are more likely to enunciate values dealing with self-direction, such as freedom, individualism, initiative, creativity, and self-actualization; while blue-collar parents are more likely to stress values of conformity to external standards such as orderliness, neatness, and obedience. Kohn, in fact, did find that the white-collar and blue-collar parents he studied did differ in this expected direction: WC parents were more likely to value in their children *internal* standards for governing one's relations with other people and with one's self, such as consideration, curiosity, and self-control; BC parents, on the other hand, were more likely to emphasize characteristics reflecting conformity to *external* constraints in their children. Parental values, then, tend to be extensions of the modes of behavior that are functional for parents in their occupational structures, and they become apparent in the context of socialization.[1]

Kohn also maintained that these value orientations are reflected in the style or circumstances of parental discipline. Because of the greater emphasis white-collar parents place on self-direction and internal standards of conduct, they are more likely to discipline the child on the basis of their interpretation of the child's *intent* or motive for acting as he does. Blue-collar parents, on the other hand, placing greater stress on conformity, are more likely to react on the basis of the *consequences* of the child's behavior. They are apt to punish the child when his behavior is annoying, destructive, or disobedient (Kohn, 1969:104).

Evidence for this hypothesis comes primarily from Kohn's Washington, D.C. study (*cf.* Kohn, 1969, Chapter 6), which was based on a sample of 339 mothers and a subsample of 82 fathers and children. Kohn specified a number of conditions or situations under which mothers and fathers punish children.[2] Parental responses to the child's behavior for each situation were then coded into five categories: (1) ignore behavior, (2) scold and admonish child to be good, (3) separate child from others or divert attention, (4) isolate child or restrict activities, and (5) punish physically.

Kohn found that middle-class parents (especially mothers) were quite discriminate in the use of physical punishment depending on whether the child's behavior was defined as "wild play" or "loss of temper." They were much more likely to use physical punishment in the latter situation because, Kohn argues, this represents to the parent the child's loss of self-control, a valued characteristic. Lower-class mothers, on the other hand, reported the use of physical punishment with equal frequency in both situations—it is the consequences of the child's behavior, *i.e.*, disruptive behavior in this case, which are most likely to elicit the parent's response.

We are able to address this theoretical issue by comparing parental responses to the child's misbehavior in situations pointedly differing in one respect, the child's *intent*. Parents were asked what they would do under two sets of circumstances: (1) when the child accidentally breaks something that the parent values, and (2) when the child intentionally disobeys the parent. These behavioral circumstances are not identical to those posed by Kohn, but they are comparable to the two situations that he isolated for special attention (in the sense that they reflect different motives): (1) "When the child plays wildly," and (2) "When he loses his temper." And, if Kohn's reasoning is correct, these two situations should differentiate similarly between the responses of middle-class and lower-class parents. According to Kohn's hypothesis, middle-class parents should be more discriminating in their responses to the child between situations one and two, while lower-class parents should be more uniform in their responses across the two situations.

METHOD

Sample and Procedure

A 20 per cent random sample was drawn from all parents of children in the third grade of the public and parochial schools in a medium-sized county (Yakima) of the State of Washington. A separate questionnaire was developed for each spouse. Both were mailed jointly to husband and wife with a cover letter explaining the purpose of the study and soliciting their help. Separate return envelopes were enclosed so that neither spouse would have to handle the form completed by the other. Spouses were asked not to discuss the questions or their answers with each other, but there was no way to enforce that request. Usable returns completed by both husband and wife were obtained from about 46 per cent of those sampled (after eliminating those who had moved leaving no address, those with no spouse in residence, and those who could not read English). Some returns were received (48 from wives, 11 from husbands) in which the spouse did not return a questionnaire. Two-hundred ten couples returned usable forms and analyses are based on these respondents.

Since data were gathered during 1970, sample characteristics can be compared appropriately with the 1970 Census for the State of Washington and for the United States as a whole. Since the males in this study were in the 30-50 age range, the Census category 35-45 years of age is used for comparison purposes. Income data are for married men, spouse present; education and occupation data are for all men aged 35-45. Limited Census data are for all men aged 35-45. Limited Census data are available from Yakima County, but not separately for the age group under consideration (Bureau of the Census, 1972).

Our sample more closely approximates the State of Washington census than the United States. For education completed, the sample corresponds very closely to the State. The sample includes a substantially larger proportion of couples with incomes under $10,000 (42 per cent compared to 29 per cent for Washington and 35 per cent for the United States). This difference reflects the substantially lower income in the County compared to the rest of the state and to the United States as a whole.

Occupationally, the sample includes more proprietors and managers and more farm owners and workers than State or U.S. and fewer craftsmen. The greater proportion of farm and lesser proportion of craftsmen largely reflect differences between the County and the State. Eleven per cent of the employed males in Yakima County work in agriculture—the same proportion as in the sample. The County has fewer craftsmen but a precise figure is not available because the *City and County Data Book* (1972) combines craftsmen with operatives. Insufficient data are available as to whether there are more businesses per thousand population in Yakima County than in the State as a whole, so we cannot determine whether the higher proportion in that category reflects a population difference or a higher than average return from that occupational category.

In general, then, the sample represents the State quite well except at points where the County is known to differ. Both the sample and the State differ at points from the United States. Therefore, appropriate caution in generalizing from the results is called for.

Measures of Parental Behavior

To get at the issue of style of parent-child interaction, we asked parents how they would respond to the child under three sets of circumstances stated as follows: (1) "What kinds of things do you do to get your child (age 8-10) to do something you want him to do?" (2) "If your child is playing and accidentally breaks something that you value, what would you do?" and (3) "If your child intentionally disobeys after you have told him to do something, what would you do?" The first question was designed to determine the positive strategies parents use to obtain the child's compliance. Questions two and three were aimed at eliciting the kinds of behaviors parents employ in dealing with the child's disruptive behavior or his disobedience.

The first situation was stated as an open-end question allowing the respondent to write in an answer. These answers were subsequently coded into the most frequently appearing categories (constructed on the basis of an initial content analysis of the responses). The final set of response categories for situation one was as follows: (1) ask or request; (2) tell child to do it; (3) explain or reason with child; (4) reward or bribe; (5) threaten or scold; (6) spank; (7) restrict privileges; (8) assign, write down, set time; and (9) other methods.

Situations two and three (accidental and deliberate disobedience) were precoded and the respondent was asked to check as many categories as applied from the following list: (1) scold and/or yell; (2) reduce allowance or fine child; (3) ignore behavior; (4) don't punish but discuss problem; (5) make child feel guilty; (6) keep reminding him not to do it; (7) restrict privileges; (8) spank; (9) slap; (10) withdraw affection; (11) isolate the child; and (12) other. In the data analysis, some of these response categories, which received very low frequencies were either combined or placed in the "Other" category.

Measure of Social Class

Our principal indicator of social class was husband's occupation. We coded this variable in two ways: (1) using the census occupation categories, and (2) using Duncan's social prestige scale (*cf.* Reiss, 1961: 263-275). Since the results were very similar for the two occupation scales, we have presented our analyses only for the census categories. Also, since we were only interested in a two-category occupation measure to correspond with the concepts "lower class" and "middle class" we collapsed the census occupation categories into "blue-collar" and "white-collar" occupations. The "blue-collar" category ranges from unskilled workers and farmers to technicians and craftsmen, while the "white-collar" category ranges from clerks and salesmen to doctors and business executives (similar to Kohn's social class dichotomy).

FINDINGS

.... The four most frequent response categories for fathers and mothers are to "ask or request the child," to "tell him," to "reason with him and explain why he should do it," and to "bribe by giving a reward or promising one" (these categories are not mutually exclusive). An interesting difference between the responses of fathers and mothers is that the most frequent strategy for mothers is to ask their children to do something (51 per cent), while fathers are most likely to tell them to do something (37 per cent). Mothers are also more likely to reason with the child than are fathers. For that matter, mothers use more strategies in getting the child's compliance than do fathers. For all but two of the response categories they showed higher frequencies, while fathers were more limited in their responses and also appeared somewhat more authoritarian.

Comparing white-collar and blue-collar parents in the strategies they use to elicit the child's compliance we find white-collar parents more frequently indicating that they "ask or request" the child as well as explain the reasons for the request when they want him to do something. But blue-collar mothers are not too different from the white-collar respondents in their pattern of responses—they also rely heavily on request and reason with their child. Blue-collar fathers, on the other hand, seem the most limited in the range of their responses to the child and the most authoritarian. "Telling the child" to do something was their most frequent response category (36 per cent) compared to "asking the child" (23 per cent) and "explaining the reasons for the request" (8 per cent).

. . . . On the question of what would the parent do if "your child is playing and accidentally breaks something that you value?" over 50 percent of mothers and fathers indicated that they would not punish the child, but would discuss the problem with him. Slightly more fathers (26 per cent) than mothers (19 per cent) said they would use physical punishment, *e.g.*, spank or slap the child. But the most frequent response of the mothers under this circumstance is to scold or yell at the child (61 per cent), which was a comparatively frequent category for the father as well (45 per cent). Scolding and yelling as well as discussing the situation with the child may be viewed as reprimanding the child for an act that may not be his fault. They represent relatively lenient reactions.

The second circumstance, however, is viewed by parents as a more serious transgression. The question as posed asked: "If your child intentionally disobeys after you have told him to do something what would you do?" Sixty-eight per cent of the fathers and 61 per cent of the mothers said that they would physically punish the child. Another 50 per cent of the parents would punish by restricting the child's privileges (51 per cent of fathers and 59 per cent of mothers). A surprisingly low proportion of parents (2 per cent of fathers and no mothers) said that they would use withdrawal of affection as a means of punishing the child. This is surprising considering the amount of attention this technique has received by scholars in this area, and the extent to which it has been used to describe child discipline practices of American families (see, for example, Bronfenbrenner, 1970; and Green, 1960).

. . . We find further support for the claim that middle-class parents are more verbal in disciplining their children and are more likely to use reason with the child than are lower-class parents. This is especially true of white-collar mothers. For both disciplinary situations they were the most likely of the four groups of respondents to scold and yell at the child (75 per cent and 20 per cent across the two situations). Blue-collar parents were somewhat more likely to use physical punishment in disciplining the child. This difference was more pronounced for situation one in which the offense was unintentional.

But now we might ask, how different are parental responses to the child depending on the circumstances of the child's behavior? Following Kohn's argument we hypothesized that there would be a greater difference in the responses of middle-class parents between situations one and two, which differ in terms of motive for the child's behavior, than there would be for lower-class parents. Our findings . . . give modest support to this hypothesis. Combining the percentage differences between circumstances one and two for the five most common response categories, we find that the differences are greater for white-collar parents than for blue-collar parents. In other words, the responses of white-collar parents are slightly more discriminating with regard to the circumstances of the child's behavior than are those of blue-collar parents. The largest difference score was found in the responses of middle-class mothers (176 percentage points). In general, wives were more discriminating than husbands (which Kohn also found).

Looking at the specific response categories we find that the largest percentage differences for both classes and sexes of parents occurred in the "punish physically," the "discuss problem," and to a lesser extent the "restrict privileges" categories. In the situation where the child accidentally breaks something, parents are much more likely to discuss the event without punishing the child—this is especially true of middle-class mothers. But when the child intentionally disobeys a parent, he is more likely to receive physical punishment or restriction of privileges. Again, these differences are greater for middle-class parents than for lower-class parents.

The differences found between blue-collar and white-collar parents in response to the child's behavior are paralleled by differences between parents of different educational levels. There is a tendency for college-educated wives and their spouses to discuss the problem with the child when his behavior is accidentally disruptive and, in general, to more frequently reason with the child as a strategy of behavior control. Wives with high-school education or less, and their spouses, were more likely to resort to physical punishment and scolding the child under these circumstances.

Comparison of education levels gives even stronger support to Kohn's hypothesis than was the case for occupation, *e.g.*, there is a greater difference between parental responses to the child in situations one and two for college-educated parents than for those of high school education. The highest difference score, for five of the most frequent response categories, is found for college women (summary difference = 197); the lowest is found for husbands of high-school wives (D = 126). The difference is larger for women than men, a difference of 65 points between the summary scores of wives in these two education categories versus a difference of 34 points for husbands.

SUMMARY AND CONCLUSION

Kohn (1969) has proposed that parents in different social classes, by virtue of experiencing different occupational requirements and realities, emphasize different values in the socialization of their children. White-collar parents, he argued, stress the development of *internal* standards of conduct in their children and thus are more likely to discipline the child on the basis of their interpretation of the child's *motives* for a particular act, while blue-collar parents are more likely to emphasize values of conformity to external standards and therefore are more likely to react on the basis of the consequences of the child's behavior.

Our findings give modest support to Kohn's. We predicted and found greater differentiation in the responses of white-collar parents than in those of blue-collar parents between two contexts of the child's behavior differing in one essential respect—the child's intentions or motives. There was a greater difference in the way white-collar parents acted toward the child when he "accidentally breaks something" versus when he "intentionally disobeys," than there was for blue-collar parents. Differences in parents' educational level produced the same results: college-educated parents were more discriminating in their responses depending on the behavioral situation than were parents with high school educations or less.

The differences, however, like Kohn's, were not very great, and we certainly would not conclude from these findings that lower-class parents are insensitive to the circumstances of the child's misbehavior or to his intentions in disciplining him. We do conclude, however, that middle-class parents are more finely attuned to these considerations and probably for the reasons discussed by Kohn.[3]

Our examination of sex and class differences in styles of parental discipline has also shown that mothers more frequently use reason and request in order to get the child to do something, while fathers more often tell the child to do it. In circumstances where the child engages in disruptive behavior or intentionally disobeys the parent, mothers are more likely to be verbal in their response (scolding and yelling at the child) while fathers rely more on physical punishment. Mothers also appear to express a wider range of responses to the child in these situations than do fathers. This was also the pattern of differences between middle- and lower-class parents. Middle-class parents were more prone to verbal reprimands of the child, while lower-class parents were more limited in range of responses and more physical, giving support to previous descriptions of social class differences in parent-child interaction.

FOOTNOTES

[1]When Kohn further analyzed the occupation categories in terms of the three conditions considered conducive to (or restrictive of) the exercise of self-direction in work (*i.e.*, closeness of supervision; dealing with people, data, or things; and complexity of work), he found these characteristics each highly related to differences in value orientations.

[2]Eight situations were specified by Kohn: (1) when the child plays wildly; (2) fights with brothers or sisters; (3) fights with other children; (4) loses his temper; (5) refuses to do what you tell him; (6) steals something; (7) smokes cigarettes; (8) uses language you disapprove of.

[3]It should also be mentioned that Kohn found this relationship between social class and values reflected in child socialization to be extremely stable and relatively invariant—it was only slightly affected by such major

structural variables as race, nationality, religion, size of community of residence, family size, age and sex of child, and it held cross-culturally (U.S. and Turin, Italy). Therefore, it should not be taken lightly or dismissed as insignificant.

REFERENCES

Baumrind, Diana. 1971. "Current patterns of parental authority." Developmental Psychology Monograph Vol. 4, No. 1, Part 2.

Becker, W. C. 1964. "Consequences of different kinds of parental discipline." In M. L. Hoffman and L. W. Hoffman (eds.), Review of Child Development Research. Vol. 1. New York: Russell Sage Foundation.

Bronfenbrenner, Urie. 1958. "Socialization and social class through time and space." In Elaine E. Maccoby, T. M. Newcomb, and E. L. Hartley (eds.), Readings in Social Psychology, New York: Holt.

Gecas, V. 1971. "Parental behavior and dimensions of adolescent self-evaluation." Sociometry 34:466-482.

Hess, Robert D. 1970. "Social class and ethnic influences on socialization." In P. H. Mussen (ed.), Carmichael's Manual of Child Psychology. 3rd Ed. Vol. 2. New York: John Wiley and Sons.

Kohn, Melvin. 1969. Class and Conformity. Homewood, Ill.: Dorsey Press.

Kohn, Melvin. 1963. "Social class and parent-child relationships: an interpretation." American Journal of Sociology 68 (January):471-480.

Reiss, A. J. 1961. Occupations and Social Status. New York: The Free Press.

U.S. Bureau of the Census. 1972. County and City Data Book. Washington: Government Printing Office.

U.S. Bureau of the Census. 1973. 1973 Detailed Census Characteristics: (U.S. Summary). Washington: Government Printing Office.

Wolfenstein, Martha. 1963. "Fun morality: an analysis of recent American child-training literature." Chapter 10 in M. Mead and M. Wolfenstein (ed.), Child in Contemporary Cultures. Chicago: University of Chicago Press.

18

father-infant and mother-infant
interaction in the first year of life

michael e. lamb

Research on infant sociopersonality development has flourished in recent years, stimulated by the formulation and presentation of the ethological theory of Ainsworth (1969, 1972) and Bowlby (1969). Two related deficiencies have become apparent, however: the paucity of normative, observational data, and the lack of research on attachment figures other than mothers (see Lamb 1976e).

The longitudinal project undertaken by Ainsworth and her colleagues (Ainsworth & Bell 1969; Ainsworth, Bell, & Stayton 1969, 1972, 1974; Ainsworth & Wittig 1969; Bell & Ainsworth 1972; Stayton & Ainsworth 1973; Stayton, Ainsworth, & Main 1973; Tracy, Lamb, & Ainsworth, 1976; Blehar & Lieberman, Note 1) has yielded extensive data concerning feeding, physical contact, and early face-to-face interaction, similarities between home and strange-situation behavior, and greeting, separation, and approach behavior, but the focus has been on mothers and nonattachment figures. These investigators have not yet published quantitative data concerning the display of other attachment and affiliative behaviors. The present investigation, therefore, was focused on the display of attachment and affiliative behaviors toward, and the nature of the interaction with, both parents and a relatively unfamiliar investigator.

There is near unanimity among theorists that infants are capable of attachment only after they have developed cognitively to such an extent that they have appreciation of the independent and permanent existence of others (cf. Bell 1970; Piaget 1937/1954; Spitz 1950) and, consequently, most consider that attachment relations begin around 7-8 months of age (Ainsworth 1973; Bowlby 1969; Schaffer 1971; Yarrow 1972). Accordingly, the present study was designed to trace the development of parent-infant attachments in the 6-month period immediately succeeding the emergence of attachment relations.

Though several recent studies have investigated parental preferences, the results have been somewhat inconsistent. One consistent finding has been that American infants do not protest separation from either parent more often—neither at home (Ross, Kagan, Zelazo, & Kotelchuck 1975) nor in structured laboratory settings (Cohen & Campos 1974; Kotelchuck, Zelazo, Kagan, & Spelke 1975; Spelke, Zelazo, Kagan, & Kotelchuck 1973; Kotelchuck, Note 2). Separation and reunion behaviors do, however, reflect preferences for mothers over strangers (e.g., Corter 1973; Stayton et al. 1973), suggesting that these behavioral measures distinguish attachment from nonattachment figures. However, the fact that some studies (e.g., Cohen & Campos 1974) have found that separation protest fails to reflect preferences apparent on other measures implies that this is an insensitive measure. Consequently, it is unwise to interpret the absence of parental preferences in the occurrence of separation protest as a strong indication of "equal attachment" to both parents.

Feldman and Ingham (1975) and Willemsen, Flaherty, Heaton, and Ritchey (1974) found that, in the Ainsworth Strange Situation (Ainsworth & Wittig 1969), infants organized their behavior similarly around whichever parent was with them and showed no preference for either. In contrast, Cohen and Campos (1974) reported that 10–16-month-olds showed significant preferences for their mothers over their fathers. Subsequent studies by Lamb (1976a, 1976f) indicated that the inconsistency between Cohen and Campos's results and those of Feldman and Willemsen resulted from differences in the degree of stress involved and in the procedures employed. Lamb concluded that in stress-free circumstances infants show no preference for either parent in the display of attachment behaviors. In the event of stress, infants intensify the display of attachment behaviors to whichever parent is with them (Feldman & Ingham 1975; Lamb 1976f; Willemsen et al. 1974), though when both parents are available, infants are more likely to seek comfort from their mothers (Lamb 1976a, 1976f).

On both theoretical (Bowlby 1969; Bretherton & Ainsworth 1974) and empirical (Lamb 1976a; Tracy et al. 1976) grounds, it is necessary to distinguish between attachment and affiliative behaviors in research on infant social relations. Affiliative behaviors are those (e.g., smiling, vocalizing) which, while they may be in the service of the attachment behavior system described by Bowlby, are also essential for interaction with friendly nonspecifics to whom the infant is not attached. Preferences in the display of such behaviors are difficult to interpret and tell the investigator little about the infant's enduring relationships or affective preferences. The attachment behaviors, on the other hand, occur more frequently or almost exclusively in interaction with attachment figures. These are behaviors most closely related to physical contact and the desire for it. Preference in the display of these behaviors would indicate that the infant was attached to only one of the persons or was "more attached" to one of them. In the present study, consequently, we should find that, while infants show no preference for either parent in the display of attachment behaviors in the stress-free home environment, they show clear preferences for the parents over the unfamiliar investigator on these measures. Confirmation of this hypothesis, and demonstration that at home, as in structured laboratory situations, infants give evidence of being attached to both parents would have considerable import for theorizing concerning the breadth of the infant social world, which is traditionally depicted as a two-person (mother-infant) system (Bowlby 1969; Freud 1948; Maccoby & Masters 1970).

However, the fact that infants are attached to both parents may be of little significance for sociopersonality development if one relationship is simply redundant. The implicit or explicit assumption of those who urge that attention be focused on father-infant as well as mother-infant relationships (Biller 1974; Lamb 1975; Lynn 1974; Nash 1965) is that these two relationships differ qualitatively, and hence have differential consequences for personality development. Accordingly, one goal of the present investigation was to determine whether mothers and fathers engage in significantly different types of interaction with their infants.

To this end, the focus was placed on all sequences of interaction involving physical contact (holding) or play. Not only do these categories incorporate much of the adult-infant interaction that takes place at this age, but in addition, they are both types of interaction that are stressed by social developmentalists (Ainsworth et al. 1972, 1974; Millar 1968; Ainsworth, Bell, Blehar, & Main, Note 3; Main & Ainsworth, Note 4). Physical contact is particularly important, since, representing as it does an ultimate degree of proximity, this is regarded as the goal of the attachment behavior system. Furthermore, the analysis of play and holding allows the categorization of patterns of dyadic interaction: the nature of the response of one individual is considered in the context of a particular action or initiative on the part of another. It has become a truism in developmental psychology that the monadic measures commonly reported (e.g., rates of display of attachment behaviors) cannot adequately depict the nature of dyadic interaction.

The goals of this study were thus fourfold. First, the aim was to examine the patterns of preferences in the display of attachment and affiliative behaviors. If the infants were attached to both parents, there should be no preference for either parent over the other in the display of attachment behaviors, while validity of the measures would be demonstrated by preferences for both parents over the investigator. Second, the aim was to provide normative data on the interactions which young infants have with their mothers and fathers in the home. The third, intricately related, issue concerned the patterns of interaction with mothers and fathers. Here we expected to find evidence that mother-infant and father-infant interaction differ qualitatively. Finally, the longitudinal design permitted investigation of the development of the parent-infant relationships in the 6-month period immediately succeeding the emergence of attachment relations.

METHOD

Subjects

The subjects were 10 boys, 10 girls, and their parents, recruited from the birth records of the Yale—New Haven Hospital by means of an introductory letter, followed by a telephone call. Forty-six percent of the families contacted agreed to participate and were offered payment for their cooperation. The social status of the families was assessed by means of Hollingshead's (Note 5) two factor index of social position; the mean rating on this scale was 29.3. There were six families (three infants of each sex) in Social Class I (major professionals), two boys and two girls in each of Classes II (lesser professionals) and III (small business owners, white collar workers), and six (three of each sex) in IV (skilled manual laborers). There were no families in Class V (unskilled manual laborers). All the subjects were white. Four of the mothers worked or studied part time—and three of them scheduled these activities so that the fathers could attend to the infants. In all but one of the families, the mother was the primary caretaker. Only four of the fathers regularly took primary responsibility for the child for any length of time. Only one family made regular use of extrafamilial substitute caretakers. Three of the boys and five of the girls were firstborns. Seven boys and three girls were second-borns; two girls were third-borns. In most cases, the siblings were not present during the observations. Nine of the girls, but only five of the boys, were capable of independent locomotion at 7 or 8 months of age. All were mobile in the 12- and 13-month visits.

While the sample was heterogeneous with respect to parental occupation and ordinal position and sex of the infant, it could be described as a representative sample of young, intact, and stable lower- to upper-middle-class families within which parental and marital roles were traditionally allocated.

Procedure

The infants were observed in their homes when both parents were present. Each family was observed when the infant was 7, 8, 12, and 13 months old. Each visit lasted between 1 and 2 hours. For purposes of analysis, the 7- and 8-month visits are considered together as the early series, while the 12- and 13-month visits, thus combined, are called the later series. This procedure was adopted in order to maximize stability and representativeness. On the average, each infant was observed for a total of 153 min in the early series, and 199 min in the later series. The visits were scheduled at the parents' convenience, the only stipulation being that both parents be home. Consequently, most visits were made in the evenings, over weekends, or on days when the parents were not working. Fifteen of the babies were visited regularly on weekends or days off work, while five were visited on weekday evenings. The parents were encouraged to continue with their routines, even if this involved leaving the room to perform chores, though they were asked to remain in the same room as the child most of the time. In a questionnaire completed by the parents after this series of visits, 90% of the parents stated that the investigators were observing the normal interaction between the infant and its parents. Two sets of parents stated that they felt inhibited by the presence of the investigators and were not as affectionate with the infants as they would have been normally. The infants' routines were not disturbed.

All visits were made by the same two persons. One of them, a female assistant referred to as the visitor, attempted to interact with the parents and the child in the same manner as would any visitor to the home. Her purpose was to alleviate the parents' anxieties about being observed and to offer the infant the choice between interaction with the parents or with a responsive and participative stranger. She did not attempt to focus attention on the child. The second person, the male observer, dictated into a tape-recorder a detailed narrative account of the infant's behavior and the contingent behaviors of the other persons present. The observer used a microphone sensitive enough to record his dictation at a level that was barely audible and thus minimally obtrusive. He detailed the infant's response to attempts by the adults to initiate interaction and took special care to record each instance of any of the following social behaviors being directed to one of the persons present: smiling at, vocalizing to, laughing or giggling in interaction with, touching, requesting to be picked up by, fussing to, or reaching to the adult. In the later series, the observer noted each time the infant offered, pointed out, or showed something to one of the adults. These instances of proferring did not occur in the early series. The observer continually reported the distance between the child and the other four persons (mother, father, visitor, observer) and noted when the infant was being held by one of them. When the infants were being held, the observer noted whether there was any positive (reflected by smiling, vocalizing, or giggling, or by jiggling or bouncing happily) or negative (reflected by fussing or stiffening) response. The adult behaviors recorded were vocalizations to the infant (later series only) and instances of playing with or holding the infants. In the two last-mentioned categories, the parent and infant behaviors were described in sufficient detail to permit analysis of the context, type of interaction, and infant affective response. Further details are given in the section headed Play and Physical Contact Interaction. In all cases, the observer's explicit function was to detail the behavior of the participants; categorization and coding judgments were subsequently based on the dictated narratives. While the observer was dictating, a timer was automatically marking on the tape the passage of each 15-sec period. The detailed accounts were subsequently transcribed by a typist, and the transcripts were thoroughly checked against the tapes for their accuracy before being analyzed.

Attachment and affiliative behaviors. The data reported in the first section of the Results were derived from those portions of the visits when the visitor, observer, mother, and father were all present in the same room as the child. With this restriction applied, each infant was observed for a mean of 122 min in the early series and 158 min in the later series. One of three trained coders tabulated each instance of the attachment and affiliative behaviors, noting to whom the behavior was directed. In addition, in each 15-sec unit it was noted whether the child was within proximity (3 feet) of any of the persons—being within proximity was considered an attachment behavior.

Smiling, vocalizing, looking, laughing, and proferring (later series only) are referred to as the affiliative behaviors. The other child behavior measures (proximity, touching, approaching, seeking to be held, fussing, and reaching) are collectively considered the attachment behaviors.

The definitions employed in the observations and in the coding are identical to those provided by Lamb (1976b, 1976f) to which the reader is referred for further details.

In the two later visits, the observer recorded and the coders tabulated instances of the adults speaking to the child.[1] These instances of adult vocalization ranged from whole sentences to single word utterances. The frequency of adult vocalization was considered to be a reliably observable index of the degree of adult activity in interaction with the infant. This index was used as a covariate in some of the subsequent analyses.

With two exceptions, all measures were frequency counts—that is, the behaviors were recorded once each time they occurred. Both proximity and touching were duration measures. Figures in these categories refer to the number of 15-sec units over which the proximity or touching extended.

Play and physical contact interaction. For purpose of the analyses reported in the second and third sections of the Results, one of three trained coders searched the transcripts for each occurrence of physical contact or play with the mother, father, or visitor. "Physical contact" was defined as the contact implicit in the infant being held—the infant had to be raised off the ground and supported by the adult. "Play" interactions were difficult to define concisely. They were the occasions when the adult engaged in interaction with the infant or attempted to stimulate the infant, other than by simply vocalizing, smiling, or engaging in caretaking activities. Since episodes of both play and physical contact often extended across brief separations from the other parent, or began when one parent was not present, it was decided that the analysis should be based on the entire transcripts, rather than solely on those periods when both parents were present throughout the interaction.

Having defined the instances of physical contact, the coder then noted: (*a*) by whom the infant was held; (*b*) the duration of the hold, measured by the number of 15-sec units over which the hold extended; (*c*) the nature of the infant's response; (*d*) the purpose of the hold.

The nature of the infant's response was rated on a seven-point scale with each point behaviorally defined.[2] The points were as follows: (1) very negative (cry, fuss, or squirm to be put down); (2) negative (stiffen); (3) neutral (no observable positive or negative response); (4) content (sink in, cuddle); (5) mildly positive (smile, vocalize, or stop fussing); (6) positive (scramble, squeal with delight); (7) very positive (laugh, jiggle, or bounce). If the response was mixed (both positive and negative), the two extreme scores were averaged. In fact, such mixed responses were rarely observed. Only 7% of the holds were so coded.

The purpose of the hold was classified as being either for *caretaking* (transport to or from changing, feeding, or bathing, being held for feeding, etc.); *discipline/control* (carrying the infant from forbidden activities); *play* (picking up the infant in order to engage it in play); *soothing* (picking up the infant when it is distressed for the purpose of comforting it); *affection* (picking up the infant simply to kiss, cuddle, or hug, etc.); and a residual category, *other* (all holds that could not be categorized in any of the previous five categories; many of these holds occurred because the babies simply wanted to be held).

Having defined each instance of play, the coder then noted: (*a*) with whom the interaction took place; (*b*) the duration of the play episode; (*c*) the nature of the infant's response; (*d*) the type of play activity; (*e*) who initiated the play.

The nature of the infant's response was rated on a seven-point scale, with each point behaviorally defined (see n. 2). The scale was as follows: (1) very negative (fuss, cry); (2) negative (fuss-face); (3) neutral (no positive or negative response); (4) content (happy face, participation in the play); (5) mildly positive (smile, vocalize); (6) positive (squeal, protest termination); (7) highly positive (laugh, jiggle, or bounce). If the response was mixed (both positive and negative), the two extreme scores were averaged. Only 2% of the play bouts were so coded.

The play activity was classified as one of the following types: *conventional* (peek-a-boo, pat-a-cake, so-big); *physical* (rough and tumble and wrestle type, usually involving holding the infant off the ground); *minor physical* (tickling, pretending to nibble the infant; unlike physical games, these typically did not involve holding the infant); *toy-mediated* (all play in which a toy or other physical object was used to mediate the interaction); and *idiosyncratic* (all those activities that could not be classified into the previous categories).

Interobserver Reliability

It was difficult to assess the reliability of the observations made by the observer, since the use of two observers was deemed likely to disrupt the natural flow of interaction in most families.

Consequently, the reliability was computed by recruiting an additional group of infants who were observed solely for the purpose of establishing the reliability of the observer's dictation, as well as by arranging for additional visits to the homes of several of the infants in the study. Seven visits were made to the home of different 7–13-month-olds. In addition, three visits were made to the homes of 15- and 19-month-olds; since the reliability on these visits was comparable, all visits are considered together for the purposes of exposition. Both of the coding assistants were involved in observer reliability trials, and the average coefficients of agreement were similar for both.

On these visits, the observer and an assistant dictated parallel but independent accounts of the child's behavior and its interaction with the parents and the visitor. The observers tried to position themselves as inconspicuously as possible and attempted to be far enough removed from one another so as not to overhear the other's dictation. This meant that their perspectives were usually different, increasing the probability of disagreement. The transcripts were then coded in the manner described above,[3] and the results obtained from analysis of the two transcripts were compared.

Attachment and affiliative behaviors. Interobserver reliability was determined by comparing the total frequency of occurrence of each behavior in each visit to each adult. Coefficients were computed to express the proportion of the total number of occurrences of each behavior reported by one observer that were correctly reported by the other observer. These coefficients were found to provide more conservative estimates of degree of agreement than did product-moment or rank-order correlations. The mean level of agreement was .81, and the median was .80 (range .75 [smiling, looking] to .93 [proximity]). Degree of reliability was consistent across persons, visits, and observers.

Play and physical contact behaviors. The two transcripts of each visit were independently coded and then compared with one another. Degree of reliability was determined by computing the proportion of the total number of episodes, the average duration, and the average responses within each category on which there was complete agreement. In all categories, and for all adults, interobserver agreement exceeded .85. There was near-complete agreement in identifying the initiator.

Another estimate of reliability is available from a related study (Lamb 1976f) involving observations of adult-infant interaction in a laboratory situation. Interobserver agreement in the occurrence of the attachment and affiliative behaviors was about .90 on all measures except one when coefficients were computed in the manner described above.

In sum, assessments of observer reliability in different situations consistently demonstrated that the behaviors and patterns of interaction considered in the present investigation could be observed and recorded with sufficient reliability to permit confidence in the data base.

Intercoder Reliability

All of the transcripts were coded by one of three persons. One of the coders was the author and main observer; the other two were involved in the observer reliability tests, since they were trained on the categories and behavioral definitions. They were unaware of the author's hypotheses throughout the time they were involved in either coding or observation.

Coefficients of intercoder reliability were computed in the same way as interobserver reliability coefficients. All coders trained on these and similar transcripts until agreement averaging .90 across all categories was achieved. The coefficients of agreement were above .85 in all categories. Once this criterial level was attained, coding of the transcripts for the study began. During the course of coding, transcripts were periodically recoded in this way. The median coefficient of agreement remained at .89, while coefficients for the individual categories were all greater than .85. With respect to the play and physical contact interaction, the coefficients of interrater agreement were above .85 in all categories.

Finally, multi- and univariate analyses of variance were computed to determine whether there was any coder effect, or any coder X adult interaction. None even approached significance.

In all cases, the reliability of the coding and of the observations was equivalent for the mother-, father-, and visitor-infant interaction.

RESULTS

Attachment and Affiliative Behaviors

For the purpose of all analyses reported in this section, the scores for each infant were converted to rates per minute of observation. This equalized the contribution of each infant to the group data and normalized the distribution of scores so that transformations were not necessary.

A comparison of the data obtained in the early series (7 and 8 months) showed no significant changes over time, either in the preferences or in the rate of display of the attachment and affiliative behaviors to any of the adults. Consequently, the data from the two visits were combined for the purposes of analysis. The same was true of the data from the 12- and 13-month observations. Likewise, preliminary analyses revealed no significant sex or social class differences. Consequently, in the analyses reported below the subjects were collapsed across these two factors. Finally, comparison of the infants who were, with those who were not, mobile in the early series revealed no significant differences between these groups, which were therefore combined for the analysis. . . .

A repeated measures age X adult multivariate analysis of variance (MANOVA)—using as variables the rates of smiling, vocalizing, looking, laughing, touching, fussing, reaching, seeking to be held, approaching, and proximity to all three persons in both the early and late series—was computed to assess whether there was a consistent preference for any person, and determine whether there were significant age effects, or age X adult interactions. The test of significance employed here, as in the other MANOVAs reported below, was the Wilk's lambda criterion. The approximate F was derived using Rao's approximation (Harris 1975).

The MANOVA indicated significant age ($p < .001$) and adult ($p < .001, p < .002$) effects, and a significant age X adult interaction ($p < .05$; second root N.S.).

The age effect. There were significant changes with age in the occurrence of both attachment and affiliative behaviors to all three persons (p's $< .001$). Inspection of [data] suggests that the older infants were significantly more likely to direct most behaviors to all adults than when they were younger. The most notable exceptions were that they were less likely to be close to any person when they were older, and that they smiled less often to their mothers and to the visitor.

The adult effect. Since the initial MANOVA indicated a significant adult effect ($p < .001, p < .002$), subsequent analyses were computed to compare the mothers with the fathers, the fathers with the visitor, and the mothers with the visitor. MANOVAs were computed to determine preferences using all behavioral measures and then using the attachment and affiliative behaviors separately. . . . Inspection of [data] reveals clear preferences for the parents over the visitor on the attachment behavior measures at both ages. When the data from both series were combined, however, neither the multivariate test nor any of the univariate tests showed a preference for either parent over the other on these measures. On the other hand, affiliative behaviors were far more likely to be directed to the fathers than to the mothers, while preferences for the parents over the visitor on these measures were inconsistent: though the fathers were preferred to the visitor, the infants directed more affiliative behaviors to her than to their mothers.

. . . . In general, the same preference patterns emerge for the two age points as emerged overall. However, the mother-father comparison on the attachment behavior measures in the early series produced somewhat ambiguous and misleading results. The multivariate test showed a significant ($p < .05$) preference for the fathers, though only one of the univariate tests even approached significance (reaching, $p < .10$). The standardized discriminant function coefficients in this analysis were such as to weight most heavily reaching—a variable showing preference for the fathers—while weighting negatively requests to be picked up and proximity—two measures showing nonsignificant preferences for the mothers. The resulting canonical variable correlated most highly with reaching. Unfortunately, the measures cannot be considered equally adequate indices of a desire for proximity or contact. Reaching is a more equivocal index of proximity seeking than wishing to be picked up, fussing, or touching—none of which showed significant preferences for either parent. Consequently, it seems misleading to attribute psychological significance to the statistical preference for the fathers. It is more parsimonious to conclude simply that infants are attached to both parents as early as 7 months of age. The data demonstrate quite clearly that the infants are attached to both parents but not to the visitor. They are quite willing, though, to engage in extensive affiliative interaction with the visitor, choosing to interact with her more often than with their mothers.

In the later series, an index of adult activity in interaction with the infant was obtained, namely, the frequency with which the adults vocalized to the infants. Both parents vocalized to the infants far more often than the visitor (p's $<$ .001), though neither spoke more often than the other. Since it is likely that the amount of interaction an infant has with an adult is dependent, at least in part, on the responsiveness and activity of the adult, the analyses were recomputed using the amount that the adult vocalized to the child as a covariate.

Use of the covariate had the effect of reducing the levels of significance of all preferences for the parents over the visitor, although most of the measures which showed preferences without the covariate showed similar preferences when it was employed. The notable exception was that use of the covariate removed all but one of the preferences for fathers in the display of affiliative behaviors, and the multivariate statistics showed no preference for either parent over the visitor on these measures. Thus when the relative activity of the adults is taken into account, preferences for parents over the visitor in the display of affiliative behaviors are equivocal. Regardless of their activity, however, there are significant preferences for the parents over the visitor in the occurrence of attachment behaviors (mother $>$ visitor, $p <$ .001; father $>$ visitor, $p <$ .05 with covariate), and no preference for either parent over the other on these measures (p's $>$ .7).

The age $\times$ adult interaction. This interaction was significant overall, as well as in two of the contrast comparisons. In the father-visitor comparison, there was a significant ($p <$ .05) multivariate interaction effect in the occurrence of attachment but not of affiliative behaviors. In the mother-visitor comparison, the interaction in the occurrence of attachment behaviors approached significance ($p <$ .10), though again, there was no significant interaction on the affiliative behavior measures. In the mother-father comparison, however, neither of the interactions was significant. The significant interactions reflected the fact that the degree of preference for either parent over the visitor, as expressed on the attachment behavior measures, increased with age. As the infants grew older, therefore, they were increasingly likely to restrict attachment behaviors to interaction with their parents only, though the degree of affiliative interaction was not similarly affected.

Play Interaction

All comparisons in this section and the next were performed using matched t tests.

Analyses were computed to determine whether there were significant differences in the types of play within the mother-, father-, and visitor-infant dyads, when the data from the four visits were combined. . . . They indicate that, while there are few differences between the types of mother-infant and father-infant play, there are rather substantial differences between parent-infant and visitor-infant play. Similar patterns emerged when the two series were considered separately.

The average response to play with the fathers was significantly more positive than to play with the mothers ($p <$ .001). The response to the fathers was more positive even when the analyses were recomputed to exclude play bouts to which the response was either negative (coded as 1 or 2) or mixed. Thus it was not that the babies responded negatively to their mothers' play; rather, the fathers were more likely to elicit the more highly positive responses. The infants also responded far more positively to play with their fathers than with the visitor ($p <$ .001). There was only a tendency for the response to the mothers to be more positive than the response to the visitor ($p <$ .10). All play in the early series and 80% of the play bouts in the later series were initiated by the adult.

[Regarding] . . . the changes that occurred in the types of play observed in the early and later series, [data show] . . . that, for mothers, fathers, and the visitor, there were many more instances of play in the later series, though this may be at least partially explained by the fact that the infants were observed for longer in the later series, so there were more opportunities for play to occur. The proportion of play that was toy-mediated increased dramatically for both parents, and to a lesser extent for the visitor, as the infants grew older. The proportion of play that involved physical stimulation decreased for all three persons, while idiosyncratic and minor physical play were also less frequent components of father-infant interaction.

Physical Contact Interaction

Analyses were computed to determine whether there were significant differences in the reasons why the parents picked up the infants. Unfortunately, the visitor held the infants so rarely that comparable analyses involving her were not possible. Both parents held the babies far more than did the visitors (p's < .001) and for far longer (p's < .001).

The analyses revealed that mothers and fathers held their babies for very different reasons. The fathers were far more likely to hold the babies simply to play with them (p < .001), while the mothers were far more likely to hold them for caretaking purposes (p < .001). Similar patterns emerged when the early and later series were considered separately. The different purposes may well explain why the average response to being held by the fathers was significantly more positive than the average response to the mothers (p < .001). Again, the difference remained even when the analysis excluded all holds to which the response was mixed or negative.

. . . . Infants were picked up more often by both parents, particularly fathers, in the later series, though this may be partially artifactual: they were observed longer in the later series. Further, the amount of time they were held by the two parents did not change significantly.

As the infants grew older, a predictable reduction in the proportion of the holds needed for caretaking and soothing occurred. The improved locomotor competence of the older infants allowed them more often to investigate forbidden areas from which they had to be retrieved—hence the trend toward more frequent discipline/control holds in the later series.

It should be noted that changes in the amount of time (duration) accounted for by each category were fewer, and where significant changes occurred, they were less dramatic, though the changes were always in the same direction.

DISCUSSION

These results yield information relevant to all of the issues raised in the Introduction. Although the attachment behavior measures clearly differentiated between attachment and nonattachment figures, there was no preference for either parent over the other apparent on these measures. The absence of preferences was evident even when differences in the level of adult activity were taken into account by covariation procedures. This implies that, in the 6-month period immediately succeeding the time when attachment relations are presumed to emerge, infants are attached to both parents. Other investigations have shown that 1-year-olds do, in fact, show preferences for their mothers in more stressful situations (Cohen & Campos 1974; Lamb 1976f). Without contesting this conclusion, which is consistent with Bowlby's (1969) notion of monotropy, I would argue that this demonstration of preference should not obscure the fact that infants are attached to both parents and that research is needed on the nature and consequences of both relationships. Indeed, it is clear that the circumstances in which preferences are demonstrated are not yet understood: the results of the present study showed that infants fussed to their fathers as often as to their mothers and were soothed by them in times of distress quite as often as by their mothers. Further research is needed to identify the types or degrees of stress which cause infants to turn to their mothers and the situations in which this occurs. All relevant data have been gathered in structured laboratory settings, and this may be a critical parameter.

The changes over time in the display of attachment and affiliative behaviors were consistent for all three adults, but only partially supported Lewis's "transformational" hypothesis, which suggests that, with age, the "distal" mode (i.e., vocalizing, looking) comes to replace the "proximal" mode (i.e., touching, being near) (Lewis & Weinraub 1974; Lewis & Ban, Note 6). The developments observed in the present study may be more simply explained: changes in the frequency of vocalizing and proximity may reflect, respectively, improved communicative and locomotor competence, while the increases in the frequency of most other attachment behaviors reflect the fact that responsibility for maintenance of proximity and contact shifts with age from adult to infant (Hinde & Atkinson 1970; Hinde & Spencer-Booth 1967).

The age X adult interaction effects also have important developmental implications. The interactions suggested that, over the 6-month period, the degree of preference for the parents over the visitor in the display of attachment behaviors widened. There was thus an increasing focalization of these behaviors on both parents, presumably as the attachment relationships developed. Evidence gathered in other studies suggests that around 1 year of age the increased differentiation of the parents from strangers on attachment behavior measures parallels the emergence of a hierarchy of attachment figures, such that, under stress, 1-year-olds turn to their mothers preferentially (Lamb 1976f). This does not happen in 8-month-olds (Lamb 1976d) or in 24-month-olds (Lamb 1976c), while the effect is considerably muted in 18-month-olds (Lamb 1976a). It appears, in sum, that the period from 7 to 13 months of age is marked by the emergence and consolidation of attachment relations, coupled with the appearance of a demonstrable hierarchy among attachment figures which fades over the next year, presumably as the father-infant relationship strengthens (Schaffer & Emerson 1964; Kotelchuck, Note 2).

In addition, this study provided evidence to support the hypothesis that the mother-infant and father-infant relationships involve different kinds of experiences for the infants. Analysis of the physical contact interaction showed that the mothers most often held the babies to perform caretaking functions, while the fathers most often held the babies to play with them. These patterns were similar in both the early and later series. It is of interest that, while the older infants were held proportionately less often by their mothers for caretaking, there was no corresponding increase in the frequency of holding for play.

On the other hand, a detailed analysis of the play interaction revealed few differences between father-infant and mother-infant play. Since others have argued that differences between mother- and father-child play do exist (Burlingham 1973; Lynn 1974), we must conclude either that the differences were not captured by the categories used in the present analysis, or that differences may be evident only when parents are alone with their children, but not when they are both present, as in this study. Radin (1976), for example, has argued that fathers may behave differently in the presence or absence of their wives, and Parke and O'Leary (1975) reported that fathers were more active in interaction with their neonates when their wives were present. In contrast, I have found that, in 12-, 18-, and 24-month-olds, both parents interact more with their infants when alone with them than when both parents are present, while infants, too, are more active in the dyadic than in the triadic situation (Lamb 1976a, 1976f, 1977; Lamb, Note 7).

On the basis of presently available evidence, it is possible to conclude that infants are attached to both parents from the beginning of attachment relations and that, in at least one important mode, the nature of mother-infant and father-infant interaction differs qualitatively and consistently. Perhaps, then, fathers are not simply occasional mother substitutes, as most have assumed (Bowlby 1969; Corter 1974; cf. Lamb 1975), for they interact with their infants in a unique and qualitatively differentiable manner. The fact that mothers and fathers consistently engage their infants in different types of interaction suggests that infants may be able to distinguish the two parents on behavioral as well as perceptual criteria. Further, inasmuch as their experiences with the two parents differ, it is plausible to argue that infants develop different expectations and learn different behavior patterns from each parent and thus that the two relationships have differential consequences for socio-personality development. Developmental psychologists have long believed (see Mussen 1967) that mothers and fathers play different roles in the socialization of older children, and the data indicate that these differential roles may be continuous from early infancy. Yogman, Tronick, Brazelton, Als, and Wise (Note 8) have reported that the nature of father-infant and mother-infant interaction differs in infants as young as 2 months of age. It is not possible at this stage, however, to show differential cause-effect relationships. Further research is needed to specify the differences between mother- and father-infant interaction, and to investigate the association between these patterns and the later personality of the child. Only when the nature of parent-child interaction is clearly described will it be possible to identify the particular characteristics of interaction with the dyads or triad that are of importance for socialization and personality development. Clearly, in our future researches, we must consider the multiplicity of potential social influences and avoid reverting to the previously common practice of considering mothers as the sole important influences on infant sociopersonality development.

FOOTNOTES

[1] In the early series, adult vocalizations were reported by the observer only when they were in response to a bid by the infant, or elicited an infant response. Thus many instances of adult vocalization were not recorded—for example, occasions when the infant ignored the adult. The new procedure (reporting all adult vocalizations, regardless of their influence on the infant) was adopted for the later series when it became apparent that the earlier practice yielded data of limited usefulness. Consequently, adult vocalizations were coded and analyzed only in the later series.

[2] Like Brazelton (Brazelton, Tronick, Adamson, Als, & Wise 1975), we rated the nature of the baby's response on a continuum. However, since some researchers (e.g., Sroufe, Waters, & Matas 1974) have criticized the practice of averaging over positive and negative responses, analyses comparing responses to different persons were computed both with and without the negative responses (1, 2) included.

[3] These transcripts were not coded by the individual who made the observation so as to avoid contamination of the reliability estimates.

REFERENCE NOTES

1. Blehar, M. C., & Lieberman, A. E. Individual differences in infants' facial interaction with mother and stranger as related to later quality of attachment. Paper presented at the meeting of the Society for Research in Child Development, Denver, April 1975.
2. Kotelchuck, M. The nature of the child's tie to his father. Unpublished doctoral dissertation, Harvard University, 1972.
3. Ainsworth, M. D.; Bell, S. M.; Blehar, M. C.; & Main, M. B. Physical contact: a study of infant responsiveness and its relation to maternal handling. Paper presented at the meeting of the Society for Research in Child Development, Minneapolis, April 1971.
4. Main, M. B., & Ainsworth, M. D. Physical contact as signal of maturity. Manuscript in preparation, 1976.
5. Hollingshead, A. B. The two factor index of social position. Unpublished manuscript, 1957. (Available from the author, Department of Sociology, Yale University, New Haven, Connecticut 06520.)
6. Lewis, M., & Ban, P. Stability of attachment behavior: a transformational analysis. Paper presented at the meeting of the Society for Research in Child Development, Minneapolis, April 1971.
7. Lamb, M. E. The development of mother-infant and father-infant attachments in the second year of life. Unpublished manuscript, 1977.
8. Yogman, M.; Tronick, E.; Brazelton, T. B.; Als, H.; & Wise, S. Development of infant social interaction with fathers. Paper presented at the meeting of the Eastern Psychological Association, New York, April 1976.

REFERENCES

Ainsworth, M. D. Object relations, dependency, and attachment: a theoretical review of the infant-mother relationship. *Child Development,* 1969, 40, 969-1025.

Ainsworth, M. D. Attachment and dependency: a comparison. In J. L. Gewirtz (Ed.), *Attachment and dependency.* Washington, D. C.: Winston, 1972.

Ainsworth, M. D. The development of infant-mother attachment. In B. M. Caldwell & H. N. Ricciuti (Eds.), *Review of child development research 3.* Chicago: University of Chicago Press, 1973.

Ainsworth, M. D., & Bell, S. M. Some contemporary patterns of mother-infant interaction in the feeding situation. In J. A. Ambrose (Ed.), *Stimulation in early infancy.* London: Academic Press, 1969.

Ainsworth, M. D.; Bell, S. M.; & Stayton, D. J. Individual differences in strange situation behavior of one-year-olds. In H. R. Schaffer (Ed.), *The origins of human social relations.* London: Academic Press, 1969.

Ainsworth, M. D.; Bell, S. M.; & Stayton, D. J. Individual differences in the development of some attachment behaviors. *Merrill-Palmer Quarterly,* 1972, 18, 123-143.

Ainsworth, M. D.; Bell, S. M.; & Stayton, D. J. Infant-mother attachment and social development: socialization as a product of reciprocal responsiveness to signals. In M. P. M. Richards (Ed.), *The integration of a child into a social world.* Cambridge: Cambridge University Press, 1974.

Ainsworth, M. D., & Wittig, B. A. Attachment and exploratory behavior of one-year-olds in a strange situation. In B. M. Foss (Ed.), *Determinants of infant behaviour IV.* London: Methuen, 1969.

Bell, S. M. The development of the concept of the object as related to infant-mother attachment. *Child Development,* 1970, 41, 291-311.

Bell, S. M., & Ainsworth, M. D. Infant crying and maternal responsiveness. *Child Development*, 1972, 43, 1171-1190.

Biller, H. B. *Paternal deprivation: family, school, sexuality and society.* Lexington, Mass.: Heath, 1974.

Bowlby, J. *Attachment and loss.* Vol. 1. *Attachment.* New York: Basic, 1969.

Brazelton, T. B.; Tronick, E.; Adamson, L.; Als, H.; & Wise, S. Early mother-infant reciprocity. In *CIBA Foundation Symposium 33: Parent-infant interaction.* Amsterdam: Elsevier, 1975.

Bretherton, I., & Ainsworth, M. D. Responses of one-year-olds to a stranger in a strange situation. In M. Lewis & L. A. Rosenblum (Eds.), *The origins of fear.* New York: Wiley, 1974.

Burlingham, D. The preoedipal infant-father relationship. *Psychoanalytic Study of the Child*, 1973, 28, 23-47.

Cohen, L. J., & Campos, J. J. Father, mother, and stranger as elicitors of attachment behaviors in infancy. *Developmental Psychology*, 1974, 10, 146-154.

Corter, C. M. A comparison of the mother's and a stranger's control over the behavior of infants. *Child Development*, 1973, 44, 705-713.

Corter, C. M. Infant attachments. In B. M. Foss (Ed.), *New perspectives in child development.* Harmondsworth: Penguin, 1974.

Feldman, S. S., & Ingham, M. E. Attachment behavior: a validation study in two age groups. *Child Development*, 1975, 46, 319-330.

Freud, S. *An outline of psychoanalysis.* New York: Norton, 1948.

Harris, R. J. *A primer of multivariate statistics.* New York: Academic Press, 1975.

Hinde, R. A., & Atkinson, S. Assessing the role of social partners in maintaining mutual proximity as exemplified by mother-infant relations in rhesus monkeys. *Animal Behaviour*, 1970, 18, 169-176.

Hinde, R. A., & Spencer-Booth, Y. The behaviour of socially living rhesus monkeys in their first two and a half years. *Animal Behaviour*, 1967, 15, 169-196.

Kotelchuck, M.; Zelazo, P.; Kagan, J.; & Spelke, E. Infant reactions to parental separations when left with familiar and unfamiliar adults. *Journal of Genetic Psychology*, 1975, 126, 255-262.

Lamb, M. E. Fathers: forgotten contributors to child development. *Human Development*, 1975, 18, 245-266.

Lamb, M. E. Effects of stress and cohort on mother- and father-infant interaction. *Development Psychology*, 1976, 12, 435-443.

Lamb, M. E. Interactions between eight-month-old children and their fathers and mothers. In M. E. Lamb (Ed.), *The role of the father in child development.* New York: Wiley, 1976. (b)

Lamb, M. E. Interactions between two-year-olds and their mothers and fathers. *Psychological Reports*, 1976, 38, 447-450. (c)

Lamb, M. E. Parent-infant interaction in eight-month-olds. *Child Psychiatry and Human Development*, 1976, 7, 56-63. (d)

Lamb, M. E. The role of the father: an overview. In M. E. Lamb (Ed.), *The role of the father in child development.* New York: Wiley, 1976. (e)

Lamb, M. E. Twelve-month-olds and their parents: interactions in a laboratory playroom. *Developmental Psychology*, 1976, 12, 237-244. (f)

Lamb, M. E. Infant social cognition and "second-order" effects. *Infant Behavior and Development*, 1977, 1, in press.

Lewis, M., & Weinraub, M. Sex of parent X sex of child: socioemotional development. In R. Richart, R. Friedman, & R. Vande Wiele (Eds.), *Sex differences in behavior.* New York: Wiley, 1974.

Lynn, D. B. *The father: his role in child development.* Monterey: Brooks/Cole, 1974.

Maccoby, E. E., & Masters, J. C. Attachment and dependency. In P. H. Mussen (Ed.), *Carmichael's manual of child psychology* (3d ed., vol. 2). New York: Wiley, 1970.

Millar, S. *The psychology of play.* Harmondsworth: Penguin, 1968.

Mussen, P. H. Early socialization: learning and identification. In T. M. Newcomb (Ed.), *New directions in psychology III.* New York: Holt, Rinehart & Winston, 1967.

Nash, J. The father in contemporary culture and current psychological literature. *Child Development*, 1965, 36, 261-297.

Parke, R. D., & O'Leary, S. Father-mother-infant interaction in the newborn period: some findings, some observations, and some unresolved issues. In K. Riegel & J. Meacham (Eds.), *The developing individual in a changing world.* Vol. 2. *Social and environmental issues.* The Hague: Mouton, 1975.

Piaget, J. *The construction of reality in the child.* New York: Basic, 1954. (Originally published 1937.)

Radin, N. The father and academic, cognitive, and intellective development. In M. E. Lamb (Ed.), *The role of the father in child development.* New York: Wiley, 1976.

Ross, G.; Kagan, J.; Zelazo, P.; & Kotelchuck, M. Separation protest in infants in home and laboratory. *Developmental Psychology*, 1975, 11, 256-257.

Schaffer, H. R. *The growth of sociability.* Harmondsworth: Penguin, 1971.

Schaffer, H. R., & Emerson, P. E. The development of social attachments in infancy. *Monographs of the Society for Research in Child Development*, 1964, 29 (3, Serial No. 94).

Spelke, E.; Zelazo, P.; Kagan, J.; & Kotelchuck, M. Father interaction and separation protest. *Developmental Psychology*, 1973, 9, 83-90.

Spitz, R. A. Possible infantile precursors of psychopathology. *American Journal of Orthopsychiatry*, 1950, 20, 240-248.

Sroufe, A.; Waters, E. C.; & Matas, L. Contextual determinants of infant affective response. In M. Lewis & L. A. Rosenblum (Eds.), *The origins of fear.* New York: Wiley, 1974.

Stayton, D. J., & Ainsworth, M. D. Individual differences in infant responses to brief everyday separations as related to other infant and maternal behaviors. *Developmental Psychology,* 1973, 9, 226-235.

Stayton, D. J.; Ainsworth, M. D.; & Main, M. Development of separation behavior in the first year of life: protest, following, and greeting. *Developmental Psychology,* 1973, 9, 213-225.

Tracy, R. L.; Lamb, M. E.; & Ainsworth, M. D. Infant approach behavior as related to attachment. *Child Development,* 1976, 47, 571-578.

Willemsen, E.; Flaherty, D.; Heaton, C.; & Ritchey, D. Attachment behavior of one-year-olds as a function of mother vs father, sex of child, session, and toys. *Genetic Psychology Monographs,* 1974, 90, 305-324.

Yarrow, L. J. Attachment and dependency: a developmental perspective. In J. L. Gewirtz (Ed.), *Attachment and dependency.* Washington, D.C.: Winston, 1972.

19   structural problems of the one-parent family

paul glasser

elizabeth navarre

INTRODUCTION

Recent concern about the problems of people who are poor has led to renewed interest in the sources of such difficulties. While these are manifold and complexly related to each other, emphasis has been placed upon the opportunity structure and the socialization process found among lower socio-economic groups. Relatively little attention has been paid to family structure, which serves as an important intervening variable between these two considerations. This seems to be a significant omission in view of the major change in the structure of family life in the United States during this century, and the large number of one-parent families classified as poor. The consequences of the latter structural arrangements for family members, parents and children, and for society, is the focus of this paper.

One-parent families are far more apt to be poor than other families. This is true for one-fourth of those headed by a woman. Chilman and Sussman summarize that data in the following way:

> About ten percent of the children in the United States are living with only one parent, usually the mother. Nonwhite children are much more likely to live in such circumstances, with one-third of them living in one-parent families. Two-and-a-quarter million families in the United States today are composed of a mother and her children. They represent only one-twelfth of all families with children but make up more than a fourth of all that are classed as poor. . . .
>
> Despite the resulting economic disadvantages, among both white and nonwhite families there is a growing number headed only by a mother. By 1960 the total was 7½ percent of all families with own children rather than the 6 percent of ten years earlier. By March 1962 the mother-child families represented 8½ percent of all families with own children (4, p. 393).

When these demographic findings are seen in the context of the relative isolation of the nuclear family in the United States today, the structural consequences of the one-parent group takes on added meaning. It may be seen as the culmination of the contraction of the effective kin group.

> This "isolation" is manifested in the fact that the members of the nuclear family, consisting of parents and their still dependent children, ordinarily occupy a separate dwelling not shared with members of the family of orientation. . . . It is, of course, not

Reprinted, by permission, from *Journal of Social Issues*, 1965, *21*, 98-109. Copyright ©1965 by The Society for the Psychological Study of Social Issues.

uncommon to find a (member of the family of orientation) residing with the family, but this is both statistically secondary, and it is clearly not felt to be the "normal arrangement" (9, p. 10).

While families maintain social contact with grown children and with siblings, lines of responsibility outside of the nuclear group are neither clear nor binding, and obligations among extended kin are often seen as limited and weak. Even when affectional ties among extended family members are strong, their spatial mobility in contemporary society isolates the nuclear group geographically, and increases the difficulty of giving aid in personal service among them (2, 6).

Associated with the weakening of the extended kinship structure has been the loss of some social functions of the family and the lessened import of others. Nonetheless, reproduction, physical maintenance, placement or status, and socialization are still considered significant social functions of the modern American family although they often have to be buttressed by other institutions in the community. At the same time, however, the personal functions of the family including affection, security, guidance and sexual gratification have been heightened and highlighted (3, 9). These functions are closely and complexly related to each other but can serve as foci for analysis of the consequences of family structure. In the one-parent family neither reproduction nor sexual gratification can be carried out within the confines of the nuclear group itself. But more importantly, the other personal and social functions are drastically affected also, and it is to these that this paper will give its attention. A few of the implications for social policy and practice will be mentioned at the end.

While it is recognized that all individuals have some contact with others outside the nuclear group, for purposes of analytic clarity this paper will confine itself to a discussion of the relationships among nuclear family members primarily. Two factors will be the foci of much of the content. The age difference between parent and children is central to the analysis. Although it is understood that children vary with age in the degree of independence from their parents, the nature of their dependence will be emphasized throughout. The sex of the parent and the sex of the children is the second variable. Cultural definitions of appropriate behavior for men and women and for girls and boys vary from place to place and are in the process of change, but nonetheless this factor cannot be ignored. Since the largest majority of one-parent families are headed by a woman, greater attention will be given to the mother-son and mother-daughter relationships in the absence of the father.

STRUCTURAL CHARACTERISTICS OF ONE-PARENT FAMILIES AND THEIR CONSEQUENCES

Task Structure

The large majority of tasks for which a family is responsible devolve upon the parents. Providing for the physical, emotional, and social needs of all the family members is a full-time job for two adults. If these tasks are to be performed by the nuclear group during the absence or incapacity of one of its adult members, the crucial factor is the availability of another member with sufficient maturity, competence, and time to perform them. The two-parent family has sufficient flexibility to adapt to such a crisis. Although there is considerable specialization in the traditional sex roles concerning these tasks, there is little evidence that such specialization is inherent in the sex roles. It is, in fact, expected that one parent will substitute if the other parent is incapacitated and, in our essentially servantless society, such acquired tasks are given full social approval. However, in the one-parent family such flexibility is much less possible, and the permanent loss of the remaining parent generally dissolves the nuclear group.

Even if the remaining parent is able to function adequately, it is unlikely that one person can take over all parental tasks on a long term basis. Financial support, child care, and household maintenance are concrete tasks involving temporal and spatial relationships, and in one form or another they account for a large proportion of the waking life of two adult family members. A permanent adjustment then must involve a reduction in the tasks performed and/or a reduction in the adequacy of performance, or external assistance.

In addition to limitations on the time and energy available to the solitary parent for the performance of tasks, there are social limitations on the extent to which both the male and the female tasks may be fulfilled by a member of one sex. If the remaining parent be male, it is possible for him to continue to perform his major role as breadwinner and to hire a woman to keep house and, at least, to care for the children's physical needs. If, however, the solitary parent be a female, as is the more usual case, the woman must take on the male role of breadwinner, unless society or the absent husband provides financial support in the form of insurance, pensions, welfare payments, etc. This is a major reversal in cultural roles and, in addition, usually consumes the mother's time and energy away from the home for many hours during the day. There is little time or energy left to perform the tasks normally performed by the female in the household and she, too, must hire a female substitute at considerable cost. The effect of this reversal of the sex role model in the socialization of children has been a matter of some concern, but the emphasis has been upon the male child who lacked a male role model rather than upon the effect of the reversal of the female role model for children of both sexes. In both cases, the probability seems great that some tasks will be neglected, particularly those of the traditionally female specialization.

The wish to accomplish concrete household tasks in the most efficient manner in terms of time and energy expenditure may lead to less involvement of children in these tasks and the concomitant loss of peripheral benefits that are extremely important to the socialization process and/or to family cohesion. Some tasks may be almost completely avoided, especially those which are not immediately obvious to the local community, such as the provision of emotional support and attention to children. A third possibility is to overload children, particularly adolescents, with such tasks. These may be greater than the child is ready to assume, or tasks inappropriate for the child of a particular sex to perform regularly.

Females are often lacking in skills and experience in the economic world, and frequently receive less pay and lower status jobs than men with similar skills. The probability of lower income and lower occupational status for the female headed household are likely to lower the family's social position in a society which bases social status primarily upon these variables. If the family perceives a great enough distance between its former level and that achieved by the single parent, it is possible that the family as a whole may become more or less anomic, with serious consequences in the socialization process of the children and in the remaining parent's perception of personal adequacy.

Communication Structure

Parents serve as the channels of communication with the adult world in two ways; first as transmitters of the cultural value system which has previously been internalized by the parents; and secondly, as the child's contact with and representative in the adult world. Except for very young children, the parents are not the sole means of communication, but for a large part of the socialization process, the child sees the adult world through the eyes and by the experience of his parents, and even his own experiences are limited to those which can be provided for him within whatever social opportunities that are open to his parents. More importantly, to the extent that the child's identity is integrated with that of the family, he is likely to see himself not only as his parents see him but also as the world sees his parents.

Since sex differences have been assumed in the ways men and women see the world and differences can be substantiated in the ways that the world sees men and women, the child can have a relatively undistorted channel of communication only if both parents are present. Therefore, whatever the interests, values, and opinions of the remaining parent, the loss of a parent of one sex produces a structural distortion in the communications between the child and the adult world and, since such communication is a factor in the development of the self-image, of social skills, and of an image of the total society, the totality of the child's possible development is also distorted.

The type and quality of experiences available even to adults tend to be regulated according to sex. In the two-parent family not only is the child provided with more varied experiences, but the parent of either sex has, through the spouse, some communication with the experiences typical of the opposite sex. Thus, the housewife is likely to have some idea of what is going on in the business or sports worlds even if she has no interest in them. The solitary parent is not likely to be apprised of such information and is handicapped to the extent that it may be necessary for decision making. The female who has taken on the breadwinner role may be cut off from the sources of information pertinent to the female role as she misses out on neighborhood gossip about the symptoms of the latest virus prevalent among the children, events being planned, the best places to shop, etc.

Finally, the solitary parent is likely to be limited in the social ties that are normal channels of communication. Most social occasions for adults tend to be planned for couples and the lone parent is often excluded or refuses because of the discomfort of being a fifth wheel. Her responsibilities to home and children tend to never be completed and provide additional reasons for refusing invitations. Lone women are particularly vulnerable to community sanctions and must be cautious in their social relationships lest their own standing and that of the family be lowered. Finally, the possible drop in social status previously discussed may isolate the family from its own peer group and place them among a group with which they can not or will not communicate freely.

Power Structure

Bales and Borgatta (1) have pointed out that the dyad has unique properties and certainly a uniquely simple power structure. In terms of authority from which the children are more or less excluded by age and social norms, the one-parent family establishes a diadic relationship, between the parent and each child. Society places full responsibility in the parental role, and, therefore, the parent becomes the only power figure in the one-parent family. Consequently, the adult in any given situation is either for or against the child. Some experience of playing one adult against the other, as long as it is not carried to extremes, is probably valuable in developing social skills and in developing a view of authority as tolerable and even manipulable within reason rather than absolute and possibly tyrannical. In the one-parent family the child is more likely to see authority as personal rather than consensual, and this in itself removes some of the legitimation of the power of parents as the representatives of society.

Even if benevolent, the absolutism of the power figure in the one-parent family, where there can be no experience of democratic decision making between equals in power, may increase the difficulty of the adolescent and the young adult in achieving independence from the family, and that of the parent in allowing and encouraging such development. Further, the adult, the power, the authority figure, is always of one sex, whether that sex be the same sex as the child or the opposite. However, in contemporary society where decision making is the responsibility of both sexes, the child who has identified authority too closely with either sex may have a difficult adjustment. The situation also has consequences for the parent, for when the supportive reinforcement or the balancing mediation which comes with the sharing of authority for decision making is absent, there may be a greater tendency to frequent changes in the decisions made, inconsistency, or rigidity.

Affectional Structure

The personal functions of the family in providing for the emotional needs of its members have been increasingly emphasized. There is ample evidence that children require love and security in order to develop in a healthy manner. Although there is nearly as much substantiation for the emotional needs of parents, these are less frequently emphasized. Adults must have love and security in order to maintain emotional stability under the stresses of life and in order to meet the emotional demands made upon them by their children. In addition to providing the positive emotional needs of its members, the family has the further function of providing a safe outlet for negative feelings as well. Buttressed by the underlying security of family affection, the dissatisfactions and frustrations of life may be expressed without the negative consequences attendant upon their expression in other contexts. Even within the family, however, the expressions of such basic emotions cannot go unchecked. The needs of one member or one sub-group may dominate to the point that the requirements of others are not fulfilled, or are not met in a manner acceptable to society. To some extent this danger exists in any group, but it is particularly strong in a group where emotional relationships are intensive. Traditionally, the danger is reduced by regulating the context, manner, and occasion of the expression of such needs.

Family structure is an important element both in the provision and the regulation of emotional needs. The increasing isolation of the nuclear family focuses these needs on the nuclear group by weakening ties with the larger kin group. Thus, both generations and both sexes are forced into a more intensive relationship; yet the marital relationship itself is increasingly unsupported by legal or social norms and is increasingly dependent upon affectional ties alone for its solidity. Such intense relationships are increased within the one-parent family, and possibly reach their culmination in the family consisting of one parent and one child.

In a two person group the loss of one person destroys the group. The structure, therefore, creates pressure for greater attention to group maintenance through the expression of affection and the denial of negative feelings, and in turn may restrict problem solving efforts. In a sense, the one-parent family is in this position even if there are several children because the loss of the remaining parent effectively breaks up the group. The children have neither the ability nor the social power to maintain the group's independence. Therefore, the one-parent family structure exerts at least some pressure in this direction.

However, where there is more than one child there is some mitigation of the pattern, though this in itself may have some disadvantages. In a group of three or more there are greater possibilities for emotional outlet for those not in an authority role. Unfortunately, there are also greater possibilities that one member may become the scapegoat as other members combine against him. In spite of the power relationships, it is even possible that the solitary parent will become the scapegoat if the children combine against her. This problem is greatest in the three person family as three of the five possible sub-groups reject one member (Figure 2). The problem is also present in the four person family, although the possible sub-groups in which the family combines against one member has dropped to four out of twelve (Figure 1). The relation of group structure to emotional constriction has been clearly expressed by Slater:

> The disadvantages of the smaller groups are not verbalized by members, but can only be inferred from their behavior. It appears that group members are too tense, passive, tactful, and constrained, to work together in a manner which is altogether satisfying to them. Their fear of alienating one another seems to prevent them from expressing their ideas freely. (Emphasis is ours.)
>
> These findings suggest that maximal group satisfaction is achieved when the group is large enough so that the members feel able to express positive and negative feelings freely, and to make aggressive efforts toward problem solving even at the risk of antagonizing each other, yet small enough so that some regard will be shown for the feelings and needs of others; large enough so that the loss of a member could be tolerated, but small enough so that such a loss could not be altogether ignored (11, p. 138).

Interpersonal relationships between parents and children in the area of emotional needs are not entirely reciprocal because of age and power differences in the family. Parents provide children with love, emotional support, and an outlet for negative feelings. However, while the love of a child is gratifying to the adult in some ways, it cannot be considered as supporting; rather it is demanding in

SUB-GROUP CHOICES AMONG GROUPS OF VARYING SIZES*

Figure 1: The Four Person Group

1. A,B,C,D	5. B,C,D	9. B,D
2. A,B,C	6. A,B	10. A,D
3. A,B,D	7. C,D	11. B,C
4. A,C,D	8. A,C	12. All persons independent; no sub-group

Figure 2: The Three Person Group

1. A,B,C	3. A,B	5. All persons independent; no sub-group
2. B,C	4. A,C	

Figure 3: The Two Person Group

1. A,B	2. Both persons independent; no sub-group

*Persons designated by letter.

the responsibilities it places upon the loved one. Support may be received only from one who is seen as equal or greater in power and discrimination. Nor can the child serve as a socially acceptable outlet for negative emotions to the extent that another adult can, for the child's emotional and physical dependency upon the adult makes him more vulnerable to possible damage from this source. The solitary parent in the one-parent family is structurally deprived of a significant element in the meeting of his own emotional needs. To this must be added the psychological and physical frustrations of the loss of the means for sexual gratification. In some situations involving divorce or desertion, the damage to the self-image of the remaining parent may intensify the very needs for support and reassurance which can no longer be met within the family structure.

The regulation of emotional demands of family members is similar in many ways to the regulation of the behavior of family members discussed under power structure. As there was the possibility that authority might be too closely identified with only one sex in the one-parent family, there is the similar danger that the source of love and affection may be seen as absolute and/or as vested in only one sex. Having only one source of love and security, both physical and emotional, is more likely to produce greater anxiety about its loss in the child, and may make the child's necessary withdrawal from the family with growing maturity more difficult for both parent and child. Again, as in the power structure, the identification of the source of love with only one sex is likely to cause a difficult adjustment to adult life, particularly if the original source of love was of the same sex as the child, for our society's expectations are that the source of love for an adult must lie with the opposite sex.

One of the most important regulatory devices for the emotional needs of the group is the presence and influence of members who serve to deter or limit demands which would be harmful to group members or to group cohesion, and to prevent the intensification of the influence of any one individual by balancing it with the influence of others. Parental figures will tend to have greater influence in acting as a deterrent or balance to the needs and demands of other family members because of their greater power and maturity. The loss of one parent removes a large portion of the structural balance and intensifies the influence of the remaining parent upon the children, while possibly limiting the ability of this parent to withstand demands made upon her by the children. There is also a tendency for any family member to transfer to one or more of the remaining members the demands formerly filled by the absent person (8). There would seem to be a danger in the one-parent family that:

1. The demands of the sole parent for the fulfillment of individual and emotional needs normally met within the marital relationship may prove intolerable and damaging to the children, who are unable to give emotional support or to absorb negative feelings from this source, or

2. The combined needs of the children may be intolerable to the emotionally unsupported solitary parent. Since the emotional requirements of children are very likely to take the form of demands for physical attention or personal service, the remaining parent may be subject to physical as well as emotional exhaustion from this source.

When emotional needs are not met within the family, there may be important consequences for the socialization of the children and for the personal adjustment of all family members. Further, fulfillment of such needs may be sought in the larger community by illegitimate means. The children may exhibit emotional problems in school or in their relations with their play group. A parent may be unable to control her own emotions and anxieties sufficiently to function adequately in society. When there are no means for the satisfaction of these demands they may well prove destructive, not only to the family group and its individual members, but to society as well.

The consequences of the problems discussed above may be minimized or magnified by the personal resources or inadequacies of the family members, and particularly the solitary parent in this situation. But, the problems are structural elements of the situation, and must be faced on this level if they are to be solved.

IMPLICATIONS FOR SOCIAL POLICY AND PRACTICE

The Introduction describes the growth of the number of one-parent families during the last generation. Chilman and Sussman go on to describe the financial plight of many of these families.

> The public program of aid to families with dependent children (AFDC) that is most applicable to this group currently makes payments on behalf of children in nearly a million families. Three out of every four of these families have no father in the home. Less than half of the families that are estimated to be in need receive payments under the program and, "... with the low financial standards for aid to dependent children prevailing in many states, dependence on the program for support is in itself likely to put the family in low-income status. ... The average monthly payment per family as reported in a study late in 1961 was only $112. ...
>
> "The overall poverty of the recipient families is suggested by the fact that, according to the standards set up in their own states, half of them are still in financial need even with their assistance payment" (4, p. 394; 10).

There is increasing evidence that both the one-parent family structure and poverty are being transmitted from one generation to the next.

> "A recently released study of cases assisted by aid to families with dependent children shows that, for a nationwide sample of such families whose cases were closed early in 1961" more than 40 per cent of the mothers and/or fathers were raised in the homes where some form of assistance had been received at some time. "Nearly half of these cases had received aid to families with dependent children. This estimated proportion that received some type of aid is more than four times the almost 10 per cent estimated for the total United States population..." (4, p. 395; 10).

If poverty and one-parent family structure tend to go together, providing increases in financial assistance alone may not be sufficient to help parents and children in the present and future generation to become financially independent of welfare funds. Under the 1962 Amendments to the

Social Security Act states are now receiving additional funds to provide rehabilitation services to welfare families, and these programs have begun. Creative use of such funds to overcome some of the consequences of one-parent family structure is a possibility, but as yet the authors know of no services that have explicitly taken this direction.

A few suggestions may serve to illustrate how existing or new services might deal with the consequences of one-parent family structure:

1. Recognition of the need of the mother without a husband at home for emotional support and social outlets could lead to a variety of services. Recreation and problem focused groups for women in this situation, which would provide some opportunities for socially sanctioned hetero-sexual relationships, might go a long way in helping these parents and their children.

2. Special efforts to provide male figures to which both girls and boys can relate may have utility. This can be done in day-care centers, settlement house agencies, schools, and through the inclusion of girls in programs like the Big Brothers. It would be particularly useful for children in one-parent families to see the ways in which adults of each sex deal with each other in these situations, and at an early age.

3. Subsidization of child care and housekeeping services for parents with children too young or unsuitable for day-care services would provide greater freedom for solitary mothers to work outside the home. Training persons as homemakers and making them responsible to an agency or a professional organization would reduce the anxiety of the working parent, and provide greater insurance to both the parent and society that this important job would be done well.

More fundamental to the prevention of poverty and the problems of one-parent family status may be programs aimed at averting family dissolution through divorce, separation and desertion, particularly among lower socio-economic groups. Few public programs have addressed themselves to this problem, and there is now a good deal of evidence that the private family agencies which provide counseling services have disenfranchised themselves from the poor (5). The need to involve other institutional components in the community, such as the educational, economic and political systems, is obvious but beyond the scope of discussion in this paper (7). Increasing the number of stable and enduring marriages in the community so as to prevent the consequences of one-parent family structure may be a first line of defense, and more closely related to treating the causes rather than the effects of poverty for a large number of people who are poor.

SUMMARY

One-parent families constitute more than a fourth of that group classified as poor, and are growing in number. Family structure is seen as a variable intervening between the opportunity system and the socialization process. The task, communication, power and affectional structure within the nuclear group are influenced by the absence of one parent, and the family's ability to fulfill its social and personal functions may be adversely affected. Some of the consequences of this deviant family structure seem related to both the evolvement of low socio-economic status and its continuation from one generation to the next. Solutions must take account of this social situational problem.

REFERENCES

1.   Bales, R. F. and Borgatta, E. F. Size of group as a factor in the interaction profile. In Hare, Borgatta and Bales (Eds.) *Small Groups.* New York: Knopf, 1955.
2.   Bell, W. and Boat, M. D. Urban neighborhoods and informal social relations. *Amer. J. Soc.,* 1957, 43, 391-398.
3.   Bernard, J. *American Family Behavior.* New York: Harper, 1942.
4.   Chilman, C. and Sussman, M. Poverty in the United States. *J. Marriage and the Family,* 1964, 26, 391-395.
5.   Cloward, R. A. and Epstein, I. Private social welfare's disengagement from the poor: the case of family adjustment agencies. Mimeographed, April 1964.
6.   Litwak, E. Geographic mobility and extended family cohesion. *Amer. Soc. Rev.,* 1960, 25, 385-394.

7. Lutz, W. A. Marital incompatability. In Cohen, N.E. (Ed.) *Social Work and Social Problems*. New York: National Association of Social Workers, 1964.

8. Mittleman, B. Analysis of reciprocal neurotic patterns in family relationships. In V. Eisenstein (Ed.) *Neurotic Interaction in Marriage*. New York: Basic Books, 1956.

9. Parsons, T. and Bales, R. F. Family socialization and interaction processes. Glencoe, Illinois: The Free Press, 1954.

10. *Poverty in the United States*. Committee on Education and Labor, House of Representatives, 88th Congress, Second Session, April 1964. U. S. Government Printing Office, Washington, D. C.

11. Slater, P. E. Contrasting correlates of group size, *Sociometry*, 1958, 6, 129-139.

20 single-parent fatherhood: an emerging life style

dennis k. orthner

terry brown

dennis ferguson

Fatherhood is receiving increased attention in the popular and professional literature. This seemingly new discovery that paternity and parenthood are reconcilable has been hailed by some as an important answer to the perceived decline in family stability. Nevertheless, this developing concern over fatherhood almost universally lies within the context of his role as a supplementary, or at best, complementary, parent. The status of primary parent is in little jeopardy of being dislodged from the mother, even if she shares in the provider responsibility for the household (Poloma & Garland, 1971; Holmstrom, 1972).

But in nearly a half-million families in the United States, the father is the primary parent because there is no mother present in the household. These men represent a growing dimension of both fatherhood and parenthood—the single parent father. Suggestions that single parenthood may be a pathological environment for childbearing are not new nor do they appear to have declined markedly. The concern in most cases, however, has been discussed and analyzed in terms of single mothers. The focus of the present paper is on the situation of the single parent father, some of the reasons why this phenomenon is growing, the strengths and stresses he faces, and the kinds of resources he needs to successfully meet his personal and parental responsibilities.

By definition, a single parent family consists of one parent and dependent children living in the same household. The resident parent may be single due to widowhood, divorce, separation, non-marriage, and more recently, single parent adoption. In the United States, there are over 4.5 million families with children under 18 headed by a single parent (U.S. Census Bureau, 1975). Approximately 90 percent of these families are headed by women and 10 percent are headed by men. These figures do not include those single parents who live with a relative or someone else who may be the head of the household. In general, fathers appear to represent a minority of single parents but this may be changing.

FACTORS CHANGING SINGLE-PARENT FATHERHOOD

There are several different means by which a male may receive exclusive custody over minor children—death of his spouse, court designated custody of his children, and adoption. Each of these factors is undergoing considerable change and may result in a different pattern of single-parent fatherhood emerging.

Maternal Mortality

Over history, it has not been unusual for either men or women to be single parents. But prior to the twentieth century, the major cause of single-parenthood was the death of the marital partner.

Because of the combination of a higher average age at marriage and a longer childbearing period with a higher adult mortality rate, many mothers and fathers were forced to rear their children without the other parent. While mortality rates were generally lower for women, men were not spared the combination of widowerhood and parenthood.

One of the most critical periods in the adult life cycle for women used to be the childbearing years. A casual glance at tombstones in old cemeteries reveals that many women died in childbirth, leaving the remaining children to their husbands. As recently as 1935, the maternal mortality rate was 58 deaths per 10,000 live births, which compares to today's rate of approximately 2.5 deaths per 10,000 births (U.S. Bureau of Census, 1975). Rapid advances in medical technology, improved methods of contraception, and more widespread access to prenatal medical attention and nutrition have largely accounted for this decline in maternal mortality. A by-product of these innovations has been a decline in the proportion of fathers who become single parents because of the deaths of their wives.

Custody Arrangements

The most significant influence on the recent acceptance of single parent fatherhood has been a change in the legal custody arrangements for minor children. Prior to 1960, very few fathers were awarded custody of their children and then, only in unusual circumstances. Fathers rarely contested the assumption of mother custody and if they did, the courts demanded that they prove the mother "unfit" for parenthood. Also, the backlog of divorce settlements rarely allowed a judge the luxury of carefully selecting between the two parental alternatives. This kind of social and legal process probably led Goode to make the following conclusion from his study of divorced women:

> There are many factors to make us believe that the father actually does approve of the custody arrangement that gives care of the child to the mother. Most of these factors may be classified under the headings of (a) the social role of the father; (b) male skills; and (c) allocation of time to occupation ... These factors operate to make husband custody neither easy nor very desirable (to husbands) in our time. Consequently, we are inclined to believe our respondents when four out of five claim that their husbands agreed to the custodial arrangements, which almost always gave the custody to the wife (1956, 312-313).

It has been suggested by some persons in and outside the legal profession that certain "presumptions" may ease the strain of child custody contests. One such opinion that has received considerable attention was rendered by Ellsworth and Levy and prepared for the National Conference of Commissioners on Uniform State Laws:

> A uniform divorce act should contain a presumption that the mother is the appropriate custodian—at least for young children, and probably for children of any age ... Since wives will, under most circumstances, be awarded custody regardless of the statutory standard, and since it seems wise to discourage traumatic custody contests whenever possible to do so, the act should discourage those few husbands who wish to contest by establishing a presumption that the wife is entitled to custody (1970, 202-203).

In contrast to these rather traditional perspectives, which may be valid in many cases, fathers who legitimately feel they have a right to custody of their children are beginning to get their day in court. No-fault divorce legislation, which has passed in some form in at least 41 states (Rosenberg & Mendelsohn, 1975) often includes increased rights to negotiation for children on the part of fathers. A provision in the statutes of Colorado was designed to give both fathers and mothers equal rights to their children after divorce (Ellsworth & Levy, 1970). The spirit of these new regulations is summed up well in the report of the California Governor's Commission on the Family:

We believe that the Court should make a custody disposition which as nearly as possible meets the needs of the child, and that it should be able to do so with minimum harm to all parties involved ... The role of the women in today's society is substantially different from what it was when the preference [for the mother] was formulated; and we agree with the Assembly Committee on Judiciary that in a substantial number of cases, the preference prevents the father from asserting his custodial right and leads to a result incompatible with the child's best interest (California Assembly Reports, 1966, 154-161).

The new roles of women are also having their effect on fatherhood. The wife-mother "drop-out" or desertion phenomenon is beginning to be noted in the popular literature. Women are demanding more opportunities in the world outside the home and many are placing more emphasis on these goals than on parenthood. In light of this, the courts are now giving more favorable attention to fathers receiving exclusive child custody if their partner rejects the child, even if they are not married (Schlesinger, 1966). In Illinois, a state-statute had held that unmarried fathers were unfit to have custody of their children. However, in the case of Stanley vs. Illinois, the U.S. Supreme Court held that this law was unconstitutional, breaking further ground for the rights of single-parent fathers.

There is some evidence that these legal and social changes are beginning to be seen in the single-parent statistics. While the proportion of men who were granted legal custody of their children during the 1950's was about 10 percent (Goode, 1956), it now appears that men are increasing this percentage. Between 1965 and 1972, a period of rapidly rising divorce rates, the number of independent divorced and separated mothers heading households increased by 58 percent but the number of divorced and separated fathers heading households alone increased by 71 percent over that period ("Rising Problems of Single-parents," 1973). This difference in rate of increase means that by 1972, over 13 percent of the single parent households resulting from divorce or separation were headed by fathers. By comparison, the number of single-parent households that resulted from spouse mortality only increased from 1965 to 1972 eight percent for fathers and three percent for mothers, comparable to the rise in the size of overall population. Undoubtedly, divorce and separation are rapidly replacing death as the major cause of single-parenthood, even among fathers.

Single-Parent Adoption

At the present time, adoption is only a minor factor in single-parent fatherhood. With the decline in the birthrate and rise in abortions, demand for adoptable children by intact families, the preferred choice of the agencies, far exceeds the supply. Nevertheless, regulations are changing and the number of single adoptive parents is increasing. Between 1968 and 1974, there were 50 recorded in New York City but this is only indicative of a nationwide trend ("Single Adoptive Parents Unite," 1974). Typically, single persons can only adopt children who are hard-to-place, i.e., those who are older, mixed racially, or handicapped (Kadushin, 1970). Male single parents, who make up only a small minority of these adoptions, are almost routinely limited to male children.

CHARACTERISTICS OF SINGLE-PARENT FATHERS

There is surprisingly little information in the literature on the life-style of single-parent fathers. In an attempt to partially remedy this situation, lengthy semi-structured interviews were conducted with 20 of these fathers from the Greensboro, North Carolina area. The fathers were studied as part of a larger investigation of the overall situation of male and female single-parents. The sample is not considered to be necessarily representative of all single-parent fathers, but because of a deliberate attempt to locate fathers from different socioeconomic backgrounds, we do have some idea of the breadth of the experiences they represent. Each of the fathers studied has custody of the children who are living with him. Preschool children between the ages of 18 months and five years are found in 10 of the households, while the remaining 10 have school-age children between the ages of six and 17 years.

Nine of the men are living with one child, nine with two children, and two with three children. The youngest father is 25 years of age and the oldest is 64, while the average age of the fathers is 37 years.

The fathers in this study represent a variety of reasons for single-parenthood, with the exception of single-parent adoption. Only three of the men are widowers which supports the decline of female mortality as a factor in single-parenthood. Fifteen of the fathers in the sample have their children as a result of divorce or separation. A highly unusual phenomenon is the situation of the never married father, yet two of our respondents fall into this category.

It is not too surprising to find that the average social status level of the single-parent fathers is above the norm. For a man to get custody of minor children, he has to demonstrate a degree of resource availability that will be respected by the courts, his peers, and perhaps his former spouse. Twelve of the men we interviewed are in professional or managerial positions, another is in sales. There are only five blue-collar men in the sample and the remaining two included a student and a previous manager who is unemployed. Sixteen of the fathers had some post-high school education; 13 held college degrees and nine had advanced or professional degrees. Their average annual income exceeded $18,000. Concerted but comparatively unsuccessful attempts to locate lower income single parent fathers suggests that their frequency is lower in the population and that they may remarry faster than those men with higher incomes.

Even though these fathers appear to have the resources that will enable them to be competent fathers, a majority of the 15 divorced or separated fathers received custody because their former wives did not want or were unable to care for the children. It is difficult to tell if this is the pattern nationally but in this sample, fathers reported getting the children because of desertion, mental illness, drug and alcohol abuse, or general instability of their wives. Many of the men, in short, received custody of their children on the basis of spouse allocation rather than adjudication.

Adult Life Style

Almost all of the fathers interviewed reported an active social life. Without a spouse in the house, this is a primary means by which single parents are able to derive adult companionship. While half of the men restricted most of their activities to their children, female friends, or themselves, the other half indicated a substantial amount of interest in activities with their male friends. It might be anticipated that male friends of the single-parent fathers would also be single but there was no indication that acquaintances were limited to other singles. In fact, while female single-parents are sometimes given derisive labels such as "wife snatcher" or "she devil" (Burgess, 1970), single fathers do not appear to feel these same negative images. Perhaps, by being male, they are perceived as having the traditional freedom for initiating social contact with women and are not considered to be as threatening to intact marriages as women who more passively attract a male suitor.

An important part of the life-style of single-parent fathers is dating. All but one of the fathers reported some recent dating activity and most of the men considered themselves to be "dating around" rather than seeing one person exclusively. This was somewhat surprising since, on the average, these fathers had been single parents for almost three years. We had anticipated some desire to remarry, if for no other reason than just to alleviate their parental strain. But, contrary to our expectations, these fathers considered themselves to be quite satisfied with their lifestyle and in no hurry to once again marry. Only half of the sample considered marriage in their future plans with the remainder unsure of marriage and presently committed to remaining single.

Sex is one area of their adult social life that generated some concern on the part of the fathers. One-third of them indicated rather frequent sexual contacts and others may have been less inclined to discuss this. Part of their sensitivity emerged when they were asked about their attitudes on cohabitation. Over two-thirds of the fathers viewed this as totally unacceptable for themselves and in direct contradiction to their parental responsibility to be sexually discrete. The majority felt that "living together" is an acceptable means for other persons to test their relationship prior to marriage but they could not see themselves so involved. In addition to the felt need for sexual discretion, the fathers commonly rejected cohabitation on the grounds that it would "lack permanence" and that "children need someone they can count on."

Parental Responsibilities and Attitudes

The professional literature commonly states that a two-parent environment does not automatically insure good childrearing and conversely, a one parent family does not mean an inadequate childrearing situation (e.g., Hill, 1968; Nye, 1957). The majority of the interviewed single-parent fathers have come to believe this and, defensively, they state that one parent is often better than two *if* the two cannot live together happily. Most seem to feel, nevertheless, that the best situation for the child is a stable two parent relationship.

The efficacy of daughters being reared by their fathers has frequently been questioned. The courts have traditionally looked askance at this and rarely in a contested case do judges grant a father custody of a girl. The fathers we interviewed were somewhat split on the issue of whether boys and girls should be brought up the same or differently; 12 felt they should be reared the same and eight, differently. But the fathers who had daughters were more likely to note the need for differences in socialization. Two of the fathers had daughters who were going through puberty at the time and they expressed considerable dismay about having to give them "proper" sex education. This should not be taken to mean that these fathers felt less competent in rearing daughters. Many mothers, in fact, share the same concerns. The fathers in question considered problems such as this to be situational, not continual and, overall, they felt they were quite successful in rearing their daughters.

The majority of the problems in adjusting to single parenthood come from harmonizing parental and adult roles and responsibilities. In many ways, the feelings of these fathers are similar to those expressed by many working mothers who also have to reconcile their adult and primary parent roles. Common problems mentioned by the fathers are lack of patience and time for their children, making decisions alone, and having to be away from their children more than they want to be. The fathers generally felt they demanded more independence in their children than other parents might.

An interesting change in attitude about parenting seems to have taken place in many of the fathers, particularly among those who had previously held more traditional role expectations. Since becoming single parents, these fathers became much more appreciative of the responsibilities of being the primary parent. In particular, they had become less discipline oriented, more concerned about the adequacy of day care, more interested in education, and more protective of their children. One case was particularly striking. A father of a preschool child was the president of a small textile firm. He had never been very concerned about the child care responsibilities of his female employees; he took it for granted that plenty of facilities were available. But when he became a single parent, he too faced the plight of finding adequate day care. Now he is thinking in terms of operating a professionally run day care center at his plant as a benefit for his employees.

Parent-Child Relationship

It is difficult to tell what the "real" relationship is between two or more persons when only one person is queried. But it is strikingly evident that the fathers we interviewed feel they have good parent-child rapport. All of them report a relationship with their children which is "close" and "affectionate." Two-thirds of the fathers feel that their children are having family experiences similar to those of most other children their age.

The desire to compensate for being the only parent by giving as much time as possible to their children was a common theme. The list of recent activities they participated in included everything from camping trips to regular attendance at local plays. All but two of the fathers reported that at times they even take their children along on dates. This gives their children some idea of the kind of woman they enjoy being with and serves to approximate, for an afternoon or an evening at least, something like an intact family.

THE USE OF ROLE COMPENSATING SERVICES

The single parent father's situation is such that he requires special services rendered from a variety of sources. His needs are special since a single parent, by virtue of his situation, must somehow compensate for the roles lost or shared with a marital partner. Areas from which this compensation may come include child care arrangements, government assistance, single parent organizations, domestic help, and kinship networks.

Child Care Arrangements

Single parent fathers are usually employed and rarely do they receive alimony or child support. Since all but one of our fathers were employed, this necessitated establishing some kind of care arrangements for their children during working hours.

The most commonly used arrangement by fathers of preschool children involved day care centers or nursery schools. Only one child was cared for by a relative, in this case, the father's sister. Another father placed his child in a half-day nursery school program, with a live-in nanny for afternoon care. These arrangements are consistent with the finding that most of our fathers preferred group care to at home care by a friend, relative, or nanny. A majority felt that the teaching program was the most important criterion in selecting a child care arrangement; safety and security came second. When asked if they preferred male or female caregivers, or both equally, the answers were evenly split between preferring both equally and preferring female caregivers.

For most of the fathers, child care has not presented a major problem to their employment. When they were asked if child care problems had interfered with their work, 88 percent said no. In one case, however, a father did lose his job because of his new parental responsibilities. Because of interruptions in his work schedule to see teachers periodically, take the child to a physician, or other such responsibilities, he began to get unfavorable evaluations and, in a tight economy, was fired.

One half of the fathers in the sample had children of school age. After-school care for these children varied from fulltime housekeeper, female relative, or older sibling to no supervision at all. Those with children over the age of nine provided no supervision for the period between the end of a school day and the end of the father's working day.

Caregiving services utilized by single parent fathers, other than during working hours, were minimal. With the exception of dating, most of the fathers reported taking their children shopping, on short errands, and visiting friends. Only four fathers reported taking their children on evening dates or to club meetings. Child care for those situations was arranged with babysitters, friends, relatives, or older siblings.

Government Assistance

There are a variety of governmental assistance programs that can help subsidize the income of single-parents. These include such things as food stamps, child care scholarships, social security, G.I. Bill, public housing, Aid-to-Families of Dependent Children (AFDC), and so on. Programs such as AFDC, however, are much more likely to go to single-parent mothers than fathers, according to local and state sources. Again, the higher average income of most of these fathers does not make them as dependent on public support but part of the reason is also the matter of demonstrating their independence and competence as parents; sometimes this is required if they are to maintain custody of their children.

This independence was particularly evident in the sample of fathers we interviewed. One-third received some form of public assistance, including social security, G.I. Bill, and food stamps, but rarely was this tied to their being a single-parent. Funds which some might have received in the form of child care subsidies of AFDC were not requested. When asked if they felt the government should help them financially because they were single parents, a majority of the fathers responded negatively. Of the seven who answered affirmatively, five specified tax breaks as the area in which the government should provide assistance. One respondent mentioned that any school experiences through college should be tax deductible.

Single-Parent Organizations

There are several different types of organizations which serve the needs of single parent fathers. Recreational and dating opportunities are the primary draw of the singles and solo parent clubs that abound in this and other areas. Informational programs on single parenthood are run by the Family Life Council and other community and religious agencies. Parents Without Partners, which had just been organized locally prior to our investigation, attempts to provide for both the informational and social needs of single-parents.

The question of the effectiveness of these organizations in meeting the needs of single parent fathers drew mixed reactions. Half of the fathers had attended meetings of some singles oriented group and half of these found them therapeutic and emotionally supportive. Organizations such as Parents Without Partners were considered to be especially beneficial and informative. One problem that is evident, however, is the lack of supportive organizations for the lower income single-parents. Many of the men who do not participate do not go because they find babysitting money hard to come by or they are uncomfortable in the "status-seeking" (which might be called "independence-assertiveness") that goes on in most of these organizations.

The sex ratio in singles organizations also has its advantages and disadvantages for the single-parent father. Since women far outnumber men, the men find it easy to meet a variety of women. But at the same time, the men find themselves uncomfortable being in the minority and "being chased" by their more aggressive counterparts. One father expressed his feelings this way: "I'll never go to another one of those meetings. All those women want is a father for their children and they'll do anything to get me!" This is not a unique reaction and this "fear of being trapped" kept several of the non-participants away.

Household Services

It may be assumed that the single parent, especially the single parent father, would seek help in doing household duties. However, three-fourths of the fathers reported no help with housework. Of those receiving help, only one had a full-time housekeeper. The remaining employers of housekeepers had this service on a part-time basis only.

Since a majority of the fathers reported receiving no help with the housework, one might suspect the fathers encourage their children to do household chores. When asked if their children ever help out at home, most fathers said they did. The preschool children were usually responsible for picking up their toys, and the older children helped with the preparation of meals. In essence, the older the child, the more help he provided around the house.

Kinship Support

Parents of single parents were found to be generally supportive, providing emotional assurance, child care, financial and housekeeping assistance. Two-thirds of the fathers reported that their parents supported them with one or more of the aforementioned functions (the parents of four of the interviewed fathers were deceased). The majority have contact with their parents weekly or more than weekly; only two reported having no contact with parents who were living. Relatives were commonly used for child care during periods when the father needed time to adjust to new situations; sometimes this lasted for several months. When family problems arise, the majority of fathers contact their relatives, especially their parents. The next most consulted group consists of friends, then professional counselors. One father reported that he also discussed problems with his minister.

CONCLUSION

It is difficult to generalize from the limited data we have presented to all single-parent fathers, but the issues that have been raised and the results considered appear to be representative of the concerns these fathers express. We have tried to go beyond most research on fatherhood and actually ask the fathers themselves about their lifestyles, their problems and successes. We also tried to avoid using only a clinical population that might have biased our results toward a pathology of parenthood. In general, we feel that each of these fathers represents a different, unique situation with an underlying thread of commonality.

If there is one most impressive conclusion we can make from our interviews with single-parent fathers, it is this: these fathers feel quite capable and successful in their ability to be the primary parent of their children. The confidence they express and the satisfaction they seem to derive in fatherhood is very difficult to deny. We had anticipated a significant problem with role strain and adjustment to being the primary parent but we found little evidence that this is a major handicap. All of the fathers experienced some problems but these were not unlike the difficulties experienced in most families. The sense of pride in being able to cope with the challenge of parenthood and seeing their children mature under their guidance is a major compensating force.

Single-parent fathers appear to be taking advantage of the trend toward allowing men to be more nurturing. Some of them received custody because they felt they were more nurturing than their wives, and others were allocated their children because their wives felt less capable of being a nurturing parent. Hopefully, the notion that fathers are the instrumental leaders of the family while mothers control the expressive roles (Parsons & Bales, 1955) has been laid to rest. Most of the fathers expressed some concern over their ability to be a nurturing parent; they wanted to know if they spent enough time reading and playing with their children, if they were understanding things at the child's level, and if they should get more involved in their children's education. But these concerns are similar to those of most parents and, overall, the single-parent fathers felt quite comfortable in their expressive roles.

Some recent attempts to examine fatherhood have suggested that single-parent fathers may tend to over-use "mother substitutes" (Biller & Meredith, 1975; Weiss, 1975) to the detriment of the child. We did not find this to be the pattern at all. Day care was almost universally used but evening and weekend time was quite carefully allocated to their children. There were exceptions to this at times, but these were exceptions, not the rule.

In those areas where the single-parent fathers do indicate strain, solutions could be forthcoming if some of the following recommendations are considered:

1.   **Day care facilities that extend services into the evenings.** Several of the fathers found that they sometimes had to work late and the hours of most day care centers put them into uncomfortable dilemmas in their jobs. Other fathers would have liked knowing that there were facilities for taking care of their children in the evenings when they had spur-of-the-moment opportunities to go out for dinner or something else. Locating a babysitter at the last minute is a commonly repeated problem.

2.   **Child care facilities in shopping centers.** This is an extension of the first recommendation. With small children, shopping can be very burdensome and for single-parents particularly, having child care available at the shopping center would shorten the time required and make the experience less frustrating for all concerned.

3.   **Organizing of babysitting cooperatives.** Most fathers do not know how to operate a babysitting cooperative and many might be interested in its cost-saving advantages. Several of the fathers expressed a desire for this kind of service.

4.   **Transportation of children to and from day care centers.** It is often difficult for a working parent to transport children from school to an after-school child care center. There are other times when, because of location of the work situation, a father would prefer to have a child

returned home from the child care center to the care of an older sibling or someone else until he arrives.

5. **Classes on single-parenthood.** Most of the fathers expressed considerable dismay over their lack of preparation for parenthood. Rarely did they have the time to learn what to expect from their children. They had depended on their wives for that. Lack of information raised their anxiety and some orientation course would have been helpful. The seminars on this subject that are presented in the local community are very well attended but they need to be made available to even more persons, particularly fathers with lower incomes.

6. **"Big sisters."** A counterpart to "Big brother" type organization is needed for those fathers who are rearing daughters. In many cases, these are arranged informally and it is probably easier for fathers to find adult female companions for the daughters than for mothers to find male companions for their sons. But not all fathers find it easy to locate women who really want to help their daughters instead of finding a husband.

These recommendations are not exclusive to single-parent fathers. Most of them also apply to single-parent mothers and other persons as well. Leadership in implementing these and other suggestions might fruitfully be undertaken by local Family Life Councils, churches, community agencies, and single-parent organizations.

Single-parent fathers, themselves, seem to have demonstrated the willingness and ability to competently handle parenthood. If the support and resources they need can be garnered, there is every reason to believe that they can and will rear responsible children. There is little doubt that the number of single-parent fathers will grow, because of their own demands and the gradual shifting of responsibilities in the family. Now is the time to develop the programs and leadership to help fathers better adapt to their changing roles and relationships.

REFERENCES

Biller, H. & Meredith, D. *Father power.* New York: Anchor Press/Doubleday, 1975.

Burgess, J. The single-parent family: A social and sociological problem. *Family Coordinator,* 1970, 19, 137-144.

California assembly reports, 1963-1965. Sacramento, California State Assembly, 1966.

Ellsworth, P. & Levy, R. Legislative reform and child support adjudication. *Law and Society Review,* 1970, 4, 166-225.

Goode, W. *After divorce.* New York: Free Press, 1956.

Hill, R. Social stresses on the family. In M. Sussman (Ed.), *Sourcebook in marriage and the family,* (3rd ed.). Boston: Houghton, 1968.

Holmstrom, L. *The two-career family.* Cambridge, Mass.: Schenkman, 1972.

Kadushin, A. Single-parent adoptions: An overview: Some relevant research. *Social Science Review,* 1970, 44, 263-274.

Nye, I. Child adjustment in broken and unhappy homes. *Marriage and Family Living,* 1965, 27, 333-343.

Parsons, T. & Bales, R. *Family, socialization, and interaction process.* New York: Free Press, 1955.

Poloma, M. & Garland, T. The married professional woman: A study in the tolerance of domestication. *Journal of Marriage and Family,* 1971, 33, 531-540.

Rising problems of single-parents. *U.S. News and World Reports,* July 16, 1973, 32-35.

Rosenberg, B. & Mendelsohn, E. Legal status of women in the council of state governments. In *The book of the states,* 1974. (Available from the U.S. Women's Bureau.)

Schlesinger, B. The one-parent family: An overview. *Family Coordinator,* 1966, 15, 133-138.

Single adoptive parents unite. *New York Times,* July 22, 1974, 24.

U.S. Census Bureau. Washington, D.C.: Government Printing Office, 1975.

Weiss, R. *Marital separation.* New York: Basic Books, 1975.

the psychological effects
of divorce on adolescents
arthur d. sorosky

As of 1972 nearly one American child in 10 lived in a one-parent home and about 7.5 million families were headed by unmarried adults. The incidence of divorce has continued to rise, both as a result of liberalized legislation and a breakdown in the traditional view of marital commitment. Many studies have looked at the psychological effects of divorce upon the children involved but few authors have addressed themselves to the specific reactions of adolescents. This becomes particularly significant when we note that divorce tends to peak at three different stages of child rearing: when the children are infants, when they reach the ages of 7 to 10 and finally when they reach adolescence. This paper will attempt to provide a review of the existing literature on the psychological effects of divorce on adolescents and to summarize the impressions of a child psychiatrist in private practice in an upper middle class suburban community.

It is impossible to generalize as to the psychological effects of divorce upon adolescents as a whole. Their reactions will vary according to many factors: a) The psychodynamics of the family prior to the divorce, including the severity of marital discord; b) the nature of the marital breakup; c) the post-divorce relationship of the parents; d) the age or stage of development of the youngster at the time of the divorce and e) the personality strengths and coping skills of the adolescent. Furthermore, the outcome must be evaluated according to both immediate and long-term effects.

Family dynamics prior to the divorce

Despert (6) stated that an "emotional divorce" in which the parents remain together, even though incompatibly, is probably more damaging to the children involved than the legal event of divorce. Anthony (1) described how the nature of the marital conflict prior to the divorce influences the type of psychological reactions manifested in the children. A hostile parental relationship results in children with increased irritability and aggressiveness; whereas, a neurotic parental relationship leads to unconsciously transmitted feelings and excessive guilt in which the children are frequently exploited as pawns, scapegoats, go-betweens, spies, informers, manipulators and allies of the battling parents. The "devitalized marriage" in which there is a gradual loss of feeling, without overt hostility, creates an emotionally flat reaction in the children. The so-called "good divorce," in which the parents make every effort to hide their conflicts and to remain friends, creates considerable confusion in the minds of the children, often resulting in an internalization of conflict with somatic symptomatology.

Another factor which influences the emotional outcome of the children is the mental health of the parents prior to the divorce. Blumenthal (3) claimed that 65% of the reasons cited as causes of the divorce were suggestive of psychiatric disturbance in at least one of the divorcing partners. Furthermore, Briscoe (4) cited that 3/4 of divorced women and 2/3 of divorced men had, or currently have, a psychiatric disease. Although it can be debated as to whether these problems are primary or secondary to the marital stress, they must be seen as contributing to a sense of insecurity in the children, which may or may not be alleviated by the divorce.

Nature of the marital break-up

In most cases the divorce comes as no great surprise to the adolescent. Undoubtedly, there have been months or years of emotional turmoil and the youngster may have wondered why the parents remained together when they were so unhappy with one another. When the divorce is announced the child may actually experience a sense of relief, feeling that some action is being taken to make his/her life more stable and secure. What is harder for the teenager to adjust to is the abrupt dissolution which occurs following the discovery of an extra-marital affair or a heated argument in which neither party is willing to compromise. In still other cases the conflict state has resulted not as much from marital incompatibility per se but from a displacement of personal psychological problems onto the marriage or from a projection of these problems from one spouse to the other.

Today we are witnessing a number of men and women going through the classic "middle-age crisis" who are being encouraged by liberalized divorce laws and societal acceptance to impulsively escape from their marital commitments. These people are attempting to suprpress and block out their frustrations and responsibilities by regressing back to a second adolescence. Their hedonistic pursuits are reinforced by the ready availability of willing sexual partners and the comfort provided by the ever present singles' apartment complexes. As parents, they have a particularly hard time conveying to their children why their marriage has failed because they don't really know the answer themselves.

Parents' relationship after the divorce

Westman (26) described divorce as a process rather than an event. Divorce only alters the form of the family relationship rather than causes the comparatively abrupt loss of bereavement with its associated grief and guilt. He stated that 1/3 of divorces are followed by turbulence that could be pathogenic for the affected children. The types of conflict situations include: a) parent-centered post-divorce turbulence—in which the parents perpetuate the same conflicts in their relationship that existed beforehand; b) child-centered turbulence—in which the children manipulate the parents to bring about a continuation of the parental conflicts or to promote the reuniting of the parents; c) parent and child turbulence—in which one parent and a child team up to produce an effect on the parent, e.g., to make the other one jealous and, d) relative induced turbulence—in which there is a stirring up of conflicts by relatives and in-laws.

Many authors have discussed the need for post-divorce parent counseling, not only for the benefit of the affected children, but also to help the divorced parents with significant adjustment problems (23, 27). Some have recommended that these counseling sessions become mandatory in order to provide the child with an advocate who is looking out for his/her best interests. It would also be helpful if divorcing parents would avail themselves of the opportunity to read some of the available books which discuss ways to prepare a child for divorce (9).

Age of the child at the time of divorce

"The younger the adolescent is when the divorce takes place, the more likely he/she will experience it as a personal abandonment and loss of the parents' love. The young adolescent is also more likely to feel guilty, with an egocentric sense of responsibility for the marital breakup, as well as having a more difficult time in handling the ambivalent feelings elicited toward either or both of the parents." Wallerstein and Kelly (25) described the following reactions to divorce in young adolescents: a) a temporary interference with entry into adolescence with regressive, dependent behavior; b) a prolonged interference with entry into adolescence with evidence of serious developmental disturbance and c) pseudo-adolescence with accelerated sexual and aggressive acting-out.

In contrast, the older adolescent is less likely to feel responsible for the divorce and be better able to approach the crisis from a reality perspective. He/she is generally involved in the divorce discussions and more likely to be told the true nature of the marital conflicts. Unfortunately, this can create a tremendous burden on the youngster and a sense of responsibility for his/her parents' welfare. It is important that divorcing parents try their best to avoid the temptation to look to their adolescent youngster for companionship and fulfillment of their own frustrated needs.

Coping skills of the adolescent

There is a great deal of variation among adolescents as to their ability to cope with the stress of divorce. Youngsters who cope best are those who possess an innate temperament of adaptability to change (24), those who have a minimum of residual separation anxiety and those who have successfully resolved the Oedipal conflict. Previous losses are also significant as they tend to be cumulative with the reactions intensifying with each experience. In this regard, adopted youngsters are more likely to view the divorce as yet another loss or abandonment similar to their relinquishment by the biological parents (22).

Immediate vs. long range effects of the divorce

Following the divorce, the initial affect experienced by the adolescent is usually grief associated with guilt. Later responses include shame coupled with resentment (1). In certain cases the feeling of guilt for causing the divorce can be seen as a warding off of the more terrifying thought that the youngster has no control or indeed no influence on the course of events in his/her environment (25). Some teenagers will act cool and detached at first, only to break down and admit their hurt feelings at some later date. One of the most specific responses to the divorce experience is the "neurosis of abandonment" described by Anthony (1) in which every new relationship is approached apprehensively with the expectation of being left, rejected or of losing love.

Adolescents affected by divorce may demonstrate a wide range of psychological reactions including behavior disorders, neurotic conflicts and psychotic breakdowns. Behavior problems include an abrupt decline in academic performance, aggressive acting-out at home and school, drug abuse, truancy, running away, sexual acting-out and group delinquent behavior. Neurotic conflicts include anxiety reactions, separation fears with school phobia, obsessive-compulsive symptoms with pervasive guilt, depersonalization experiences and psychophysiologic reactions, especially eating disorders. The stress of divorce can also be instrumental in precipitating a schizophrenic reaction.

Some authors have argued that divorce is not really the direct cause of emotional disorders and that as a group the children affected by divorce show no greater overall incidence of emotional problems, often functioning better after the divorce (5, 11, 19). It is apparent, however, that the experience of divorce may be highly traumatic for some adolescents. Still others may show no adverse effects initially but problems may manifest themselves later in life as a profound fear of marital failure (1, 3) or as adult psychiatric problems (1).

ADOLESCENT DYNAMICS AND THE DIVORCE EXPERIENCE

The crises encountered in normal adolescence can be divided roughly into two psychodynamic categories: internal (intrapsychic) and external (environmental) conflicts. The internal conflicts include the acceptance, expression and control of aggressive and sexual impulses, as well as emerging identity concerns. The external conflicts include dependency-independency issues, peer acceptance and social approval, as well as growing concerns about the future. Experiencing the divorce of one's parents during the adolescent years can intensify these conflicts, serve as a means of inhibiting their expression and resolution, or stimulate a premature attempt at mastery.

Aggression conflicts

During adolescence there is a great deal of inner turmoil and a need for external firmness, consistency and setting of limits. Divorced parents seem to have special difficulty in accomplishing these environmental controls for their children because of a preoccupation with their own problems, guilt secondary to their own acting-out and a fear of losing their child's favor to the other parent. Furthermore, there is often a sabotaging of disciplinary efforts by the other parent. The end result of this parental permissiveness is a deep sense of insecurity on the part of the youngster involved. He/she becomes caught in the classic vicious cycle of testing limits, going beyond the limits without restriction, feeling guilty and retesting the parents in a futile attempt to find a source of punishment and retribution.

Prior to the divorce the teenager often carries the burden of trying to hold the parents together and when that fails his/her frustration may be directed at the ungrateful parents with a vengeance (16). In certain cases the anger is directed at the mother for not being able to stop the child's father from leaving home or going off with another woman (17). Ultimately, this angry frustration may result in a breakdown of the adolescent's emerging capacity to accept his/her own ambivalence with a resulting lack of fusion of love and hate. The child thus becomes afraid of the potential destructiveness of his/her own anger and rage (20).

Some adolescents affected by divorce walk around with a "chip on their shoulders." They are sullen and irritable and ready to jump on anyone who crosses them. They are highly cynical and feel disillusioned with life. In some cases, the pent-up frustration and hostility is released in destructive, criminal behavior. McDermott (15) illustrated how the type of acting-out often correlates with the description of the absent parent, suggesting an identification with a part or fantasized part of the parent as a way of dealing with the loss experienced. Furthermore, the anger expressed in some male adolescents may represent a defense against threats to their masculinity elicited by the divorce experience (1).

Sexual conflicts

Blos (2) described adolescence as a second edition of childhood with an accompanying resurgence of Oedipal issues. Laufer (14) and Neubauer (18) demonstrated how the death or absence of the opposite-sex parent can interfere with Oedipal reality, intensifying and complicating the final resolution of the conflict. Miller (17) showed how the father leaving the home can be viewed as a sexual rejection by his adolescent daughter. Also, the teenage boy who is placed in a surrogate husband role after the father has departed has an especially difficult time dealing with the uncomfortable incestual feelings aroused by the closeness of the relationship with his mother.

Unfortunately, some parents tend to use the adolescent as an unconscious extension of themselves, thereby encouraging sexual acting-out. Furthermore, the parents may have a difficult time setting limits for sexual behavior because they feel they are being hypocritical, in light of their own extra-marital sexual activities. Another source of conflict is the situation in which the mother grows to resent her daughter's attractiveness, youth, sexuality and open future, causing her to react in a punitive, restrictive manner which is likely to incite defiant sexual acting-out.

Indeed, the parents' sexual needs and behavior are thrown into prominence and the child is flooded with revelations about the parents' sex lives which he/she might not have experienced if not for the divorce (20). The parents are no longer safe objects. For example, the father may be dating a girl close to the child's age, putting both in an uncomfortable pseudo-peer relationship with a breakdown of healthy generation boundaries. One way that adolescents may attempt to deal with these uncomfortable feelings is by becoming overly moralistic (27) or turning to the defenses of ascetism and intellectualism described by A. Freud (8).

Problems can also result from the accusations that either or both parents have made in the adolescent's presence about their ex-spouse's sexual inadequacies or infidelities. The child has a propensity to identify with the parent of the same sex and to fear that he/she also is destined to become a sexual failure or incapable of controlling sexual impulses (17, 25). Sexual acting-out may then become a counterphobic attempt at working through these fears or perpetuating a self-fulfilling prophesy of poor impulse control. In a related sense, girls brought up without fathers tend to be more seductive in their behavior (12) and may be inclined to act-out a search for their "lost father" through sexual relationships with older men or an early pregnancy and marriage (27).

Identity conflicts

Erikson (7) described the essential task of adolescence as the development of a sense of identity and showed how the failure of this process results in a state of identity confusion. In part, this identity is established through an identification with the parents, especially the one of the same sex. In the case of divorce this process is complicated by the absence of at least one of the parents from the home and the parents' struggle with their own concurrent identity crises (2). In desperation the child will often react by splitting the parents into good and bad (17, 20), by idealizing one parent and devaluing the other.

Sometimes there is a conscious or unconscious collusion between the parent and child to recreate the lost parent through the child's identification with the other parent's traits. This can lead to parent-child struggles which are similar to the ones that existed previously between the mother and father (1, 15). In other situations the mother may force the male child to identify with her, creating anxieties and marked defensiveness in the child (1). In contrast, the remaining parent is often manipulated by the child into playing the role of the absent parent (1). Every effort should be made to avoid this type of role playing and confused identifications.

Dependency-independency conflicts

Anna Freud (8) described the typical adolescent struggle as centering around denying, reversing, loosening and shedding the ties to the infantile objects. Blos (2) pointed out that the process of detachment from the parents during adolescence is accompanied by a profound sense of loss and isolation equivalent to the experience of mourning. He described the fear of the adolescent girl of regressing to pre-genital dependency; whereas, in the boy there is a fear of returning to the passive Oedipal stage of development. In this sense, adolescence is seen as a second stage of individuation from the parents. During this phase the youngster vacillates regularly between denying dependency needs and regressing to infantile levels with a desperate search for dependency gratifications.

The divorce experience results in an actual object loss, in contrast to the symbolic loss experienced by the adolescent as he/she emancipates him/herself from the family. In some respects the divorce-induced loss is harder to accept than losing a parent through death because there is a concomitant feeling of loss of love (17). The experience also tends to accelerate individuation of the parents with the child forced to prematurely relate to them as separate entities, often with a need to align with one of them for a sense of protection and security (25).

Children of divorce may fear abandonment by the custodial parent as well. Some may be seen to stick close to home in order to keep close watch on the parent. In contrast, some youngsters become over-involved with their peers and avoid any family ties and activities. This distancing and withdrawal can be interpreted as a defense against experiencing the pain of the family disruption (25).

The adolescent's sense of security is further undermined by extraneous pressures created by the divorce situation. Resulting financial pressures may lead to a change in life style, a new neighborhood and transfer of schools. Also, in many families the mother is forced to go to work for the first time creating a further sense of loss and feeling of abandonment. Some youngsters will react to all of these pressures with insecurity and a regression to more immature levels of behavior. On the other hand, some may become precociously mature about worldly matters, taking on numerous paying jobs and developing an intense concern about money and financial security.

Social conflicts

During adolescence the child gradually transfers interests and emotional attachments from the family to the outside world. Acceptance by peers and sexual attractiveness take precedence among the youngster's priorities. The child of divorce often feels embarrassed by the new status and may attempt to keep it a secret from peers. In some cases the youngsters actually experience a rejection from their old friends when they learn about the divorce. It is not unusual, therefore, that children from broken homes often seek out friends in a similar predicament to spare them the painful feeling of being stigmatized as different. In a healthier sense, these relationships provide mutual support and an opportunity to share and work through feelings with peers who are capable of empathizing with one another.

Dating is another experience which is adversely affected by divorce. The youngster is afraid of getting too close to a companion because of an unconscious fear of being hurt or abandoned— becomes cynical of the meaning of "love." Furthermore, there is particular difficulty in resolving the usual conflicts that arise in a courtship because of the lack of models of constructive conflict resolution. In contrast, some youngsters may become totally consumed in a love relationship as a means of escape, or in an attempt to find a security lacking in their broken home.

Future conflicts

The older adolescent becomes more concerned about the future. He/she begins to think about getting into college or making a vocational choice. There is a sense of fear and uncertainty about the adult world. There are major decisions to be made and the older adolescent, in contrast to the younger one, is more likely to turn to parents for objective advice and support. The teenager from the divorced home may fail to find that assistance from his/her parents. The parents are often too preoccupied with their own problems to be available to the youngster, or even too threatened by his/her emerging independence to offer any help. Youngsters with lesser ego strength may find this period of adolescence to be highly troublesome, resulting in an extreme sense of despair and panic.

In addition to vocation and career choice the older adolescent is beginning to think about the prospects of marriage in the near future. Many children from broken homes are outspoken about not wanting to marry and repeat the mistakes made by their parents. They seem to have a pervasive fear of marriage failure which may serve as a self-fulfilling prophesy if and when they marry later on. It is a known fact that divorce has a tendency to repeat itself through the generations.

Custody and Visitation

In most cases it is the father who moves out of the home and leaves the children in the custody of the mother. After he has moved out it is not unusual for the adolescent to feel a deep concern and sense of guilt about the father's newly acquired modest living arrangements. The youngster may become overly protective about the father's health and financial well-being. Many fathers enjoy and even encourage this pampering, especially from their teenage daughters, as this serves as an antidote for loneliness and unmet needs.

In his new role of visiting parent the father has an opportunity to play the role of "good guy" because he is not involved in the day-to-day disciplinary disputes. Furthermore, he has an easier time keeping his personal social life removed from the children, thus avoiding their resentment. In contrast, the mother is forced to make many of the major disciplinary decisions and then finds herself a further target for her child's hostility and jealousy when her dates begin to pick her up at the home. Many mothers react with intense resentment and envy of their ex-husband's position of freedom from childrearing pressures and easy opportunity to resocialize without intrusion. When the youngster becomes aware of mother's frustrations, he/she may play on her vulnerabilities by threatening to leave and move in with father. This occasionally results in an impulsive change of custody which is agreed to, not necessarily in the child's best interests, but to provide the beleaguered mother with a sense of relief or the father with a feeling of victory over his ex-wife. Such power struggles can lead only to further insecurity in the youngster. There are cases, of course, in which the child's best interests can be served by a change in custody from one parent to the other.

New concepts about custody and visitation have been provided by Goldstein, Freud and Solnit (10). They feel that in regard to custody consideration, primary concern should be given to the welfare of the child, both emotionally and physically, with the parents' interests being considered as secondary. They emphasize that there should be a continuity of care in the child-parent relationship. Once it is determined who will be the custodial parent it is that parent, not the court, who should have the power to decide under what conditions he or she wants to raise the child. Thus the non-custodial parent should have no legally enforceable right to visit the child, and the custodial parent should have the right to decide whether it is desirable for the child to have such visits. This approach was designed by the authors to protect the integrity of an ongoing relationship between the child and the custodial parent. These ideas are especially pertinent to the younger child affected by divorce and have lesser significance for the adolescent who may require contacts with the non-custodial parent for healthy identity resolution.

Reaction to Parents' Dating and Remarriage

After the divorce, the adolescent must learn to cope with the parents' dating and possible remarriage. The youngster can't help but make comparisons and feel mixed loyalties (21). In many cases the child's unresolved hostility toward one of the parents is displaced onto the date or step-parent of the same sex which ultimately recreates many of the same intra-familial conflicts experienced prior to the marital breakup.

Some adolescents will become adept at playing the parents' companion against the other parent: "Dad's girlfriend is much nicer than you. She's like a real friend to me." Such tactics provide the youngster with a sense of power and control in an attempt to defend against deep feelings of insecurity and helplessness. Unfortuantely, some parents will reinforce such patterns by encouraging their dates to win the child over, as yet another means of getting back at their ex-spouse.

One of the most difficult tasks of the divorcing parents is to avoid over-stimulating their adolescent youngsters by making obvious their sexual liaisons with dating partners. Even though the teenagers may seem to be highly sophisticated about sexual matters, they generally have a strong need to deny their parents' extra-marital relations. They are usually successful unless their parents' sex life is flaunted at them. The resulting discomfort is rarely verbalized but often acted-out in behavior designed to punish the parents. In general, it is best for the parents to keep their sexual activities removed from their teenage children, even if its means telling them "little white lies" such as spending the weekend with a same sexed friend rather than a date. Such dishonesty is really protective and is usually respected as such by the youngsters even though they may suspect the truth. On the other hand, when the parent has established a meaningful heterosexual relationship, with the prospects of remarriage, it is easier for the youngster to accept the notion that sleeping or living together is a means of two people getting to know one another in order to avoid another marital failure which would be deleterious to all concerned.

The remarriage of parents is a difficult adjustment for children of all ages, especially adolescents. It is crucial that the youngsters be given ample opportunity to work through their feelings, but not given the power to influence the parent's decision or choice of mate. After the marriage it is important to differentiate the roles of parent and step-parent. The biological parent will always have an essential role in providing the child with a sense of geneological identity, even though the step-parent may play an increasingly important role in the youngster's psychological development. Every effort should be made to include the non-custodial biological parent in celebrations and important milestone events in the teenager's life.

There are those situations in which the non-custodial parent has demonstrated no genuine concern and interest in the youngster following the divorce. In these cases, the prospects of adoption by the step-parent becomes an issue. Such a major decision should be arrived at gradually, with lengthy discussions and sharing of feelings by all involved. If it appears that the youngster is merely attempting to gain revenge against the departed parent, the adoption should be discouraged as it is likely to leave him/her with considerable guilt in later years. In general, adoption is a more pertinent issue with the preadolescent child who requires a sense of familial intactness and stability for healthy identifications and emotional development. For the adolescent, who is so close to adult legal status, a change of name and identity can be very unsettling and create further conflicts. In a few selected situations, however, adoption by the step-parent may be the healthiest alternative and provide the youngster with the sense of security necessary to continue the unfinished work of adolescence.

Discussion

It can be argued that the anger, bitterness and tension associated with a bad marriage or an "emotional divorce" causes more damage to a developing adolescent than the legal act of divorce itself. Although this is true in many cases, experiencing parental divorce can be seen to create certain psychological vulnerabilities in affected adolescents: 1) a fear of abandonment, rejection or loss of love; 2) an interference with the resolution of the typical adolescent conflicts and 3) an intense fear of personal marital failure. In addition, the contemporary trends toward the "good divorce" and the impulsive marital breakup leave the involved youngsters with considerable confusion and disillusionment.

The greater likelihood of the products of divorce having an unsuccessful marriage of their own is a serious issue which needs further study and consideration. For the most part, these persons seem to have identified with the parental failure and approach their own marriage with either an expectation of failure or an overdetermination to succeed. With some, the fear of divorce makes every argument with their spouse seem like a major crisis resulting in an avoidance of necessary confrontation and expression of feelings.

If for no other reason, the tendency toward "hereditary divorce" makes it crucial for the divorcing couples to do everything they can to minimize the trauma and long-lasting effects on their children. Even though they are unable to resolve the hostility that exists between them, they must make every effort to avoid using their children as pawns and to treat them as individuals with personal needs and concerns. What these youngsters are looking for, more than anything else, is a reestablishment of "generation boundaries" in which they can relate to their parents as authority figures, not friends. The parents, including step-parents, must work together, as best they can, to provide loving support as well as firm limits and controls. This will enable their adolescents to continue growing toward individuation; acceptance, expression and control of aggressive and sexual impulses; identity formation; security in the peer world and a healthy, positive attitude toward the future.

Divorcing parents, in particular, need to be aware of the dynamics and typical reactions of adolescents so that they can separate out the divorce-related issues. This can be accomplished by reading books on the subject and attending special parent group meetings. Such programs are frequently offered at community mental health centers, child guidance clinics and religious institutions. The affected teenagers can also benefit from sharing their personal feelings and experiences with other youngsters experiencing parental divorce. This is accomplished on an informal basis when children of divorce seek each other out as friends, but professionally or para-professionally run rap-groups can be very beneficial as well. It is our impression that both the immediate psychological problems and the long range difficulties, namely adult psychological conflicts and marital failure, can be minimized by preventive measures designed to counter the tendencies of grieving victims of divorce to internalize their conflicts and thus avoid a healthy working through of their problems.

Mental health workers must continue to study the etiology of marital failure and provide guidelines for its prevention. Parents must be taught the importance of mutual respect and open communication among family members. Children must be shown how to resolve interpersonal conflicts through discussion and compromise. Furthermore, they must be helped to appreciate the importance of self-discipline and fulfillment of personal commitments. Youngsters who grow up cherishing these basic values are more likely to achieve marital success in their own lives and thus diminish the risk of transmitting divorce-related conflicts to their offspring.

REFERENCES

1. Anthony, E. J. "Children At Risk From Divorce: A Review," in *The Child In His Family: Children At Psychiatric Risk,* Vol. 3, E. J. Anthony and C. Koupernik, eds. New York: John Wiley, 1974, pp. 461-477.
2. Blos, P. *On Adolescence.* New York: Free Press, 1962.
3. Blumenthal, M. D. "Mental Health Among the Divorced," *Arch. Gen. Psychiat.,* Vol. 16, No. 5, 1967, pp. 603-608.
4. Briscoe, C. W. et al. "Divorce and Psychiatric Disease," *Arch. Gen. Psychiat.,* Vol. 29, No. 1, 1973, pp. 119-125.
5. Burchinal, L. G. "Characteristics of Adolescents From Unbroken, Broken and Reconstituted Families," *Jour. of Marriage and the Family,* Vol. 26, 1964, pp. 44-51.
6. Despert, J. L. *Children of Divorce.* Garden City, New York: Doubleday, 1962.
7. Erikson, E. E. *Identity Youth and Crisis.* New York: W. W. Norton, 1968.
8. Freud, A. "Adolescence," *Psychoan. Study of the Child,* Vol. 13, 1958, pp. 255-278.
9. Gardner, R. A. *The Boys and Girls Book About Divorce.* New York: Jason Aronson, 1970.
10. Goldstein, J., Freud, A., and Solnit, A. J. *Beyond the Best Interests of the Child.* New York: Free Press, 1973.
11. Goode, W. J. *After Divorce.* Glencoe, Ill.: Free Press, 1956.
12. Hetherington, E. M. "Girls Without Fathers," *Psychology Today,* Vol. 6, 1973, pp. 47-52.
13. Landis, J. T. "The Trauma of Children When Parents Divorce," *Marriage and Family Living,* Vol. 22, 1960, pp. 7-13.
14. Laufer, M. "Object Loss and Mourning During Adolescence," *Psychoan. Study of the Child,* Vol. 21, 1966, pp. 269-293.
15. McDermott, J. F. "Divorce and its Psychiatric Sequelae in Children," *Arch. Gen. Psychiat.,* Vol. 23, No. 5, 1970, pp. 421-427.
16. Milgrim, S. A. "The Adolescent in Relation to His Separated Yet Inseparable Parents," in *Children of Separation and Divorce,* I. R. Stuart and L. E. Abt, eds. New York: Grossman, 1972, pp. 37-53.
17. Miller, D. *Adolescence: Psychology, Psychopathy and Psychotherapy.* New York: Aronson, 1974, pp. 383-385.
18. Neubauer, P. "The One Parent Child and His Oedipal Development," *Psychoan. Study of the Child,* Vol. 15, 1960, pp. 286-309.
19. Nye, F. I. "Child Adjustment in Broken and Unhappy Unbroken Homes," *Marriage and Family Living,* Vol. 19, 1957, pp. 356-361.
20. Rogers, R. R. et al. "Roundtable: Divorce," *Medical Aspects of Human Sexuality,* Vol. 10, No. 1, 1976, pp. 55-80.
21. Schlesinger, B. and Stasiuk, E. "Children of Divorced Parents in Second Marriages," in *Children of Separation and Divorce,* I. R. Stuart and L. E. Abt, eds. New York: Grossman, 1972, pp. 19-35.
22. Sorosky, A. D., Baran, A., and Pannor, R. "Identity Conflicts in Adoptees," *Amer. Jour. of Orthopsychiat.,* Vol. 45, No. 1, 1975, pp. 18-27.
23. Steinzor, B. *When Parents Divorce.* New York: Pantheon, 1969.
24. Thomas A., Chess, S., and Birch, H. G. *Temperament and Behavior Disorders in Children.* New York: N. Y. Univ. Press, 1969.
25. Wallerstein, J. S. and Kelley, J. B. "The Effects of Parental Divorce: The Adolescent Experience," in *The Child in His Family: Children at Psychiatric Risk,* Vol. 3, E. J. Anthony and C. Koupernik, eds. New York: John Wiley, 1974, pp. 479-505.
26. Westman, J. C. et al. "Role of Child Psychiatry in Divorce," *Arch. Gen. Psychiat.,* Vol. 23, No. 5, 1970, pp. 416-420.
27. Westman, J. C. "Effect of Divorce on a Child's Personality," *Medical Aspects of Human Sexuality,* Vol. 6, No. 1, 1972, pp. 38-55.

22

myths that intrude on the
adaptation of the stepfamily

gerda l. schulman

This article will focus on certain phenomena that the writer has repeatedly observed in stepfamilies in which at least one of the stepchildren had overt problems severe enough to prompt the family to seek help. Although all families—natural as well as reconstituted ones—share some social and interpersonal characteristics, the stepfamily has certain unique problems which tend both to intensify the normally existing family conflicts and tensions and to create some new ones that stem from the joining of two family groups in which the children are biologically related to only one parent.

It is not the writer's intent to indicate in any way that all stepfamilies are or have to become problem families; most reconstituted families, however, are more susceptible to particular culturally accepted and fostered myths, and most of these families have lived through considerably more trauma than has the average family. It is thus clear that they seem to be more vulnerable and susceptible to trouble.

The nonproblem and the problem stepfamily share certain characteristics. The difference between them lies more in the degree of the distortions and rigidification of the myths. The distortions and rigidification concern the existence of such compensatory factors as the health of the new parental pair and of the stepchildren and the age and sex of the stepchildren.

There are two kinds of recurring myths in the reconstituted family that seem to be generic because they have occurred in different countries and cultures from time immemorial and have been handed down from generation to generation through fairy tales, sayings, and proverbs. They are the myth of the "bad stepmother" and the countermyth of "instant love" that is expected from the stepparent as well as from the stepchild.

Moreover, in the stepfamily as in the natural family, difficulties can also arise because of certain outer realities or as a result of inner realities that are related to transferentially influenced wishes, fantasies, and hopes—all of which tend to cause overexpectation and disappointments. In the reconstituted family, however, fantasies and hopes play larger parts than in the ordinary family and projection tends to occur and be played out more intensively and in a more complicated way. This projection is due in large measure to the fact that the child has already incurred a loss that not only creates greater vulnerability in him but tends to increase and stimulate the fantasy of the perfect mother (or father). The adult stepparent, who is a figure in the fantasy, tends to react irrationally to the messages inherent in the child's behavior partly because he too is vulnerable. Like the stepchild, he has experienced abandonment and rejection and finds himself especially in need of emotional nurture and support at the very time when he has to assume a new role. On the other hand, the ready-made family has a special appeal for individuals who, for a number of reasons, have been delayed in their development and are attracted to a partner with children.

Reprinted, by permission, from *Social Casework*, 1972, *53*, 131-39. Copyright ©1972 by Family Service Association of America.

The writer has observed that when these troubled new families are brought together in family treatment, myth and reality are subtly interwoven in the family system and that patterns evolve which distinguish these families from other families. Although the purpose of this article is not to deal with the treatment process per se . . . , the importance of family sessions for diagnostic as well as for treatment purposes should be stressed. The family therapist needs to be aware of and sufficiently free of the myths in order to intervene in the system by making manifest what occurs and separating myth from reality. Only then can the therapist help to effect changes that will bring about genuine cohesiveness in the new family. If the therapist is too bound by the taboos and not able to deal with the resistance, the family members will be unable to resolve their basic difficulties.

For the purpose of differentiation, these families may be grouped as follows: (1) families with a stepfather who has no children of his own and who marries a woman with a child or children; (2) families with a stepmother who has no children of her own and who marries a man with a child or children; and (3) families in which both the man and the woman have children of their own from a previous union and now establish a family in which the man and the woman are both a natural and a stepparent. This type of family will be referred to as a "combination family."[1]

In any of these groups, a child may subsequently be born to the marital pair because of usually existing strong strivings to cement their union. Depending on the depth and relative health of the family's relationships, the natural child of this union may provide either added closeness (communality of interests) or additional strain. In at least one family with whom the writer worked, the child of the new union was placed out of the home in foster care, although the mother's two older children, who were brought by her into the new marriage, also had serious problems. The mother was overprotective of them and never permitted their stepfather to play a significant role, although she complained that he showed no interest in them. Partly as a result of this parental behavior, their child was neglected, developed problems, and, as sacrificial lamb, became the expendable member in the family.

PREVIOUSLY UNMARRIED STEPFATHER

In the great majority of families in which a previously unmarried man becomes a stepfather, the man was very dependent on his family of origin (usually his mother) and, therefore, not only married late but liked the thought of a woman with children and thus, in a way, married a "mother." In his relationship with his stepchild, he is both identified with the child and in rivalry with him. The other type of man in this category is one who in his early years was an "antifamily" man (prematurely independent, acting-out adventurer, or a prison-type character) but later settled down and wanted to make up for the loss of time, unconsciously hoping for respectability and stability.

The dependent mother's boy is usually unsure of and not very active in pursuits of his role. He is more interested in his wife's capacity to mother him than in being a strong father—a characteristic that causes special complications in relation to boys. With girls, these men usually have more positive, often teasing-flirtatious relationships, which tend to threaten the mothers especially when their daughters reach adolescence. If the mother fights or struggles, this type of man often relinquishes his role as father to pacify the wife.

The second type of man appears much stronger and acts in an autocratic manner because by the time he settles down, he has had to repress his antisocial or infantile impulses. He now rejects any childlike or acting-out behavior on the part of his stepchild. The mother of the child is often intimidated by, but in need of, the man and sacrifices the interest of the child to keep peace in the marriage. Although these two types of men are different and consequently behave differently as husband and stepfather, certain fantasies and fears that exist in all these families are related to their roles rather than to their personalities.

There are two potent fantasies that seem to be played out differently and contribute to a different myth. The first is similar to the one in families in which there is a stepmother, although being a stepfather does not carry with it the same expectation as being a stepmother, largely because in our culture love and nurturing is expected less from a man than from a woman. Thus, there are no fairy tales of a "wicked stepfather," but there exists, nonetheless, a tendency to idealize the natural father. "If only he would be my real father" is a frequently heard statement. Both stepfather and stepchild want closeness and acceptance of the other. Their object of comparison is a fantasy rival and, as all wishful fantasies, is idealized. Conversely, the stepfather thinks, "If she were my real daughter (son), she (he) would love and obey me." The child thinks, "If he were my real father, he would adopt me, stick up for me, protect me."

The writer discovered that in one of the families she treated, the stepdaughter had always wanted to be adopted by her stepfather and interpreted his failure to do so as a clear sign of his lack of caring. When she was about nine years old, her stepfather approached her one day and in his customary teasing way asked her whether she wanted to be adopted by him. The little girl did not think he meant it and angrily said, "No." The stepfather understood her answer as a blatant rejection and never asked her again. Nine years later, this incident came to light in a family therapy session.

The second fantasy exists only in families with stepfathers and stepdaughters and is more in the nature of a fear on the part of the mother; namely, that the stepfather will find the stepdaughter more desirable than the mother. This fear is often expressed in vague anxieties and allusions and is projected onto the outside, but underneath lies the very potent rape fantasy. In some families the mother's rejection of, or even expulsion of, her daughter during adolescence is related to this fantasy, as is the stepfather's withdrawal and overcritical attitude during the period of the girl's growing up. At best, the stepfather often finds himself caught between his wife's wanting him to show interest in her daughter and his fear that such interest will be misconstrued or that his impulses will not stand the strain of closeness. The oedipal situation is more overt because the incestual taboos are not as applicable.

THE "WICKED" STEPMOTHER

Contrary to the popular myth, most stepmothers are neither wicked nor cruel, nor do all families who have stepmothers have serious problems. If a woman who marries a man with a child has sufficient ego strength and has the genuine support of a husband, the stepmother-stepchild relationship can grow into a mutually enriching and satisfying one. However, if the stepmother is a person with shaky self-esteem and in need of support and the husband chooses her (albeit unconsciously) to mother him rather than his child, the relationship is bound to become problematic, no matter what the overt intention is. In fact, many women who choose such a relationship are moved by genuine desire to "mother" an "orphan" because in their childhood they themselves missed mothering, actually or psychologically. The very experience that motivates them makes them, at the same time, poorly suited to assume a role that is bound to reawaken earlier feelings.

In some instances, the new marriage is contracted under the pretense that children of the man's first marriage will not join the household. To the surprise of the new wife, subsequent circumstances create a coercive situation in which the wife has little choice but to take the children into her home, lest she lose the affection or esteem of her husband. Added to this problem is the cultural expectation that the natural father should give a home to his child in the absence of the child's mother. The relatively frequent occurrence of the collapse of arrangements that have held for long periods of time prior to the new marriage leads this writer to suspect that collusive messages may have been set into motion between the child's father and the child's caretaker (grandparents, foster parents, institutions, or even the child's own mother) at the time of the father's remarriage, culminating in the child's joining the new household.

Even if there are no messages on the part of the parents, the child himself is aware of the fact that circumstances have changed and that there is now a possible home for him. His yearnings to become part of the new family may drive him to act in such a way that the natural parent, as well as the stepparent, have no choice but to let the child join them. In this context, it frequently happens that a child who has adjusted to a placement facility suddenly begins to act out and forces action both by the institution and the parents.

In both types of families, the new wife who chooses or is forced into the role of stepmother may have doubts about the real motivation for the husband's marrying her, although the degree of doubts may differ. Was she chosen for herself or just to take care of his children? The stepmother as well as the stepchild, therefore, can suffer from the Cinderella myth. This kind of feeling is aroused and accentuated if the husband (the natural father of the children) is not genuinely supportive of and giving to his wife. Although it is true that any mother's ability to give to and be related to her child is at least partially dependent on the "nurturing" she gets from her mate, a stepmother is even more dependent on and in need of her husband's support. The reason for this need is that the stepmother is a newcomer to an already formed relationship and is seen both as a rescuer as well as an intruder into the father-child dyad. Indeed hers is a most complicated position. She has, or feels she has, to make up for the child's past hurt inflicted by the natural mother, while at the same time the child projects onto her anger that really belongs to his now idealized natural mother. In such a situation all family members clearly feel insecure and vulnerable and engage in a great deal of mutual testing.

In the F family the stepmother complained of the clinging, demanding behavior of her stepson, who needed to be reassured repeatedly that she loved him. This need in turn created guilt in Mrs. F, who could not admit her own resentment and concomitant anger toward the child. The more she assured him and the therapist that she loved the child "as if he were her own," the more guilty she felt and the more the child, sensing her real feeling, pressed for reassurance. Mr. F, the father, was torn between his identification with the child and his need to appease his wife and was unable to assume the kind of responsibility that would be reassuring and strengthening both to his wife and his child. As so often happens in conflicting situations, he tried to accomplish both at once and therefore did neither well. He bullied the child and scolded him for being a nuisance, and he subtly undermined his wife's role by not supporting her and by joining the child, implying that the stepmother was indeed lacking affection and understanding. Being a basically passive person, he reverted to his usual pattern of withdrawal, which only left his wife feeling embittered and overwhelmed.

Because the stepmother role and status is so dependent on the support of the husband, it is the passive, weak, and excessively dependent man who most often lets his wife and child down. Families and often even professionals confuse the seeking and forming of alliances or merging with genuine support—another distortion that needs to be dispelled by the therapist. "I always agree with my wife" is a frequently made statement that implies blind alliance against the child, fostering the child's feeling that his father has betrayed and sacrificed him and adding to his angry and hateful feelings toward the stepmother. The wife, on the other hand, senses the husband's underlying feelings or sees through his actions, and she feels increasingly alone, helpless, and overwhelmed by the responsibility.

By virtue of his passivity, the child's father keeps out of the area of significant transactions with his child—a position that allows him to criticize his wife no matter what she does with the child. The stepmother is thereby often cast in the position of being the disciplinarian, whereas the father by default emerges as the softer, kinder parent. The predicament of her role adds to the stepmother's helplessness and engenders anger that is usually turned against the child, and the vicious cycle is completed.

There are many variations of this theme affecting the troubled stepfamily's transactions. In family treatment sessions, the existing undercurrent and conflict must be brought to the surface so that it can be modified. If modification does not occur, the newly formed family often breaks up either through divorce of the parents or placement of the child. In either case, if the problem is not worked through, the resulting damage is not only in the second trauma but in the residual anger and guilt experienced by the dyad that has stayed together.

Thus far this article has dealt with the kind of constellation occurring in a stepfamily which tends to intensify aspects of the *Cinderella* and *Hansel and Gretel* myth in which both the stepmother and the stepchild are caught. Both feel unloved, misunderstood, exploited, and mistreated; both are caught in a situation that forces them to act in a certain way because of circumstances and a competitor against whom nobody can win. In dreams, daydreams, and fantasies of the wishful or anxiety-arousing variety and in hopes, fears, and expectations, the stepchild compares the stepmother unfavorably with the natural mother, who becomes endowed with qualities she may never have had. The stepmother, who at best operates within a difficult reality, is sensitive to the comparison because of the myth of the bad stepmother, which the father, as the spokesman of the culture, often reinforces.

The stepchild, who already feels discriminated against, is often exposed to unrealistic hopes and expectations of the stepmother, which complicate the relationship, especially when the child is seen as a symbol rather than as a real person. Behavior difficulties of the stepchild are often considered by the stepmother as conformation of her shortcomings (proof of her "badness"). In instances that occur more frequently between a stepmother and an older stepchild, difficulties may arise when the stepmother is intent on infantalizing a child who is at a period when he needs freedom to grow up and separate.

This issue became serious in the R family. Mrs. R, the stepmother, showed considerable tolerance and love for her younger stepson, but did not value or encourage independent strivings of her older seventeen-year-old stepson. For instance, she refused him the use of the washing machine to wash his soiled underwear (the young man suffered from encopresis). His desire to do his own washing was a step on his part toward assuming self-responsibility. In general, she complained less about this serious symptom than about his not calling her "mother" and his "not being good and doing as I tell him to." The father felt some warmth and pity for his son, but always allied himself with his wife in an effort to keep her satisfied and pleased. The young man's excellence in school and responsibility in his part-time job were overlooked by both father and stepmother.

THE COMBINATION FAMILY

In this kind of family, each parent is at the same time a natural parent and a stepparent. Many of the transactions, patterns, and myths thus far described also exist in such a family. Because each parent and each child is cast in and carries both roles, however, there seems to be more room for reality testing, and dilution that counters and decreases fantasies can take place. For instance, if a stepchild feels mistreated and neglected by his stepmother or indifferently treated by his stepfather, but he sees similar behavior toward the natural child, the stepchild feels somewhat reassured. He no longer feels that he is hated because he is not the real child, and he can view the stepparent more realistically as a human being with shortcomings. More significantly, because each child in such a family is in the same position, empathy and mutual support develop more easily among the stepsiblings and can be utilized profitably in treatment.

The combination family, however, is often characterized by a good deal of competition and rivalry and an inclination to use one's own children as models and the other parent's children as weapons or targets so that the children are often caught in a crosscurrent of misuse and exploitation, which finally erupts in a free-for-all battle among the children, who find it safer to fight one another than to fight the parental person. Although this fighting can also occur in a family with many children, the stimulus and approbation for such actions are much greater in a stepfamily.

Divisions and alliances that often result in "cleavage patterns"[2] are more likely expressed in the status and the behavior of subgroups, which are often made scapegoats in much the same way that individuals are in ordinary families. This syndrome has a diluting effect and makes for mutual support in the subgroup.

Although the combination family consists of two existing family units, one subgroup is usually considered the basic family and is accorded the dominant position. The difference in status does not appear to depend on whether the subgroup is headed by the mother or the father, but rather on whose house becomes the new family's home and which of the parents is the dominant partner. Because each of these subgroups finds itself in a new situation, the members try to protect each other against what is experienced as alien and perhaps hostile. The communication style between subgroups is usually defensive-aggressive and expressed in such statements as, "My children are better behaved than yours; they have fewer problems; they are more considerate than yours."

The older siblings in each subgroup may become inordinately protective of their younger brothers or sisters and consequently critical of attitudes and actions of the stepparent, especially the stepmother. This type of behavior most frequently occurs if the older sibling had operated as a parent substitute prior to the remarriage. Although he may feel somewhat relieved and freed of a burden, he now also feels deprived of gratification and status; he may especially resent it if the stepparent, joined by his natural parent, once again treats him like a child. The stepparent in turn senses the older stepchild's critical appraisal, which is more often than not also carried by the kinship of the absent parent. Grandparents, who have often been called upon to substitute for the absent parent, stand similarly to lose and often sabotage from the outside the tenuous position of the stepparent.

Another subgroup consists of the marital pair, each of whom, as already stated, may use the children in the battle against the marital partner but, nonetheless, tends to join the other in the feeling that "if not for the children all would be well." Thus, although each child has to relinquish his parent to a stranger, he finds some solace in the fact that the other children have feelings similar to his own and an empathetic camaraderie tends to develop.

The youngest child in these families is usually favored and becomes more quickly absorbed by the stepfamily. Accordingly both the marital alliance and the "adoption" of the youngest child cut across original family boundaries and represent significant movement toward the becoming of a "new family."

The L family consists of Mr. L and his three children and Mrs. L and her two children. Jeannie, the youngest daughter of Mr. L, soon became Mrs. L's pet. Jeannie's status was equally resented by both sets of children for different reasons. They inclined alternately to gang up against Jeannie or spoil her. Their actions, however, gradually produced some linkage in all the older children, which eventually turned into closeness. Conversely, and unhappily for the child who had the greatest number of problems, both sets of children began to treat twelve-year-old Henry as the scapegoat, and they acted in amazing unison in relation to him.

As we can see, subgrouping occurs increasingly as the new family begins to have its own history together. The family therapist needs to be aware of the fact that in the process that welds two families together, even making a scapegoat of one of the subgroup members may at times represent a positive, unifying force that can not and should not be treated like the rigidified scapegoat pattern that exists in the original biological family. The family therapist may therefore choose to emphasize that at long last all children seem to agree on certain issues and even become friendlier with one another, rather than only to challenge the treating of one child as a scapegoat.

Similarly, feelings, such as sadness over the interest the parents have in each other causing the children to feel excluded, on the one hand foster resentment against the adult authorities, but on the other hand produce positive feelings among the peers (shared sadness). Because each child has either lost or has had to give up a parent, stepsiblings are often able to identify with such syndromes as loyalty conflict and resentment against the stepparent. Such peer support thus hastens the process of identification among the children; if it is utilized in the therapeutic situation, it represents a mighty force against competition and rivalry.

Because the combination family usually has to accommodate several children of different sexes and ages and with different needs, personalities, and past experiences, the questions of "Is there enough to go around?" and "How can one be fair?" become crucial issues which, if not resolved, make for great conflicts. Bedtime, allowances, privileges, and responsibilities are the issues most used in the conflict that hides much more basic questions, feelings, and needs.

Although similar issues may also develop in the natural family, natural parents seem to have greater ability to deal with their children in a rational way. They seem to respond more to their children according to the needs and rights that are dictated by age and sex differences, whereas in the combination family, issues are more likely to be dealt with in an irrational fashion. A stepchild often feels that he has to do more chores or is receiving less not because he is older but because he is loved less. In turn, the stepparent, equally needy, seems to expect from the stepchild more gratitude and acknowledgment, which are rarely shown. Even appropriate but unequal treatment is considered unfair by stepchildren. Some stepparents, joined by their spouses, are likely to counter these reactions by becoming rigidly "fair" in an effort to treat all children alike.

In one of the families treated by the writer, a fifteen-year-old stepson was not permitted to visit the parents of his deceased mother. They lived out of town and offered to pay for the trip because it would be "unfair" to the other children in the family, who were not in such a "favorable" position. The fact that this boy, who had lost his mother in a tragic accident (a circumstance very different from those of the other children whose father was living), had been moved around among various relatives prior to his father's remarriage was not given consideration by anyone and did not affect the decision. The degree of dissociation in relation to this child's "unequal" past life experience was phenomenal. The rationalization for the decision was that "in our family all children are treated the same."

One of the goals in family therapy with these families is to counteract this artificial equation and the existing clichés by eliciting and stressing the differences in feelings and attitudes and to treat them with the understanding that differences not only exist but are in order. What is needed is honesty about one's feelings rather than denial, which only adds to guilt and projection and makes it less possible to deal rationally with children. If the stepparent is freed from the impossible expectation that he love another person's child as his own or love him at all, it will be possible to insist that appropriate treatment is required by each individual in the family so that the family can function and an individual can grow.

PREMARITAL AND PREPARENTAL PREPARATION

Discussion thus far has centered on some of the existing myths, misconceptions, and distortions in reconstituted families and the ways in which they affect subsequent relationships within the new family. Because they are handed down in one way or another from generation to generation, they cannot be dealt with as if they were only symptoms of a particular family's pathogenicity, but it is necessary also to challenge the cultural misnomers and clichés. This challenging can be done best before a new family is formed because the framework of discussion can still be a relatively objective one. Problems that are likely to arise can be foreseen and certain issues can be examined theoretically. The difference, for instance, between allowing a child whose parent is planning to get married to make the decision for the parent and allowing the child to respond to the impending event cannot be emphasized enough. However much a child resents or welcomes his parent's remarriage, he should never be put into the position of assuming responsibility for the decision itself. Marriage is a contract between adults and not between a child and an adult.

Adults who put a child in this abnormal position only create problems for themselves and the child, regardless of whether the marriage eventually takes place. Although a marital partner is chosen by the parent, the child *becomes* a stepchild. Family therapy during such crucial time enables the members of the family-to-be to get to know one another with greater honesty than is possible in a social situation. Therapy gives the child the opportunity to express his feelings regarding an event over which he has not—and should not—have control; however, he is given a chance to become part of a meaningful process of preparation.

Although part of a parent's natural motivation in contemplating remarriage may be to secure a substitute parent for his child, there is often an underlying requirement for instant love and devotion on the part of both the child and the stepparent-to-be, which turns the healthy motivation into something unrealistic and possibly pathogenic. No other relationship is burdened by such an expectation. Even men who become fathers are permitted to go through an adjustment period. Different from a man and a woman who can have subsequent mates, a child can only have *one* real parent. This obvious fact is denied even though some cultures, such as the French, tend to beautify the relationship by calling the stepmother *belle mère* (beautiful mother). No wonder then that the name by which a stepparent is called is endowed with such importance. The name "mother" will not necessarily make the wish come true and bestow on the relationship something that in reality never can be.

The issues of choice, as well as opportunity for the development of what is at best a complex and conflicting relationship for all members who eventually will form the nucleus of a new family, have a greater chance to be resolved at least partially if they are dealt with before the new marriage takes place. Under the best of circumstances the actual life-together experience will evoke feelings that will have to be worked out later. The new family has to assume tasks that the natural family does not have to undertake. There is not time for marital adjustment before the children come. At least three, and often more, individuals have to make a rather abrupt operational adjustment to each other. The fact that only positive feelings are expected of the stepchild and the stepparent complicates rather than facilitates the matter.

Family therapy as a treatment modality can be particularly useful to the reconstituted family both during the time of planning and when the new family is already living together. Because mythical as well as real expectations, hopes, and fears are shared by most family members and because they are culturally reinforced, the family therapist has an important role in challenging and decreasing them. Moreover, because we are dealing with at least two distinct subgroups which have to learn to live together, family treatment, with its emphasis on genuine communication, often enables the family fragments to move from pseudo wholeness and unity through the stages of difference and differentiation to achieve genuine unity. Instead of feeling second best, they begin to appreciate and value their uniqueness.

SUMMARY

The writer has attempted to show how the adjustment problems existing in the reconstituted family are complicated by the existence of certain myths and expectations that put undue stresses on the family. Wishful expectations and fears are aroused in all members of a new family, but, to the extent that they are reinforced by our culture, they become less accessible to change. Even therapists unwittingly contribute to the myths; it is not uncommon to hear therapists referring to the stepparent as "your father" or "your mother" or acting as if a child has always lived in his new family, thus denying the child's special identity.

Like other families, the reconstituted family has to deal with the issues of idealization and projection; however, because all members have lived through either abandonment or expulsion, or sometimes both, they are considerably more sensitive to criticism and rejection. They also are more likely to experience feelings of worthlessness than are other families, whether they deal with these feelings through denial or acting out. Although certain phenomena are shared by all types of reconstituted families, significant differences are apparent and depend on the sex of the substitute parents and the child and whether children of one or both former unions join the new family.

The writer has used data of reconstituted families that have developed sufficiently serious problems to require therapeutic intervention. Like natural families, a great majority of the reconstituted families manage their lives with reasonable success. The syndromes described here, albeit to a lesser degree, occur in and affect all reconstituted families, although they need not lead to pathogenic interaction. The writer believes that family treatment is a particularly helpful modality for the troubled reconstituted family because it emphasizes genuine communication and enables a family to engage in the kind of process that encourages differentiation rather than competition and fragmentation and that eventually leads to a new and unique alignment.

FOOTNOTES

[1] Anne W. Simon, *The Stepchild in the Family: A View of Children in Remarriage* (New York: Odyssey Press, 1964), p. 201.

[2] Jessie Bernard, *Remarriage: A Study of Marriage* (New York: The Dryden Press, 1956) cited in footnote by Simon, *Stepchild in the Family*, p. 203.

23   alternatives in child rearing in the 1970s

bernice t. eiduson

jerome cohen

jannette alexander

Since 1965 there is considerable journalistic and informal evidence that many variants of the two-parent nuclear family have been appearing on the American middle-class scene.[7,12,13,26,40,42,66] Many of these alternative family styles grew out of the "counter-cultures," which were vocally and visibly alienated from society. As many of the social scientists who studied the original middle-class, turned-off adolescents and young adults in the middle and late 1960s had noted, members of these groups had come from cultured, sophisticated, economically advantaged homes, and had been carefully reared by mothers (often well-educated and trained) who had assumed traditional roles and who had taken their child-rearing functions seriously and devotedly.[1,6,21,34,35,36,63,68,69]

The members of the counter-cultures thus were themselves educated and sophisticated. In the values they espoused—their search for humanism, for meaningful personal relationships, for non-violent solutions, for direct and uninhibited gratifications, for maximizing individual potential and respecting individual difference—their anti-authority and anti-Establishment attitudes were focal. Since these counter-culture people were of child-bearing age, it raised the question of how children in alternative family styles were being reared.[8,24,50,57,60,64]

Children had been mentioned superficially and in an off-handed way in most of the writing on the counter-cultures. The bulk of the lively journalistic and social science interest in alienated young people had been devoted to their struggles to separate themselves and to be separated from the Establishment;[10,11,15,32,38,41,51,52,55] to their value systems and beliefs; and to the life styles they set up to better express both their values and their outrage at traditional and "system-bound" ways of living.[9,16,23,33,39,44,56] The most telling reports have come from journalistic documentation, often self-revelatory.[14,59,61,62,65] These books compare in interest, if not depth, with the fascinating historical research accounts of earlier attempts in American history to cope with difference, disappointment, frustration, and denial by the majority of society.[22,29,67] In these latter, the role of children is given some attention, particularly as the structure of the groups, as intentional communes, aimed at complete self-sustenance and isolation from involvement with formal institutions in the outside community. Then, planning for the children's upbringing and education and roles grew out of a need to formalize structures and responsibility, out of a sense of commitment to the group, and a desire to guarantee its perpetuity.[50,67]

In accounts of current alternative life styles, children have generally been more casually treated, an indication perhaps of their more informally developed roles. In a pilot study undertaken by the UCLA Project, all references to children in twelve volumes on alternative life styles were collated, and a content analysis of specific dimensions related to demographic and behavioral characteristics—

Reprinted, by permission, from *American Journal of Orthopsychiatry*, 1973, *43*, 720-31. Copyright ©1973 by the American Orthopsychiatric Association, Inc.

number involved, activities, roles, caretaking arrangements to which they were exposed, eating, sleeping, and play arrangements.[18,19,33,39,42,44,50,54,59,67] These volumes dealt primarily with communes, but also included bibliographies on single mothers who establish one-parent families by keeping their infants, and group marriage arrangements.

It was evident from these accounts, admittedly more journalistic than scholarly, that children were by and large a secondary source of concern. That is, the life styles had been entered into by parents because of their own needs, desires, motivations, and preferences; the needs of children had usually been thought afterward to be also well-met. This is not to say that no thought was given to child care and to optimizing the child's environment in line with what parents regarded as valuable psychological and physical nutrients for growth; in some cases this was indicated in these accounts. In subsequent pilot work undertaken by this project, through detailed, standardized depth interviews and home observations, this had been shown not only to be the case, but to exist to a degree scarcely matched in other than highly sophisticated day-care centers or kibbutz-like family models.[49,58] Furthermore, in these reports, the meshing between parent needs and child needs often appeared very skillful, so that it was arbitrary to try to say how the arrangement was actually effected, or why.

Nevertheless, this content analysis did direct our project's attention to the more peripheral role of the child at this early stage in the development of alternate family styles, when a good deal of pioneering experimentation was taking place. To understand the implications of this for the child's growth and development, to learn how counter-culture values were being transmitted to children, and to obtain data on accessibility of these groups to study, the UCLA group continued with a year of pilot studies. This work involved detailed depth interviews with the parent, focused on child-rearing practices and child growth. From these we obtained insights into the philosophy of these groups and their attitudes toward child rearing, and could contrast these findings with data obtained from young parents of the 1970s who are living in the more traditional two-parent families.

First, some background data on the alternative groups studied:

THE UNMARRIED MARRIEDS

These were defined as a two-parent family whose structure existed as a social, rather than a legal contract. The literature, and subsequently our pilot work, suggested that this group did in many ways share the philosophy of the "turned-off" middle-class counter-cultures.[32,40,51] Living together as "unmarried marrieds" has little similarity with the "shacking up" of previous generations, or with the large number of "common law" marriages found among the poor who experience constraints and problems associated with legal marriage. Rather, this alternative form of "marriage" involves an ideological commitment to a relationship rather than to joint living by virtue of a new legal status. Rejection of the concept of legal marriage is fundamentally a conviction that the bond of love and trust that holds them together is much more important and stronger than the legal bond authorized by church and state could be.[9]

In the family setting, parents spend long periods of time with one another and share the same emotional exchanges of closeness and rejection, desire and repulsion, and certainty and uncertainty about each other as are found in more traditional marriages; yet there is a frankness and openness about their status. They do not hide their approach to life; frequently they display both of their names on the mailboxes.

Since the possible instability of the relationship might be critical in a child's development, we explored parental motivations for this life style. While some are not officially married because they refuse to accept the civil contract that attests to the fact that they are now anointed by the establishment—secular or religious—others simply do not accept the relevance of the marriage contract to their relationship as it exists for them at the moment, wishing no structural constraints to their "splitting" if things change between them. Still others seek to avoid evident unhappiness and misery of many legal marriages, especially those in which they grew up. By contrast, living together is seen as representing true maturity in an acceptance and faith they place in one another.[13,51]

Many of the unmarried marrieds are either students or ex-students living close to campus environments, but apparently large numbers of persons are also living in such arrangements outside of campus environments (personal communication, Bureau of the Census, 1971).

In our feasibility studies, "unmarried married" couples appeared to share a value system with a strong emphasis on personal relationships and humanism. This and the women's consciousness and liberation movements play a strong philosophical role in determining child-care patterns and attitudes. In all our pilot cases, the father was present at birth and enjoyed an active role in early child-caring activities and play with the child. The choice of having the child appeared even more determined than in the traditional family, in as much as the option of termination of pregnancy was freely available without the guilt associated with such termination in the traditional family. From this aspect, and on the basis of data about child care that are elaborated below, we regard this family style as a form of very motivated parenting by two parents, at least during the early periods of development. Children seem to have a close and intimate contact starting in infancy, when they are often strapped to the mother's back, accompanying her in all her activities, even school classes. There are few times the child is left with others; the more customary practice is to build the child's activities and caretaking to mesh with the parents' availability. Fathers alternate with mothers in staying home—and share almost all the activities that have to do with the child. In fact, in one family studied in the pilot group, the child called the father "Mama Tom." The intimacy of the family group also extends to encouraging with the child the same affection and openness and expression of sensuous pleasures. This is in line with the rationale of personal commitment and enjoyment for the "unmarried married" relationship.

THE SINGLE MOTHER

The single, or unmarried, mother is far from a new phenomenon in our society. Yet there has been a significant change reflecting this alternative way of bearing and raising children in society today.[46,47,48] It has not only been the "pill" that has emptied the adoption agencies of children available for adoption at birth but also a new perspective on the part of many single parents who keep their children and raise them without the guilt associated with that circumstance in previous generations. (The institutionalized acceptance of the single parent is also evident in their acceptability to agencies as adoptive parents for older, "harder to place" children.[28]) The women's movement and the "turned off" middle-class student were forceful agents in making parenthood a viable option for a woman, whether she is married legally or not. Young women from middle-class families in increasing numbers are allowing their pregnancies to continue and keeping their children.[2,27,45] Under such conditions a variety of styles of mothering have emerged, since a single mother requires a variety of supports if she is to have some opportunity to become economically independent and socially involved.

Among the family styles that our pilot work encountered as ways frequently chosen by single mothers were small group homes, or boarding homes where a number (4-10) of single mothers live together with their children; foster homes for mother and child; and living alone in an apartment. The actual physical arrangements for the child differ among residences but, in general, mother and child have a room or apartment-like set-up for their own sleeping, and then share common dining and living room quarters with the larger family unit in group homes. A parent alone usually lives in a small apartment, but many prefer to share a house with a like parent and child. The possibility of children's eating and playing together, sharing toys, etc., is usually considered one of the advantages for children in group living arrangements.

In addition, some communities have developed programs that facilitate a young mother's return to school or work so that she can gain skills necessary for an independent existence.[20] Although the programs are still largely educational, some are experimental in providing child-rearing training and social exchanges, suggesting that the Establishment recognizes that complex needs of the "parent in adolescence" must be met in order for the child to grow up in a healthy way. Child care facilities, caretaking arrangements in high schools, training centers, and infant caretakers in group home settings reflect the kinds of assistance the community has developed, which means that most children of single parents are exposed to multiple caretaking as early as six weeks of age.

Societal recognition of this family arrangement has also encouraged single parents to move toward developing organizations and social networks that provide them with some of the personal contacts that the early responsibilities of single parenthood might reduce. Persons who have opted for single parenthood see themselves as progressive and experimental.[25,43] The expansion of organizations, such as Momma League and La Leche League, into activity programs, information and training centers, as well as consciousness-raising efforts, also suggests how sensitive the middle-class single mother is to her needs, and how different from the largely lower-class single mother of yesteryear. A good deal of the organizational activity centers around programming for children, so mothers exchange views as to how to rear them in line with their anti-sexist philosophy, and develop social arrangements that may compensate for nonexistent siblings and fathers. Out of those exchanges grow a variety of family arrangements and residences on a more or less temporary basis. Therefore this population provides ample opportunity for observing an alternative in family style that has voluntarily, and proudly, turned its back on the "Establishment" nuclear family.

COMMUNES

Creating a communal alternative to isolated nuclear family living is not in itself a new experience in this country. Some Americans have always sought a new start, along with an expression of dissent against the status quo. Causes of their dissent and ways they chose to organize their new communal existence varied in past generations as it does for today's communards. Some were based upon religious convictions and others upon economic idealism and a rejection of gross economic inequalities. Some rebelled against authority, and attempted to establish a model of governing based upon an absence of central authority; others sought a strict structure with clear lines of hierarchical authority and ultimate rejection from the community of those who would not yield to such authority. Some have relatively long histories, such as the Bruderhof, while others such as the intellectual community "Brook Farm" in Massachusetts, rather rapidly dissolved.[29,51,67] The life styles displayed by the current commune movement are perhaps even more varied than the well-known historical models, making definition of this alternative life style problematic; communes vary today in type of membership, organizational structure, and general purpose.[26,37] Some are involved in agricultural subsistence, seeking a closeness to the land characterized by the early close-knit communities reported to have existed in our past history, while others are composed of middle-class young professionals who do not wish to disengage from the urban scene or its various technological comforts. They vary in size from twelve or less to hundreds. A significant number are based upon religious commitments of various persuasions. Many of the new religious communes are steeped in Eastern philosophy and culture; others are part of the new "Jesus movement," searching for a new way to live out traditional Judeo-Christian convictions. Communes are often formed around common interests, crafts, or some unifying goal. They begin with people who find each other, like each other, and share a similar value system. The sharing of political views and convictions is often an important aspect of these intentional communities. Some communes are in fact composed of political activists who see their alternative life styles as a reflection of the social revolution they believe in and the beginning of a radical change in everyday life starting with family organization.

Some communes are reported to be group-marriage oriented, but there appears to be an extremely small number of these. One such group, called "The Family," lives in Taos, New Mexico, and has a life style in which they share in common the children of the group, not knowing or caring which individuals have been biologically responsible for the union of sperm and ovum. A similar commune exists nationally, with a sizable base in Los Angeles. Other groups are oriented as extended families, with couples remaining essentially monogamous in their own private quarters, although the partners may change from time to time. Still others live together under a community concept rather than as a family unit, sharing those things that seem to them more effectively achieved in multiple family cooperatives, such as expenses, household chores, and child care responsibilities. The organization of such groups has been given particular impetus by the women's consciousness movement.

The lifespan of current communes varies considerably. Some stay together only for the initial glow of comradery, while others, in increasing numbers, develop a stable group of committed members with more long-lasting aspirations for their community. Such issues as organization of work and other aspects of living, interpersonal relationships, economic feasibility, and ability to buffer or cope with outside community harassment have been suggested as germane to the stability of communal arrangements.[4, 30, 31, 53]

The residential arrangements often determine to a large extent adult-child relationships. Living arrangements show variety and ingenuity: tents and cabins in rural areas, apartment houses and motels in cities. Eating and sleeping arrangements for adults and children vary with the specific commune. As the 1970 Census found (personal communication, 1972), their usual criteria of common entry-hall and kitchen proved inadequate to the task of categorizing group living arrangements, and many were coded as boarding houses! Separate family houses, children's houses, baby nurseries, and other unit arrangements are common as community houses. Structures vary from lean-to's and buses to elaborate frame and stone buildings.

The number of children varies from commune to commune. In general, the adult-child ratio of 2½:1 cited by Fairfield[19] and Cavan[8] seems to hold. The adults are conscious of the population explosion, and therefore few parents with more than three biological children are evident; but "families" with eight to ten children are not infrequent. Birth, pregnancy, and children are esteemed and joyously regarded as an expression of a natural, ecologically-appropriate experience.

Adult-child relations are often determined by proximity of living, and particularly of sleeping, quarters. Relations with biological parents may be infrequent when children are physically separated from adults and caretakers assigned, as they are in some instances. A child's relationship with other adults is also related to the extent to which a hierarchical structure of relations or responsibilities exists.[8, 26, 50] Interestingly, a family multiple dwelling arrangement can permit a child to move among households, as when he is in conflict with other household members, lonely for peers, or when his family is "splitting" for a time.[8]

Interview data during pilot work elaborated the wide range of child-rearing practices found among communes in relation to caretaking. Detailed interviews with commune parents about their own and their children's life styles permitted us to look for common denominators among practices, and for dimensions in the "family" structure and philosophy that might account for differences. A number of dimensions stood out as possibly salient: age of the child; number of caretakers; area in which the commune existed, such as rural or urban; accessibility to resources in the outside community; residential mobility of the immediate family; creedal or non-creedal affiliation;[5] and conscious concern with planning (although not "scheduling") for a child's daily activities vs. a laissez-faire attitude toward child activities.

These three family styles, then, the unmarried marrieds; single mothers; and communes were selected for comparison with the two-parent nuclear family of today.

VALUES AND ATTITUDES IN REGARD TO CHILD-REARING

Data from detailed interviews were analyzed to provide a picture of current child-rearing practices, attitudes, and value systems of parents from each population. The children around whom the interviews were focused ranged from one month to four years. Interviews provided such data as demographic and personal background information on parents; marital and work status at time of child's birth; current living arrangement; birth; medical and developmental history of the child; attitudes and practices concerning eating, sleeping, discipline, sex, rules, scheduling; child problem areas; social and emotional development; aspirations for the child, etc.

Data were categorized and scaled for comparative analysis of environments and child-rearing practices and attitudes. Findings showed some similarities in practices that had been attributed solely to some counter-cultures. Breast feeding is now routine in young mothers, for example. Also, in all groups, babies are carried on the mother's back and accompany her most of the time, so there is almost constant physical proximity between mother and child in the first year of life. In most areas, however, there was considerable range in practices stemming from shared attitudes and values, so that family groups could be ordered in terms of frequency with which specific practices are adopted. Some of the attitudes and value-systems commonly found in experimental groups that are likely to effect a child's development are as follows:

1. Intense mother-child relationships from birth through the first two or two-and-a-half years, with a clear break in this pattern in the direction of independence and self-reliance at two-and-a-half or three years. The latter comes at a time when the youngster has been weaned (breast-feeding may extend until this time), and is mobile, and when the mother begins to think of herself and her own needs and wishes to return to previous activities.

2. At the same time that an intense attachment to a single caretaker is fostered, there is also an attempt to develop in the child a generalized sense of trust to other caretaking adults. This may be through the use of multiple caretakers, or in the switching of infants among young mothers for breast feeding. Multiple caretakers sometimes have differences in perspectives around caretaking, making for inconsistencies. In fact, commune members report that differences over child-rearing are a common source of family difficulty.

3. Good health, in line with a desire for wholesomeness and a oneness with the environment, assumes important proportions. Many experiences, like childbirth, are considered to be "natural," rather than "illnesses." Natural foods comprise the bulk of the diet; in most cases children's dietary input is restricted in regard to sweets and other "junk" food. Dependence on institutionalized medical and dental services is limited to emergencies, with self-help medical and pharmocological expertise encouraged. Few preventive interventions are sought.

4. While non-violence is generally espoused among counter-culture groups, certain dissonant practices are seen in regard to the handling of aggressive behaviors between children, and in parental disciplinary attitudes and practices. In line with parental desires for each child to be assertive (and particularly for girls, upon whom a "passive role has been foisted by stereotypic cultural attitudes"), children are generally allowed to work out relationships with peers without adult interference; in fact, direct interrelations are fostered. Only the demands of safety take precedence. Again, in regard to discipline, although the perpetration of violence is seen as a violation of individuality—and the child is seen as having rights as an individual—parents acknowledge that there are times when their own needs take precedence over the child's and they impose discipline, even physical punishment. Disciplines cover the spectrum, from total nonviolence to "an eye for an eye."

5. Humanistic and interpersonal relationships and the direct expression of affectional needs are highly valued. In line with this, there is a desire to cast off artificial repression of sexuality and intimacy. For the child this means exposure to adult nudity and observation of sexual activity, and a certain permissiveness around instinctual drives, which may or may not go with opportunities for acting out. There are differences among and within family styles in regard to the latter, but in general parents aim for more freedom in their children and for earlier sophistication.

6. Child-peer relationships become potent socializing agents, since early independence from mother often moves a child into "juvenile groups" as replacement. Peers are depended upon for support and decision, and age mates are closely modeled.

7. Early decision-making is encouraged in the child, in line with the philosophy that a child has individual rights and has a role in participatory democracy. In some family groups, conscious politicization of children is encouraged. Group decision-making by parents is modeled by children as an important mode for solving problems.

8. Parents are ambivalent about serving as models for identification. They shrink from "putting their trip" on the child; yet they admit to value and life style preferences, and thus reinforce those behaviors of the child that are consonant with their attitudes. They also resist serving as identification models because of their more or less consistent acceptance of an anti-sexist philosophy; thus, mothers are not willing to have their girls identify with them as not-completely-emancipated women; similarly with boys and males.

9. Achievement striving is played down, except for the desire to become competent and thus fulfill individual potential and creativity. Competition as a motivational force is repressed. Sensory impressions, intuition, the occult as opposed to the rational, are appropriate data for the enhancement of creativity. Children are expected to be able to distinguish what is appropriate behavior within the "family" and in the "outside world."

10. Because materialistic values are tied in with technological advances and non-humanistic goals, dependence on possessions and material objects is minimized whenever possible. Children have few toys. Personally-owned objects are minimal as compared with objects that are shared by the group, when the child is in a "group family." Also, children see some adults proudly "ripping off" the outside world, and ignoring social contracts involving personal ownership. The variability found in the alternative family groups in implementing these general child-rearing attitudes made it evident that systematic studies of these groups must take account of the variety or extremes in child-rearing practices within the populations.

One of the other findings from the pilot data is that many of the attributes and practices of counter-culture families are also found in contemporary two-parent families. Pilot data suggest that the alternative life styles represent a concentrated form of attitudes, values, and behaviors that are broadly represented in contemporary society, but not recognized as such because they are more amorphous and poorly crystallized. Even at a superficial level it is clear that much that passes through the communication media—TV, movies, magazines, books, newspapers—finds a more logically consistent expression in some of the "alternative life styles" than in the bulk of society, and yet elements seem to be broadly based in general society.[3] This appears to be the case with child-rearing practices, too, for pilot work showed that many of the parental behaviors and values in regard to children that had been attributed to the counter-cultures in literature, journalism, and popular myth, were in actuality also found to be characteristic of parents living in the nuclear two-parent family today. To note a few examples: breast feeding was the only mode of feeding in control and experimental samples; independence and self-reliance were fostered in all children as they reach pre-school age, with many of the same practices being used across populations to encourage this characteristic; meaningful interpersonal relationships were valued over the encouragement of intellectual resources.

CONCLUSION

The changes in the child-rearing values and practices that now are manifest in embryonic and ambiguous form, sometimes as apparently isolated events, may well be auguring new directions of child-rearing in the mainstreams of society in the future. It is important and timely, therefore, to discuss and study what the implications of such changes will be for the infant and growing child.

What is the likely impact of multiple caretaking and multiple models on the child's social and emotional development? Of non-differentiated roles of father and mother in parenting? Of the fluid family with its combination of fixed and transient members? Of frequent early and purposeful exposure to intimacy and sexuality? Of the humanist perspective? Of an ambivalent and even hostile interfacing with established institutions? Of the parental conflicts around freedom and control that go with a permissive and laissez-faire "do your own thing" orientation?

What is the impact of natural food, health-oriented diets, changes in customary sleeping and eating arrangements, and of the disavowal of established medical practices of the child's physical growth and development? How do parental non-achievement and non-intellectual attitudes and practices influence cognitive growth and intellectual development of the child?

A host of such questions is readily generated from new value systems and practices. The answers are not readily forthcoming. In fact, one colleague remarked that this is an area in which the most sophisticated of us has a difficult time predicting results in advance. It is this challenge, this fascinating, provocative, and compelling problem to which we are addressing ourselves today.

REFERENCES

1. Allen, J. and West, L. 1968. Flight from violence: hippies and the green rebellion. Amer. J. Psychiat. 125:120-126.
2. Baizerman, M. et al. 1970. Pregnant adolescents: a review of literature with abstracts: 1960-1970 Supplement, Sharing.
3. Bartell, G. 1971. Group Sex: A Scientist's Eyewitness Report on the American Way of Swinging. Wyden, New York.
4. Berger, B. 1967. Hippie morality, more old than new. Trans-Action 5(2):19-23.
5. Berger, B. 1971. Child-rearing practices of the communal family. Progress report presented to N.I.M.H., University of California, Davis.
6. Block, J., Haan, N. and Smith, M. 1967. Activism and apathy in contemporary adolescence. *In* Contributions to the Understanding of Adolescence, J. Adams, ed. Allyn and Bacon, Boston.
7. Blois, M. 1971. Child-rearing attitudes of hippie adults. Dissertation Abstracts 31:3329-3330.
8. Cavan, S. 1971. Hippies of the redwood forest. Scientific Analysis Corporation. Berkeley, Calif. (mimeo)
9. Coffin, P. 1972. The young unmarrieds. *In* Intimate Life Styles: Marriage and Its Alternatives, J.S. and J.R. Delora, eds. Goodyear Publishing, Pacific Palisades, Calif.
10. Constantine, L. and Constantine, J. 1970. Where is marriage going? The Futurist 4:44-46.
11. Cooper, D. 1970. The Death of the Family. Vintage Books, New York.
12. Corrigan, E. 1971. Child-rearing practices of unwed mothers. Dissertation Abstracts 31(9A):4893.
13. Delora, J.S. and Delora, J.R. 1972. Intimate Life Styles: Marriage and Its Alternatives. Goodyear Publishing, Pacific Palisades, Calif.
14. Diamond, S. 1971. What the Trees Said. Dell, New York.
15. Editors of Life Magazine. 1972. The marriage experiments. Life 73 (Apr. 28).
16. Estellachild, V. 1972. Hippie communes. *In* Intimate Life Styles: Marriage and Its Alternatives, J.S. and J.R. Delora, eds. Goodyear Publishing, Pacific Palisades, Calif.
17. Fairfield, R. 1970. Updated directory of communes. Modern Utopia. v. 4.
18. Fairfield, R., ed. 1971. Communes, USA. Modern Utopia, v. 5.
19. Fairfield, R. 1972. Communes, USA. Penguin, Baltimore.
20. Gershensen, C. 1972. Child development, infant day-care, and adolescent parents. Sharing, pp. 1-10.
21. Gillman, R. 1971. Genetic, dynamic, and adaptive aspects of dissent. J. Amer. Psychoanal. Assoc. 19(1):122-130.
22. Gollin, G. 1967. Moravians in Two Worlds. Columbia University Press, New York.
23. Gross, H. 1968. The Flower People. Ballantine, New York.
24. Haughey, J. 1972. The commune: child of the 1970's. *In* Intimate Life Styles: Marriage and Its Alternatives, J.S. and J.R. Delora, eds. Goodyear Publishing, Pacific Palisades, Calif.
25. Heimel, J. 1972. Youth—on identity as a woman. J. Clin. Child Psychol. 1:14-16.
26. Houriet, R. 1969. Getting Back Together. Coward, McCann, & Geoghegan, New York.
27. Howard, M. 1971. Pregnant school-age girls. J. School Hlth 41(7):361-364.
28. Kadushin, A. 1970. Adopting the Older Child. Columbia University Press, New York.
29. Kanter, R. 1972. Commitment and Community: Utopias and Communes in Sociological Perspective. Harvard University Press, Cambridge.
30. Kanter, R. 1968. Commitment and social organization: A study of commitment mechanisms in utopian communities. Amer. Sociol. Rev. 33:499-517.
31. Kanter, R. 1972. Getting it all together: some group issues in communes. Amer. J. Orthopsychiat. 42:632-643.
32. Karlen, A. 1969. The unmarried marrieds on campus. New York Times Magazine (Jan. 26).
33. Katz, E. 1971. Armed Love. Holt, Rinehart, & Winston, New York.
34. Kaufman, J., Allen, J. and West, L. 1969. Runaways, hippies, and marijuana. Amer. J. Psychiat. 126(5):163-166.

35. Keniston, K. 1970. Student activism, moral development, and morality. Amer. J. Orthopsychiat. 40:577-592.
36. Keniston, K. 1965. The Uncommitted: Alienated Youth in American Society. 3rd ed. Dell, New York.
37. Kinkade, K. 1972. A Walden Two Experiment: The First 5 Years of Twin Oaks Community. Morrow, New York.
38. Linney, T. 1972. Youth—on alternatives to the family. J. Clin. Child Psychol. 1:5-7.
39. Lyman, M. 1971. Mirror at the End of the Road. American Avatar, Roxbury, Mass.
40. Lyness, J., Lipetz, M. and Davies, K. 1972. Living together: an alternative to marriage. J. Marr. Fam. 34(2):305-311.
41. Macklin, E. 1972. Heterosexual cohabitation among unmarried college students. The Family Coordinator 21:463-467.
42. Melville, K. 1972. Communes in the Counter Culture. Morrow, New York.
43. Momma League, a magazine for single mothers.
44. Mungo, R. 1970. Total Loss Farm. Bantam, New York.
45. Osofsky, H. 1968. The Pregnant Teenager: A Medical, Educational and Social Analysis. Charles C. Thomas, Springfield, Ill.
46. Osofsky, H. and Osofsky, J. 1970. Adolescents as mothers: results of a program for low-income pregnant teenagers with some emphasis upon infant's development. Amer. J. Orthopsychiat. 40:825-834.
47. Pakter, J. et al. 1961. Out-of-wedlock births in New York: I—sociological aspects. Amer. J. Pub. Hlth 51:683-696.
48. Pakter, J. et al. 1961. Out-of-wedlock birth in New York City: II—medical aspects. Amer. J. Pub. Hlth 51:846-865.
49. Rabin, A. 1965. Growing Up In the Kibbutz. Springer, New York.
50. Roberts, R. 1971. The New Communes: Coming Together in America. Prentice-Hall, Englewood Cliffs, N.J.
51. Rogers, C. 1972. Becoming Partners: Marriage and Its Alternatives. Delacort Press, New York.
52. Schulterbrandt, J. and Nichols, E. 1972. Coming of age to young Americans. J. Clin. Child Psychol. 1:28.
53. Schulterbrandt, J. and Nichols, E. 1972. Ethical and ideological problems for communal living: a caveat. The Family Coordinator 21:429-433.
54. Schaffer, H. 1969. Communal Living: Editorial Research Reports. (no. 5) Congressional Quarterly, Washington, D.C.
55. Skolnick, A. and Skolnick, J. 1971. Family in Transition: Rethinking Marriage, Sexuality, Child-rearing, and Family Organization. Little Brown, Boston.
56. Smith, D. 1970. The group marriage commune: a case study. J. Psychedelic Drugs 3:1-3.
57. Smith, D. and Sternfield, J. 1970. Natural childbirth and cooperative child-rearing in psychedelic communes. J. Planned Parenthood Assoc. 5:1-5.
58. Spiro, M. 1958. Children of the kibbutz. Harvard University Press, Cambridge.
59. Steiner, S. and Maran, M. 1971. Chamisa Road With . . . Paul and Meredith: Doing the Dog in Taos. Random House, New York.
60. Trainer, D. 1968. When hippies become parents. Redbook 130:66 ff.
61. Wells, T. and Christie, L. 1972. Living together: an alternative to marriage. *In* Intimate Life Styles: Marriage and Its Alternatives, J.S. and J.R. Delora, eds. Goodyear Publishing, Pacific Palisades, Calif.
62. West, L. 1971. Flight from violence II: the communes. Paper presented at American Psychiatric Association Meeting, Washington, D.C.
63. West, L. and Allen, J. Three rebellions: red, black, and green. *In* The Dynamics of Dissent, J. Masserman, ed., Grune & Stratton, New York.
64. Williams, T. 1972. Infant Care. Consortium on early childbearing and childrearing, Research Utilization and Information Sharing Project, Office of Child Development, Washington, D.C.
65. Wolfe, B. 1968. The Hippies. Signet, New York.
66. Wright, H. 1965. 80 unmarried mothers who kept their babies. State of California Department of Social Welfare.
67. Zablocki, B. 1971. The Joyful Community. Penguin, Baltimore.
68. Zwerling, I. 1967. Psychological consequences: the phenomenology of alienation. Paper presented at the Richmond Professional Institute, Richmond, Va.
69. Zwerling, I. 1967. Socio-cultural antecedents: the etiology of alienation. Paper presented at the meeting of the Richmond Professional Institute, Richmond, Va.

24

working with abusive parents: a psychiatrist's view

brandt f. steele

The actions of parents or other caretakers which result in abuse of infants and children do not fall into any standard diagnostic category of psychiatric disorder, nor should they be considered a separate specific psychiatric disorder themselves. Yet to consider child abuse as a derailed pattern of childrearing rather than as a psychiatric disorder does not mean that abusing or neglecting parents are free of emotional problems or mental illness. They may have many psychiatric disorders, much the same as the general population.

Abusing or neglecting parents have about the normal incidence and distribution of neuroses, psychoses and character disorders which exist rather independently and separately from the behavioral patterns expressed in abuse of their offspring. Such psychiatric conditions may warrant appropriate treatment in their own right regardless of the coexistence of patterns of abuse.

There is a small group of abusive parents (less than 10 percent of the total) who suffer from such serious psychiatric disorder that they may be either temporarily or permanently unavailable for treatment of the more subtle problems of abuse. Among such conditions are schizophrenia, serious postpartum or other types of depression and incapacitating compulsive neuroses, with or without phobias. Ideally, such persons should be screened out of the regular treatment program and given inpatient or outpatient care as necessary. Also in this group are those parents who suffer from severe alcoholism, abuse of narcotic and non-narcotic drugs or from significant sexual perversion, and those who have been involved repeatedly in serious antisocial violent or criminal behavior. Such troubled persons need much more intensive, prolonged psychiatric care and social rehabilitation than can be provided in the usual child protective program. Until such measures have been accomplished, it is futile to try to alter the pattern of abuse.

It is obvious, then, that psychiatric consultation should be available in all situations where workers are dealing with the problem of child abuse and neglect. Proper psychiatric screening procedures ensure that the most troubled parents will receive the appropriate type of care and also protect workers from spending enormous amounts of time and energy on problems which require other special kinds of intervention. Working with such disturbed parents should never be delegated to the usual worker in child protective agencies. It is unfair to child, parent and worker, and the results are usually unhappy for all concerned.

A few words must be said about the socioeconomic status and racial background of abusing families. Unfortunately, because so many of the early reports and descriptions of child abuse came through welfare agencies and municipal hospitals it became a common belief that abuse and neglect of infants were associated with racial minorities and poverty-stricken groups of people. Such ideas still persist in many quarters, despite the increasing knowledge that child abuse and neglect occur among families from all socioeconomic levels, religious groups, races and nationalities. These facts

Reprinted from *Children Today* (U.S. Department of Health, Education, and Welfare), 1975, *4*, 3-5, 44.

should not be interpreted to deny the profound effect which social and economic deprivation, housing problems, unemployment, and subcultural and racial pressures have on the lives and behavior of the caretakers who abuse and neglect their children. Any stress can make life more difficult, and the ramifications of poverty can make anything worse than it would otherwise be. Such factors may be, and often are, involved in one way or another or in varying degree in many cases of abuse. They must be considered in every program of treatment of the families in which abuse occurs and appropriate actions and remedial measures undertaken through social case work, psychotherapy, counseling, vocational rehabilitation, financial aid, or any other method available to the agencies involved with the family.

A word of caution is appropriate, however: no matter how necessary and useful it might be to improve the socioeconomic status of parents, this should not in any way be confused with treating the more deeply seated personal character traits which are involved in abusive behavior. It is well recognized that individual acts of abuse may occur when the parents are faced with a crisis in relation to finances, employment, illness and so forth, but such crises cannot be considered adequate causes for abuse. Crises of this kind are equally common in the lives of many people who never display abusive behavior and, on the contrary, abuse can occur in families who are wealthy, well educated and well housed. The role of crisis as a precipitating factor in abusive behavior is an important one, however.

WORKING WITH THE PARENTS

The first task faced by all those who try to work in the area of child abuse, regardless of professional background or lack of it, is that of coming to peace with one's own attitudes toward the problem of abuse and neglect of infants and small children. It is very emotionally disturbing to see a seriously injured or neglected baby, and we usually respond in either of two ways when confronted with the situation. We may disbelieve that such a thing could actually be true. We deny that parents could really have attacked their own offspring and that some other explanation for the situation must be found. Alternatively, if we do believe actual facts of what has happened we tend to have a surge of righteous anger and feel disposed to scold and punish the parents. Obviously, neither of these attitudes is useful in trying to do something to better the situation and help the parent improve his method of child care. Denial precludes any chance of dealing with the problem, and long experience of many people has indicated over and over again that criticism and punitive attack of the parents have adverse effect and no real therapeutic value.

Most useful in eliminating to the highest degree possible an attitude of anger toward the parents is a knowledge of how the parent's own life and difficulties help in understanding why he happened to become an abusive parent. Probably the thing which is most helpful in producing an understanding non-punitive stance in the one who is working with the abusive parent is to realize that one is not working with an abusive parent as much as one is working with a grownup person who was in his own early life a neglected or abused child himself. This one basic premise is probably the most important thing to keep as an organizing principle in the back of one's mind as one is trying to understand and work with abusive parents, regardless of one's own professional training or type of approach.

CHARACTERISTICS AND PROBLEMS OF ABUSIVE PARENTS

For most abusive parents their immaturity and dependency is essentially functional in nature and related to the emotional deprivation endured in early life. Hence it can be remedied to a significant degree by more rewarding and more satisfying experiences in adult life, especially those occurring during carefully managed therapeutic working relationships. However, it is necessary to keep in mind another cause for the inadequacy and inept parenting behavior. A small but significant number of children who were abused or neglected in their earliest years suffered organic brain damage due either to head trauma or to malnutrition during critical growth periods. As a result they had perceptual defects, diminished IQ and significant delay in language development. These deficits may produce in later adult life a condition characterized by significant lack of basic knowledge and attitudes of helplessness, immaturity and dependency.

If such organic causes of difficulty are suspected by the worker, careful evaluation by appropriate psychological testing and psychiatric examination should be undertaken. Such parents who are organically impaired will not respond easily, if at all, to the usual methods of working with abusing parents, whereas those whose immaturity and dependency are essentially functional in origin are much more responsive to interventions. If parental dysfunction due to brain damage is documented, therapeutic goals can be appropriately revised and limited, thereby preventing the expenditure of much unproductive effort by the worker.

THE CONSTELLATION OF PSYCHOLOGICAL CHARACTERISTICS

No two abusive parents are exactly alike, of course, but in general all of them share certain characteristics to some degree in a variety of combinations. The main components of this constellation of factors involved in abuse may be summarized as follows: the special form of immaturity and the associated dependency in its various manifestations; the tragically low self-esteem and sense of incompetence; the difficulty in seeking pleasure and finding satisfaction in the adult world; the social isolation with its lack of lifelines and reluctance to seek help; the significant misperceptions of the infant, especially as manifested in role reversal; the fear of spoiling infants and the strong belief in the value of punishment; and the serious lack of ability to be empathically aware of the infant's condition and needs, and to respond appropriately to them.

The cumulative effect and dynamic interactions of these various factors make it extremely difficult for the parent to maintain equanimity and be successful as he or she tries to meet the demanding tasks of child care. The daily care of infants and small children requires large amounts of time, physical energy and emotional resources. The caretaker needs to have much patience, ingenuity, empathic understanding and self-sacrificing endurance—the very things which we see tragically lacking in abusive parents.

These parents have never had their own needs satisfied well enough to provide the surplus which would enable them to give to the infants under their care. With good reason they often doubt their own ability to do even a minimally acceptable job and they do not know where or how to seek help. In contrast to averagely successful parents, they do not have an adequate support system of spouse and extended family, or helpful neighbors, friends, pediatricians and so forth. Probably most important of all, they do not have a background of life experience which has enabled them to get pleasure out of life and to trust other people. They have no storehouse of spare emotional energy but live a precarious hand-to-mouth emotional life, without a built-in cushion of hope, or available contacts to tide them over tight spots and crises. It is because of this that crises are crucially important in the lives of abusive parents and are often the precipitating factor in single events of abuse.

TREATMENT MODALITIES

The matching up of parent, worker and treatment modality is difficult and usually managed on a less than ideal scientific basis. Abusive parents are unique individuals, often with great reluctance to become involved in any form of treatment. Hence the type of treatment may be selected under great influence of what the parent will go along with at the given moment, rather than because of any theoretical preference for a specific method. It is equally true that the selection of a worker or a mode of treatment will be influenced by availability rather than theoretical principles. There is at present no data derived from thorough comparative studies which indicate how or why any one modality of treatment is more effective than another for particular kinds of parents. It is known, on the other hand, that even in the face of rather haphazard selective mechanisms, remarkably good results have come for parents who have been treated by many different methods.

By far the greater part of the burden of caring for abusive parents is carried by public and private social agencies. Although the traditional values and methods of social case work are maintained in such agencies, there is also an increasing use of other techniques and of para-professional workers under supervision. Social workers in health-based child protective services have also been active in developing innovative techniques of working with abusive families and social workers in many different kinds of programs have been active in developing services and training people in the areas of lay therapy, parent aides and homemakers.

Many different modes of psychotherapy have been used in the care of abusive parents and their families. A few parents have been successfully treated by classical psychoanalysis, but the general character structure and lifestyle of most abusive parents make this procedure quite impractical and probably unsuccessful. Psychoanalytically oriented dynamic psychotherapy in the hands of skilled experienced therapists has been extremely successful in many cases. With most abusive parents, the therapist must be more willing to adapt to patient needs and to allow more dependency than is ordinarily considered appropriate. Intensive psychotherapy which skillfully utilizes the transference, with avoidance of the development of a full transference neurosis, can stimulate great growth and deep structural change in these patients despite their severe immaturity and developmental arrest. In general, abusive parents respond best when psychotherapy is accompanied by supportive adjuncts associated with a cooperative child protective service or provided by individual social workers, lay therapists or group therapy. Skilled and experienced psychologists can also work successfully as counselors and therapists in both individual and group situations.

There is increasing use of group therapy as a mode of working with abusive parents, but as yet there is a dearth of published reports describing fully either techniques or long-term results. Groups may be composed of the single parent who has done the actual abusing or of mothers or of couples. Most groups are formed and led by professionally trained group therapists such as psychologists, psychiatrists or other mental health workers, although social workers in protective agencies have also taken up this pattern of treatment. It is thought by some that it is always wise to have at least two leaders, preferably a man and a woman, and especially if there is an attempt to develop a couples group the leaders must be male and female. A rapidly growing and extremely important movement is the development of self-help groups formed under the titles of Parents Anonymous and Families Anonymous. Organized on a voluntary basis by abusive parents themselves, with sponsorship and guidance from a professional worker, these groups provide a haven of safety and help for people who might otherwise be unable—out of fear and anxiety—to relate to any other kind of treatment program. After some time of working in such self-help groups the participants may be able to enter into other more extensive programs.

For those parents who have the courage and ego strength to enter into group programs, the process helps them express their emotions more openly, and also to become desensitized to criticism. They find out they are not alone in their troubles and their self-esteem is improved. As an especially important benefit the group provides channels for developing contacts into the wider community, first with group members and later with others, a kind of relationship in which the abusive parent has been woefully lacking. Experience suggests that even though group therapy may be the chief mode of treatment involved in caring for abusive parents, it may not be sufficient by itself. Contacts outside the group, either with group leaders on an individual basis or with other workers from other agencies or disciplines, are often necessary for the patient's best development and improvement.

Couples groups can help solve the common difficulty of getting both spouses involved in treatment. Husbands are notoriously reluctant to get help, but the presence of male workers leads some of them to accept either group or individual treatment programs. It is important for both partners in the marriage to be involved in rehabilitative efforts if at all possible, regardless of which one was the actual abuser. Abuse is always, in part, a family problem with one parent actively abetting or condoning the abusive behavior of the other, even though not actually participating in the abusive acts.

Behavior modification techniques have been used to obtain changes in the attitudes and actions of abusive parents in a relatively short time. Whether this technique has validity for long-term rehabilitation is not yet clear.

Other modes of dealing with abusive parents have used "role modeling" and techniques derived from learning theory. These modes are at least partly based on the assumption that the parent is in difficulty because he has not been given proper opportunity and material to develop adequate parental attitudes and actions. To some extent this is true, but these modes are based essentially upon the provision of material for cognitive learning whereas the deepest deficit in abusive parents is in the emotional or affective sphere. There is apparently a small group of parents who are neglectful or only mildly abusing, who can profit by the chance for cognitive learning of good parental techniques. However, the fallacy of believing this can be a standard method is demonstrated most clearly by the fact that in many cases, even those of serious abuse of a child, the parents are able to take care of other children in the family perfectly well. It is evident in such situations that it is not lack of factual knowledge which hampers the parents but the emotional difficulties involved with specific attitudes and misperceptions of the parent toward an individual child.

Psychiatric understanding of the tragic long-term troubles of abusive parents can provide a perspective on the place which child abuse takes in their lives, and their attempts to adapt to their world. It offers a rational framework which enables workers from many disciplines—and who use various modalities of treatment—to help parents grow and to develop new and better patterns of childrearing. The most valuable ingredients, over and beyond intellectual insight, which enable parents to grow and develop are the time, attention, tolerance and recognition of the worth of an individual human being which the worker can provide.

25

parent-child relationships of
male and female high school students

nick stinnett

joe ann farris

james walters

INTRODUCTION

Various research studies indicate that parents have a differential impact upon their children according to the sex of the child (21). The indication that boys may be more susceptible than girls to parental influence is reflected in the findings of a closer association between the perceptions of parents and the adjustment of male children, as well as a closer association between intelligence in male children and maternal behavior (1, 12, 17).

Very little is known concerning why parent-child relationships differ according to sex of both parent and child (21). Perhaps one of the most effective ways of finding answers to this question is to obtain more recent, specific information about the differences in the perceptions of boys and girls concerning several aspects of their parent-child relationships.

The review of literature has revealed the following observations concerning differences in parent-child relationships according to the sex of the child:

1. Parents exert more power and are less permissive toward their same sex children than toward their opposite sex children (6, 16).
2. Girls tend to receive more love, affection, nurturance, and praise from both parents than do boys; while boys tend to see themselves as being treated in more hostile, negative ways by both parents (2, 5).
3. Boys receive sterner discipline (2).
4. Girls reflect more positive perceptions concerning parent-child relationships than do boys (3, 8).
5. Both boys and girls tend to view the mother as being more nurturant than the father (4, 9).

The specific purposes of this study were to compare the perceptions of male and female high school students concerning each of the following aspects of parent-child relationships:

(a) Type of discipline received from father during childhood.
(b) Type of discipline received from mother during childhood.
(c) Degree of closeness of relationship with father during childhood.
(d) Degree of closeness of relationship with mother during childhood.
(e) Source of most discipline during childhood.
(f) Degree of praise received during childhood.
(g) Source of most affection during childhood.
(h) Degree to which family participated in recreation together during respondent's childhood.
(i) Degree to which father found time to do things together with respondent as a child.

Reprinted, by permission, from *The Journal of Genetic Psychology*, 1974, *125*, 99-106, slightly abridged. Copyright ©1974 by The Journal Press.

(j)   Degree to which mother found time to do things together with respondent as a child.
(k)   Degree to which parents expressed affection toward respondent as a child.
(l)   Source of greatest parental influence in determining the kind of person the respondent is.
(m)   Source of greatest general influence in determining the kind of person the respondent is.
(n)   Degree to which the respondent feels free to talk with parents about problems and other concerns.

METHOD

Subjects

The subjects for this study were eleventh and twelfth grade students enrolled in home economics classes at seven selected high schools in the state of Oklahoma. A total sample of 499 students was obtained. Cover letters explaining the research, assuring anonymity to the students, and including directions for administration of the questionnaires were sent to nine teachers representing the seven high schools in the state. The data were obtained during the month of February, 1971.

The sample consisted of 56 percent white and 36 percent black students. Seventy-two percent of the subjects were female, and 28 percent were male. Eighty percent of the subjects were Protestant. As determined by the McGuire-White Index of Social Status (11), the sample was primarily from the upper-lower (43 percent) and lower-middle (27 percent) socioeconomic classes. Forty-six percent of the respondents indicated their place of residence for the major part of life as being a small town under 25,000 population, while 25 percent reported having lived on a farm for the major part of life. The largest percentage of the subjects (64 percent) indicated that their parents were living together; 16 percent indicated their parents were separated or divorced with no re-marriage. A majority of the students (52 percent) in the sample reported that their mothers had been employed for a major part of their childhood. Of the total, 27 percent indicated part-time employment of the mother, and 25 percent indicated full-time employment.

Instrument

The questionnaire was composed of fixed alternative type questions and included (a) a general information section in order to obtain such background data about the subjects as race, sex, and religious preference, and (b) several questions designed to obtain knowledge of the students' perceptions of relationships with their parents. The McGuire-White Index of Social Status (11) was used to determine the socioeconomic classification of the students.

RESULTS

The chi-square test was utilized to examine the hypotheses in order to determine if significant differences existed between male and female high school students' perceptions concerning various aspects of their parent-child relationships. No significant differences were found to exist in the perceptions of males and females concerning (a) type of discipline received from father during childhood, (b) type of discipline received from mother during childhood, (c) degree of closeness of their relationship with father during childhood, (d) degree of closeness of their relationship with mother during childhood, (e) degree to which family participated in recreation together during respondent's childhood, (f) degree to which father found time to do things together with respondent as a child, (g) degree to which parents expressed affection toward the respondent as a child, (h) source of greatest general influence in determining the kind of person the respondent is, and (i) degree to which the respondent feels free to talk with parents about problems and other concerns.

The results indicated that significant differences existed in the perceptions of male and female high school students concerning each of the following aspects of parent-child relationships:

Source of most parental discipline during childhood (significant at the .001 level). The greatest difference was found to exist in the category of *father*, where more than twice as many males (30.7%) as females (14.2%) reported *father* to be the primary source of parental discipline during childhood.

Degree of praise received during childhood (significant at the .001 level). The greatest difference was found to exist in the category of *often*, with more than twice as many female students (26.7%) as male students (10%) reporting they received praise *often* during their childhood.

Source of most affection during childhood (significant at the .02 level). A greater proportion of male students (56.1%) than female students (42.3%) perceived *mother* to be the source of most affection during childhood, while more female students (40.1%) than male students (25.9%) reported *both mother and father about equally* as the source of most affection during childhood.

Degree to which mother found time to do things together with respondent as a child (significant at the .05 level). Almost equal differences were found in two categories, *very often* and *rarely*. A greater number of female students (21.5%) than male students (12.9%) indicated that mother *very often* found time to do things together with them as a child, while more male students (22.1%) than female students (13.3%) reported that mother *rarely* found time to do things together with them as a child.

Source of greatest parental influence in determining the kind of person the respondent is (significant at the .001 level). The greatest difference was found to exist in the category of *father*, with more than twice as many male students (25.5%) as female students (10.8%) reporting that *father* was the greatest parental influence in determining the kind of person they are. Also, a larger proportion of female students (57.5%) than male students (41.5%) perceived that *mother* was the greatest source of parental influence.

DISCUSSION

The findings that twice as many males as females reported *father* to be the primary source of parental discipline during childhood would seem to indicate that, as perceived by the students, fathers play a more active role in the disciplining of sons than they do with daughters, and may be related to research (7) indicating that fathers emphasize sex role learning for male children more than for female children. Perhaps the father's interest in his son's acquiring the masculine traits causes him to be involved more in providing discipline and in assuring that he adopts the behavior necessary for the male role. This present finding is also supported by Bronfenbrenner's (2, p. 249) finding that "boys are subjected to greater pressure and discipline, again mainly from their father."

The finding that more than twice as many female students as male students reported receiving praise often during childhood is supported by Bronfenbrenner's (2) report that girls seem to receive affection, attention, and praise more often than boys. This finding, in addition to the findings that the majority of the boys reported the *mother* as the source of most affection and that boys were much less likely than girls to report that affection came from *mother and father about equally* would seem to reflect a cultural expectation that it is more appropriate for fathers to express affection and praise toward female children than toward male children. Such a cultural expectation and practice may account in large measure for the fact that numerous studies have indicated that there is a higher frequency of stuttering, delinquency, schizophrenia, and reading and behavior problems in boys (13, 21).

The finding that a greater proportion of males than females perceived the mother to be the source of most affection during childhood is not surprising, since it seems an accepted value in American society for females to have freedom in expressing affection to both sexes and males to have less freedom in expression of affection and especially so in expression of affection toward male children. Showing affection is part of the "mothering" role, but is not as closely associated with the father role. This finding, as well as the finding that the greatest proportion of both males and females perceived the *mother* to be the greatest source of most affection, is related to various research reports showing that children tend to perceive the father as more punitive and the mother as more nurturant (9, 21). In one study (9) the girls, in comparison with the boys, perceived the father as being both more punitive and more affectionate. The present findings also coincide with the observations of Smart and Smart (18, p. 461) who state that "father tends to react expressively with his daughters, enjoying, praising, and appreciating them as feminine creatures, while with sons he is more demanding, exerting pressure and discipline, insisting upon successful interaction with the outside world."

The finding that a greater proportion of females than males reported that the mother *very often* found time to do things together with them as a child is not surprising when one considers that many of the activities in which mothers participate with daughters are ones which may be part of her daily activities and would not require as much extra effort as would the activities more suited for the male child.

The finding that more female students (57.5%) than male students (25.2%) reported greatest parental influence from the *mother,* while a greater proportion of male students reported the greatest parental influence to be from the *father* is consistent with the cultural expectation that children will identify with the same sex parent. However, the findings that the greatest proportion of both males and females reported the *mother* to be the greatest influence in their lives reflects the greater role the mother assumes in child rearing and provides support to the thesis that the mother exerts a greater influence than does the father upon the lives of the children. The finding that the greatest proportion of male students (41.5%) reported the *mother* to be the greatest influence can be explained by the previously mentioned finding that the source of most affection for the majority of the male students was the *mother* and also by the research indicating that children tend to identify with the parent whom the child perceives as more rewarding and affectionate (15, 21, 22). This finding is also related to the thesis that both sexes identify with the mother in very early years (10). The fact that the boy later has to shift his identification to the father, while no such shift is required of the girl, suggests that the male's identification process is more difficult than the female's.

The finding that no significant difference was found in the perceptions of male and female high school students concerning the degree to which parents expressed affection toward the respondent as a child is in contradiction to other research indicating that girls receive more love, affection, and nurturance from both parents than do boys (2, 5). This finding is undoubtedly related to another finding in this study that both males and females listed the mother as the major source of affection. When this is considered along with the fact that mothers have freedom in expression of affection to both sexes and the fact that "in early childhood the mothers assume primary responsibility for child rearing" (14, p. 695), the present finding is not too surprising.

One major conclusion of this study is that parents have a decidedly different effect on the lives of their sons and daughters and that mothers have greater influence than do fathers upon the children. Another tentative conclusion is that adolescent girls seem to have more positive and supportive parent-child relationships than do boys.

That boys have somewhat less positive and supportive parent-child relationships may offer a partial explanation as to why boys seem to be more susceptible to parental influence. This possibility is related to the research of Stevenson (19) and Stevenson, Keen, and Knight (20) which supported the thesis that the supportive behavior of parents toward their children tends to generate satiation effects. Their research indicated that parents exerted less influence upon their children's performance of motor tasks than did strangers. It is possible that because girls tend to experience more positive and supportive parent-child relationships, they also experience more satiation effects of this supportive behavior and therefore tend to be less susceptible than are boys to parental influence.

The findings that adolescent males and females perceive their parental relationships as different again indicates that parents respond to the sexes differently because of different sex role expectations. The male, having a more constricted sex role with which to identify, is subject to more restrictive action from parents (especially in the form of discipline from fathers), whereas the female with less rigid role expectations receives positive reactions (such as praise) more often from both parents.

Perhaps the great importance that the father feels for early sex role identification by the son places a pressure on the parent-son relationship early in life, which after the relationship has been formed in this manner, may not have the opportunity to develop into the more relaxed and less pressured interaction that exists with daughters.

REFERENCES

1. Bayley, N. Research in child development: A longitudinal perspective. *Merrill-Palmer Quart. Devel. & Behav.*, 1965, 11, 183-208.
2. Bronfenbrenner, U. Toward a theoretical model for the analysis of parent-child relationships in a social context. In *Parental Attitudes and Child Behavior*, John Glidewell (Ed.). Springfield, Ill.: Thomas, 1961.
3. Croake, J. W., & Know, F. H. Changing attitudes toward parents and university personnel. *Coll. Stud. Survey*, 1970, 4, 60-64.
4. Dahlem, N. W. Young Americans' reported perceptions of their parents. *J. of Psychol.*, 1970, 74, 187-194.
5. Droppleman, L. F., & Schaeffer, E. S. Boys and girls reports of maternal and parental behavior. *J. Abn. & Soc. Psychol.*, 1963, 7, 648-654.
6. Emmerich, W. Variations in the parents' role as a function of sex and the child's sex and age. *Merrill-Palmer Quart. Devel. & Behav.*, 1962, 8, 3-11.
7. Goodenough, E. W. Interest in persons as an aspect of sex difference in the early years. *Genet. Psychol. Monog.*, 1957, 55, 287-323.
8. Hawkes, G., Burchinal, L. G., & Gardner, B. Pre-adolescents' views of some of their relationships with their parents. *Child Devel.*, 1957, 28, 393-399.
9. Kagan, J., & Lemkin, J. The child's differential perception of parental attributes. *J. Abn. & Soc. Psychol.*, 1960, 61, 440.
10. Lynn, D. B. Sex differences in identification development. *Sociometry*, 1961, 24, 372-393.
11. McGuire, C., & White, G. D. The measurement of social status. Research Paper in *Human Development No. 3* (rev.). Austin: Univ. Texas, 1955.
12. Medinnus, G. R. Adolescents self-acceptance and perceptions of their parents. *J. Consult. Psychol.*, 1965, 29, 150-154.
13. _____. Readings in the Psychology of Parent Child Relations. New York: Wiley, 1967.
14. Medinnus, G. R., & Johnson, R. C. Child and Adolescent Psychology. New York: Wiley, 1969.
15. Payne, D. E., & Mussen, P. H. Parent-child relations and father identification among adolescent boys. *J. Abn. & Soc. Psychol.*, 1956, 52, 358-362.
16. Rothbart, M. K., & Maccoby, E. E. Parents' differential reactions to sons and daughters. *J. Personal. & Soc. Psychol.*, 1966, 4, 237-243.
17. Schaefer, E. S., & Bayley, N. Maternal behavior, child behavior and their intercorrelations from infancy through adolescence. *Monog. Soc. for Res. in Child Devel.*, 1963, 28, 127.
18. Smart, M. S., & Smart, R. C. Children: Development and Relationships. New York: MacMillan, 1972.
19. Stevenson, H. W. Social reinforcement with children as a function of CA, sex of experimentor and sex of subject. *J. Abn. & Soc. Psychol.*, 1961, 63, 147-154.
20. Stevenson, H., Keen, R., & Knight, R. M. Parents and strangers as reinforcing agents for children's performance. *J. Abn. & Soc. Psychol.*, 1963, 67, 183-186.
21. Walters, J., & Stinnett, N. Parent-child relationships: A decade review of research. *J. Mar. & Fam.*, 1971, 33, 70-111.
22. Winch, R. F. Identification and Its Familial Determinants. New York: Bobbs-Merrill, 1962.

26   adolescent orientations toward parents and peers: variations by sex, age, and socioeconomic status

russell l. curtis, jr.

One of the most important processes during the period of adolescence is the choice of significant others for sources of information, orientation and guidance. The dynamics of these choices are typically interpreted in the literature as "reference group" functions and are viewed as reaching their most turbulent or variable stage during adolescence. There are several reasons for this. Those commonly cited include adolescent experiences with shifting organizational settings (different schools, summer jobs and camps, matriculation to college, etc.), conflicting value sources (the media, the school, parents, friends, etc.) and the rapid social and physical maturation processes which call for a variety of adjustive mechanisms. These dynamics as well as the patterns of shifting reference sources are items of central interest in the study of adolescents, especially in the American literature.

The purpose of this paper is to examine adolescents' shifts in orientations toward and respect for their friends, mothers and fathers from the 7th through the 12th grades. These grades correspond to the age-levels of 12-13 through 17-18 (with few exceptions). The major contributions of this paper consist of describing these orientations toward and respect for these three reference sources for a large number of students (9,056) of both sexes and from different socioeconomic levels. The findings are related with a large body of previous findings which are described below.

Previous Findings

Socioeconomic Variations

A large number of studies have found significant class differences in parental attitudes, parental childrearing behaviors and the perceptions of parents and other adults by children and adolescents (cf. the extensive reviews by Bronfenbrenner, 1958; Kohn, 1963, 1969; and Kerckhoff, 1972). Several contributions to these differences have been identified. Kohn suggested that occupational experiences and conceptions of "getting ahead" contributed to a developmental orientation with an emphasis on internal controls among middle class parents and a traditional, collectivist perspective with an emphasis upon external controls among lower and working class parents. Bronfenbrenner's analysis of changing childrearing patterns from 1930 to 1955 identified a greater willingness on the part of the middle *vis a vis* lower SES groups to refer to experts for childrearing advice. The process was viewed as influencing middle more than lower class mothers toward a greater emphasis on independence training, creative explorations, and permissiveness; during the period, some class differences were observed to be reversed, especially with respect to permissiveness.

Some typical findings for differences in parental behaviors are that middle class parents are more permissive, less punitive, and less likely to employ coercive suggestions, negative verbal sanctions, severe penalties (especially physical) and restrictive regulations (Walters and Crandall,

1964; Sears, Maccoby, and Levin, 1957; Bayley and Schaefer, 1960). Relatedly, children and adolescents perceive their parents in ways which are consistent with these childrearing patterns. On the basis of perceptual data, lower class parents (*vis a vis* middle class) have been reported to be more autocratic and rejecting (Elder, 1962), less willing to discuss issues in a democratic manner (Psathas, 1957), and less competent, less interested in their children and less secure in their own endeavors, especially in the case of fathers (Rosen, 1964). Part of these differences may be due to differential family size (Elder and Bowerman, 1963; Sears, Maccoby and Levin, 1957; Hart, 1957) which has been found to detract from the quality of parent-child relationships. For the period covered in the above research (backdating by age of children), lower and working socioeconomic groups maintained larger birth rates.

These patterns also appear to be generalized to other adults—teachers, policemen, etc. Singer (1971) in a study of a large sample (N = 4,440) of 10th and 11th graders, found a larger percentage of high status adolescents to be "adult oriented" than low status adolescents. Family size was also found to be inversely associated with an adult orientation.

Extending the implications of the Singer study, and linking them with other observations on class differences in attitudes and interpersonal orientations, the possibility of constellations of judgments about the significance of others which is closely associated with socioeconomic positions becomes a tenable consideration. This is related with the view that judgments of the self (self concept, self esteem, etc.) influence one's view of others and, further, that others may be defined in similar ways (e.g. competent, honest, etc.) Cox (1962), for example, found that boys' positive attitudes toward fathers were associated with competent and warm relations with peers. Following Rosenberg's findings that adolescent self-esteem was inversely associated with socioeconomic status, it may be that lower status adolescents tend to view all significant others in a more unfavorable light than do middle or upper status adolescents.

Sex Variations

Several studies of U.S. children and adolescents conclude that females are more congenial and are more likely to display strong affiliation needs than are males (Lynn, 1962; Kahn and Fiedler, 1961; Harris and Tseng, 1957). Females have also been found to be less aggressive (or more pro-social aggressive—Sears, 1961), more likely to conform to immediate models (Costanzo and Shaw, 1966) and more likely to maintain an adult orientation (Singer, 1971) than males.

With these differences, we would expect females to respect the opinions of their parents and friends more than males and to report more satisfactory relationships with each of these reference sources. This appears to be the case. In studies by Gardner (1947), Hawkes, Burchinal and Gardner (1957) and Kahn and Fiedler (1961), boys have been found to be more critical of parents and to hold less favorable attitudes toward both parents and friends. Such differences, however, must be qualified by sex of parent as well as by age (discussed below). In general, mothers are reported to be more nurturant, warm, responsive, etc. and, in some research, to be the preferred parent. (Harris and Tseng, 1957; Dubin and Dubin, 1965; Gardner, 1947; Kagen, et al., 1961). Other research, however, indicates that the same-sex parent is preferred (Stevenson, et al., 1967).

Finally, an interesting qualification to some of the above patterns can be added. This is the tendency for a larger proportion of females than males to develop preferences for the role of the opposite sex. This has been reported in the research by Harris and Tseng (1957) and by Tuddenham (1951). Several explanations are available for this pattern but the most powerful in my opinion is that of Lynn (1966) who hypothesized these trends of differential attraction to sex roles on the basis of sex-based status and power differentials which favor the male in our society. For the present study, this consideration takes on immediate relevance for girls' valuations of friends as reference sources since the latter are likely to be female during this age-range (cf. Gordon, 1957). Indirectly, it might also interact with valuations of parents.

Age Variations

Several changes occur as a person moves through childhood and adolescence in our society. Those which have been of most interest to social scientists, and which are the primary focus here, are the changes in interpersonal relationships (i.e., variable attractions to different persons) which appear during this period of physical, social and intellectual growth. The most accepted generalization is that the child moves away from parents and toward peers once play groups and school-based settings become viable interaction options. When and how much are questions which have not received specific answers, however. Costanzo and Shaw (1970) found that peer influences increased during the elementary school years, reaching a peak around ages 11-13. Other sources also support the view that peer influences crest in the early junior high years. If we are to accept the general thesis that adolescents are forced to choose between parents and peers for models, for orientations, etc., then it is conceivable that a rise in the importance of one of these sources *could* be accompanied with a fall in the value of the other. From this point of view, the findings of Harris and Tseng (1957) and of Gardner (1947) that adolescents' valuations of parents remained rather constant during the junior high and high school years and tended to increase during late high school would suggest that peers do not become more influential after the beginning of teenage years, or at least would argue that they do not continue to erode the value of parental opinion.

In a larger context, these changing social orientations can be seen as reflections of shifting patterns of conformity. Hamm and Hoving (1961) found an increasing tendency for children to conform to both peer and adult models between grade-levels two, five and eight; only the shifts toward peers, however, were statistically significant. For approximately the same age-period, (i.e., 7-13) Costanzo and Shaw (1966) found increasing conformity to erroneous responses for both males and females; beyond age 13, however, there was a decrease. In this regard, the study by Harris and Tseng (1957), noted above, showed childrens' favorable attitudes toward peers, mothers and fathers to decrease from the 3rd grade through the middle years (5th through 8th grades) but, for each of these three reference sources, to remain relatively constant (or increase slightly) beyond that grade-level. This period of independence or anti-conformity could also create difficulties for parents whose reactions, in turn, would alter adolescents' perceptions of them as reference sources. The finding by Blood and Wolfe (1960: 247-248) that the conflicts between husbands and wives about child discipline were greatest during the adolescent age would be a relevant consideration here.

Summary of Previous Findings

From this selective but representative review, child and adolescent judgments of parents and friends (or peers) as reference sources were found to be: more favorable toward mothers than fathers, more favorable toward all three in the view of females, more favorable toward all three on the part of middle than of lower class children and adolescents, unlikely to change appreciably toward friends (or peers) beyond early adolescence, and likely to become more positive toward parents in late adolescence. Lacunae in the literature are the interaction of sex, age, and class on the valuations of these reference sources, and, even when available in a limited form (say, age and sex), the small sample size which was employed. For example, the differences between lower class female and male adolescents' valuations of friends and mothers and how these differences, (whatever they might be) change in time have not been described in the literature. This analysis focuses upon these questions from data from a large number of respondents.

Data

The data here came from an adolescent survey of 18,664 adolescents from unbroken homes in North Carolina and Ohio during April and May of 1960. The original study was conducted by Charles E. Bowerman. A sub-sample is employed for this analysis. This consists of 9,056 respondents from grade-levels 7 through 12 in 24 public schools in which students from all classes were present on the day the questionnaires were administered and which contained all students wtihin a single building structure and an average of 40 or more students per grade-level. Few differences exist between the parent and sub-samples other than that the latter excluded many small, rural schools where grade-level N's were quite small (less than 40). The exclusion of schools with missing classes (excursions, etc.) attentuate a possible region-by-representation sampling bias.

Data for this analysis are from three eight-item scales: orientations toward father, mother, and friends. These scales were comparable in all respects with exception of the designated "others." The scale values are interpreted here as measures of the extent to which these others were important as reference sources. The items tapped such dimensions as the extent to which the other's (i.e. father, mother, friends) opinions were valued, their advice was sought, etc. Face or construct validity constitute no interpretative difficulties here. As Guttman-like scales, a reproduceability of approximately .80 was achieved for each. Scale values are dichotomized at 06 and higher for "high valuations" and 05 and lower for "low valuations." Data are presented as the percentages with "high valuations."

Socioeconomic distinctions were made on the basis of a preliminary search for the point of greatest differences in students' orientations as related with fathers' occupation. These were dichotomized by fathers' occupations as Lower (Operatives and kindred, Service, Farm Laborers) and Middle-and-Working (Professional and Managerial, White Collar, and Skilled Labor). No racial distinctions were made since the percentage of minorities (less than 5%) was quite small.

RESULTS

Overall Attractions to Fathers, Mothers and Friends

The distributions of percentages of students with high valuations appear in Table 1. Derivations from Table 1 show the differences when controlling for sex and for socioeconomic status. The most obvious differences are the sex variations in valuations of friends and the general preferences for mothers and fathers *vis a vis* friends.

The percentages of females with high valuations of friends are almost twice as great as those for males; these differences are clearly due to sex and not to age (by grade-levels) or to socioeconomic status. These findings for valuations of friends as reference sources strongly support the conclusions of other studies (above) that females are more sociable and, perhaps, have a higher affiliation motive than do males.

The contrasts between friends and parents, however, clearly depart from many other observations. Parents are clearly more important here as reference sources than are friends. The exception to this would be lower status females whose attractions to fathers and friends were approximately equal. The valuations for both parents, however, do decrease with ascending grade-levels. A floor threshold is reached around grades 10 and 11 (corresponding generally to ages 16 and 17) and, in the case of valuations of fathers by middle and working class students, an increase occurs between grades 11 and 12.

So, while parental opinions are clearly preferred to those of friends, it is also true that parental opinions become devalued during the adolescent life-cycle of these respondents. Thus, rather than moving from one set of reference figures to another, these data show that a gradual independence from parental perspectives is achieved while the influence of friends remains relatively consistent (between ascending grade-levels), but rarely more important (various contrasts within sub-groups across same grade-levels), than that of parents. A similar conclusion has been reached by Turner (1964) and by Campbell in their observations on the pulls of parent and peer systems for teenagers.

Of the two parents, mothers are preferred at every grade-level for three of the four sub-groups, lower females and males and middle-and-working females. The differences are much larger for the two female sub-groups than for lower status males. For middle-and-working males, attractions to fathers

TABLE 1. PERCENTAGES OF STUDENTS WITH HIGH VALUATIONS OF FRIENDS, FATHERS, AND MOTHERS

Sex and Occupational Status of Father	Grade-Levels					
	Seven	Eight	Nine	Ten	Eleven	Twelve
Valuations of Friends						
Middle & Working						
Male	27.4% (694)	28.4% (543)	29.8% (503)	26.6% (497)	27.8% (472)	28.2% (478)
Female	51.0 (730)	51.7 (536)	57.0 (506)	59.8 (493)	58.9 (452)	55.2 (455)
Lower						
Male	24.7 (259)	28.0 (189)	23.1 (186)	29.4 (255)	29.2 (205)	27.1 (155)
Female	50.9 (301)	47.4 (251)	56.1 (228)	54.1 (242)	49.2 (236)	52.6 (190)
Valuations of Mothers						
Middle & Working						
Male	85.0% (694)	73.3% (543)	68.0% (503)	68.0% (497)	59.7% (472)	59.4% (478)
Female	87.7 (730)	84.9 (536)	82.2 (506)	76.3 (493)	76.1 (452)	75.6 (455)
Lower						
Male	76.4 (259)	66.6 (189)	71.6 (186)	64.5 (255)	63.4 (205)	51.0 (155)
Female	80.7 (301)	78.1 (251)	74.7 (228)	72.8 (242)	70.3 (236)	73.7 (190)
Valuations of Fathers						
Middle & Working						
Male	81.6% (694)	77.3% (543)	70.8% (503)	65.0% (497)	60.4% (472)	68.2% (478)
Female	76.2 (730)	68.7 (536)	65.6 (506)	58.2 (493)	59.7 (452)	64.0 (455)
Lower						
Male	73.0 (259)	63.5 (189)	68.3 (186)	54.5 (255)	55.6 (205)	46.5 (155)
Female	59.5 (301)	54.6 (251)	50.7 (228)	54.2 (240)	50.0 (236)	51.6 (190)

are slightly larger in only four of the six grade-levels. In short, previous findings (above) of preferences for mothers over fathers, though often differing on the dimensions of valuation (e.g. warmth, helpfulnesss, source of orientations, etc.) than that reported here, are upheld for three of four SES-by-Sex sub-groups of adolescents. Again, higher SES males are an exception.

Sex, SES, and Age (by Grade-levels) Variations

One sex difference has already been reported: the greater attractions to friends' opinions on the part of females. Another important sex variation can also be observed. Differences for attractions to mothers' opinions, favoring females, are larger than the differences for fathers' favoring males. This is true for all six grade-levels for middle-and-working students and four of the six for lower status students. This is another indication of the sexual differences in interpersonal relationships which were noted earlier: the greater sociability, in general, and successful relationships with parents, in particular, on the part of females.

The expected socioeconomic differences (i.e., greater respect for the opinions of parents and friends by higher status adolescents) obtain for females. Only the valuations of fathers were in the directions anticipated from previous research for this male sample. The latter is consistent with Rosen's (1964) findings that class differences were more significant for valuations of fathers than of mothers. Rosen's sample, however, was all-male (9-11 yrs. of age). Here, the class differences in valuations of fathers are even larger for females in four of the six grades.

Predominant variations by age (or grade-levels) have already been described. Another one which deserves attention is the slight increase in the attractions to fathers between the 11th and 12th grades by middle-and-working class students. The immediate explanation for this shift would be that fathers play an important stabilizing and resource-provision (information, financial aid, etc.) role in the anticipated movement away from school, and perhaps home, on the part of 12th graders. Fewer resources are available in the lower class home and, notably, the same pattern does not obtain.

Are there any sex-by-SES interaction effects? From other studies as well as many of the results here, we would expect higher SES females to be most attracted and/or respectful of the opinions of others and lower status males to be least likely to display these orientations. In the case of middle-and-working females in this sample, there is some evidence for this. In all six grade-levels, larger percentages of middle-and-working females have high valuations of friends and of mothers than do any of the other sub-groups. This does not obtain for fathers, however. And, further, lower class males are not consistently the lowest sub-group in the percentages with high valuations for any of the three reference figures.

CONCLUSIONS AND IMPLICATIONS

The findings in this study are consistent with many conclusions which have been reached in previous research on adolescents' attractions to parents and to friends as reference sources. These include the greater attraction to parents by higher SES adolescents and a greater attraction and/or dependence on friends' opinions by females. The preference for the same-sex parent, an observation which has been offered elsewhere, was found for females in this research. Finally, attractions to parental opinions and orientations were found to decrease, though not continuously, from early junior high throughout the late high school years.

Other findings, however, differ from conclusions or implications from previous research. First, preferences for the same-sex parent (in comparisons between same grade-levels) were not discernible for males. Fathers and mothers were equally attractive. Second, both parents were clearly preferred over friends at each grade-level by all of the sub-groups (class by sex) of adolescents. Third, while there was a strong indication of a growing independence from parental perspectives with ascending grade-levels (and increasing age), this was not accompanied by an increasing attraction to friends as reference sources. Fourth, among upper status adolescents (here, middle-and-working), there was an indication of an increase in respect for fathers' opinions between the 11th and 12th grades. And, finally, class differences in the valuations of parents were generally found to be larger for females' valuations of fathers than for males' valuations of either parent. This was not consistent across all grade-levels, however. All of these findings are fruitful grist for future research.

The large size of this sample (9,056) contributes to the reliability of these data. And, while these data are cross-sectional rather than longitudinal, there is little reason to believe that significant historical effects would have operated during the relatively short, six-year age-range. On the other hand, these data were gathered before the recent changes in sex-related attitudes and behaviors, especially within marriage, and the need for current, comparable research is obvious.

FOOTNOTE

[1]Tests of Statistical significance are not presented because small differences are often significant at the .05 level (or less) as a result of the large cell N's. The substantive foci, here, are the *patterns* of differences between sub-groups (sex and socioeconomic status) and how these shift with ascending grade-levels.

REFERENCES

Bayley, Nancy and Earl S. Schaefer. "Relationships between Socioeconomic Variables and the Behavior of Mothers toward Young Children," *Journal of Genetic Psychology*, 1960, 96 (March): 61-77.

Blood, Robert O., Jr. and Donald M. Wolfe. *Husbands and Wives.* New York: Free Press, 1960.

Bronfenbrenner, Urie. "Socialization and Social Class through Time and Space," in Eleanor E. Maccoby, Theodore M. Newcomb and Eugene L. Hartley (eds.) *Readings in Social Psychology.* New York: Henry Holt and Company, 1958, pp. 400-425.

Costanzo, Philip R. and Marvin E. Shaw. "Conformity as a Function of Age Level," *Child Development*, 1966, 37 (December):967-975.

Cox, F. N. "An Assessment of Children's Attitudes toward Parent Figures," *Child Development*, 1962, 33 (December):821-830.

Dubin, Robert and Elisabeth R. Dubin. "Children's Social Perceptions: A Review of Research," *Child Development*, 1965, 36 (September):809-838.

Elder, Glen H. Jr. "Structural Variations in the Child Rearing Relationship," *Sociometry*, 1962, 25 (September): 241-262.

_____ and Charles E. Bowerman. "Family Structure and Child-Rearing Patterns," *American Sociological Review*, 1963, 28 (December):891-905.

Gardner, L. Pearl. "An Analysis of Children's Attitudes toward Fathers," *Journal of Genetic Psychology*, 1947, 70 (March):3-28.

Gordon, C. Wayne. *The Social System of the High School.* New York: Free Press, 1957.

Hamm, Norman H. and Kenneth L. Hoving, "Conformity in Children as a Function of Grade-Level, and Real versus Hypothetical Adult and Peer Models," *Journal of Genetic Psychology*, 1971, 118 (June):253-263.

Harris, Dale B. and Sing Chu Tseng. "Children's Attitudes toward Peers and Parents as Revealed by Sentence Completions," *Child Development*, 1957, 28 (December):401-411.

Hart, I. "Maternal Child-Rearing Practices and Authoritarian Ideology," *Journal of Abnormal and Social Psychology*, 1957, 55 (September):232-237.

Hawkes, G. R., L. B. Burchinal and B. Gardner. "Pre-adolescents' Views of Some of Their Relationships with Their Parents," *Child Development*, 1957, 28 (December):393-399.

Kagen, Jerome, Barbara Kosken and Sara Watson. "Child's Symbolic Conceptualization of Parents," *Child Development*, 1961, 32 (December):625-636.

Kerckhoff, Alan C. *Socialization and Social Class.* Englewood Cliffs, New Jersey: Prentice-Hall, Inc., 1972.

Kohn, Melvin L. "Social Class and Parent-Child Relationships: An Interpretation," *American Journal of Sociology*, 1963, 68 (January):471-480.

_____. *Class and Conformity.* Homewood, Illinois: Dorsey Press, 1969.

Kohn, A. Robert and Fred E. Fiedler. "Age and Sex Differences in the Perception of Persons," *Sociometry*, 1961, 24 (June): 157-164.

Lynn, David B. "Sex-Role and Parental Identification," *Child Development*, 1962, 33 (September):555-564.

_____. "The Process of Learning Parental and Sex-Role Identification," *Journal of Marriage and the Family*, 1966, 28 (November):466-470.

Psathas, George. "Ethnicity, Social Class and Adolescent Independence from Parental Control," *American Sociological Review*, 1957, 22 (August):415-423.

Rosen, Bernard C. "Social Class and the Child's Perception of the Parent," *Child Development*, 1964, 35 (December):1147-1153.

Sears, Robert R., Eleanor E. Maccoby and Harry Levin. *Patterns of Child Rearing.* New York: Harper and Row, 1957.

_____. "Relation of Early Socialization Experiences to Aggression in Middle Childhood," *Journal of Abnormal and Social Psychology*, 1961, 63 (November):466-492.

Singer, Eleanor. "Adult Orientation of First and Later Children," *Sociometry*, 1971, 34 (September):328-345.

Stevenson, Harold W., Gordon A. Hale, Kennedy T. Hill and Barbara E. Moely. "Determinants of Children's Preferences for Adults," *Child Development*, 1967, 38 (March):1-14.

Tuddenham, R. D. "Studies in Reputation: (I) Sex and Grade Differences in School Children's Evaluations of Their Peers, (II) The Diagnosis of Social Adjustment," *Psychology Monographs*, 1951, 66 (No. 1):1-39.

Walters, Elinor and Vaughn J. Crandall. "Social Class and Maternal Behavior from 1940 to 1960," *Child Development*, 1964, 35 (December):1021-1032.

27

parental views on teenage
sexual behavior

roger w. libby

gilbert d. nass

In the present study parents' views of appropriate rules and behavior in teenage courtship were examined. Consideration was given to differences between democratic and autocratic attitudes concerning dating rules and teenage sexual behavior.

Reiss (1967) has emphasized the importance of the liberal-conservative ethos as a predictor of courtship attitudes. He contended that a liberal or conservative life style was more important than social class in determining the degree of sexual permissiveness (Reiss, 1965). Reiss' findings emphasize the relevance of identifying subjects' liberal and conservative attitudes. Reiss also reported that equalitarianism with a departure from double standard adherence was approved by the majority of both his student and adult samples, but that a female's close ties to the family institution function as support to non-equalitarianism. Another of his specific findings was that in groups with lower levels of sexual permissiveness, social forces will have a greater likelihood of altering the individual's level of sexual permissiveness than in groups with higher levels of sexual permissiveness. The legitimacy of the proposition was questioned by Heltsley and Broderick (1969). Using religiosity as a measure of social forces they disputed this general finding and suggested the quality of the particular factor, in this case religion, influenced sexual permissiveness. The effective rejoinder by Reiss (1969) still leaves the proposition as one to consider in further research. Wake (1969, pp. 170-177) asserted that the double standard was nearly nonexistent for his sample of middle to upper socio-economic status mothers and fathers. Those parents were described as equally permissive toward sons' and daughters' sexual experiences. However, a progressive decrease in permissiveness was reported by the mothers and fathers when the sexual activity approached and involved coitus. Bell (1966, pp. 34-35) indicated that most parents probably assume that their offspring accept traditional sexual values. He suggested that parent-child conflict in the sexual area may decrease with the increase of the liberal view of sexuality in America.

In the present research, data concerning parents' views of courtship norms were secured as part of a larger study of parental attitudes toward public high school sex education. Items regarding courtship norms were analyzed. The proposed relevance of the liberal-conservative life style in the cited literature led to the reanalyses of the data. The life style measure used was based on the "Traditional Family Ideology Scale (TFI)" that Levinson and Huffman (1958) developed to assess genotypical democratic-autocratic ideology. The re-analyses incorporating basic life style as an independent variable were guided by the general hypothesis that the democratic-oriented parents would hold a considerably different set of norms than more autocratic-oriented parents regarding selected aspects of teenage courtship. Specifically, it was hypothesized that: 1) democratic parents, compared to autocratic parents, would allow teenagers significantly more freedom in their courtship decision-making; 2) democratic parents, compared to autocratic parents, would evidence significantly less endorsement of the double standard of sexual morality; and 3) democratic parents, compared to autocratic parents, would evidence significantly less stringent courtship rules for girls.

METHODS

Two hundred and fifty parents (125 couples) in Manchester, Connecticut comprised the sample. Manchester, with a population of 46,800, essentially served as a satellite city to Hartford, the state capitol. An attempt was made to secure parental couples for simultaneous interviews while also obtaining a sample representative of Manchester's social class, age, and religious composition.

Sampling Procedure and Distribution

Random sampling procedures were used with census tracts and city blocks serving as the sampling frames. A total of 601 housing units were contacted. Sixty-one percent (369) of the housing units contacted failed to provide sample eligible or physically accessible couples, e.g., single-parent homes, non-parent homes, no one home, and couples on different work shifts. Of the 232 "eligible" parent couples, 54% (125) volunteered to participate. Of the 46% (107) refusing to participate, a large majority (88%) indicated a lack of time or interest in the study. Thirteen of the refusal couples stated they did not wish to discuss sex or sex education because they disapproved of sex education.

Selection procedures produced a sample which closely approximated the general population in social class, religion and age composition (Libby, 1969). Race was not a factor, as Manchester had less than twenty non-whites over the age of twenty in 1960 (U.S. Census, 1961:21).

Interview Procedures

The interview method was selected as the most efficient way to collect the data. Its chief advantages, as contrasted with mailed questionnaire research, were considered to be maximizing subjects' participation, flexibility in utilizing several open-ended questions, and developing rapport— all were seen as increasing the study's validity (Sax, 1968, p. 202).

The interviewers were a male graduate student in his mid-twenties and a female college graduate in her mid-fifties. Each of the interviewers interviewed an equal number of mothers and fathers, so that the effect of the sex and age differentials of the interviewers were balanced. Participating fathers and mothers were interviewed both separately and simultaneously by the interviewing team. To further control bias, the interviewers alternated the sex of their subject at each consecutive interview.

Questionnaire Interview Schedule

The interview, which included over 70 items, took about an hour to complete. Included were several items relevant to understanding parental views of courtship behavior. Also included was a modified version of the Traditional Family Ideology Scale (TFI) which was used as a measure of democratic-autocratic ideological attitudes (Levinson and Huffman, 1958). The TFI has appeared frequently in the literature as a reasonable measure of an individual's position on a "democratic" to "autocratic" continuum (Dreyer and Rigler, 1969).

FINDINGS

First, decision-making in establishing courtship rules was examined. Seventy-two percent of the parents responded that "parents and teenagers should work out the rules together—50-50," 28% asserted that "mostly parents" should make up the rules, while no parents responded that "mostly teenagers" should decide dating rules.

When asked whether the dating rules should differ for girls, 51% of the parents (126) indicated that rules should differ, and 49% (123) responded that rules for girls should not differ. Parents desiring different rules for girls were then asked *how* the rules should differ. All would place greater restrictions on the girl than the boy. Parents were then asked why they felt that rules either should or should not differ for girls. Among parents contending that rules should differ for girls, 65% (81) felt that girls are more vulnerable and have more to lose (pregnancy, reputation), while boys are more responsible or are better able to take care of themselves; 10% (13) said the girl sets the standards of behavior and has the larger responsibility; 11% (14) believed the rules should differ because it was appropriate by cultural standards or was the way they were taught; and 14% (17) gave "other" reasons, which most often involved the idea that parents have more control over the girl, therefore rules should center on the girl. Of the parents (119) responding with reasons why the rules should not differ for girls, 66% (79) indicated that there was a mutual trust toward offspring of both sexes; 8% (10) just accepted the situation and stated that "they're together anyway"; and 25% (30) said that boys should be restricted as much as girls.

Two hundred and thirty-seven parents responded to the open-ended question, "What do you feel a parent should do, if anything, if he or she realizes an 18-year-old daughter is having sexual relations before marriage?" Forty-three percent (103) of the parents stated they would try to change the daughter's behavior by showing their disapproval and using discussion to convince her that such behavior is wrong; 17% (40) would actively disapprove by restricting, punishing, and breaking the relationship; 4% (10) of the parents would force marriage; 16% (37) would consult outside help (such as a minister, social worker, psychologist, etc.); 5% (12) would approach it situationally and say it "depends on the circumstances"; 10% (23) would try to understand and would provide support, but would "find out why"; while 5% (12) would give contraceptive advice.

Parents were then asked if "the situation should be different for an 18-year-old boy" having sexual relations before marriage. Eighty-six percent responded "no."

The type of sex education these parents felt was appropriate for their children's courtship stage was obtained by asking them, "In what ways are you approaching (or have you approached) sex education in your family?" The great majority of subjects were "proscriptive-oriented" (87%) rather than "discussion-oriented." Even so, of the two hundred fifty respondents, 59% (147) replied "no" when asked whether their own sex education was satisfactory. When considering "how is your approach different from the approach of your parents," 88% stated they were more open about sex than were their parents.

Items questioning appropriate sources of sex education, teenage contraceptive knowledge, the effectiveness of negative instruction in preventing teenage intercourse, also provided information about parental norms for courtship behavior.

An item eliciting parents' views toward teenage contraceptive knowledge was "Teenagers are better off not to know about contraceptives, because such information might lead to sexual experimentation." The total sample responded as follows: 2% "strongly agree"; 16% "agree"; 6% "undecided"; 66% "disagree"; and 9% "strongly disagree." Thus 75% of the parents appeared to agree that contraceptive knowledge alone does not lead to sexual experimentation.

Parental assessment of the effectiveness of negative sex instruction was obtained by asking, "Would you agree or disagree that discussing the dangers of venereal disease and premarital pregnancy is an effective way to prevent premarital intercourse amongst teenagers?" Seventy-three percent (179) agreed with this negative approach, while 27% (67) disagreed. Parents were then asked *why* they agreed or disagreed with the effectiveness of such an approach. Of parents agreeing with the negative approach, 49% believed that the *fear* of consequences or a combination of education and fear would be effective; 43% agreed because they felt education of possible consequences would be enough to stop premarital intercourse; and 8% agreed because such an approach "has worked in the past" or for other reasons. Eighty percent of the 67 parents disagreeing with the effectiveness of the negative approach felt that discussion won't change behavior, as teenagers will do what they want to anyway; 7% felt such instruction must come from the church or home, or that "morals" were a greater deterrent; and 13% felt the negative approach was ineffective because such things as contraceptive availability to control venereal disease will override fear.

TFI Findings

The general hypothesis guiding the special data analyses was that democratic-oriented parents and autocratic-oriented parents, as measured by the Traditional Family Ideology Scale (TFI), would hold considerably different sets of norms regarding teenage courtship. For the analyses a mean split on the TFI was used, dividing parents into two groups, democratic-autocratic. The major result showed both democratic and autocratic parents holding similar courtship standards. The two groups of parents were not statistically significantly different on any of the courtship norm items previously discussed in the findings section. Thus, the general hypothesis was not given support.

Democratic and autocratic parents showed significant differences in their questionnaire responses on only three sex education items. The three items on which the parental groups differed were: 1) Have you approached sex education with your children in much the same way as your parents did with you? 2) Was your own sex education satisfactory? and 3) Teenagers are better off not to know about contraceptives. In comparing their own "teaching" of sex with that which they received from their parents, the majority of both democratic and autocratic parents indicated they did not use the same approach as their own parents. However, 24% of the autocratic versus 13% of the democratic parents did use their parents' approach and this difference was statistically significant at the .05 level. Fifty percent of the autocratic parents were not satisfied with their own sex education while 68% of the democratic parents were not satisfied. This difference was statistically significant at the .01 level. Parental response to the final discriminating item, "Teenagers are better off not to know about contraceptives because such information might lead to sexual experimentation," had 75% of the total sample disagreeing. However, the differential response of democratic and autocratic parents was statistically significant at the .001 level. The direction of difference is indicated by the fact that 16% of the democratic parents versus 2% of the autocratic parents "strongly disagreed" and 7% of the democratic parents versus 25% of the autocratic parents "agreed."

Three more specific hypotheses were also tested with TFI data: 1) democratic parents, compared to autocratic parents, would allow teenagers significantly more freedom in their courtship decision-making; 2) democratic parents, compared to autocratic parents, would evidence significantly less endorsement of the double standard of sexual morality; 3) democratic parents, compared to autocratic parents, would evidence significantly less stringent courtship rules for girls. The findings show that on the items relevant to these hypotheses democratic and autocratic parents provide similar responses and no statistically significant differences were found. Therefore, the data did not provide support for the three specific hypotheses.

Additional Analyses

Because the democratic-autocratic family ideology distinction did not differentiate the parents regarding their norms concerning teenage dating, additional analyses were performed employing available variables which could possibly account for the existing set of parental courtship norms (Rosenberg, 1968). These included sex of parent, social class, and religion.

Sex of Parent. The only items for which the independent variable "sex of parent" was statistically significant was the question of who should decide dating rules for teenagers. Mothers (36%) were more apt than fathers (20%) to contend that "mostly parents" should decide dating rules, rather than having parents and teenagers decide together (p < .01).

Social Class. Social class as an independent variable provided a statistically significant result on the single item involving assessment of what the parent should do, knowing that their 18-year-old daughter was having sexual intercourse before marriage. Although a significant chi square (p < .05) was obtained it should be noted the direction, e.g., from highest to lowest social class, was not always linear (Nass, 1964, pp. 133-136; Duggan & Dean, 1968). The overall response showed the lower class parents were slightly more restrictive. For example, "forced marriage" was advocated by 9% of the upper-lower parents, 3% of the lower-middle, while only one upper-middle and no upper class parents advocated such a course of action. "Active restrictions and punishment" were advocated most frequently by lower-middle class parents (21.4%), upper-lower class parents (19.7%) and least by upper and upper-middle class parents (7.4%). "Showing firm disapproval" was highest for upper-middle class parents (50.9%), followed by upper-lower (46.5%), lower-middle (38.8%) and upper class parents (27.3%). "Try to understand" was advocated most by the upper class parents (27.3%) followed by upper-middle (14.0%), upper-lower (9.9%), and lower-middle (5.1%). The response, "consulting outside help, such as psychiatrists, ministers, etc.," also reflected the non-linear social class pattern. Outside help was suggested by 21% of the lower-middle class parents, 18% of the upper-middle, 9% of the upper-lower and by none of the upper class parents.

Religion. Religious affiliation was statistically significant for two questions. Not a single "Humanist-Agnostic-Atheist" or Jew agreed that "Teenagers are better off not to know about contraceptives." However, 29% of Catholic parents and 27% of Protestant parents held such a view, with the difference between the four groups statistically significant at p < .01. For the second question, "Humanist-Agnostic-Atheist" parents were least satisfied with their own sex education (77%), followed in order by Protestants (64%), Catholics (52%) and Jews (36%) (significant at p < .05).

Frequency of church attendance was not statistically significant for any of the questions utilized in this report. Thus, parents responded very similarly even though they were classified as attending church every week, or once a month, or a few times a year, or never.

DISCUSSION

The data indicated that parents, whether evidencing a democratic or autocratic life style by their response on the Traditional Family Ideology Scale, essentially expressed conservative attitudes regarding courtship behavior. These predominant norms included disapproval of complete autonomy of young adults in deciding courtship rules, considerable disapproval of both their daughters' and sons' nonmarital sexual involvement, and approval of a fear technique to deter teenage sexual exploration by emphasizing dangers of venereal disease and nonmarital pregnancy. For example, typical responses of parents included:

> *I try to keep them from knowing too much; I approach it the same as my parents did. My parents did not tell me about it. I don't discuss it either. I think sex education corrupts the minds of 15-16 year olds! There is absolutely no communication between parents and kids about sex. Kids know too much already. I just tell them to behave and keep their eyes open."*

> *"I never discussed sex with my kids and they never asked questions, and my parents were the same way."*

The data also indicated that parents with a democratic life style, as compared to autocratic parents, tended to show less satisfaction with their own sex education and expressed greater willingness for adolescents to have considerable sex education exposure. Thus, by differentiating parents into democratic-autocratic life style categories the data showed these two groups to be quite similar regarding courtship norms but somewhat different in their response to various sex education approaches. Perhaps parents showed greater ambiguity in their attitudes regarding sex education because this area was a recent arrival on the public scene. Thus, they possibly were less able to easily apply prior norms. These parents often expressed some uncertainty over the role of the school as juxtaposed to parental responsibilities. Given the general state of flux and ambiguity regarding sex education, the basic flexible life style of the democratic parents probably emerged and came into play more readily. Therefore in the sex education area the democratic parents presented different attitudes than did the autocratic parents. However, in the courtship area the existing conservative normative system encompassed both autocratic and democratic parents. Both types of parents tended to refer to personal experiences of their own younger days, and combined with a dramatic feeling of responsibility to get their children to do "right," they did not exhibit much variation from the existing deeply ingrained conservative norms.

Parental uncertainty in the sex education area poses several dilemmas. For example, the finding that autocratic parents were also more satisfied with their own sex education, together with data that they also were more likely to approach sex education as did their parents, raises the issue of their willingness to accept new knowledge and programs. Thus, developing strategies for breaking through traditional norms becomes a major objective for those proposing new programs.

Parents seemed to know what kind of "end product" they wanted in the way of life style for teenagers. Also, their espousal of conservative norms allowed them to overwhelmingly endorse the effectiveness of the "fear approach." Typical parental responses included:

"If they know dangers, they will avoid intercourse, and have a fear of the Lord."

"The fear tactic has worked in the past few generations; a lack of fear promotes promiscuity."

"G.I. fear movies worked for me."

"It brings to notice of the boy or girl the possibilities of terrible happenings in later life."

However, the great majority of parents also disagreed that "teenagers are better off not to know about contraception. . . ." Thus, even though parents desired to appear certain, calm and pleased with their current beliefs and the wisdom of their approach, their responses indicated considerable ambiguity.

The overall picture showed parents struggling with the determination of the amount of freedom to be entrusted to teenagers in deciding their dating limits and advocating the existence of a conservative single standard in regard to courtship rules. The data demonstrated a lack of a double standard and would seem to support literature evidencing the passing of the double standard (Reiss, 1965). However, the data indicated, as did Reiss (1965; 1967) and Bell (1966), that adults preferred to replace the double standard with a "conservative single standard," although youth are more prone to adapt a single standard of "permissiveness with affection." Though the parents did not support a double standard, a general impression derived from the interview data indicated that they thought as if the double standard was prevalent among adolescents and therefore justified their sex education approaches on the supposed existence of the double standard among teenagers.

Even though most parents viewed themselves as more open than their own parents in the sex education of their children, the fact that nearly all parents took a "traditional" rather than a "liberal" approach to the sex education of their children is probably typical of many cities and suburban communities. It appeared that parents were seeking "an answer" to changing sexual standards. While not wanting to appear "old fogies" a good many parents very clearly believed in "traditional" sexual values, and expected their children to believe and follow the same values. They were seemingly searching for some way to "put the lid back on" while maintaining some degree of "democratic" procedure with their adolescents.

REFERENCES

Bell, Robert. Parent-Child Conflict in Sexual Values. *Journal of Social Issues, 22:*34-45, 1966.

Dreyer, Albert and David Rigler. Cognitive Performance in Montessori and Nursery School Children. *Journal of Educational Research, 62:*409-416, 1969.

Duggan, Thomas J. and Charles W. Dean. Common Misinterpretations of Significance Levels in Sociological Journals. *The American Sociologist, 3:*45-46, 1968.

Heltsley, Mary E. and Carlfred B. Broderick, Religiosity and Premarital Sexual Permissiveness: Re-examination of Reiss' Traditionalism Proposition. *Journal of Marriage and the Family, 31:*441-443, 1969.

Levinson, Daniel and Phyllis Huffman. Traditional Family Ideology and Its Relation to Personality. In Don Dulany, Jr. *et al.* (eds.), *Contributions to Modern Psychology.* New York: Oxford University Press, 1958.

Libby, Roger. Liberalism-Traditionalism and Demographic Correlates of Parental Attitudes Toward High School Sex Education Programs. M.A. Thesis, University of Connecticut, Storrs, Connecticut, 1969.

Nass, Gilbert D. Friendship Formation: An Empirical Test of Balance Theory. Ph.D. Dissertation, University of Iowa, 1964, 133-136.

Reiss, Ira L. Social Class and Premarital Sexual Permissiveness: A Re-Examination. *American Sociological Review, 30:*747-756, 1965.

Reiss, Ira L. *The Social Context of Premarital Sexual Permissiveness.* New York: Holt, Rinehart and Winston, 1967.

Reiss, Ira L. Response to the Heltsley and Broderick Retest of Reiss' Proposition One. *Journal of Marriage and the Family, 31:*444-445, 1969.

Rosenberg, Morris. *The Logic of Survey Analysis.* New York: Basic Books, Inc., 1968, 238-239.

Sax, Gilbert. *Empirical Foundations of Educational Research.* Englewood Cliffs, New Jersey: Prentice-Hall, Inc., 1968, 202.

Simon, Julian L. *Basic Research Methods in Social Science: The Art of Empirical Investigation.* New York: Random House, Inc., 1969, 40-43.

United States Bureau of the Census. Census of Population: 1960 (Vol. 1), Characteristics of the Population (Part E—Connecticut) Washington, D.C., 1961.

United States Bureau of the Census. U.S. Census of Population and Housing: 1960. Final Report (PHC-1-1961, Census Tracts: Hartford, Connecticut)' Washington, D.C., 1961.

Wake, Frank R. Attitudes of Parents Toward the Pre-Marital Sex Behavior of Their Children and Themselves. *Journal of Sex Research, 5:*170-177, 1969.

Wright, Virginia. An Independent Study Account. Unpublished paper, Department of Child Development and Family Relations, University of Connecticut, Storrs, Connecticut, 1968.

28

runaway adolescents' perceptions
of parents and self

stephen wolk

janet brandon

The purpose of the present paper was a verification of predicted familial interactions and self-perception correlates of the adolescent behavior of running away from home. The correlates selected for assessment are represented in the body of theory and research concerning child and adolescent development which has indicated the importance of parental treatment and the self-concept of a child and adolescent to behavior.

Research considering parental antecedents of emotional, social, and intellectual development of children, converges in suggesting that varying degrees of parental warmth, acceptance, and support are salient dimensions of influence (22). As a specific example Peterson (19) in a study of adolescents, found that adolescent perception of parents as more or less controlling and interested predicted the presence or absence of delinquency, happiness, school achievement, and peer friendship. Other investigators (16; 9; 6; 18) would also support the generalization that the nature of parent-child interaction plays a strong role in the psychological development and social responses of children and adolescents, both for socially desirable development (school achievement) as well as conventional anti-social behavior (delinquency).

In an effort to extend the relationship of parental antecedent behavior to the less conventional adolescent response of running away the following prediction was offered: relative to non-runaway adolescents, runaways will perceive and report their parents as less *supportive,* more *controlling,* and more *punishing.* This prediction assumes that the act of running away stems from a type of parental-adolescent relationship that can be characterized as restrictive and punitive. Medinnus (15) and Peterson (19) have found that adolescents who exhibit problem behavior tend to have parents who are extremely rejecting, punitive, and neglectful.

An additional and related question concerns whether the sex of the child and parent interact to influence differentially the perceptions of runaways and non-runaways. Bronfenbrenner (5) and Devereux (8) have argued that boys require high level of support and authority from fathers for satisfactory development to proceed. On the other hand girls may often suffer, developmentally, from too much paternal control and restrictiveness. This research, as well as that by Peterson (19) seems to suggest that the role of the father is crucial in socialization but of differing importance to males and females. In the context of the present study possible different perceptions of fathers and mothers were considered as a function of the sex of the child and the decision to run away from home.

The dimension of the individual's perception of self as playing a role in adjustment and development has been taken as an axiom by many psychologists. Self-perceptions have been related to studies of achievement, delinquency and vocational choice (7; 6; 17). Very little systematic research has covered possible self-concept conditions of runaway adolescents. Yet the self-concept and aspects of the self, such as ego control, anxiety, and self-esteem, have been identified in the causality or consequence of maladjustment. Thus, Scarpetti (20) found that adequacy of the self-concept clearly differentiated delinquents from non-delinquents. Levinson (13) in one of the few empirical studies of male runaways, found a lack of self-acceptance to be characteristic of this group, who reported themselves as dull, weak and sad. From this research it is tentatively hypothesized that runaway adolescents, relative to non-runaways, would manifest a more negative self-concept.

It is this latter prediction which hopefully reflects the importance of a systematic study of a fairly undefined clinical phenomenon, i.e., running away. While the phenomenon of running away from home apparently is increasing among adolescents, relatively little in the way of objective systematic information exists, suggesting causes, or at the minimum, correlated conditions. It is not uncommon to encounter popular discussions of the phenomenon in which the runaway adolescent is considered to be responding for mature and adaptive reasons, or out of desperation and in response to inadequate ego strength and/or punitive familial interaction. These alternative conceptualizations grow out of the vested interests of specific societal agencies and therapeutic approaches employed to rehabilitate the runaways. It would seem important that objective and unbiased data be brought to bear upon an intriguing and equally confusing behavioral response common to adolescence.

METHOD

Sample

Runaways. Adolescent runaway male and female subjects were solicited for participation from runaway houses in the suburban Maryland Area. Six locations were identified and a total of 47 subjects from these locations (female = 26, male = 21) participated in the study. These runaway houses represented a non-directed, family oriented type assistance extended to runaways who voluntarily had placed themselves in the houses. The age distribution of the group was: 13 years (4), 14 years (10), 15 years (12), 16 years (16), 17 years (5). Only those subjects who had both parents present in the home during their childhood constituted the final data producing sample. The entire sample was Caucasian.

Non-runaways. A control group of 47 non-runaway adolescents (female = 26, male = 21) were paired with the runaway subjects as a function of sex, age (maximum of 6-month age difference) and race. Additionally, the non-runaways were selected from the same neighborhoods from which the runaways had originated, neighborhoods fairly homogeneous with regard to socioeconomic status, and considered to be in the lower two-thirds of the middle class.

Procedure

Contact with runaway subjects was made by the counselors at the runaway houses, who arranged for participation of volunteers. Subjects responded anonymously to the questionnaires.

Non-runaway adolescents participating in after school activities were contacted for voluntary participation. These activities were not related to academic or sports achievement, but rather represented more informal club-type meetings.

Instrumentation

Cornell Parent Behavior Description (CPBD). The CPBD was chosen to depict a subject's perception of parental treatment. The instrument consists of 30 items which are responded to for each parent. The CPBD yields six subscale scores for each parent. Those scores of relevance to the hypotheses of the study were:

Support (parent available for counseling, support, and assistance); **Punishment** (use of physical and non-physical punishment); **Control** (demanding, protecting, and intrusive). The validity of the scale has been established in the research literature (1; 8), including correlations with direct observation of parent-child interaction. Additionally, cross cultural studies of parental behaviors have made ample use of the CPBD (10). Seigelman (21) and MacDonald (14) report reliability coefficients for the total scale that range from .70 to .81 and for individual subscales that range from .48 to .82. Additionally, reliability estimates were calculated for both groups in the present study (alpha coefficient) for each subscale by parent. These coefficients ranged from a high of .90 (Father-Support) to a low of .56 (Mother-Control).

Adjective Check List (ACL). The ACL afforded an assessment of adolescents' perceptions of self. The instrument consists of 300 adjectives commonly used to describe personal attributes. Thirteen of the total 24 indices of self-concept were selected for study and are related to the hypotheses. These are (attributes in parentheses): *total number of adjectives checked* (relative presence of repressive tendencies); *defensiveness* (tendency to be anxious, apprehensive, and critical of self); *number of favorable adjectives checked* (anxiety, self-doubt); *self-confidence; personal adjustment; achievement* (dubious about the rewards coming from effort); *affiliation; exhibition* (lack of self-confidence); *number of unfavorable adjectives checked* (lack of control over hostile aspects of self); *lability* (impelled toward an endless flight from perplexities); *abasement* (self-punishing to ward off external criticism); *counseling readiness* (pessimism concerning ability to resolve problems). The subject was instructed to check the items which best describe him as he really is. The score for each index is determined by subtracting the number of contra-indicative (negative) from indicative (positive) items. Raw scores are converted to standard scores ($\overline{X} = 50.0$; SD = 10.0). Previous use of the ACL both for basic research and counseling has been extensive (3). Gough and Heilburn (12) report reliability coefficients of from .61 to .75 between judges using the ACL to describe a group of subjects; the same authors report coefficients of correlation between each index and the total number of adjectives checked that argue for the discriminant validity of each index.

Statistical Treatment of Data

A three-way analysis of variance (Runaway/Non-runaway X Sex of Subject X Sex of Parent) with repeated measurements on the last factor assessed the effects upon adolescent perception of parents. The dependent variables were represented by total raw scores for Support, Punishment, and Control of the CPBD.

A one-way multivariate analysis of variance (Runaway/Non-runaway) was employed to assess overall differences between the two groups in regard to their self-perceptions. The dependent variables were represented by standard scores for the selected 13 indices of the ACL. As a follow-up procedure univariate F-tests were conducted on each of the thirteen scores, for which the alpha level was set at $p < .004$. This allowed rejection of the null hypothesis of no self-concept differences between groups to be made at $p < .05$, since this follow-up procedure involved 13 individual comparisons.

RESULTS

It was predicted that runaway adolescents compared to non-runaways, would report their parents to be more punishing and controlling, and less supporting. For the variables of support ($F (1,90) = 26.69$, $p < .01$) and punishment ($F (1,90) = 19.00$, $p < .01$) such main effect differences were obtained and are reflected in the pattern of mean scores reported in Table 1. No difference existed between groups for the variable of control. The only interaction effect observed involved the sex of the child and the decision to run away. Runaway girls, relative to runaway boys, reported more control on the part of both parents; the difference between non-runaway boys and girls was slight and non-significant (see Table 1). Additionally runaway boys perceived less control of both parents than any of the other groups of subjects. Two unpredicted main effects were also observed. For the variable of support, all subjects reported less support from father than mother ($F (1,90) = 6.65$, $p < .05$); in regard to punishment, girls reported more punishment by both parents than boys ($F(1,90) = 9.44$, $p < .01$).

TABLE 1. MEAN SCORES FOR THE VARIABLES OF SUPPORT, PUNISHMENT, AND CONTROL BY CLASSIFICATION OF SUBJECT AND PARENT.

	RUNAWAY		NON-RUNAWAY	
	Girls	Boys	Girls	Boys
Support				
Mother	22.31	21.95	28.08	29.38
Father	19.69	17.71	26.50	28.33
X̄t		20.48	27.99	
Punishment				
Mother	23.81	17.71	18.23	18.31
Father	24.15	21.29	16.81	15.48
X̄t		21.98	17.32	
Control				
Mother	28.42	23.38	27.54	27.05
Father	27.92	22.90	26.62	26.52
X̄t		25.93	26.95	

TABLE 2. SUMMARY OF THE ANALYSES OF VARIANCE OF THE DEPENDENT VARIABLES OF SELF-PERCEPTION AND MEAN SCORES BY GROUP.

	RUNAWAY	NON-RUNAWAY	F
Variable			
Total Checked[b]	50.34	47.36	1.09
Defensiveness[b]	41.13	47.34	8.94[a]
Favorable Checked[b]	40.81	48.87	13.54[a]
Unfavorable Checked[c]	56.72	52.70	1.41
Self-Confidence[b]	45.85	49.19	4.32
Self-Control[b]	39.89	42.85	2.56
Lability[c]	50.81	51.34	.08
Personal Adjustment[b]	39.53	46.70	11.48[a]
Achievement[b]	43.92	48.34	5.22
Affiliation[b]	42.49	48.71	9.07[a]
Exhibition[b]	54.60	56.75	1.86
Abasement[c]	49.64	48.26	.79
Counseling Readiness[c]	51.21	45.53	10.11[a]

[a] Represents a difference between means at $p < .05$ for 13 tests.
[b] Low score indicates negative self-concept.
[c] High score indicates negative self-concept.

A multivariate analysis of variance (least likelihood ratio) was conducted on the 13 measures of self-perception. This test results in an F value of 2.58 ($p < .005$), indicating that runaways held a distinctly different self-perception from non-runaways. In order to define this difference more fully, univariate F tests examined the variations between groups for each index of self-concept singly. The results of these tests, in addition to mean scores for each group are presented in Table 2.

Five of the 13 indices of self-concept significantly (p < .05) distinguished runaways from non-runaways: defensiveness, total favorable adjectives checked, personal adjustment, affiliation, and counseling readiness. Therefore, runaway adolescents, compared to non-runaways, manifest a self-concept that is more defensive, self-doubting and less trusting. It is a self-concept that also reflects a difficulty in maintaining interpersonal relationships and a preoccupation with and a pessimism for resolving personal problems.

DISCUSSION

It appears that the runaway adolescents in the present sample report less favorable perceptions of parents on two of the three predicted variables: support and punishment. This finding is consistent with other research which has found that runaways experience frequent punishment and describe their parents as rejecting (2). Such perceived negative parental treatment might well influence the decision to run away as a reaction to family stress. Blood and D'Angelo (2) report that runaways identified more items as conflicts with parents and suggested that deficiencies in positive reinforcement accounted for this. The runaways did not differ from the non-runaways in regard to perceived parental control. Had the runaways perceived more parental control than non-runaways, it might have been reasonable to surmise that the runaway act is a reaction to over control by the parent, as some popular accounts do argue. Rather, some runaways have frequently stated that running away represents an effort to make the parents notice them, as several counselors have noted to the authors. Perhaps the finding of more reported punishment and less support, in conjunction with the absence of control differences, suggests the parent of the runaway, relative to the non-runaway, may be responding more punitively and arbitrarily.

For the variable of control, runaway girls did perceive significantly more parental control than any other group. Runaway boys, on the other hand, perceived less parental control than any other group. Thus, the predicted difference between runaways and non-runaways in regard to parental control was to some extent further contingent upon the sex of the child. It may be that for girls the presence of added punishment, reported by all runaways, in conjunction with excessive parental control, differentially directed toward females, makes the decision to run away a reaction to a punitive, restrictive family atmosphere.

A somewhat different explanation may be offered to explain why runaway boys report the lowest levels of parental control. Bronfenbrenner (4) found that relatively high amounts of discipline and authority were necessary to cultivate traits of responsibility and leadership in boys. To the extent that runaway behavior can be considered immature it may not be surprising that the runaway boys in the present study reported less control than the non-runaway boys. For boys, when a necessary degree of control and parental restriction is absent, behavior may proceed to develop immaturely and nonadaptively, resulting in a high incidence of running away. For girls, to whom control may be generally more often directed by parents, an excess of such parental action may lead to conflict and a sense of hopelessness.

The literature on adolescent development frequently has focused on the adolescent's struggle to achieve psychological autonomy from parental values and controls. Douvan and Adelson (11) have employed this concept in extensive research with adolescents. Furthermore, these authors and others have distinguished two dimensions to adolescent autonomy: associational autonomy (friendship, activities) and normative autonomy (ethics, attitudes). It has been established in this research that adolescents strive for and achieve more autonomy in the associational than the normative area, suggesting that both parents and peer groups exert influence in different areas of adolescent development. In considering the findings of the present study it could be argued that the report of more punishment and less support by runaways on the part of their parents suggests some deviation and conflict from the norm of adolescent-familial interaction. Parental punishment, for the runaway, may be impinging upon the adolescent's quest and success for associational autonomy; parents may be negatively reinforcing behavior related to the development of this type of autonomy. Similarly, the report of less parental support by adolescent runaways could imply that these parents do not supply the kind of guidance in the normative area that adolescents apparently do seek. The runaway act may then be interpreted as an extreme form of response to what is perceived by the adolescent as a lack of validation of the struggle for autonomy, when compared to the more typical adolescent experience. However, the findings concerning parental control might also suggest a further dimension to running away, concerning a motivation for the act, for males and females. To the adolescent girl, running away represents a desperate reaction to familial restrictiveness; to the adolescent boy, running away may be indicative of relative normlessness represented in the failure of parents to exert enough control over the more aggressive actions of males.

One of the strongest findings of the present study concerns the overall and specific differences in perceptions of self between runaways and non-runaways. It was the case that runaway adolescents held much less favorable perceptions.

The lower scores of the runaways on the defensiveness scale can be interpreted that they are anxious, critical of themselves and others and given to complaints about their circumstances. Such an individual not only has more problems than his peers, but tends to dwell on them and put them at the center of his attention. For the index of number of favorable adjectives checked, the lower scores of the runaways characterize them as experiencing anxiety, self-doubts, and perplexities, while often being headstrong, pleasure seeking, and original in thought and behavior. Personal adjustment defines a positive attitude toward life more than an absence of problems or worries. The relatively lower score of the runaway adolescent suggests he or she sees himself or herself at odds with other people and as dissatisfied. Others see the runaway as defensive, anxious, inhibited, worrying, and withdrawn. The difference between runaways and non-runaways on the scale of affiliation suggests that the former are less trusting of others and more restless and unsuccessful in interpersonal situations. The final scale which differentiated runaways from non-runaways was counseling readiness. Runaways scored significantly higher than non-runaways on this scale. The person who is "ready" for counseling must have a certain degree of motivation for change and improvement if counseling is to be effective. This scale functions as an aid in identifying counseling clients who are ready for help and who seem likely to profit from it. The runaway who goes to a runaway house may be more likely to profit from counseling techniques. The segment of runaway adolescents who seek out some type of counseling setting or interim residence, as in the present study, could be manifesting such a readiness for counseling.

In summary, the five indices of self-concept which significantly differentiated runaways from non-runaways are consistent with an interpretation of runaway behavior as stemming from negative self-development. Popular accounts describing or defining running away as behavior reflective of a well-adjusted adolescent fleeing intolerable, over-demanding social and familial environments, are not fully congruent with the present data. Although it was found that the present sample of adolescents reported less support and more punishment by parents, it was also found that runaway boys may be responding to the absence of sufficient control, while runaway girls are repelled by too much control.

Several areas of practical significance appear appropriate to explore toward the goal of improved and effective counseling for runaways. At least two dimensions of parent behavior in the lives of runaways who come to runaway houses for assistance appear substantiated. It would be useful for counselors to know on what dimensions to focus their attention when considering treatment for runaways. The possible role of a counselor as a parent surrogate would be enhanced should he/she be aware that it is quite likely the runaway is seeking support and encouragement. Additionally, recognition of the varying perceptions of parental control by male and female runaways would seem of value to the direction and techniques of counseling. The findings of the study also suggest that counseling for runaways should consider employing techniques which are effective in developing more positive perceptions of self. It might be worthwhile to consider that the finding concerning counseling readiness indicated that some runaways are motivated in such a way that they will benefit from the counseling experiences they encounter.

Of considerable importance to the results and interpretations of the present study, are apparent methodological limitations. The use of volunteers for both groups studied, and, in particular, the runaways, may restrict inferences and generalizations that can be drawn. It is conceivable that runaways who respond to personal inventories and questioning possess a personality and self-concept distinctly different from those who opt not to volunteer. While one can only speculate on such a notion, it would be methodologically positive if future research could survey a wider spectrum of runaways in halfway or runaway houses. It may also be accurate to acknowledge that a study of only those runaways who seek interim settings cannot generalize its findings to all groups of runaways. Perhaps these runaways represent a type more favorably disposed to a reestablishment of familial ties (as evidenced by a greater need or readiness for counseling). If this is so then the differences between runaways and non-runaways observed in the present study represent a conservative estimate of the self-concept and parental antecedent correlates of adolescents who choose to leave home. Finally the obvious limits of retrospective reports of family interactions need to be acknowledged. Perhaps it could be argued that the differing perceptions of parents, by runaways and non-runaways, represents the attempt of runaway adolescents to rationalize their behavior. Thus, what may be taken as antecedent conditions to the act of running away may, in fact, be a consequence of the need to justify an extreme act, i.e., establish some fault with parents. No correlational study, in the present case, can establish a cause-effect relationship. However, excluding a longitudinal approach that could develop data files early in childhood to which subsequent adolescent reactions, including acts of running away might be related, the adolescent phenomena of running away seems destined to be studied retrospectively. However, from a basic research point of view the understanding of the adolescent act of running away represents a small but important extension to a full definition of adolescent development. Adolescent running away is also a phenomenon that deserves continued delineation for counselors and mental health specialists who desire firm conceptual grounds upon which to develop a rehabilitative program.

REFERENCES

1. Barker, R. G., and L. S. Barker. "Social Actions in the Behavior Streams of American and English Children," in *The Stream of Behavior* edited by R. G. Barker. New York: Appleton-Century-Crofts, 1963.

2. Blood, L., and R. D'Angelo. "A Progress Research Report on Value Issues in Conflict between Runaways and Their Parents," *Journal of Marriage and the Family* (August), 1974, 486-491.

3. Buros, O. K. (Ed.). *The Sixth Mental Measurements Yearbook.* Highland Park, N.J.: Gryphon Press, 1965.

4. Bronfenbrenner, Urie. "Some Familial Antecedents of Responsibility and Leadership in Adolescents," in L. Petrullo and B. M. Bass (Eds.), *Leadership and Interpersonal Behavior.* New York: Holt, Rinehart, and Winston, 1961a.

5. Bronfenbrenner, Urie. "Toward a Theoretical Model for Analysis of Parent-Child Relationships in a Social Context," in J. Glidewell (Ed.), *Parental Attitudes and Child Behavior.* Springfield: Charles C. Thomas, 1961b.

6. Cervantes, L. *The Drop Out: Causes and Cures.* Ann Arbor: University of Michigan Press, 1965.

7. Coopersmith, S. "A Method for Determining Types of Self-esteem," *Journal of Educational Psychology,* 1959, (59) 87-94.

8. Devereux, E. C., and Urie Bronfenbrenner. "Child-rearing in England and the United States," *Journal of Marriage and the Family,* 1969, (31) 257-270.

9. Elder, Glen H. "Parental Power Legitimation and its Effect on the Adolescent," *Sociometry,* 1963, (26), 50-65.

10. Devereux, E. C., Urie Bronfenbrenner, and G. S. Suci. "Patterns of Parent Behavior in the United States of America and the Federal Republic of West Germany," *International Social Science Journal,* 1962, (14), 488-506.

11. Douvan, Elizabeth, and J. Adelson. *The Adolescent Experience.* New York: John Wiley, 1966.

12. Gough, H. G., and A. B. Heilbrun. *The Adjective Check List Manual.* Palo Alto: Consulting Psychologist's Press, 1965.

13. Levinson, B. M. "Self-concept and Ideal Self-concept of Runaway Youths: Counseling Implications," *Psychological Reports,* 1970, 871-874.

14. MacDonald, A. P. "Internal-external Locus of Control and Parental Antecedents," *Journal of Consulting and Clinical Psychology,* 1971, (39), 141-147.

15. Medinnus, Gene R. "Delinquents' Perceptions of their Parents," *Journal of Consulting Psychology*, 1965, (29), 592-593.
16. Morrow, W. R., and R. C. Wilson. "Family Relationships of Bright, High Achieving and Underachieving High School Boys," *Child Development*, 1961, (32), 501-510.
17. Offer, Daniel. *The Psychological World of the Teenager.* New York: Basic Books, 1969.
18. Peck, R., and R. Havighurst. *The Psychology of Character Development.* New York: John Wiley, 1960.
19. Peterson, Evan T. "The Adolescent Male and Parental Relations." Paper read at the National Council on Family Relations annual meeting, New Orleans, (October), 1968.
20. Scarpetti, Frank R. "Delinquency and Non-delinquency, Perception of Self, Values, and Opportunity," *Mental Hygiene*, 1965, (49), 399-404.
21. Seigelman, M. "Evaluation of Bronfenbrenner's Questionnaire for Children Concerning Parental Behavior," *Child Development*, 1965, (36), 163-174.
22. Walters, J., and N. Stinnett. "Parent-Child Relationships: A Decade Review of Research," *Journal of Marriage and the Family*, 1971, (2), 70-111.

part 3

sibling relationships

INTRODUCTION

Part 3 of this book examines an often neglected aspect of the study of family relationships—sibling relationships. A large body of literature has accumulated in connection with studies of birth order, ordinal position, sibling position, and position in the family constellation, and with studies which correlate these variables with almost every other variable imaginable. However, there have been very few studies that actually examine the interaction of siblings within the family. Because of this lack, Part 3 features readings on ordinal position and sibling interaction in hopes that an exploration of these topics will contribute to a broader understanding of sibling relationships.

The first research to focus on siblings appeared during the 1930s (Chapin, 1932; Krout, 1939; Sletto, 1934); however, Alfred Adler had identified the importance of position in the family constellation in 1927 [cited in *(29)*]. Sears (1950) wrote on ordinal position as a psychological variable, and even today it is the psychologists more than the sociologists who appear to study more ordinal position seriously.

During the 1950s, popular books were written in order to give parents and teachers guidance in helping children with their sibling relationships (for example, Neisser, 1951). Bossard and Boll (1954, 1955, 1956*a*, 1956*b*; Bossard, 1959) studied sibling relationships from a sociological perspective whereas Koch (1954, 1955*a*, 1955*b*, 1956*a-e*, 1957) studied them from a psychological one.

Despite the efforts of Bossard and Boll, Koch, and numerous other researchers, Irish (1964) concluded that sibling interaction was an aspect that had been neglected in family-life research. In his article, which affords a review of salient research pertaining to sibling relationships, Irish identified the following as factors impeding sibling research. (1) The overemphasis of Freudian thought, which stresses the impact of parents on childhood socialization, has led to an enormous amount of research on the parent-child relationship and very little on sibling relationships. (2) Sociologists are usually pressured to explore topics related to mate selection and early marital adjustment because these are topics of tremendous interest to their college students, who are themselves concerned with early adult relationships. (3) Sibling relationships do not take place in all families. Whereas the birth of the first child is often studied vigorously to see what impact it has on the marital relationship, the arrival of each additional child is rarely studied to determine the degree to which established patterns are further modified. (4) Unfortunately, those who are trained to work with children, i.e., teachers, day-care directors, etc., are rarely trained as researchers. Those who have the ready access to children that is needed for sibling study are not very likely to be interested in or capable of carrying out such research. (5) The residential patterns which exist in our society are not conducive to the study of adult sibling relationships. Adult siblings live in their own households, often separated by hundreds or thousands of miles from the siblings with whom they once lived as children. (6) There are real practical problems with research methodology. First, there are all the problems of terminology *(29)* and, second, there are all the variables which must be carefully controlled for in designing the study *(30)*.

Factors such as the age of siblings, the age-spacing of siblings, the sex of siblings, the birth order of siblings, and the size of family (i.e., the total number of siblings) make for a whole host of complex factors which must be considered from the very beginning of the research design. How else can all of these factors be controlled for in the sample-selection process? Furthermore, if one wants to study actual sibling interactions, how can one observe sibling relationships without having one's presence alter the nature of the interactions?

Keeping the shortcomings of early sibling research in mind, one can readily appreciate the specific information on sibling relationships offered by the four readings that are included in this section. The first article *(29)* by Manaster, originally appeared as an introduction to a special issue of the *Journal of Individual Psychology* (May, 1977) which contained birth-order research reports. In it, Manaster defines many of the terms necessary to an understanding of birth order and sibling research.

The second article *(30)*, by Falbo, is a thorough review of the literature pertaining to the only child. This reading is significant because the declining birthrate in our society means that there may well be an increase in the proportion of families with only one child and these children will not experience sibling relationships. Also, Falbo reviews much of the research on sibling relationships through comparisons made between only children and children who have siblings. The third reading *(31)*, by Sutton-Smith and Rosenberg, is an example of a carefully designed study in the field of sibling research.

The topics which have been studied by sibling researchers are numerous and varied. Sibling studies run the gamut from studies of sibling position and intellectual or cognitive abilities (Cicirelli, 1973, 1974, 1976; Marjoribanks, 1976; Marjoribanks and Walberg, 1975a, 1975b; Zajonc, 1976; Zajonc and Markus, 1975), to associations with personality in general (Croake and Hayden, 1975; Croake and Olson, 1977; Toman, 1969), to how children from the same family manage their money (Phelan and Schvaneveldt, 1969). See Forer (1977) for a listing of all birth-order studies already published during the 1970s. Sutton-Smith and Rosenberg (1970) are among the best-known sibling researchers, probably because of their book *The Sibling,* which reviews much of the information that has been gathered on siblings.

The final reading in this section *(32)*, an article by Bank and Kahn which is based on their clinical experiences, reviews much of the outstanding research on sibling relationships and also examines some of the special roles played by interacting siblings *(32)*.

One recent textbook (Smart and Smart, 1976) has identified the following sibling roles: 1) playmates and companions, 2) teacher-learner, 3) protector-dependent, and 4) adversaries. Additional sibling roles might include model-imitator and leader-follower, however, there is no one all-inclusive list of sibling roles available at present.

In a recent research report, Pfouts (1976) reports the results of a study of fifty two-boy families which were white, intact, urban, and middle class. She identified the following types of sibling relationships: 1) the happily ambivalent relationship, 2) the problematic relationship, 3) the stressful relationship, and 4) the tragic relationship. Her findings "generally supported the hypothesis that when children differ significantly in highly valued characteristics, the less well-endowed will show more hostility toward siblings than will the more favorably endowed" (Pfouts, 1976:202).

Throughout the research literature greater emphasis seems to be placed on the adversary role through studies of sibling rivalry (Croake and Hayden, 1975; Schachter, Shore, Feldman-Rotman, Marquis, and Campbell, 1976) than on the companionate or affectionate roles (Bowerman and Dobash, 1974). More research is needed on all of the roles played by siblings.

Furthermore, Bigner (1971) found evidence that sibling position influences self-description. Since self-concept has been identified as a variable that plays an important role in all interpersonal relationships, more attention should be paid to the sibling relationship. Also, Toman (1969) hypothesized that experiences gained in sibling role-relationships may have an influence on marital relationships, since mates selected from certain sibling positions made better matches with mates of certain other sibling positions. For example, the older-sister-of-brother would be a suitable match for a younger-brother-of-sister. Although some research studies have been carried out in order to test Toman's theory, more research of this type is needed in order to determine whether the theory should be refuted or not (Birtchnell and Mayhew, 1977). Also, more research is needed on adult sibling relationships since the findings of studies on sibling solidarity differ considerably (Cumming and Schneider, 1961; Rosenberg and Anspach, 1973).

REFERENCES

Bigner, J. J. Sibling position and definition of self. *The Journal of Social Psychology 84* (1971):307-8.

Birtchnell, J., and Mayhew, J. Toman's theory: Tested for mate selection and friendship formation. *Journal of Individual Psychology 33* (1977):18-36.

Bossard, J. H. Large and small families: A study in contrasts. *American Society of Chartered Life Underwriters Journal 13* (1959):222-40.

Bossard, J. H. S., and Boll, E. S. Security in the large family. *Mental Hygiene 38* (1954):529-44.

Bossard, J. H., and Boll, E. S. Personality roles in the large family. *Child Development 26* (1955):71-78.

Bossard, J. H., and Boll, E. S. Adjustment of siblings in large families. *American Journal of Psychiatry 112* (1956*a*):889-92.

Bossard, J. H. S., and Boll, E. S. *The large family system: An original study in the sociology of family behavior.* Philadelphia: University of Pennsylvania Press, 1956*b*.

Bowerman, C. E., and Dobash, R. M. Structural variations in inter-sibling affect. *Journal of Marriage and the Family 36* (1974):48-54.

Chapin, F. S. The experimental approach: The advantages of experimental sociology in the study of family group patterns. *Social Forces, 11* (1932):200-07.

Cicirelli, V. G. Effects of sibling structure and interaction on children's categorization style. *Developmental Psychology 9,* (1973):132-39.

Cicirelli, V. G. Relationship of sibling structure and interaction to younger sib's conceptual style. *The Journal of Genetic Psychology 125* (1974):37-50.

Cicirelli, V. G. Sibling structure and intellectual ability. *Developmental Psychology 12* (1976):369-70.

Croake, J. W., and Hayden, D. J. Trait oppositeness in siblings: Test of an Adlerian tenet. *Journal of Individual Psychology 31* (1975):175-78.

Croake, J. W., and Olson, T. D. Family constellation and personality. *Journal of Individual Psychology 33* (1977):9-17.

Cumming, E., and Schneider, D. Sibling solidarity: A property of American kinship. *American Anthropologist 63* (1961):498-507.

Forer, L. K. Bibliography of birth order literature in the 70's. *Journal of Individual Psychology 33* (1977):124-41.

Irish, D. P. Sibling interaction: A neglected aspect in family life research. *Social Forces 42* (1964):279-88.

Koch, H. The relation of "primary mental abilities" in five- and six-year-olds to sex of child and characteristics of his sibling. *Child Development 25* (1954):209-23.

Koch, H. The relation of certain family constellation characteristics and the attitudes of children toward adults. *Child Development 26* (1955*a*):13-40.

Koch, H. Some personality correlates of sex, sibling position, and sex of sibling among five- and six-year-old children. *Genetic Psychology Monographs 52* (1955*b*):3-50.

Koch, H. Attitudes of young children toward their peers as related to certain characteristics of their siblings. *Psychological Monograph, 70,* whole no. 426 (1956*a*).

Koch, H. Children's work attitudes and sibling characteristics. *Child Development 27* (1956*b*):289-310.

Koch, H. Sibling influence on children's speech. *Journal of Speech Disorders 21* (1956*c*):322-28.

Koch, H. Sissiness and tomboyishness in relation to sibling characteristics. *Journal of Genetic Psychology 88* (1956*d*):231-44.

Koch, H. Some emotional attitudes of the young child in relation to characteristics of his sibling. *Child Development 27* (1956*e*):393-427.

Koch, H. The relation in young children between characteristics of their playmates and certain attitudes of their siblings. *Child Development 28* (1957):175-202.

Krout, M. H. Typical behavior patterns in twenty-six ordinal positions. *Journal of Genetic Psychology 55* (1939):3-29.

Marjoribanks, K. Sibsize, family environment, cognitive performance, and affective characteristics. *The Journal of Psychology 94* (1976):195-204.

Marjoribanks, K., and Walberg, H. J. Birth order, family size, social class, and intelligence. *Social Biology 22* (1975*a*):261-68.

Marjoribanks, K., and Walberg, H. J. Family environment, sibling constellation and social class correlates. *Journal of Biosocial Science 7* (1975*b*):15-25.

Neisser, E. G. *Brothers and sisters.* New York: Harper and Brothers, 1951.

Pfouts, J. H. The sibling relationship: A forgotten dimension. *Social Work 21* (1976):200-204.

Phelan, G. K., and Schvaneveldt, J. D. Spending and saving patterns of adolescent siblings. *Journal of Home Economics 61* (1969):104-9.

Rosenberg, G. S., and Anspach, D. F. Sibling solidarity in the working class. *Journal of Marriage and the Family 35* (1973):109-13.

Schachter, F. F., Shore, E., Feldman-Rotman, S., Marquis, R. E., and Campbell, S. Sibling deidentification. *Developmental Psychology 12* (1976):418-427.

Sears, R. R. Ordinal position in the family as a psychological variable. *American Sociological Review 15* (1950):397-401.

Sletto, R. F. Sibling position and juvenile delinquency. *American Journal of Sociology 39* (1934):657-69.

Smart, M. S., and Smart, L. S. *Families: Developing relationships.* New York: Macmillan, 1976.

Sutton-Smith, B., and Rosenberg, B. G. *The sibling.* New York: Holt, Rinehart, and Winston, 1970.

Toman, W. *The family constellation: Its effects on personality and social behavior.* New York: Springer, 1969.

Zajonc, R. B. Family configuration and intelligence. *Science 192* (1976):227-36.

Zajonc, R. B., and Markus, G. B. Birth order and intellectual development. *Psychological Review 82,* no. 1 (1975):74-88.

29

birth order: an overview

guy j. manaster

Birth order, an integral concept in Adlerian theory, has been used extensively by Adlerians in clinical and assessment settings. It would be safe to say that Adlerians have made greater use of birth order information than have any other school or group in psychology. And yet considerable research and theorizing on birth order exists in the greater field of psychology aside from Adlerian psychology. This research has proven to be far from conclusive, but strong, active proponents persist in the face of equally strong and persistent criticism. . . .

This article will introduce Adler's general position on birth order, and speak to criticisms of birth order research. Lastly, the article will discuss the most difficult and confusing problem of terminology, nomenclature in this field . . . and recommend definitions in an attempt to bring order, if not standardization, to the use of terms in the field.

ALFRED ADLER'S VIEW OF BIRTH ORDER

Adler first presented his views on birth order in 1918 (Ansbacher & Ansbacher, 1956, p. 382). Their importance as one facet of the family constellation is illustrated by Dreikurs' (1950) pronouncement of "the only fundamental law governing the development of the child's character: he trains those qualities by which he hopes to achieve significance or even a degree of power and superiority in the family constellation" (p. 41). Adler drew "attention to the fact that before we can judge a human being we must know the situation in which he grew up. An important moment is the position which a child occupied in his family constellation" (1927, p. 149).

A multitude of factors impinge on the child in the family. The personalities of both parents, their relationship, their cooperation as partners and as parents, the health of all family members, socioeconomic status, religiosity, etc., all influence the individual child, as does his or her birth order position. Adler insisted "that the situation is never the same for two children in a family; and that each child will show in his style of life the results of his attempts to adapt himself to his own peculiar circumstances" (1932, p. 108).

The assumption is that particular birth order positions have in common presses or demands which influence the child's view of his or her position in the family and life, and increase the likelihood of the child developing attitudes and styles of behavior in correspondence with his or her perceived position. For example,

> *Every oldest child has experienced for some time the situation of an only child and has been compelled suddenly to adapt himself to a new situation at the birth of the next*

Reprinted, by permission, from *Journal of Individual Psychology*, 1977, *33*, 3-8, slightly abridged. Copyright © 1976 by The American Society of Adlerian Psychology, Inc.

oldest . . . Other children may lose position in the same way; but they will probably not feel it so strongly . . . The second child is in a quite different position, . . . Throughout his childhood he has a pacemaker. There is always a child ahead of him in age and development and he is stimulated to exert himself and catch up . . .

All other children have followers; all other children can be dethroned; but the youngest can never be dethroned . . . He is always the baby of the family and probably he is the most pampered . . . And yet, . . . the second largest proportion of problem children (after oldests) comes from among the youngest . . .

The only child has a problem of his own. He has a rival, but his rival is not a brother or sister. His feelings of competition go against his father. An only child is pampered by his mother. (Adler, 1932, pp. 108-113).

We assume then that children might, or might probably, rise to the common challenges of their own birth order positions. Therefore similarities may be found among persons occupying each birth order position and differences may be found between holders of the various birth order positions. . . .

However, numerous variants must be accounted for in birth order research. Birth order position is not identical to ordinal position. "The situation counts, not the mere order of birth. In a large family a later child is sometimes in the situation of an oldest" (Adler, 1932, p. 111). "If there is a big space of years between the birth of children, each child will have some of the features of an only child" (Adler, 1932, p. 114). "An only boy brought up in a family of girls has a hard time before him . . . In a rather similar way, an only girl among boys is apt to develop very feminine or very masculine qualities" (Adler, 1932, pp. 114-115). Adler thus spoke to the very difficult problems of use of birth order in assessment, therapy and research posed by variations in family size, birth spacing, and sex of siblings. Yet Adlerians reaffirm that "the siginficance of a child's place in the family cannot be denied, but in each case it must be examined like a piece in a puzzle, i.e., only in connection with all the other factors that determine character formation" (Sperber, 1974, p. 103).

CRITICISMS OF BIRTH ORDER RESEARCH

The most damning, and referenced, recent criticism of birth order research surveyed

the relationships between birth order and various normal and abnormal psychological characteristics in three ways: (a) looking at the prevalence of different birth ranks in various relevant populations, (b) comparing the characteristics of individuals of known birth rank, and (c) examining parents' reports of their treatment of children of different birth ranks (Schooler, 1972, p. 171),

concluding that "the general lack of consistent findings revealed by this review leaves real doubt as to whether the chance of positive results is worth the heavy investment needed to carry out any more definitive studies" (1972, p. 174). The "heavy investment needed" refers to aspects of analyses frequently overlooked in the existing literature which must be accounted for in future studies.

Overlooked in the "prevalency" studies have been changes over time in birth rate and family size. Hare and Price (1969) showed that these changes alter population proportions of first borns (increased when more new families are starting) and/or last borns (increased when family size is decreasing—more families having their last child). As family size has been related to socioeconomic status, and socioeconomic status has been related to achievement, studies of birth rank prevalence must control these factors. Schooler further suggests that studies of characteristics of individuals of known birth ranks might be strengthened considerably if family density and sex of siblings were taken into account. Interestingly, then, with the exception of the effects of family demographic changes on birth rank frequency in populations, Adler long ago indicated the refinements necessary to working with birth order that Schooler echoed.

In the face of Schooler's skepticism, birth order research continues with significant results in specified areas (Breland, 1973) and with increased respectability when the various critical factors noted above are controlled (examples: Zajonc, 1976; Zajonc & Markus, 1975).

BIRTH ORDER TEMINOLOGY

Birth order, order of birth and ordinal position are oftimes used synonymously and interchangeably, in other instances they have different and exact meanings which may be contradictory.

Family constellation, family configuration and sibship also suffer in usage with considerable overlap at times and distinct definitions at other times. . . .

The following definitions, or descriptions, of the key terms in the birth order field are recommended:

Ordinal position (order of birth)—"Ordinal, *adj.*, being of a specified order or rank (as sixth) in a numberable series." "Ordinal number, *n.*, a number designating the place (as first, second, third) occupied by any item in an ordered sequence." These definitions from Webster's (1968) clearly indicate the basis in mathematics of the term ordinal. Ordinal position and order of birth should be used when indicating the numerical place of an individual's birth in the order of births in his or her family, as in first of two, or third of five.

Birth order most frequently implies the following definition of order: "a category, type, class or kind of thing of distinctive character or rank." Birth order terms (only, oldest, second, middle and youngest) refer to categories or types of persons whose distinctive character may be known, described and, theoretically, empirically demonstrated. These birth order terms may also refer to rank in the numerical order sense, hence the confusion. However they need not do so, as in the instance where two children in a family are spaced closely together, say two years apart, followed eight years later by two more siblings spaced closely. This sibship could be variously described as (1) oldest, second, middle and youngest; (2) oldest, two middles and youngest; or, and I think this a preferable description of psychological birth order, (3) oldest, youngest, oldest, youngest. Obviously, using birth order as herein defined demands operational definitions by each researcher.

Sibship—"the quality or state of being a sib or a member of a sib," "a group of sibs." Investigations of all children in the family, which go beyond ordinal position or birth order as defined above, as when sex of siblings is also studied, may be said to be sibship research.

Family configuration should, perhaps, refer to analyses of the structural and identifiable social characteristics of the family, such as any or all of the above, intactness, parents' age, socioeconomic status, race, etc. This use is based on the definition of configuration as "relative disposition or arrangement of parts; interrelationships of constituent elements."

Family constellation—the relevant definitions of constellation include "a determining, differentiating, or individualizing pattern or grouping," "a group of consciously related, especially emotionally significant ideas," "an assemblage or configuration of stimulus conditions or factors affecting behavior and personality development." Family constellation is the broadest, most inclusive term in this listing. It may denote aspects of all of the above-defined terms and may also refer to individualizing, emotionally significant stimulus factors, as it is used by Adlerians. When Adlerians use the term family constellation in its fullest sense they include such factors as the personality of each parent; their cooperation; other significant relatives, like a grandmother living with the family; and the theme, or code, or motto of the family—the emotionally significant ideas individual to the family which may influence development within the family.

CONCLUSION

The problems of birth order research are numerous. The technical-statistical problems are manageable, and the definitional problems may be reduced by their discussion in this article. Adler noted or implied concerns regarding family size, density and sex of siblings in reference to birth order, and birth order as a factor in family constellation. It is apparent that the time has come to integrate his concerns into contemporary birth order research. Birth order and family constellation information may be extremely useful. Empirical justification for their use is still needed. . . .

REFERENCES

Adler, A. *Understanding human nature.* New York: Greenberg Publisher, 1927.
Adler, A. *What life should mean to you.* London: Unwin Books, 1932.
Ansbacher, H. L., & Ansbacher, R. R. *The individual psychology of Alfred Adler.* New York: Harper Torchbooks, 1956.
Breland, H. M. Birth order effects: A reply to Schooler. *Psychological Bulletin,* 1973, *80*(3), 210-212.
Dreikurs, R. R. *Fundamentals of Adlerian psychology.* Chicago: Alfred Adler Institute, 1950.
Price, J. S., & Hare, E. H. Birth order studies: Some sources of bias. *British Journal of Psychiatry,* 1969, *115,* 633-646.
Schooler, C. Birth order effects: Not here, not now! *Psychological Bulletin,* 1972, *78*(3), 161-175.
Sperber, M. *Masks of loneliness: Alfred Adler in perspective.* New York: MacMillan, 1974.
Webster's Third New International Dictionary of the English Language Unabridged. Springfield, Mass.: G. & C. Merriam, 1968.
Zajonc, R. B. Family configuration and intelligence. *Science,* 1976, *192,* 227-236.
Zajonc, R. B., & Markus, G. B. Birth order and intellectual development. *Psychological Review,* 1975, *82*(1), 74-88.

30

the only child: a review

toni falbo

Most of the research on birth order is based on the principle that the birth order situation in which a child develops is determinative of that individual's behavior as an adult (Ansbacher & Ansbacher, 1956; Schachter, 1959; Sutton-Smith & Rosenberg, 1970; Zajonc & Markus, 1975). It is theorized that experiences associated with a particular birth order situation establish relatively enduring personality characteristics, and that the presence of siblings can bring about positive characteristics like sharing and cooperation as well as negative characteristics such as aggression and competition. However, in the case of only children, the assumption is that their lack of siblings has only negative effects. Only children are popularly conceived to be selfish, lonely, and maladjusted (Thompson, 1974). Little popular or scientific attention has been paid to the positive aspects of not having siblings. The main reason for this oversight is that both the general public and the behavioral science community have acquired the pronatalist ideology of our culture (Peck & Senderowitz, 1974; Russo, 1976). That is, both groups have unconsciously accepted the social norm that all healthy adults should have children. The purpose of the present paper is to review the literature about only children to see if the popular assumptions about their characteristics, and the negative consequences of not having siblings, survive scientific study.

Only a few articles directly focusing on the only child have appeared (Almodovar, 1973; Arlow, 1972; Burke, 1969; Campbell, 1933; Dyer, 1945; Falbo, 1976; Fenton, 1928; Guildford & Worcester, 1930; Hooker, 1931). Frequently, only children have been combined with first borns (for example, Greenberg, 1967; Hoyt & Raven, 1973; Schachter, 1959; Toman & Toman, 1970) in studies of birth order. As a result of this relative lack of information, many questions about only children are not answered. This review will be limited to those areas of research that have received a reasonable amount of attention. These areas are: intelligence, achievement, interpersonal orientation, and sex role development.

INTELLIGENCE

One area where only children have received a fair amount of attention is research on intelligence. Research conducted by the Scottish Council on Research in Education (1933, 1949, 1953) reported that only children had as much as a 22 point IQ advantage over children who came from families with five or more children. Wark, Swanson, and Mack (1974) found that only and first borns scored higher on intelligence measures than did second, third, fourth, fifth, and even sixth borns. Payne (1971) found that the verbal aptitude scores for only and first borns were higher than for later borns. Similarly, Horrocks (1962) reported a greater verbal precocity in adolescent only children. Zajonc

(1976) and Claudy (1976) found that only children, on average, had higher IQs than did children from large families, especially later borns. However, this rosy picture of the intelligence of only children is somewhat dimmed when we compare them to either first or second borns from small families. Rather than having the highest IQ, as would be predicted from their family size, only children have been found to score lower than first or second borns of two or three child families and most like first borns in four child families. This result holds across socioeconomic groups (Claudy, 1976) as well as cross-culturally (Belmont & Marolla, 1973). Zajonc (1976) suggested that only children's scores reflect their lack of opportunity to tutor younger siblings, which he believes fosters intellectual development. This explanation is bolstered by the finding that last borns are the other exception to the generally linear relationship between birth order, family size, and intelligence. Like only borns, last borns score lower than would be predicted from the linear relationship.

Thus, only children have an IQ advantage over children from large families. However, perhaps because only children have less of an opportunity to tutor younger children, they have an IQ disadvantage relative to first or second borns of two or three child families.

ACHIEVEMENT

In general, past research has supported the conclusion that onlies, like first borns, achieve more than later borns. Disproportionate numbers of first and only borns have been found among eminent men (Ellis, 1904), the faces on *Time* covers (Toman & Toman, 1970), psychologists (Roe, 1953), and other groups presumably representing achievement. Consistent with these findings, several investigators have found greater academic achievement among only and first borns (Guilford & Worcester, 1930; Jones, 1954; Lees & Steward, 1957; Oberlander & Jenkins, 1967; Skouholt, Moore, & Wellman, 1973).

The conclusion that first and only borns achieve more has been contested. Schooler (1972) persuasively argued that many, if not most, of the reported birth order effects are due to socioeconomic or other characteristics of the samples. Schooler (1972) provided several examples of birth order effects in achievement which were eliminated when socioeconomic and frequency of certain birth order groups, were controlled.

However, Breland (1974) subsequently demonstrated that even when parents' education, family income, and mother's age were covaried, significant birth order effects in the National Merit Scholarship Qualification test were found. Breland's results also indicated that there are achievement differences between only and first borns similar to those reported for intelligence; that is, only borns score less well than first borns of two, three and even four child families, but higher than later borns of four or more child families. The fact that Breland's measure of achievement is similar to measures of intelligence probably accounts for the similarity in findings. Further work comparing only and first borns with other measures of achievement is needed.

There are several possible explanations for the birth order effects in achievement. The first most obvious explanation is that only and first borns may achieve more than later borns because they are more intelligent than later borns. A second explanation shows it is economically more feasible for a family with one child to send that child to college than it is for a family with several children. Thus, only borns may achieve more in the United States because they are more likely to obtain higher education. Indeed, Bayer (1967) found that only borns were the most overrepresented birth order group among college students.

Third, achievement-related personality characteristics may develop as a result of childhood experiences within the family. One personality characteristic relevant is achievement motivation. There is remarkably little research on birth order and need for achievement and none of it has systematically compared only and first borns. Measuring need for achievement with the Edwards Personal Preference Schedule (Edwards, 1963), Sampson and Hancock (1967) and Angelini (1967) found that first and only borns scored higher on need for achievement than did later borns. Rosen

(1961) used a projective measure of need for achievement and found that among the higher socio-economic groups, only and first borns scored higher than did later borns from medium and large families. In contrast, Rosenfeld (1966) used a projective measure of need for achievement and found no birth order effects.

Searches for the factors affecting the development of achievement motivation have frequently focused on the standards of child behavior expected by parents. Rosen and D'Andrade (1959), in agreement with Winterbottom (1958), found that achievement motivation is fostered by parents imposing relatively high standards of mature behavior on their children at earlier ages. There is evidence that first borns receive greater pressure for more mature behavior from parents than do later borns (Clausen, 1966; Kammeyer, 1967). Furthermore, first borns probably have even higher standards of behavior expected of them than do only borns because the presence of young siblings forces adult caretakers to spend more time attending to younger children.

There is one factor special to only children that could enhance their achievement: their uninterrupted relationship with their parents. The acquisition of adult-like behavior is probably accelerated in only children because they have solely adult models of behavior in their family environment. Children with siblings are exposed to both child and adult models of behavior and this may slow these children's acquisition of adult-like behavior. Guilford and Worcester (1930) support this speculation, reporting that only children are more adult-oriented than are children with siblings. Further, what research there is on this subject supports the relative importance of parents for only children. Gewirtz and Gewirtz (1965) found that mothers of only children interacted with their children twice as much as did mothers of last borns. Falbo (1976) found that among undergraduates, 40% of the only children reported that their parents were "the most influential person in making them the person they are," as compared to 3% of first, 2% of middle, and 7% of last borns.

A final explanation for the greater achievements of first and only borns is that they acquire personality predispositions conducive to the exercise of leadership (Adler, 1930). Thus, one would expect only and first borns to be overrepresented in positions of leadership. A recent test of this hypothesis among military officers failed to support it for only children. Farley, Smart, and Brittain (1974) found that first borns were more likely to be officers in any branch of the military than were only, second, or third borns. A study of firemen, however, found that both first and only borns were more likely to take the leadership role in large work groups than were later borns (Smith & Goodchilds, 1963).

In summary, the relative achievements of only and first borns are not completely documented. In terms of the acquisition of achievement-related behavior, only borns have the advantage of greater financial resources and uninterrupted parent-child relationships. The disadvantages for only children are that they are not pushed to mature behavior by the presence of younger siblings as are first borns.

INTERPERSONAL ORIENTATION

A third major area of research about only children concerns interpersonal orientation: affiliation, interpersonal styles, and mental health.

Affiliation. In early research on affiliation, Schachter (1959) reported that only and first borns were more likely than were later borns to choose being with another person while waiting for anticipated discomfort. This research has been replicated in the field (Hoyt & Raven, 1973) as well as with role-playing techniques (Greenberg, 1967). All three of these studies combined first and only borns into one category because no significant differences between only and first borns were found.

Two studies of *need* for affiliation have considered only children separately from first borns. Using projective techniques, Conners (1963) found that only children demonstrated less affiliation deprivation than did people from two child families. Likewise, he found that only children scored higher on the FIRO-B (Schutz, 1958) affection scale than did people with siblings. Conners (1963) interpreted these findings as support for his hypothesis that only children suffer less affection deprivation than do children with siblings and that this results in lowered need for affiliation. Consistent with these results, Rosenfeld (1966) compared the need for affiliation scores of first and only borns and found first borns to have significantly higher needs for affiliation than only borns have.

A recent study of affiliation has found differences between only and first borns in self-reported affiliation. Surveying undergraduates, Falbo (1976) found that only children reported having fewer friends and belonging to fewer clubs than did people who had siblings. However, these same only children reported having a comparable number of close friends and leadership positions in clubs. There were also no differences between onlies and nononlies in terms of their reports of the amount of time spent alone daily and in their felt popularity.

In the same study, Falbo (1976) used a group dynamics exercise, the NASA exercise (Pfeiffer & Jones, 1969), to measure further aspects of affiliation. She found that only borns were much more likely than subjects with siblings to make personal decisions independent of group decisions. Furthermore, only children exhibited this autonomy without reporting discomfort during the group decision process.

Thus, although the evidence is sparse, it seems likely that in some measures of affiliation, only and first borns can be distinguished. Perhaps, as Conners (1963) suggests, only children have lower needs for affiliation because they experience less affection deprivation. This may explain why only children exhibit greater autonomy in decision-making without experiencing discomfort during the group decision process, and why they report having fewer friends and joining fewer clubs while not perceiving themselves as unpopular (Falbo, 1976). Research is needed investigating the relationship between number of siblings, affection deprivation, and autonomy.

Styles of interaction. Another area of interpersonal orientation which has been related to only children is styles of interaction. This area is potentially important because siblings are generally considered to be primary agents in the development of interpersonal behavior (Sutton-Smith & Rosenberg, 1970). In a study of sociometric choices within the classroom, Miller and Maruyama (1976) found that last borns were selected more frequently as playmates and someone to sit close to than were earlier borns. Likewise, teachers of these students rated those who were later borns as being more sociable than were those who were early borns. Furthermore, this birth order difference in social skills was found regardless of family size or socioeconomic status. Miller and Maruyama suggested that because only and first borns, between whom there were no differences, do not have older siblings, they acquire more autocratic, less interactive interpersonal styles and that this has negative consequences for peer popularity.

Contradictory results about only children were observed in an earlier study of peer popularity. Sells and Roff (1963) obtained likeability ratings from the same sex grade school classmates and found that only and youngest borns received the highest ratings. A possible reconciliation of these discrepant findings derives from the fact that they measure peer popularity differently. Likeability ratings (Sells & Roff, 1963) do not necessarily measure the same aspects of peer acceptance as do playmate and seating selections (Miller & Maruyama, 1976). It may be that last borns have acquired a more compliant disposition than have only borns, thus making last borns better choices for someone to play with or sit next to in class. However, this does not necessarily mean that only borns are less well liked generally or that they are socially unskilled.

Both the Miller and Maruyama (1976) and the Sells and Roff (1963) studies infer interpersonal behavior from peer popularity. Very little research directly studying the interpersonal styles of only and nononly children has been conducted. What evidence there is suggests that only children have different interpersonal styles than do children with siblings. Falbo (1976) employed a two play Prisoner's Dilemma Game (Deutsch, 1960) to examine the difference between only children and people with siblings. No differences between only and nononly borns were found in the initial move. However, when subjects made a second move, in response to a bogus cooperative play of an unknown other person, only borns were more likely to respond with a cooperative move than were people who had siblings. Falbo explained her results in terms of sibling rivalry. She argued that because only children lack sibling rivalry, they acquire a more trusting style of interaction. Sutton-Smith and Rosenberg (1970) arrived at a similar conclusion. They reasoned that because only children continuously receive help and nurturance from their parents, only children develop the expectation that others are helpful and rewarding. In contrast, children with siblings do not have this expectation about parents (in the case of later borns); or they have it shattered when younger siblings appear (in the case of first borns).

Mental health. A theme underlying the stereotype of the only child concerns the presumed mental health problems of only children. Only children are popularly conceived to be "generally maladjusted, self-centered and self-willed, attention seeking and dependent on others, temperamental and anxious, generally unhappy and unlikeable, and yet somewhat more autonomous than a child with two siblings" (Thompson, 1974, 95-96). Given the strength of this negative stereotype, it is surprising that little research has been devoted to assessing the mental health of only children. In general, on a variety of mental health variables, no differences have been found between only and nononly children (Burke, 1969; Howe & Madgett, 1975). In fact there is some evidence that only children are underrepresented among psychiatric or other clinical clients (Blatz & Bott, 1927; Corfield, 1968; Kurth & Schmidt, 1964; Tuckman & Regan, 1967). However, there is also evidence that only children are more likely to be referred for clinical help (Hough, 1932; Ko & Sun, 1965), and to repeat visits to the clinic (Howe & Madgett, 1975). However, in all three studies (Hough, 1932; Howe & Madgett, 1975; Ko & Sun, 1965) the investigators suggested that the major reason for this relatively high referral and repeat rate was the overprotective attitude of the parents.

An area of research relevant to mental health is self-esteem. Two early studies of self-esteem and only children (Fenton, 1928; Goodenough & Leahy, 1927) compared teacher ratings of only vs. nononly children and found that the two groups differed in the traits of "conceit" and "self-confidence." Only children were given higher ratings than were nononlies in both traits. However, in these studies, the birth order of the children and the purpose of the study were not conscientiously concealed from the teachers. Therefore, it is possible that the teacher ratings were contaminated by the teachers' application of the stereotype about only children.

More recent studies of self-esteem and birth order have come up with contradictory information about only children. Zimbardo & Formica (1963) found that later borns had higher self-esteem than did only borns. In contrast, Rosenberg (1965) reported that only borns were more likely to be classified as having high self-esteem than were nononly borns. However, no test of significance for Rosenberg's data was computed and the apparent difference between only and nononly borns existed mainly for males, especially Jewish males. Coopersmith's (1967) study of adolescent males found that only and first borns were overrepresented in the high self-esteem group. On the other hand, Kaplan (1970) measured the self-esteem of a representative sample (N=500) from Harris County, Texas, and found no difference between only and nononly borns. Instead, Kaplan (1970) found that last borns were more likely to be in the high self-esteem group than were middle or first (and only) borns. Further tests of Kaplan's findings indicated that it held up only for white males from higher social class groups.

Obviously, more research with large and representative samples spanning all age groups is needed before conclusions about the mental health of only children can be justly made. Future research in this area should focus not only on the birth order and family size of the child, but also on the characteristics of the parents. If only children are prone to certain types of adjustment problems, the cause of this disorder may not be their lack of siblings, but rather to some special characteristic of the parents.

There is reason to believe that parents of only children are unusual. Census information (U.S. Bureau of Census, 1970) indicates that among completed families, divorce or death of one parent is more common among one child families than among two to four child families. Also, it is possible that there is a psychological self-selection process operating among parents of one child. These parents have already demonstrated their willingness to deviate from the norms of American society by virtue of their having just one child. Studies of American family size norms indicate that a two child family is the lower limit of social acceptability (Blake, 1974).

In addition, researchers in this area should be wary that their results are not contaminated by the social stereotype of the only child. Researchers should be sensitive to the likelihood that labeling a client as an only child will influence the diagnosis.

SEX ROLE DEVELOPMENT

Investigations of the origins of sex role identification have frequently indicated that the sex role behavior of parents is determinative of the sex role identification of their offspring (Hetherington, 1967; Lynn, 1969; Vogel, Broverman, Broverman, Clarkson, & Rosenkrantz, 1970). Other investigators have expanded this familial influence on the development of sex role identification to include the birth order and sex composition of the siblings. Rosenberg and Sutton-Smith (1968) contend that the sex composition of the family brings about alterations in the sex role identification of all family members. For example, in two child families, where both children are female, Rosenberg and Sutton-Smith (1968) found that the fathers had relatively high masculinity scores. They attributed this to a contrast effect. As interesting as the Rosenberg and Sutton-Smith analysis is, other investigations have failed to obtain similar relationships between sex composition, birth order, and the masculinity-femininity of family members (Landers, 1970; Vroegh, 1971). Thus, it is currently far from certain what the effects of the sex composition of the family are on development of sex role identity in children.

A question which has arisen in this area of research is: where do only children fit in? Since only children come from an unusual family composition, what can we expect about their sex role identification? The answers available in the literature are few, but the sparsity of information has not discouraged Sutton-Smith and Rosenberg (1970) from concluding: "There are other data to show that the only boy is more feminine than other males, and the only girls more masculine; moreover, that the deviation in these opposite-sex directions leaves them with a greater tendency toward sex deviations consonant with these tendencies" (p. 153).

Sutton-Smith and Rosenberg (1970) cited four references in support of this statement (Gundlach & Riess, 1967; Heilbrun & Fromme, 1965; Hooker, 1931; Rosenberg & Sutton-Smith, 1964). An examination of these studies, however, indicates that they provide little or no support for the Sutton-Smith and Rosenberg statement. In three of the four studies cited, no measure of sexual deviancy was included in the research. These three studies contained various measures of conformity to American sex role norms. Hooker's (1931) research concerned teacher ratings of the classroom behavior of elementary school students. Among other findings, Hooker reported that teachers rated only children as more likely to "show signs of being sissies or tomboys" (p. 126). In the Rosenberg and Sutton-Smith (1964) study, only the only child boys demonstrated an unusual sex role pattern. These boys (N=12) scored high on both masculinity and femininity scales. Furthermore, in the Heilbrun and Fromme (1965) study, the masculinity/femininity scores of only children did not differ significantly from those of children with siblings. Thus, the evidence cited by Sutton-Smith and Rosenberg does not give much support to the conclusion that only children are more likely than others to be more cross sex typed on measures of masculinity and femininity.

The fourth reference cited by Rosenberg and Sutton-Smith does, in fact, deal with the relative frequency of birth orders in a sample of lesbians and nonlesbians. However, this study did not find that only children were more likely than others to be found among the lesbian sample. Instead, Bundlach and Riess (1967) reported that a disproportionate number of only children, first borns of a two child family, *and* later borns from large families were found among the lesbian sample, although they had no explanation for this finding. It was especially perplexing to them because just the reverse had been found about the frequency of only children among male homosexuals (Bieber et al., 1962).

A likely explanation for the Gundlach and Riess result lies in errors associated with the sample, rather than something intrinsic to birth order. This sampling error could be brought about by the smallness (N=217) and self-select nature of the lesbian sample, and the questionable selection procedure undertaken in obtaining the nonlesbian sample.

The Sutton-Smith and Rosenberg (1970) statement about sex deviancy of only children is not supported by the literature they cite. Given the paucity of information about sex role development of only children, conclusions about their sex role identification or sexuality are currently unwarranted.

Only children can provide a valuable comparison group for investigators studying the effects of sibling sex status on the development of sex role identity. A good example is the study by Bigner (1972). He compared only children to children of the same sex who had one male or female older sibling, thereby ascertaining the effects of having an older male or female sibling upon the sex role identity of children. Bigner's results suggested that one of the sources of sex role androgyny is the presence of an older opposite sex sibling. More research employing only children as a comparison group would be useful in future research on the effects of siblings on sex role development.

SUMMARY AND CONCLUSIONS

Intelligence is the only topic area in which consistent and reliable results about only children are available. The IQ scores of only children are located between first borns from small families and later borns from large families. One of the reasons offered to explain why only children do not score as well as one would predict from their small family size is that they lack a younger sibling to tutor. If this peer tutoring hypothesis is correct, then one of the major disadvantages of not having siblings is a dampening of intelligence below what it would be if a younger sibling were present.

Other than for intelligence, very few conclusions about only children can be drawn. Nonetheless, it should be noted that there is no evidence that supports the popular belief that only children are selfish, lonely, or maladjusted. Furthermore, some research evidence suggests that the absence of siblings can have beneficial effects on the development of children.

REFERENCES

Adler, A. *The education of children* (1930). Chicago: Regnery, 1970.
Almodovar, J. P. Existe-te-il un "syndrome de l'enfant unique?" *Enfance,* 1973, *3-4,* 233-249.
Angelini, H. B. Family structure and motivation to achieve. *Revista Interamericana de Psicologia,* 1967, *1*(2), 115-125.
Ansbacher, H. L., & Ansbacher, R. R. *The individual psychology of Alfred Adler.* New York: Basic Books, 1956.
Arlow, J. A. The only child. *Psychoanalytic Quarterly,* 1972, *41*(4), 507-536.
Bayer, A. E. Birth order and attainment of the doctorate: A test of economic hypotheses. *American Journal of Sociology,* 1967, *72,* 540-550.
Bieber, I., Dain, H. I., Dince, P. R., Drellich, M. G., Grand, H. G., Gundlach, R. H., Kreiner, M. W., Rifkin, A. H., Wilbur, C. B., & Bieber, T. B. *Homosexuality: A psychoanalytic study.* New York: Basic Books, 1962.
Bigner, J. J. Sibling influence on sex-role preference. *Journal of Genetic Psychology,* 1972, *121*(2), 271-282.
Blake, J. Can we believe recent data on birth expectation in the United States? *Demography,* 1974, *11,* 25-44.
Blatz, W. E., & Bott, E. A. Studies in mental hygiene of children: I. Behavior of public school children—a description of method. *Journal of Genetic Psychology,* 1927, *34,* 552-582.
Breland, H. M. Birth order, family configuration, and verbal achievement. *Child Development,* 1974, *45,* 1011-1019.
Burke, M. O. A search for systematic personality differentiate of the only child in young adulthood. *Journal of Genetic Psychology,* 1969, *60,* 41-45.
Campbell, A. A. A study of the personality adjustments of only and intermediate children. *Journal of Genetic Psychology,* 1933, *43,* 197-206.
Claudy, J. G. *Cognitive characteristics of the only child.* Paper presented at the 84th Annual Convention of the American Psychological Association, Washington, D.C., 1976.
Clausen, J. A. Family structure, socialization, and personality. In L. W. Hoffman & M. L. Hoffman (Eds.), *Review of child development research, 2.* New York: Russell Sage Foundation, 1966.
Conners, C. K. Birth order and needs for affiliation. *Journal of Personality,* 1963, *31*(3), 409-416.
Coopersmith, S. *The antecedents of self-esteem.* San Francisco: Freeman, 1967.
Corfield, V. K. The utilization of guidance clinic facilities in Alberta, 1961. *Alberta Psychologist,* 1968, *9*(3), 15-45.

Deutsch, M. Trust, truthworthiness, and the *F* scale. *Journal of Abnormal and Social Psychology,* 1960, *61,* 138-140.

Dyer, D. T. Are only children different? *Journal of Educational Psychology,* 1945, *36,* 297-302.

Edwards, A. L. *Edwards Personal Preference Schedule.* New York: Psychological Corporation, 1963.

Ellis, H. A. *A study of British Genius.* London: Hurst & Blackett, 1904.

Falbo, T. *Folklore and the only child: A reassessment.* Paper presented at the 84th Annual Convention of the American Psychological Association, Washington, D.C., 1976.

Farley, F. H., Smart, K. L., & Brittain, C. V. Birth order, rank and branch of service in the military. *Journal of Individual Psychology,* 1974, *30*(2), 227-232.

Fenton, N. The only child. *Journal of Genetic psychology,* 1928, *35,* 546-556.

Gewirtz, J. L., & Gewirtz, H. B. Stimulus conditions, infant behaviors and social learning in four Israeli child-rearing environments: A preliminary report illustrating differences in environment and behavior between 'only' and 'youngest' child. In B. M. Foss (Ed.), *Determinants of infant behavior III.* New York: Wiley, 1965.

Goodenough, F. L., & Leahy, A. M. The effect of certain family relationships upon the development of personality. *Journal of Genetic Psychology,* 1927, *34,* 45-71.

Greenberg, M. S. Role playing: An alternative to deception? *Journal of Personality and Social Psychology,* 1967, *7* (2 Pt 1), 152-157.

Guilford, R. B., & Worcester, D. A. A comparative study of the only and nononly child. *Journal of Genetic Psychology,* 1930, *38,* 411-426.

Gundlach, R. H., & Riess, B. F. Birth order and sex of siblings in a sample of lesbians and nonlesbians. *Psychological Reports,* 1967, *20,* 61-62.

Heilbrun, A. E., & Fromme, D. K. Parental identification of late adolescent and level of adjustment: The importance of parental model attributes, ordinal position, and sex of child. *Journal of Genetic Psychology,* 1965, *107,* 49-59.

Heatherington, E. M. The effects of familial variables on sex typing on parent-child similarity, and on limitation in children. *Minnesota Symposia on Child Psychology,* 1967, *1,* 82-107.

Hooker, H. F. The study of the only child at school. *Journal of Genetic Psychology,* 1931, *39,* 122-126.

Horrocks, J. E. *The psychology of adolescence.* Boston: Houghton and Mifflin, 1962.

Hough, E. Some factors in the etiology of maternal over-protection. *Smith College Studies of Social Work,* 1932, *2,* 188-208.

Howe, M. G., & Madgett, M. E. Mental health problems associated with the only child. *Canadian Psychiatric Association Journal,* 1975, *20*(3), 189-194.

Hoyt, M. P., & Raven, B. H. Birth order and the 1971 Los Angeles earthquake. *Journal of Personality and Social Psychology,* 1973, *28*(1), 123-128.

Jones, H. E. Environmental influence on mental development. In L. Carmichael (Ed.), *Manual of child psychology* (2nd ed.). New York: Wiley, 1954.

Kammeyer, K. Birth order as a research variable. *Social Forces,* 1967, *46,* 71-80.

Kaplan, H. B. Self-derogation and childhood family structure. *Journal of Nervous and Mental Disease,* 1970, *151,* 13-23.

Ko, Y., & Sun, L. Ordinal position and the beahvior of visiting the child guidance clinic. *Acta Psychologia Taiwanica,* 1965, 1016-1062.

Kurth, E., & Schmidt, E. Multidimensional examinations of stuttering children. *Probleme and Ergebnisse der Psychologie,* 1964, *12,* 49-58.

Landers, D. M. Sibling sex status and ordinal position effects on females' sport participation and interest. *Journal of Social Psychology,* 1970, *80,* 247-248.

Lees, J. P., & Stewart, A. H. Family or sibship position and scholastic ability: An interpretation. *Sociological Review,* 1957, *5,* 173-190.

Lynn, D. B. *Parental and sex role identification.* Berkeley: McCutchan, 1969.

Miller, N., & Maruyama, G. Ordinal position and peer popularity. *Journal of Personality and Social Psychology,* 1976, *33*(2), 123-131.

Oberlander, M., & Jenkins, N. Birth order and academic achievement. *Journal of Individual Psychology,* 1967, *23,* 103-109.

Payne, D. L. Birth-order, personality and performance at the Air Force Academy. *Journal of Individual Psychology,* 1971, *27*(2), 185-187.

Peck, E., & Senderowitz, J. (Eds). *Pronatalism: The myth of Mom and apple pie.* New York: Crowell, 1974.

Pfeiffer, J. W., & Jones, J. E. NASA exercise: Seeking consensus. *Handbook for Structured Experiences for Human Relations Training.* Iowa City: University Associates Press, 1969.

Roe, A. A. Psychological study of eminent psychologists and anthropologists and a comparison with biological and physical scientists. *Psychological Monographs,* 1953, *67*(2, Whole No. 352).

Rosen, B. C. Family structure and achievement motivation. *American Sociological Review,* 1961, *28,* 574-585.

Rosen, B., & D'Andrade, R. C. T. The psychosocial origins of achievement motivation. *Sociometry,* 1959, *22,* 185-218.

Rosenberg, M. *Society and the adolescent self-image.* Princeton University Press, 1965.

Rosenberg, B. G., & Sutton-Smith, B. Ordinal position and sex-role identification. *Genetic Psychology Monographs,* 1964, *70*(2), 297-328.

Rosenberg, B. G., & Sutton-Smith, B. Family interaction effects on masculinity-femininity. *Journal of Personality and Social Psychology,* 1968, *8* (2), 117-120.

Rosenfeld, H. Relationships of ordinal position to affiliation and achievement motives: Direction and generality. *Journal of Personality,* 1966, *34*(4), 467-479.

Russo, N. F. The motherhood mandate. *Journal of Social Issues,* 1976, *32*(3), 143-154.

Sampson, E. E., & Hancock, F. R. An examination of the relationship between ordinal position, personality and conformity: An extension, replication and partial verification. *Journal of Personality and Social Psychology,* 1967, *5,* 398-407.

Schachter, S. *The psychology of affiliation.* Stanford: Stanford University Press, 1959.

Schooler, C. Birth order effects: Not here, not now! *Psychological Bulletin,* 1972, *78,* 161-175.

Schutz, W. C. *FIRO: A three dimensional theory of interpersonal behavior.* New York: Rinehart and Company, 1958.

Scottish Council for Research in Education. *The intelligence of Scottish children: A national survey of an age group.* London: University of London Press, 1933.

Scottish Council for Research in Education. *The trend of Scottish intelligence.* London: University of London Press, 1949.

Scottish Council for Research in Education. *Social implications of the 1947 Scottish mental survey.* London: University of London Press, 1953.

Sells, S. B., & Roff, M. Peer acceptance-rejection and birth order. *American Psychologist,* 1963, *18,* 355.

Skouholt, T., Moore, E., & Wellman, F. Birth order and academic behavior in first grade. *Psychological Reports,* 1973, *32*(2), 395-398.

Smith, E. E., & Goodchilds, J. D. Some personality and behavioral factors related to birth order. *Journal of Applied Psychology,* 1963, *47*(5), 300-303.

Sutton-Smith, B., & Rosenberg, B. G. *The sibling.* New York: Holt, Rinehart, and Winston, Inc., 1970.

Thompson, V. D. Family size: Implicit policies and assumed psychological outcomes. *Journal of Social Issues,* 1974, *30* (4), 93-124.

Toman, W., & Toman, E. Sibling positions of a sample of distinguished persons. *Perceptual and Motor Skills,* 1970, *31*(3), 825-826.

Tuckman, J., & Regan, R. A. Size of family and behavioral problems in children. *Journal of Genetic Psychology,* 1967, *111*(2), 151-160.

U.S. Bureau of the Census, Census of Population: 1970, Subject Reports, Final Report PC(2)-3A, *Women by number of children ever born.*

Vogel, S. R., Broverman, L. K., Broverman, D. M., Clarkson, F. E., & Rosenkrantz, P. S. Maternal employment and perception of sex roles among college students. *Developmental Psychology,* 1970, *3,* 384-91.

Vroegh, K. The relationship of birth order and sex of sibling to gender role identity. *Developmental Psychology,* 1971, *4*(3), 407-411.

Wark, D. M., Swanson, E. O., & Mack, J. More on birth order: Intelligence and college plans. *Journal of Individual Psychology,* 1974, *30*(2), 221-226.

Winterbottom, M. R. The relation of need for achievement to learning experiences in independence and mastery. In J. W. Atkinson (Ed.), *Motives in fantasy, action, and society.* New Jersey: Van Nostrand, 1958.

Zajonc, R. B. Family configuration and intelligence. *Science,* 1976, 192, 227-236.

Zajonc, R. B., & Markus, G. B. Birth order and intellectual development. *Psychological Review,* 1975, *82*(1), 74-88.

Zimbardo, P., & Formica, R. Emotional comparisons and self-esteem as determinants of affiliation. *Journal of Personality,* 1963, *31,* 141-162.

sibling consensus on power tactics

brian sutton-smith

b. g. rosenberg

INTRODUCTION

The majority of studies of power within the family focus on the power of the parents. Attempts are made to discover which parent has the most power for which function (economic, child rearing, etc.), and various consequences for child identification, child achievement, etc., are shown to follow (5, 6, 8, 18). The traditional and usually implicit theoretical model behind such approaches is one that attempts to explain events within a social system (in this case, the family) in terms of the actions of predominantly one type of agent within that system: the parents. Yet, as any adequate social system theory would demand, and as any harried parent could volunteer, the other members of the family system—the children—also have power.

The present paper is one of a series in which the types of power shown by children and their parents in only- and two-child families are being investigated. Earlier studies of college students have shown, for example, that children in two-child families perceive themselves as having more power *vis-a-vis* their parents than do children in only-child families, and that first- and second-born siblings show consensus on seeing the firstborns as using more high power tactics and the second-borns as using more low power tactics (22). Where these previous investigations used adults as subjects, the present study uses children. If the power differences shown among the various types of siblings in the earlier work have any generality, their antecedents should be manifested at the child as well as at the adult level. From this earlier work with adults, it can be predicted that children who are firstborns will be perceived more often as commanding, reprimanding, scolding, and bossing, and reciprocally that second-borns will more often plead, whine, sulk, and appeal for the help of others. Again, the firstborns will use more physical power, while secondborns will show more anger, stubbornness, and harassing tactics.

In addition to this replication of the adult data at the child level, the present study is also concerned with the generality of these power tactics in other social situations. In an earlier study with children, for example, it was shown that although firstborns are the most bossy at home, they are less bossy than secondborns when both groups are playing with their best friends (20). In that study, it was inferred that the second-borns are more bossy with their friends than are the firstborns because they model after the arbitrary power of their older siblings. In the present study, therefore, it is predicted also that second-borns will be perceived by their classmates as more often using high powered tactics than do firstborns.

Reprinted, by permission, from *The Journal of Genetic Psychology*, 1968, *112*, 63-72, slightly abridged. Copyright ©1968 by The Journal Press.

METHOD

As the concept of *influence* has perhaps been the most pervasive of the various approaches which have been made to the study of power (9), the present study was initiated inductively with two simple pilot questions to children: "How do you get your sibling to do what you want him (her) to do?" and "How does your sibling get you to do what he (she) wants you to do?" Preliminary inquiries of elementary school children led to the development of two 40-item inventories reflecting the most frequently mentioned responses to these questions.

On each form, the child wrote his own name and the name and age of the sibling to whom he was making reference. "This is the way I get _____ to do what I want him (her) to do," or "This is the way _____ gets me to do what he (she) wants me to do." Firstborn children wrote in the names of their immediately younger siblings, and later-borns wrote in the names of their immediately older siblings. For each item, the child was asked to circle the frequency with which that item was employed on a one- (never) to five- (always) point scale.

Subjects in the present study were 95 preadolescent fifth and sixth grade children at Kenwood School, Bowling Green, Ohio. Children in this school are of predominantly middle to upper middle class status. There were 51 girls and 44 boys, of whom 33 were firstborn and 62 later-born. The mean age difference between the firstborns and their stated siblings was 2.48 years and between the later-borns and their stated siblings was 2.72 years. There was no significant difference between the two means. Only subjects with siblings within four years of their age were used in the study. Firstborns were distributed across two-child, three-child, four-child, and larger than four-child families in the proportions 10:15:6:2. The distribution for later-borns across these family sizes was 7:22:26:6. An assumption of the present study based on a successful earlier demonstration (20) was that the power relationships between the dyads would not be affected by these differences in family size. The distribution of subjects across the eight ordinal dyads was as follows: 13 boys with younger brothers (M1M), five boys with younger sisters (M1F), nine girls with younger sisters (F1F), six girls with younger brothers (F1M), 16 boys with older brothers (MM2), 10 boys with older sisters (FM2), 21 girls with older sisters (FF2), and 15 girls with older brothers (MF2).

The types of items used in the inventories are illustrated in [the data]. Because a novel scale of this sort is susceptible to as yet unanalyzed response sets, it was decided to begin analysis by attention only to those items on which the siblings of complementary ordinal relationships indicated consensus. For example, if the older sibling rated himself as more bossy than the younger and rated the younger as less bossy than himself, and then the younger also stated that he was less bossy than the older and the older was more bossy than he, there was said to be a consensus across the four responses to the one item "bossy." The statistical technique used to arrive at such consensus between siblings was a factorial analysis for unequal cell frequencies with repeated measures using an unweighted means solution (25).

To investigate the hypothesis that there would be a reversal in power trends from sibling to peer group relations, all the children who were a part of this inquiry also responded to a six-item sociometric on which they filled in the names of those in their class who got others to do what they wanted (a) by being bossy; (b) by asking for help; (c) by wrestling or hurting; (d) by asking for sympathy; (e) by tricking or threatening; and (f) by flattering, bribing, or bargaining. These items had proven to be salient in the earlier inquiry with college students. This sociometric was administered several months after the sibling inventories. All scores were converted to standard scores and subjected to a factorial analysis for unequal cell frequencies, unweighted means solution.

To control for the possibility that sociometric power attributions would reflect simple popularity which might already vary between ordinal positions as has been indicated in some ordinal research (3, 17), all children were asked to list the names of their five best friends. Each child's attributions were converted to standard scores and differences compared across all ordinal positions in terms again of a factorial analysis for unequal cells.

RESULTS

.... Each dyad is considered separately; older brother and younger brother (M1M and MM2); older sister and younger sister (F1F and FF2); older brother and younger sister (M1F and MF2); older sister and younger brother (F1M and FM2). Levels of significance as low as $p < .25$ are occasionally indicated because they parallel differences of the same content but higher significance level for some of the other dyads.

The greatest consensual agreement in the results is that firstborns are perceived both by firstborns and second-borns as more bossy: M1M ($p < .001$), F1F ($p < .001$), F1M ($p < .05$), M1F ($p < .25$). Of similar consensus is the tendency of nonfirstborns to show what is presumably a low power procedure of appealing to others outside the sibling dyad for help, crying, pouting, sulking, or threatening to tell tales or using prayer. Thus, MM2 ask other children ($p < .02$), complain to the parent ($p < .10$); FF2 ask parents for help ($p < .01$), tell tales ($p < .05$); MF2 ask parents for help ($p < .05$), complain to parents ($p < .001$), ask other children ($p < .05$). Crying and pouting is also common to MM2 ($p < .01$), FF2 ($p < .05$), and MF2 ($p < .01$). Only the boy with an older sister does not seek help outside the dyad, nor does he sulk or pout. Apparently, the younger brother with an older sister does not show the same degree of powerlessness as the other nonfirst categories, a finding which replicates a difference for these boys in an earlier study (20). His use of bribery, blackmail ($p < .05$), breaking things ($p < .05$), taking things ($p < .05$), making the F1M (his reciprocal in the dyad) feel guilty ($p < .05$) are unique amongst the second-borns.

Physical power tactics appear to vary with sex. Thus, beating up, belt and hit (M1M, $p < .01$), and wrestle and chase (FM2, $p < .05$) are ascribed to boys. But scratching and pinching (FF2, $p < .02$; MF2, $p < .02$) and tickling (F1M, $p < .05$) are ascribed to girls. The direct physical power of M1M and FM2 on their sibling opposites apparently has a strong effect, as their partners are the only ones who score higher on getting angry, shouting, and yelling (MM2, $p < .05$; F1M, $p < .05$).

The polite and perhaps strategic techniques of explaining, asking, and taking turns are attributed only to firstborn girls (F1F, $p < .05$; F1M, $p < .01$).

The firstborn boy with the younger sister is not as clearly characterized as the others, but his attributes (directional, but nonsignificant) are similar to those of the other firstborn boy (M1M)— boss, wrestle, play tricks, and spook.

The results for the sociometric study did not confirm the hypothesis.... However, there is a tendency for the ordinal positions noted to reverse the sibling findings, as predicted. Thus, second-borns, not firstborns, show a tendency to be seen as more bossy; and firstborns, not second-borns, to ask more often for help ($p < .25$). Sex differences were significant throughout, with males more often seen as bossy, wrestling, or hurting and tricking or threatening; and females as asking for help and asking for sympathy.

Results for the popularity study were also nonsignificant. The only tendency was for second-born boys and firstborn girls to be seen as more popular, a cross-sibling reversal paralleling several other studies in the literature (19, 23).

DISCUSSION

The results indicate considerable consensus between first- and second-born children that firstborns are of higher power and that second-borns are of lower power: that is, if being bossy can be regarded as an index of high power and appealing to others for help, crying, pouting, and sulking an index of low power. Perhaps the sex differences in which males are more often seen as bossy and females as more often appealing for help can be taken as supporting such a proposition. This difference between the ordinal positions, which has the advantage of fitting common sense notions, has support in the literature on ordinal position and dominance (14), and has furthermore been replicated in work with college students of strict ordinal positions (23). In the college study which dealt with the eight ordinal positions in the two-child family, rather than with older and younger siblings in various size families as in the present inquiry, the firstborns were also seen as more bossy, reprimanding, and scolding; and the second-borns reciprocally as pleading, sulking, appealing for help and sympathy from the firstborn and from others. Again, the college firstborns also used more physical restraint, although in the present study with children the firstborns use more actual physical attack: that is, beating up, wrestling, and hurting. The difference between the children and college students lies in the children's statement that they use such direct aggressive physical techniques. Firstborn college students also give more rewards and deprive of more privileges than do second-borns. The second-borns respond by getting angry, being stubborn, and by harassing, pestering, and bothering the firstborns. The literature on ordinal position seems to support this finding that the nonfirstborns are actually more aggressive and quarrelsome (14).

In sum, the consensus about power techniques established by the present child study is similar to findings in the general ordinal position literature and in the earlier college level study with more carefully controlled ordinal groups. Either the subjects of both age levels are engaging in mutually similar stereotyped responses to these inventories, or there is a continuity of power relationships from childhood through college age levels. The authors favor this latter interpretation because of their earlier findings of enduring sibling effects across the age levels from childhood through college (13, 22).

Returning to the introductory materials in which the authors stressed the importance of considering sibling as well as parent power influences, it can be said that some of the differences agreed upon by siblings in the present study would appear to derive from parental sources and that some would appear to derive from the character of the sibling interaction itself. Taking first those characteristics of the firstborns that appear to be modelled after their parents, the older girls' use of explaining, giving reasons, and asking may be said to be modelled after their mothers with whom the firstborns have closer relations than do the second-borns, at least in conversation (3). Again, "excluding" and "taking turns" might perhaps be regarded as "affiliation" strategies, assuming that those (firstborns) who are more concerned and anxious about affiliation (15) learn to develop such devices for its management.

Some of the other findings, however, are perhaps best interpreted in terms of the intrinsic characteristics of high and low power relationships generally, rather than in terms of the relationships between the siblings and their parents. No matter whether the group be an animal or human one, those who are larger in size and ability usually exercise dominance (bossiness) in order to ensure themselves of greater access to the available rewards. Dominance exercised by the more powerful, and anger and resentment (shouting, yelling) exercised by the less powerful may be regarded as universals across social systems. In the human family system, of course, one of the available rewards is the intangible affection of the parent so that the exercise of power by the firstborn may be greatly increased by his jealousy of the nonfirstborn as baby. A long literature of sibling rivalry attests that such jealousy can instigate increased dominance by the firstborn (1, 12). The point being made, however, is that although this peculiarly human jealousy increases the dominance of the older, it is not the origin of such dominance. The accident of birth creates size and ability differences and these no less than size differences in lower species lead to the institution of a pecking order. We may assume the less powerful younger siblings will fight back with all the powers at their command. The younger brother's relative strength when he has only an older sister to contend with may be taken as an illustration of this view. Usually, however, younger siblings seem to have to be content with the exercise of greater power outside their own sibling groups (10, 19, 20, 24). Perhaps, as Henry (7) has said, power needs (if not relations) are symmetrical: that is, those seriously overpowered have needs to repeat the treatment to some other persons less powerful than themselves. Much of the literature on the authoritarian personality could be derived from such a premise (2).

Again, looking at the sibling group as a miniature social system, the appeal by the nonfirstborns for the support of their parents (threaten to tell, complain to parent, ask parent for help, ask other children) parallels the tendency in politics and in small group research for the weak to ally themselves with a stronger third force. This strategy appears to have much generality as a group relational characteristic, though a hardly advisable one in politics according to Machiavelli. In the family this characteristic is, in part, supported by the parents being more indulgent with the younger children and thus implicitly encouraging their appeal for help (4, 11).

Yet another way of looking at the sibling social system is to consider it with its dominance hierarchy as a system in a state of balance. As long as older and younger stay with their respective powers, there is a minimum of fighting. According to Scott, this is one of the functional virtues of pecking orders at the animal level (16). They minimize conflict. Yet, if we pay attention to the harassing of the younger ones, to their attempts to appeal for assistance, we can add that they seem to be attempting some of the time to destroy this system of balance with their siblings. Thus, if they can prove more suffering (by complaining, crying, etc.), they can usually get the parents, as a third party, to interfere and at least temporarily upset the system. And they can often do this by first teasing and pestering the older ones until losing their self-control; the older ones make use of excessive power so that appeal by the younger to their parents is then legitimized. If this is the correct description of the state of affairs, we may perhaps postulate as a law that if dominance hierarchization reduces overt hostilities endogenously, at the same time it induces in the low-powered members exogenous counter coalitional activity, aimed at upsetting the established order.

In sum, the intrinsic characteristics of small groups with unevenly divided power appear to provide the greatest explanatory coverage for the present sibling data.

SUMMARY

Unlike most studies on power within the family, this study concentrates on the powers exercised by siblings on each other, rather than on the powers exercised by the parents. Subjects are 95 preadolescent children divided into four dyadic relationships by ordinal position (older brother-younger brother; older sister-younger sister, etc.). Consensual responses to two 40-item power inventories indicate that the older siblings are perceived as more powerful; and that younger siblings are perceived as showing more resentment and appealing to parents for help. Sociometric trends support the view that the younger siblings more often exercise stronger power outside the family group. Results are interpreted in social structural terms, which suggest that there are limitations to the customary unidirectional model of parent-child relationships.

REFERENCES

1. Adler, A. Understanding Human Nature. Greenwich, Conn.: Fawcett, 1959.
2. Adorno, T. W., Frenkel-Brunswik, E., Levinson, D. J., & Sanford, R. N. The Authoritarian Personality. New York: Wiley & Sears, 1964.
3. Bossard, J. H. S., & Boll, E. Personality roles in the large family. *Child Devel.*, 1955, 26, 71-78.
4. ———. The Large Family System. Philadelphia, Pa.: Univ. Pennsylvania Press, 1956.
5. Bowerman, C. E., & Elder, G. H. Variations in adolescent perception of family power structure. *Amer. Sociol. Rev.*, 1964, 29, 551-567.
6. Droppleman, L. F., & Schachter, E. S. Boys' and girls' reports of maternal and paternal behavior. *J. Abn. & Soc. Psychol.*, 1963, 67, 648-654.
7. Henry, A. F. Sibling structure and perception of disciplinary roles of parents. *Sociometry*, 1957, 20, 67-74.
8. Hess, R. D., & Torney, J. V. Religion, age, and sex in children's perception of family authority. *Child Devel.*, 1962, 33, 781-789.
9. Janda, K. F. Towards the explication of the concept of leadership in terms of the concept of power. *Hum. Rel.*, 1960, 13, 345-363.
10. Krout, M. H. Typical behavior patterns in twenty-six ordinal positions. *J. Genet. Psychol.*, 1939, 54, 3-29.
11. Lasko, J. K. Parent behavior towards first and second children. *Genet. Psychol. Monog.*, 1954, 49, 97-137.
12. Levy, D. M. The hostile act. *Psychol. Rev.*, 1941, 48, 356-361.
13. Rosenberg, B. G., & Sutton-Smith, B. Ordinal position and sex role identification. *Genet. Psychol. Monog.*, 1964, 70, 297-328.

14. Sampson, E. S. The study of ordinal position: Antecedents and outcomes. In B. Maher (Ed.), *Progress in Experimental Personality Research*. New York: Academic Press, 1965.
15. Schachter, S. The Psychology of Affiliation. Stanford, Calif.: Stanford Univ. Press, 1959.
16. Scott, J. P. Animal Behavior. New York: Doubleday, 1963.
17. Sells, S. B., & Roff, M. Peer acceptance—Rejection and birth order. *Amer. Psychol.*, 1963, 18, 355.
18. Sigel, I. E., Hoffman, M. L., Dreyer, A. S., & Torgoff, I. Influence techniques used by parents to modify the behavior of children: A case presentation. *Amer. J. Orthopsychiat.*, 1957, 27, 356-364.
19. Singer, J. E. The use of manipulative strategies: Machiavellianism and attractiveness. *Sociometry*, 1964, 27, 128-150.
20. Sutton-Smith, B. Role replication and reversal in play. *Merrill-Palmer Quart.*, 1966, 12, 285-298.
21. Sutton-Smith, B., & Rosenberg, B. G. Age changes in the effects of ordinal position and sex role identification. *J. Genet. Psychol.*, 1965, 107, 61-73.
22. _____. Sibling perception of power styles within the family. Paper presented at American Psychological Association, Chicago, Illinois, September, 1965.
23. Sutton-Smith, B., Roberts, J. M., & Rosenberg, B. G. Sibling association and role involvement. *Merrill-Palmer Quart.*, 1964, 10, 25-38.
24. Veroff, J. Development and validation of a projective measure of power motivation. *J. Abn. & Soc. Psychol.*, 1957, 54, 1-8.
25. Winer, B. J. Statistical Principles in Experimental Design. New York: McGraw-Hill, 1962.

32   sisterhood-brotherhood is powerful: sibling sub-systems and family therapy

stephen bank

michael d. kahn

PROBLEMS WITH EXISTING THEORY: UNDERRATING OF SIBLING IMPORTANCE

Current theories of family interaction focus almost exclusively on the influence of the parents on the psychosocial development of their children. Thus, family therapy has usually focused on correcting the parenting process. Transmission from parents to children downward, less frequently upward from children to parents, is the cornerstone of most major family theories. When interaction between members of the same generation has received attention, it has been mainly with the marital or parenting pair that family therapists have worked most comfortably. A notable example exists in the work of Virginia Satir (23) who conceptualizes most family problems as an outgrowth of marital disappointment. This leads to a therapy in which children are seen in order to improve their relationship with their parents and to communicate more openly about the parents' marital difficulty. Satir's theory and therapy deal almost not at all with sibling relationships.

That sibling relationships have, at best, been seen as products of the interaction *between* each child and the parents rather than *among* the children themselves is evident from a review of most major texts of family therapy. For example, Boszormenyi-Nagy and Spark in their detailed investigation of family loyalties (6) discuss sibling dynamics only in terms of ways in which parents assign an adult-like role to a well child. The well brother or sister is seen then as the parents' representative. But the authors give no description of the well sibling's contributions to his disturbed sister's or brother's problems. Nor is there any indication that siblings may influence *each other* for better or worse. This is particularly surprising because loyalty, the central concept of the book, is the keystone of sibling relationships. Similarly, most recent books of readings on child and family relationships ignore the sibling sub-system and what to do about it.

The neglect of the "sibling underworld," as one author has called it, is notable, too, in much of the in-depth clinical study of family behavior. For example, Lidz and his co-workers (14) refer to the fact that the "normal" sibling is often far from well-adjusted, but this is as far as the observation goes. In the same vein, Hoover and Franz (11) focus on the non-schizophrenic siblings in families in which there is one schizophrenic child. While they were able to describe the adaptations of these non-schizophrenic children as "firm, contented, isolated, struggling, near miss, or delinquent," development was seen only in terms of how successfully or unsuccessfully the non-schizophrenic children avoided the patterns established between the schizophrenic sibling and his *parents*. No observations were made directly of the relationships among the siblings themselves. More rigorous experimental family studies (18), which have brought families into laboratory conditions, use siblings for their value as "normal controls" rather than for any specific relationship property among the siblings. Here, normal siblings are used only for the contrast they make with their disturbed brothers or sisters.

In all fairness, the general under-emphasis of sibling status is common to our entire culture, and not just to family therapists. In contrast with other cultures, as Caplow points out (7), Europeans and Americans emphasize the romantic aspect of family life, namely husband-wife relationships and the product of that union, the children. But in African cultures south of the Sahara, paths between generations are de-emphasized, fraternal solidarity is more important than romantic love, and loyalty and the control of rivalry among brothers are the cornerstones of family stability. In contrast, in Western technologically advanced societies, brotherhood, sisterhood, and sibship in general no longer have the particular real status they once had. This fact appears to be the result of the attenuation of traditional distinctions among siblings, whereas in pre-industrial times a sibling's birth order gave him a right to certain forms of power. The ancient tradition of primogeniture, which entitled the first-born male to receive all the family's resources, has been replaced by a more egalitarian sibling group in which power and influence are more subtly worked out. Levirate and Sororate, ancient traditions that decreed a brother and sister would marry his or her sibling's spouse in the event of the sibling's death have not been practiced for many years. In addition, shrinking family size has made the sibling sub-group and sub-groups within the sibling sub-group less visible.

STUDIES OF SIBLING RELATIONSHIPS: RETROSPECTIVE ACCOUNTS

While Riskin and Faunce (22) recently noted the lack of research on sibling interaction in the family therapy literature, we have been able to unearth several scattered islands of research and theory in this largely unexplored area. The following synopsis summarizes work in which verbal report or indirect methods of assessing sibling relationships were used.

Alfred Adler's theory of sibling power struggles (1) was based on the reports he obtained from individuals about their perceptions of, and interactions with, siblings. Basically the Adlerian theory views sibling rivalry as an outcome of the order of birth; it is engendered by a struggle for the love of one or both parents. The focus on dominance, hierarchical aspects of the sibling power struggle, and on rivalry itself is exemplified in a number of studies conducted in the 1930's (13), but few of these studies focus directly on live observations of whole sibling groups. Rabin (21), in his study of Kibbutz children versus non-Kibbutz children, suggests that sibling rivalry may be a function, as Adler suggested, of the child's having been taught early in life to seek or not to seek the affection of parents. Again, however, the data on rivalry are obtained by post-hoc testing procedures rather than "live" observation of behavior.

A large body of work investigates child and adult personality as a function of the sibling sex status, birth order, and family size. This work is thoroughly summarized in Sutton-Smith and Rosenberg's book *The Sibling* (24). Birth order and its interaction with sexual role has demonstrable and clear connections with personality and personal functioning. A whole range of variables, including Machiavellianism, success in war situations, academic success, and cognitive style, are related to distinct sibling position profiles. Toman (25), basing his thinking on the reports of patients from individual therapy sessions, makes a number of testable predictions about personality style, mate selection, and marital adjustment, again on the basis of birth order and the interaction of sexual role with birth order. One's previous experience with sibling power relationships and the experience that one develops adapting to members of the opposite or same sex among one's sibs serve as the crucial developing ground for marital adjustment. Unfortunately, many of Toman's hypotheses have not been tested, and those that have been tested have been only partially confirmed with no replication. However, Toman does suggest obtaining a complete sibling history in diagnostic interviewing, and while he does not talk in terms of family therapy, his hypotheses would lead to a definite emphasis on sibling relationships in individual therapy. Bowen (5) cites Toman's concepts frequently. As part of Bowen's theory of differentiation of self, differentiation from the sibling group as well as the establishment of a personal relationship with one's sibs is considered important in the de-detriangulation process.

J. Gerstl (8) interviewed 150 brothers and sisters who comprised 50 sibling triads in which the youngest sibling was at least 10 years old. The author found 23 coalitions where all three siblings of the triad were in agreement that a coalition was present. Twenty-one of 23 coalitions involved siblings of the same *sex*. The large majority of coalitions were between siblings who were close in *age*. This study confirms much more informally gathered impressions that siblings team up on the basis of likeness and similarity. Caplow (7) developed an interesting theory of power relationships within families. On the basis of theory (with little experimental substantiation to this date) Caplow makes a set of predictions that describe the conditions under which sibling coalitions are likely to form:

> *When the parental coalition is so solidary that no child is ever allowed to form a winning coalition with one parent against the other, we may expect to see strong coalitions among the children, and even a condition of general solidarity uniting all the children of a large family. When one parent is clearly dominant, a . . . coalition is likely to form between the weaker parent and a child, which may lead in turn to the formation of sibling coalitions against the favored child or to other very complicated patterns in a sizeable family. When father and mother are nearly equal in power, but do not have a strong parental coalition, sibling rivalry will be intense and bitter as the children compete among themselves for the shifting coalition opportunities offered by their parents. (p. 99)*

Bossard and Boll (4), in what stands as a highly original contribution, interviewed one hundred adult siblings from one hundred large (more than six siblings) families. Through an interview and questionnaire, they obtained retrospective accounts of what it was like to be a member of a large family. While the data take in the perception of only one member of each family, they do suggest in a rich way the pervasiveness and extent of the sibling influence. This book, which has largely been ignored by family therapists, is packed with dynamic and factual data. We can summarize Bossard and Boll's conclusions:

Retrospectively, siblings saw each other as much more fair to one another than the parents had been to them. While 44 per cent of siblings voiced resentment of parental discipline, only 11 per cent voiced resentment of discipline by parental siblings. Siblings, the authors note, have better judgment about what really constitutes misbehavior; children understand the persistence of misbehavior more accurately.

Sibling phenomena are especially visible in large families because of the necessity for division of labor and the complexity of role allocations. As the size of the family increases, the importance of sibling sub-structure seems to increase. As playmates, almost all the informants indicated that they played primarily with their sibs, and happily so. The emphasis on sacrifice, on the group rather than on the self, was striking. Sibling rivalry and conflict appeared to have been minimal, forgotten, and secondary to the primary bond of loyalty in the sibling sub-group. Siblings were seen as making a concentrated effort not to embarrass each other and toward regulating each other in a way that would preserve the good image of the sibling group. In later life, sibling relationships were described by the informants as close in two-thirds of the cases; when contacts were not close in later life, it was because of wide spacing in birth time or because children did not have an opportunity because of hardship to play with each other in early years. Ninety-seven out of the 100 informants agreed that in large families siblings have a primary socializing function for each other, that the learning of fair play, self-control, sharing, being able to listen as well as talk, were all important functions played by the sibling system.

Finally, "intra-sibling combines" were described in some detail. Like other authors, Bossard and Boll discovered that dyads are the preferred sub-unit of large sibling groups, that there are sub-systems within the sibling system, and that these sub-systems are formed usually in groups of two, less frequently in groups of three. These sibling combines are drawn together by complementarity of interests, mutual needs, or narrow political interests that serve the group of two or three within the family matrix.

The interactive effects of one sibling upon another have been studied in depth by Lidz, *et al* (14) in their article on ego differentiation in schizophrenic symptom formation in identical twins. The detailed case presentation noted that after hospitalization of one twin, the co-twin who remained at home became acutely disturbed. Using a review of case notes obtained by each of the twin's individual therapist, as well as a review of the family history as seen through the parents' eyes, they pieced together a crucial ego psychological function played by one sibling for the other. Other in-depth case studies include that of Newman (19) who studied three younger brothers of three schizophrenic patients. The guilt experienced by the younger siblings for allowing the older brother to become the sacrificial lamb of the family and for not rescuing the older brother was examined in detail.

STUDIES OF SIBLING RELATIONSHIP: LIVE OBSERVATIONS

We have located only four scattered studies in which the researchers made live observations of on-going sibling interaction. Greenbaum reports (9) a clinical diagnostic procedure in which two siblings are interviewed together or are watched playing together. The purpose of this procedure is to give the therapist a more balanced view of the child in his natural sibling ecology and to make more natural the therapist's contact with the identified sibling. Greenbaum's procedure is oriented more toward understanding the identified patient rather than re-working any aspect of the sibling sub-system. Furthermore, the procedure involves only two siblings (the identified and the well sibling) and may exclude other important sibling coalitions and sub-formations.

As part of the massive, in-depth, experimental and clinical study of the schizophrenic Genain quadruplets, Quinn and Stein (20) studied the social interaction patterns of the quads with one another as well as with outsiders. Their findings are interesting not only because of what they discovered about the Genain sisters but because they used careful observations, time-sampling techniques, reported inter-rater reliability, and applied a theory (Simmel's theory of coalition in triads) to explain their findings. Among their observations: The quads interacted with one another far less than they did with outsiders; they were not a particularly cohesive group; and there were clear pairings within the group as well as differences in the extent to which siblings initiated contact with one another. Myra, perhaps the healthiest of these schizophrenic sisters, was demonstrated to isolate herself forcefully from the sibling group. Individuation from the undifferentiated mass of siblings was seen as an important maturational process.

By far the most extensive direct observations of whole sibling sub-systems, theory-making, and application of theory to therapy lie in the work of Minuchin, Montalvo, and their associates (16, 17). In their first book, *Families of the Slums,* Minuchin, Montalvo, *et al.* interviewed and treated large, fatherless, poverty families in which the allocation of power to the siblings and the disorganization of parental functioning made recognition of sibling sub-system imperative. Both in this work and in Minuchin's more recent *Families and Family Therapy,* the following points emerge about sibling interaction and the role of the therapist.

1. Siblings give reflected self-appraisal, and this is crucial for the development of the identity. Sibs turn to each other for protection when parents are disorganized. Siblings can, and do, form cohesive defensive groups when one is attacked by an outsider. Sibs can act as socializers for each other, interpreters of the outside world for each other. They can bring intense pressure to bear upon one another. And finally, they can activate "rescue squads" requiring differentiated roles within the sibling pack. (One child may call the police, another child may hide a younger child, etc. See Bossard and Bell (4) previously cited for description of similar functions in non-clinical large families.)

2. Therapeutic interventions described as conflict-resolution family therapy and structural family therapy include the following:

(a) Boundary-making between the sibling sub-system and the parental system: There seems to be a definite effort directed toward letting parents function as parents and children function as children. The therapist's job is to restore executive power to the parent, if possible. As part of this process, the sibling sub-system itself can be modified.

(b) Strengthening the sibling sub-system by allowing siblings to communicate more effectively and educably with each other.

(c) Reducing the power and influence of parental siblings in such a way as to increase the power of the parent.

The present authors have drawn this synopsis of the Philadelphia Child Guidance group's approach to the place of siblings in family therapy from many scattered references in the two books previously mentioned (16, 17). In the present paper we expand on this and other works cited to present a more comprehensive view of this aspect of family functioning and therapy. We suggest different and additional methods of conceptualizing sibling influence and a therapy format that emphasizes the family therapy of siblings.

THE AUTONOMY OF SIBLING SYSTEMS

It is clear that parents supervise and monitor sibling relationships, but there is a limit to the influence of parents over the sibling system. In our view, siblings are not merely representatives to each other of their parents' wishes and expectations. Siblings exert power, exchange services, and express feelings in a reciprocal way with one another that is often not revealed explicitly in the presence of parents. In our experience, siblings are much more spontaneous when we see them separately from the older generation: They are more direct with each other, less competitive, and "tuned in" to each other in ways that are strikingly empathic. This should not be surprising. In a study currently in progress (3), preliminary data indicate that siblings (brother-brother dyads age 4 and 6) spend more than twice as much time alone with each other than with parents in a sample of middle-class families. Siblings live in their sub-system according to specific sub-system "rules" just as other sub-systems, e.g. marriages, have *their* own sets of rules. Siblings define for each other, as do marriage partners, how far each other may go and in what direction each may go. Sibling status and power, which may be monitored directly by parents when the family is interacting as a whole, may take a very different direction when parental management is not directly present. While an eldest sibling can be invested with powers and privileges in the public view of parents, a coalition between his younger brother and sister can demolish his effective power on the playground where there is a world of children not monitored by parents. There is wide variability in the autonomy of sibling sub-systems from the parental system. As children mature and as they increase in age, their activities can be less and less effectively monitored by parents. The extreme limiting case of this, of course, is in the post-parental sibling sub-system when parents are sick or deceased. The sibling relationship lasts through a life time, often fifty to eighty years as compared with the child-parent relationship which is usually from thirty to fifty years in duration. It may well be that the sibling system, as in the case of aging parents who need nursing care, has a more powerful effect upon parents than vice versa. Here the action in the sibling group becomes primary. Sibs are, in this situation, no longer a sub-system: they are the primary system.

SIBLING FUNCTIONS

What are the functions that siblings serve for one another relatively free of parental monitoring?

1. **Identification and Differentiation.** In our view, identification and differentiation occur between siblings as well as between child and parent. The strength of sibling identification is often revealed when one sibling leaves or dies (see section on sibling mourning) and the remaining sibling

either incorporates or idealizes the image of the departed one. The process by which one child sees himself in the other, experiences life vicariously through the behavior of the other, and begins to expand on possibilities for himself by learning through a brother's or sister's experience is a powerful phenomenon. Identification is the "glue" of the sibling relationship. In a sense the possibilities for identification with brothers and sisters are more abundant than the possibilities for parent-child identification, but the motivation for identification (love, protection, belief of guilt) may be less. Thus, sibling identifications may be less compulsive and freer of the "driven" qualities that often characterize parent-child identifications. If this is so, then it suggests that family therapy may take judicious advantage of this identification process, especially when adequate parental models are absent.

Differentiation, the other side of the coin, is another key process among sibs. Without adequate sibling differentiation, a dangerous process of fusion can block the growth of each child.

> *In a family treated by one of the authors, the younger of two teen-age brothers became quite imitative of his brother upon his mother's having abandoned the family. The older brother who had a history of psychotic ideation, hallucinogenic drug involvement, and serious acting-out behavior became for the younger a desperate replacement for the close relationship that had existed with the mother. If the older brother bought records by the latest rock group, the younger would soon follow suit. If the older dated a girl at a church gathering, we could be certain that the younger would soon be imitating this. The fusion between the two brothers became so pronounced that when the older announced, again, that he had been hearing the voice of God, the younger converted to a Fundamentalist sect and claimed that he too could communicate with God. This is particularly significant because, prior to the mother's leaving, the younger boy had been maturing in a surprisingly successful fashion. For him the identification with, fusion with, and lack of differentiation from the older brother resulted in his placement in a mental hospital a month after the older brother's admission.*

Each sibling can be the touchstone for the other's concept of what he would *not* like to be. Such a phenomenon is paraphrased by the statement, "I am *not* going to be like you!" or, "I was once like you, and I will *not* be any more." Frequently there is a defensive aspect in this differentiation suggesting that the sibling who rejects another sibling secretly fears that he may be like his brother or sister. Among other siblings, the "I am not at all like you" process stands as a fragile distancing maneuver which suggests that siblings *do* indeed have much in common. Differentiating serves, then, as a way of externalizing or projecting deeply felt needs or anxieties. Projective identification between siblings can have all the force and power that it does between parents and children.

2. Mutual Regulation. Siblings serve as sounding boards for one another; they provide a safe laboratory for experimenting with new behavior where new roles are tried on, criticized, encouraged, or benevolently acknowledged before being used either with parents or non-family peers. Siblings provide an "observing ego" for one another that can exert an effective and corrective impact upon, and for, each other. The mutual regulatory process among brothers and sisters proceeds on the basis of fairness and honesty, a relationship among relative equals. Because siblings have fewer emotional obligations and experience relatively less guilt about each other, they naturally can influence and even counsel each other in a non-possessive way characteristic of effective psychotherapy.

> *A striking example of this was noted when one of the authors treated a family in which the 18-year-old daughter, the third of four girls, had become pregnant illegitimately and was one month away from having a baby of mixed racial parentage. Both older sisters and younger sister provided continuous emotional support combined with very direct and*

spontaneous questions about their sister's future. This process continued day and night for nearly two weeks. The sisters hardly emphasized the "damage" to family's reputation and reported to the therapist that they steered clear almost entirely of the question of whether having a black child would "hurt" mother and father. They focused instead on the question of how she could enjoy life, have a baby, and attend college at the same time. Their sympathetic concern regarding the boyfriend's possible rejection by other whites was cited by the girls as a major factor in prompting their sister to seek adoption for the baby.

In another case, the therapist invited two sisters of a suicidal college student to join the family therapy session. Relatively immobilized in the presence of the anguished mother and depressed father, the sisters became verbal, direct, and achieved noticeable rapport with their sib once their parents left the room. Shortly after, the girl began a significant reconstruction of her life with the continued instrumental assistance of her sisters who found her a new job, took her out shopping, and in general kept her active and goal-oriented.

3. Direct Services. Both within the family and outside, siblings perform valuable, tangible services for each other. In the every-day sibling ecology, brothers and sisters can make life easy or difficult for one another; they can be quiet, facilitative, sloppy and obstructive, or neat and cooperative. They teach each other skills, lend each other money, manipulate powerful friendship rewards for one another, and serve as controllers of resources; introduction to a new friendship group often depends on the kind auspices of one sibling to another. Brothers and sisters can act as buffers for each other, interposing themselves between their sib and the outside world. The exchange of goods and services among siblings in the emotional autonomy of the sibling underworld is in continuous flux and is subject to subtle and continuous negotiation, balancing, and change.

One sibling pair, brothers 11 and 8, describe their exchange of services this way. The older provided protection for the younger on the way to school. His large physical stature and willingness to stand up to anyone who picked on the younger boy provided safety. The 8-year-old, when asked if he felt he could pay his brother back in any way remarked that he "would never rat on him to his parents." When the parents found a knife they had not purchased in the 11-year-old's drawer, the younger brother stated that it was he rather than his brother who had taken it. This willingness to face down the parents served as a form of exchange with his older brother's willingness to run interference for him against other children. Such exchanges are seldom negotiated directly or explicitly, although siblings will sometimes make "deals" with one another e.g. "You let me borrow your records and I'll do your paper route for you tomorrow morning."

We are impressed with the ability of siblings to negotiate and bargain effectively with each other in a manner that would be instructive for most warring married couples!

4. Dealing with Parents: Coalitions. Siblings hold an enormously powerful trump card. One can benefit or harm another simply by the way in which their relationship with the parent is managed:

(a) An important function is that of *balancing* the power of the parents. In one family we observed that whenever the alcoholic father would become abusive toward the older brother, the sister would suggest that she and her brother play cards, get out of the house, or go for a walk. In the delicate set of family checks and balances, siblings can protect one another from parental-executive "abuse of power."

(b) *Joining* is another important function. Siblings together can negotiate with more strength against the parents than one of them acting alone. At the same time, if both sibs are misbehaving, neither sibling can be seen as the only offending party.

Two brothers, 18 and 16, were brought to family therapy because of repeated school truancy. A careful inquiry showed that John, the older, had been relatively stable until six months after his brother began acting out. He told the therapist in a separate session he hated to see his brother be singled out for so much criticism. Through misbehavior, he admitted that he was trying to balance the skewed pattern of criticism that was being leveled at his brother by attempting to draw notice to himself.

(c) *Secrets and Tattling.* Siblings know in many cases much more about one another's behavior than either of the parents. Tattling can be an important lever in the relationship between siblings. We have seen numerous siblings at war with one another because one sibling acted as an informer on the other's behavior to the parents. In other sibling groups, there is a conspiracy of silence, which the parents report to the therapist as an unbreakable understanding of the children from which the parents feel isolated and excluded. Siblings are the guardians of each others' private worlds. Willingness to make and maintain each other's privacy often serves as a powerful bond of loyalty among the children.

(d) *Translating Functions.* Siblings serve as a bridge for one another between their world and that of the adults. While Minuchin, *et al.* have referred to the fact that the oldest and healthiest child in disorganized families often serves as an interpreter to the siblings of external reality, we wish to make a somewhat different point. We see the siblings playing out what Gerald Zuk (27) has called the go-between process. In this process siblings mediate between one another; they mediate the outside world for their parents and may mediate the parents' relationship.

In particular, in families of young children we see the parents often rely upon one sibling to translate the meaning of another's silence or non-verbal gesture. When one sibling shrugs, grimaces, or falls silent, parents may ask another sibling, "What was that?" We have also noted that in families with young children the verbal behavior of the youngest is often intelligible to the older siblings whereas the parents cannot understand. In another family in which a child, aged 4, had a serious speech impediment, the 8-year-old brother provided an almost simultaneous translation of what the younger brother was saying to the parents who admitted their frustration at translating the 4-year-old's pathetic attempts at speech.

Siblings also serve as translators for one another for the behavior of their parents. They alert one another to punishment that may be forthcoming, signal each other about parents' moods and attitudes and warn each other about the consequences of transgressing against the parents. Finally, we see siblings as a group performing genuine educative functions for the parents. In numerous families we have observed children returning home to educate their parents about changes in the wider culture from which the parents may have been insulated. Siblings, in groups, can bring educational pressure to bear on parents, as is the case when the eldest has gone away to college, smokes marijuana, returns home, informs the parents who are aghast. Six months later his younger sister, a senior in high school, smokes marijuana, and the 14-year-old younger brother admits to the parents that he has tried it. The parental reaction to the smoking is much less than their initial horror. It seems frequently to be a function of what we call "educational pressure tactics" by the siblings who operate together as a cohesive force.

(e) A related function is *pioneering*. *Pioneering* seems to occur when one sibling initiates a process thereby giving permission to the others to follow accordingly. While the negative side of the scapegoating coin says, "If he does it, then I won't do it," the positive side says, "If he does it, then I can do it." We have observed many instances in which one sibling feels justified in continuing certain behaviors or maintaining a new value because the other sibling has "broken the ice" with the parents. The leader or "pioneer" generally feels satisfaction at having another sib emulate what he has begun, while the follower feels justified in that a pattern, which he claims no responsibility for, has already been set. These pioneering patterns include breaking explicit family rules, staying out late, smoking dope, driving the family car, spending allowance on the "wrong things," or taking new developmental pathways—e.g. leaving the family (or) adopting different morals/political codes, and lifestyles unimaginable to the parents.

> *In a recent family case, one of the sisters successfully terminated her prolonged empty marriage of eight years one year after a similar decision by her older sister. In confronting the parents' criticism, the theme, "If she can do it, I can do it," was very much in the air.*
>
> *This also happens in less dramatic ways in everyday life. Recently one of the author's daughters, age 12, began dancing provocatively to some contemporary music while her 13-year-old sister joined with her parents in laughing somewhat uneasily at the developmental implication of the dance. Two days later the pioneering daughter was joined in dance by her previously quiet sister and both laughed at the parents who sat, shaking their heads and smiling, aware that there was little to do about such an unfolding phenomenon once the "trail had been blazed."*

MOURNING AND LOSS: THE DEPARTURE OF SIBLINGS

The power of sibling relationships is most clearly demonstrated when a fundamental change in the structure of the sibling group occurs. These structural changes have enormous consequences. Trauma, such as the marriage or death of a sibling, the onset of illness, or even the divorce of a sibling from a spouse, can jolt a brother or sister. Normal separations can have profound consequences in that the support and other important processes that buttressed the sibling relationship are no longer taking place or have changed. Hospitalization, leaving home for school, marrying, and moving away all may be important precipitants of psychological disturbance in another sibling. This suggests that a complete history of sibling departure should be a significant focus for both the family and individually oriented therapists.

Beyond mourning, an internal process, the separation of siblings through life-cycle events can remove the buffer that the remaining sibling has between himself and his parents.

> *For the moment let us consider a system in which there were only two siblings. A college student who had been seen by one of the authors in individual therapy reported: "When my older brother left for college I had a terrible lump in my throat when he got on the bus. I felt that I had lost my best friend. In fact, I think he really is my best friend. After all, who else is there to shoot the bull with around the house? We used to double date and do all kinds of things together. I haven't felt the same since he left. And now all I do is sit around and listen to my mother mope, and you know what a drag that is." This student also reported that he felt much more confident when his brother was home. His brother radiated confidence and support in contrast to the parents who were chronically depressed.*

Sibling departures, then, can mean the loss of emotional support for the remaining siblings at home and also put the remaining sibling in a "naked" position with respect to the parents. The relationship with both parents, therefore, becomes overloaded for the remaining sibling, who often wishes that the departed sibling would return.

> *A 21-year-old borderline girl who had always functioned relatively well with the advice and assistance of her brother suddenly decompensated when her brother left home to go to Viet Nam. At this point she had to transact for herself (rather than through the*

brother) her relationship both with the parents and with the outside world. When referred for psychiatric help, she refused to accept treatment until her brother was present during a furlough from the Army. In the meantime, her relationship with both parents had been exposed as an angry one, frought with disappointment on the part of both the parents and her. Until that time, the realities of her disorientation had never been clear both because the brother had supported her and also because the family's attention had been focused upon her brother.

Siblings continue to influence one another even when they are not physically together and even when they have had little or no communication. The circumstances under which a sibling departs quickly can become mythologized both by the remaining sibling and the parents. This myth often serves as a legacy or object lesson that guides the family's relationship with the remaining sibling and influences the remaining sibling's conception of himself. It should be pointed out that sibling reputations are normal processes, that they may be facilitative as well as negative, as in the situation in which a successful older brother leaves in his wake the expectation by teachers and by the younger sister that the younger sister will do well. As a self-fulfilling prophecy this turns out to be so. But there are many examples, more frequently seen by family therapists, of the negative impact of sibling mythologies. In several cases in which we have seen the entire family, we have noticed that adolescents who appear to be emotionally paralyzed, afraid of taking risks, involved in only half-hearted efforts at differentiation, and who have substantial underlying depression, have older siblings who had previously experienced difficulties repeatedly needing psychiatric intervention. These older sibling legacies, serving as a morality play filtered by the parents, seem to produce paralysis. Because the sibling has often identified with the deviant unsuccessful one, he prematurely closes off options that he might otherwise have explored.

In two strikingly similar cases in which parents brought their 14-year-old sons in for therapy for a pattern of under-achievement and moderate depression, we obtained a history of an older sister who had been both abusing drugs and living a promiscuous life style that had ultimately led to prostitution. The families' reactions to both these boys had been extremely tentative, despite their progressive acting-out. It was as if a kid-glove approach was being used as a feeble effort to limit these boys' attempts to test the limits. In both family therapy situations, the parents expressed the fear that the departed, wayward daughters had influenced the remaining sons (despite clear evidence that the remaining sons were functioning better than their older sisters). Both families lived in the fear that if they "rocked the boat" with the younger male sibling, they could cause him to follow in the sister's footsteps. In a sense, the tail end of the hurricane of the previous sibling's disturbance paralyzed the attempt of the subsequent sibling to experience a clear rebellion against the parents, to act forcefully with the family on his own behalf during his adolescence. The fathers of both these boys, in reporting their difficulties, expressed the feeling, "Oh, no, not again!"

THE REACTION OF THE "WELL" SIBLING TO THE PSYCHOLOGICAL DISTURBANCE OF THE "SICK" ONE

How does a well sibling respond to brothers or sisters who become dysfunctional? With whom does he side in the family war? Genuine emotional neutrality is probably impossible in family relationships, and this principle certainly applies to the relationship between siblings. The well sibling is an involved participant in the crisis of the sick sibling. As a spectator and as a participant, he is witness to the wounds in both parents and in his sibling. The well sibling is then confronted with choices. "With whom shall I side, and what are the costs to me of side-taking?" There appear to be four general well-sibling strategies for dealing with the disturbance of the sick sibling.

Strategy No. 1. Flight and Avoidance. By far the most frequent strategy employed by the well sibling is to detach himself from the sick sibling *without* obviously siding with the parents. The well sibling tries to chart a course between the Scylla of the parents' need for support and the Charybdis of the disturbed sibling's need for friendship and coalition. He may feel sorry for, and angry at, the parents and the sick sibling simultaneously. His flight from both the sick sibling and the family is an attempt at resolving feelings of helplessness and paralysis. The well sibling leaves the family with relief, realizing that he could pay a high price for embroilment in family politics. He seeks coalition with other well siblings, peers, and people outside the family system who can offer more reward. The relief upon fleeing that the avoidant well sibling experiences is often mixed with guilt.

A 24-year-old young man who had a lifelong history of conflict with parents, school adjustment problems, and chronic depression, included, at the therapist's request, his 26-year-old sister. The therapist asked her why her brother was the one who had all the problems and what her view of this had been as a child. Her answer suggests the experience of the avoidant sibling. Well sibling: "I felt sorry for all of you: there was so much screaming and yelling between you and Mom and Dad. But I guess I just got out of the way, you know, I'd go up to my room and lie on my bed and listen. I used to wish that you could run away to another family where you could get along better. I always felt lousy for not standing up for you then. I was miserable, but never told anyone." Therapist: "So what did you do?" Well sibling: "I got married early, at 18. I came home as little as possible. I only started coming back to see Mom and Dad once you had gone off to college."

Another patient, 14 years old, a boy residing at an adolescent treatment unit, had run away from home and had been placed in the institution at his own request. His three brothers remained in an urban slum with alcoholic, and probably psychotic, parents. His own adjustment was healthy. He expressed to his counselor, however, a strong sense of guilt regarding what he called his "copping out on my brothers." He eventually began to AWOL from the institution, each time returning by himself from his home visits. His explanation was that his returns home were "check-ups" to make certain that his brothers were still alive and well; he said he bore some responsibility to see that things did not get worse. This boy, like the sister in the previous example, seemed to be burdened with the question: "By what right do I survive while the others suffer so much?" (Robert J. Lifton, in his book Death in Life *(15) refers to the survivors of holocausts such as Hiroshima as being burdened with survivor guilt. Well siblings may experience some of the same feelings.) Well siblings of the type described here often involve themselves in family therapy sessions with a sense of energy verging on urgency as if to expiate themselves from the guilty yoke they seem to carry.*

Stretegy No. 2. Well Sibling Sides with Parents Against Sick Sibling. If the parents seem to have developed a strong, rewarding emotional bond with the well sibling *and* well sibling has played an earlier policeman-like, parental role with the sick sibling, the well sibling often appears as a "white sheep." He has little to gain by supporting the deviant brother or sister. In the eyes of the sick sibling, the well sibling appears too good, somewhat smug, and his behavior toward the sick sibling may appear self-righteous and impatient. If the sick sibling's symptoms become directed against the well sibling (as well as the parents) the sudden fury of the scapegoating process of the triad, well sibling plus parents against sick sibling, can take on considerable force. The addition of an unsympathetic well sibling to the scapegoating can make scapegoating total, the isolation profound. Like the subjects of Asch's early conformity experiments, the sick sibling loses his only ally in the family when he attacks his sibling, and this may place sick sibling in a weak and pressure-prone position with respect to the demands of the family. The attack of well sibling upon sick sibling is not necessarily an obvious process.

Without an obvious coalition with the parents, the well sibling can join the parents in a *de facto* way. The well sibling by quietly aggravating his disturbed brother or sister produces an unacceptable explosion in the sick sibling that leads to parental criticism of the sick sibling. The well sibling remains silent, but his neutrality and manipulation serve as an acknowledgement that he is really on the parents' side.

> *For example, a 7-year-old boy who knows his younger brother is extremely sensitive to noise plays his record player too loud. The younger boy attacks the older, while the "subtle aggravator" manages an air of innocence.*

Incidents of this kind can produce, over time, a shadow coalition between the well siblings and the parents. Over many years, if the well sibling gives the sick sibling "enough rope to hang himself," the sick sibling achieves the scapegoat status previously described.

Strategy No. 3. Well Sibling Forms a Friendly Coalition on the Side of the Sick Sibling. Siblings often find strength in unity. We have worked with numerous sibling pairs in which the sick sibling and the well sibling act out together with force of tandem action, overwhelming the parent or parents. The effect is to nullify and cancel out some of the parental scapegoating of the sick sibling.

> *Thus, in one case, a relatively well older adolescent sister began joining her brother on his drinking binges, defying the parents and staying out beyond a reasonable hour. The older sister had much resentment of her own, until now unexpressed, which became directed toward the parents through her coalition with her brother. The brother and sister, in family therapy sessions, joked openly with each other about their exploits, while the parents helplessly looked on. Here the alliance between the well and sick sibling served both siblings' need for support in a power struggle with the parents. Rebellion, as well as differentiation from parents, was served by a mutual egging-on process.*

We have found such coalitions *against* parents usually serving other important needs of both siblings. One example would be active protection of the sick sibling by the well sibling who identifies with the sick one's plight. Through coalition with the sick sibling, the well sibling can vicariously relieve and rework personal issues cut off by avoidance in previous years.

> *Another older sister, 30, joined family therapy sessions for her "kid" brother, 16, with whom she had very little contact for three years. An instant coalition was formed with the sister taking the brother's side and arguing for more time and interest to be shown to him. Her own older struggles with the parents, she admitted, were being expressed through the brother: "This time," she told her father, "bring up one of your kids the right way."*

Frequently, well sibling-sick sibling coalitions are of a more "undercover" or subtle variety with the well sibling supporting the sick sibling without risking going public with this support—i.e., letting the parents know. We have seen frequent instances of the well sibling providing comfort and direct support for the sib who had been embroiled with the parents.

> *A 25-year-old woman in individual treatment reported that her older well sister could never criticize her parents when all four of them were together. The older sister found public siding with the "sick" sister risky. But the older sister was clearly supportive when seen by the therapist alone with her "sick" sib. She advised her how to avoid fights with the parents, how to stand her ground, and how to keep out of parental arguments. By siding quietly, the older sister maintained a warm rapport with her "sick" sib and maintained a cordial though bland and inoffensive relationship with their parents.*

Strategy No. 4. Well Siblings and the Go-Between Process. The go-between process described by Zuk (27) describes this particular well sibling strategy. By playing the role of the "interested third," he or she tries to mediate in the quarrels in the family and assumes the role of peacemaker. He might be described as a parental sibling in the following sense. He is parental both to his own disturbed sibling and also toward his parents' anxious and immature ways of responding to the sick sibling. Constantly acting as oil on troubled waters, providing a buffer for all family conflicts, this sib keeps the family stuck in its comfortable misery. The family therapist must often be involved in helping this kindly mediator to remove himself from the family embroilment. The therapist must skillfully remove this sibling who represents, to the therapist, a pseudo-therapeutic rival. The procedures by which the therapist works with this go-between sibling are somewhat delicate and will be described in the next section.

SIBLINGS IN FAMILY THERAPY

We make sibling relationships an important focus in family therapy, wherever possible, no matter what the age of the identified patient might be. In childhood and in the teenage years, one of the principal reasons for referral is trouble in the sibling system: children are fighting with one another, are unfraternal, are ganging up against the parents, etc. While there is often less action in the sibling sub-system during the middle adult years (25-50), action resumes as the parents grow older and siblings must turn to each other for the care of sick and aging parents. After parents die, sibs offer the only ties to their family of origin.

Using Sibling Concepts to Relabel Family Problems. Both in individual and family therapy, we take a complete anamnesis of sibling relationships. We ascertain, as does Toman, the sibling status relationships of all members of the family. This diagnostic information can prove valuable in the kinds of interpretations used in family therapy.

> A father and mother, the parents of two boys 10 and 8, were seen with their children because the children were reported to be fighting viciously with one another. The parents felt both embarrassed and guilty about the obstreperous behavior of their offspring and seemed at a loss for any effective action other than screaming at them and breaking up the conflict. This parental interaction usually resulted in more fighting between the children.
>
> As a way of connecting in a positive and non-guilt-inducing manner with both parents, the therapist, after taking a history, pointed out these facts: (a) that the mother had been an only child and therefore lacked experience in dealing with sibling conflict; (b) that the father had been separated by six years in age from his only other sibling; (c) that the two boys were very close in age and in physical stature, which normatively meant there would be a struggle for power and balance. These comments gave the family a view of this situation as a normal and explainable process and permitted the therapist to make his next observation, which involved removing the parents from the sibling fighting system so that the children could be left to establish their own ways of resolving conflict.

Siblings as Consultants. We routinely try to ascertain from the identified patient which siblings he or she sees as helpful. We try to "import" these siblings into individual and family therapy, usually on a brief basis, using them in order to move the therapy in certain strategic directions. At times, we hold a separate meeting with one or more siblings of the identified patient, usually *not* in the presence of parents, because siblings tend to demonstrate their loyalties more openly when free of the need to choose sides with the parents present. We have had repeated experiences of "importing" absent siblings from afar to provide a new context for the family's symptoms. This is especially useful during a crisis or when the family appears to be reaching an impasse with the therapist. With considerable drama, the therapist may announce that a geographically distant sibling is essential for the progress of the therapy. We try to build this drama so that, when the absent sibling comes into the family session, the family hopes are high and their anxiety is raised to the point of representing a useful crisis.

A 14-year-old girl and her parents were seen for three sessions when the girl, who was over-involved in a relationship with an older boy, became despondent and rather manipulatively threatened suicide. She refused to talk with either parent in the therapist's presence, and the therapy seemed to be going nowhere. Having ascertained that her brother, Bill, who was at a university on the opposite coast, had been her closest compatriot during her growing-up years, the therapist asked the family's permission to bring Bill home across a distance of 3500 miles to participate in the family therapy session. Having obtained this permission, the therapist, in his office, on the spot, phoned Bill, and he agreed to be on the first plane out the next morning. Within 24 hours, he had returned home for his first visit in a year, and a three-hour meeting was held the same day with the 14-year-old and the older brother. What ensued was typical of such meetings. The imported sibling, as an outsider, shed significant light on the family's functioning, was able to speak directly and openly to his sibling, duly expressed support for her but also expressed constructive criticism, and acted as a consultant for the therapist about the family. He simultaneously drew some of the parents' heat away from the spotlighted sister.

This process must not be abused by the therapist. The imported sibling is willing to serve as a consultant largely because he knows he can return to a safe place outside the family. The family appreciates his viewpoint because he often has a privileged status. But at the same time, the therapist must not pressure the imported sibling into damaging his own relationship to the family by revealing too many secrets. The therapist must make certain that he does not use the imported sibling in a parental way. It must be remembered that the imported sibling must get something for himself from this session too. We usually take pains to ensure the sibling-guest-consultant a chance to verbalize something of his own unmet needs. Another caution we have learned is not to over-burden already over-taxed siblings. This can have disastrous consequences for the therapy.

In a large, lower-class family of six children in which the symptomatic child was retarded and presented behavior problems, the therapist assigned several tasks to the oldest daughter to carry out. Week after week the family would return with the tasks accomplished, a not unusual finding in families in which the oldest daughter is quite competent. Upon the assignment of yet another task, the oldest daughter finally stood up and said that she was sick of having to take care of everybody in the family and walked out of the session. The family did not return to the therapy because the daughter's participation and presence was considered by them as an essential keystone in their functioning. Parental children usually resent their statuses, and if the therapist decides to employ them in working on a sibling relationship, he must make certain that he simultaneously frees the parental sibling for a more rewarding life.

Sibling Rehearsals. We have noted that siblings often rehearse behaviors with their brothers and sisters that they later try out on parents and in the outside world. We have capitalized on this fact in our therapy format by inviting siblings in for a session so that the patient's rehearsal of important new behavior can take place. Because siblings are usually less threatening to the identified patient than parents or other people and because other siblings are more receptive, we find this provides a good warm-up.

A severely obese, unhappy, young woman in her late 20's came to the realization that she was, if not homosexual, then bi-sexual in her orientation. Terrified of announcing this to her parents, she was encouraged to discuss it first with her sisters by bringing them in to therapy sessions. At a later time she was then able to get enough courage to announce this to her parents in the presence of her sisters, whose support had been garnered. Interestingly, the women in this family, three sisters and the mother, began holding their own consciousness-raising sessions after the family therapy stopped, discussing intimate sexual matters with one another and then achieving a closeness not hitherto attained.

Sibling Rallies.[1] We frequently call a meeting of the entire sibling group, with the parents temporarily excluded. The purpose of the sibling rally is to foster encouragement, support, greater honesty, and understanding within the sibling sub-group. At times our purpose is to help the identified sibling patient live down his scapegoat or mental-patient status with siblings present; at other times it may be to work out a specific issue in which the sibling patient feels that he or she has been treated unfairly.

Doreen, 34, the mother of three children, and a single parent, was repeatedly called upon to take care of her alcoholic and aging parents. Her parents came to her house only at Christmas and Thanksgiving, required her continuous care when they were drunk, and when illness struck, she was the one (the only member of her sibling group—she had an older brother and younger sister) who cared for the parents. The therapist, who was seeing Doreen with her three children, obtained this information almost accidentally. Because of the tremendous strain the grandparents were placing on Doreen, it was clear that her capacity to mother her own children was sorely limited. At this point the therapist called for a sibling rally. The older and younger siblings gladly came in for two sessions in which the patient raised, with some bitterness, the issue of her status as the one who was over-responsible. Her brother and sister agreed that she had over-functioned but at the same time criticized her for making it impossible for them to take a role with their parents. After a period of heated conflict among the siblings, new balance was achieved in which the labor of caring for the parents was more equally divided.

In another situation, a 19-year-old boy who had been hospitalized twice for psychotic kinds of episodes was feared by both parents who, despite intensive family therapy, clung to their worry that he was permanently mentally ill. This was despite the fact that the patient demonstrated clearly that his two hospitalizations had been induced by LSD rather than any longstanding schizophrenic process. The therapist felt that the patient had been mis-diagnosed at the hospital in which he had been placed and that the image of chronic schizophrenic had been accepted by the family. While it was impossible to unlabel this young man with his parents, we called for a sibling rally in which his siblings warmly responded to the patient's progress and admitted how "fixed" Mother and Dad seemed to be about his being a mental patient. Steve, the identified patient, felt that the meetings with siblings had given him greater pride and renewed confidence in himself; the approval of parents became less important.

Sibling Exile. In many families we find there is a well sibling who serves (see section on well sibling-sick sibling relations) as an interested third party, mediating between the parents and the disturbed sibling. This sibling keeps the family on an uneasy but stable balance, and we see his sibling role as too brotherly, too parental, and his role with the parents as too parentified. In order for the necessary conflict to occur between the sick sibling and his parents, we try to find a way to extract the mediator sibling from the conflict.

Mother brought her teen-age, 17-year-old son in for therapy. They lived on a modest income with the older brother, aged 21. The mother was extremely concerned about depression in the younger son and about the possibility of violence at home. The younger boy's angry feelings were directed continuously toward his older brother who acted as an agent of mother, as a replacement for the dead father.

The therapist felt that the proper direction for the 17-year-old's conflict would by toward the mother, but this could not happen until we helped the older boy to leave home. In a family therapy session in which the older sibling was included, we pointed out that there was a difference between a brother and a father, that the older brother could be a good brother but not a father, and that we empathized with the older brother because of his "stunted" life. When he inquired what we meant by stunted life, we pointed out that he was missing a lot of fun by playing "junior therapist" to mother and brother. It was suggested to the older brother that mother had had the wisdom to hire herself and her younger son a therapist so that perhaps the older boy could now afford to retire from his position of unlicensed family therapist and live his own life. The following week he made tentative plans to move out of the house, and the conflict between the mother and the younger sibling increased. This was viewed by the therapist as a healthy increase of tensions. At this point the normal adolescent conflict between son and mother could be worked with directly without undue interference from the older brother.

CONCLUSIONS

One writer suggests that adults, and the present authors would add family therapists, may have an "adultomorphic" perception of the world of children. ". . . if the younger generation were to conduct inquiries concerning family life, their perception of members' roles would quite likely be quite different . . . Museum examples of household rooms constructed to fit the eye level perspective of young children suggests how a 'view from below' might considerably alter the assessment of the relative importance of parental, sibling, and peer influences (12, p. 284)." Family therapists, perhaps because of their own middle position in their life cycles, with heavy involvement in the rearing of their own children, have paid too little attention to observation, theory, and research in the area of sibling interaction and sibling psychotherapy. As we have all heard in another context: "Sisterhood-brotherhood is powerful."

FOOTNOTE

[1] A video interview (a Sony 3600) of a sibling rally can be obtained on request from Dr. Stephen Bank, 109 Broad Street, Middletown, Conn. 06457.

REFERENCES

1. Adler, A. *Understanding Human Nature*, New York, Premier Books (Fawcett Publications), 1959.
2. Anthony, E. J. and Koupernik, C. (Eds.). *The Child in His Family, Vol. I*, New York, Wiley-Interscience, 1970.
3. Bank, S. A Study of the Time Spent by Same-Sex Siblings With One Another, in preparation.
4. Bossard, J. H. S. and Boll, E. S., *The Large Family System*, Philadelphia, University of Pennsylvania Press, 1956.
5. Bowen, M., "Toward the Differentiation of Self in One's Own Family," pp. 111-174, in J. Framo (Ed.), *Family Interaction: A Dialogue Between Therapists and Researchers*, New York, Springer, 1972.
6. Boszormenyi-Nagy, I. and Spark, G. M., *Invisible Loyalties*, Hagerstown, Md., Harper & Row, 1973.
7. Caplow, T., *Two Against One: Coalition in Triads*, Englewood Cliffs, New Jersey, Prentice-Hall, 1968.
8. Gerstl, J., *Coalitions in the Sibling Triad*, Minneapolis, University of Minnesota, Dept. of Sociology, mimeograph, 1956.
9. Greenbaum, M., "Joint Sibling Interview As a Diagnostic Procedure," *J. Child Psychol. Psychiat.* 6:227-232, 1965.
10. Grossman, F., *Brothers and Sisters of Mentally Retarded Children*, Syracuse, N.Y., Syracuse University Press, 1972.

11. Hoover, C. and Franz, J. O., "Siblings in the Families of Schizophrenics," *Arch. Gen. Psychiat.,* 26:334-342, 1972.
12. Irish, D. P., "Sibling Interaction: A Neglected Aspect in Family Life Research," *Social Forces,* 42:269-288, 1964.
13. Levy, D. M., *Sibling Rivalry,* American Orthopsychiatric Association Research Monograph No. 2, 1937.
14. Lidz, T., Fleck, S., and Cornelison, A., *Schizophrenia and the Family,* New York, International University Press, 1965.
15. Lifton, R., *Death in Life: Survivors of Hiroshima,* New York, Random House, 1967.
16. Minuchin, S., Montalvo, B., *et al., Families of the Slums,* New York, Basic Books, Inc. 1967.
17. Minuchin, S., *Families and Family Therapy,* Cambridge, Mass., 1974, Harvard University Press.
18. Mishler, G. and Waxler, N., *Interaction in Families.* New York, John Wiley & Sons, 1968.
19. Newmann, G., "Younger Brothers of Schizophrenics," *Psychiatry,* 29:146-151, 1966.
20. Quinn, O. and Stein, J., "The Social Interaction Patterns of the Quadruplets" in D. Rosenthal, (Ed.), *The Genain Quadruplets,* New York, Basic Books, 1963.
21. Rabin, A. I., *Growing Up in the Kibbutz,* New York, Springer, 1965.
22. Riskin, J. M. and Faunce, E. E., "An Evaluative Review of Family Interaction Research," *Fam. Proc.,* 11: 1972, 365-455.
23. Satir, V., *Conjoint Family Therapy,* Palo Alto, California, Science & Behavior Book, 1967.
24. Sutton-Smith, B. and Rosenberg, B. G., *The Sibling,* New York, Holt, Rinehart & Winston, 1970.
25. Toman, W., *Family Constellation,* New York, Springer Pub., 2nd ed., 1969.
26. Vogel, N. and Bell, W., "The Emotionally Disturbed Child as the Family Scapegoat" in: *A Modern Introduction to the Family,* The Free Press, New York, 1968, pp. 412-427.
27. Zuk, G., *Family Therapy: A Triadic-Based Approach,* New York, Behavioral Publications, 1972.

part 4

extended-family relationships

INTRODUCTION

This part on extended family relationships focuses primarily on in-law and intergenerational relationships. In our society when people marry, they are supposed to shift their primary loyalty from their original family to their newly formed conjugal relationship and the new family that may arise from it. In-law and intergenerational relationships can be studied together under the heading of extended-family relationships. What constitutes an in-law relationship for one spouse is often an intergenerational relationship for the other. An understanding of in-law and intergenerational relationships is central to the understanding of interpersonal relationships within the family.

No attempt has been made in this section to consider the broader concept of kinship. Those who might question the importance of extended-family relationships in contemporary industrial society are referred to Brasher's (1970) article on kinship in our time. In fact, whole books have been written on the subject of kinship. The interested reader would also do well to examine the works of Farber (1966, 1968, 1971, 1977), since he is one of the most outstanding authors of kinship studies. In one of his studies, he explains: "Kinship is not simply an extension of family relationships: it defines the ways in which nuclear families are expected to interact with one another and places constraints on interaction with families. Kinship thus exists as a context in shaping familial behavior" (Farber, 1971:5).

The research that has been conducted on in-law relationships has been exceedingly limited. The most thorough exploration of in-law relationships was reported by Duvall (1954) in a very readable book and was based on the results of an investigation of an adult sample of 5,020 men and women. Much of what Duvall discovered about interpersonal relationships with in-laws probably still holds true for contemporary in-law relationships.

One of Duvall's more outstanding findings was the fact that women appeared more likely than men to be involved in in-law problems. Duvall suggested that women were more often reported as difficult in-laws to get along with and women themselves reported having more difficulty in getting along with their in-laws because the family roles of women more frequently emphasize close interpersonal relationships within the family. Research results yielded the following ranking, from high to low, in terms of the frequency of reports of problems with specific in-laws: mother-in-law, sister-in-law, brother-in-law, and father-in-law. The most frequently voiced complaints regarding mothers-, sisters-, and fathers-in-law were the same—"meddles, interferes, dominates, intrudes on our privacy, etc.," whereas the primary complaint offered about brothers-in-law cited incompetence or inability to do a job well. Difficulties with mothers-in-law were reported by 491 subjects, with sisters-in-law by 272 subjects, with brothers-in-law by 72 subjects, and with fathers-in-law by 52 subjects. Out of the total sample, 345 subjects gave specific reasons why their in-laws were not a problem. From these data it was learned that a feeling of acceptance and a lack of meddling and interference were present in the majority of problem-free in-law relationships. Since the conjugal relationship is highly valued in our society, any member of either family who intrudes on the autonomy of the married couple runs the risk of being perceived as a difficult in-law. However, since many subjects reported no in-law problems, in-law relationships are not necessarily problematic.

The reading by Leader *(33)*, which examines the place of in-laws in the marital relationship describes the various kinds of in-law relationships which prevailed among the clients Leader was seeing in a therapeutic setting. These kinds of in-law relationships, however, may not be as common throughout the general population.

Another research study that dealt with in-law relationships was conducted by Spicer and Hampe (1975), who interviewed 62 divorced men and 42 divorced women in a study of kinship interaction after divorce. They found that interpersonal relationships with former affinal kin were more likely to be maintained by divorcées who had custody of the children. These individuals were more likely to maintain interpersonal relationships with their former spouse's relatives in order to allow their children to continue interacting with members from both sides of the family. The influence of our bilateral lineage system apparently plays a significant role here. For both consanguine and affinal kin, continued interfamily visiting after divorce is highest for parents, next for siblings, and considerably lower for other kin. The percentages are consistently higher for visitation with consanguines than affines and higher for those with children than for those without.

We often hear that our society is very neglectful of the elderly. Shanas (1973) studied family-kin networks and aging from a cross-cultural perspective. Data for the United States were compared with comparable data for Denmark, Britain, Yugoslavia, Poland, and Israel. One measure of the socio-emotional distance between kin is the frequency with which they see each other. For the United States it was found that among persons aged 65 and over who were not living with a child, 52 percent had seen a child in the last 24 hours and 78 percent had seen a child within the last week. These findings were quite similar to those for the other industrialized nations studies. In all of those countries, Shanas pointed out that there was a recognition of the right for the aged to live separately from their adult children. Still, a majority of the aged parents in the United States live with or within ten minutes' distance from a child.

The findings reported by Johnson and Bursk in their article *(34)* on the relationships between the elderly and their adult children echo much of what was reported earlier by Shanas. However, it should be pointed out that there is considerable variation as to how much contact the elderly have with their adult children. Arling (1976) and Bild and Havighurst (1976) reported significant variation among subgroups of the elderly in their samples. They also found that the degree of extended-family interaction depended upon the health status and economic resources of the elderly. Those with good health, physical mobility, and ample economic resources interact more frequently with their children and other members of the extended family.

Extended-family relationships vary by social class and upper-class families are better able to remain actively involved in an extended family because of the economic assets and prestige. When they travel, they are able to cover considerable distances without major financial sacrifice. Upper-middle-class families tend to have greater geographic mobility, but they can afford to keep in touch by telephone and travel by airplane. Because extended families tend to be separated by greater geographical distances, patterns of support frequently take the form of financial assistance rather than child care or home nursing. Since, in general, the upper-middle-class elderly are quite secure financially, financial support is usually provided by the older generation to the younger one. For the working class, relationships between adult children and their parents depend on residential proximity (Komarovsky, 1962; Young and Wilmott, 1962). If working-class parents move away from their extended families during retirement, this can bring about a reduction in extended-family interaction. Members of the lower social class usually do not leave home to get ahead in the occupational world. They are not involved in the pursuit of upward social mobility, which is accomplished by going where the jobs are located, and they do not have the economic resources to provide much in the way of financial support. Consequently, members of lower-class families are more actively involved in the exchange of personal services between the generations.

Readers who are interested in an account of the plight of the elderly are referred to Johnson's (1971, 1977) research. Johnson found that, among working-class retirees who lived in a trailer-court community, neighbors often performed tasks generally associated with extended-family roles. Arling (1976), in a study of elderly widows, showed that white widows saw more of their adult children whereas black widows were more active in organizations and knew more of their neighbors. He concluded that some groups resisted isolation by means of extended-family contacts whereas others relied more heavily on friends.

Many of the elderly live in semi-isolated situations, and those who are poor and disabled or diseased do not have the physical or economic ability to remain actively involved in extended-family relationships. For the less-advantaged elderly, contacts are more easily managed with friends and neighbors than with members of the extended family.

Turner's *(35)* article offers a brief review of nine theoretical models used to explain the patterns of intergenerational exchange. In the article, Turner concludes that the "younger adult generation" (or middle generation) emerges as the center of control or power in the patterns of three-generation-family exchange. A similar view is offered in an article by Robertson, who found considerable support for the "postulate that parents act as mediators between the grandparent and grandchild generations in socializing both into their relationship" (Robertson, 1975:103).

One classical study which has made a significant contribution to intergenerational research is a study of three generations of the same families conducted by Hill and his associates (1970). Their findings, which support many of the previously stated conclusions regarding the importance of extended-family relationships in our contemporary society, led them:

> To conclude that although intergenerational transactions do appear to be governed in part by the norm of reciprocity that two other norms are even more apparent, namely the norms of filial obligation and of noblesse oblige. These latter norms appear to be sufficient to motivate an optimum level of kin keeping activities designed to maintain viable modified extended family networks [Hill, et al., 1970:80].

In another study that utilized three generations from the same family as subjects, Bengtson (1971) examined inter-age perceptions and the generation gap, using a sample of 84 three-generation families. The average age of the grandparents was 75 years, that of the parents was 44 years, and that of the grandchildren was 17 years. Bengtson reported that the age of the respondent made a considerable difference in terms of the degree to which a generation gap was perceived. The youngest age-group, the grandchildren, saw a larger gap between the generations than did either the parental or the grandparental groups. These findings were seen as support for the "developmental stake" theory, which indicates that, whereas the younger generation has its reasons for emphasizing intergenerational differences, the parental and grandparental generations have their reasons for minimizing such differences.

In the final reading of this section, Robertson focuses on the special roles often associated with grandparents in our society *(36)*. Although this article is a report of research based upon the perceptions of young adult grandchildren, Robertson (1977) has also researched the topic from the perspective of grandmothers. This reading was chosen because it examines the significance of grandparental roles in general and does not focus on the roles of either sex in particular.

REFERENCES

Arling, G. Resistance to isolation among elderly widows. *International Journal of Aging and Human Development 7*, no. 1 (1976):67-86.

Bengtson, V. L. Inter-age perceptions and the generation gap. *The Gerontologist 11*, nos. 4, 2 (1971):85-89.

Bild, B. R., and Havighurst, R. J. Senior citizens in great cities: The case of Chicago. *The Gerontologist 16,* nos. 1, 2 (1976):4-88.

Brasher, R. E. Kinship in our time. *Family Perspective 5,* no. 1 (1970):4-9.

Duvall, E. M. *In-laws: Pro and con.* New York: Association Press, 1954.

Farber, B. *Comparative Kinship Systems.* New York: Wiley and Sons, 1968.

Farber, B. *Kinship and class.* New York: Basic Books, 1971.

Farber, B., ed. *Kinship and family organization.* New York: Wiley and Sons, 1966.

Farber, B. Social context, kinship mapping, and family norms. *Journal of Marriage and the Family 39,* (1977):227-40.

Hill, R., Foote, N., Aldous, J., Carlson, R., and MacDonald, R. *Family development in three generations.* Cambridge, Mass.: Schenkman, 1970.

Johnson, S. K. *Idle heaven: Community building among the working-class retired.* Berkeley: University of California, 1971.

Johnson, S. K. Maintaining contact with sons and daughters: A problem of the elderly. In *People as Partners,* edited by J. P. Wiseman, pp. 325-33. 2nd ed. San Francisco: Canfield Press, 1977.

Komarovsky, M. *Blue-collar marriage.* New York: Random House, 1962.

Robertson, J. F. Interaction in three generation families, parents as mediators: Toward a theoretical perspective. *International Journal of Aging and Human Development 6,* no. 2 (1975):103-10.

Robertson, J. F. Grandmotherhood: A study of role conceptions. *Journal of Marriage and the Family 39* (1977):165-74.

Shanas, E. Family-kin networks and aging in cross-cultural perspective. *Journal of Marriage and the Family, 35* (1973):505-11.

Spicer, J. W., and Hampe, G. D. Kinship interaction after divorce. *Journal of Marriage and the Family 37* (1975):113-19.

Young, M., and Willmott, P. *Family and kinship in east London.* Rev. ed. Baltimore: Pelican Books, 1962.

33   the place of in-laws in marital relationships

arthur l. leader

When a person matures and separates from his parents, eventually creating his own family, he will ordinarily have gradually enlarged his circle of social contacts, responsibilities, and ties. In entering marriage as part of a new phase of the life cycle, he takes on a special relationship that creates a new demand for sharing and reciprocity. Although he has separated from his original home and family, he continues to have some kind of relationship with them, the quality dependent in large part upon the previous texture of the relationship. In addition to maintaining these ties—indeed embedded in them through a matrix of social and family values and affects—he works out some adaptation to the family of his spouse that is determined in part by his relationship to his family of origin.

Therefore, the beginning marital relationship—in addition to requiring a variety of new adjustments by the couple, for which courtship and engagement had, it is hoped, partially prepared them—involves a complex set of new relationships to one's own family and to the spouse's family. Each family, of course, must also make its own adaptation to the moving out of a child and the advent of an incoming daughter- or son-in-law.

The readiness of the marriage partner to take on and to form significant ties to his in-laws can be viewed as an additional step toward maturity. It is a challenge and a difficult task to relate simultaneously to one's family of origin, a new partner, and a new in-law family, especially when the couple's personalities, careers, and interests are not always fully formed.

In family therapy, one becomes increasingly aware of the importance of intergenerational connections and the linkages between families of origin and the in-law families. One of the few relevant references indicates that "it is . . . of paramount importance to understand the unity and/or disharmony between one's original family system and its in-law system."[1]

The varieties of meaning that the in-laws have for the spouse sometimes include, surprisingly, a value that transcends the importance of the marital relationship itself. In fact, some spouses go through one or more marriages looking for but never able to find the "proper" in-laws. In a sense, for them the marriage serves as a bridge that attempts, unsuccessfully, to span the unresolved gulf between themselves and their own family.

This article discusses some of the meanings that in-laws represent for the spouse. The focus is on this phenomenon largely because there seems to be little coverage of it in the literature, yet expanded exploration in family therapy indicates wide variety in the search for family substitutes and repopulations, which have great power and impact concurrently upon several generations.

Literature, both fictional and professional, is full of analyses of the profound phenomena—psychological, social, and cultural—that draw two people into marriage. The predominant psychological forces are often subtle and unconscious, based to some extent on the concept of transference.

Reprinted, by permission, from *Social Casework*, 1975, *56*, 486-91. Copyright ©1975 by Family Service Association of America.

Many people in looking for permanent alliances are attracted to important figures reminiscent of their past who have had significant positive or negative meanings for them. It is not uncommon to seek out as a partner of the opposite sex a very similar, or very different, parent substitute. Most often the key figure from the past is of the opposite sex, but not always. For example, a wife may be looking for a mother figure through the kind of husband she unconsciously selects. By the same token, as viewed through the concept of complementarity, the husband has his own need to be more of a mother than a father to his wife. Again, this may be an accepting or rejecting mother figure or an ambivalent one.

OLD PROBLEMS, NEW FAMILIES

This article is concerned with that group of people who in entering a marriage are also attempting unconsciously either to express or to work through old problems within their original families, not so much through the marital partner as through the partner's family, and often through one parent. That parent may be the mother or the father, an accepting or rejecting figure, or both. Because a family is more than the sum of its parts, the significant, unconsciously sought object may be a particular kind of family with a special kind of status, constellation, size, atmosphere, or style.

The importance of the family in meeting basic needs and in shaping values and personality is fundamental, and the power of family continuity and ties is universal. Thus, it is natural for individuals leaving their own families for marriage to carry with them a deep sense of family. It is natural for a person contemplating marriage, or even leaving home without marrying, to seek, usually unconsciously, the kind of family he will be joining. If his is a healthy emancipation from his own family, he may tend to seek a family that fits complementarily with his own. If he still has unresolved conflicts with his family upon leaving home for marriage or other reasons, he may also be alert to the kind of family he will be acquiring. In the latter situation, he is apt to look for a family like his own, so that unconsciously he may continue the neurotic pattern, although a few seek partners with an opposite type of family in an attempt to receive what they did not have before. These people are, in a sense, unconsciously using the spouse in a new socially acceptable manner as a way of making substitute connections to significant others. Unfortunately, this selection process seldom seems to work. Some individuals and couples need a strong tie to the past; the striving is toward some sense of family continuity and fulfillment. Others, needing a distant connection, are able to achieve a sense of family by creating their own new families.

In the selection of foster homes, of course, agencies deliberately attempt to make up for the traumas or deficits within the original family. In other family-like arrangements as well as alternate life-styles including communes, where there is no formal marriage, there seems to be a strong effort to capture or reproduce the essential ingredients of family bonds and living. Even if parents or parental substitutes are not designated, authority, leadership, and caretaking figures do tend to emerge, providing either the battleground on which to attempt to continue old wars or new opportunities for gratifying old needs. Some families seem tailor-made either in their replication of or contrast to the original family. As the importance of these acquired connections to the partner is understood, it can be appreciated how the marital relationship, serving as it does as a conduit to something more rooted and primitive, may become secondary and thereby a source of great conflict to the marital pair, often without their knowing why.

For many individuals who are enmeshed in conflict with their parents, marriage sometimes seems to hold out the promise of finding new family experiences or correcting old ones. It holds the attraction of apparent opportunities for physical and emotional separation, a new home, and, most important, a new family with a new set of ready-made parents. However, most of these marriages are doomed to failure because the neurotic use of in-laws can seldom resolve old conflicts. The in-laws are sometimes sought for the following primary purposes: (1) to assist in the continuation of a happy family life through an extension to in-laws as part of the life cycle as described above; (2) to find the love, affection, and approval through one or both in-laws not found in the original home; (3) to meet the need for social climbing and financial support; or (4) to prove that one or both new parents, like the original ones, are rejecting and cold, thereby insuring and reinforcing the repetitious pattern in yet another arena.

Many relationships, marital and other, flavored to some extent with transference phenomena, work out well. Seeking satisfactions within the family of in-laws is a natural and healthy extension. Many partners are able to obtain gratification through their spouses and their families on many levels so long as there is a reciprocal arrangement—or a complementary fit among most members. Conflict arises when the partner seeks but does not find what he needs, either beacuse the in-laws are unwilling or unable to meet the need or because the method of expressing the need unwittingly alienates them. There may be other complicated reasons why at a particular stage in their life cycle the in-laws are unable to make sufficient room for a new member of the extended family. Conflict may also arise when the partner does find what he needs but in the finding revives or creates rivalry within his mate.

Fantasy plays an extensive role in the subsequent extreme disillusionment and frustration that develop. The person who propels himself into marriage as a means of fleeing from his family with the expectation that he will acquire a different family is generally doomed to a poor relationship with his wife and both families. He becomes not only angry at the in-laws but tends to blame his wife for not making things better between them. She, in addition to feeling caught between him and her parents, sometimes feels, not unrealistically, that she has been used for something beyond her.

CASE ILLUSTRATIONS

The wife of one young couple who applied for marital counseling referred to her depression and loneliness. Without denying the importance of the marital relationship, she focused on her inadequacy as a mother of two young children and her related fear that she would end up like her own mother—unable to generate confidence.

She then said that her feeling of rejection was particularly keen in her relationship with her father- and mother-in-law with whom she had attempted to achieve a close relationship, but to no avail. She felt that her mother-in-law, who was very different from her own mother, was the kind of woman from whom she could learn a good deal. Despite her attempts at being friendly, her mother-in-law visited their home infrequently. When she took the children to them, the father-in-law made fun of the stuttering of one child. She had discussed with her husband her need to get close to her mother-in-law but, she complained bitterly, he gave her no support in facilitating a connection.

Despite her strong wish, the support and approval she sought from her mother-in-law were no more forthcoming than from her own mother—not an uncommon phenomenon. Her anger and blame toward the husband are also a familiar consequence.

In another case in which concern for a four-year-old child brought a family to the agency, the focus soon shifted to a severe marital conflict.

The husband complained bitterly about his wife's lack of warmth and femininity. He expected his wife to be the mother he never had. It was not until he married that he really began to move ahead as an architect and to achieve, for the first time in his life, a real sense of belonging. This improvement seemed related, however, more to his mother-in-law than to his wife; he spoke in the warmest terms about his mother-in-law in whom he had found the mother that he never had. He had moved in with his wife and her family nine months before their marriage and basked in the warmth of his mother-in-law. He said that this was the only real home he had ever known. He described his mother-in-law as the "kindest and warmest person."

It was ironic that when his wife was eventually more prepared to offer these gifts to him, he had trouble accepting them from her. The missing mothering from an older woman proved to be crucial for him.

In another case, the primary importance of the need for the surrogate family was at the expense of the marriage and was reinforced by the complementary role played by the in-laws.

Following a divorce, Lila sought help with problems with her own family and in making a life for herself. The marriage of brief duration apparently failed because she suddenly discovered that there was no husband-wife relationship. Upon her husband's insistence, they had moved into the home of her family who promptly took over their support. He treasured this arrangement and refused to move even into an available separate apartment within the house. He had no desire to work and his major concern was to be taken care of. His mother had died when he was a child, and his father had never been available to him. He had finally found the mother and father he never had. His in-laws, in their turn, had a strong need to infantilize their new son-in-law as they did their daughter. Although, in the beginning, the wife had her own need to condone this arrangement, she eventually decided to extricate herself from it.

The following illustration is similar, but it underscores the setting off of intense negative interaction between siblings.

In marrying Jane, Mark had found not only a wife but parenting as well; her father proved to be more of a father to him than his own had been. Unfortunately, this relationship was at the expense of Jane, for the warmer the relationship became, the more she began to feel left out by her father. The situation was further sadly complicated by the fact that when she had a child, somewhat reluctantly under some pressure from her husband, she lost out further to her father when he became more affectionate to the granddaughter than to her. At one point, everyone was intensively competing for the affection of each other—three generations rivalrous with each other.

The following situation also illustrates a paramount need for a substitute mother complicated by the wife's exclusion from a tightly possessive relationship between her husband and his mother.

Gail complained so bitterly and aggressively about her husband that it took time to locate the terrible hurt she experienced at the hands of her new mother-in-law. Gail had tried hard to win her approval in ways that were mainly appropriate, but to no avail. She had to deal with a rivalrous and possessive mother and a son who was caught between the two women, but leaning in favor of his mother. In a moving family session involving them all, it became clear that Gail had a strong need for approval from a mother she had not had. Before marriage she had looked up to her future mother-in-law, whom she considered intelligent, cultured, and talented, but she found herself being looked down on by her mother-in-law with arrogance and belittlement. Fairly typically, her fury with her husband mounted because he could do nothing to improve the relationship. Furthermore, her retaliation took the form of restricting the visits of the mother-in-law to their young child. In the interview, Gail cried when she realized how much she still needed a mother figure.

In a number of these cases, the wish to be taken in by the spouse's family is almost equivalent to the wish to be adopted, with the subsequent emergence of "sibling" rivalry between the marital pair. There is a reference to this phenomenon in Ivan Boszormenyi-Nagy and Geraldine M. Spark: One fascinating aspect is the wish to be adopted by one's in-laws. This phenomenon may introduce such ramifications as unconsciously placing an excessive demand on the aged in-laws and rivalry with one's mate for sharing his parents. It can also be used as a defense for not working through or facing one's commitments and responsibility to one's own family of origin. A double blow may be experienced by the marital pair when the "adoption myth" is exploded by the nonadoption of the in-laws.[2]

Spouses with a pathological history of rotation through foster homes and institutions and severe deprivation may never recover from their scars. Even though they are persistently searching for some substitute parent-like nurturance, they are unfortunately seldom able to find or accept it. It was so with Eva, illegitimate herself, who had a long history of placements, alcoholism, depression, and psychotic episodes. When she finally found a husband, she became furious that she was unaccepted by her husband's parents.

Sometimes it is not so much the kind of parent-in-law that is important as the kind of family. Sometimes what is sufficient is the existence of a warm loving family that can provide an anchor or a new sense of belonging. To a varying degree, most people seem to need some connection to an external force larger than themselves—a sense of continuity and belonging that extends beyond the self and the simple dyad. Some people hunt for a family considered important because of status, wealth, profession, and so forth. For example, one socially ambitious actress married into a famous family. Because the husband was the "black sheep," a fact she knew prior to marriage despite her fantasy, she never became any more acceptable than he, and she continued to be furious with both the family and him.

Another young woman, Shirley, sought security from her in-laws. The couple was on the verge of a divorce, and the husband accompanied his wife to the first interview with the social worker with extreme reluctance. It became clear in this interview that Shirley had entered the marriage looking for a family. She came from a traumatic background that included the suicide of her father and promiscuity of her mother. She viewed Joe's family as warm and closely knit, and she assumed that Joe and his family could give her security and protection. In fact, they had been living together in his parents' house even before their marriage. At one point, within the context of a symbiotic relationship, Joe's mother was reported to have said to Shirley, "You think that I'd let you take my son away from me!"

When Joe's parents were included in an early family interview, the worker found them to be very disturbed persons who, far from offering any security to or acceptance of Shirley, rejected her outright. Shirley kept pleading with Joe not to divorce her. His response, backed by his family, was to pack her belongings and send them to a distant city where she was visiting her family because of a crisis there.

This behavior was a replication of her being thrown out of her own house by her mother at the age of nineteen, and it revived her feeling of being homeless, abandoned, and worthless. She made one final fruitless effort to find support from her own mother. When the finality of Joe's decision had sunk in, she settled down to work out her many problems as a single woman through the relationship of a warm supportive worker. In the next four years, still unmarried, she sought out the same worker on two occasions for brief help at times of crisis. During the last period, she was placed in a short-term therapy group and, not unexpectedly, managed to make the group her family.

RECIPROCAL PROCESS

Just as the selective process often operates in the choice of an in-law, there may be a reciprocal process operating for the in-law out of his own need. Courtship is a period for testing out not only the primary premarital relationship but also family values and potential sources of support and affection. It is a two-way system. In-laws can exert a powerful influence on the process, overtly or subtly, by the kind of messages they communicate to their child and their prospective son- or daughter-in-law. Their approval or disapproval can be critical not only to the life or death of the relationship but also, following marriage, to the kind of liaison that develops between in-laws. Family background and connections on the part of each prospective in-law are still an important concern. One could make a claim for lessened importance in a modern urban society. On the other hand, because it creates increased depersonalization and anomie, there may be an even greater longing to find through someone else's family a firm anchor point and a surer sense of belonging. In literature as in life, we come to know, sometimes with raised eyebrow, of classic attachments between generational in-laws that exceed the fire and intensity of the marital relationship. Through marriage, in-laws sometimes achieve new heights of gratification in acquiring for the first time the substitute son or daughter or the kind of child they never had.

Just as a son-in-law may seek out a parent-in-law for healthy or neurotic reasons, a parent-in-law may seek out a son-in-law for reasons ranging from extending the arm of nurturance, to punishing a figure from earlier life, to infantilizing a very infantile son-in-law. It is not uncommon for a married couple and the in-laws to get caught in a never-ending cycle of financial and emotional dependency, with reciprocal reverberating resentment on both sides that fastens them further into a helpless bind.

Some sons-in-law are taken into the business of their fathers-in-law. Some do very well and some do not. Some become natural members of the family with a real sense of belonging that matches, supplements, compensates for, or replaces their own family. Others are in constant or chronic turmoil. One of the reasons seems to stem from old smoldering conflicts that are kept alive through the replication of an earlier rebellious child-parent relationship. The needs are generally complementary on both sides. What sometimes makes matters worse is that, despite the two-generational battle, the in-laws find the grandchildren very acceptable, thereby contributing to additional feelings of rejection and hurt on the part of the married couple.

CONCLUSION

An attempt has been made in this article to draw attention to the importance of the spouse's family. The power and influence of family connections and continuity are so universal that individuals leaving their own families for marriage carry over to the in-laws a strong sense of family—positive or negative. Although it is natural to continue to have close relationships after marriage to both one's own family and the spouse's family, conflicts arise when the spouse seeks through his partner's family, usually unconsciously, to express or work through old problems within his original family. Excessive needs from earlier lack of fulfillment that fuel either a replication of old conflicts or a search for new gratifying substitutes can result, in some instances, in disturbing the marital relationship or relegating it to a secondary place. In-laws, too, have their own needs and complementary roles in adapting to new members of the family. The resultant conflicts tend to contribute to excessive marital friction as well as to intergenerational turmoil in ever-widening circles.

FOOTNOTES

[1] Ivan Boszormenyi-Nagy and Geraldine M. Spark, *Invisible Loyalties* (New York: Harper & Row, 1973), p. 222.

[2] Ibid., p. 224.

relationships between the elderly and their adult children

elizabeth s. johnson

barbara j. bursk

The goals of the research reported on in this paper were: (1) to explore the affective quality of relationships that elderly people have with their adult children from the perspective of both persons and (2) to understand the social, psychological, and environmental variables which influence the affective quality.

This study grew out of a concern with the way in which the family integrates its elderly members into a psychologically extended family structure. By psychologically extended family, we mean one in which there is supportive interaction between the generations but where the generations do not necessarily live within the same household. This process is clearly important for the individuals involved. Familial ties between elderly parents and their adult children cannot be regarded in isolation but are part of the total pattern of aging in our society. One aspect of this aging process involves the way that cultural norms, values, and roles affect the expectations of older people regarding their lives, which include relationships with adult children.

However, it is also true that in today's society there are no cultural guidelines, no specific norms, for behavior in the area of inter-generational relationships between elderly parents and their adult children. There is no socialization mechanism available for aiding elderly parents or adult children with their new roles at this life stage. Knowledge about the affective quality of existing relationships between adult children and elderly parents as well as greater understanding of the factors which currently influence those intergenerational relationships, would facilitate the development of intervention strategies for use where improvement in intergenerational relationships is desirable.

An extensive literature review of factors related to the elderly parent-adult child relationship turned up only one empirical study of the affective quality of the relationship (Simos, 1973). No studies were identified in which both the elderly parent and an adult child(ren) were interviewed.

OVERVIEW OF FAMILY RELATIONSHIPS
BETWEEN ELDERLY PARENTS AND ADULT CHILDREN

In contrast to the lack of societal guidelines for relationships between elderly parents and their adult children, Puner (1974) feels that the importance of family involvement with the elderly has not only *not* diminished but that the affectional and supportive functions of the family emerge as crucial integrative mechanisms for the elderly in American society. Troll's (1971) review of the literature led her to the conclusion that these family ties are the last social stronghold to which the elderly adhere.

Reprinted, by permission, from *The Gerontologist*, 1977, *17*, 90-96, slightly abridged. Copyright ©1977 by the Gerontological Society.

Sussman and Burchinal's (1962a) assessment of the relationships between generations suggests that people, as they age, become more involved with their families than with non-kin or other types of activities. They feel that the family's extended kin network is an extensive link between elderly parents and adult children and functions in indirect economic and social ways, such as the mutual exchange of services, gifts, advice, and financial assistance between the generations in as many as 93% of families.

In a second position paper, Sussman and Burchinal (1962b) suggest that sociological and demographic changes in society have *not* changed the importance of family relations in the lives of the elderly, especially in times of illness, difficulty, or crisis, or on ceremonial occasions. They also suggest that emotional support by the adult children has replaced physical support and care of the elderly individual. Close intergenerational ties are based upon mutual affection, interdependence, and reciprocal giving. Puner (1974) suggests that the importance of the family is further demonstrated by the fact that the 10-12% of the aged who have no family or close relationships with kin are those individuals who constitute the caseloads of social agencies.

Satisfying relationships between the elderly and their children do not appear to be dependent on geographical proximity but are related to communication between parents and children. Both original research (Britton, Mather & Lansing, 1961; Shanas, Townsend, Wedderburn, Friis, Milhoj, & Strehouwer, 1968) and articles based on the research of others (Brody, 1970; Troll, 1971) have suggested that many of the elderly want to remain as independent as possible, preferring to live in their own homes, a choice which enables them to maintain their sense of autonomy. However, choices available often depend upon the social strata of the elderly; more choices are available for the elderly in the middle-class family (Smith, 1954).

Summaries of other people's research (Butler & Lewis, 1973; Puner, 1974) suggest that in the United States, 80% of all older people have living children and 75% of them live either in the same household or 30 minutes away. Kosa, Rachiele, and Schoomer (1960) found that one-third of all widowed, single, divorced, and separated males shared a home with their children, whereas half of all widowed, divorced, and separated females shared a home with their children.

Shanas (1960) found that the poorer the health of the older person, the more likely he/she was to be living in the same household with at least one child. Brody (1966) has reported on applicants to a geriatric institutional facility for whom the actual precipitating factor in the request for admission appeared to be only the last in a series involving the interpersonal relationship between the elderly person and his/her family. This factor tipped the balance so that the family (often also aging) could no longer sustain the elderly relative outside of an institution. Puner (1974) suggests that family relationships are more stable when separate households are maintained. As previously noted, separate households may depend on the health of the parent.

Brody (1970), Cottrell (1974) and Stern and Ross (1965) suggest that affect bonds with their children are very important for the aged. Hence, it is in the sphere of emotional and social gratification that the elderly parent derives much from his/her family relationships, even though the aged parents may be less integrated into the physical, day-to-day living pattern of their families.

DEFINITION OF VARIABLES

On the basis of an extensive literature review completed by project staff (Ananis et al., 1976), four categories of variables appeared to have potential as correlates of the affectional quality of the relationship between the elderly parent and the adult child. These life areas were: health, living environment, finances, and attitude toward aging. Indicators were constructed for each of these four areas as well as for family relations. Questions included within an indicator were based on our informed (from the literature and experience) beliefs as to those aspects of the life area which had potential for influencing the affective quality of the relationship between elderly parent and adult child.

The family relations indicator included questions addressed to both the parent and the child about the openness of communication between them, their enjoyment of each other's company, their ability to count on each other, and an actual rating of the relationship.

The health indicator included questions about the parent's mobility outside of the home, the extent of medication usage, activity level, and rating of the parent's health.

The finances indicator included items about objective and subjective income adequacy, and problems between parent and child caused by finances.

The living environment indicator included questions about privacy, whether close friends live nearby, convenience to transportation, reason for moving to the present location, fearfulness in the home, and general attitude toward the surroundings.

The attitude indicator included questions about the parent's current happiness, the difficulty of his/her life, and general life satisfaction.

Our hypothesis was that a high over-all rating in each of these four life areas would contribute to a high over-all affective quality in the elderly parent-adult child relationship.

SAMPLE SELECTION

Working under the direction of the first author, 18 (17 females, 1 male) second year social work graduate students each selected three elderly parent-adult child pairs to interview. The total number of elderly parent-adult child *pairs* in this nonprobability convenience sample was 54. The three elderly parents selected by each interviewer had to have at least one characteristic in common (e.g., ethnicity, religion, living situation, etc.). Attention was directed to insuring that a wide range of characteristics of the elderly parents were represented.

Given the importance of research in the area (Kaplan, 1975), and the desirability of obtaining a fairly large sample, it was preferable to use a nonprobability sample for this study than the much smaller probability sample which could have been obtained for the same time and cost effort. In addition, given the high refusal rate which was expected when the participation of two persons was required, it was not cost-effective to use a probability sample. In fact when nonresponse rates are high (28 individuals, evenly divided between parents and children, refused to participate in this survey), what was intended as a probability sample is more accurately considered a nonprobability sample.

The geographical area from which interviewees were drawn encompassed greater Boston and the surrounding suburbs. The sample was limited to white, noninstitutionalized elderly persons, aged 65 and over. The adult children were all 21 years old or older. Participants in the survey were not known to have sought therapeutic help around their parent-child relationship. The sample cannot be considered representative of the elderly population at large, nor can the relationship be viewed as typical of all elderly parent-adult child relationships. However, it is important to note that there are great difficulties in attempting to recruit two individuals, who do not necessarily live in the same household, for a study of this type.

. . .

Our sample was older, more female, more suburban, and financially better off than the elderly population in the USA. The dominant white ethnic and religious groups of the area were well-represented. A majority of the elderly parents lived alone.

. . .

INSTRUMENT DESIGN

The data collection instrument was a structured interview schedule which included both closed and open-ended questions. With a focus on the elderly parent, questions were developed in each of the following areas, general background information, family relationships, health, living environment, finances, and attitude toward aging. Emphasis was placed on certain practical considerations such as easily understood questions and amount of time to complete an interview, i.e., no more than an hour and a half. A second instrument, based on the pretested parent questionnaire, was constructed for use in interviewing the adult child.

QUESTIONNAIRE ADMINISTRATION

Each potential participant was contacted by telephone or in person in order to arrange a mutually convenient time for the interview. Because the interview was conducted in the homes of the participants, the atmosphere was a positive, comfortable, and relaxed one. The interviewer asked the questions, interpreting unclear questions only when necessary. The elderly parent and the adult child were interviewed separately.

While receptivity to participation was an important factor in the inclusion of subjects for this study (resulting in restricted generalizability), one positive benefit was the good cooperation of the interviewees.

Each question was asked exactly as it was worded and the same order of the questions was maintained for all participants. Each interviewer was responsible for recording the participants' responses and for writing a profile of the relationship.

DATA ANALYSIS

As previously noted, indicators for each of the five areas, finances, health, attitude toward aging, living environment, and family relationships were constructed from selected questions in the interview schedule. Each question was subjectively evaluated for its association with the affective quality of the parent-child relationship. Responses were coded as to their assumed positive, in between, or negative contribution to the affective quality of the relationship.

The hypothesis that the four indicators selected, finances, health, attitude toward aging, and living environment, would be associated with the affective quality of the relationship between elderly parents and their adult children was explored by analysis of the data from the 108 questionnaires. The quantitative analyses included (1) correlations, (2) regression of the family relations indicator on the four life area indicators, and (3) regression of the single dependent variable, the parent's rating of the relationship with the interviewed child, on a selected variable from each of the four specified life areas. In addition to the quantitative data analyses, a more qualitative analysis was done of the profiles of the relationship pairs which were written by the interviewers.

While many correlations were carried out between the variables, those that were statistically significant (many more than would have been expected by chance), for the most part represent cross validation of variables. However, one interesting finding was the fairly high agreement ($r = .55$) between the responses of the elderly parents and adult children to the question, "how would you rate your relationship with your parent (child)?"

A multiple regression technique was used to identify the independent contributions of each of the four life area indicators to the affective quality of the family relationship indicator.

Using this multiple regression technique, the health and attitude toward aging indicators were statistically the most significant correlates of family relationships. The better the elderly parent's health (beta = .30, $p < .01$), the better the relationship between parents and child. Similarly, the better the elderly parent's attitude toward aging, the better the relationship between elderly parent and adult child (beta = .27, $p < .01$). The other two indicators, living environment and finances, were not statistically significantly related to the family relationship indicator. The amount of variance in the dependent variable, family relationships, accounted for by the four independent variable indicators was 25%.

A separate regression analysis was carried out using using simply the parent's rating of the relationship with the interviewed child as the dependent variable. The independent variables (all based on parent responses) were the parent's perceived income adequacy, the parent's general attitude toward his/her housing, the parent's satisfaction with life; and the parent's rating of his/her health. In this case the only variable which was statistically significantly (beta = .24, $p < .05$) related to the parent's rating of the relationship with the interviewed child was the parent's perceived income adequacy. The more positively perceived was income adequacy, the more positively perceived was the parent-child relationship. The amount of variance in the parent's rating of the relationship which was accounted for by the independent variables (16%) was less than with the composite indicators.

From the profiles of the interviewed pairs we tried to delineate certain trends or themes within the four life areas which related to family relationships. These themes were:

(1) When parents and children shared similar values, and had a relationship based on mutual respect and trust, with realistic perceptions of the other, as seen by the interviewer, the pair seemed to give the quality of their relationship a higher rating. Less contact, with less shared values led to lower rating scores.

(2) In rating the quality of their relationships, the elderly person tended to rate the relationship with the interviewed child at least as high, often higher, than did the adult child. In only one instance did a child rate the relationship higher than the parent. When the interviewer perceived that there were difficulties in the parent-child relationship by rating it with a lower score, the child's rating score tended to coincide more with the interviewer's subjective rating than did the elderly parent's.

(3) A surprising majority of elderly parents were satisfied with their living environment, whether the living situation was dictated by circumstances of health, financial necessity, or their family's ability to accommodate them. When a move was involved, and the elderly parent accepted the reason for their moving as valid, the elderly parent expressed satisfaction with his/her living environment. When the elderly parent had moved fairly recently, a loss of familiar friends was often mentioned.

(4) Felt financial security, not level of income, seemed of importance, but its impact was difficult for the interviewer to assess in terms of family relationships.

(5) Better quality relationships usually existed when the elderly parent was fairly engaged and kept busy in various activities. At the same time, these active elderly parents maintained regular contact with their children. This contact was felt to be warm and supportive. In general, the better perceived relationships were associated with parents who were in better health; not restricted in choice of daily activities; and independent.

(6) When health was more seriously impaired, and when the family relationship had already been perceived to be strained, the parental illness strained it more so.

Analysis of the data showed that the health and attitude toward aging indicators were statistically the most important correlates of the affective quality of the relationship between elderly parents and their adult children. The substantive importance of health as a factor in the affective quality of relationships between elderly parents and their adult children receives indirect support from the fact that health has consistently been viewed as a prime correlate of more general life satisfaction (Adams, 1971; Brand & Smith, 1974; Gubrium, 1970; Ryser & Sheldon, 1969; Spreitzer & Snyder, 1974). In addition, the analysis of the profiles completed *before* the statistical analysis had been carried out supported the results of the regression analysis using the life area indicators: health and attitude toward aging were perceived by the interviewer to be important correlates of the over-all affective quality of the family relationship.

Individuals in good health are not as likely to experience problems adjusting to old age. Elderly persons who are in poorer health not only experience general difficulties in adjusting to old age, but it appears that they may also experience problems in their relationships with their children. In addition, society's negative attitudes regarding the aging body may contribute to the diminished self-image that all elderly persons experience and which elderly persons in ill health may experience to an even greater degree. The resulting lowered self-esteem of the elderly person may result in increased family friction when these conditions are present.

This study also suggested the potential that parent's perceived income adequacy has as a possible source of family friction, at least from the parent's perspective.

However, it is important to note that when more complex indicators were used as both independent and dependent variables, i.e., when both the elderly parent's and the adult child's perceptions of: their relationship, the parent's health, the parent's finances, the parent's attitude toward aging, and the parent's living situation were included in the regression analysis, the results were completely different than when less complex variables and only the parent's point of view were used. In fact, when other regression analyses were carried out using only single response independent and dependent variables rather than the composite indicators, there was a great deal of fluctuation in the results. When slight modifications were made in the variables included in the composite indicators, there were minor fluctuations in the beta weights but the health and attitude toward aging indicators remained statistically significant at the $p < .01$ level.

IMPLICATIONS

This study found a significant association between a positive elderly parent-adult child relationship and health and attitude toward aging factors associated with the elderly parent. Although replications using paired data from a larger sample of elderly parents and their adult children are needed in order to generalize the findings of this study to the greater elderly parent-adult child population, when the findings of other related research are considered, some preliminary implications about the results of the present study can be made.

While a better health-care delivery system for older persons (and people of all ages) stands by itself as a necessary national goal for our society, this study also suggests that good health for elderly people can be an important variable in how elderly parents and their adult children regard their relationship. This association between good health and good relationships indicates that intervention strategies for elderly who do experience poor health should not only be developed but should be considered essential given that poor health may exacerbate poor family relationships, and poor family relationships have implications for the institutionalization of the elderly parent as Brody (1966) suggests.

While improved preventative health care is a necessary societal goal for elderly (and all) persons, until this goal is realized, greater attention should be paid to intervention strategies which are aimed at ameliorating the relationship between poor health and a poor relationship between elderly parent and adult child. At present, poor health can increase the elderly parent's dependency on the adult child with an increase in resentment by the adult child (often caught between caring for his/her own children and caring for the elderly parent), and increasing frustration of the parent, with an over-all poorer relationship between parent and child as the result. To the extent that poor health is a factor in the elderly person's life, we as practitioners and as policy makers must try to find ways to alleviate the burden of the family through services which offer respite to the family and independence to the parent without resorting to institutionalization except as a last resort.

While elderly day-care centers and home-care corporations have begun to appear, their continued existence is often dependent on their ability to demonstrate that they cost less than institutional care.

The idea of respite care, whether for a few days per week, for a weekend, for vacations, or in an emergency, is an interesting concept (available in some other countries), and one which offers support to families who have an elderly member with health problems. Time away from the work and responsibility involved in the care of an aging parent who has health difficulties, is often as much of a necessity for the adult child as it is for the parent with preschool children. The result of a convenient, socially sanctioned breather in the form of a respite care program might mean an increase in the family's ability to maintain the important relationship with the aging parent and also potentially reduce the incidence of institutionalization.

In addition, other supportive services for elderly persons such as convenient transportation to shops, medical, and other facilities, as well as home medical services should be developed for all elderly, not just for those who are in the extremely low income group. Services for elderly which take some of the burden away from their children may enhance better relationships between the generations and facilitate more involvement between elderly parents and adult children if and when more serious problems develop.

Finally, as both a cautionary note and as a possible intervention strategy, we feel that future studies should take into consideration the possible effects of the interview process on the relationships of the elderly parent and adult child (Rubin & Mitchell, 1976). The actual interview process could be the first step, for some of the participants, in thinking about the quality of their relationship. It is important that resources be made available to those interviewees who want assistance in discussing and/or dealing with their relationship, as a result of their thoughtful participation in the research.

REFERENCES

Ananis, R., Bursk, B., Flanzbaum, M., Gershman, L., Hartz, S., Isenberg, L., Karpinski, J., McPherson, D., Memolo, S., Motenko, A., Peck, E., Plaut, E., Reedy, J., Schley, H., Scobie, C., Streeter, S., Weiss, G., & Winer, B. *The quality of relationships between elderly parents and their adult children*. Master's thesis, Boston Univ., 1976.

Adams, D. L. Correlates of satisfaction among the elderly. *Gerontologist*, 1976, *11*, 64-68.

Brand, F. N., & Smith, R. Life adjustment and relocation of the elderly. *Journal of Gerontology*, 1974, *29*, 336-340.

Britton, J. H., Mather, W. G., & Lansing, A. K. Expectations for older persons in a rural community: living arrangements and family relationships. *Journal of Gerontology*, 1961, *16*, 156-162.

Brody, E. The aging family. *Gerontologist*, 1966, *6*, 201-206.

Brody, E. The etiquette of filial behavior. *Aging & Human Development*, 1970, *1*, 87-94.

Butler, R., & Lewis, M. *Aging and mental health*. Mosby, St. Louis, 1973.

Cottrell, F. *Aging and the aged*. William Brown Co., Dubuque, IA, 1974.

Gubrium, J. F. Environmental effects on morale in old age and resources of health and solvency. *Gerontologist*, 1970, *10*, 294-297.

Kaplan, J. The family in aging (editorial). *Gerontologist*, 1975, *15*, 385.

Kosa, J., Rachiele, L. D., & Schoomer, C. Sharing the home with relatives. *Marriage & Family Living*, 1960, *22*, 129-131.

Puner, M. *To the good long life: What we know about growing old*. Universe Books, New York, 1974.

Rubin, Z., & Mitchell, C. Couples research as couples counseling: Some unintended effects of studying close relationships. *American Psychologist*, 1976, *31*, 17-25.

Ryser, C., & Sheldon, A. Retirement and health. *Journal of the American Geriatrics Society*, 1969, *17*, 180-190.

Shanas, E. Family responsibility and the health of older people. *Journal of Gerontology*, 1960, *15*, 408-411.

Shanas, E., Townsend, P., Wedderburn, D., Friis, H., Milhoj, P., & Stehouwer, J. *Old people in three industrial societies*. Atherton Press, New York, 1968.

Simos, B. G. Adult children and their aging parents. *Social Work*, 1973, *18*, 78-85.

Smith, W. Family plans for later years. *Marriage & Family Living*, 1954, *16*, 36-40.

Spreitzer, E., & Snyder, E. E. Correlates of life satisfaction among the aged. *Journal of Gerontology*, 1974, *29*, 454-458.

Stern, E. M., & Ross, M. *You and your aging parents*. Harper & Row, New York, 1965.

Sussman, M. B., & Burchinal, L. Parental aid to married children: Implications for family functioning. *Marriage & Family Living*, 1962, *24*, 320-332. (a)

Sussman, M. B., & Burchinal, L. Kin family network: Unheralded structure in current conceptualizations of family functioning. *Marriage & Family Living*, 1962, *24*, 231-240. (b)

Troll, L. E. The family of later life: A decade review. *Journal of Marriage and the Family*, 1971, *33*, 263-290.

35   patterns of intergenerational exchange:
a developmental approach

joseph g. turner

FAMILY STRUCTURE AND FUNCTION

Current theories of family structure and function have been greatly influenced by earlier theories of social differentiation. One theoretical viewpoint held that the nuclear family in American society was a relatively isolated unit with little or no contact with other kin families (Linton, [1]; Parsons and Bales, [2]; Wirth, [3]). Sussman [4] challenged this view, documenting that families are an interdependent kinship system, tied together by networks of activity and mutual assistance. Accordingly, social exchange occurs between, as well as within, related families.

One model which attempts to explain the dynamics of this exchange (Richer, [5]) postulates that people who hold or control valued resources rise to power in a social system. Power accelerates under two conditions: when those who need the resources do not have alternative sources of supply, and/or when they do not have a resource of equivalent value with which to reciprocate. If both conditions prevail, the person without social exchange value is likely to display deference in order to ensure access to further resources in the future.

Parental and Filial Dependency

During the early months of life, an infant unilaterally depends upon his parents or parent surrogates for all resources (Blau, [6]). This disproportionate balance of power does not normally remain static over time but rather shifts to accommodate gains in the resource repertoire of the child. As children grow older, they depend less upon their parents, thereby decreasing the power within the older adult generation (Goldfarb, [7]; Thomas, [8]).

According to Hill [9], older parents see themselves as meager givers and high receivers and label their status as dependent, contrasted with younger adults who see themselves as high in giving and modest in receiving. Eventually, as physical and mental powers wane and economic resources become depleted, the older person's exchange power decreases even further, and he becomes unilaterally dependent upon his offspring. At any given point in time, therefore, the degree of power vested in the adult generation will depend on his resources and the dependency needs of the other generations in his family (Hill, [9]; Macdonald, [10]; Sussman, [11]; Waller and Hill, [12]).

However, it cannot be presumed that all older people are without resources. Support by older parents of their children continues in many families for long periods of time, so that more younger adults according to the 1960 Census, live with their parents than the reverse. The older adult attempts to maintain an independent status as long as possible (Streib and Thompson, [13]), utilizing his accrued assets and pensions from private employees or from government programs of support. When these resources are no longer sufficient, the older parent then most frequently turns to his children,

Reprinted, by permission, from *The International Journal of Aging and Human Development*, 1975, 6, 111-15.

more often to a daughter than to a son (Macdonald, [10]; Shanas, [14]; Smith, [15]).

Research by Winch [16] gives a possible explanation for this pattern of behavior. He found that mother-son ties are strong, so that emancipation problems are greater for the son than for the daughter. Not only must the son break his major identification with his mother, but has to shift from dependence when he marries. On the other hand, daughters continue to identify with their mothers, carrying over their dependency role as they leave their family of orientation. Komarovsky [17] concurs with Winch, stating that the different training received by girls and boys with respect to emancipation creates strong and lasting ties to the girl's family of orientation. Since neither changes of identity nor dependency has occurred with their daughter, parents are more likely to turn to her than to their more independent son. Townsend [18] has noted that British family mores intensify this tendency.

Schorr [19] has contended that support for an aging parent most often is given because of a sense of filial duty, corresponding to his feelings of love and warmth for parents. Rautman [20] has noted that accepting the help of children requires of the older person a special proficiency in role reversal. On the other hand, Goldfarb [7] sees the phenomenon as the developmental working out of a dependent relationship rather than as a new imbalance of power. According to him, persons manifest dependency throughout their lives in a variety of ways, contingent upon changing personal needs and situational demands. There is no "child-parent" reversal, but rather a new and clearer opportunity to express dependency. It is not necessary to postulate that persons regress to previous modes of adaptation and look to their children as if they were parents. Instead, manifestations of a dependent relationship are more transparent at some times than at others, since they no longer need to be disguised or denied. Goldfarb has characterized the older person as being engaged in "a motivated search for dependency."

Streib [21] has suggested that social relationships between aged parents and their children continue to follow patterns established in the period when children leave home to seek education, careers, and marriage.

CONDITIONING BY INGRAINED RITUALS

Bossard and Boll [22] concluded that patterns of interaction in families are the consequence of long ingrained rituals established in childhood. These rituals become the bases for mutual areas of satisfaction which can be participated in, enjoyed, and perpetuated by family members of all ages. Rituals set limitations and controls by which behavior is regulated, resulting in minimal stress to the individuals concerned. Sussman [23] found that a kinship pattern established prior to the onset of an illness continues beyond the time the parent is fully incapacitated.

Krasner [24] has considered the family dynamics of the special case when institutionalization of an older parent has become necessary. If there is a healthy, positive attitude between the adult and his aging parent, affection may grow in this difficult situation. If the relationship is characterized by neurotic or negative feelings, a cyclic pattern of interaction develops, with guilt, anxiety, and resentment common to both parties but for differing reasons. The younger adult resents the demands that the dependency of his parent imposes upon him but feels guilty about this resentment. If he acts ignobly toward his parent, it poses a threat to his own self concept, both as a responsible adult and as a supportive child. Anxiety breeds added resentment toward his parent. Simultaneously, the older person fears that his attempts to ease the burden upon the child may be misinterpreted or unappreciated. Feelings of being a burden result in guilt on his part; as anxiety about the interaction increases, he tends to withdraw. He may feel, also, that the sacrifices he made for his child are being repaid with rejection. This pattern of anxiety and rejection has a tendency to spiral the older adult into deeper dependency.

Whatever their genesis, there are established patterns of intergenerational activity and mutual assistance which appear to function within a system of exchange, with the younger adult generation eventually emerging as the center of power.

REFERENCES

1. Linton, R. The natural history of the family. In R. N. Anshen (Ed.), *The family: Its function and destiny.* New York: Harper-Row, 1959, pp. 30-52.
2. Parsons, R. & Bales, R. F. *Family socialization and interaction process.* Glencoe, Ill.: The Free Press, 1955.
3. Wirth, L. Urbanism as a way of life. *American Journal of Sociology,* 1938, *44,* 1-24.
4. Sussman, M. B. The isolated nuclear family: Fact or fiction? *Social Problems,* 1959, *6,* 333-340.
5. Richer, S. The economics of childrearing. *Journal of Marriage and Family,* 1968, *30,* 462-466.
6. Blau, P. M. *Exchange and power in social life.* New York: John Wiley, 1964.
7. Goldfarb, A. I. Psychodynamics and the three generation family. In E. Shanas, & G. F. Streib (Eds.), *Social structure and the family: Generational relations.* New Jersey: Prentice-Hall, 1965.
8. Thomas, W. I. *Primitive behavior: An introduction to the social science.* New York: McGraw-Hill, 1937.
9. Hill, R. Decision making and the family life cycle. In E. Shanas, & G. F. Streib (Eds.), *Social structure and the family: Generational relations.* New Jersey: Prentice-Hall, 1965.
10. Macdonald, R. W. Intergenerational family helping patterns. Unpublished doctoral dissertation, University of Minnesota, 1964, No. 65-15, 316.
11. Sussman, M. B. The help pattern in the middle-class family. *American Sociological Review,* 1953, *18,* 22-28.
12. Waller, W., & Hill, R. *Family: A dynamic interpretation.* (Rev. ed.), New York: Dryden Press, 1951.
13. Streib, G. F., & Thompson, W. E. Personal and social adjustment in retirement. In W. Donahue, & C. Tibbitts (Eds.), *The new frontiers of aging.* Ann Arbor, Mich.: University of Michigan Press, 1957, pp. 180-197.
14. Shanas, E. *The health of older people.* Cambridge, Mass.: Harvard University Press, 1962.
15. Smith, W. M. Family plans for later years. *Marriage and Family Living,* 1954, *16,* 36-40.
16. Winch, R. F. Interrelations between certain social background and parent-son factors in a study of courtship among college men. *American Sociological Review,* 1951, *16,* 784-795.
17. Komarovsky, M. Functional analysis of sex roles. *American Sociological Review,* 1950, *15,* 508-516.
18. Townsend, P. The family life of old people. Glencoe, Ill.: The Free Press, 1957.
19. Schorr, A. *Filial responsibility in the modern American family.* Washington, D.C.: U.S. Department of Health, Education, and Welfare, 1960.
20. Rautman, A. L. Role reversal in geriatrics. *Mental Hygiene,* 1962, *46,* 116-120.
21. Streib, G. F. Family patterns in retirement. *Journal of Social Issues,* 1958, *14,* 46-60.
22. Bossard, J. H. S., & Boll, E. Rituals in family living. *American Sociological Review,* 1949, *14,* 463-469.
23. Sussman, M. B. Relationships of adult children with their parents in the United States. In E. Shanas & G. F. Streib (Eds.), *Social structure and the family: Generational relations.* New Jersey: Prentice-Hall, 1965, pp. 62-92.
24. Krasner, J. D. The reaction of the adult child to the institutionalization of the aged parent. Institute of Gerontology; the University of Michigan, *Living in the multigeneration family.* 1969, pp. 83-89.

36

significance of grandparents: perceptions of young adult grandchildren

joan f. robertson

Despite the proliferation of investigations focusing on interaction in three-generation families, little attention has been focused on the role of grandparenthood with regard to its significance to young adult grandchildren. In the absence of empirical data, myths are erringly perpetuated. One such myth is the view that grandparenthood provides a source of emotional gratification for grandparents and young grandchildren, but that grandparents are not very influential in the lives of young adult grandchildren.

The few studies which indicate something about young adults' perceptions of grandparents are very limited in scope. The ambiguity and contradictory nature of their findings make it impossible to generate hypotheses to test the significance of grandparents for this age group. The one exception (Gilford & Black, 1972) focuses on the grandparent-grandchild relationship from the perspective of the young adult grandchild and provides a basis for testing the hypothesis that parents assume a mediating role between the first and the third generations. Other studies indirectly touch on the significance of grandparenthood to the young adult. Robins and Tomanec (1962), for example, report that college students feel closer to grandparents than to aunts, uncles, and cousins. Adams (1968) ranked uncles and aunts slightly above grandparents and cousins in importance. Looft (1971), in a somewhat different, but thought-provoking vein, asked respondents of different ages across the life-span to name significant others that acted as principal sources of knowledge about how to get along in the world. Interestingly, parents and peers were viewed as informational transmitters and no mention was made of grandparents.

The objective of this research, a pilot study, was to gather data which could be used to generate hypotheses which could be put to test in a subsequent study to continue our ongoing efforts to study the significance of grandparenthood from a three-generation perspective. Drawing from our previous research (Robertson, 1971; Wood & Robertson, 1975), this study explored five areas of inquiry; (1) attitudes and expectations grandchildren hold regarding grandparents; (2) grandchild's perceptions of the appropriate and/or expected grandparent behavior; (3) grandchildren's responsibilities toward grandparents; (4) grandchildren's perceptions of the degree of parental influence in their relationships with grandparents; and (5) conceptions of the *ideal* grandparent.

ITEMS USED TO ASSESS SIGNIFICANCE OF GRANDPARENTS TO YOUNG ADULT GRANDCHILDREN

Data for this study were obtained from responses to a highly structured group-administered instrument. A series of Likert-type, range of choice, and yes-no items were used to measure the five areas of inquiry. Likert-type items were used to assess attitudes and expectations held regarding grandparents. Perceptions of appropriate and/or expected grandparent behavior were obtained by forcing respondents to respond to a range of choice items detailing a number of expressive and instrumental behaviors which grandchildren expect of grandparents. Grandchildren's responsibilities toward grandparents were assessed by a series of Likert-type items and one range of choice item detailing a series of specific behaviors. Perceptions of the degree of parental influence in relationships with grandparents and conceptions of the ideal grandparent were measured by a combination of Likert-type, range of choice, and yes-no items. Examples of these items will be detailed in the discussion section of this paper.

Since this was a pilot study for the explicit purpose of generating hypotheses, our findings have been analyzed on a simple descriptive level.

STUDY POPULATION

The study population consisted of 86 young adult grandchildren ranging from ages 18 through 26. As one might expect from a young adult sample, over 3/4, i.e., 83% of the respondents were single as opposed to 16.3% who were married. The majority, 58%, were 21-23 years old with slightly over 1/4, 26%, ranging from ages 18-20. Using parental occupation as an index of socioeconomic status, more than half of the respondents, i.e., 57% of the males and 56% of the females, indicate that they came from stable blue-collar backgrounds. Most of the respondents were either Lutheran Protestants or Catholics. Finally, there was a disproportionate number of female respondents, since they accounted for slightly over 2/3 of the study population.

YOUNG ADULT GRANDCHILDREN'S RESPONSES TO SIGNIFICANCE OF GRANDPARENTS TO THEM

Attitudes and expectations regarding grandparents. Contrary to popular notions, young adult grandchildren espouse a series of very favorable attitudes toward grandparents. For example, of the respondents, 92% indicate that "a child would miss much if there were no grandparents when he was growing up." According to 90% of the respondents, grandparents are not "too old-fashioned or out of touch to be able to help their grandchildren." Eighty-six percent report that "a good grandparent does not spoil grandchildren" and 72% indicate that grandparents have much influence on grandchildren. Noteworthy is the finding that approximately 71% of the respondents emphasize that grandparents would rather spend time with their friends of their own age than with their grandchildren or that 70% indicate that teenagers do not feel grandparetns are a bore. It is also important to point out that approximately 42% of the respondents felt "grandparents should be more like a friend than a respected elder." In contrast, 35% disagreed with this statement, and 22% had no opinion on the matter.

We found variation in intensity of agreement and disagreement between sexes on some of the items. For example, over half of the women respondents strongly disagreed with the statement that a child would miss much if there were no grandparents around when he was growing up in contrast to 42% of the males who responded in a similar way. In response to the item "a grandparent should be more like a friend than a respected elder," half of the males agreed, in contrast to 36% of the women who disagreed. Both men and women feel grandparents should discipline grandchildren, although more women (55%) accept this as permissible than men (46%). Finally, 2/3 of the males as opposed to slightly more than half of the women disagreed with the statement "grandparents don't usually have much influence on their grandchildren."

Perception of the appropriate and/or expected grandparent behavior. As indicated in Table 1, adult grandchildren expect very little from grandparents by way of explicit behavior other than some giftgiving or grandparents acting as bearers of family history. They do not expect grandparents to be

TABLE 1. PERCEPTIONS OF APPROPRIATE AND/OR EXPECTED GRANDPARENT BEHAVIOR

Item	Response Categories % Distribution (N=86)			
	Yes	No	NA*	Total
Somebody who gave you gifts of money or took you places	59.3	36.0	4.7	100
Somebody to whom you could go to for advice	31.3	64.0	4.7	100
Somebody who kept you informed of family heritage rituals, news, folklore, etc.	55.8	39.5	4.7	100
Somebody who you could rely on for emotional comfort	40.7	54.6	4.7	100
Somebody who understood you when nobody else did	27.9	67.4	4.7	100
Somebody who was a liaison between you and your parents	29.0	66.3	4.7	100
Somebody to whom grandchildren can turn to for personal advice	23.3	55.8	21.9	100
Somebody who aids in financial support	8.1	69.8	22.1	100
Somebody who aids in rearing of my children	43.0	34.9	22.1	100
Role model—somebody whose occupation I can imitate	23.3	54.7	22.0	100

*NA — Non-applicable.

liaisons between them and parents, to be somebody they turn to for personal advice, to understand them when nobody else does, to be one who aids in their financial support, to be somebody who acts as a role model, or to be somebody whose occupation they might choose to imitate.

These findings bring to question the research of others (Faris, 1947; Neugarten & Weinstein, 1964; Streib & Thompson, 1960; Sussman, 1962; Sussman & Burchinal, 1962, a, b) who report that grandparents serve such functions for families. The notion conveyed by those studies is that grandparents serve unique functions for family systems, i.e., grandchildren, and these functions facilitate the development of qualitative relationships between generations. These findings suggest that adult grandchildren expect little by way of concrete behaviors from grandparents except for emotional gratification, and corroborate our findings from the grandparent populations (Robertson, 1971, 1973; Wood & Robertson, 1975) which indicate that grandparents engage in 10 out of 12 behaviors with grandchildren with very little frequency. Thus, for both young adult grandchildren and grandparents, the most significant and appropriate behavior is that which builds or sustains emotional gratification. It is important, however, to make clear that emotional gratification means more of a nurturance than should it convey the idea that grandchildren expect specific behaviors to be the basis of such gratification.

Grandchildren's responsibility toward grandparents. Contrary to popular impressions stemming out of the generation-gap literature, young adult grandchildren feel definite responsibilities toward their grandparents. Roughly 2/3 of the respondents agreed that "grandchildren should feel obliged, as soon as they are old enough, to help their grandparents if they need help." Further, 62% indicated that "grand-children should not expect money for helping grandparents." Slightly more than half of the respondents, 54%, indicated that grandparents were "somebody I feel I should visit and give emotional comfort." More than half claimed they visited with grandparents because they genuinely enjoyed being with them or loved them. This is in contrast to 20% who visited with grandparents because their parents did or 11% who did so because it was expected of them.

Perceptions of degree of parental influence. Almost 2/3 of the respondents agreed that their parents set the pace for grandparent-grandchild relationships. This appears to be done in a variety of ways. For example, 18.6% indicate that parents' attitudes and behaviors transfer to grandchildren, whereas 8.1% indicate that a grandchild's relationship with grandparents is influenced by their parents' relationship with their parents, and 22.1% stress that parents make grandchild and grandparent interaction physically possible. In so doing, they make the relationship an available one. Some, 16.3%, agreed that parents act to set the pace of the relationship, but gave no indication as to why.

Conceptions of the ideal grandparent. According to the majority of the respondents, the ideal grandparent is "one who loves and enjoys grandchildren, visits with them, shows an interest in them" or, next in importance, is one "who helps grandchildren out when they can, when asked or needed." Grandparents possess a number of characteristics which have been rank ordered from the most important signifying elements of the ideal grandparent to the least important which can be construed to represent the least ideal grandparent. Important characteristics ranked were grandparents as loving, gentle, helpful, understanding, industrious, smart, a friend, talkative, and funny. The least important characteristics in their order indicated were laxy, childish, dependent, mediators, companions, or teachers.

CONCLUSION

When we scrutinize the preceding findings for the purpose of generating hypotheses for further study, it becomes clear that we must scrap the findings of many of the earlier studies and negate the functionality of grandparents to young adult grandchildren in all areas except that of gift givers, bearers of family history and tradition, and emotional gratification. It is important to point out that when young adult grandchildren view emotional gratification as an appropriate or expected behavior from grandparents, they appear to relate to this as a given. Perhaps, this conveys the perspective that grandparenthood is one of the few roles available to older adults which has not concrete behavioral expectations associated with it.

While young adult grandchildren clearly espouse attitudes which indicate that grandparents are not too old-fashioned and out of touch to be able to help them or that a child would miss much if he did not have grandparents, it is interesting to note that they do not choose to use grandparents as companions, advice givers, liaisons between them and their parents, role models, or somebody who financially supports them. Thus, there is an incongruence between what grandchildren think and feel about the significance of grandparenthood and the behaviors they expect from grandparents. Further research must account for these distinctions.

Finally, it is important to note that grandchildren feel definite responsibilities toward their grandparents. This includes emotional support, tangible help wherever possible, and visiting. For young adult grandchildren, visiting with grandparents is more qualitative rather than ritualistic. This negates Rosow's (1967) perspective that visiting patterns for grandchildren generations may take on more of a ritualistic than qualitative function. This does not appear to be the case for this age group of grandchildren.

The finding that young adult grandchildren feel definite responsibilites toward their grandparents tends to dispute prevalent myths and stereotypes stemming from the generation-gap issues. Or, since this was a predominantly stable blue-collar sample, this group may reflect parental values of concern and filial responsibility when the need be. Whatever the reasons, these data, however preliminary and descriptive, lead us to conclude that grandparents are significant to young adult grandchildren. This is clearly reflected, we think in the younger generation's willingness to intervene to assist grandparents wherever possible—a perspective of young adults which runs counter to popular impressions, which portray this age group as relatively independent of extended family concern.

REFERENCES

Adams, Bert N. *Kinship in an urban setting.* Markham, Chicago, 1968.

Faris, R. E. L. Interaction of generations and family stability. *American Sociological Review,* 1947, *12,* 159-64.

Gilford, R., & Black, D. 1947. The grandparent-grandchild dyad: Ritual or relationship? Paper presented at 25th annual meeting of Gerontological Society, San Juan, Dec. 17-21, 1972.

Looft, W. R. Perceptions across the life span of important informational sources for children and adolescents. *Journal of Psychology*, 1971, *78*, 207-211.

Neugarten, B., & Weinstein, K. The changing American grandparent. *Journal of Marriage & the Family*, 1964, *26*, 199-204.

Robertson, J. F. *Grandparenthood: A study of role conceptions of grandmothers*. PhD thesis, School of Social Work, Univ. Wisconsin-Madison, 1971.

Robertson, J. F. Interaction in three-generation families; parents as mediators: Toward a theoretical perspective. *International Journal of Aging & Human Development*, 1975, *6*, 103-110.

Robins, L. N., & Tomanec, M. Closeness to blood relatives outside the immediate family. *Marriage & Family Living*, 1973, *24*, 340-346.

Rosow, I. *Social integration of the aged*. Free Press, New York, 1967.

Streib, G. F., & Thompson, W. E. Adjustment in retirement. *Journal of Social Issues*, 1958, *14*, (whole issue).

Sussman, M. B. Kin family network: Unheralded structure in current conceptualizations of family functioning. *Marriage & Family Living*, 1962, *24*, 231-240.

Sussman, M. B., & Burchinal, L. Parental aid to married children: Implications for family functioning. *Marriage & Family Living*, 1962, *24*, 320-332. (a)

Sussman, M. B., & Burchinal, L. Parental aid to married children: Implications for family functioning. *Marriage & Family Living*, 1962, *24*, 231-240. (b)

Wood, V., & Robertson, J. The significance of grandparenthood. J. Gubrium (Ed.), *Time, roles, and self in old age*. Behavioral Publications, New York, 1975.

part 5

toward a total view of family relationships

INTRODUCTION

The readings contained in this part of the book examine the complexity and diversity of family interaction, and it is hoped that their inclusion will guide the reader toward a more comprehensive view of family relationships. The readings have been selected to increase one's awareness of the numerous factors influencing the study of family interaction. These factors include: subcultural variation, the composition and life-style of the family, the impact of social stress, the simultaneous study and treatment of more than one dyadic relationship, the recent advances in the field of marriage and family counseling, and the potential impact of social change on family relationships.

A number of readings in other parts of this book have stressed the importance of the variable of social class and its influence on family relationships [*(2)*, *(4)*, *(16)*, *(17)*, and *(26)*], but few have mentioned the potential influence of racial, religious, and ethnic variations within the population. More studies of specific minority groups should feature a control for the variable of social class. Some minority-group studies have offered in-depth examinations of only one strata within a given minority group (Liebow, 1967), whereas others have compared family-related behavior patterns of several social-class groups within a specific minority group, such as the work done with black families by Willie (1974) and with Italian-American families by Gans (1962).

Since little mention has been made in this book of the variable of religion, an article has been included which shows how family relationships differ between black Muslims and black Christians in the United States. This article *(37)*, by Edwards, illustrates why social characteristics of families, including religious identification, should be controlled for in studies of family interaction. Also, Turner (1973) has shown that attitudes toward aging parents vary according to religion and this influences the nature of the adult-child/aged-parent relationship.

More than 30 years ago, Bossard (1945:293) developed the following mathematical formula:

$$X = \frac{Y^2 - Y}{2}$$

where X equals the number of paired interpersonal relationships and Y equals the number of people in the family. Using this formula, it is easy to see that family relationships can be dramatically influenced by the size of the family. However, this formula for family interaction does not encompass the total complexity due to size of family because there can also be interpersonal relationships consisting of three, four, or more persons, all occurring at the same time. Kephart (1950) dealt with this problem, and Rodgers pointed out that by using Kephart's formula one discovers "a family of five has a potentiality of from four to ninety different interpersonal relationships" (1973:45). Rodgers also indicated that neither Bossard nor Kephart's mathematical formulas take into consideration the adjustments that a family makes to increases or decreases in its size. Bossard and Kephart's work helped to define family size as one aspect contributing to the complexity of family interaction.

In addition to family size, the composition of the family and the various life-styles of its members are other key factors which are important to the understanding of the complexity and diversity of family relationships. Some of the readings [(19), (20), (21), (22), (29), (30), (31), and (32)] have emphasized the fact that the composition of the family can influence the nature of family relationships. In the article by Kanter, Jaffee, and Weisberg (38), the study of the adult-dyad and parent-child dyad within an urban communal setting helps to explain how important it is for researchers to identify the kind of family they are studying. Intact nuclear families, one-parent families, reconstituted families, families headed by a homosexual pair, families living in communes, and families with three generations residing together are just a sampling of the variety of family forms present in contemporary society.

Some aspects of family interaction may remain the same regardless of a family's size, specific membership, or pervasive life-style, whereas other aspects may· differ significantly from one kind of family to another. We need more research on family relationships in both traditional and nontraditional family settings. We know far more about marital and parent-child relationships than we do about sibling and intergenerational relationships in a variety of settings.

The article by Hill is a classical work which has been included in this section because it indicates that patterns of family interaction are altered when a family is subjected to stress or involved· in a crisis situation (39). Some previous readings have already mentioned two significant family-crisis situations, namely divorce [(19), (20), and (21)] and child abuse (24). Since Hill's early theoretical paper about social stresses on the family was originally published, many studies of family crisis have been reported, with topics ranging from the effects of stress on marital interaction (Bahr, 1971) to the crisis of dealing with personal or familial bankruptcy (Siporin, 1967). Glasser and Glasser (1970) have pulled much of this research together. Nevertheless, Hill's article was chosen over the more recent articles because it offers a general introduction to the topic of family crisis and also because it is important as a classical work.

Olson and Sprenkle's article (40) on emerging trends in family treatment is included for a couple of reasons. First, it is an appropriate choice for a book about family relationships because it permits one to assess the present state of the marriage and family counseling profession. Secondly, and more importantly, the article is a worthwhile choice in that it addresses the recent move in treatment towards working with the family as a whole.

It should be realized that patterns of family interaction are actually far more complex than any of the readings suggest. Most of the readings in this book examine a dyadic relationship between spouses, between parent and child, between siblings, or between generations. However, a more comprehensive view of the complexity of family relationships sees each paired-dyad relationship as having an impact on the other dyadic relationships. In other words, family relationships should not be thought of as occurring in isolation from each other. They occur concurrently and can influence each other. For example, it can be assumed that the degree of satisfaction with the marital relationship will influence the nature of the parent-child relationship. For example, the character of the marital relationship can determine how well parents adjust to a parent-child relationship with a handicapped child (Farber, 1962). Furthermore, the birth of a second child has been shown to have an influence on the parent-child relationships involving the first-born or older sibling (Taylor and Kogan, 1973) and Ihinger's (1975) theory regarding sibling conflict suggests that the parent as referee influences sibling interaction.

As early as the 1960s, Handel (1965, 1967) stressed the importance of the psychological study of whole families. To date there are few reports of any research which has dealt with the true complexity of family interaction by studying more than one dyadic relationship at a time to determine the influence of one upon another. Rodgers (1973), in the conclusion of his book on family interaction and transaction, does assess the status of research from a developmental perspective.

Another issue of concern to contemporary family researchers is that of external forces and their influence on the internal climate of the family. Since the primary purpose of this book was to examine the internal relationships of family members, very little emphasis has been placed on the external family relationships between the family and the economy, the government, or the community. The family's interaction with these external systems has been covered elsewhere (Bell and Vogel, 1968; Eldridge and Meredith, 1976). External relationships of the family have been addressed in this book only when a discussion of them naturally arose due to their impact on the nature of the internal family processes—for example, the interface of the worlds of work and family.

Just as Olson and Sprenkle's article is helpful in assessing the status of the field of marriage and family counseling, the articles by Nye *(41)* and by Glick *(42)* permit an assessment of the present status of the family in a rapidly changing society. Social change is another factor that is bound to influence the kinds of family relationships which exist. The articles by Nye and by Glick were chosen over the other articles in the burgeoning volume of literature on the future of the family because so many of the other articles are purely speculative in nature and lack any empirical base. Nye has studied emerging and declining family roles, which have a direct bearing on what is expected in family interaction. Glick's research position in the population division of the U.S. Census Bureau has uniquely qualified him for analyzing demographic data to identify present trends and their potential impact on the American family. Of this much we can be sure, the present population statistics point out important trends which are likely to have considerable impact on the interpersonal relationships of those living in both traditional and nontraditional family environments. The decline in the marriage rate, the postponement of marriage, the postponement of parenthood, the decline in the birth rate, the increase in the divorce rate, and the increase in the numbers of people who adhere to nontraditional life-styles are all bound to influence the nature of family relationships in the future.

REFERENCES

Bahr, S. J. The effects of stress on marital interaction. *Family Perspective 5*, no. 2 (1971):36-44.
Bell, N. B., and Vogel, E. F., eds. *A modern introduction to the family* Rev. ed. New York: Free Press, 1968.
Bossard, J. H. S. The law of family interaction. *American Journal of Sociology 50* (1945):292-94.
Eldridge, E., and Meredith, N., eds. *Environmental issues: Family impact.* Minneapolis: Burgess Publishing Company, 1976.
Farber, B. Marital integration as a factor in parent-child relations. *Child Development 33* (1962):1-14.
Gans, H. J. *The urban villagers.* New York: Free Press of Glencoe, 1962.
Glasser, P. H., and Glasser, L. N., eds. *Families in crisis.* New York: Harper and Row, 1970.
Handel, G. Psychological study of whole families. *Psychological Bulletin 63* (1965):19-41.
Handel, G., ed. *The psychosocial interior of the family: A sourcebook for the study of whole families.* Chicago: Aldine-Atherton, 1967.
Ihinger, M. The referee role and norms of equity: A contribution toward a theory of sibling conflict. *Journal of Marriage and the Family 37* (1975):515-24.
Kephart, W. M. A quantitative analysis of intragroup relationships. *American Journal of Sociology 55* (1950):544-49.
Liebow, E. *Tally's corner: A study of Negro streetcorner men.* Boston: Little, Brown, 1967.
Rodgers, R. H. *Family interaction and transaction: The developmental approach.* Englewood Cliffs, N.J.: Prentice-Hall, 1973.
Siporin, M. Bankrupt debtors and their families. *Social Work 12* (1967):51-62.
Taylor, M. K., and Kogan, K. L. Effects of birth of a sibling on mother-child interactions. *Child Psychiatry and Human Development 4* (1973):53-58.
Turner, J. G. The influence of religion on family attitudes toward aging parents. *Family Perspective 8*, no. 1 (1973):27-31.
Willie, C. V. The black family and social class. *American Journal of Orthopsychiatry 44* (1974):50-60.

black muslim and negro
christian family relationships

harry edwards

The notion that the Nation of Islam has possibly exerted positive as well as negative influences upon its members became the originating idea out of which the major questions for this study emerged. Specifically, the study focused upon a comparison between Muslim and lower-class Negro Christian families.

Due largely to the work of Frazier, many Americans became aware of the chaos and instability extant within many lower-class American Negro families. Frazier portrays the lower-class Negro family as matriarchal in structure, often common-law in nature, and characterized by an adult male figure functioning almost solely in a procreative capacity.[1]

Although there have been many studies that have enlarged upon some of the specific aspects of Frazier's work, in the nearly two decades since its publication, there has been no study done on the lower-class American Negro of comparable scope or sociological import. Since the surprisingly rapid expansion of an isolated incident aboard a bus in Montgomery, Alabama, into what has become known as the "Negro Revolt" and the occurrence of other significant events, it is doubtful that the nature and structure of the lower-class Negro family, as described by Frazier, have remained unchanged. Indeed there is some recent evidence, albeit controversial, that tends to substantiate the oft voiced speculation that the Negro family is in the process of still further deterioration.[2] Many students of the race problem in America are becoming more aware of the role the instability of the lower-class Negro family plays in hindering the implementation of some practical solutions to the problems involved.

Although the civil rights movement has, for the most part, had as a goal integration of the black American into the existing social fabric, it has also given rise to an abundance of what have been termed "black Nationalist" organizations. These organizations have not stressed the need for a racially integrated society but have advocated the development of a racially and socially plural society—as in the case of several so-called Afro-American organizations—or they have pushed for complete racial separatism—physical and social—as is the case with the Nation of Islam. Most of these black Nationalist organizations have developed special programs of study and training to prepare themselves to assume roles in their unique version of the "great society." One aspect of this training and preparation has been the attempt to alter the pattern of family relationships characterizing the lower-class Negro family. There are increasing signs, particularly in large urban centers, that these attempts have been at least partially successful.

METHODOLOGY

The basic design for the study involved the comparison of matched pairs of families—one group of families affiliated with the Nation of Islam, the other group affiliated with lower-class Negro Christian Churches. The major technique employed was the focused interview supplemented by a great deal of participant observation and the occasional use of informants. The interviews focused on four specific areas of family relations: husband-wife, extended kinships, parent-child, and family-community.

The sample consisted of 14 families from each group. They were matched for mean spouse educational attainment, mean spouse income, race, and the factor of having a minimum mean time of four years in active affiliation with their respective religious organizations. The highest level of educational attainment for the families was 12 and one-half years. Most were considerably lower. The bulk of the spouses were educated in southern public schools. The yearly family income ranged from about $2,000 to a high of $5,500. All members of the sample lived in the same geographical area and were phenotypically Negroid.[3] Each family had at least a minimum mean time in active affiliation with its church or mosque of four years; however, the Muslims as a group averaged five and one-half years while the Christians' average was 11 years. The lesser mean active affiliation time among families of the former group may be due to a number of factors among which are the traditional religious posture of the American Negro and the more recent proselytizing success of the Nation of Islam.

Although detailed information of all the families involved in this study is not presently readily available, there are sufficient data to substantiate the following brief statements regarding the general occupational and family profiles of the Muslim and Christian groups.

On the whole, Muslim families were wage-earning families in contrast to Christian families which tended to be non-wage earners. The types of jobs held by the Muslims ranged from low-income jobs—selling papers and manual part-time labor—to relatively high-income jobs—steady factory work and fork-lift operations. Those Muslims holding low-income or part-time jobs usually held more than one job. For instance, it was not unusual to find a Muslim selling papers during morning work hours and busing dishes during the afternoon work hours.

In the Christian families, by contrast, the modal condition was one of unemployment. The female spouses typically earned what steady wage income came into these families. The jobs held were low-income ones; part-time jobs were held also. These were usually jobs of a service nature—waitress, domestic, and hair-straightener. In the cases of both Muslim and Christian families, the higher paying jobs were held by persons with relatively high rank in the two religious organizations (e.g. incomes over $4,000 were earned by assistant ministers and student ministers in the Christian and Muslim groups, respectively).

The Christian spouses were, on the average, older than the Muslim spouses. They also had a greater number of children than did the Muslims. However, the Muslim families were characterized by a stair-step succession of births, whereas the Christian families were less intensively prolific. There is evidence to support the contention that the discrepancy between these two contrasting birth patterns may have been due to differing attitudes toward birth control. Also, the fact that working female spouses would have been considerably inconvenienced by a continuous succession of nine-month gestation periods was probably a factor of some impact in determining this discrepancy.

All of the families involved in this study lived in the same geographical area—an area characterized by dilapidated housing, rats, or high unemployment rate, as well as other conditions typical of the black ghettos across the United States.

RESULTS

The results will be reported for each of the four areas of family relations. In each instance, the responses of the Muslim group will be compared to those of the Christian group.

Husband-Wife Relationships

The questions in the area of husband-wife relationships were directed toward ascertaining those role functions of each spouse that involved work, money authority, decision making, and the use of leisure time. The literature is replete with references to the characteristic tendency toward the use of physical expression, often in the form of violence, among lower-class Negroes. This violence is often also present in husband-wife relationships, particularly as these relationships revolve around such fiscal problems as the procurement and allocation of money.

For the Christian families, the state of one spouse's financial and material affluence as perceived by the other played a greater role in determining the degree of stability of their relationship than did the same situation among the Muslims. All but one Christian case responded with at least a qualified "yes" to the question of whether they thought the female spouse should work. They indicated a "balance of authority" between themselves and their spouses. Through contributing a portion of money to the family income equal to or greater than that of their husbands', the Christian females felt themselves to be more justified and secure in expressing or seeking the realization of their own individual desires, opinions, and decisions in the marriage situation. Though not all of the Christian females worked the majority did bring money into the family. This was primarily due to welfare and child support payments from previous relationships. In light of this, it would appear that the welfare system is indirectly perpetuating the matriarchal family structure among these lower-class Negroes by making welfare aid and child support payments payable directly to the female spouse in the household.

The Muslims' opinions regarding the desirability of married females working were the exact opposite of those expressed by the Christian groups. In fact, the Muslims were against any female holding an income-producing job, whether married or not. They felt that a woman's place was in the home and the task of earning a living was the sole responsiblity of the adult male. This conviction was expressed adamantly by both male and female spouses. The majority of these Muslim women seemed to believe that their main task in life was to be good wives and mothers ("good" being synonymous with Muslim). Most, if not all, authority was vested in the role of the male. Consonant with this authority, the Muslims reported that all major decisions affecting the family were made by the male. In the majority of cases, such decisions as where to live and what purchases to make, as well as when to make them, were made by the Muslim male. This is in contrast to the Christian families wherein the females made these decisions. The responses of the Christian families relative to decision making and authority, both of which were anchored in the female's role because of income production, tended to lend substantial validity to the notion that the lower-class Christian families functioned within a matriarchal structure. The Muslim families, by contrast, through family role definition prescribed by Black Muslim dogma, have established for themselves a more patriarchal family system. This role clarity appeared to reduce intrafamily conflict considerably for the Muslim families.

For the most part, Muslim respondents regarded intrafamily conflict of any type as totally unnecessary and avoidable. By contrast, the Christian respondents thought such conflict to be unavoidable and some physical violence inevitable "if two people lived together long enough." The Muslim mechanism for avoiding trouble involved a use of the fundamental teachings of their religion in the face of impending conflict. Statements were often made to the effect that, when conflict threatened, the spouses concerned merely "got on the side of Islam" and the wrong fell of its own weight. No such responses came from the Christian, nor was there any evidence of their gravitating toward religious fundamentals in time of impending conflict between spouses.

The duties of each Muslim spouse in the marriage situation were outlined in astonishingly minute detail and taught in training sessions held specifically for this purpose. The female was trained to fulfill her principal duties—those of mother and housewife. She was taught, among other things, how to cook, what to cook, how often to cook, how to sew, and how to keep house. She was trained in home economy and maintenance. The male spouse likewise was taught his responsiblities and how to fulfill them. These predetermined responsibilities and the activities that they generate were so calculated as to avoid a conflict. They further placed the Muslim male spouse in the position of the productive, contributing breadwinner and protector of his family. By contrast, the typical Christian response to questions as to who held what responsibilities was: "It depends."

Another contrast between the two types of families was in the extent of "idling" activity. The Christian male spouses participated in this "idling" or "killing time" far more than did the Muslims. Not once did the author find a Muslim male in any of the local "hangouts" or in an idling situation. First of all, most of the idling places were also places where drinking and smoking were common pastimes. Muslim ideology forbids the use of either alcohol or tobacco. There were two other factors which contributed to this lack of an idling custom among Muslims. First, due to the Muslims' overt enthusiasm for their religion, they were often unwelcome at idling places. Their constant tendency to emphasize the decadent and useless behavior of the "regulars" of such places made them unwelcome, even on the occasional "fishing expeditions" to hangouts frequented by the "dead" (see below). Secondly, the Muslims did not have free time to participate in idling. After fulfilling a predetermined schedule of activities, the Muslim males would spend a great proportion of their leisure time on "fishing expeditions." These expeditions were considered part of their duties as Muslims. They believed that the final hour for North America was near. They, likewise, believed it to be their duty to save as many black men as possible.[4] Not to make an attempt to do so was considered behavior unworthy of a Muslim.

Family-Extended Kin Relationships

A number of situations determined the break between the Muslim spouses and their relatives. In those cases where the parents and in-laws of the Muslim spouses lived within the area, "uniting with" the Nation of Islam was contrary to their wishes of these relations. This assumes added significance since the majority of these parents and in-laws belonged to Christian churches. Also of significance in the break between Muslim spouses and their parents was the inflexibility of the Muslim spouses in their adherence to the behavioral codes of the Nation of Islam. It was found that conscientious Muslims did not smoke, drink, or curse, nor did they tolerate these prohibited indulgences within their homes. Since many of the Muslims' relatives did in fact indulge in these habits, a situation of mutual intolerance and estrangement soon followed. Of relevance here also were the reactions of the parents and in-laws to the Muslims, particularly as these reactions focused upon the behavior and activities of the Muslim female spouse. Muslim females never straightened their hair or wore make-up of any kind. The resulting appearance of the female was often a point of criticism and mockery from relatives, particularly it seemed from the female spouse's mother. This situation, too, was intolerable. No Muslim tolerated criticism or mockery of moral directives emanating from the Honorable Elijah Muhammed—especially not in his own home, which is next to the mosque in its sanctity.

The Christians, by contrast, maintained continual, if not stable, relationships with their relatives. Generational ties were particularly characteristic of the Christian female spouses and their mothers. In only a few cases did the mothers of the female spouses actually live in the same homes with them. However, even though the physical propinquity was not there, psychosocial closeness was very much in evidence. The telephone was the major medium for contact. The majority of Christian females indicated that their primary confidants, creditors, and advisers were their mothers. Several Christian female spouses noted that their mothers were the first to learn of their pregnancies, plans to work, and other such important occurrences.

Among the Muslims, no such relationships existed. In discussions with the female spouses at the mosque, it was made abundantly clear that the primary, and often the only, confidants for these women were their husbands. There were apparently never any occasions for these Muslim females to borrow goods or money from anyone, since such decisions were typically made by the male spouse. And for the female to do so "over the head" of the male spouse would have been in direct opposition to Muslim directives regarding her proper role in the family.

Parent-Child Relationships

The responses of the Christian spouses show that they conformed more closely to the generally held lower-class Negro subcultural attitudes and practices with regard to children and child rearing than did the Muslim spouses. The differences between the two groups' relationships with their children did not begin with the actual socializing effects of home life on the child, but with the parents' attitudes towards birth control.

The Muslim subjects expressed indignation and disgust at the queries on birth control methods. Not a single Muslim respondent reported that any methods of birth control, "natural" or otherwise, had been used by either spouse since they became serious adherents to the ideology of the Nation of Islam. The Christian respondents, on the other hand, not only stated that they had used or were using various birth control devices, but several subjects also reported that they regretted not having practiced birth control more often and more consistently. While the Christians had more children than did the Muslims, the spacing of the children in the latter group was characterized by a stair-step succession of births, whereas child births in the former group were erratically spaced. Apparently the desire for children also helped determine to a large extent parents' interaction with the child. By removing any question of the desirability of children, regardless of circumstance, the Muslims also removed one potential source from which a child's emotional and social maladjustment might arise. In doing so, they quite possibly may have opened the door to other problems, such as poverty-stricken families and lack of adequate living space, which could have equally as damaging effects on the child as the lack of proper parent-child emotional relationship. However, the Muslims felt that poverty and "overpopulation" were merely manifestations of what they considered to be the white man's intrinsically evil nature and his criminal use of the world's resources. As such, these afflications would pass away with him. The act of practicing birth control because one does not desire children was, on the other hand, viewed as an act against the Nation of Islam and, therefore, against Allah.

Given the birth of a child, the Muslim and Christian groups also exhibited differing attitudes with regard to child-rearing practices. These differences involved the acceptability and effectiveness of various disciplinary practices as well as the manner in which these practices should be carried out. The Christians had few reservations concerning the use of physical punishment. Generally they held the opinion that, after the age when a child knows that what he is doing is wrong, other forms of punishment are only minimally effective.

The Muslims generally indicated that they held the use of physical punishment in close reserve, to be used only at those times when all other forms of chastisement failed. The reasons were very similar to those given for not advocating the use of physically coercive measures between spouses. They also indicated that there was seldom any need for physical punishment because of the effectiveness of Muslim child-rearing methods and the example of proper behavior provided by the parents.

Of significance in the area of disciplinary practices were the subjects' responses to questions pertaining to youths who get into trouble. Their differing points of view began with their ideas concerning the concept of "trouble" itself. The Christians' responses tended to indicate they they considered a child to be in trouble when (and if) he was caught in a compromising situation. The Muslims, on the other hand, considered any individual to be in trouble when a transgression was conceived, regardless of whether he actually committed the act, must less, whether he was caught. They reasoned that such an idea was indicative of a more deep-seated anomaly which at best could give rise to more un-Muslimlike behavior. In short, the Christians considered the onset of trouble to be the point at which relevant authority figures become aware of the act and the person responsible for it, whereas the Muslims considered the commencement of trouble to be that point at which the idea for the act was consciously conceived. Consistent with their varying conceptions of trouble were the two groups' opinions as to what types of trouble young people "inevitably" get into. The Christians felt that it was inevitable that youth would get into trouble because of a spirit of curiosity and the need to experiment. Among these acts were included sexual offenses and thefts of varying degrees of seriousness. The Muslims, on the other hand, considered only one type of trouble as inevitable—that which a black man might encounter as a Muslim in a white man's society. They saw sexual offenses, thefts, and other law violations as inexcusable and, hence, intolerable. They argued that such behavior was only the consequence of the black man's attempt to imitate the white man.

While the Christian respondents did not endorse premarital sexual relations, neither did they express violent opposition to it. Instead, their responses indicated that their main effort was directed towards the preparation of their offspring to "protect themselves because you sure can't stop them." The Christians also permitted their offspring to begin the use of cosmetics and other such accoutrements at an earlier age than the general society would consider as appropriate. The Muslims abhorred the use of any cosmetics at any time and any age.

Although the Christian subjects, as a group, had greater educational aspirations for their children than did the Muslims, the latter group took more positive steps toward the fulfillment of their more limited aspirations. The Muslims expressed an intense determination that their children should finish school. This determination originated primarily from the Muslims' belief that knowledge, from whatever source, is "the key to all things." They felt that knowledge acquired within the walls of the white man's schools had value when interpreted within the context of Muslim ideology. Their respect for the law and their determination to adhere to its dictates were also chief factors underlying their efforts to keep their children in school. However, they were extremely hostile towards higher education and its more specialized knowledge. While adamantly insisting on an absence of truancy and on rigorous study habits for their offspring through high school, they felt just as strongly against their children continuing in the existing system of higher education. Among the reasons for these anti-college feelings were criticisms of the curriculum in history and science. It was felt that these subject areas did not acknowledge the works of Allah and the original black man before the dawn of the white man's recorded history. It was also thought that the white man has left out of his history and science books those contributions and achievements made by black individuals and nations and, in some cases, that he had even claimed these achievements and contributions as his own. Finally, the Muslims reported that the black youth who was away from his own people while attending these institutions would find it difficult not to believe "the white man's lies," primarily because he would have no one to explain to him how and why these lies were being propagated.

The Christians by comparison, who were much less strict about the school attendance and study habits of their children, placed a high value on college for their offspring. However, they apparently had little notion of the sacrifices necessary if these aspirations were to be realized.

Though the Muslims' educational aspirations for their children were more limited than those of the Christians, the Muslims' aspirations were, nevertheless, more realistic with respect to their prevailing economic and social situations. The probability of their attaining these limited goals would appear to be much higher than the Christian group's chances of realizing the educational goals to which they aspire for their offspring. In general, then, the Christians advocated the use of the severest form of punishment for their offspring, but were very lenient and permissive with regard to their children's engaging in the illicit forms of behavior which, at the very least, might prompt such punishment. Their only justification for this inconsistency would appear to be that the punishment is not administered for the commitment of the act, but for being caught. They also held high educational goals for their offspring but did little to attain them.

Family-Community Relationships

An analysis of responses pertaining to family-community relations revealed that the Muslim families had almost no contact with any institution other than that to which they maintained religious ties. The Christians, by comparison, reported an array of extra-religious institutional contacts and commitments. Overwhelmingly the most common contact was that reported to have taken place with various welfare institutions. Of the Christian families, 93 percent had applied for and received some type of public aid within a three-year period as opposed to 21 percent of the Muslim families. Likewise, 64 percent of the Christian families reported that they had had contact with some branch of the local law enforcement system as opposed to 21 percent of the Muslim group.

Considering the Christian families' reports as to their attitudes towards "trouble"—especially that most characteristic of juveniles—and these families' economic situations and work habits, their reports of institutional contact with respect to welfare and law enforcement agencies were strikingly consistent. Likewise, the Muslims' institutional contacts of the sort discussed above followed more or less consistently from their expressed views on trouble and their values on industriousness and the economic independence of the family.

The two groups were diametrically opposed to one another on the question of the desirability of social clubs for either adults or youths. While the Christians thought that such clubs were highly beneficial, the Muslims viewed any type of social club with intense suspicion and distrust. Not all of the Christians belonged to social clubs, only a little over one-half. However, even among those Christians not belonging to clubs, such membership was not considered undesirable. While no Muslims belonged to any social club, neither was there any consistent answer given as to why such was the case. This suggests that the Muslims possibly had no direct policy against such affiliation but may have discouraged it through more indirect means. Among these means might have been the prohibition against the consumption of liquor, the preparation of relatively rigid activity schedules for members, and the declaration that time should not be used wastefully ("wasted time" being defined as all of that time not used in Muslim goal attainment).

The Muslims were also concerned with economic and social "welfare." There were two facets to the Nation of Islam's approach to changing the economic and social situation of the black man in the ghetto. First of all, there was no need for the potential Muslim to apply separately for material aid and then for aid in adjusting socially and psychologically to his responsibilities. When a person applied to and was accepted by the Nation of Islam, as a Muslim, regardless of what the precipitating factor behind his decision to apply was (be it economic hardship or the need for spiritual security), he is exposed to the entire program. That is, efforts were immediately initiated by the Muslims to ascertain and at least partially satisfy his economic needs; efforts were made to secure work for him that he was qualified to do or to train him for the types of jobs that were available; and he was resocialized to the Muslim orientation to life. Secondly an attempt was made by the Muslims to show the convert that his social and psychological orientations to life were inextricably interconnected with his poverty stricken or socially deteriorating situation and that to change the latter would inevitably change the former. This task was made easier by the fact that the same individuals who gave him aid and found him a job were also the people who attempted to resocialize him—his "Muslim brothers." Material aid and resocialization were both administered by the same people, under the same roof, and at the same time. It is perhaps through this technique that the Muslim convert may have come to see economic betterment and security as part and parcel of religious, social, and psychological change.

DISCUSSION

In the family relationships of the two groups, there is evidence of two differing foundations for authority. The first of these foundations is manifest in the relationships observed among Muslim families. It derives its legitimization from a basis of respect on the part of the female spouse for the role and position of her husband and the acceptance of her role as a supporting one. This female role is not, however, without its relative advantages. Since, traditionally, the lower-class Negro family has not been organized on a foundation of primary authority, it would appear that the Nation of Islam has had some success in narrowing the gap between the family structure and interactional patterns of its members and those of American middle-class society.

The Christians' family relationships may be characterized as deriving from a second basis of authority. These relationships appear to have been grounded in the spouses' desires for physical comfort, economic security, and a subtle type of respect that emerges from conflict situations. As the economic situation changed, there apparently also occurred commensurate changes in the balance of authority and the overall status of the marriage relationship.

The Muslims approximated the dominant group's values concerning family relationships to a far greater extent than did the Christians. The same general statement holds for the Muslims' relationships with their children. It seems that the Muslims anchored the appropriate role characteristics with the appropriate sexes as prescribed within the context of traditional American values. The Muslim male earned a living, protected his family, and was chief representative of his family in outside social dealings, while the Muslim female concentrated her efforts primarily in the area of child rearing and housekeeping. This is in contrast to the typical lower-class American Negro family life style, where, because of the social heritage and the disadvantaged position of Negroes in American society, there developed a matriarchal family type which has become extremely unstable. If we are in fact moving more and more toward an urban, neolocal, nuclear family type, the Muslims would appear to be less deviant than the lower-class Negro Christians. Also in the area of family-community relationships, the Muslims typified the wage-earning, noncriminal, middle-class ideal to a greater extent than did the Christians.

On the basis of these findings, there would appear to be some questions as to the accuracy of the popular notion concerning the degree of social and psychological nonconformity extant within the Nation of Islam. From the perspective of the uninformed public, the Muslims are seen as in a state of rebellion—as totally rejecting the values and goals of this society and replacing them with their own values and goals. Because of their separatist ideology and their refusal to participate in various institutions of the society, persons who are fairly well informed might view the Muslims as an organized group of either rebels or retreatists. However, the results of this study tend to portray the Muslims as, again in Merton's terminology, primarily ritualists who have adopted and "black-washed" a version of American middle-class values and goals while simultaneously rejecting the institutionalized means to their attainment.

Although the Muslims are shown to be lower class in terms of income, education, and general environment, they are very middle class in many other respects—especially with regard to such issues as sex practices, the value put upon education (with some qualifications), personal hygiene and grooming, the high value placed upon work and industriousness, and their intense interest in developing and maintaining a high degree of mental and physical alertness. These are clearly not the characteristics typically found to exist throughout the lower-class Negro subculture.

In conclusion it seems clear that the Muslims were not only more conforming than the Christians in their adherence to what appear to be traditional American values regarding intrafamily behavior, but also that there exists a narrower gap between the Muslims' ideational values and their normative behavior.

Although a severe access problem exists with regard to researching the Nation of Islam and its membership, it is hoped that much research will be forthcoming, particularly since it is only through this means that accurate social and psychological portraits of this significant group can be obtained.

FOOTNOTES

[1] E. F. Frazier, *The Negro Family in the United States,* New York: Citadel Press, 1948.

[2] Evans and Novak column entitled, "The Moynihan Report," *New York Herald Tribune,* August 18, 1965; Benjamin F. Payton, "The President, the Social Experts, and the Ghetto: An Analysis of an Emerging Strategy in Civil Rights," unpublished paper, pp. 1-9; Peter Goldman, "The Splintering Negro Family—A Confidential Report," *News Week,* (August 9, 1965).

[3] Both the Muslim and Christian religious bodies, however, numbered among their memberships persons of other racial extraction.

[4] The Muslims ignore completely the traditional grouping of homo sapiens by race. Hence, any nonwhite by Muslim definition is a "black brother" (these racial brothers include such racially diversified people as Chinese, Filipinos, Mexicans, Indians [Eastern], North American Indians, Arabs, Negroes, Africans, Japanese, Eskimos, etc.).

38 coupling, parenting, and the presence of others: intimate relationships in communal households

What happens to the most intimate human ties when the territory of the relationship is shared with others? What happens to couple and parent-child relationships in the presence of other adults who have equal claims on the household? What is the structure of the environment for couples, parents, and children when family space is public rather than private, when others are present as audiences, claimants on the intimate territory, and sources of alternative ties? We have studied urban communal households—domestic collectives—in an attempt to answer these questions about the nature of important relationships in the presence of others. Rather than focusing on the group as the unit of interest, then, we are focusing on how specific relationships are affected and changed by sharing a household with other adults. Although the setting for this research is a particular kind of family experiment in the 1970's, many of the results can be generalized to any situation in which outsiders are present in the intimate space of a relationship, whether the "others" are relatives, boarders, close friends, or professionals such as family therapists. The study of relationships "in the presence of others" also highlights, by contrast, a variety of taken-for-granted family dynamics.

The major effects can be summarized as an initial shift in the locus of social control. When relationships are conducted in the presence of "others," couples and parents experience a loss of control, both over their territory and over their partner. The "others" change the relationship by their presence as an audience, direct intervention, their availability as potential coalition partners, and their claims over the intimate space. Couples experience pressures toward individuation, autonomy, and egalitarianism, as well as a loss of sovereignty. Parents experience diminishing abilities to make and enforce rules and increased self-consciousness about child rearing, as well as important help in many of the tasks of parenting. Children, of ages five to eleven, who gain additional adult relationships, are also the recipients of increased rule making by other adults. And, paradoxically, while both couples and parents report a loss of control, they still tend to have more power in the household than other adults uninvolved in relationships, so that while they report their *lack* of control, other household members report the "unfair" control of people in couple or parent-child relationships. These effects are strongest in the early stages of communal involvements; over time satisfactory accommodations tend to be made.

Our research has involved field work, interviews, and instrumented data collection with members of 35 urban and suburban communal households in the Boston and New Haven areas since March 1972, fifteen of which include children under twelve. Single people outnumbered both couples and parent-child units, with few households containing more than one couple or one parent. A majority of the parents were single parents, thus making the analysis of the parent-child relationship in communal houses as a "dyad with others present" even more meaningful. The culture of the

Reprinted, by permission, from *Family Coordinator*, 1975, *24*, 433-52. Copyright ©1975 by the National Council on Family Relations.

households was solidly avant-garde middle class rather than hippie or student. They were generally located in a large old house in middle class areas; relatively few were in hip-bohemian-student areas of the city. Mean household size was 9.6. Interviewed in depth were couples, parents, and children who had lived in a private household at least six months before beginning to live communally; most of the couples studied were married.

THEORETICAL BACKGROUND

Georg Simmel's work on the significance of numbers for social life and theories of coalition formation that derived from it provides one framework for understanding the significance of the "presence of others" (Simmel, 1950; Caplow, 1968). Simmel asserted that a dyadic relationship is completely different in form from a relationship between three or more people and, in fact, that the change from two to three-or-more parties is one of the most significant numerical leaps. The two-person relationship is a union, two complementary and unique parts coming together; it may come to depend upon a division of properties such that persons experience their own incompleteness without the contribution of the other. Each one constitutes the relationship; it would not exist if either one left. The person least involved may have the most power, according to the "theory of least interest" derived from this analysis, because if either person leaves, the relationship by definition ends. Each person is a majority, so the power pattern is normally one of dominance-submission. Equality is hard to achieve if there are two opposing interests clashing.

With the introduction of a third person, the relationship may drastically alter. The third party provides an audience for the initial dyad and merely by watching may alter the relationship in a number of ways: by serving as a representative of "society" or interests beyond the dyad (a reminder of social norms), and thereby increasing the self-consciousness of the pair as they interact and increasing the pressure for image-maintenance; by serving as a witness and potential swing vote should the dyad engage in dispute; and by becoming privy to "family secrets," thereby reducing the space in which one important solidifier of relationships can be maintained. As coalition theory suggests, a third party also makes possible coalitions and power blocs other than the original couple, thus dramatically altering the power structure, since it is now possible for any two to form a coalition against any third person or one person to set another two against one another. Power cannot as easily be unilaterally exercised by one dyad member over another because of the threat of third party intervention or the forming of a superior coalition with the victim.

The nature of group dynamics differs in additional ways in three-person versus two-person groups. Relations of three or more, Simmel theorized, are based on what members have in common rather than their unique properties emphasizing a union of commonality instead of the union of opposites of the dyad and de-emphasizing polarization. Finally, Simmel proposed that relations of three or more have a "superindividual" reality such that any one of the members can leave but the relationship, the unit, the group, will still exist. Unlike the situation of the dyad, members can be replaced without totally changing the unit's character. The three-person group is thus theoretically immortal, and the "principle of least interest" that gives power to the member threatening withdrawal is no longer automatically operative.

If the larger group is a potential threat to the freedom, sovereignty, power configuration, and division of properties of the dyad as an exclusive and excluding relationship, the two-person intimate alliance may also be a potential threat to the solidarity of the larger group. Several analyses suggest that, particularly when the need or desire for collective commitment to "superindividual" entities is high, exclusive relationships such as couples and parent-child bonds may threaten the group because they represent competition for members' emotional energy and loyalty; because they may be self-sufficient in themselves, not needing the group and leaving it behind, withdrawing their resources and shutting others out; and because they may represent a natural power bloc within the group with the advantage in coalition formation of easier access to and knowledge of one another (Kanter,

1972a, 86-7; Slater, 1963; Coser, 1974). When things are difficult in a group, people in committed subgroup relationships may also have the advantage over nonrelated people because they do not "need" the total group to the same extent; such inequalities may threaten group cohesion and satisfactory resolution of the dispute. In a variety of past and present communes, for example, groups developed a number of practices to reduce the importance of biological family ties and increase the number of functions served by the whole group rather than the small unit (Kanter, 1972, 1973). Philip Slater (1963) has described the mechanisms by which society in general intrudes on couples and families, reasserting control over them and pulling them back into the social fabric when they threaten withdrawal and secret behavior free of social constraints.

Thus, intervention into the relationship of a couple or parent-and-child may not only be *made possible* by the presence of others but may also be *actively sought* by the others in order to reduce the threat of dyadic withdrawal and maintain the cohesiveness of the larger unit all comprise. Several propositions follow. For example, helping one dyad member with a responsibility involving the other is also a way of intervening in the relationship and indicating the potential replaceability of a partner, thus undercutting both the exclusiveness and the self-sufficiency of the dyad. In collective households, then, the amount of helping people do with each other's needs and obligations, from babysitting to providing company while the partner is out, serves both a manifest function of reducing burdens and a latent function of helping prevent dyadic withdrawal. Further, we can propose that when others intervene in a dyadic relationship, they are likely to try to maximize keeping both members actively available to the group—supporting the weaker member against the stronger so that the stronger will not "destroy" the weaker, and supporting the one who is being pulled into withdrawing against the one who is pulling. Finally, when collective commitment is important and the dyad is not necessary as a fundamental building block of the collective, we can propose that when third parties serve as audiences representing social norms, the norms of which they remind the pair are likely to be norms *against* dyad unity and fusion.

This theoretical overview makes apparent a fundamental asymmetry between how dyad members and third parties would view their joint relationship in a three-or-more person group. While pair members may experience the loss of control over their relationship and joint space and the control of third parties, the "others" may themselves feel out of control of the situation in the presence of the "natural coalitions." Paradoxically, while dyad members may feel they do not have enough power in the presence of others, the others may see them as too powerful. While dyad members may feel they give up control, the others may instead feel they take control. This situation engenders a number of tensions in the group and an atmosphere in which dyad members are continually aware of working on contradictions and balancing pulls.

The analysis thus far is relevant to any relationship of three-or-more roughly equal participants containing committed dyads. But we suggest that these phenomena are exaggerated in communal households and therefore more visible. First, urban communal households intentionally develop a public character that makes others potentially present for generally all family events but sleeping, sexual intercourse, and bathroom use. Group members also have access to and claims on all household territory except a member's single private room, and sometimes even that place if the door is not closed or the resident not present (Kanter, 1974).

Secondly, communal households generally stress negotiated as opposed to institutionalized norms. Since there are few precedents for organizing collective households and often explicit values favoring shared power, members must come together in a period of initial chaos, high expectations, and sometimes conflict and confusion, to create a household organization. House meetings at weekly or biweekly intervals are often the first process established. The emphasis on negotiation—which we suggest will be characteristic of most families in the future—stems from the ideology of alternative families as well as the structural consequences of joint residence by many equal, unrelated adults. House meetings and other public negotiations aid shared power and meeting on common ground, even if there are age or resource differences. The existence of egalitarian norms means that when others intervene in a dyad they are as likely to support the weaker as the stronger member.

Finally, the household's division of labor is also the result of an explicit small group negotiation process. It is likely to be determined on the basis of fair sharing of the load rather than skill or ascribed characteristics, and it is likely to involve every member, often including children, as an individual rather than as a member of a unit. (Job sharing, indeed, is another way in which collective commitment can be enhanced. See Kanter, 1972.) This and other structural and other ideological characteristics of communal household increase and channel the effects of the "presence of others" on couples and parents.

COUPLES: DIMINISHED SOVEREIGNTY

When a couple moves from their own place into a public household, their initial experience is a loss of power and sovereignty, combined with an opening up of their relationship to others. Since the couple members are not the sole proprietors of the house, they have less autonomy, privacy, power and freedom to set rules than if they lived alone. This can be stressful, but some people also find it a positive experience, especially if it is in line with one's ideology, as it was for this woman:

> *I learned a lot about sharing. I had lived five years in a couple and had really got into some privatistic things. Control things like always knowing what's in the refrigerator; little things that psychologically make a lot of difference. Taking control of the house and knowing what had to be done, and planning around that. At first it was difficult for me to lose that control, although it was also liberating. I sometimes didn't have input into what we ate, which brought back bad memories of my parents' house. Or we would get a lot of magazines, which we would save. But in the commune they would get lost, and I had to change my feelings about those pieces of property.*

As a subunit of the house, one's couple is not identical with the whole, but is subject to observation, as well as checks and balances by other people.

> *Having an audience can be disconcerting at first, as this man felt: I wasn't convinced that I wanted to have other people observing my idiosyncracies and challenging me, wondering aloud why I did x or y. Suddenly all of my routines were subject to scrutiny, things that the other member of the couple would just let by. Like my fixing everything in the house, which would now become issues, because suddenly it wasn't my house. I didn't have to be responsible for everything, because others wanted to know how to take care of the house too. So in the process we started to question these roles.*

The audience alters the way one deals with a mate as well. One person reported that in his nuclear household he could go on a unilateral strike, as by refusing to talk to the other in the face of repeated demands to take out the garbage. In a communal household, the presence of an audience witnessing this "childish" behavior and able to step in the breach, potentially isolating the agressor, makes this strategy less effective.

In a communal household, couple members cannot control all inputs and outputs for themselves and each other—whether material or emotional. This makes the couple boundary more permeable and intimacy more diffused. The limited exchange of interpersonal goods and services within the couple is replaced by a marketplace, in which different possible relationships and experiences are available from a variety of others. Some of the couples were at a stage where they felt their relationships were becoming stale, boring, routine and depressing. New people represented an injection of energy, and forced them to re-evaluate their relationship, as this man found:

Initially I had two distinct feelings. First that I was losing my family. I was afraid of that. I liked the family set-up, the closeness to the children. I felt the nuclear feeling, closeness, was going to be gone forever, and that has turned out to be true. The other feeling was one of camaraderie. Here were people I loved setting out on a frightening, glamorous, together thing. We had a chance of really experiencing close friendship we couldn't get in other ways. So there was fear and optimism at the start.

Almost every couple interviewed remarked that living collectively resulted in their learning that if and when their mate cannot meet a particular need, there are others who can. They find that many of the conflicts they had as a nuclear couple are less intense, because the other no longer represents a unique and irreplaceable resource. This both takes pressure off their relationship, and decreases its intensity—a potential gain and a potential cost.

The loss of sovereignty and opening up to new relationships that couples experience creates an element of risk which is not shared by single commune members. Since the commune upsets the balance of the relationship, opening it up to new inputs and sources of control, and diffusing the focus of couple members on each other for gratification, one is testing the relationship when one enters a commune. There is always the possibility that the relationship will be totally replaced, or cease to be useful within a communal context. The commune removes barriers to temptation and change, and a relationship that cannot stand comparison will probably not stand up to communal living. This factor probably accounts for the high number of couples who split up within the first few months of communal living (nearly 50%) and the very low number of splits that occur later (Jaffe and Kanter, 1975). Couple members who split up after moving into a commune usually report that the commune hastened or catalyzed a seemingly inevitable process, or gave them the support to leave the relationship or invest in new ones. An empty shell couple has little reason to remain together within a commune.

Interventions and Coalitions: Heightened Conflict Expression

Other household members can actively intervene or form supportive coalitions with one member of the couple; thus there is opportunity and pressure for the couple member to open up conflicts. Said one woman:

When there's other people around, you can express that conflict, your difficulty, whereas when there's just the two of you you have these old patterns, like you get angry and it doesn't affect anyone else, you're just angry for a couple of days, and the other person learns to ignore it. You don't talk about it or try to realize what's making you angry. When you're living with other people they are affected by it so you have to be more critical about what's happening to you emotionally, and the effects of your behavior on other people.

In many groups, couple issues that cause strain for others are resolved either by house members talking to the couple privately, or being sought out as mediators by the couple. Couples who feel that their relationship is only their business are usually those who withdraw from the house in other ways, and soon move out of communal settings.

Conflict expression and seeking support outside the couple is facilitated by living with others of one's own sex, since same-sex coalitions are more or less "natural" alliances (Caplow, 1968). Almost all of the people we interviewed had been affected by the women's movement, especially its aim to allow women to gain a sense of themselves by breaking down a woman's identification with her man. Most of the women in communes, and many of the men, have been in women's or men's consciousness raising groups, and through such groups they learn to identify and seek support from people of their own sex, which breaks down dependency on one's mate for such support. Many of the communes had women's groups, meeting intermittently or regularly. One commune separated its house meetings into men's and women's groups. The women began to talk about how the married and single women were competitive and jealous, and how this inhibited their closeness because they were still into societal roles of either protecting their man or feeling bad because they didn't have men. The men, meanwhile, had to deal with the ways in which they used women to deal with feelings, to bring up issues around feelings and generally to keep the social life of the house together. They began to take initiative around these areas, discussed problems in their couples, and began to do things together.

Pressure for Individuation and Autonomy

Since there are usually single people, and since almost everything from deicsion making to task allocation is expressed in terms of individuals, one of the major effects of a communal environment on a couple seems to be that it shifts their definition of themselves from being "part of a couple" to "individual member of the commune." Couple members thus lose control over their partner at the same time that they lose their special couple sovereignty over their household.

This changes both the way each member of the couple sees himself/herself and the way he/she behaves. Couple members reported that previous to living communally they felt treated as an inseparable twosome: they were viewed as part of a couple, rarely went places or maintained friends alone, the wife expected to identify and gain status not from her own but her husband's achievements, and the two were taken as a single conversational unit, in which the opinion of one was assumed to stand for both. Several couples mentioned the difficulty of keeping single friends, the norm being you have another couple over [for] dinner and maintain a very structured relationship with them, rather than drop in or maintain individual friendships. One woman mentioned that she felt guilty if she went out, because she would be leaving her husband alone to babysit. Also, many traditional couples have a norm that they cannot disagree or neglect to support the other person in the presence of others, even though they may later disagree violently.

The communal house seems to reverse each of these fusing processes, by structurally reinforcing the autonomy and individuality of each member of the couple. Couple members feel freer to come and go, develop relationships, and act without their mate. For example, if one member of a couple is at work, the other who might be in the commune with the children will be relating individually to other commune members. People can go out without feeling that their mate will be all alone, so there is no longer pressure, for example, to go to movies or concerts or parties which one does not care for, just because the mate is going. Of course this process does not go smoothly.

One husband talked about the change in their relationship, which occurred in the year they began to live communally, after many years of very traditional marriage and child rearing:

> *We began more and more doing things on a completely individual basis, following our interests whether or not they included the other. Like, quite recently the weekly women's meeting began, and Elaine has had long talks and strong friendships with people here that don't involve me. . . . The biggest change is this recognition of each of our individual lives outside of our relationship. I have recognized that there is less of my life tied up with her, whereas before I was married 24 hours a day, my entire life was in relation to her, whether something was happening or it wasn't. Now there are parts of my life that she doesn't enter.*

As a couple they have had conflicts over her feeling that he puts his relationship to the community above her—something he admitted and tried to moderate. He felt that they had been at a point where they had little in common, and now that they recognize their separateness, they can also recognize what they share.

Communal households reinforce individuation by making membership and citizenship available only to individuals. Each person joins individually, and usually states individual reasons for wanting to join. When a house member forms a couple with someone outside, it is never automatically expected that the new person will move in; the new person must ask for membership individually, or in one household has the special status of "consort" until he or she becomes a member. There is also pressure for couple members to make decisions and participate in house meetings individually. As people get to know them individually, and under the conflictual lens of house meetings, the facade of couple agreement can no longer be maintained. Many house members talked about how they welcomed times when one member of a couple was away, because that was a way of getting to know the other person separately. Couple members likewise valued time around the house when their mate was absent as a time for forming individual relationships to others. Couple members reported that when they behaved as a traditional couple—sitting together at meals, performing house duties for each other, always agreeing, cutting each other off in conversation, or immediately going to the mate when they come home, expecting them to stop what they are doing—they are apt to be confronted by others, who feel left out or uncomfortable at such closed boundaries.

At the extreme pole of individuation lies the couple that substitutes membership in the community for couple membership. Although only a few couples reported that they joined communes with the intention of making the relationship to the commune primary, simply drifting away from a couple relationship is one possible consequence of individuation. A woman tells of how she moved out of an unfulfilling couple:

> Al was particularly concerned with privacy when we were having a discussion or argument or anything personal between us. Much more so than I. And he didn't really want to go into the conflicts we were having, but just to sweep them under the rug. Since both of us were pretty involved in community things it became harder to nourish our relationship. We didn't work at it hard enough. Our expectations and our interests diverged. We looked in the community to each follow our separate interests, so we didn't have to share. That was happening so nicely that we were spending less and less time together. Our time together would be with other people around so it wasn't time for us but for community, and didn't help our relationship. It became a substitute for the relationship.

Each of them eventually became involved with other people who more closely shared their interests. She spent a summer traveling, and then returned and took a separate bedroom. Neither of them felt an immediate need to resolve their relationship, which existed in a state of separateness and ambiguity until a year later, when they formally acknowledged their separation as a permanent fact, and began living with other people.

This is just one extreme example of how communal settings may even support a complete severing of the relationship: one may remain part of a "family" while leaving a couple, continuing the relationship to the group. In many houses each individual has his or her own room, so that in some cases a split does not even necessitate a room change. There were several instances where both members of the former couple remained in the house after severing their relationship, though not without tension.

Pressure for Egalitarian Relationships

While the pursuit of autonomy and stress on individuation is a force toward equality, there are additional ways in which the structure of the urban communal household promotes male/female equality and a decrease of sex role differentiation among couples. Ideology supports structure: all the communes we studied are explicitly against male dominance (in contrast to some spiritual and rural communes), and are actively trying to equalize sex role related behavior around the house (see Kanter and Halter, 1973). A communal household does not automatically allow the institutionalized slipping into complementary roles and functions—a rigid division of labor based on sex—which can easily occur between two people whose relationship may depend on such division. In many cases neither member of the couple likes housework, and the communal environment decreases the total amount of work each person must do, so that "oppression" of the female via unwanted housework is not simply replaced by male drudgery. Also, people report that many people working together cleaning the house for a few hours a week is more pleasant than working alone. There is less work for all, so when men are asked to participate the demands are not so onerous. The group negotiation process also makes it difficult to maintain a sex-related division of labor. One man reported:

> *Sex roles have become less important here. People all do certain things and the roles are becoming less and less defined. Some women like to work around the house, and all the men help cook, and clean. It wasn't so for us before. I worked and she took care of the kids. At times I took over some of what I always considered to be "her" work. Now I don't see it as hers any more, we simply help each other. I never did much cooking, but here I do it regularly. It is my contribution to the community rather than me giving her a hand, which incidentally, I always needed to be thanked for, because I was doing a favor, something I didn't have to do.*

The presence of a same sex reference group enables many groups to resolve couple role conflicts in favor of greater sharing and equality. Many groups use the word "struggle" in connection with this process of sex role redefinition among couples, and in general among men and women living together. They use group meetings to deal critically with the meaning of equality, to give feedback to others who are not aware of the implications or meaning of their behavior, or are not changing in ways that the house had agreed to. Thus, change of behavior in a communal setting can be monitored constantly. Couples who might have difficulty resolving sex role conflict, or might agree in principle but argue over pathways toward their goals, now participate in a forum which clarifies goals and can judge the degree to which they are met.

Couple Power and Couple Boundaries

Although couple members experience a loss of control, they may still end up with more power than single people in a communal household. Couples retain some control over their own relationship, and there are several ways in which their existence as a couple (particularly in the majority of houses which are largely populated by single people) can gain them disproportionate power.

In some groups, for example, there is a "first family," a couple that takes on some characteristics of a set of parents. They may attain such status because they own the house, or initiated the household, or because they are the oldest members (in age or time lived communally), or simply because they are the only couple. Such "parent trips" in communal households are often a source of conflict and difficulty. Incidents such as the male member of the only married couple handling all the financial affairs, with the others periodically complaining about this but not initiating an alternate plan, demonstrate the tendency for communes to break down into conventional sex role behavior, despite ambivalence about it. Thus, in some houses the existence of a parental couple is a source of comfort, with members differentially seeking them out for advice and support, while in others "parent trip" is an accusation, a protest against the real and imagined authority of a couple. The symbolic role of a couple, especially one with children, is such that members of a couple were routinely the most influential in their communes.

Couples have the advantage of not needing the group for emotional sustenance to the same extent that others may; couple "withdrawal" is thus often a reality as well as a threat. Couples may often experience their communal life as a fluctuation between periods of withdrawal into nearly exclusive focus on their couple relationship, and periods of involvement in community activities such that the couple is nearly absorbed into the household, with each member pursuing his or her own activities. The other members would obviously prefer the latter pole, but due to threat, preference or mutual commitment, couple members often feel they have to withdraw into the couple, forming in a sense a mini-nuclear family within the group.

Couple withdrawal is especially threatening in households where there are single people who do not have the option of withdrawing into a couple for emotional support or relief from the community. According to one woman in a couple:

> *For us, a couple, the commune was wonderful, a dream. It was shitty for single people. There were only two of them. The other couple were having problems, so they became sort of clingy when they were together. Sharon had her insecurities and not being in a couple heightened that, and there was no way to deal with that. Single people don't enjoy it. You have an issue that you talk about around the table that's really heavy, and then I could go back to the bedroom and talk with Ron, so I have three hours of support to work it through. Sharon would have no idea even what the issues are and no support. Sometimes she hears about the issue, but mostly she doesn't know whether because of privacy or simply time. So I have double support. The upshot is that Sharon will live in a woman's house next year.*

In several houses which contained two couples and a fifth single person, that person was always peripheral to the community, feeling lonely and usually developing an outside relationship and having a very low commitment to the commune.

Couples in communal settings also derive power from the ways in which they maintain their boundaries and thus exclude others. The couples we studied set limits to the diffusion of intimacy. While there are many needs that others can satisfy, there are many ways in which the intimacy of the community are expressed, multiple sexual relationships are hard to maintain, and are a regular part of very few of the communes we studied. Our findings contradict the media view of sexual libertarianism as a central feature, at least of urban communes. Nearly all of our communes show a preference for couple members not developing sexual relationships with their housemates. After a while most groups develop an "incest taboo," which seems to be a source of stability, and sexual experimentation for couples occurs largely outside the commune. Similarly, single people who attempt multiple relationships within a commune seem to drift into couple relationships. At present it seems that the family-like intimacy that is the goal of communes does not include shared sexual relationships, probably because the jealousy and comparisons which occur tend to disrupt the weaker of the relationships even more dramatically than other forms of sharing, leading to one of the participants leaving the commune.

The couple may also maintain other limits: emotional and informational as well as sexual shared "secrets" and private knowledge, including the knowledge that stems from private discussion behind closed doors, are important mechanisms of exclusiveness and solidarity. Couple members generally have several sources of intentional and unintentional private knowledge such as how the other feels about an issue before it is openly discussed; they may also have a longer shared history. their knowledge of each other—sexual, psychological, biographical—is generally greater than that of other members. And couples may also deliberately generate their own "secrets."

While the other members are privy to much of the couple's personal and emotional life, the traditional norm against a couple discussing their relationship with outsiders, or when one member does, for the outsider to feign ignorance, still looms large in many communal houses. In only a few households, primarily those with a radical feminist orientation and those having several couples, do couple members make a commitment to be open with the commune about conflicts and issues within their relationship. Maintaining the confidentiality of the couple seems to be a homeostatic mechanism, which is usually broken only in times of great stress and conflict. For example, in one commune it was obvious that one of the couples had a very traditional relationship in which the woman was passive, dependent, and powerless, but this was never mentioned openly. Then, another woman in the commune got into a conflict with the male member of that couple around his disrespect for her own autonomy and dismissal of her as a person, which in turn exposed both weakness and strain in his couple relationship, and led to a process which eventually ended in the woman receiving support from the other members of the house to ask her mate to leave.

But usually the process of becoming aware of a couple's relationship is more circuitous, and extends the stress that the couple is under to other members of the house. Either the couple gives out signs of stress, depression, or anger, such as by making biting comments or not doing their housework, or else one member of the couple may seek out another house member. (Interestingly, both men and women in couples tend to confide in other women, perpetuating another sex role related dynamic.) The other person is then in the difficult situation of knowing something, yet facing a norm against communicating either their knowledge or their own feelings of helplessness or discomfort. This may cause strain for the whole community.

Finally, when it will help a couple gain its private ends, couples may approach the rest of the group as a power "bloc." The couple has several weapons: to claim superior "need" to the extent that more people or more complex situations are involved; or to threaten withdrawal (emotional or physical) if the group is not responsive to couple demands. Such levers may enable the couple to gain privileges or concession, as when couples routinely claim the best rooms or have more influence over guest policy. Couples have the knowledge that if they maintain some of their own boundaries, they can always simply reform their isolated unit, excluding the others, when things go poorly.

Much of the behavior of others toward couples may thus be seen as a response to couple power. Although the households we studied, unlike traditional or religious communes (Kanter, 1972, 1973), did not develop formal mechanisms to regulate couples and place them under the control of the group, they do exert group pressure on couples not to withdraw and to form relationships (coalitions) with others. This pressure may occur even in relatively loose households around casual couples. One member reported:

> There were subtle hostilities from almost everyone being directed at their partial withdrawal from the rest of us into their own world. It came out in criticisms of their relationship by various people . . . It's true that if you start to get into a heavier-than-usual relationship with anyone, you should have every freedom to let it develop. Living in a commune, however, carries with it a responsibility to maintain a certain amount of awareness of where everyone else is at and how what you are doing is affecting the total group.

The Delicacy of Couple Existence

Many couples thus find that the issue of their withdrawal versus the commitment and participation in community activities is their first confrontation with the meaning of communal life to their relationship. Experiencing the withdrawal of the privacy and psychic space they may have been accustomed to, many couples report an initial defensive overreaction. Their first encounter with the super-individual entity "the commune," which makes claims on them, makes them feel they have given too much up already, while their housemates paradoxically feel they have not yet given enough. Some couples react to these demands by trying to reestablish autonomy over a smaller space. They may fix up and spend time in their private living space as though it were a separate complete home—in several cases with small kitchen units and private phone so that the couple could reduce its need to leave its own quarters. Couples may create informal barriers to entering their rooms except at certain times or under certain conditions, or do their household chores together. But if they ideologically desire to deprivatize their relationship, and not enter the commune as a unit called a "couple," they will also face additional pressure to live up to their beliefs.

PARENTS: THE DILEMMAS OF SHARING RESPONSIBILITY

Parent-child relationships are affected by the structure of a communal household in many of the same ways male-female couples are, by the parents' diminished sovereignty over the household, the presence of an audience and potential coalition partners, and pressures for individuation and autonomy. For parent-child units as well as couples, the communal household replaced the nuclear family's limited exchange of goods and services with a market place. Since the family's exchange is usually one-sided, with many more goods and services flowing from the parent to the child than in the other direction, many parents, indeed, come to communal households seeking the market place: a sharing of child care responsibilities, a provision of inputs from other adults, the presence of others to take over when the parent is depleted—that is, a change from obligatory exchange, in which the parent *must* give to the child, to a free market, in which the parent can choose when and how to give the child because he or she is one of a number of resource-holders. One reported:

> *The house took the pressure off. When I was the only Mommy I lost my temper a lot more. There was no relief. Living alone with them I was terrified that I'd get sick. There was absolutely no one else. Here if I have some problem there is always someone to take care of them. So relating to the children is a lot freer. I do it because I want to, not because I have to.*

Generally others helped through casual babysitting, performing household tasks in the communal division of labor, and distracting children's attention. While the diffusion of dependence helped parents with their burdens, it also provided children with numerous and easily available alternative relationships within the home, as a mother indicated:

> *It's a very positive thing. Children should be raised this way; they shouldn't be isolated. Adults aren't isolated, even in the nuclear family. But the child is in a prison. . . . Communes are the feeling of neighborhood that there used to be; you had your groups of kids after the day in school. You don't see it in suburbia; you don't see it too much anywhere. But here we have it.*

Rarely did parents report in interviews that they had as much help as they wanted. One single father, for example, felt that he did "98%" of the child care in his household, even though others frequently took care of his four-year-old daughter when he went out. But it is also clear from our interviews that the parents themselves often erected barriers to the involvement of others during the initial stages of communal involvement. The diffusion of responsibility and intimacy seems to be threatening for communal parents perhaps even more than for communal couples, who may be consciously or unconsciously looking for ways to disengage. The parents we studied were concerned about the loss of control and loss of intimacy that sharing child care might entail. One woman who had lived alone with her husband and four children before creating a communal household indicated that she found it much harder to let go of parent-related jobs than other domestic chores she had enjoyed performing, even when the jobs were routine and inconvenient, like getting the children's bath at night. A woman in another house seemed to exude ambivalence. She expressed a desire to give up her "fused identity" with her child but indicated pleasure over the strength of the bond that created:

> *I'm trying to loosen possessive feelings around a kid, giving up some of that. Letting other people parent her, the decision to give up my total investment in her creation, was hard. I can no longer project myself and invest in making her my ideal. It's risky in a way, to give up some control.*

The presence of others complicates parent-child relationships and diminishes parental sovereignty at the same time that it offers relief from exclusive task responsibility.

Audience Effects and "Reflected Identity"

The presence of others affects parental control in several ways. First, others act as a virtually ever-present audience to parent-child interactions, especially at meals and in play situations. Many communal parents report greater self-consciousness about rule-making and rule-enforcing when others are there to witness them. They indicate a greater concern with demonstrating consistent, reasoned discipline, in part because of awareness that the child may have a champion if the parent mistreats him/her. For some parents, this means that they hold back, try to control their anger, and refrain from disciplining or restricting the child as severely as they might without an audience. Often the issue of reflected identity arose even among people experimenting with a new culture. One mother reported her feelings that what her son does reflects on her:

> *Every time Jonathon (three years old) spills milk I feel I have to get in there and wipe it up fast. I consider it my responsibility; it's a test of my ability as a mother to try to teach him not to do it.*

Another woman indicated she was sensitive to other adults' opinions of and expectations for her child; at first she tried unsuccessfully to put pressure on him to behave better in front of the others.

A concern for the opinions of others may sometimes cause a parent to over-react to a child's actual or imagined misbehavior, particularly if those others have equal claims on the household territory. This story was told by the veteran of several communal situations about her first experience:

> *Dan (nine years old) was the oldest child. He moved in with a new child who was just crawling and getting into things. He had had a separate room, and then he had to share. Gary was 1½ years younger than Dan. They were different kinds of kids—Gary was more energetic, Dan more long-term and concentrated. Everyone had expectations of Dan as the older kid: to be the intermediary between adults and kids, to take care of the younger ones, to be super. He began to make hideouts to hide in, to get away from the pressure. One day Dan and Gary were playing wildly in the living room, and Gary fell and hurt his head. Dan said he had fallen. Leslie, Gary's mother, said Dan had pushed him. I believed her. I didn't see where Dan was coming from, as he maintained for months that he hadn't pushed Gary. I went crazy at the time. One night Leslie and Fred (Gary's father) and another person in the house persuaded me to take Dan to a child therapist and to go to one myself—I was so invested in other people's opinions.... I later understood that Leslie's fears of Gary getting hurt were a protection of her own violence. I also found out long after, from another adult, that Dan was telling the truth.*

Parental identification with children's images in the presence of others, then, sometimes means that parents experience their limited control more acutely. The audience makes them aware by reflection of what control they can and cannot exercise over their children.

If the presence of an audience, then, heightens issues of "reflected identity"—the concern that one family member will be "judged" by the behavior of another, it also makes possible new alliances that affect parent-child relations. The others represent potential coalition partners for both parent and child and make possible a number of relationship configurations. First, the others may attempt to gain influence over either the parent or the child—in the first case by indicating that the parent should exert *more* control over the child, in the second, *less.* To the extent that a parent desires a positive relationship with a third party, then, he or she may be relatively easily induced to occasionally turn against his or her child, to "side with" the other against the child, in order to make the child's behavior acceptable to the other so that the parent herself will be acceptable.

Separate Relationships and Multiple Rule-Makers

Parents also experience loss of control over the child's experiences, environment, and relationships. Parents were no longer the principal rule-makers and rule-enforcers for their children. Other adults had the right to make and enforce rules for the joint household, to make demands on the children, to provide experiences for them, and form relationships with them. In a few instances, though rare, other members of the household encouraged the child to do something that contradicted parental rules or behaved toward the child in ways that violated the spirit of the parents' desires. Parents could avoid this only to the extent that they could control the other adults in the household—an unlikely occurrence among a group of adults valuing egalitarian participation. Thus, for parents to remain in force as principal rule-makers and rule-enforcers for their children, they must also have power in the commune, be able to enforce rules for the other adults. What in the private family is a relative simple (structurally) matter of negotiation between two parents or a strong stand by one in order to define norms affecting a child becomes in the commune an even more complicated political situation.

In a political context, the demands or requests of parents concerning their children may, indeed, sometimes be seen as power moves on their part, as a way to gain special privilege or undue influence in the group and may in extreme cases be responded to in political ways regardless of the real needs of the child. More than one parent in houses with relatively few kids reported his or her difficulty convincing others in the house that the children were not just miniature adults but had special needs and required special kinds of behavior. For example:

> We have been easier on the kids than the other adults in the house would believe we should be, in terms of sharing responsibility. . . It's been a disagreement between us and the other adults about whether a six- or seven-year-old child is capable of doing an adult's share or any very substantial share of a large household's chores.

Some of this difficulty could have resulted from the ignorance of nonparents and/or their unwillingness to engage in special efforts; but part of it may also be attributable to a reluctance to acknowledge the special status of child and, by implication, parent. In houses with relatively more children and parents—so that the threat of special status was reduced—parents did not report the same phenomenon.

Parents generally had strong feelings about the ways others related to their children; their reactions to the relationships sometimes included frustration at their lack of control. Complaints about others' behavior toward a child were frequent; overt expressions of jealousy about anothers' *positive* or *strong* relationship with a child were rare and far from automatically being the child's emissary and intermediary to others outside the family, in some cases, parents may not even be the first to know what issues occur around their children, and they may be limited in their ability to effect change.

One outcome is that children gain more autonomy and a measure of individuation similar to that occurring for couples when third parties are available to form relationships outside of the intimate dyad. Children quickly learn what resources and relationships exist for them in the house and, often, how to manage them themselves. Sometimes other adults besides the parent may intervene on the child's behalf, and it is not at all clear that final authority or final knowledge always rests with the parent. Children themselves choose which adult to confide in or ask for advice. In one group, an 11-year-old formed a strong friendship with a woman in her twenties, who replaced the mother as principal "expert" on what was happening with Monica and what would be best for her. Under such circumstances parents occasionally felt that other people could influence their children more readily than they could. According to one report:

Keith was in the five-year-old demand stage. Two other women decided they didn't want to be ordered around. They taught him to say please *and* thank you. *They accomplished this—a nonparent can do this more easily—in the space of about ten days.*

Competition and conflict over what kinds of child rearing standards would prevail was frequent. In one household, two mothers with young daughters fought about child rearing strategies; one felt the other too permissive, the other thought the first too strict. The feeling that permissiveness or authority in the other is bad for a child is hard to deal with for people with a rhetoric of freedom. Since the two mothers shared child care, they also had to cope with the results of the other's style. One of them finally moved out, saying that while she intended to continue living communally, she wanted to be the *only* parent next time, pointing up the politics of the situation. Another household broke up over the issue. Two couples had infants and were uncomfortable with the personal style of the other set of parents and what impact that style would have on their ability to influence their child as they wished. In a third case, the conflict between parental styles resulted in different sets of rules being enforced for the children of each set of parents, causing the groups' major issue of the first year. One parent unit was very strict and controlling, making demands on the children to work; the other felt that kids could decide all things. Their children shared a room, and over time the conflict built up. One child would have to go to sleep while the other sat outside and watched TV. This situation was resolved by the children forming a coalition to defeat *both* sets of parents.

Parental Domains

We have already indicated that some parents retain, willingly or unwillingly, a number of child care responsibilities, but over all of the groups studied, it becomes clear that it is not particular duties and chores that distinguish parents from nonparents in communal households. Depending on the household, nonparents are likely to be found at any time with children, and children are likely to form close relationships with at least one person other than a parent. What *does* distinguish the domain remaining more exclusively in parental hands is the parents' legitimate involvement with the general boundaries of relationships and experiences for the child. Parents tend to reserve for themselves the rights to protect their children and to punish them.

The kinds of protection reported included speaking up for children when they were unfairly treated (one mother called it "running defense for my child"), trying to get them the extra things they needed from the house or others, or defending children against the criticism of others. Parents often preserved a space and time of the day that was known to be exclusively for the parents and children to be together, alone and safe from interruption—often in the children's room just before bedtime, when other house members would have retreated to private activities and the house was quiet, or in the parents' room if the children's room was shared with nonsiblings. The specialness of these times of safety and closeness is manifest in interviews with communal children.

Only in cases where the parent had explicitly conferred the privilege of invoking sanctions against children upon certain adults was such an adult activity permitted. The bestowal of this privilege occurred rarely. In only one household did the mother specifically allow certain male communal members to invoke sanctions with her children. These male members exercised this privilege in telling children in cases of rule violations to go to their rooms and to leave the table at dinnertime. But it was clear that they were acting for the mother.

Parenting in the presence of others, then, is complex and, like coupling, involves its own delicate balances: help with child care versus retention of the exclusiveness of parenting; concern for the child versus concern for the reactions of others; children's separate relationships with others versus parents' desires to protect their children; letting go of burdens versus losing control. Parents both applaud their children's exposure to a variety of relationships and styles and mourn the loss of parental sovereignty. A single father said:

> *In comparison to a nuclear family, the fact that communes bring a child in contact with a variety of people of different styles, ages, tastes, makes communal upbringing better. But there are times when communes seem to leave out extreme love and tight relationships; I feel these are important in a person's life. The multiplicity of relationships of the nuclear family. Fay (his daughter) and I have gained a great deal, and also we've lost a little too.*

CHILDREN: MULTIPLE RELATIONSHIPS AND MULTIPLE RULE-MAKERS

The presence of others appears to offer a number of freedoms and skills for children while adding other constraints. (We include in the category of "children" ages four-twelve.) Children have a variety of adult relationship partners, and, in forming multiple relationships, learn to make choices and learn to express themselves easily to grown-ups. Children themselves become the audience for a number of adult-adult exchanges over the dinner table or at house meetings, including conflict between their own parents and the others. Parents and other adults become demystified by this process; their own weaknesses and norm violations are exposed. Urban communal households shield children from sex and drugs (though drug use itself is infrequent) and occasionally from heavy or late house meetings—but not from discussion about these matters or other affairs or adult life. Aware of house conflicts, children also become aware of times when their own parents are in the wrong or have mispleased others or have failed to get their way on issues; the "front" of parental strength is more difficult to maintain. Older children may even form coalitions on the side of others rather than their parents. In addition, the presence of others and therefore the enlarged size and complexity of the households mean that children have to learn to "speak up" in order to be heard, to be persuasive and interpersonally skilled in order to get something they want. In a comment that echoed other parents, one mother said of her five year old who had lived communally for a year:

> *He's more sophisticated, less of a baby. He's more aware of dynamics between people. It's easier for him to talk to people and to express himself in words—between parents and children, there's a lot of nonverbal stuff. With the others, he's learned a lot about expressing himself, and he's exposed to so much.*

The possibility for multiple relationships and observation of adults in communal households also brings the possibility for constraints—particularly when children are scarce and the household is numerically as well as socially adult-dominated. As parents lose exclusive control, other adults gain the right to impose control over their relationships with children and the household. More people in the house may also mean more people telling the child what to do, observing deviance, and imposing constraints as well as providing knowledge, company, and support.

The "Cinderella Effect": Children and Rule-Making

Children of four-twelve almost universally experienced communal living as a situation involving "too many bosses" or "too many people saying 'stop that' "—especially in houses with few other children and crowded quarters. We can call this the "Cinderella effect" ("Cinderella do this; Cinderella, do that") to capture the experience of multiple rule-makers and rule-enforcers. As one child explained:

> *Sometimes it's not so fun to live here because there's a lot of people that chase you around and tell you what to do. . . Like they tell me sometimes when I'm sneaking food, they say 'stop eating all the food, it's almost dinnertime.' And sometimes they say, 'don't stand on the chairs, that chair is very weak,' or 'don't run around the dining room table when we're eating because it shakes and spills all the coffee and the milk and the water.'*

Soon after entry, new communal residents generally formulate rules governing his or her private space. These rules often pertain to adults; but, given the presence of children in the commune, they invariably govern specific usage of the space by the child. These rules specify whether the individual's room may be used by children, under what conditions (if any) it may be used by children (to watch TV, to play in), at what times of the day it may be used by children, if the owner must be present or must be absent during the usage period, whether prior permission must be requested, to whom one must request permission (to the owner or in the case of absence, to a parent), and how one requests such permission (by knocking or orally). Generally such rules clarify the meaning of such territorial boundary markers as the closed door—whether this signal means the room is completely off limits, or whether it means that the child may knock to request permission to enter.

In addition to rules about private space, each communal member may formulate rules governing use of private property—e.g., possessions both in the private space and in the communal spaces. Following an individual's move into a communal household, he or she often 'donates' property temporarily (usually in the form of furniture, kitchenware, TV's, or stereos) to the group. However, usage, maintenance, and control of the property, is still a prerogative reserved by the individual owner and is frequently exercised whenever such property is being misused. As children have often not yet learned the taken-for-granted adult usage patterns of property, rules for children's property use are frequently formulated.

Because of their limited mobility, resources, and short 'work' day, children often spend considerable time at home and are frequent users of communal space. This frequency and the quantity of paraphernalia involved (toys, games, paper, crayons, and so forth) means that kids are frequently violators of rules of neatness and spatial order. Or, as one parent explained:

One of the problems here with Sherri that is abrasive is the mess she makes and how responsible she is for cleaning up after herself . . . being forgetful and people not liking that, particularly so in the TV room which is a commonly used room by a lot of people. There's sort of a trail of Sherri throughout the house. We've tried keeping boxes in certain places where she could keep all her stuff, but other people, aside from me and Dick (her father) get after her if it's annoying to them.

In meetings, rules are formulated setting forth explicit expectations for children in terms of their maintenance of the communal space. In some houses it was after the pressure of several communal members that the rotation of household tasks came to specify the degree of participation required of kids. As the mother of several children explained:

The kids' lack of responsibility got to some of the people, especially to two particular adults who were annoyed that the kids did not do much around the house. Since all the people here had shared responsibilities the adults felt that the children too should have shared responsibility, cleaning the house and picking up after themselves. Previously the kids had had no stated responsibilities—they were occasionally asked from time to time to do certain chores, but they were not included in the rotation of household responsibilities. So we had a group meeting and decided that the children should be included at the next meeting since we were talking about responsibilities in the house for them.

Divisions of labor involving children in household maintenance tasks were commonly found in urban communes. And, children frequently voiced their awareness of the expectation of adult communal members that they 'do their chore' for the week.

Group meetings are also settings for rule-making about children's usage of communal space. The primary spatial violation by children concerns noise. Often rules specify the types of noise permitted and in which areas, the hours when noise is prohibited (early morning, late at night), the types of noise-generating activities (parties, fighting) prohibited.

Rules may also define when the child must stop using communal space; bedtime is a time when children must vacate the communal areas. Although bedtime decisions are most often formulated by parents, occasionally others make such decisions at group meetings. One parent of several children reported:

> *Children here were very much brought up by the group in that decisions even relative to bedtime were reached by the community. Bedtime has been a big bone of contention with the children . . . they have a very natural curiosity to be part of whatever is going on in the evening, at which point myself and the rest of the people had just had enough of kids. Most people here were not working 9 to 5 and instead worked in the house . . . they would be here in the afternoon when the children got home from school, and so by evening, they had had enough of kids.*

In group meetings, rules are conveyed and made more explicit to children, and the role of nonparent others in controlling children's experiences is supported. If, for example, an adult has told a child not to enter a room without knocking, at a group meeting the adult may reinforce the rule publicly to the child. Often too, group meetings are settings where rules are evaluated—those which have been formulated and made explicit may be judged to have failed, and new rules are then formulated to better deal with the issue. As a nine-year-old boy explains what happened to him:

> *I'm not allowed to walk in people's room if their door's closed . . . But, if you do one mistake and then you do it again, maybe you do a mistake when you didn't know that rule and you say, 'I didn't know it.' And so they say, 'well, now you know it.' And then if you break it then, then they bring it up in the next meeting and then they talk about it and then they get an even bigger rule, like you can't even go into this room if the door's open.*

Rule-Enforcing

The presence of many adults in the home territory ensures a large number of adults engaged not only in rule-making but also in rule-enforcing. Methods of rule-enforcing may include constant repetitions of the rule to the child, and the use of threats or sanctions. Repetition of a rule was the most common means of enforcement: "don't stand on chairs," "don't eat all the food before dinner," "don't interrupt," "pick up your things in the TV room and put them in your room." Threats frequently contained a contingent-responsibility clause: "If you break that, you'll have to pay for it (or fix it)" or "if you mess up my room when you come in here, then you'll have to clean it up." The threat generally functioned sufficiently as a deterrent so that threats tended to be rarely enforced. More severe sanctions, as we mentioned earlier, were reserved to parents.

The existence of the "Cinderella effect," having multiple rule-makers and rule-enforcers, may create various problematical situations for children, including inconsistency, ambiguity, and contradictions. Difficulties arise because each adult communal member has a different set of expectations concerning what is appropriate child behavior and each adult has different definitions of what constitutes an infraction. The noise issue highlights the different adults' sets of expectations and definitions of what constitutes "too much noise" on the part of the children. What is an appropriate or acceptable noise level for children to many adults is often considered excessive noise by others. One mother said:

> *There are adults here who react differently than I would. I can see encounters that are handled differently than I would handle them. Sometimes people are stricter or often less patient with noise. For instance, when the girls are making noise, someone might say 'you're making noise, you'll have to go do that somewhere else,' at a time when I probably wouldn't have even bothered to say that.*

Different expectations and definitions may result in inconsistent rule-enforcement. Thus, what a parent might consider an activity or action that falls within an acceptable range of child behavior, another communal adult may not. The child is faced with an inconsistency: the definition of the rule varies from adult to adult and similarly, the definition of their adherence to the rule varies from adult to adult. Rule-enforcement thus becomes a highly arbitrary process for children—fixed at the whim of many different adults. Children often adjust to this and learn that adult standards differ and, depending on their ages, may also use these differences to make choices about which set of standards to ignore. But because adults have more power, children are likely to be called on all of their norm violations. In fact more authoritative behavior seems to come out around kids than any other area of communal life—the release of authoritarian tendencies in a democratic social structure.

Rule-enforcement may also be contradictory. What some adults have explicitly allowed, others may have prohibited. Thus, a child may be permitted to watch television in one adult's room while the same act may be explicitly prohibited by another adult in the latter's room. Similar contradictory rule-enforcement arose for a 4½-year-old-boy when his father was out one evening. His bedtime had been established by his father as 8 p.m. Another member, a woman whom the father had asked to put the boy to bed, enforced a 7 p.m. betime rule despite the boy's protestations to the contrary. In such situations the child is very often caught between "Scylla" and "Charybdis"—maneuvering the waters between the "great powers" can be a frustrating task.

Another consequence of the presence of others as rule-makers and rule-enforcers is the likelihood that children will experience the conditions of 'double jeopardy'—having an infraction noticed more than once and being reprimanded more than once for the same offense. The large number of adults living in the communal home territory increases the likelihood that many will be present in the home territory at the same time. This simultaneously increases the likelihood that more than one adult will notice a child's rule-breaking offense during a short time period. Often then, more than one adult reprimands a child for the same offense—scolding a child or asking him to follow a rule without realizing that another adult, just a few moments before, may have cited him for the same offense.

A variation on the theme of 'double jeopardy' arises when the child may be reprimanded by one adult to follow one rule (such as picking up his toys in the living room) moments after another adult has reprimanded him to follow a different rule (to clean up his mess in the kitchen). This epitomizes the consequences of the "Cinderella effect"—"Cinderella, do this!" "Cinderella, do that!" "No, Cinderella, do this!" A child's response to this situation is described by a six-year-old's mother:

> What really drives Ethan crazy is if someone says to him 'Ethan, do this,' and somebody else has just said to him previously, 'Ethan, do this,' and he's in the process of doing that thing when somebody says, 'do this.' That really flips him out. That must be one of the most difficult experiences for him here.

Recourse to a higher court of appeal (e.g., parent) is rare for communal children; parents themselves make the decision to protect their children only in extreme circumstances and do not intercede for children unless greatly provoked. When another adult makes a rule or reprimands a child as rule-enforcement, that adult's word is law—and generally not subject to amendment or reversal. One of the desires most frequently expressed by parents in communes with children and adults is that each communal adult member have a distinct relationship with the children. Parents encourage other adults to have 'their own' relationships to each child. This functions especially in terms of gripes—that parents prefer adults to deal directly with the child rather than express it to them as middlemen. As one mother explained: "The norm here is if that child is bothering you, it's your problem, not mine. I don't want to hear about it. Deal with the child." Depending on their age, children *may* come to house meetings and complain of unfair treatment, just as any member can bring up a grievance; occasionally children have influenced a change of rules.

It must be recognized, of course, that the participation of each adult in rule-making and rule-enforcement for children depends on a number of variables, including length of time as communal resident, time spent daily in the home territory, familiarity with children in general and with those specific children, familiarity with child's parents, and view of children (as a special category or as little adults). The extensiveness of communal constraints on children and whether children face arbitrary adult domination varies also with the number of children and the degree of crowding in the household. More children and more space reduce the continual control fewer children in more cramped quarters face, partly because children gain their own territory and become a more critical mass for the household, so that their own status as children can be more easily acknowledged and incorporated into household routine. With more children, kids can form their own coalitions.

It should also be noted that there can be areas of freedom as well as constraint for kids in communal houses: differentiation from parents, demystification of parents, multiple relationships with those adults available to children, and the ability to effectively use the disagreements between adults to gain freedom. Further, the wider visibility of adult behavior in such households and the generally more experimental behavior and permissive norms means that communal children often have behavioral freedoms their neighbors lack despite rules about use of space and property; one mother reported that her kids' friends find the commune a very free place "where they are allowed to swear."

But in general the presence of a large number of adults in the children's home territory, then, increases the likelihood of a large number of adults participating in rule-making and rule-enforcing vis-a-vis these children—what has been here termed the "Cinderella phenomenon." This phenomenon consists of arbitrary, inconsistent, and contradictory rule-enforcement where situations of 'double jeopardy' (reprimands for the same offense) are likely to occur and where the child has no recourse to a higher court of appeal. Under such circumstances parents are not the dominant sources of social control for their children in the household.

CONCLUSION

We have explored some of the impacts of the presence of others on the most intimate human relationships: those of couples and parents and children in communal households. The shift from essentially dyadic to larger group relations in the home adds a number of complex phenomena: audiences, alternative resources, coalition partners, interventions, and political jockeying. In each kind of relationship the primary tie may remain central for many people while they balance availability and responsibility to the others. The major effects in both cases involve a shift in the locus of social control. There are both greater opportunities for wider intimacy, more ties, sharing of chores and responsbilities, autonomy, and egalitarianism and a series of new issues with which couples, parents, and children must cope.

Some of these issues arise as a function of an ideology and culture particular to American communal households in the 1970's, but others are structural effects of the "presence of others." We would expect similar structural effects in other circumstances in which intimate relations are conducted on more public territory, whether extended family households, utopian communities, multiple family therapy, close-knit urban neighborhoods with minimal private space, or families with boarders or lodgers.

REFERENCES

Caplow, Theodore. *Two Against One: Coalitions in Triads*. Englewood Cliffs: Prentice-Hall, 1968.
Coser, Lewis A. *Greedy Organizations*. New York: Free Press, 1974.
Jaffe, Dennis T. Couples in Communes. Unpublished doctoral dissertation, Yale University, 1975.
Jaffe, Dennis T. and Rosabeth Moss Kanter. Couple Strain in Communal Households: A Four-Factor Model of the Separation Process. *Journal of Social Issues*, 1976, 32, 169-191.

Kanter, Rosabeth Moss. *Commitment and Community: Communes and Utopias in Sociological Perspective.* Cambridge: Harvard University Press, 1972a.

Kanter, Rosabeth Moss. Communes in Cities. *Working Papers for a New Society,* 1974, 2, 36-45.

Kanter, Rosabeth Moss. The Family and Sex Roles in American Communes. In Rosabeth Moss Kanter (Ed.), *Communes: Creating and Managing the Collective Life.* New York: Harper and Row, 1973.

Kanter, Rosabeth Moss. Getting It All Together: Some Group Issues in Communes. *American Journal of Orthopsychiatry,* 1972b, 42, 632-43.

Kanter, Rosabeth Moss and Marilyn Halter. Dehousewifing Women, Domesticating Men: Equality between the Sexes in Urban Communes. Presented at the 1973 Meetings of the American Psychological Association.

Slater, Philip E. On Social Regression. *American Sociological Review,* 1963, 28, 339-64.

Simmel, Georg. *The Sociology of Georg Simmel.* Kurt Wolff (Ed.). Glencoe, IL: Free Press, 1950.

Weisberg, D. Kelly. Children and Communal Life. Unpublished doctoral dissertation, Brandeis University, 1975.

social stresses on the family:
generic features of families under stress
reuben hill

Two streams of research concerned about social stresses and the family have been running parallel for some time. . . . I refer to the research on crisis-proneness in families carried out by family sociologists and the cumulating work of latter-day social work researchers on the properties of the "multi-problem family." To facilitate further the merger of these two professional groups, I shall undertake in this paper to summarize the major issues and findings in family crisis research as seen by family sociologists. I shall first attempt to provide the broad outlines of the conceptual framework most used by family sociologists in the study of family crises. Second, I shall attempt to catalog the stressful events that have been studied and those that remain unstudied, using classifications developed to differentiate crises into types. Third, our chief findings to date will be listed, indicating types of families which thrive and which wilt under stress. Fourth, the generic phases and modes of adjustment to stress will be demonstrated. Fifth, the short-run and long-run effects of stress on families will be assessed. I shall conclude with speculations about the implications of these findings for agency policies and practices.

A CONCEPTUAL FRAMEWORK FOR
VIEWING FAMILIES IN CRISIS

The conceptual scaffolding on which the research to be summarized in this paper has been built makes frequent use of three variables: family, crisis-provoking event, and meaning attached to the event. Let us begin by identifying the major conceptual properties of the family.

The Family as an Interacting and Transacting Organization

Family sociologists have come to view the family as a small group, intricately organized internally into paired positions of husband-father, wife-mother, son-brother, and daughter-sister. Norms prescribing the appropriate role behavior for each of these positions specify how reciprocal relations are to be maintained as well as how role behavior may change with changing ages of the occupants of these positions.

Viewed externally, the family often appears to be a "closed corporation," particularly in urban areas where the nuclear group of father, mother, and their children is clearly differentiated from the kinship extensions of maternal and paternal grandparents and collateral relatives. Such a family performs like a closed corporation in presenting a common front of solidarity to the world, handling internal differences in private, protecting the reputation of members by keeping family secrets, and standing together under attack. Nevertheless, the closed nature of the family is selectively opened for

Reprinted, by permission, from *Social Casework*, 1958, *39*, 139-50. Copyright © 1958 by the Family Service Association of America.

transacting business with other agencies, including kin and professionals. These agencies can be ranked on their accessibility to the interior of the family: immediate kin highest, family friends and neighbors next, the family physician, the family pastor, the family lawyer, and so on. Other agencies enter the family with greater difficulty and often through the intermediation of individual family members who act as liaisons for the family: the school, the employer, the health clinic, the casework agency, and other such formal agencies. Recent research has suggested that the more open the community (as in the modern city), the more likely the family is closed in form; and the more closed the community (as in the isolated mountain village), the more open are the doors and windows of the family to non-family members.*

Compared with other associations in the society, the average family is badly handicapped organizationally. Its age composition is heavily weighted with dependents, and it cannot freely reject its weak members and recruit more competent team mates. Its members receive an unearned acceptance; there is no price for belonging. Because of its unusual age composition and its uncertain sex composition, it is intrinsically a puny work group and an awkward decision-making group. This group is not ideally manned to withstand stress, yet society has assigned to it the heaviest of responsibilities: the socialization and orientation of the young, and the meeting of the major emotional needs of all citizens, young and old.

When the family is viewed historically, we can see that it is more dependent today than it was formerly on other agencies in society for fulfilling its purposes. Once a self-contained economic and social unit buttressed by kinship supports, the family now has interdependent relations with many other associations in working out its problems. I have elsewhere[14] described the ways in which the family functions in equilibrating troubles of its members:

> The modern family lives in a greater state of tension precisely because it is the great burden carrier of the social order. In a society of rapid social change, problems outnumber solutions, and the resulting uncertainties are absorbed by the members of society, who are for the most part also members of families. Because the family is the bottleneck through which all troubles pass, no other association so reflects the strains and stresses of life. With few exceptions persons in work-a-day American return to rehearse their daily frustrations within the family, and hope to get the necessary understanding and resilience to return the morrow to the fray.
>
> Thus, the good family today is not only the focal point of frustrations and tensions but also the source for resolving frustrations and releasing tensions. . . . Through its capacity for sympathy, understanding, and unlimited support, the family rehabilitates personalities bruised in the course of competitive daily living. In that capacity the family is literally love in action.

In sum, the concept of the family which we have identified above is that of an arena of interacting personalities, intricately organized internally into positions, norms, and roles. When viewed externally it can be seen as an organized group engaged in transactions with other associations. It is not new to trouble. Indeed, problems and exigencies beset American families from wedding day to dissolution day. Most families have had a long history of troubles and have worked out procedures and a division of responsibility for meeting problematic situations as they arise. These can be viewed broadly as the family's repertory of resources for dealing with crises which we shall have occasion to return to later.

---

*In this connection, see the reports of European research by C. D. Saal of Holland and Elizabeth Bott of England, in *Recherches Sur La Famille*, published by UNESCO Institute of Social Science, Cologne, 1956, pp. 29-69, 229-247.

The Crisis-Precipitating Event

The second major concept in our scaffolding is the *stressor,* or crisis-provoking event. A stressor in this context is a situation for which the family has had little or no prior preparation and must therefore be viewed as problematic.[26] It is often difficult empirically to disentangle the problematics and the hardships of the stressful event from the definitions the family makes—the meaning aspect of the event. To make the distinction conceptually is one step in the direction of doing so empirically. Actually the hardships of the event lie outside the family and are an attribute of the event itself, constituting a distinct variable requiring separate attention.

No crisis-precipitating event is the same for any given family; its impact ranges according to the several hardships that may accompany it. We might take, as an illustration, the dismemberment of a family through conscription of the husband-father into the armed services in wartime—an event that appeared to be uniform, striking, as it did, hundreds of thousands of families in America in World War II. Hill and Boulding,* studying this phenomenon, found the number of hardships accompanying the event ranging from none to six, including sharp changes in income, housing inadequacies, enforced living with in-laws or other relatives, illness of wife or children, wife's having to work and be both mother and father, child-discipline problems stemming from the father's absence. There were, on the other hand, families where the war separation event produced father-substitutes who were an improvement on the absentee, improved housing, increased income, and a more relaxed family life. Similarly the catastrophic event of a tornado strikes unevenly as a crisis-precipitating event. Some families lose not only property but life and limb too; many experience reduced income only; still others suffer fright and anxiety, but in the short run make net gains financially because of the moratorium on debts and the grants from relief agencies which often accompany severe catastrophes.[15] Clearly, the stressor event must be seen as a variable rather than as a constant in family crisis research.

Since no stressor event is uniformly the same for all families, but varies in striking power by the hardships that accompany it, the concept of hardship itself requires some additional attention. Hardships may be defined as those complications in a crisis-precipitating event which demand competencies from the family which the event itself may have temporarily paralyzed or made unavailable.

Definition of the Event as Stressful

It has always puzzled observers that some families ride out the vicissitudes of floods and disasters without apparent disorganization, whereas most families are at least temporarily paralyzed by such catastrophes. The key appears to be at the "meaning" dimension. Stressors become crises in line with the definition the family makes of the event.

A boy caught stealing in one neighborhood may be ostracized and bring his family shame and disgrace, while a boy in a different social grouping may well achieve standing within his family and in his neighborhood through an identical act. To transform a stressor event into a crisis requires an intervening variable that has been variously termed, "meaning of the event" or "definition of the event."

Placing this final variable in an equation with the other elements in our conceptual framework, we get a formula as follows: A (the event) → *interacting* with B (the family's crisis-meeting resources) → *interacting* with C (the definition the family makes of the event) → *produces* X (the crisis). The second and third determinants—family resources and definition of the event—lie within the family itself and must be seen in terms of the family's structures and values. The hardships of the event, which go to make up the first determinant, lie outside the family and are an attribute of the event itself.

*In *Families Under Stress,*[14] Chapt. IV, pp. 50-97.

This threefold framework enables us to ask the proper questions to account for crisis-proneness in families, identifying as it does the interplay of the most important explanatory variables. We turn now to our findings about the stresses studied to date, the properties of the crisis-prone, and the phases of adjustment characteristic of families under stress.

A CLASSIFICATION OF STRESSOR EVENTS

Three systems of classification of family troubles have been used by investigators in cataloging crises: (1) by source, whether extra-family or intra-family, (2) by effects upon the family configuration, which combine dismemberment, accession, and demoralization, and (3) by type of event impinging on the family.

Source of Trouble

If the blame for the stressor can be placed outside the family, the stress may solidify rather than disorganize the family. Crises differ in their sources—some originate within, others outside the family. Crises that arise as a result of economic depression or of war, both of which are beyond the individual family's control, present quite different problems from the crises arising out of the interpersonal relations within the family such as infidelity, non-support, or alcoholism. The loss of life's savings due to bank failure during a depression will induce a crisis for most families, but consider the impact created by the loss of life's savings through the improvidence of an alcoholic father, which event was in turn precipitated by a serious rift in the affectional relations within the family. It is not the loss of life's savings in this instance so much as it is the interpersonal relations which constitute the matrix of trouble.

Classified by source of trouble, stressor events divide into three categories: (1) extra-family events which in the long run tend to solidify the family, such as war bombings, political persecutions, religious persecutions, floods, tornadoes, hurricanes, and other "acts of God," defined as stressful but solidifying because external to the family; (2) intra-family events such as illegitimacy, non-support, mental breakdown, infidelity, suicide, and alcoholism, which are defined as stressful but usually are more disorganizing to the family because they arise from troubles that reflect poorly on the family's internal adequacy; and (3) some extra-family events that are often not defined as critically stressful and are assimilable because other persons are in the same situation or worse, or events similar to others the family has previously undergone, such as some war separations, some war reunions, loss of home in a disaster, forced migration, sudden decrease in income during a depression, and premature births (see especially Caplan[5]).

Combinations of Dismemberment-Accession and Demoralization

A second type of classification first suggested by Eliot[9] and expanded by Hill[26] involves the combination of loss of family member (dismemberment) or addition of an unprepared-for member (accession) and loss of morale and family unity (demoralization), or all three. (In the chart on page 362, crises that have already been studied are starred, suggesting areas in which there is demonstrable need for further research.)

Closely allied with this classification are stressor events that do not result in dismemberment in the sense of a change in the plurality pattern of the family, but do bring marked changes in the family configuration. Those family situations where roles are involuntarily vacated through illness, or are not fulfilled at all as in families with mentally retarded children, might be cited as examples (see the work of Bernard Farber and his associates in the Institute for Research on Exceptional Children, the University of Illinois). Families experience significant strains when members become diabetics, rheumatic fever patients, or experience congestive heart failure and demand special considerations over prolonged periods. Such illnesses require a reallocation of the patient's roles to others within the family and a standardization of his role on a more or less indefinite basis.[22]

A CLASSIFICATION OF FAMILY CRISES OF
DISMEMBERMENT-ACCESSION AND DEMORALIZATION

Dismemberment Only
*Death of child, spouse, or parent
*Hospitalization of spouse
*War separation

Accession Only
Unwanted pregnancy
Deserter returns
Stepfather, stepmother additions
*Some war reunions
*Some adoptions, aged grandparents, orphaned kin

Demoralization Only
*Nonsupport
Infidelity
*Alcoholism
Drug addiction
Delinquency and events bringing disgrace

Demoralization Plus Dismemberment or Accession
*Illegitimacy
Runaways
*Desertion
*Divorce
Imprisonment
Suicide or homicide
*Institutionalization for mental illness

Most crises of dismemberment, accession, and crippling illness sooner or later involve *de-morale-ization*, since the family's role patterns are always sharply disturbed. Dismemberment creates a situation in which the departed one's roles must be reallocated, and a period of confusion-delay ensues while the members of the family cast learn their new lines. The addition of a new member resulting from the marriage of a divorced or widowed person strains the resources of a family that "closed ranks" too well.[3][11]

Types of Impact of Stressor Events

Ernest W. Burgess[4] has added two categories for further classifying family crises: (1) sudden change in family status, and (2) conflict among family members in the conception of their roles.

A sudden upturn in economic and social status may constitute a crisis quite as disruptive as that of economic loss or social disgrace. The price of upward mobility for some families may be family breakdown. We are only beginning to learn something of the conditions under which the family survives or goes to pieces when there is a swift change from poverty to riches or from obscurity to fame. More usually we think of stressor events bringing sudden changes downward in status. The variety of crises of this type is well known. The large number starred in the list below suggests that many of these crises have already been studied systematically by family sociologists.

TYPES OF STRESSES INVOLVING STATUS SHIFTS
*Sudden impoverishment
*Prolonged unemployment
Sudden wealth and fame
*Refugee migrations, political and religious
*Disasters, tornadoes, floods, explosions
*War bombings, deprivations
*Political declassing, denazification

Many of the difficulties that build up into crises involve differences in conception of their respective roles by family members. Conflicts between parents and children should be understood and studied in terms of their differences in the role expectations. Koos[19] finds the adolescent-parent relationships to be a focal point of crisis in the middle-class family. In upward-mobile families, the appropriate roles for wife and mother differ by socioeconomic groups, and the work-a-day housekeeper roles of one's original class may have to be unlearned and the hostess roles of the next class may have to be learned to fit the changed expectations of husband and children.

The current crisis of desegregation in the South is a stressful event for both white and Negro families, largely because of the great differences in role expectations held by parents and children. As the schools are integrated, children of both groups tend to forget color as the individual personality shines through. They make friends on the basis of congeniality rather than color alone. Parents and some teachers lag behind the children in this respect. Parents try to limit friendships and home associations, thus producing conflict with their volatile adolescents. Dating, dancing, and contact games become focal points of disagreement, since these activities violate the Southern mores which parents feel obliged to perpetuate. The children may only partially accept these mores and resent their parents' restrictions. Conflicts develop between families whose restrictions differ, since styles for adolescents are often set by the freedoms that the most permissive parents allow their children. Thus the full-blown dimensions of a family cirsis are experienced until a new set of norms accepted by both generations develops.[13]

With this background of the range of types of stressful events spelled out, we turn to a consideration of the factors making for crisis-proneness and freedom from crisis among families. It has been suggested that crisis-proneness runs in families as does accident-proneness. What support can be adduced for such a proposition? We know that some families can handle stress better than other families. In what ways do they differ from the crises prone?

FACTORS MAKING FOR CRISES-PRONENESS IN FAMILIES

We can profitably take advantage now of an equation that summarizes the conceptual framework of most of the family crisis research I am reporting: A (the event) → interacting with B (the family's crisis-meeting resources) → interacting with C (the definition the family makes of the event) → produces X (the crisis). Crisis-proneness is in effect the phenomenon of experiencing stressor events (A) with greater frequency and greater severity and defining these (C) more frequently as crises. In other words, crisis-prone families appear to be more vulnerable to stressor events of the types we have just cataloged, and more likely because of meager crisis-meeting resources (B) and failure to have learned, from past experience with crisis, to define these events as crisis-provoking. The explanation for crisis-proneness therefore lies primarily in the B and C factors in our equation.

Note the differences in vulnerability when families are assessed on a class basis alone. To the lower-class family, living up to and even beyond its income, there may be a quality of desperation in a financial crisis that is lacking for the middle-class family with reserves upon which it can draw. The lower-class family not only is restricted in income, but in health, energy, space, and ideas for coping with crisis—owing to its hand-to-mouth existence, it lacks defense in depth. Conversely, the lower-class family with little to lose in the way of prestige or status and little opportunity to climb upward may be able to react more favorably to endangered reputation than can the respectability-focused, middle-class family.

Crisis-Meeting Resources, the B Factor

The vulnerability of the lower-class family, however, is no greater to certain stressor events than that of the middle-class family. Each has its characteristic Achilles heel. Robert C. Angell[1] was the first among family sociologists to seek for the B factor in our equation, a set of resources in family organization which, by their presence or absence, kept the family from crisis or urged it into crisis.

His findings go beyond the points of vulnerability identified above by class. He employed two concepts—family integration and family adaptability. By the first he meant the "bonds of coherence and unity running through family life, of which common interests, affection, and a sense of economic interdependence are perhaps the most prominent." By the second he referred to the family's capacity to meet obstacles and shift courses as a family. He was trying to get at the family's latent predisposition to action in the face of challenges to its usual mode of existence. These latent action patterns, which are most clearly observable at times of crisis, are integrated, in turn, by the values held by the family. Angell found it possible to explain the different reactions of crisis-proof and crisis-prone families to sharp decreases in income during the depression by these twin factors of integration and adaptability, with a restudy of the cases suggesting the greater importance of family adaptability.

Cavan and Ranck[6] and Koos[20] used somewhat different concepts but were in essential agreement. To these researchers a crisis-proof family must have agreement in its role structure, subordination of personal ambitions to family goals, satisfactions within the family obtained because it is successfully meeting the physical and emotional needs of its members, and goals toward which the family is moving collectively. Having all of these, the family is adequately organized. Lacking them, the family is inadequately organized and likely to prove vulnerable to crisis-precipitating events. In both the Cavan-Ranck and Koos studies, the B factor is, in effect, adequacy-inadequacy of family organization.

Social workers have long employed the term "problem family" to designate the crisis-prone family. Early social work viewed problem families primarily as reactors to the conditions of poverty, and saw a shoring up of the economic resources as all-important. Subsequently the shift to a more psychological emphasis established that parents and children in problem families were maladjusted individuals in need of individual treatment. Problem families became not so much victims of a poor distributive order as aggregates of neurotic or psychopathic individuals. More recently the work of Community Research Associates with problem families emphasizes the importance of the distortions of the marital axis, the incompatible combinations of personalities which make for divided and incompetent family headship.[7] Such families are "disorganized" social failures when judged against generally accepted family objectives,[8] and tend to be *multi-problem* families collecting attention and services from public and private agencies all out of proportion to their number in the community.

English researchers have written considerably on problem families, labeling them as deviant, antisocial, and lower class. Irvine[16] stated that "Problem families can be most usefully defined as socially defective families characterized by child neglect and squalor, which defeat current efforts at rehabilitation." Stephens[25] observed that the most obvious common feature of these families is the disorder of their lives. Baldamus and Timms[2] see them as having defective standards of behavior: "The more extreme cases of disorganization and inefficiency in problem families approach a situation of retreatism, as defined by Robert Merton. Conformity to established values is virtually relinquished, especially in respect to standards of behavior."

Max Siporin,[24] in summarizing the work on the problem family, has made the cogent observation that present-day American social workers and sociologists, in constrast to our English colleagues, have preferred to concentrate on the processes of family maladjustment rather than to focus on the stereotyping of families with the use of such epithets as hard-core, inadequate, and disordered. Behind the use by these Americans of terms like "disorganized" is a theory of disorganization and recovery which they seek to study further. This is evident in the attempt we shall make below to link together crisis-meeting resources of family organization and the definitions the family makes of a stressor event in accounting for its crisis-proneness.

Family Definitions, the C Factor

The C factor in our equation has received attention only recently from students of the family. Hill and Boulding,* studying war separation and reunion crises, perceived three possible definitions of

*See first footnote of this article.

the crisis-precipitating event: (1) an *objective* definition, formulated by an impartial observer, (2) a *cultural* definition, formulated by the community, and (3) a *subjective* definition, provided by the family. The most relevant definition in determining a family's crisis-proneness is the third, that provided by the family. The researcher and the community stand outside the situation looking in, but the family members are on the inside, and the family's attitudes toward the event are all-important in this connection.

A family's definition of the event reflects partly the value system held by the family, partly its previous experience in meeting crises, and partly the mechanisms employed in previous definitions of events. This is the *meaning* aspect of the crisis, the interpretation made of it.

Not infrequently families with objective resources adequate to meet the hardships of sickness or job loss crack under the stress because they define such hardship situations as insurmountable. Accident-proneness is disproportionately high among individuals who lack self-confidence and are characterized by anxiety. Crisis-proneness in families also proves related to outlook—to whether or not the event is defined as challenging or crisis-provoking.

Crisis-Proneness, a Function of Both B and C Factors

If we combine deficiency in family organization resources (the B factor) and the tendency to define hardships as crisis-producing (the C factor) into one concept of family inadequacy, we may analyze its major features in a polygon wheel of interacting forces which we reproduce below from the work of Koos and Fulcomer.[21] As they explain it, there is sometimes an initial cause that tends to create tensions in other areas of family life, which, in turn, become conflicts themselves. For example, cultural disparity may cause a lack of sexual satisfaction because of the differing ideas and standards of sex behavior, which in turn may lead to suspicion of the mate and lack of co-operation as breadwinner or homemaker, which in turn may create conflicting roles in the family and draw individual members into new positions of responsibility in the family at the expense of other members. The accumulation of these tensions so weakens the affectional relationships and integration of the family as to render it unable to meet even a simple departure from its ordinary life patterns. The result, when an out-of-ordinary event occurs, is a crisis.

A SCHEMA FOR DEPICTING THE INTERPLAY OF STRESSOR EVENT,
CONTRIBUTING HARDSHIPS, AND FAMILY RESOURCES IN PRODUCING A FAMILY CRISIS

CAUSES

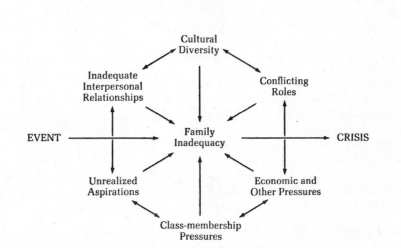

ADJUSTMENT TO CRISIS

Koos and Fulcomer's ingenious diagram, if carried another step into the adjustment of the family to the crisis, would reveal again an interplay of many of the same factors reflecting family adequacy-inadequacy which made families prone to crisis originally. Causation is just as complex in adjustment as it is in the definition of, or sensitivity to, crisis.

Adjustment to a crisis that threatens the family depends upon the adequacy of role performance of family members. As we have already shown in our discussion of the conceptual framework, the family consists of a number of members interacting with one another, and each member is ascribed roles to play within the family. The individual functions as a member of the family largely in terms of the expectations that other members place upon him; the family succeeds as a family largely in terms of the adequacy of role performance of its members. One major effect of crisis is to cause changes in these role patterns. Expectations shift, and the family finds it necessary to work out different patterns. In the process the family is slowed up in its affectional and emotion-satisfying performances until the new patterns are worked out and avenues for expressing affection are opened once more.

The Course of Adjustment

What can we say about the course of adjustment to crisis? We know that it varies from family to family and from crisis to crisis, but the common denominator may be charted in the truncated form of a roller-coaster. As a result of meeting a crisis, the family members are collectively numbed by the blow. They may meet friends, at first, as if the blow had not fallen. Then, as the facts are assimilated, there follows a downward slump in organization, roles are played with less enthusiasm, resentments are smothered or expressed, conflicts are expressed or converted into tensions that make for strained relations. As the nadir of disorganization is reached, things begin improving, new routines arrived at by trial-and-error or by thoughtful planning and sacrificing are put into effect, and some minimum agreements about the future are reached. The component parts to the roller-coaster profile of adjustment to crisis are: crisis → disorganization → recovery → reorganization.

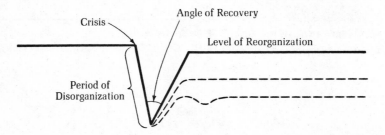

Refinements of this basic pattern have been worked out by Hill[14] on adjustments to war separation and by Jackson[17] on adjustments to alcoholism. Jackson identifies seven stages of adjustment: (1) attempts to deny the problem, (2) attempts to eliminate the problem, (3) disorganization, (4) attempts to reorganize in spite of the problem, (5) efforts to escape the problem: the decision to separate from the alcoholic spouse, (6) reorganization of the family without spouse, (7) reorganization of the entire family. These stages parallel closely the stages of adjustment and recovery to bereavement. An analysis of what happens as the family breaks old habits and organizes new routines during the downhill and uphill part of the roller-coaster figure above shows some interesting changes in family organization.

Generic Effects of Crisis on Family Behavior

In one of the most sensitive areas of family life, the sexual area, sharp changes are noted. The frequency and pattern of sexual relations change, ceasing altogether for some couples.[18] In crises involving interpersonal recriminations, where the crisis is regarded as the fault of any one member, the position of that member is greatly devaluated.[19] Personality changes in members reflect the anxiety and feelings of insecurity engendered by the crisis, and in a sense each responsible member experiences a roller-coaster pattern of personal shock, disorganization, recovery, readjustment. Particularly is this evident in bereavement, where the adjustments of family members follow a course of disbelief → numbness → mourning → trial-and-error adjustments → renewal of routines → recovery.

Changes in parent-child relations are frequently reported in adjustment to crisis. In well-integrated families, Angell[1] found few changes in relative position of parents and children as a result of the crisis of impoverishment, but did find changes in less well-integrated but more adaptable families.

In summarizing the impressions of disaster workers and making inferences from the relatively scanty firsthand information from families experiencing such catastrophes as tornado, hurricane, or flood, we find a confirmation of the roller-coaster pattern at the beginning of the crisis experience. In the immediate recovery period, however, there is an almost euphoric increase in family solidarity (with high solidarity also in the network of neighbors and friends) in the first weeks after the disaster.[15]

Inter-family activities vary as a result of crisis. Some families withdraw from all activities until the "shame" is over and become more than ever closed systems. Others become quite outgoing in their open-window policy during the troubled period.[1]

These are all *short-time* effects of crisis. The evidence concerning the long-time effects of crisis on families is conflicting. Cavan[6] found that, if the families were well organized before the crisis of impoverishment, they tended to remain well organized; moreover, it seemed that previous successful experiences with crisis were predictive of recovery in a new crisis. Angell[1] found well-integrated and adaptable families invulnerable to crisis; that is, they took it in stride without marked changes in their organization or role structure. Helmut Shelsky,[23] studying post-World-War II German families who had experienced severe bombing and the post-war deprivations of denazification and under-employment, found families in general more solid as a consequence. He explains the phenomenon of higher family solidarity as a reaction to the unstable larger society in which home and family are made into a haven from the uncertainty and insecurity of the post-war world. Kent Geiger,[10] studying refugee families from the U.S.S.R. in Europe and the U.S., found families that had been terrorized politically by the regime to be more frequently solidified than disorganized by the experience. The impact of economic deprivation on these families, however, was seen to be detrimental to interpersonal solidarity within the family. Thus, from Geiger's study, political persecution appears to be positively, and deterioration of material living conditions to be negatively, related to family unity. Koos, focusing on the troubles of low-income families in New York City over a two-year period, found among those initially disorganized by crisis evidence of permanent demoralization, a blunting of the family's sensitivity, and a tendency to be more vulnerable in future exposures. "Once having been defeated by a crisis, the family appears not to be able to marshal its forces sufficiently to face the next event; there is, in other words, a permanent defeat each time."[20]

If the conflicting evidences were to be reconciled, the synthesis would follow these lines: Successful experience with crisis tests and strengthens a family, but defeat in crisis is punitive on family structure and morale.[12]

TYPES OF FAMILIES BEST EQUIPPED TO MEET TROUBLES

In this brief discussion of family adjustment to stress, there may be some merit in listing the attributes of family organization, modes of adjustment, and factors making for adjustment which have grown out of the studies of families in crisis and which have been confirmed in an entirely new context by Hill in an analysis of family adjustments to war separation and reunion. In it the findings of earlier studies were treated as hypotheses to be tested in the as-yet-unstudied crises of war separation and reunion. The findings of this analysis divide between factors making for adjusment to crisis and a confirmation of generalizations about modes of adjustment that work out best in the face of crisis (see especially Table 28 in Hill[14]).

Factors Conducive to Good Adjustment to Crisis

Family adaptability, family integration, affectional relations among family members, good marital adjustment of husband and wife, companionable parent-child relationships, family council type of control in decision-making, social participation of wife, and previous successful experience with crisis were all confirmed as important factors in enabling families to adjust to crisis.

Rather fully corroborated within the new contexts of war separation and reunion were the following generalizations from previous studies:

1. Crisis-proneness, the tendency to define troubles as crises, is distributed disproportionately among families of low family adequacy.

2. The course of adjustment is a roller-coaster pattern of disorganization–recovery–readjustment (corroborated as modal pattern for separation but not for reunion).

3. Family reactions to crisis divide between short-time immediate reactions and secondary long-time adjustments.

4. Demoralization following a crisis usually stems from incipient demoralization before the crisis.

5. The length of time a family continues to be disorganized as a result of crisis is inversely related to its adequacy of organization.

6. Unadaptable and unintegrated families are most likely of all to be unpredictable deviants in adjusting to crisis.

7. Foreknowledge and preparation for a critical event mitigates the hardships and improves the chances for recovery.

8. The effects of crisis on families may be punitive or strengthening depending on the margin of health, wealth, and adequacy possessed by the family.

IMPLICATIONS FOR AGENCY POLICIES AND PRACTICE

My statement of implications for agency policies and practices is offered most tentatively. It attempts to answer two questions: (1) How does research on families under stress change our views of family organizational needs? (2) How might practices be changed in line with these needs?

Family Organizational Needs

We find families increasingly vulnerable as they are shorn of kin, neighbors, and friends. Centered as they are about the husband and wife and their one or two children, modern American families are highly mobile, precariously small, and poorly structured units to survive life's stresses—death, unemployment, war separations, infidelity, desertion, and so on.

The goal of self-sufficiency, of families' being capable of surviving by themselves, may have had some merit in pioneer days when the family groups were large and included several relatives besides the children. Today the myth of family self-sufficiency requires discrediting. To replace it we bring the concept of interdependence of families within communities. This concept will need to be implemented in our communities with appropriate organization, to be sure, if it is to have any meaning to people.

In my war-separation study the families who adjusted least well and most slowly were frequently solitary families characterized by past mobility and transiency, or they were families whose relationships with relatives and neighbors had become tenuous. In either case, these families lacked the nests of supporting families with which to share their troubles and were, therefore, forced to live *alone* in an enforced anonymity. Left to their own devices, crisis-stricken families in a new neighborhood withdraw into their narrow family circles and fester inwardly rather than risk being rebuffed.

Several studies have offered evidence that families whose economic well-being is marginal are more vulnerable to crisis. Koos[20] eloquently portrays the marginality of living in such families:

> As the investigator strips off the outer layers of low-income urban existence he becomes increasingly aware of its hand-to-mouth quality. Only the things that must be done managed to get done. There are no sheltered reservoirs within which man can store up his surplus thoughts, energies and products—and not surprisingly, because for people living under these conditions there are no surplus thoughts and energies and products. They need all of their energies and every cent they can earn in order to meet the day-by-day demands, and they know that their environment will make endless demands upon them whichever way they turn. Life under such conditions takes on a nip-and-tuck urgency that belies our culture's middle-class ethos of a reasoned calculation of one's future.
>
> Individuals and whole families of individuals suffer from these pressures. Housewives lament that they can buy only for the next meal because there is no place in which to store additional foods. Wage earners know that every cent they make is mortgaged in advance simply to keep up with basic expenditures, and they curse and worry because they cannot save for a rainy day. Adolescent girls have no place in which to entertain the "boy friend" because home offers no opportunity for privacy. Only the youngest members of the family can dawdle and dream beyond life's immediacies, and they, too, suffer indirectly.

IMPLICATIONS FOR FAMILY SERVICES NEEDED

The high mobility of young families results in feelings of "aloneness" as they move into new communities or join the stream moving out of the central city into the suburbs. Separated from kin and hometown neighbors, to whom do they turn for counsel and help when they want to spill their troubles? How do they become integrated into a new neighborhood or community? The challenge for social work is to develop institutions less commercial than the "welcome wagon" and more neighborhood oriented. We need community organization and neighborhood development activities in this direction, such as Milwaukee supported in its department of health for a time. We need to institutionalize the status of "newcomers" and utilize it to provide orientation and welcoming activities into neighborhood and community.

It is noteworthy that those families that best succeeded in meeting the crisis of wartime separation made frequent mention of the accessibility of relatives, neighbors, and friends. They rarely mentioned, we are sad to report, the churches, the family agencies, or other welfare groups that claim in their annual bid for contributions from the community that they provide services of this kind to families in trouble.

In shaping a community program that is more family-centered, we need to face the fact that many families that once received help and comfort from kin and neighbors have now lost contact with them and live in anonymity. We must recognize that their problems are often such that they do not know which, if any, social agency could or would help if asked. We need to reorganize our agency offerings to meet families at their own level of need. As we have seen the need among the families in the studies reviewed here, help might often have consisted simply of providing an opportunity to ventilate their anxieties, share their woes, and ask for reassuring, simple advice about problems occasioned by the absence of the husband and father, or the changed regulations for children attending schools in double shifts. There are, at the present time, few agencies to which families willingly turn for help on the more superficial levels of life.

Even if social workers were willing to extend such superficial services broadly, there are only a few hundred family service agencies in the entire United States, and marriage counseling services are limited to the metropolitan centers and to a few college campuses. The professional services for nonindigent families in trouble must be drawn mainly from the family physician, the teacher, the minister, the family lawyer, and the occasional child welfare worker with the public welfare department. To these professionals, the following suggestions from the researches I have summarized appear justified:

1. Professional services will make their greatest contribution if they are made with the total family context in mind. Particularly is this true in the case of crises of dismemberment and demoralization.

2. Families, like combat teams and other collectivities, have a morale and *esprit de corps* to maintain if they are to be effective. Physicians have found that illnesses that yesterday were called psychosomatic are today regarded as products of family aggravations.

The helping professionals will need to approximate family group workers, serving the child's family *as a family* rather than serving the child solely as a personality. This involves becoming an artist in relationship therapy, keeping all the family relationships healthy.

3. Families need to be kept intact and relatively self-sustaining.

Both war separations and peacetime separations render a net disservice to most families, although many ride them out successfully. Voluntary separations should not be undertaken without serious thought as to the consequences. Employers should know that transferring an employee to a position in a distant community where tight housing prevents his taking the family along is doing the employee a serious disservice. However, if separation is forced upon the family, our research shows that it is much more easily assimilated if prepared for well in advance. Making this fact known widely may greatly mitigate the untoward effects of separation because of employment, hospitalization, institutionalization, and even imprisonment.

4. Counseling and casework become patchwork remedies unless a strong program of preventive social work and education is undertaken by agencies.

We know that families of various types are capable of meeting crises, that we do not have to stamp out uniform models. Successful families, however, share the resources of good marital adjustment, family adaptability, and, to a lesser degree, family integration. Their communicative lines must be kept open through frank discussions and the use of the consultative process in arriving at family decisions. Caseworkers will see the challenge to train young people, and they will seize the opportunity through parent education to reach young parents, to encourage the development of patterns of family organization which make for survival in the face of trouble. To date, few programs have attempted, even experimentally, to produce students competent to exercise family leadership in flexible family organizations of this sort. Here lies the challenge of preventive social work and family life education of tomorrow.

REFERENCES

1. Angell, Robert C. *The Family Encounters the Depression,* Charles Scribner's Sons, New York, 1936.
2. Baldamus, W., and Timms, Noel, "The Problem Family: A Sociological Approach," *British Journal of Sociology,* Vol. VI, No. 2 (1955), pp. 318-327.
3. Bernard, Jessie, *Remarriage,* Dryden Press, New York, 1956.
4. Burgess, Ernest W., "The Family and Sociological Research," *Social Forces,* Vol. XXVI, No. 1 (1947), pp. 1-6
5. Caplan, Gerald, and associates, Harvard School of Public Health, "Some Comments on Family Functioning in Its Relation to Mental Health," 1956 (unpublished).
6. Cavan, R. S., and Ranck, K. H., *The Family and the Depression,* University of Chicago Press, Chicago, 1938.
7. Community Research Associates, *Classification of Disorganized Families for Use in Family Oriented Diagnosis and Treatment,* New York, 1954.

8.   _____, *The Prevention and Control of Disordered Behavior in San Mateo County, California.* New York, 1954, p. 15.

9.   Eliot, Thomas D., "Handling Family Strains and Shocks," in *Family, Marriage and Parenthood,* Howard Becker and Reuben Hill (eds.), D. C. Heath, Boston, 2nd ed., 1955, p. 617.

10.   Geiger, Kent, "Deprivation and Solidarity in the Soviet Urban Family," *American Sociological Review,* Vol. XX, No. 1 (1955), pp. 57-68.

11.   Goode, William J., *After Divorce,* The Free Press, Glencoe, Ill., 1956.

12.   Hill, Reuben, "The American Family: Problem or Solution," *American Journal of Sociology,* Vol. LIII, No. 2 (1947), pp. 125-130.

13.   _____, "Families and the Prospect of Educational Integration," in *The Implications of Desegregation for Family Life in Virginia,* Virginia Council on Family Relations, Richmond, 1955, pp. 2-10.

14.   _____, *Families Under Stress,* Harper & Brothers, New York, 1949.

15.   _____, and Rayner, Jeanette, "Observations of Family Adjustments in the Kansas City Tornado," unpublished memorandum in preparation, 1957.

16.   Irvine, Elizabeth E., "Research into Problem Families: Questions Arising from Dr. Blacker's Investigations," *British Journal of Psychiatric Social Work,* No. 9 (1954), p. 32.

17.   Jackson, Joan K., "The Adjustment of the Family to Alcoholism," *Marriage and Family Living,* Vol. XVIII, No. 4 (1956), pp. 361-369.

18.   Komarovsky, Mirra, *The Unemployed Man and His Family,* Dryden Press, New York, 1940.

19.   Koos, Earl L., "Class Differences in Family Reactions to Crisis," *Marriage and Family Living,* Vol. XII, No. 3 (1950), pp. 77-78.

20.   _____, *Families in Trouble,* King's Crown Press, New York, 1946.

21.   _____, and Fulcomer, David, "Families in Crisis," in "Dynamics of Family Interaction," E. M. Duvall and Reuben Hill (eds.), Women's Foundation, New York, 1948, Chapt. 8 (mimeographed).

22.   Parsons, Talcott, and Bales, Robert F., *Family, Socialization and Interaction Process,* The Free Press, Glencoe, Ill., 1955.

23.   Shelsky, Helmut, *Wandlunger in der Deutschen Familien in der Gegenwart,* Enke-Verlag, Stuttgart, 1954.

24.   Siporin, Max, Baylor University College of Medicine, Texas Medical Center, "The Concept of the Problem Family," 1956, p. 8 (unpublished).

25.   Stephens, Tom, *Problem Families,* William S. Heinman, New York, 1947.

26.   Waller, Willard Walter, *The Family: A Dynamic Interpretation,* rev. by Reuben Hill, Dryden Press, New York, 1951, Chapt. 21, "Family Crises and Family Adjustment."

emerging trends in treating relationships
david h. olson
douglas h. sprenkle

In the last decade, the growth and development of the profession of marriage and family counseling has mushroomed. Not only has the number of professional publications increased dramatically, but the demand for relationship-oriented treatment by couples and families has grown to the point that most mental health facilities are adding this service. Work with couples and families is no longer a practice carried out in private for highly selected cases, but it is becoming the treatment choice of a wide range of emotional (intrapersonal) and relationship (interpersonal) problems.

This paper reviews some of the major trends in the fields of marital and family counseling since the first author's extensive review article (Olson, 1970). That paper explicated the history of marriage counseling and family therapy, described major trends in clinical practice and theory development, and reviewed the status of research in these fields. Much of the recent work on the cutting edge of the field both conceptually and empirically is presented in a recent book entitled *Treating Relationships* (Olson, 1976a).

In the past review (Olson, 1970), marriage counseling and family therapy were described as young "fraternal twins" developing along parallel but surprisingly separate lines. While the benefits of interchange would seem obvious, the relative autonomy of the two fields was seen in their separate training centers, their divergent literatures, sources of theory, clientele, and professional affiliations of their practitioners.

Not unlike many youth, these two related fields were also depicted as developing with a great amount of vigor but without a sufficient amount of rigor. They had experienced enormous growth and hard won acceptance in the previous decades, but that growth spurt resulted in limited conceptual or empirical grounding. Specifically, the main features of clinical practice could best be described as each therapist "doing his own thing." Both fields could still be depicted as techniques in search of a theory (Manus, 1966), and such theory that did exist was generally only tenuously related to practice. Well designed research, especially in family therapy, was virtually nonexistent.

Other review articles which summarized research trends through the early 1970s, reached similar discouraging conclusions. Goodman (1973) assessed the status of marriage counseling as a developing science on the basis of research published through 1968. She concluded that most investigations were conducted as an adjunct to the activities of professionals whose primary identifications were with fields other than marriage counseling. There was no core of research professionals in the field, and there was little programmatic effort. Most investigators published only once, and no one bothered to replicate their work. Gurman's (1973; 1975a, 1975b) and Beck's (1976) careful and thorough reviews of the outcome research in marital therapy found most of the investigations deficient with regard to such criteria as specificity, therapist sample size, control groups, independent rating, and multidimensional assessment. Well, Dilkes, and Trivelli (1972) examined outcome research in family therapy through 1971. It is noteworthy that only 18 family therapy studies could be located. Of those, only two were considered of adequate quality in terms of sample, design, and methodology.

Since the publication of those reviews, certain trends have begun to emerge around the country which we shall categorize under the headings A) conceptual and programmatic and B) research and evaluation. All of the latter and most of the former can be envisaged as bright spots in the rather cloudy state of the fields. While they remain a long way from being well developed sciences, marriage and family counseling are showing encouraging signs of maturity.

CONCEPTUAL AND PROGRAMMATIC TRENDS

1) There are fewer clear distinctions and more synergetic interplay between marriage and family counseling. Increasingly, the meaning and distinctions of the fields called marriage counseling and family therapy are becoming more blurred and less distinct. As professionals from a variety of fields such as social work, psychiatry, psychology, and the ministry have entered and continue to enter the field of relationship-oriented counseling, the distinction between counseling versus therapy is rapidly fading. Increasingly, professionals are identifying themselves as marriage *and* family counselors rather than by the nature of their initial training.

The aforementioned relative professional autonomy of the marriage and family fields is clearly breaking down. No doubt this trend was abetted when the American Association of Marriage Counselors (AAMC), founded in 1942, became the American Association of Marriage and Family Counselors (AAMFC) in 1970. The number of centers offering training in marriage *and* family counseling is growing and as of this writing there are five doctoral programs with this dual emphasis. The *Journal of Marriage and Family Counseling* began publication in 1975 and *Family Process*, since 1962 the unofficial organ of the family therapy movement, regularly carries articles with a couple as well as family emphasis. Articles relevant to both thrusts are also found regularly in the National Council on Family Relations' *Family Coordinator* and *Journal of Marriage and the Family* and in the National Alliance for Family Life's *Journal of Family Counseling.*

2) The structural distinctions between marriage counseling and family therapy are also fading as there is increasing focus on treating all types of relationships, including unconventional ones. The structural distinctions that marriage counseling always involves both the husband and the wife and no other family members in all the sessions is rapidly breaking down.

Many practitioners who primarily identify themselves as marriage counselors now include the children or grandparents in treatment for one or more sessions. Conversely, the older orthodoxy that family therapists see all members of the family in all sessions is rapidly vanishing. Examining such widely read family therapy texts as Minuchin (1974), Nichols (1973), and Ferber, Mendelsohn, and Napier (1973), it is clear that family therapists are opting to work with couples and other subsystems as well as total family units. After initial sessions, many family therapists will see the parents alone and focus on their relationship even though the presenting problem was a child. Typical of this trend is family therapist James Framo's statement:

> *Although in particular situations I believe it is necessary to do* family *therapy throughout the course of treatment (i.e. including the children), I have moved more in the direction of working with the marriage relationship of the parents once the originally symptomatic children have become defocused (1975, p. 22).*

Marriage and family counseling then, is being seen more as a continuum, with the choice of treatment unit becoming more pragmatic than ideological. The synergetic interplay between the two approaches is increasingly valued.

There is also a movement today to be much more radically inclusive and to appeal to variant family forms and lifestyles. This is happening more at some university marriage and family counseling centers which often have a thriving clientele of couples "living together" or significantly involved in each other's lives. Such relationships may be same sex or opposite sex. The relationships of singles and those involved in alternative life styles, such as communes and group marriages, are being treated by those who call themselves marriage and family counselors. While these trends are emerging, many practitioners are opposed to counseling those involved in alternative life style arrangements (Knapp, 1975).

   3) The need for specialization within relationship-oriented treatment is being recognized. Ironically, there are specialists as well as generalists emerging in this field. One of the components of a maturing profession is the development of specializations within the field. In his Presidential Address to the American Association of Marriage and Family Counselors, Clark Vincent (1975) called upon the membership to consider this issue. Just as physicians, lawyers, and other professionals have recognized that the complexities of their fields mandated limited areas of expertise, so too must marriage and family counselors realize that they cannot be competent in all areas. In the Yellow Page advertising in large city telephone directories, the same counselor sometimes offers help with marital, sexual, parent-child, financial, and personal adjustment problems even though each of these areas has a growing body of literature and related set of skills that could provide the basis for a specialty (Figley, Sprenkle, & Denton, 1976).

   At least one treatment area, human sexuality, has helped to spawn a separate professional organization—The American Association of Sex Educators and Counselors. While most marriage and family counselors remain "general practitioners" we predict that more and more therapists will develop specialized expertise. Another emerging arena of relationship counseling is divorce counseling (Nichols, 1973; Fisher, 1973, 1974; Brown, 1976). The focus is initially on helping the couple to work on an amenable divorce settlement and then to work with the individuals in developing a satisfactory independent life style.

   4) There is an increasing application of social learning theory, general systems theory, and Rogerian client-centered variables to treating relationships. A rapprochement of theory and practice in marriage and family counseling is being abetted by the increased integration of certain theories into treatment programs. Examples of this integrative approach will be briefly reviewed.

Social Learning Theory

   Social learning theory has made a rather dramatic effect recently because its basic tenets are probably most readily translatable into treatment modalities and techniques. Behavior theorists have conceptualized marital distress as a breakdown in mutual reinforcement (Stuart, 1960), an imbalance in reinforcing exchanges (Patterson & Reid, 1970), and as a type of coercive interaction, sustained by mutual reinforcement, in which partners dispense aversive stimuli to control the behavior of their mates (Patterson & Hops, 1972). Although these formulations vary somewhat, all theorists conclude that intervention is most effective if focused on increasing positive acts and decreasing negative ones. It is believed that these behavioral changes will produce positive changes in feelings and cognitions about relationships.

   Gerald Patterson, Robert Weiss, and their colleagues at the University of Oregon (Patterson, 1976; Weiss, Hops, & Patterson, 1972; Patterson, Hops, & Weiss, 1975) are among the leading behavior theorists and researchers in the marriage and family fields. They have utilized a social learning model to assess the differences between distressed and non-distressed couples (Birchler, Weiss, & Vincent, 1975; Vincent, Weiss, & Birchler, 1975) and have developed a behavioral exchange reinforcement program for couples which helps them to reinforce certain target behaviors and extinguish others. The Patterson group (Patterson, 1976) has recently reported the work of a ten-year program for the treatment of disturbed children by means of a social learning approach. Both parents and the children's school teachers were utilized as change agents on the assumption that they were crucial to the children's social environment. Socially aggressive children not only changed in school and home but results generalized to the entire family.

Richard Stuart's "Operant Interpersonal Approach" (Stuart, 1976) has been another pioneering effort in the behavioral treatment of couples. Stuart developed an eight stage model which has as its central theme the acceleration of positive behavioral change. Couples initially complete a Marital Pre-Counseling Inventory (which may be used for research purposes) in order to help pinpoint target behaviors, and help the therapist plan the treatment program efficiently. The program stresses developing behavioral contracts, negotiating role responsibilities, and learning how to maintain behavioral change. Stuart has treated over 750 couples in the past 10 years utilizing these methods.

Other significant behaviorally oriented programs include the work of James Alexander and his colleagues at the University of Utah with families of delinquents (Alexander, 1976; Alexander & Barton, 1974; Parsons & Alexander, 1973) and the Behavioral Exchange Program designed to increase conflict negotiation skills (Rappaport & Harrell, 1972; Harrell & Guerney, 1976). Although not always properly identified, social learning principles such as desensitization and shaping techniques have also been a predominant theme in many sex counseling programs (i.e., Masters & Johnson, 1970; Messersmith, 1976).

General Systems Theory

A second emerging theoretical approach has been general systems theory. It is unquestionably the dominant theoretical framework in family therapy and most of the widely read theorists pay homage to it in their recent works (e.g. Bowen, 1975; Bell, 1975; Haley, 1975; Framo, 1975; Andrews, 1974; Boszormenyi-Nagy, 1973; Minuchin, 1974; Satir, 1972; Ferber, et al., 1972; Whitaker, 1975). Unlike social learning theory, the gap between systems theory and practice is rather wide and the possiblities for diverse application are numerous. Systems theory is primarily a general framework and a diverse variety of seemingly unrelated interrelated propositions have been deduced from it. Its value as a heuristic conceptual framework for viewing human behavior is its greatest asset to date. It has led, on the one hand, to relatively short term therapies emphasizing behavior change and symptom relief (e.g. Weakland, et al., 1974; Minuchin, 1974); and, on the other hand, to longer term family psychotherapy focusing on family history, insight, and/or the subjective feelings of family members.

The only unitary thread among theorists is that the family is involved in the etiology of disturbance and is the primary treatment unit. It will be up to the current generation of researcher-therapists to operationalize such systems theory concepts as "interdependence," "emergence," "circular causality," and "morphogenesis" that guide their work. Even such a commonly held assumption related to interdependence—that symptomatic behavior in children is related to dysfunctional behavior in the marital dyad—has not been adequately tested.

The communications principles derived from systems theory, originally by such pioneers as Don Jackson (1968) and further developed by Watzlawick, et al. (1967), are increasingly being integrated into treatment programs. Perhaps the most widely known of these programs is the Minnesota Couples Communications Program (MCCP) developed by Sherod Miller and associates at the University of Minnesota (Miller, et al., 1976). Originally developed for pre-marital couples in 1967, the program is now more widely taken by married couples and other dyads, such as co-therapists, who wish to enhance their communication. Such systems and communications concepts as morphogenesis, meta-communication, and feedback strongly influenced the design and evaluation of the program, which has been tested on more than 1200 groups both nationally and internationally.

James Alexander and associates (Alexander, 1976; Alexander & Barton, 1974) previously mentioned in connection with social learning theory, have also been strongly influenced by the general systems approach. Their work with delinquents was based upon some basic research which indicated that the communications patterns of delinquent families were more defensive and less supportive than patterns in normal families. Specifically, the investigators tested system reciprocity (interdependence) and found that in normal families, members tended to reciprocate supportive but not defensive communication. Conversely, families with delinquents would reciprocate defensive but not supportive communication (Alexander, 1973). The Alexander program, then, utilized both general systems and social learning approaches. Behavioral techniques were employed to increase both the rate and reciprocity of supportiveness while decreasing defensive behaviors among family members. Craig Messersmith (1976) has also proposed a model which integrates systems and social learning approaches in the treatment of sexual dysfunction.

Rogerian Client Centered Approaches

A third theoretical influence, to date used primarily with parent-child relationships and with couples, has been the Rogerian or client-centered approach. Bernard and Louise Guerney and associates at the Pennsylvania State University have been leading advocates. In 1962, when at Rutgers, the Guerneys originated filial therapy, a program designed to help parents deal with their children's problems through the use of speaking and listening skills based upon the Rogerian model of expressing feelings and empathic listening (Guerney, 1976). Rappaport (1976) has described the Conjugal Relationship Enhancement Program (CRE) which applies similar principles to enhance couple communication. The Guerneys have also applied Rogerian based skills in a program focusing on parent-adolescent relationship development (PARD). There are plans to develop similar programs for entire families. These programs have contributed to accretive knowledge since the skills taught were previously shown to be of benefit therapeutically (Rogers, 1951) and have been used in training both counselors and para-professionals (Carkhuff, 1969).

5) There is an emphasis on increasing specific skills rather than on more global treatment. The trend in many of the more current approaches is toward identifying and increasing specific communication skills. For example, rather than the diffuse goal of "improving communication" the Minnesota Couples Communication Program (Miller, et al., 1976) has identified such concrete objectives as "speaking for self," "documenting," and "making feeling and intention statements." Other counselors are training couples and families in assertiveness skills (Lehman-Olson, 1976), sexual contacting and non-demand pleasuring (Hartman & Fithian, 1972), and other techniques which focus quickly on the client's difficulties and allow researchers to assess more adequately both the process and outcome of treatment.

6) Therapists are increasingly using educational and preventative models. While marital and family therapists continue to treat troubled relationships, more programs are being developed with an educational or growth and enhancement model. Their model focus is on enabling couples and families to deal with current problems rather than waiting until the problems become more severe. In part, these programs are a reaction against the traditional model which is more concerned with rooting out pathology than with promoting higher levels of health (Vincent, 1973).

In addition to such programs as CCP, CRE, and PARD, the Association of Couples for Marital Enrichment (ACME) (Mace & Mace, 1976) has also given strong impetus to this trend. Although founded by a pioneering couple in marriage counseling, David and Vera Mace, ACME is a predominantly non-professional organization designed to facilitate marriage enrichment among participant couples and to coordinate and stimulate the development of other enrichment programs. ACME uses and endorses many of the existing communication programs such as MCCP. It also sponsors its own weekend enrichment retreats. This preventative program also emphasizes the potential value of couples as paraprofessionals.

Although most programs in the sexual area are directed toward alleviating dysfunction, there are some noteworthy sexual enrichment programs, such as the Human Sexuality Program at the University of Minnesota (Maddock, 1976). Literally thousands of couples and hundreds of parents and adolescent offspring have gone through the Sexual Attitude Reassessment (SAR) and other enrichment programs offered in Minneapolis. These efforts have also stimulated similar endeavors around the country.

7) There is greater reliance on group versus individual approaches. Whether the focus is on training or treatment, there are more couples and families involved in groups. Although there is some initial resistance by clients to enter treatment groups, they often find it beneficial. The group setting can offer a social context in which trust can develop and from which support can be drawn. Groups offer an important reference point from which couples and families can gain perspective on their own difficulties and discover that they are not unique in having problems. The group context also offers multiple models for relatedness and multiple sources of feedback.

Another important reason for the group trend is economy. Although not a new approach, multiple family therapy (Laqueur, 1973; Leichter & Schulman, 1974) continues to develop in part because seeing families together saves therapists time. It also enables them to reach a greater number and variety of clients and such group approaches are also less costly for participants.

Group treatment methods for couples on college campuses are becoming increasingly common (Smith & Alexander, 1974). Leichter (1973) describes the nature of couples groups in later stages of the life cycle as well. Many group training programs have already been cited in the communication area. Other recently reported examples are assertiveness training workshops (Lehman-Olson, 1976), parent groups (Gottschalk, 1976), and jealousy workshops (Constantine, 1976).

8) Therapists are employing short-term contracts rather than open-ended treatment. Stimulated by the behavioral approaches and educational training programs, spurred by the desire for economy, and motivated by a sincere questioning of the excessive length of much treatment, more therapists are relying on fixed time contracts. This forces both therapists and clients to pinpoint certain target concerns and to maximize their time together (Rappaport, 1976).

While brief therapy traditionally has been considered a less desirable substitute for long term treatment when the latter was not feasible, it is currently being examined as the possible treatment of choice. Weakland, et al., (1974) described the results of a six year program of rapid problem resolution in marital, family, and individual concerns at the Brief Therapy Center of the Mental Research Institute, Palo Alto, California. With treatment limited to a maximum of 10 sessions, the authors achieved significant success in meeting the agreed upon treatment goal of the clients in about three-fourths of 97 widely varied cases—a rate that compares very favorably with long term modalities. While the evaluation plan involves some clinical judgment and occasional ambiguities, the results do constitute a challenge to proponents of the more expensive treatments. The program has been influenced by some of the rapid treatment approaches of Pittman, et al., (1971), Minuchin and Montalvo (1967), and Milton Erickson (Haley, 1973).

RESEARCH AND EVALUATION TRENDS

A second set of trends reflect an intensified emphasis on research and evaluation of both the process and outcome of treatment. It is probably this emphasis which is the hallmark of the field of marriage and family counseling in the 1970s and is clearly represented in a recent edited book (Olson, 1976a). The current generation of therapist-researchers are leading a quieter revolution than those first generation mavericks who thrust an interpersonal model on a professional community obsessed with intraphychic process, but it is a revolution nonetheless. The coming decade will probably witness the death of some long held assumptions, and the questioning of many others. For one example, the widely held assumption that co-therapy leads to more effective client outcomes in marital therapy is given only negligible support in the studies reviewed to date (Gurman, 1975a, 1975b). The decade will probably also see a diminution in prestige of therapeutic gurus whose effectiveness is "assumed" from the sonorousness of their assertions or the charisma of their personalities.

This quiet revolution has gained impetus from several factors. First, the current generation is relatively free of the burden of having to fight for recognition in a hostile environment. Marriage and family counseling is no longer a covert craft to be whispered about behind closed doors at conventions. Energies formerly given to polemics can now be directed toward grounding propositions and programs. Second, the current generation is less tied to one "school" of doing marriage and family counseling. Through the burgeoning literature they are aware of multiple perspectives and that their own teachers have not necessarily found "the Holy Grail." Third, as training centers have grown, the influence of certain master teachers has often been balanced by faculty receiving training elsewhere and exposed to different input. Finally, the doctoral and postdoctoral centers are becoming increasingly populated with students with rigorous training in methodology and statistics who are unapologetically interested in the science as well as the art of counseling. They are used to asking difficult questions and are unwilling to accept testimonials as evidence of effectiveness. The specific trends follow:

1) Clearer and more researchable questions are being asked. One of the most crucial early issues in any investigation is "to render the research question researchable (Hill, 1973)." This entails clear conceptualization and rigorous operationalization. Yet most of the early research asked vague, global questions such as "Does marriage counseling increase marital satisfaction?" or "Does family therapy improve family functioning?" The latter question assumes that family therapy is a phenomenon that is both unitary and easily delimited. It further assumes that the empirical correlates of "family functioning" are readily available to the eager researcher. It is little wonder that most early investigations were inadequate. Current researchers are most likely to ask such questions as: "Does behavioral role reversal increase the frequency of the client's assertive statements?" Note also that here there is a better linkage between what the therapist is attempting to change (i.e., increase assertiveness) and what the research would measure.

2) There is an increase in systematic studies of treatment programs. The aforementioned problem (Goodman, 1973; Olson, 1976b) that research in the field was predominantly of a one-shot nature is now being rectified. Not only has the sheer quantity of research increased but also more studies are being done in a systematic and sequential manner. Not only are results replicated but the knowledge gained is accretive. The major team projects identified earlier are most representative of this trend, i.e., those associated with Sherod Miller (Minnesota), Bernard Guerney (Pennsylvania), Gerald Patterson (Oregon), James Alexander (Utah), and James Maddock (Minnesota). An additional programatic effort has been conducted by Richard Cookerly (1976) who completed four sequential large sample studies on the outcome of different marriage counseling approaches.

3) Greater rigor in evaluation research is being practiced. There has been a quantum leap in the quality of marriage and family outcome studies in the past five years (Olson, 1976a). Research is moving from unfocused single case studies, with non-independent raters, lacking in adequate measurement techniques, without control groups; to more clearly focused multi-dimensional studies, with independent raters, using a multi-method approach, and rigorous experimental designs with matched control groups. Fortunately the range and variety of evaluation methods is increasing and the description and availability of these methods is being publicized (Phillips, 1973; Cromwell, Olson, & Fournier, 1976).

4) Increased use of multi-method approaches involving both self-report and observational methods. Past research on treatment has frequently relied on a single self-report measure of change, often as reported either by the client or the therapist. While such self-report data is valuable in that it gives an "insider" or subjective view of what has transpired, it may be affected by such problems as social desirability response set, problems of recall, and other perceptual distortions (Olson, 1974). More of the recent studies are not only using several self-report measures from both the client and therapist, but they are also incorporating laboratory and home observation procedures. For example, a recent study of marital treatment (Weiss, Hops, & Patterson, 1972) utilized four self-report measures and three observational techniques: coding of 1) a structured interview for positive and negative exchanges, 2) a ten-minute videotape segment of spouses resolving conflict, and 3) three one-hour home visits. Such multi-method multi-trait studies not only increase the validity of the research but also enable one to more clearly identify what type of treatment was most effective on a variety of specific outcome dimensions.

5) There is more attention to change in both the treatment outcome and the treatment process. Although most of the research is still focusing solely on the outcomes of treatment, some attention is being given to changes that occur during the treatment process itself. This concern with process measures has been primarily stimulated by the behavioral approach which emphasizes clients keeping behavioral self-report records in their interactions with significant others at home. These "behavioral self-reports" are more objective than traditional self-report questionnaires or instruments which ask for perceptions or opinions (Patterson, et al., 1975; Olson, 1974). The former is a record of specific behavior, usually recorded on a daily basis. It alerts the therapist to the changes in client's behavior between sessions and provides concrete feedback. As an example, the Patterson group asks couples to keep a daily record of spousal behaviors which each partner finds either pleasing or displeasing. The therapists monitor this data through frequent telephone contact.

Taken together, these research trends suggest that we are finally in a position to be able to address seriously Paul's (1967) question: "*What* treatment, by *whom*, is the most effective for *this* individual with *that* specific problem under *which* set of circumstances?"

LOOKING TO THE FUTURE

Because of the preceding trends, especially those in research and evaluation, we are generally optimistic about the future of marriage and family counseling as a field. The trends are incipient, however, and the extent to which they become dominant will determine the pace of constructive change.

Two other issues, one conceptual and the other professional, will also help to determine the shape and scope of the field in the coming decade. The conceptual issue is whether the field will continue to focus primarily on intrafamily system dynamics or whether it will give more attention to the interface of family and the other systems which impinge upon it. While some therapists (Boszormenyi-Nagy & Spark, 1973) have transcended the nuclear family unit by attending to intergenerational influences, and others (Speck & Attneave, 1973) have broadened the treatment unit to include one's social network, few therapists have been concerned with the impact of economic, political, educational, and other social-cultural systems on the family, and how these affect treatment.

This parochialism is inconsistent with general systems theory which stresses that social systems such as families are "open systems." As Kantor and Lehr (1975) note: ". . . the chief characteristic of such systems is an almost continuous interchange not only within the system, but across the boundary between the inner environment and the outer environment." Such interchange is not optimal, but is mandatory for the survival of systems (Figley, Sprenkle, & Denton, 1976).

A few therapists are taking the interface of the family and these external systems seriously. Patterson (1975), as noted previously, considers what happens in the educational system as crucial to the treatment of problem children, and school as well as home intervention is included. William Taylor and colleagues at Purdue University have developed a program which utilizes the home-school interface to help families with handicapped children (Taylor, et al., 1976). Several programs are now giving attention to the interface of marriage and family counseling and the world of work (Skidmore, 1974; Skidmore & Skidmore, 1975; Figley, Sprenkle, & Denton, 1976). Still other interventionists, by considering the unique needs of certain client populations or treatment settings, are contributing to the spirit of a true ecological approach, i.e., working with low socioeconomic groups (Minuchin, et al., 1967; Foley, 1975), prisoners (Ostby, 1968), rural populations (Williams, 1975), alcoholics in treatment centers (Gallant, 1970).

The concern for competence and accountability in marriage and family counseling will also determine the development of this field as a separate mental health profession. While the establishment of training centers, specialized journals, distinct professional organizations, and codes of ethics are important and encouraging trends, there is still ground for concern. Many of the contributions to the literature, and even some of the best works cited in this review, are still being made by those who would not identify themselves as marriage and family counselors. While these contributions are no less welcomed or appreciated, the profession needs to develop more programmatic research within its own ranks, by persons whose lifelong professional commitment is to the field. Furthermore, only a small percentage of the nation's marriage and family counselors are even members of the American Association of Marriage and Family Counselors. This, in conjunction with the fact that only six states license or certify marriage and family practitioners, means that incompetence and outright quackery still abound. This can only reduce the credibility of the profession, in the eyes of other professionals, but also of the increasing numbers of couples and families seeking relationship-oriented treatment. As the profession becomes more visible, it is even more imperative that the profession must be accountable for its quality of service.

CONCLUSION

In conclusion, the field (we suggest that henceforth the singular be used) of marriage and family counseling is no longer in its infancy. Conceptually, programmatically, and empirically, it is showing signs of maturity since the decade of the 1960s. The 1970s show more evidence of theory that is both grounded and relevant, research that is linked to both general principles and application, and practice guided by both coherent rationale and the possibility of objective assessment. It appears that the future will bring greater integration of research, theory, and practice which is just beginning to demonstrate significant pay-offs for each area and for the profession (Olson, 1976c; Sprenkle, 1976).

But the field remains far from becoming fully mature. Indeed, sometimes it still appears like an adolescent, full of undirected energy and awkwardly handling the increasing demands of adulthood. However, it is becoming increasingly imperative that this youth directly deal with the difficult and complex issues of credibility and accountability before it will to be fully recognized as a more mature profession—the mental health field.

REFERENCES

Andrews, E. *The emotionally disturbed family.* New York: Jason Aronson, 1974.
Alexander, J. Defensive and supportive communication in normal and deviant families. *Journal of Consulting and Clinical Psychology,* 1973, *40,* 223-231.
Alexander, J. F., & Barton, C. Behavioral intervention with families of delinquents: Therapists characteristics, family behavior, and outcome. Paper presented at the National Convention of the Association for the Advancement of Behavior Therapy, Chicago, 1974.
Alexander, J., & Barton, C. Behavioral systems therapy for families. In D. Olson, (Ed.), *Treating relationships,* Lake Mills, IA: Graphic Publishing, 1976.
Beck, D. F. Research findings on the outcomes of marital counseling. In D. Olson, (Ed.), *Treating relationships,* Lake Mills, IA: Graphic Publishing, 1976.
Bell, J. E. *Family therapy.* New York: Jason Aronson, 1975.
Birchler, G. R., Weiss, R. L., & Vincent, J. P. Multimethod analysis of social reinforcement exchange between maritally distressed and non-distressed spouse and stranger dyads. *Journal of Personality and Social Psychology,* 1975, *31,* 349-360.
Blechman, E. A., & Olson, D. H. L. Family contract game: Description and effectiveness. In D. Olson, (Ed.), *Treating relationships,* Lake Mills, IA: Graphic Publishing, 1976.
Boszormenyi-Nagy, I., & Spark, G. *Invisible loyalties.* Hagerstown, MD: Harper & Row, 1973.
Bowen, M. Family therapy and family group therapy. In D. Olson, (Ed.), *Treating relationships,* Lake Mills, IA: Graphic Publishing, 1976.
Brown, E. M. Divorce counseling. In D. Olson, (Ed.), *Treating relationships,* Lake Mills, IA: Graphic Publishing, 1976.
Carkhuff, R. *Helping and human relations.* New York: Holt, Rinehart & Winston, 1969.
Constantine, L. L. Jealousy: From theory to intervention. In D. Olson, (Ed.), *Treating relationships,* Lake Mills, IA: Graphic Publishing, 1976.
Cookerly, J. R. Evaluating different approaches to marriage counseling. In D. Olson, (Ed.), *Treating relationships,* Lake Mills, IA: Graphic Publishing, 1976.
Cromwell, R. E., Olson, D. H. L., & Fournier, D. G. Diagnosis and evaluation in marital and family counseling. In D. Olson, (Ed.), *Treating relationships,* Lake Mills, IA: Graphic Publishing, 1976.

Ferber, A., Mendelsohn, M., & Napier, A. (Eds.) *The book of family therapy.* New York: Science House, 1973.

Figley, C. F., Sprenkle, D. H., & Denton, G. W. Training marriage and family counselors in an industrial setting. *Journal of Marriage and Family Counseling,* 1976, *2,* 167-175.

Fisher, E. A guide to divorce counseling. *The Family Coordinator,* 1973, *22,* 55-61.

Foley, V. *An introduction to family therapy.* New York: Grune & Stratton, 1974.

Framo, V. Personal reflections of a family therapist. *Journal of Marriage and Family Counseling,* 1975, *1,* 15-28.

Gallant, D. M. Group psychotherapy with married couples: A successful technique in New Orleans alcohol clinic patients. *Journal of the Louisiana Medical Society,* 1970, *122,* 41-44.

Goodman, E. S. Marriage counseling as science: Some research considerations. *The Family Coordinator,* 1973, *22,* 111-116.

Gottschalk, L. A., Brown, S. B., Bruney, E. H., Schumate, L. W., & Uliana, R. L. Parents' group in a child-center clinic. In D. Olson, (Ed.), *Treating relationships,* Lake Mills, IA: Graphic Publishing, 1976.

Gurman, A. The effects and effectiveness of marital therapy: A review of outcome research. *Family Process,* 1973, *13,* 145-170.

Gurman, A. Evaluating outcome in couples therapy. Presentation at the Annual Meeting of the American Association of Marriage and Family Counselors, Toronto, 1975a.

Gurman, A. S. Some therapeutic implications of marital therapy research. In A. Gurman, and D. Rice, (Eds.), *Couples in conflict,* New York: Jason Aronson, 1975b.

Guerney, L. F. Filial therapy program. In D. Olson, (Ed.), *Treating relationships,* Lake Mills, IA: Graphic Publishing, 1976.

Haley, J. *Uncommon therapy: The psychiatric techniques of Milton H. Erickson, M.D.* New York: Grune & Stratton, 1969.

Haley, J. Why a mental health clinic should avoid family therapy. *Journal of Marriage and Family Counseling,* 1975, *1,* 3-13.

Harrell, J., & Guerney, B. G. Training married couples in conflict negotiation skills. In D. Olson, (Ed.), *Treating relationships,* Lake Mills, IA: Graphic Publishing, 1976.

Hartman, W., & Fithian, M. *Treatment of sexual dysfunction.* Long Beach, CA: Center for Marital & Sexual Studies, 1972.

Hill, R. Strategies for designing family research. Mimeographed, The Family Study Center, The University of Minnesota, 1973.

Jackson, D., (Ed.). *Communication, family, and marriage.* Palo Alto: Science & Behavior Books, 1968.

Kantor, D., & Lehr, W. *Inside the family.* San Francisco: Jossey Bass, 1975.

Knapp, J. J. Some non-monogamous marriage styles and related attitudes and practices of marriage counselors. *The Family Coordinator,* 1975, *24,* 505-514.

Laqueur, H. P. Multiple family therapy. In A. Ferber, M. Mendelsohn, and A. Napier, (Eds.), *The book of family therapy,* New York: Science House, 1973.

Lehman-Olson, D. Assertiveness training: Theoretical and clinical implications. In D. Olson, (Ed.), *Treating relationships,* Lake Mills, IA: Graphic Publishing, 1976.

Leichter, E. Treatment of married couples groups. *The Family Coordinator,* 1973, *22,* 31-42.

Mace, D., & Mace, V. Marriage enrichment: A preventive group approach for couples. In D. Olson, (Ed.), *Treating relationships,* Lake Mills, IA: Graphic Publishing, 1976.

Maddock, J. W. Sexual health: An enrichment and treatment program. In D. Olson, (Ed.), *Treating relationships,* Lake Mills, IA: Graphic Publishing, 1976.

Manus, G. I. Marriage counseling: A technique in search of theory. *Journal of Marriage and the Family,* 1966, *28,* 449-453.

Masters, W. H., & Johnson, W. E. *Human sexual inadequacy.* Boston: Little, Brown & Company, 1970.

Messersmith, C. E. Sex therapy and the marital system. In D. Olson, (Ed.), *Treating relationships,* Lake Mills, IA: Graphic Publishing, 1976.

Miller, S., Nunnally, E. W., & Wackman, D. Minnesota Couples Communication Program (MCCP): Premarital and marital groups. In D. Olson, (Ed.), *Treating relationships,* Lake Mills, IA: Graphic Publishing, 1976.

Minuchin, S., Montalvo, B., Guerney, B. G., Rosman, B. L., & Schumer, F. *Families of the slums.* New York: Basic Books, 1967a.

Minuchin, S., & Montalvo, B. Techniques for working with disorganized low socioeconomic families. *American Journal of Ortho-psychiatry,* 1967b, *37,* 880-887.

Minuchin, S. *Families and family therapy.* Cambridge, MA: Harvard University Press, 1974.

Nichols, W. C. The field of marriage counseling: A brief overview. *The Family Coordinator,* 1973, *22,* 3-14.

Olson, D. H. L. Insider and outsider views of relationships: Research strategies. Paper presented at Symposium on Close Relationships, University of Massachusetts, 1974.

Olson, D. H. L., (Ed.). *Treating relationships,* Lake Mills, IA: Graphic Publishing, 1976a.

Olson, D. H. L. Bridging research, theory and practice: The triple threat of science. In D. Olson, (Ed.), *Treating relationships,* Lake Mills, IA: Graphic Publishing, 1976b.

Olson, D. H. L. Trends and overview: Treating relationships. In D. Olson, (Ed.), *Treating relationships,* Lake Mills, IA: Graphic Publishing, 1976c.

Ostby, C. H. Conjoint group therapy with prisoners and their families. *Family Process,* 1968, *7,* 184-201.

Parsons, P. V., & Alexander, J. F. Short term family intervention: A therapy outcome study. *Journal of Consulting and Clinical Psychology,* 1973, *41,* 195-201.

Patterson, G. R., & Reid, J. B. Reciprocity and coercion: Two facets of social systems. In C. Neuringer and J. Michael, (Eds.), *Behavior modification in clinical psychology*, New York: Appleton-Century-Crofts, 1970.

Patterson, G. R. Parents and teachers as change agents: A social learning approach. In D. Olson, (Ed.), *Treating relationships*, Lake Mills, IA: Graphic Publishing, 1976.

Patterson, G. R., Hops, H., & Weiss, R. L. Interpersonal skills training for couples in early stages of conflict. *Journal of Marriage and the Family*, 1975, *37*, 295-303.

Paul, G. L. Strategy of outcome research in psychotherapy. *Journal of Consulting Psychology*, 1967, *31*, 100-118.

Phillips, C. E. Some useful tests for marriage counseling. *The Family Coordinator*, 1973, *22*, 43-54.

Pittman, F. S., Langsley, D. G., Flomenhaft, K., DeYoung, C. D., Machotaka, P., & Kaplan, D. M. Therapy techniques of the family treatment unit. In J. Haley, (Ed.), *Changing Families: A Family Therapy Reader*, New York: Grune & Stratton, 1971.

Rappaport, A. F., & Harrell, J. A behavioral exchange model for marriage counseling. *The Family Coordinator*, 1972, *21*, 203-212.

Rappaport, A. F. Conjugal relationship enhancement program. In D. Olson, (Ed.), *Treating relationships*, Lake Mills, IO: Graphic Publishing, 1976.

Rogers, C. R. *Client centered therapy*. Boston: Houghton-Mifflin, 1951.

Rutledge, A. L. *Pre-marital counseling*. Cambridge: Schenkman Publishing Co., 1966.

Satir, V. *Peoplemaking*. Palo Alto: Science & Behavior Books, 1972.

Skidmore, R. A., Balsam, D., & Jones, O. F. Social work practice in industry. *Social Work*, 1974, *19*, 280-286.

Smith, R. L., & Alexander, A. M. *Counseling couples in groups*. Springfield, IL: Charles C. Thomas, 1974.

Speck, R., & Attneave, C. *Family networks*. New York: Pantheon, 1973.

Sprenkle, D. H. In my opinion: The need for integration of theory, research, and practice in the family field. *The Family Coordinator*, 1976, *25*, 261-263.

Stuart, R. B. Operant interpersonal treatment for marital discord. *Journal of Consulting and Clinical Psychology*, 1969, *33*, 675-682.

Stuart, R. B. An operant interpersonal program for couples. In D. Olson, (Ed.), *Treating relationships*, Lake Mills, IA: Graphic Publishing, 1976.

Taylor, W. C., Cohen, A., Black, D., & Sprenkle, D. Parent and family involvement workshops. Presentation at the Indiana Federation Council for Exceptional Children, February, 1976.

Vincent, C. E. *Sexual and marital health: The physician as consultant*. New York: McGraw-Hill, 1973.

Vincent, C. E. Isms, schisms, and the freedom for differences. *Journal of Marriage and Family Counseling*, 1975, *1*, 99-110.

Vincent, J. P., Weiss, R. L., & Birchler, G. R. A behavioral analysis of problem solving in distressed and non-distressed married and stranger dyads. *Behavior Therapy*, 1975, *6*, 475-487.

Watzlawick, P., Beavin, J., & Jackson, D. *Pragmatics of human communication*. New York: W. W. Norton, 1967.

Weakland, J. H., Fisch, R., Watzlawick, P., & Bodin, A. Brief therapy: Focused problem resolution. *Family Process*, 1974, *13*, 141-168.

Weiss, R. L., Hops, J., & Patterson, G. A framework for conceptualizing marital conflict, a technology for altering it, some data for evaluating it. Paper presented at the Fourth International Conference on Behavior Modification. Banff, Alberta, Canada, 1972.

Wells, R. A., Dilkes, T. C., & Trivelli, N. The results of family therapy: A critical review of the literature. *Family Process*, 1972, *110*, 189-207.

Whitaker, C. A. A family therapist looks at marital therapy. In A. S. Gurman, & D. Rice, (Eds.), *Couples in conflict*, New York: Jason Aronson, 1975.

Williams, A. R. Setting up a rural private practice. *Journal of Marriage and Family Counseling*, 1975, *1*, 277-280.

emerging and declining family roles

f. ivan nye

Sociologists studying the family have become accustomed to thinking of the family as an institution experiencing a continued and perhaps rapid reduction in family functions. These ideas are especially traceable to Ogburn (1938) and Zimmerman (1947). Ogburn identified seven functions as follows: economic production, status giving, education of young, religious training, recreation, protection, and affection. Of these, he said all but one, affection, are declining. Ogburn's rationale for asserting that six of the seven functions were declining was that other institutions are increasingly providing part of these services to individuals and to the society. Thus, recreation is declining because of the development of commercial recreation outside of the family.

The fallacy in this line of logic is that the total amount of recreational activity may be increasing faster than its rate of development outside of the family or, more directly, the amount of family recreation may be increasing because much recreational activity outside the home still involves family members with each other and therefore belongs within the family institution.

Parsons made one notable contribution to present issues in pointing out that all institutions are in the process of change and that change does not necessarily mean decline. Old functions may become the *raison d'être* for new social organization and existent institutions develop new specializations within and emphasis on functions. He saw continuous changes in functions and behavior as characteristic of institutions (Parsons, 1955: Chapter 1). Blood also has commented on the emergence of new patterns of family behavior. He suggests that three new roles have emerged in the family, which he called mental hygiene, companionship, and giving affection (Blood, 1964:49).

The idea then that institutions may develop new functions which become the substantive content of roles of those who occupy the positions in an institution is not entirely new but no one has done much with the perspective at least insofar as the family is concerned. It is the purpose of this paper to outline a procedure by which we can test for the presence of a new role in an institution or the absence of one which has traditionally been assigned to an institution.

NEW ROLES IN THE FAMILY

We hypothesize that three new roles are now present in the American family which have not typically been recognized and incorporated into institutional descriptions of the American family. These are recreational, therapeutic, and sexual. We think that the new recreational and therapeutic roles form segments of both the positions of mother and father. The sexual role has long been perceived as part of the position of wife but no consensus has existed that a corresponding set of duties and responsibilities existed for the husband.

Reprinted, by permission, from *Journal of Marriage and the Family*, 1974, *36*, 238-45, slightly abridged. Copyright ©1974 by the National Council on Family Relations.

We should observe here that we are referring to role in its *normative* aspect, what persons in a position should or should not do rather than the mere presence of some relevant behavior. In this respect we draw from the work of Gross, Merton and Bates in that each position involves more than one role (Gross, Mason and McEachern, 1958; Merton, 1957; and Bates, 1956). Each of them affirm that the duties and obligations attached to a position must be subdivided into segments. Bates specifies that the segments (roles) are composed of social norms. We would modify this slightly to state that the role is normatively defined in terms of a more or less internally-consistent set of duties and responsibilities. Our explication of role is close to but not identical with that of Bates (1956). It is stated in more detail in a recent volume (Nye and Berardo, 1973: chapters 1 and 10).

In some segments of the positions of father, mother, and spouse, the roles are clearly defined and generally accepted by sociologists. These include: housekeeper, child care, child socialization, provider (for husband), and a sexual role for the wife. In most societies, but possibly not in current American society, one would add a kinship role. Above, we have hypothesized that three additional ones are in fact becoming established in contemporary American society.

A PROCEDURE FOR ROLE TESTING

Various authors list different sets of roles for occupants of a given position without necessarily providing any empirical referent for the role labels. To the extent that they refer to self-evident roles concerning which consensus exists, there is no need for empirical documentation. However, for new roles not generally recognized by the society it is not sufficient to contend that a norm exists and that presumably a pattern of behavior corresponds to that norm. Therefore, we have developed a rationale and a procedure for testing for roles. The first step is to ask a sample of persons (preferably a random sample) whether persons occupying a given position have a duty to enact the role. For example, with respect to the recreational role we asked: In your opinion whose duty is it to organize and start family recreation?

    Husband entirely
    Husband more than the wife
    Husband and wife exactly the same
    Optional—it doesn't matter who does it provided it is done
    Wife more than husband
    Wife entirely
    It is no one's duty

If it is not a duty, only incidental or optional behavior, then it is not prescribed normatively and the test is decided negatively. No role exists. However, if a majority respond that it is the duty of the occupants of one or more position, then the question arises whether there are sanctions to enforce role enactment. It is our feeling that norms without sanctions are essentially meaningless because there are no constraints to follow the prescriptions or proscriptions of the norms. Therefore, we suggest that not only the existence of a norm but also evidence of the existence of sanctions to enforce the norms is necessary in determining the presence of a role. We asked: What would you think about a mother (father) who refused to help organize and start recreation with her (his) family:

    Strongly disapprove
    Mildly disapprove
    Makes no difference one way or the other
    Mildly approve
    Strongly approve

An affirmative reply that the occupants of one or more positions has a duty to enact the role *and* a statement of disapproval, especially strong disapproval for those who refused to do so, if given by a majority of the sample, is taken as evidence of the existence of the role in the population from which the sample is drawn.

In the following section we shall try to show that some sociologists have perceived norms or behavior suggestive that these roles are implicit in American society. Following that we will offer data concerning the proportion of individuals who affirm the normative content of the roles and report their own enactment of the roles.

PREVIOUS EVIDENCE OF THE ROLE: THE THERAPEUTIC ROLE

By therapeutic role we are thinking of assistance that one provides to another in the solution of any problem which may be bothering that person. The nature of the problem may be concrete, involving an occupational decision, or emotional, involving feelings or insecurity or rejection. It may originate in the family, even between the spouses, or be external to the family.

Several sociologists have noted family behavior which might be considered problem solving. These include Parsons and Zeldich's expressive role (Parsons and Bales, 1955), Levinger's Socio-Emotional Role (1964), and Blood and Wolfe's Mental Hygiene role (1960). There is also substantive content from Whyte (1952) dealing with wives of executives. Komarovsky (1962) mentions the idea of a therapeutic role and explores the related phenomenon of communication between spouses. While none of the above develop the concept of a therapeutic role, all discuss needs served by it or behavior somewhat relevant to it. Their writings provide considerable support for the belief that pressing needs are felt in the American family for a confidant and for other assistance in grappling with a range of problems and that spouses are enacting the therapeutic role. On the basis of this literature plus our personal observations, we hypothesized that a therapeutic role does exist in American society.

A RECREATIONAL ROLE

Ogburn recognized recreation as a family activity (Ogburn, 1938) although he did not treat it as a role. Bates includes it in his list of roles for the position of mother (Bates, 1956). Blood perhaps had recreation partly in mind when he suggested a companionship role (Blood, 1964). Foote (1954) emphasized recreation in suggesting that much of family interaction is now play. Blood and Wolfe (1960) reported recreation as a source of considerable husband-wife conflict. Nye (1963) found that fully employed mothers did not decrease their family recreation, even though there was much pressure on their time. Thus, recreation has frequently been discussed as an important form of family activity rather than a peripheral one and, at least in Bates' writing, it has been seen as a role. However, it has not generally entered the literature of the family as an institution possessing normative content nor have we had evidence that the public in general has viewed it as a set of duties and responsibilities. Therefore, we have treated it also as a hypothesized role.

We are thinking of recreation as an activity which an individual enters into primarily for the pleasure he expects to receive from that activity. The recreational role is viewed as a set of responsibilities incumbent on occupants of a position to facilitate the recreational resources and activities available to others. In the present project, the existence of the role in the positions of spouse and parent is investigated. This does not assume that children have no recreational responsibilities. However, that issue is left as residual to the present exploration of the role.

INTERCOURSE ROLE FOR MEN

We have assumed that the sexual role of women to meet the needs of their husbands is a long-established family role. The view that women have sexual needs or can experience sexual pleasure comparable with men is of more recent origin. As this perspective on women's sexuality becomes pervasive, rights and duties regarding marital sexuality may become equally shared by men and women. There would be no less reason to have a male than a female sexual intercourse role. Bates

(1956) assumed such a role by listing "sexual partner" in the position of husband-father. Hacker (1957) discussed problems of men in attempting to meet the sexual needs of their wives. Rainwater (1965) provided some data on the proportion of husbands who are concerned that their wives enjoy intercourse. The college texts on marriage, marriage manuals and clinical accounts of marriage all attest to the efforts (with varying degrees of success) of men to provide sexual satisfaction to their spouses. Therefore, although the literature includes minimal mention of intercourse as a male role, we hypothesized that it currently exists in the American family as a distinct role for the husband as well as the wife.

THE SAMPLE

The respondents were drawn as a random sample of parents of children in grade three of Yakima County, Washington, in 1970. Yakima County includes one city of about 50,000 population, several small towns, and a sizable rural population. Its income level was slightly lower than that of the state of Washington but about average for the United States. The 210 couples from whom data were obtained appear to average slightly higher in education and income level than the county; however, since these are married men between the ages of 28 and 50, they represent a slightly better educated and affluent group than the census categories for adult men in general. We do not yet have a comparable census listing for married males of this age group. It probably will show a closer fit between our sample and the census figures than do our present data. Data were gathered through mailed questionnaires from both husband and wife in each household. A return rate of about 50 per cent was obtained.[1]

TESTING FOR THE EXISTENCE OF ROLES

The Therapeutic Role

We asked each spouse whether: (1) he (she) felt that wives (husbands) have a duty to try to help their spouses to solve their problems, and (2) whether he (she) would disapprove of a person of his (her) own sex who would not assist the spouse with a problem. We also asked each respondent how his (her) spouse usually reacted when he (she) wanted help from the spouse with a problem. . . .

About 70 per cent of the husbands and 60 per cent of the wives responded that the spouse (of one's own sex) has a duty to try to help solve the problem. In addition, almost 30 per cent of each sex believed it is preferable that one enact this role even though these respondents do not consider it strictly a duty. A few husbands and a few more wives see such problem solving as entirely optional. Sanctions, in general, follow the feeling that a duty is involved with more than three-fifths of both sexes expressing strong disapproval for refusal to enact the role and most of the balance would disapprove failure to enact but without indicating that the disapproval is strong.

Since our role model is a normative one, it does not require that actual role behavior correspond to the norms and sanctions, yet both imply that behavior should correspond to the norms and sanctions. We found that role enactment does correspond approximately to the norms and sanctions. Eighty per cent of the husbands indicated that their wives responded "actively" to their problems with sympathy, affection and reassurance, and/or active attacks on the problem. Another 10 per cent of the wives listened without other response while 10 per cent made some negative response. Wives reported that 63 per cent of their husbands responded positively, 20 per cent listened only, and 17 per cent responded negatively.

We find that the majority of the respondents define the role normatively, indicate sanctions to support it, and actually enact it positively. These data support the hypothesis of a therapeutic role.

The Recreational Role

Respondents were asked: (1) whose duty (if anyone's) is it to organize family recreation, (2) whether the respondent would disapprove of a husband or a wife who failed to enact the role, and finally, (3) who usually did organize family recreation.

. . . [We] see a rather different normative definition of a role—one that emphasizes *parental* duty without necessarily specifying the duty as specifically that of one or the other of the parents. This is possible because either or both can enact the role. (This is not true of the sexual and therapeutic roles.) More than 90 per cent of both men and women affirm parental duty to organize and in other ways facilitate family recreation, but few attribute this "new" role especially to one or the other spouse or parent. A few wives (7 per cent) and more husbands (17 per cent), however, see the role as essentially the duty of the husband.

A majority of both sexes would disapprove of a person who refused to enact the role. However, a large proportion would not specify strong disapproval. The role enactment data show that it is a role which one or the other spouse does, in fact, enact. Only four per cent of the wives and no husbands report that neither takes leadership in organizing recreation for family members. The behavior pattern is largely consistent with the normative perceptions since husbands and wives share role enactment about equally. A few more men report themselves as more often enacting the role, but wives do not agree and report an even distribution between spouses.

The Sexual Role

Strong support was found for the hypothesis that a set of sexual responsibilities exist for the husband as well as the wife. About 90 per cent of both sexes see it as a duty to be available to meet the sexual needs of the other. However, the dissents are interesting, too, in that one wife in nine does not perceive any obligation to participate in sexual intercourse. There is strong disapproval of a spouse who "rarely or never consents" to have sexual intercourse with the spouse. . . . Again, a small but appreciable minority would not provide any sanctions for nonperformance. More men than women would invoke sanctions for nonperformance.

The behavior of husbands corresponds closely to the norms, with only nine per cent of wives indicating that the husband is usually unresponsive to their sexual interests. Wives' behavior conforms less closely, with 30 per cent of the husbands reporting their wives usually do not participate if their (the wife's) initial reaction is negative.

The data support the hypothesis for a sexual role for the husband. Both men and women give overwhelming support to the idea that spouses have sexual responsibilities. A majority of both also verbalize sanctions to enforce these duties. Men are more nearly unanimous in their support of sanctions for the enforcement of their role than are wives in supporting wifely sexual duties. Finally, few men but a sizable minority of women fail to respond to the sexual needs of their spouses.

COMPARISON WITH "ESTABLISHED" ROLES

The data shown have substantiated the hypothesis that therapeutic, recreational, and (male) sexual roles exist. But are these roles as completely accepted and enforced as are such traditional family roles as child care, child socialization, and provider? Present data suggest not. Our 210 couples were unanimous in assigning the child socialization obligation to one or both parents and provide not only disapproval for nonperformance but more than half of the respondents indicated they would not choose as close friends parents who neglect the task. The same held true for the child-care role except that two parents (one-half of one per cent) indicated that others had the obligation to take care of the children (a grandmother or housekeeper, perhaps). The provider role is likewise held with unanimity to be paternal responsibility. In addition to disapproval (93 per cent of men and 94 per cent of women would strongly disapprove of a man who preferred to see his family supported by public assistance), about 75 per cent would not be willing to have him as a close friend. Present data, then, disclose a considerable difference between the unanimity and strength of sanctions which apply to the traditional, central familial roles and what we suggest are emerging familial roles.

ARE KINSHIP AND HOUSEKEEPER ROLES DISAPPEARING?

Traditionally, housekeeping and obligations to kin have been almost as central to the functioning of the family as have the child care, socialization, and provider roles. Parsons implied the decline of the kinship role by suggesting that the American nuclear family is relatively isolated from kin and that reciprocal responsibilities are relatively limited (Parsons and Bales, 1955). While many have shown that some interaction with kin continues, and we have hypothesized a kinship role still exists, it appears to be on the decline. The same might be suggested of the housekeeper role. For decades portions of cooking, canning, clothing making and the like have moved to special manufacturing and service agencies outside the family. Therefore, we think that both the obligations to kin and the obligation of the wife to prepare meals and clean and maintain the home are in the process of disappearing. This does not mean that such behavior is likely to disappear, but that it is becoming an option instead of an obligation normatively defined and enforced by sanctions.

A majority of the respondents do see a duty to keep in touch with relatives and to assist in financial emergencies, yet over 30 per cent disagree that such duty (financial) exists and less than 40 per cent of either sex express strong disapproval of others who fail to discharge such obligations.

Almost all the respondents still see housekeeping as the duty of the wife or wife and husband jointly, although three per cent of both sexes feel it should be performed by others. We neglected to ask about attitudes toward eating meals out, having help with the housecleaning and the like which would have given a better idea of their thoughts about sharing the role with outside agencies. However, only a minority of both sexes would discriminate against a woman who was not strongly committed to the housekeeper role. About half the wives indicated that they would be glad to share their housekeeper role with a competent housekeeper.

SUMMARY AND IMPLICATIONS

Present data show the presence of three familial roles which have not usually been described by sociologists of the family as part of the normative structure of the family. These are therapeutic, recreational, and (male) sexual. A majority of the respondents affirmed that spouses do have these duties and that sanctions for nonperformance exist. Also, a substantial majority of respondents report that they do enact the role.

The data, however, show that less unanimity exists in the normative definition of these roles than is true for the child care, child socialization, and provider roles. Full consensus exists that one or both parents have duties to enact these roles, disapproval for failure to enact them is near-unanimous, and a majority of respondents would ostracize those who fail to enact them.

Two other traditional roles, kinship and housekeeper, are still normatively defined by a majority of respondents but sanctions for enforcement are relatively weak.

From the above, we conclude, tentatively, that three new roles, therapeutic, recreational, and (male) sexual, are becoming more firmly imbedded in the normative structure of the American family. Three traditional roles: child care, socialization, and provider, are firmly imbedded and strongly sanctioned; while two other traditional roles, kinship and housekeeper, are in the process of disappearing from the normative structure and may well become optional family activities.

NEEDED ADDITIONAL RESEARCH

Although the data reported here support the presence of three family roles not usually included in descriptions of the family as an institution, this does not conclusively demonstrate that they are *in the process* of emergence in the institutional structure. These roles could have long been part of the normative structure and that fact could have been overlooked by family sociologists. Too, the presence of these norms in one county of one state in the United States does not conclusively demonstrate their presence in the society as a whole. A larger sample of a broader segment of American society is needed to establish an adequate benchmark of family role-structure for the society. Then at a future date, in perhaps five or ten years, another sample should be drawn from that population, to determine whether the role is accepted by a larger or smaller proportion of the population and to determine whether supporting sanctions are stronger or weaker and whether role behavior more or less fully corresponds to the normative content of the roles. Such additional research would establish conclusively the role trends which we believe are provisionally established by research reported.

FOOTNOTE

[1] We have usually been able to obtain a considerably higher return than this. Undoubtedly one factor was the request that both husband and wife complete the instrument. Another was that it was long (16 pages for the husband, 20 for the wife) and some sections were rather complex.

REFERENCES

Bates, Frederick L. 1956. "Position, role and status: a reformation." Social Forces 34 (May).

Blood, Robert O. 1964. "Impact of urbanization on American family structure and functioning." Sociology and Social Research 49 (Jan.-Feb.):5-16.

Blood, Robert O. and Donald M. Wolfe. 1960. Husbands and Wives. Glencoe, Ill.: The Free Press.

Foote, Nelson M. 1954. "Family living as play." Paper read before the National Council on Family Relations, Oakland, California.

Gross, Neal, Ward Mason, and Alexander McEachern. 1958. Explorations in Role Analysis. New York: John Wiley.

Hacker, Helen. 1957. "The new burdens of masculinity." Marriage and Family Living 19 (August):227-234.

Merton, Robert F. 1957. Social Theory and Social Structure. Glencoe, Illinois: The Free Press.

Nye, F. Ivan and Felix M. Berardo. 1973. The Family: Its Structure and Interaction. New York: Macmillan.

Nye, F. Ivan and Lois Wladis Hoffman. 1963. The Employed Mother in America. Chicago: Rand McNally.

Ogburn, William F. 1938. "The changing family." The Family 19 (July):139-143.

Parsons, Talcott and Robert F. Bales. 1955. Family, Socialization and Interaction Process. Glencoe, Ill.: The Free Press.

Rainwater, Lee. 1965. Family Design, Marital Sexuality, Family Size, and Contraception. Chicago: Aldine.

Zimmerman, Carle C. 1947. Family and Civilization. Harper and Row.

42   a demographer looks at american families

paul c. glick

. . .

RECENT CHANGES IN
MARRIAGE AND FERTILITY

The population picture in the late 1930's was gloomy. Many marriages had been delayed, so that the average age at marriage had risen, and a near-record nine per cent of the women 50 years old had never married. Birth rates had lingered at a low level, even without today's wide variety of means for birth control and without today's high degree of acceptance of a small number of children as a desirable family goal. Lifetime childlessness was edging up toward 20 per cent, and many of the children whom some leading demographers thought were merely being postponed were never born; a speculative interpretation is that many of the women who delayed having those other children reached the point where they liked it better without them than they had thought they would.

Then came World War II, with its extensive dislocations of family life particularly among families with husbands—or would-be husbands—of draft age, extending up to around 40 years of age. Marriage and birth rates remained low, and millions of women—married as well as single—were welcomed into the labor force who would never have gone to work outside the home if the male civilian work force had not shrunk so much.

After World War II, the marriage and divorce rates shot up briefly, fell again sharply, and then subsided gradually (Glick, 1974: Chapter III). By the mid-1950's, a relatively familistic period had arrived. Couples were entering marriage at the youngest ages on record, and all but four per cent of those at the height of the childbearing period eventually married. Moreover, the baby boom that had started with the return of World War II service men reached a plateau in the mid-1950's and did not diminish significantly until after 1960. By that time, the rate of entry into first marriage had already been falling and the divorce rate had resumed its historical upward trend.

By the late 1960's and early 1970's, the familistic style of life seemed to be on the wane again. The marriage rate among single persons under 45 years old was as low as it had been at the end of the Depression. Last year, the average age at marriage was close to a year higher than it had been in the mid-1950's, and the proportion of women who remained single until they were 20 to 24 years old had increased by one-third since 1960 (U.S. Bureau of the Census, 1974). The divorce rate had soared to the high level it had reached soon after the end of World War II, and an estimated one out of every three marriages of women 30 years old had been, or would eventually be, dissolved by divorce (Glick and Norton, 1973; Glick, 1973). The birth rate in 1973 was the lowest in the country's history, 15 per 1,000 population. The total fertility rate in 1973, which shows how many children women would have if they continued having children throughout their childbearing years at the same rate as in

Reprinted, by permission, from *Journal of Marriage and the Family*, 1975, *37*, 15-26. Copyright © 1975 by the National Council on Family Relations.

1973, stood at a new low level of 1.9 children per woman. This is just one-half as many as in 1957, when the total fertility rate was 3.8 children per woman.

All of this has happened in the last 35 years, with high or low inflection points (depending on the variable) occurring near the middle of this period. It was an exciting period for a demographer to live through, because it was marked by sharp changes which called for careful measurement and perceptive interpretation. It was a period full of headaches for school administrators who had to adjust plant capacity to student load, as well as for manufacturers and distributors of products for babies or teenagers or any other functional age group because of the widely fluctuating demands by age. And it was a period when ideas were changing about the proper age for marriage, about desired family size, and about how serious it is to disrupt a marriage that does not seem to be viable. As ideas changed in one of these fundamental aspects of family life, other ideas came into question. So, we are now going through a period of change in demographic patterns that undoubtedly reflects basic, underlying attitudes toward conformity with traditional behavior, especially as such conformity comes in conflict with the development of the full potentiality of each member of the family.

SOME IMPLICATIONS OF RECENT CHANGES

During the 12-month period ending in August, 1974, the estimated number of marriages in the United States was about 2,233,000, and the number of divorces was 948,000. For the first time since soon after World War II the marriage total for a 12-month period was significantly smaller (by 68,000) than it had been in the preceding year. However, the divorce total for the 12 months ending in August, 1974, had continued to rise (by 56,000) above the level for the preceding 12 months (U.S. Center for Health Statistics, 1974a).

These current figures are the latest available in a growing series which document a slow down of marriage and a speedup of divorce. Since 1965, the annual number of first marriages has not been keeping pace with the rapid growth in the number of persons in the prime years for first marriage—those who were born soon after World War II. In fact, the number of marriages in recent years would have been even smaller if it had not been for the sharp upturn in remarriages associated with the increase in the number of divorces in this period. According to the latest information available, about four out of every five of those who obtain a divorce will eventually remarry (U.S. Bureau of the Census, 1972a).

From the peak year for births, 1957, to the present the declining birth rate has resulted in part from a decrease in the proportion of children born to women above 30 years of age and has been associated with a decrease in the median age at which women bear their children, from 25 years to 24 years. During this period there has been little change in the interval between marriage and the birth of the first child. At the same time, the proportion of first births that have occurred outside marriage has just about doubled, from 5 per cent in the late 1950's to 11 per cent in 1971.

When married women today are asked how many children they expect to have in their lifetime, those under 25 years old say they believe they will have just about enough for zero population growth (aside from immigration). And answers to this question have been generally consistent over the last few years, with more changes in replies by identical women being in the direction of fewer rather than more children. Although fertility changes during the last 35 years provide ample evidence of the capacity of American couples to change their minds about how many children to have, the general consensus among most demographers is that a repeat of the post-World War II baby boom is most unlikely in the foreseeable future (U.S. Bureau of the Census, 1974a).

RECENT DELAY IN MARRIAGE AMONG THE YOUNG

The average woman at first marriage today is 21 years old. During the approximately 15 years of the post-World War II baby boom, the average woman had been one year younger at marriage, 20 years.

Another way of showing the extent of the recent delay in marriage is to point out that a new low level of 28 per cent single was registered for women 20 to 24 years of age in 1960; but the corresponding figure for women in their early twenties in 1974 had jumped up by more than one-third to a level of 40 per cent single (U.S. Bureau of the Census, 1974b). There is no doubt about it. Young women are now postponing marriage longer than their mothers did in the late 1940's and early 1950's. (Corresponding data for men are not presented because their coverage in censuses and surveys has fluctuated as the size and location of men in the Armed Forces has varied widely since 1940.)

A delay in marriage—identified by an increase in the per cent single—has been common to young women (under 25 years old) of all education levels, but census figures show that the increase in singleness was greatest during the 1960's among young women who had not attended college. This finding is probably at least tangentially related to the sharp rise in unwed motherhood among white women during the 1960's; most unwed mothers have never attended college. Young women with a high school education but with no college training continue to be the ones with the smallest per cent single. (The situation among older women is different, as will be shown below.)

Why has this delay in marriage occurred among the young? At least a part of the answer lies in the fact that nearly three times as many women were enrolled in college in 1972 as in 1960 (3.5 million versus 1.2 million), and the college enrollment rate has more than doubled for women in their twenties during those 12 years. Another demographic factor was the "marriage squeeze"; during recent years this phenomenon has taken the form of an *excess of young women* of ages when marriage rates are highest, because women born in a given year during the baby boom after World War II reached their most marriageable age range two or three years before men born in the same year (Carter and Glick, 1970). Still other demographic factors include the sharper increase in the employment of women than men and the amazing decline in the birth rate, both of which signaled expanding roles open to women outside the home. Among the less tangible factors has been the revival of the women's movement. In fact, the excess of marriageable women in the last few years may have contributed as much to the development of that movement as the ideology of the movement has contributed to the increase in singleness.

A detailed analysis of recent marriage trends has suggested that it is too early to predict with confidence that the recent increase in singleness among the young will lead to an eventual decline in lifetime marriage. However, just as cohorts of young women who have postponed childbearing for an unusually long time seldom make up for the child deficit as they grow older, so also young people who are delaying marriage may never make up for the marriage deficit later on. They may try alternatives to marriage and like them.

EARLY MARRIAGE AND HIGH FERTILITY OF THOSE APPROACHING MIDDLE AGE

Women who are now 35 to 44 years old were born during the Depression years of the 1930's. They have been a most interesting group for demographers to study because of their many unique features: they were born when the birth rate was at the lowest level recorded up to that time (total fertility rate averaging about 2.3 children), with only the rates after 1970 being still lower; they set a record for early marriage (average about 20 years) and for high birth rates (total fertility rate peaking at 3.8 in 1957); and now they have in prospect one of the lowest proportions single on record (likely to fall below 4 per cent before they end their fifties) and one of the lowest proportions who will remain childless throughout life (10 per cent for women regardless of marital status and 6 per cent among those who ever marry). They have shared more fully than the preceding generation—and probably more than the following generation—in the process of marrying and replenishing the population.

These women, now 35 to 44 years of age, are featured here and in the discussion of divorce below because of their uniqueness in another respect. They are old enough to have experienced most of their lifetime marriages, childbirths, and divorces, and yet they are young enough to reflect recent changes in family life patterns. Because of the recent developments with regard to the delay in marriage and the fertility decline among those now in their twenties, it would have been tempting to have featured this younger age group. However, this option was not adopted because not enough time would have elapsed after school attendance for those with four or more years of college to have essentially established their lifetime levels of marriage and childbearing.

As noted above, the marriage history of women now 35 to 44 has culminated in a record low proportion single for women of that age range (now five per cent and likely to drop below four per cent by 1990). But the continuing decline in singleness for women of this age range was not uniformly distributed among the several educational groups. Although the per cent single was *rising* most rapidly among *young* college-educated women (those under 25), the per cent single was *declining* most rapidly among *older* college-educated women (those 35 to 44). Women college graduates 35 to 44 reduced their excess per cent single, as compared with all women in the age group, by a substantial one-fourth during the 1960's. Still, women college graduates with no graduate school training have continued to record a high proportion single, 10 per cent in 1960 and 8 per cent in 1970; and those with graduate school training recorded a *very* high level of 24 per cent single in 1960 but "only" 19 per cent single in 1970 (U.S. Bureau of the Census, 1967 and 1972b).

Similar socioeconomic differentials in the decline in singleness were found when the measurement was in terms of occupation and income. For example, the proportion single among women who were professional workers dropped by about one-third from the high level of 19 per cent in 1960 to 13 per cent in 1970. Moreover, women in the upper income bracket ($7,000 or more in 1960 and $10,000 or more in 1970—about the right difference in income level to adjust for the decreasing value of the dollar) had about a one-fourth decline in the proportion single between 1960 and 1970 (from the very high level of 27 per cent to the still quite high level of 21 per cent). Thus, in summary, the declines in singleness among the women in these upper socioeconomic groups consisted of tendencies for this aspect of their marital pattern to converge with—to become more like—that of women in the lower socioeconomic groups.

Why did this happen? A partial answer must be the relative *scarcity of women* of optimum age to marry during the mid-1950's, a period of affluence when nearly all men in the upper socioeconomic group were marrying. Thus, all but two or three per cent of the men in 1970 in the upper income bracket had married by early middle age; they had been at the height of their period for first marriage during the late 1940's and the 1950's. Another part of the answer must have been the greatly increasing opportunities for young women to work at attractive jobs outside the home even though they were married—a phenomenon that was far less common only a generation before 1960. It had obviously become far easier for a woman to combine a working career and marriage (Davis, 1972).

Why have not still more of the women in the upper socioeconomic groups become married? In 1970, fully 1 in every 5 women around 40 years of age with some graduate school education or with an income of $20,000 or more have not married, as compared with only 1 in every 20 women with no college education (U.S. Bureau of the Census, 1972b). Most of these women were submitted to the maximum pressure to marry during the period 10 to 20 years ago. Probably no one would argue with the interpretation that women with graduate school training have far more options for interesting roles to cultivate—including wife, mother, and/or career woman—than those with less education. But, despite the sharp increase in marriage among "fortyish" upper group women, could it be that a significant proportion of men who are also in the upper socioeconomic group still hesitate to marry a woman who expects to be a partner in an *egalitarian* marriage—or a woman who might be a serious competitor for the role of chief breadwinner of "head of the household?" It seems reasonable to expect a substantial further decline in the force of this factor as the impact of the women's movement is felt increasingly among both men and women. The expected direction of change would seem to be a growing acceptance of the situation in which the wife equals or outranks the husband in such matters—without as much of a disturbing effect on the couple's social relationships as it evidently continues to have today.

DIVERGENCE AND CONVERGENCE
OF DIVORCE BY SOCIAL LEVEL

In 1970, the proportion divorced (and not remarried) continued to be lower among men approaching middle age (35 to 44 years old) than among women of comparable age—3.6 per cent versus 5.5 per cent. This pattern results from the older average age of men at marriage, hence the shorter duration of marriage for the men, and also from the larger proportion of men than women who eventually remarry—about five-sixths versus three-fourths. The difference between men and women in the proportion currently divorced has increased substantially since 1960, when 2.6 per cent of the men and 3.8 per cent of the women were divorced (and not remarried). This divergence between the sexes may have developed because of several factors including the increasing extent to which divorced women tend to outlive divorced men.

Meanwhile, a "democratizing" development in relation to marriage patterns is reflected in the fact that the proportion divorced among men 35 to 44 years of age has tended to converge since 1960 among the educational, occupational, and income groups. Men in the upper status groups continue to have a below-average proportion divorced (but not remarried), however, the gap was smaller in 1970 than it was in 1960. More specifically, the proportion divorced increased during the 1960's by about three-eighths for all men in the age group but by a considerably larger proportion (about one-half to two-thirds) for men with 4 or more years of college, for professional men, and for men in the top income class for which data are available ($10,000 or more in 1960 and $15,000 or more in 1970).

Changes during the 1960's in the proportion divorced among women by social and economic groups were more complex than those for men. For all women 35 to 44, the proportion divorced went up, on the average, by nearly one-half during the 1960's, from 3.8 per cent to 5.5 per cent. But among women who were professional workers or in the uppermost income level—where the per cent divorced among women (unlike men) has been characteristically quite high—the per cent divorced rose by a smaller proportion (under one-third) than among other women. (The per cent divorced for professional women went up from 6.0 per cent in 1960 to 7.8 per cent in 1970; and the per cent divorced for women in the uppermost income group rose from 11.8 per cent to 15.1 per cent.) Thus, for these categories of upper group *women,* the per cent divorced was tending to converge with that for other women by increasing more *slowly* than the average, while for upper group *men* the per cent divorced was tending to converge with that for other men by increasing more *rapidly* than the average.

The pattern is especially complex when changes in the proportion divorced are analyzed for women college graduates 35 to 44 years old. Women who terminated their education with 4 years of college hold the record for the smallest per cent divorced (3.0 per cent in 1960 and 3.9 per cent in 1970). Moreover, they reinforced this position during the 1960's by being the educational group with the *smallest* proportional increase in the per cent divorced (three-tenths). By contrast, women 35 to 44 with one or more years of graduate school have had fewer years since marriage in which to obtain a divorce but still hold the record among educational groups for the largest per cent divorced (4.8 per cent in 1960 and 7.3 per cent in 1970). Moreover, they reinforced this position by having the *largest* proportional increase in the per cent divorced of all educational groups (over one-half). Thus, both women with 4 years of college and those with 5 or more years of college have tended to diverge from the general level of increase in the proportion divorced but in opposite directions.

WHY THE UPTURN IN DIVORCE?

While the number of couples experiencing divorce has been rising, many other changes have also been occurring. Some of these changes might have actually been expected to cause the divorce rate to *decline.* For example, divorce rates are generally lowest among men in the upper socioeconomic groups, and the proportion of men in the upper education, occupation, and income groups has been increasing; yet the proportion divorced has been rising most in these very same groups. One of the many plausible hypotheses for investigation in this context can be posed in the form of a question:

Was a larger proportion of men with "divorce proneness" being drawn into the ranks of upper socioeconomic groups in the two decades after World War II? This was a period when those ranks were being augmented by upwardly mobile persons who were rising from the lower socioeconomic groups; persons in the groups from which they were rising have probably always had the highest rates of marital dissolution.

This hypothesis could be examined by studying the relationship between the direction of intergenerational socioeconomic mobility and rates of marriage and divorce. Men who have been upwardly mobile by a substantial amount (defined as men whose achievement is quite perceptibly above that of their fathers) might be shown to have more initial advantage in the marriage market than their brothers with little or no such upward mobility. However, for many the advantage may not have lasted; these upwardly mobile men might have permitted "excessive achievement orientation" or complications resulting from their change of social level to interfere with the promotion of satisfaction in their marriages. Downwardly mobile persons may tend to have even more difficulty in their marital adjustment. This hypothetical relationship may be tested in the next year or so by the present author and Arthur J. Norton as a by-product of the study of "occupational change in a generation" that is being conducted by David L. Featherman and Robert M. Hauser, of the University of Wisconsin, on the basis of data from a Census Bureau survey in 1973.

Socioeconomic changes during the last decade or two that might have been expected to cause a *rise* in the divorce rate are numerous, but the contribution each has made to this rise cannot be readily demonstrated. Illustrations include the increasing proportion of young wives with small families who have succeeded in translating their higher level of education into jobs that make them financially independent of their husband; an increasing proportion of couples whose income has risen to a level at which they can afford the cost of obtaining a divorce to resolve a marriage that is not viable; the increased availability of free legal aid which may have permitted a large number of impoverished families to obtain a divorce; the war in Vietnam which complicated the transition of millions of young men into marriage or made their adjustment in marriage more difficult than it would have otherwise been.

Other changes that may have contributed in varying degrees to the increase in divorce during the last decade have less of an economic orientation. One cluster of such changes includes a greater social acceptance of divorce as a means for resolving marriage difficulties—in particular, the relaxation of attitudes toward divorce by a growing number of religious denominations; the relatively objective study of marriage and family relationships at the high school and college levels; the movement to increase the degree of equality of the sexes which is making some headway toward easing the social adjustment of persons who are not married; and the reform of divorce laws, in particular, the adoption of no-fault divorce.

NO-FAULT DIVORCE LAWS

An article entitled "Legal Status of Women," prepared at the U.S. Women's Bureau lists 23 States that had adopted "some form" of no-fault divorce by January, 1974—16 of them since 1971 (Rosenberg and Mendelsohn, 1974). The 23 states are Alabama, Arizona, California, Colorado, Connecticut, Florida, Georgia, Hawaii, Idaho, Indiana, Iowa, Kentucky, Maine, Michigan, Missouri, Montana, Nebraska, Nevada, New Hampshire, North Dakota, Oregon, Texas, and Washington. A 24th state, Minnesota, passed a no-fault divorce law in the 1974 legislative session. Moreover, the legislators in nearly all other states are in the process of considering how to incorporate this feature into their divorce laws.

Persons who have examined the divorce laws closely have cautioned, however, that the no-fault movement is not really as far along as the advocates of "true" no-fault divorce would like to see. This view was expressed to me in a letter from Lenore J. Weitzman (University of California at Davis) who, together with two colleagues, is conducting a Federally sponsored study of "The Impact of Divorce

Law Reform on the Process of Marital Dissolution: The California Case" (Weitzman, Kay, and Dixon, 1974). According to their calculations, five states have instituted true no-fault divorce by adopting the provisions of the Uniform Act; nine other states have adopted some other form of no-fault divorce. The states which have merely *added* no-fault divorce to their existing grounds for divorce should really not, according to Dr. Weitzman, be considered no-fault divorce states. Under a "true" no-fault divorce law, a couple may terminate its marriage without any expectation of punitive consequences resulting from the action; the main items to be settled are a reasonable division of joint property and arrangements for the maintenance of the children and the maintenance of one spouse on the basis of need. However, in states where no-fault is only one of several grounds for divorce, one spouse may threaten to consider the other "at fault" but settle for a no-fault divorce in the negotiation for a more favorable settlement. For this reason, the number of no-fault divorces in those states may not indicate the true number who obtained divorces without negotiations involving the adversary concept.

CHILDREN OF PARENTS WHO HAVE (OR HAVE NOT) BEEN DIVORCED

Women whose first marriage ended in divorce have been, on the average, about two years younger when they entered marriage than married women of the same age who have not been divorced (U.S. Bureau of the Census, 1973c). However, on the average, about three years elapse between divorce and remarriage. So, if the average divorcee gains a couple of years of married life through early marriage but loses three years of married life through divorce, what is the net effect on her family size? According to 1970 census data for women 35 to 39 years old, the answer varies according to her later marriage experience. First, divorced women 35 to 39 years old who had gone on to marry a man who had not been married before wound up with him and 3.1 children, on the average, or virtually the same number at the census date as that (3.2 children) for couples with both the husband and wife still in their first marriage. Second, those who were still divorced at the census date had borne a smaller number, namely, an average of 2.6 children. And third, among married couples at the census date where both the husband and the wife were divorced after their first marriage, the average number of children was intermediate, 2.9 children ever born (U.S. Bureau of the Census, 1973a).

Another way to show how many children are affected by divorce is to note that 15 per cent of all *children under 18 years of age* in 1970 were living with one or both parents who had been divorced after their first or most recent marriage. Some of these children were born after their divorced parent had remarried, but a larger number were living with a stepparent at the census date. Thus, about two-fifths of the children with a previously divorced parent were born after the remarriage and hence were living with their two natural parents; however, the other three-fifths were living with a stepparent. Besides these children of "ever divorced" parents, another 15 per cent were not living with both (once-married) natural parents. In other words, these figures imply that only about 70 per cent of the children under 18 years of age in 1970 were living with their two natural parents who had been married only once. Among black children the corresponding figure was very low, 45 per cent, but that for white children was also low, 73 per cent (U.S. Bureau of the Census, 1973b).

The proportion of *children of school age* living with both natural parents in their first marriage was even smaller than 70 per cent in 1970. Therefore, the remaining more than 30 per cent of school children were *not* living with a father and a mother who were in a continuous first marriage. This means that such children are no longer rare. Even though children of separated, divorced, or never-married parents still have many problems today, they at least have far less cause to feel unique or exceptionally deprived than similar children of yesterday. Moreover, because the birth rate has been declining for several years, the *average* number of children involved per divorce has declined since the mid-1960's (to 1.22 in 1970 and 1971); however, the *total* number of children involved in divorce was still rising in 1971, when it was 946,000 (U.S. National Center for Health Statistics, 1974b). In a country where many legal grounds for divorce have been established and used, a large number of children will inevitably be involved in separation and/or divorce. But there is no optimum proportion of children who should be thus involved, any more than there is a fixed optimum proportion of couples who should dissolve their marriage by divorce.

WHAT IS A REASONABLE AMOUNT OF LIFETIME MARRIAGE (OR DIVORCE)?

Saying that there is no fixed optimum proportion of marriages that really should not remain intact leaves much to be said about the current level of divorce and the prospective level over the next decade or two. For one thing it is now very high, in fact the highest in the world, and seems likely to remain that way. In 1972, the most recent date for which many international figures are available, the divorce rate was the highest in the U.S.A., with a rate of 3.72 per 1,000 population. Other countries with high 1972 levels of divorce were the U.S.S.R. with a rate of 2.64 and Hungary with a rate of 2.32. Cuba had a 1971 rate of 3.23 (United Nations, 1973). More recently, the U.S. divorce rate climbed on up to 4.4 per 1,000 population in 1973 and to 4.5 per 1,000 during the 12 months ending in August, 1974 (U.S. Center for Health Statistics, 1974a).

In the context of our high divorce rate, some questions worthy of exploration can be raised. How many of the divorces are desired by both parties? On the basis of experience in divorce counseling, Emily Brown, current chairman of the Family Action Section of the National Council on Family Relations, estimates that around 4 out of every 10 of the couples obtaining a divorce include one member who did not want it. But that leaves around 6 out of every 10 who did want it. Did the right couples obtain a divorce? Surely some who did so were ill-advised in this respect, whereas others with far more justification for a divorce were inhibited from obtaining one. And yet the situation may be so complex—when all of the pros and cons are considered—that even the wisest of family counselors must have difficulty in rendering objective judgment about the advisability of continuing or ending the marriages of a large proportion of those who come to them for counseling service.

A certain amount of divorce undoubtedly grows out of the fact that the supply of acceptable marriage partners is very often quite limited, and those who would be most ideal partners never meet, or if they do, they may do so at the wrong time or become unavailable to each other at the optimum time for marriage. In other words, marriage partners are typically joined through a process of chance, often involving compromise, and if the compromise element is substantial, there should be no great surprise if the marriage is eventually dissolved by permanent separation or divorce. In view of the haphazard manner in which the important step of marriage is generally undertaken, and in view of the many frailties of human adults, the surprise may be that the proportion of marriages that last—to a happy (or bitter!) end—is as large as it is.

Men at the top of the socioeconomic scale must have the most advantages in marital selection and in the means for achieving a satisfactory adjustment after marriage. Thus, a potential husband with a promising occupational future no doubt arrived at that enviable position usually—but, of course, not always—because of personal characteristics that should also make him an attractive candidate for marriage. This type of man has the widest choice of women for a potential wife—one with maximum appeal and few "hangups." And if the man's work history materializes into occupational success, his chances of keeping his marriage partner satisfied with their marriage arrangement should be accordingly enhanced—other things being equal. In fact, the statistics demonstrate that the most lasting marriages are contracted by men in the upper socioeconomic levels.

Viewed from the vantage point of the potential wife, the line of reasoning is quite similar in some key respects but has important differences. One similar feature is the great amount of competition they face in their search for men who are attractive candidates for marriage. A dissimilar feature is the somewhat different set of personal characteristics which describe an attractive woman as compared with an attractive man for selection as a marriage partner—under the situation as it has existed for a long time but under a situation that may have already started to make a wide-ranging change.

But if the most attractive men marry the most attractive women, as so often happens, is it any wonder that they turn out to have the highest proportion of continuing marriages? And, by implication, is it any wonder that other persons more often terminate their less-than-ideal matches through separation and divorce? But the situation may not be as bad as it seems, in view of the fact that this discussion relates to a band of persons on or near the diagonal of a distribution showing the marriage appeal of potential husbands cross-classified by the marriage appeal of potential wives.

Thus, a study might be expected to show that, for a given type of men in a given marriage market area, somewhere around the top 20 per cent of men in attractiveness might be considered as reasonably acceptable husbands for the top 20 per cent or so of women, with (sliding) lower quintiles of men being "acceptables" for corresponding lower quintiles of women. As the lowest 20 per cent of potential husbands and wives is approached, those in this group should theoretically be relatively satisfied with their marital partners provided they marry someone within their own range. But are they going to be all that satisfied? And what about those who either by choice or because they lost out in the competition married someone outside their optimal range? It would be logical to expect their marital dissolution rate to be substantial and to account for a disproportionately large share of all divorces. Although dissolution of marriage by divorce is by far the most likely amoung couples in the lowest economic level, undoubtedly a relatively large proportion of these same couples would still have an above-average divorce rate even if their income levels were augmented considerably.

A key variable in this context is "coping power." Presumably those of upper status have much more of it, on the average, than those who achieve only lower status. Although the development of superior coping mechanisms would ordinarily be expected to result in maintaining a marriage intact, it would also be expected to result from time to time in the firm decision that a marriage is not tolerable and should be dissolved. And yet, the kinds of talent and support that fail to elevate the standing of a person above a low level must tend to leave that person with fewer options within which to achieve satisfactory adjustment either occupationally or maritally. At least the findings for men are generally consistent with this interpretation.

For women, however, the pattern is different, with those who have the most education and the most income being generally less likely to enter marriage or to maintain continuing marriages, on the average, then those with lesser achievement in their educational background and work experience. How long this pattern for women will persist is anyone's guess, but it could last indefinitely among those who genuinely prefer being unmarried. On the other hand, it could change substantially over the next decade or two if modifications of attitudes about what constitute proper sex roles become modernized through appropriate socialization of the younger generation and resocialization of the older generations (Bernard, 1972).

RECENT CHANGES IN LIVING ARRANGEMENTS

Along with the recent decrease in fertility and increases in separation and divorce have come other developments that have shrunk the typical cluster of persons who live together as a household. Very few married couples live in with relatives as they once did. At the height of the housing shortage after World War II, fully 9 per cent of all couples were without their own house or apartment, but now only 1 per cent have to—or choose to—double up with others. In the 1940's only 1 in every 10 households was maintained by persons living alone or with a lodger or two, but now 1 in 5 households is of this type, and 1 in every 6 households consists of one person living entirely alone. As an overall measure of the shrinking family size, it is instructive to note that the average household consisted of 5 persons from 1890 to 1910, then 4 persons from 1920 to 1950, and 3 persons since 1960—with the 1974 average dipping fractionally below 3 persons, to 2.97 persons (U.S. Bureau of the Census, 1974b).

This development reflects mainly the longtime decline in fertility, but now more young adults live in apartments away from their parental home or in apartments rather than college dormitories, and more elderly persons are financially able—and evidently prefer—to live apart from their adult children. The most rapid increase in household formation since 1960 has occurred among young adults with no relative present, but the numerical increase has been much larger among elderly persons living alone. A spectacular 8-fold increase occurred during the 1960's in the number of household heads who were reported as living apart from relatives while sharing their living quarters with an unrelated adult "partner" (roommate or friend) of the opposite sex. One out of every four of these 143,000 "unmarried couples" in 1970 were women who had a male partner "living in." Among older men sharing their living quarters with nonrelatives only, one in every five shared it with a female partner (U.S. Bureau of the Census 1964 and 1973b). These older couples must include a substantial proportion of widowed persons who were living in this manner in order to avoid losing survivor benefits through remarriage.

Another "variant family form" is the commune, a type of living arrangement that has not been adequately quantified on a nationwide basis, partly because many of the communes are not welcome in their neighborhood and would rather not be identified in a census or survey.

The shrinking household size and the growing number of small households consisting of single-parent families, unmarried couples, or persons living entirely alone are evidence that large families are no longer regarded with favor by many persons and that new life styles are being tried by persons who want to learn whether the new ways are more satisfying to them than more conventional patterns. Some of the living arrangements with increasing numbers of adherents are bringing unrelated persons into closer companionship, whereas more of them are providing at least temporary relief from contacts with relatives that were regarded as too close for comfort.

But with four out of every five divorced persons eventually remarrying, the single-parent family has been in large part a temporary arrangement serving as a transition for the parent from one marital partner to another, and between parenthood and stepparenthood. New surveys will be watched for possible evidence that more of those with dissolved marriages will settle down with another unmarried person in a relatively stable union (with or) without a legal "cohabitation contract" that would have to be retracted through a court procedure if the union is to be dissolved later on.

KIN NETWORK TIES AND
NEIGHBORHOOD CHARACTERISTICS

The scattering of adult married and unmarried family members has been accelerated during recent decades through increased migration, which is related to increased amounts of higher education, among many other things. Fewer neighborhoods are now dotted by families of the same surname. Yet a substantial amount of contact is maintained with relatives, even with those who live at a considerable distance. A study under the direction of David M. Heer (on behalf of a committee established by the Family Section of the American Sociological Association) contemplates the collection and analysis of national data on the extent and nature of relationships that keep alive the kin network among persons under 40 years of age and their parents and siblings. The results are expected to quantify variations in types of communication and mutual assistance that are characteristic of "kinpersons" living different distances apart and belonging to different socio-economic groups. Funds for the support of this project are now being negotiated.

As adults move to localities that are beyond commuting distance of their close relatives, they may (or may not) become closely integrated into their new local neighborhoods. Studies are therefore needed to show the adjustment patterns of families in relation to the type of community in which they live. One study along this line is being planned by the present writer and Larry H. Long, also of the Bureau of the Census, on the basis of computer tapes available from the 1970 census. This source permits the analysis of marital and family characteristics in relation to such variables as duration of residence in the neighborhood (census tract or other small area), the ethnic composition of the neighborhood, the educational and income level of the neighborhood, the rate of turnover of population in the neighborhood, and the age and quality of housing in the neighborhood. Funding for this project may be obtained during the next year.

CONCLUDING REMARKS

The foregoing review of certain aspects of American marriage and living arrangements included some facts about what has been happening recently to family life in this country and has called attention to some areas where further research is needed. The accompanying interpretative comments were intended to add understanding to the census and vital facts that were presented. That is about as far as a demographer is expected to go in trying to help people do something about "the situation" in which so many American families find themselves today. Surely there is plenty of room for a division of labor between demographers and others who have a contribution to make in this area, including family lawyers, family counselors, socioeconomists, home economists, psychologists, social workers, religious leaders, and journalists.

However, there are undoubtedly some nondemographers who are looking for a cause to promote in this context. My personal opinion is that they might be well-advised to consider some of the following directions in which to exert their efforts:

1. The development of the contents for more practical and effective training at home, in the high schools, and in colleges about how young persons can make a wise selection of their marriage partner and how they can keep their marriage alive and healthy over a long period of time—and about how they can use reasonable criteria to decide whether it is any longer practical to keep their marriage intact (Broderick and Bernard, 1969).

2. Designing a scientifically tested and appealing system for selecting a marriage partner, for bringing together young men and women who would have a much higher probability of establishing an enduring and satisfying marriage than could be expected through the almost universally haphazard system that now exists—at the same time realizing that the rational approach must be supplemented by the strength of emotional appeal (Glick, 1967).

3. Acceptance by the public of the concept of periodic marriage checkups through visits to highly expert marriage counselors (when a sufficient supply becomes available), with these visits occurring in a manner analogous to periodic physical checkups that are voluntarily made, and with the visits considered urgent when a seemingly dangerous marital condition is developing.

4. Continuing modernization of marriage and divorce laws, which would tend to encourage couples to take much more seriously their entry into marriage but not quite so seriously as some couples do the hazards of ending a marriage that is no longer worthy of continuation.

5. Development of child care facilities staffed by highly professional personnel, so that more mothers can feel free to maximize the alternatives available for the use of their time while their children are growing up—provided that careful attention is given in choosing the ways in which the additional free time is used (Campbell, 1973; Low and Spindler, 1968).

6. Finally, programs to increase the appeal of experiencing a good marriage, including the continued collection and dissemination of knowledge about how to cultivate such a marriage—so that more emphasis can be placed on building up the positive side of married life, in a period when so many stimuli that reach the public have the effect of making nonmarriage appear to be much more desirable (Mace and Mace, 1974).

Certainly demographers cannot be counted upon—in their capacity as practicing demographers—to promote such causes as these to improve family relations in the modern world, but they can help to promote such causes indirectly by providing imaginative factual information about the types of circumstances which tend to be associated with enduring marriages and about other types of circumstances that tend to be associated with a substantial amount of seemingly inevitable marital dissolution.

REFERENCES

Bernard, Jessie. 1972. The Future of Marriage. New York: World Publishing.

Broderick, Carlfred B., and Jessie Bernard (eds.). 1969. The Individual, Sex, and Society: A SIECUS Handbook for Teachers and Counselors. Baltimore: The Johns Hopkins Press.

Campbell, Arthur A. 1973. "Population: the search for solutions in the behavioral sciences." American Journal of Obstetrics and Gynecology 116:131-152.

Davis, Kingsley. 1972. "The American family in relation to demographic change." Pp. 237-265 in Charles F. Westoff and Robert Parke, Jr. (eds.), U.S. Commission on Population Growth and the American Future, Vol. I, Demographic and Social Aspects of Population Growth. Washington, D.C.: U.S. Government Printing Office.

Glick, Paul C. 1957. American Families. New York: John Wiley and Sons.

Glick, Paul C. 1967. "Permanence of marriage." Population Index 33:517-526. Presidential Address, Population Association of America, April 1967.

Glick, Paul C. 1973. "Dissolution of marriage by divorce and its demographic consequences." Pp. 65-79 in Vol. 2 of International Population Conference, Liege 1973. Liege, Belgium: International Union for the Scientific Study of Population.

Glick, Paul C. (ed.). 1974. Population of the United States, Trends and Prospects: 1950 to 1990. U.S. Bureau of the Census, Current Population Reports, Series P-23, No. 49. Washington, D.C.: U.S. Government Printing Office.

Glick, Paul C. and Arthur J. Norton. 1973. "Perspectives on the recent upturn in divorce and remarriage." Demography 10:301-314.

Low, Seth, and Pearl G. Spindler. 1968. Child Care Arrangements of Working Mothers in the United States. U.S. Children's Bureau and U.S. Women's Bureau. Washington, D.C.: U.S. Government Printing Office.

Mace, David and Vera Mace. 1974. We Can Have Better Marriages. Nashville, Tenn.: Abingdon Press.

Rosenberg, Beatrice, and Ethel Mendelsohn. 1974. "Legal status of women." In Council of State Governments, The Book of States, 1974-75. Available through U.S. Women's Bureau.

United Nations. 1973. Demographic Yearbook, 1972. New York: United Nations.

U.S. Bureau of the Census

    1964 1960 Census of Population, Vol. II, 4B, Persons by Family Characteristics. Washington, D.C.: U.S. Government Printing Office.

    1967 1960 Census of Population, Vol. II, 4E, Marital Status. Washington, D.C.: U.S. Government Printing Office.

    1972a "Marriage, divorce, and remarriage by year of birth: June 1971." Current Population Reports, Series P-20, No. 239. Washington, D.C.: U.S. Government Printing Office.

    1972b 1970 Census of Population, Vol. II, 4C, Marital Status. Washington, D.C.: U.S. Government Printing Office.

    1973a 1970 Census of Population, Vol. II, 3A, Women by Number of Children Ever Born. Washington, D.C.: U.S. Government Printing Office.

    1973b 1970 Census of Population. Vol. II, 4B, Persons by Family Characteristics. Washington, D.C.: U.S. Government Printing Office.

    1973c 1970 Census of Population, Vol. II, 4D, Age at First Marriage. Washington, D.C.: U.S. Government Printing Office.

    1974a "Prospects for American fertility: June 1974." Current Population Reports, Series P-20, No. 269. Washington, D.C.: U.S. Government Printing Office.

    1974b "Marital status and living arrangements: March 1974." Current Population Reports, Series P-20, No. 271. Washington, D.C.: U.S. Government Printing Office.

U.S. National Center for Health Statistics

    1974a "Provisional statistics (births, marriages, divorces and deaths for August 1974)." Monthly Vital Statistics Report, Vol. 23, No. 8. Washington, D.C.: U.S. Government Printing Office.

    1974b "Summary report, final divorce statistics, 1971." Monthly Vital Statistics Report, Vol. 23, No. 8 Supplement 3. Washington, D.C.: U.S. Government Printing Office.

Weitzman, Lenore J., Herma Hill Kay, and Ruth B. Dixon. 1974. "No-Fault divorce in California: the view of the legal community." Paper presented at the annual meeting of the American Sociological Association in Montreal, August 25-29.

ch. 21-24